The Second Wave

The Second Wave

A Reader in Feminist Theory

edited by
Linda Nicholson

ROUTLEDGE
New York and London

Published in 1997 by

Routledge
29 West 35th Street
New York, NY 10001

Published in Great Britain in 1997 by

Routledge
11 New Fetter Lane
London EC4P 4EE

Printed in the United States of America
Design: Jack Donner

Library of Congress Cataloging-in-Publication Data

The second wave : a reader in feminist theory / Linda Nicholson, editor.
        p.   cm.
    Includes bibliographical references and index
    ISBN 0–415–91760–3 (hb) —   ISBN 0–415–91761–1 (pb)
    1. Feminist theory—United States. 2. Women's rights—United States.
I. Nicholson, Linda.
HQ1190. S42   1996
305.42'01—dc20

                                                          96–25168
                                                             CIP

Contents

Preface

The idea for this volume occured several years ago when I taught my first graduate course in feminist theory. No one text included many of the essays I viewed as marking important turning points in feminist theory debates. Like many teachers who encounter such a dilemma I put together a "course packet" for teaching. While there were many collections already available in Women's Studies and even in feminist theory, many of these seemed oriented to a student with less background than those I was preparing to teach. Many of these volumes offered lots of "snippets" from famous writers, rather than essays in their entirety. These kinds of volumes might be useful for a first and second year student, but seemed less appropriate for a more advanced undergraduate or graduate student who wanted to be exposed to an author's ideas in the form that the author had chosen. Also, many of the available collections seemed organized around topics, either of women's oppression or of types of feminist theory. While, again, these can be useful schemas for introducing students to the field of Women's Studies or feminist theory, they seemed less appropriate for more sophisticated students who wanted some sense of changes within feminist theory over time.

Two features of this volume follow from this original motivation. For one, most of the essays are full length essays or chapters. For the sake of producing a manageably sized book I did have to shorten a few of the longer essays. Those selections that have been shortened from their original size are: "Introduction" to

The Second Sex by Simone de Beauvoir; chapter one, "The Dialectic of Sex" from *The Dialectic of Sex* by Shulamith Firestone (a page length footnote has been eliminated); "The Unhappy Marriage of Marxism and Feminism" by Heidi Hartmann; the chapter on "Sexuality" from *Toward a Feminist Theory of the State* by Catharine MacKinnon; and "Contesting Cultures: 'Westernization,' Respect for Cultures, and Third-World Feminists" by Uma Narayan.

Secondly, the volume is organized roughly historically. In my selection and organization of the sections, I have attempted to mark out a history of debates in the second wave in the United States as these have changed over time. Because important contributions to a given discussion sometimes were published long after the point when other contributions first appeared, with different debates emerging in the interim, the individual selections do not themselves necessarily follow a strict chronological order. Overall, however, the volume is intended to convey a changing discussion over time.

Why the focus on the history of the discussion in the United States alone? This follows from my belief that there has not been one history of feminist theory debates worldwide, and to extend the focus would be to imply such a singular history. While writers in many countries have importantly affected debates in others—which is why not all of the contributors to this volume are *from* the United States—the discussions in different countries have exhibited different emphases. Thus the debates in France, England, Italy, Mexico, etc. have been marked by different concerns and have followed different trajectories. No one volume whose intent was historical could capture this diversity in the development of discussion.

I thank those who provided support as I worked on this project. Numerous people made useful suggestions that changed the shape of the volume. In this regard I specifically thank Lillian Williams as well as those anonymous reviewers who commented on one version of the table of contents. The summer of 1995 was a particularly difficult one for me and many came forward to help me through it. Two people who gave particularly large doses of support were Nancy Fraser and Pat Mills.

This book would not be here if not for Maureen MacGrogan. Maureen has deconstructed the idea of "editor" for me such that it now merges with close friend. That deconstruction has made a lot of things possible, including this book.

Finally, I wish to thank Steve Seidman. If Maureen deconstructs the idea of "editor" for me, Steve deconstructs the idea of "friend." The ways in which he has been there for me over the years is only superficially acknowledged in this kind of thank you.

Introduction

Is "the second wave" a useful concept? Scholars have raised important questions about the distinction "first wave/second wave" as a way of organizing the history of feminism. When does each wave begin and when does it end? What activities and what social groups are excluded by this distinction? What countries does it or does it not apply to? These are important questions and merit discussion. Nevertheless, I believe that something important occurred in the 1960s that is still spinning itself out. That occurrence was a new intensity in many societies in the degree of reflection given to gender relations. The political movements that came into being in the 1960s meant that a radical questionning of gender roles was being carried out not only by isolated scholars or marginalized groups, but in front of and with the attention of many national publics. The consequence has been a major restructuring of institutions worldwide. Something happened in the 1960s in ways of thinking about gender that continues to shape public and private life.

I view the beginnings of these changes in the United States in two, originally separate, political movements. The first was the Women's Rights movement, emerging early in the 1960s. This was a movement composed of largely professional women who began putting pressure on federal and state institutions to end the discrimination that women experienced in entering the paid labor force. This movement also drew on the dissatisfaction felt by many middle class housewives with their lot as housewives. But, somewhat independent of this movement was a second movement, the

Women's Liberation Movement, which emerged out of the New Left of the latter part of the 1960s. While Women's Rights has been the more politically widespread movement in the United States, expressing an ideology more in accord with that of the population as a whole, it is from the Women's Liberation Movement that most of the more theoretical works of the second wave have emerged.

The emergence of Women's Liberation out of the New Left shaped its early theoretical tasks. The major political problem that early Women Liberationists faced was in getting others in the New Left, women as well as men, to recognize the importance of women's oppression, its presence across large stretches of history and its fundamentality as a principle of social organization. This meant developing a theory that explained the origins of women's oppression and the means by which it has been sustained over time. The theory had to account both for the pervasiveness of women's oppression throughout much of history, yet also allow for the different forms this oppression has assumed in different societies. Many of the early contributors to Women's Liberation had been deeply affected by the insights of Marxist theory. Marxism provided a metanarrative of the social whole that simultaneously explained all previous societies, allowed for historical change and diversity among these, and left open the possibility of a future society where its own explanatory power would become irrelevant. Second wave theorists knew that any convincing theory they were to put forth must accomplish all of these tasks as well.

But the emergence of Women's Liberation out of the New Left meant that second wave theorists not only had to produce an account of women's oppression as theoretically compelling as Marx's, they also had to establish some relation between their theories and Marxism. Early radical feminist theorists argued that as women's oppression was prior to and more basic than other forms of oppression, it demanded a theoretical explanation more encompassing than and different from Marxism. Other theorists, more influenced by Marxism, tried to work out ways of theorizing the specificity and seriousnessness of women's oppression without discarding the insights of Marxism altogether. One common approach taken toward the latter task was to make a distinction between Marx's method and his specific analysis. Feminists, they argued, should retain the idea of "historical materialism," that is, a method of analysis that begins with a focus on how human beings act to satisfy needs in the context of social structures that change over time. The problem was that traditional Marxist theorists, in their specific analyses, had interpreted the idea of activity geared to the satisfaction of needs too narrowly, focusing on those activities more traditionally associated with men than with women. This limitation of Marxism was expressed in the narrowness of many Marxists' interpretation of the concept of "production"; feminists argued that "production" needed to be understood as including not only work geared to the creation of food and objects, but also work geared to the creation and care of human beings. The essays included in this volume reflect some of the ways this expansion has been conceptualized and some of the implications such an expansion entails for Marxist theory.

While the initial tasks of second wave theorists were to generate explanations that accounted for the fundamentality of women's oppression and to respond to Marxism, for many, new tasks began to emerge in the early 1970s. In the late 1960s and early 1970s two contradictory beliefs existed as part of the general culture: that the differences between women and men were deep and rooted in nature and, secondly, that women and men were basically the same. Second wave feminists initially drew heavily on this latter belief to press for changes in the status quo. While many, particularly "liberal" feminists, continued in this direction, those feminists who saw their politics as more radical began to focus on the differences between women and men. This focus can in part be explained by the political limitations radical and socialist feminists saw as associated with a "women and men are the same" perspective. Such a politics seemed to consist in pushing society towards accepting women in the same positions as men in an otherwise unaltered social world. But as one of the popular slogans of the period claimed: "Women who strive to be equal to men lack ambition." For radical and socialist feminists, a politics that merely strove toward placing women where men had previously been also lacked ambition. If one were to build a politics which radically altered the status quo, one needed to focus on the deep ways society differentiated the life activities and psyches of women and men. What began to emerge can be described as a "difference" feminism; because it often elaborated the meaning of differences between women and men in terms of the unique situation and characteristics of women, it has also been labelled a "gynocentric" feminism.[1]

This new focus on the differences between women and men was elaborated, however, in a variety of ways. In my selections I have identified three distinct orientations within this general turn. One way of moving away from a "women and men are fundamentally the same" perspective was to stress the depths of women's oppression. A focus on oppression led toward a view of women as victims, and to the move toward separatism found in large sections of the radical feminist community during the 1970s. The essay "The Woman Identified Woman" and the chapter from MacKinnon reflect this first elaboration of difference. A second type of gynocentrism tended toward describing the differences between women and men in more neutral terms, emphasizing both their positive and negative consequences on women's lives. The Chodorow and Gilligan essays reflect this second type of orientation. A third type, represented here in the essays by Hartsock and Collins, focused on the ways in which the distinctive positions of women—for Hartsock, women in general and for Collins, African American women in particular—provide a unique and positive standpoint for understanding society and for developing a liberatory vision.

"Difference" or "gynocentric" feminism produced an enormous amount of highly creative work. The writings of such theorists as MacKinnon, Chodorow, and Gilligan led to "aha" experiences for large numbers of people. Suddenly, patterns that many had sensed "through a glass darkly" were laid out in clear and convincing texts. This general orientation, however, suffered from one serious weakness: it tended to deny difference *among* women. The description of women's differences from men seemed too often to involve homogeneous visions of womanhood.

The tendency to deny difference among women was, in gynocentric feminism, complex. Certainly by the late 1970s, most second wave feminists were sensitive to the charges of exclusion that lesbians, women of color, working class women, etc. were making against many of the texts and demands of the movement. By this time there were few texts that were not acknowledging differences among women. However, such assertions of differences were often made in conjunction with assertions of commonalities. This combination was made possible through a number of strategies. Sometimes feminist theorists would claim that they were describing a "common" pattern, such as a separation between private and public life, which differed only in intensity among different societies. Sometimes, theorists assumed what Elizabeth Spelman has described as a type of "tootsie roll" or "pop bead" metaphysics, where individual identity was seen as a composite of the separable elements of gender, race, class, etc. Within such a metaphysics, gender could be described in singular terms, under the assumption that the effects of race, class, sexuality etc. merely "added on" to this commonality in gender.[2] Not surprisingly, when a commonality in gender was assumed, it was described from the perspective of those of privilege.

For many feminist theorists, what was needed, therefore, were not merely more assertions about differences among women, but exploration into the unarticulated premises that made the assertion of gender commonality possible even when differences were being asserted. The contributors to the section on "theorizing difference" explore these premises. Similar to Spelman, they note that the problems often stem from an understanding of the experiences of privileged women as normative or universal. Thus white women are seen as without race and their experiences as "raceless." Differences among women are not seen as relational. Moreover, contributing to the problem were certain conceptions of the subject: as unitary and preconstituted in isolation from others.

The discussion of such issues led to what became perhaps the major theoretical debate of the 1990s, around "essentialism." The way in which this debate was constructed was heavily influenced by the poststucturalist ideas of Lacan and Derrida. Central to the writings of these two theorists was a critique of autonomous, preconstituted conceptions of the subject, and of theories of language that construed meaning in representational or essentialist terms. For Lacan and Derrida, such conceptions of the subject and of language, depicted in such phrases as "phallocentrism" and "logocentrism," have reigned over large sweeps of history. For feminist thinkers influenced by these theorists, the problems of gynocentrism could be answered by developing understandings of "woman" that fell outside of such phallocentric or logocentric worldviews.

The problem, however, was that such understandings seemed to entail only negative interpretations of "woman." If "woman" were to serve as "other" to phallocentric conceptions of identity, this could only be in so far as "woman" lacked any identity of its own. But a purely negative idea of "woman" could support no positive political agenda, that is, no substance for the political project known as feminism. Did feminism demand a return to the essentialist readings of "woman" expressed by gynocentric feminists?

For many feminist theorists, the task became that of negotiating between the shoals of gynocentrism on the one hand, and certain forms of poststructuralism on the other. Certain poststructuralist ideas, such as its view of subjectivity as discursively constructed and multiple in nature were convincing: could such ideas be combined with enough of a notion of gender to allow for a feminist politics?

One response to this dilemma, reflected in the positions of several contributors to this volume, has been to endorse a pragmatic view of language and an understanding of subjectivity as discursively constituted, multiple in nature but as also capable of reflection and change. This position rejects a liberal reading of subjectivity as pre-constituted and recognizes the positionality of subjectivity within history. It recognizes power as an important dynamic in the discursive construction of identity. It thus allows that the meaning of "woman" shifts over history and over diverse contexts as this form of subject constitution intersects with other forms. It recognizes, therefore, that the political meaning of feminism cannot be derived from any pre-given concept of "womanhood" but must evolve as different political actors, men as well as woman, struggle over how gender is to be understood.

This type of position opens up a set of questions different from those that feminist theory so far has been considering. If one accepts that feminism should not attempt to base itself on the supposedly pre-given, but should recognize its own meaning as evolving out of the multiple input of actors who are diversely situated, what are the conditions in which such input should be made? How can we avoid, or at least minimize, existing inequalities of power in the construction of the very meaning of feminism? How do we conceptualize the meaning of such other constructions of identity as race, nation, or class to allow for meaningful understandings of the ways in which "woman" is multiply constituted? And, finally how do we forge political movements capable of addressing the complex ways imbalances of wealth, dignity, power, and love are reproduced? These, I believe, are the questions now facing us.

NOTES

1. Iris Young, "Humanism, Gynocentrism and Feminist Politics," In *Hypatia: A Journal of Feminist Philosophy*, issue no. 3, a special issue of *Women's Studies International Forum*, vol. 8, no. 3, 1985, 173–183.
2. Elizabeth Spelman, *Inessential Woman* (Boston: Beacon, 1988).

Early Statements

The initial tasks facing second wave theorists were to document the seriousness of women's oppression and develop theories to account for it. Simone de Beauvoir's *The Second Sex* soon became viewed as a classic because of the elegant case it made for the depth and pervasiveness of women's oppression. De Beauvoir sees in certain physiological differences between women and men, most notably men's freedom from reproductive activity, the potential for men to first define themselves as subject. Thus biology becomes elaborated into gender as woman becomes the "other" to man within a hierarchical relationship.

De Beauvoir was not alone in pointing to women's reproductive differences from men as a potential cause of women's oppression. Most notable in elaborating a full scale theory based on these differences was Shulamith Firestone's *The Dialectic of Sex*. According to Firestone, women's ties to childbearing and early childrearing caused a basic power imbalance between women and men that predated all other power imbalances. While this power imbalance has been present to some degree in all previous societies, it has been more accentuated in some depending on the specific organization of the family created. But biology need not determine. We have now reached a point in history where the sexual differences between women and men have become technologically irrelevant. Thus, we are at that point in history where genital differences need no longer matter culturally. What had been so important for all of human history can now be left behind.

Firestone's account was extraordinarily powerful, but it also left many unsatisfied. As at least one strand of Marxism had convincingly demonstrated, biology must always be understood from within a cultural context. Although Firestone acknowledged the historicity of the nuclear family, she also seemed to presuppose it in her claim that women's biology causes their dependence on men. Are not all of us dependent on each other in some way or other? The old are dependent upon the young, and the sick upon the healthy, as much as women are dependent upon men. Is it not just a specific organization of society, i.e., that associated with the nuclear family, that makes childbearing and childrearing a cause of female dependence? Can we develop a theory that is *not* grounded in biology to satisfy all of the above requirements?

One essay that appeared to do this was Gayle Rubin's "The Traffic in Women." Like Firestone, Rubin pointed to the limitations of Marxism, that its focus on the economic was too narrow. Rubin noted that the social whole includes at least three domains, the political, the economic and the sexual. While Marx had developed a powerful theory of the economic, also needed was a comparable analysis of the domain of sexuality, or as Rubin called it "the sex/gender system." As Marx's analysis was substantive enough to provide a convincing account of the moving force of economic change yet abstract enough to allow for diversity in economic forms, so too did an analysis of the "sex/gender" system need to be substantive enough to be explanatory of women's oppression across great stretches of history but also abstract enough to allow for diversity in the forms and degree of this oppression. Rubin preferred the term "the sex/gender system" to "patriarchy" as the latter seemed limited not only to one form of "the sex/gender system" but even to one form of women's oppression.

To develop such an analysis, Rubin turned to Lévi-Strauss, who had argued that the exchange of women made possible the institution of kinship, and for early societies organized around kinship, the construction of society itself. As Rubin claims, such an argument could account for the depth, pervasiveness, yet diversity of women's oppression. If kinship were based on the exchange of women, then women would be disempowered in relation to men at a very fundamental level and across a wide spectrum of societies. Moreover, diversity in the form and extent of women's oppression could also be accounted for by appeal to diversity among kinship systems.

These insights from Lévi-Strauss could also be used to explain such other cross-cultural phenomena as the incest taboo, the bipolar construction of gender and heteronormativity. If the exchange of women were necessary for the construction of kinship, what also would be required would be the cultural elaboration of sexual differences into gender differences, a societal demand for heterosexuality and a prohibition against heterosexuality within the immediate kinship group. In short, in elaborating on Lévi-Strauss' ideas, Rubin could account for the very construction of gender and its ties to heterosexuality and the incest taboo: individuals are gendered as "opposites" who sexually desire the "other" outside of the immediate kinship group in order that marriage be guaranteed and kinship, and thus social structure in general, be reproduced. Rubin added to this already elegant theory certain claims of Lacan to account for the mechanisms by which children internalize gender, heterosexuality and the symbolic power of the penis.

Like Firestone's account, Rubin's also had within it a way to explain its own potential for future irrelevance. While kinship systems were basic to early societies in organizing most features of human life, including food acquisition and dispersal, crime and punishment, ties to the past and future, etc., they have gradually become limited to organizing only sex and gender. In short, kinship has become steadily irrelevant as a structural component of the social whole. We are now at that stage in history where a genderless identity and a "polymorphous perverse" sexuality are possible. All we have to lose are the chains that keep us tied to a now functionless "sex/gender" order.

In short, the period of the first stage of second wave feminist theory was marked by the attempt to construct powerful theories that would explain women's oppression in, to use Rubin's famous phrase, its "endless variety and monotonous similarity." But congruent with such attempts was the growing awareness that the variety was not being adequately accounted for in much of the discourse and political action of the second wave as a whole. The Combahee River Collective Statement is an early representation of this awareness.

The importance of this statement exists on a variety of different levels. For one, it underscores the participation of women of color, lesbians, and working class women in second wave politics from the beginning. It signals early on in second wave theory the need for feminists to seriously relate issues of gender to those of race, class and sexuality.

The statement also made certain important theoretical moves less easily remembered today. Over the last several years, identity politics have come into question as associated with a type of isolationism and essentialism. This statement defends identity politics on the grounds that the most profound politics come out of one's own identity and argues that only black women can adequately specify their own needs. In contemporary discussions around identity politics there is a tendency to forget the strong orientation of *pre*-identity politics towards making the world better for *others*, without necessary input from those others themselves. Thus, there is the tendency to forget that identity politics originated as a reaction against this earlier, more arrogant conception of political activity. This statement reminds us of these origins. But secondly, this statement defends identity politics while also rejecting separatism. Included within the statement is not just a claim that black women cannot afford separatism because of the need to work with black men in struggles against racism, as black feminist rejections of separatism have sometimes been described. The statement rejects even the separatism of white women on the grounds that it ignores all but the gender and sexual sources of women's oppression. In short, as early as 1977, some feminists were noting that *all* women are racialized and classed, and that gender intersects with such factors so fundamentally as to negate the possibility of abstracting any one factor as a basis of self identity or political action. As early as 1977 some feminists were understanding the need for articulating identity in ways that facilitated rather than undermined coalition politics.

Most second wave theory emerged out of the "Women's Liberation" rather than the "Women's Rights" movement. Consequently, much feminist theory of the second wave has been "radical" or "socialist" in orientation. To provide some representation to a liberal perspective in this collection, I have included the essay by Wendy Williams, "The Equality Crisis: Some Reflections of Culture, Courts, and Feminism." This essay dates from 1982, and is therefore not, strictly speaking, representative of second wave's early years. But it eloquently depicts challenges liberal feminism has had to deal with throughout its history. Liberalism is built on the premise of equality before the law for all human beings. However, this premise has come into conflict with other existing conceptions of women's relationships to men such as the principle of spousal unity and the doctrine of separate spheres. Williams focuses on certain contemporary court cases that put into conflict the principle of equality with existing conceptions of women's roles. These cases represent not just a challenge to those who support the status quo but also to feminists. Are we truly committed to legal equality or do we support laws that presuppose differences between women and men? Williams argues for upholding equality in all cases. As she claims, while there are real socially constructed differences between women and men, in defending laws that presuppose such differences, we ultimately undermine women's best interests.

1

SIMONE DE BEAUVOIR

"Introduction" to *The Second Sex*

For a long time I have hesitated to write a book on woman. The subject is irritating, especially to women; and it is not new. Enough ink has been spilled in the quarreling over feminism, now practically over, and perhaps we should say no more about it. It is still talked about, however, for the voluminous nonsense uttered during the last century seems to have done little to illuminate the problem. After all, is there a problem? And if so, what is it? Are there women, really? Most assuredly the theory of the eternal feminine still has its adherents who will whisper in your ear: "Even in Russia women still are *women*"; and other erudite persons—sometimes the very same—say with a sigh: "Woman is losing her way, woman is lost." One wonders if women still exist, if they will always exist, whether or not it is desirable that they should, what place they occupy in this world, what their place should be. "What has become of women?" was asked recently in an ephemeral magazine.[1]

But first we must ask: what is a woman? "*Tota mulier in utero*" says one, "woman is a womb." But in speaking of certain women, connoisseurs declare that they are not women, although they are equipped with a uterus like the rest. All agree in recognizing the fact that females exist in the human species; today as always they make up about one half of humanity. And yet we are told that femininity is in danger; we are exhorted to be women, remain women, become women. It would appear, then, that every female human being is not necessarily a woman; to be so considered she must share in that mysterious and threatened reality known as femininity. Is this attribute something secreted by the ovaries? Or is it a Platonic essence, a product of the philo-sophic imagination? Is a rustling petticoat enough to bring it down to earth? Although some women try zealously to incarnate this essence, it is hardly patentable. It is fre-quently described in vague and dazzling terms that seem to have been borrowed from the vocabulary of the seers, and indeed in the times of St. Thomas it was considered an essence as certainly defined as the somniferous virtue of the poppy.

But conceptualism has lost ground. The biological and social sciences no longer admit the existence of unchangeably fixed entities that determine given characteristics, such as those ascribed to woman, the Jew, or the Negro. Science regards any charac-teristic as a reaction dependent in part upon a *situation*. If today femininity no longer exists, then it never existed. But does the word *woman*, then, have no specific content? This is stoutly affirmed by those who hold to the philosophy of the enlightenment, of rationalism, of nominalism; women, to them, are merely the human beings arbitarily designated by the word *woman*. Many American women particularly are prepared to think that there is no longer any place for woman as such; if a backward individual still takes herself for a woman, her friends advise her to be psychoanalyzed and thus get rid of this obsession. In regard to a work, *Modern Woman: The Lost Sex*, which in other respects has its irritating features, Dorothy Parker has written: "I cannot be just to books which treat of woman as woman . . . My idea is that all of us, men as well as women, should be regarded as human beings." But nominalism is a rather inadequate doctrine, and the antifemininists have had no trouble in showing that women simply *are not* men. Surely woman is, like man, a human being; but such a declaration is abstract. The fact is that every concrete human being is always a singular, separate individual. To decline to accept such notions as the eternal feminine, the black soul, the Jewish character, is not to deny that Jews, Negroes, women exist today—this denial does not represent a liberation for those concerned, but rather a flight from reality. Some years ago a well-known woman writer refused to permit her portrait to appear in a series of photographs especially devoted to women writers; she wished to be counted among the men. But in order to gain this privilege she made use of her husband's influence! Women who assert that they are men lay claim none the less to masculine consideration and respect. I recall also a young Trotskyite standing on a platform at a boisterous meeting and getting ready to use her fists, in spite of her evident fragility. She was denying her feminine weakness; but it was for love of a militant male whose equal she wished to be. The attitude of defiance of many American women proves that they are haunted by a sense of their femininity. In truth, to go for a walk with one's eyes open is enough to demonstrate that humanity is divided into two classes of individuals whose clothes, faces, bodies, smiles, gaits, interests, and occupations are manifestly different. Perhaps these differences are superficial, perhaps they are des-tined to disappear. What is certain is that right now they do most obviously exist.

If her functioning as a female is not enough to define woman, if we decline also to explain her through "the eternal feminine," and if nevertheless we admit, provisionally, that women do exist, then we must face the question: what is a woman?

To state the question is, to me, to suggest, at once, a preliminary answer. The fact that I ask it is in itself significant. A man would never get the notion of writing a book on the peculiar situation of the human male.[2] But if I wish to define myself, I must first of all say: "I am a woman"; on this truth must be based all further discussion. A man never begins by presenting himself as an individual of a certain sex; it goes without saying that he is a man. The terms *masculine and feminine* are used symmetrically only as a matter of form, as on legal papers. In actuality the relation of the two sexes is not quite like that of two electrical poles, for man represents both the positive and the neutral, as is indicated by the common use of *man* to designate human beings in general; whereas woman represents only the negative, defined by limiting criteria, without reciprocity. In the midst of an abstract discussion it is vexing to hear a man say: "You think thus and so because you are a woman"; but I know that my only defense is to reply: "I think thus and so because it is true," thereby removing my subjective self from the argument. It would be out of the question to reply: "And you think the contrary because you are a man," for it is understood that the fact of being a man is no peculiarity. A man is in the right in being a man; it is the woman who is in the wrong. It amounts to this: just as for the ancients there was an absolute vertical with reference to which the oblique was defined, so there is an absolute human type, the masculine. Woman has ovaries, a uterus; these peculiarities imprison her in her subjectivity, circumscribe her within the limits of her own nature. It is often said that she thinks with her glands. Man superbly ignores the fact that his anatomy also includes glands, such as the testicles, and that they secrete hormones. He thinks of his body as a direct and normal connection with the world, which he believes he apprehends objectively, whereas he regards the body of woman as a hindrance, a prison, weighed down by everything peculiar to it. "The female is a female by virtue of a certain *lack* of qualities," said Aristotle; "we should regard the female nature as afflicted with a natural defectiveness." And St. Thomas for his part pronounced woman to be an "imperfect man," an "incidental" being. This is symbolized in Genesis where Eve is depicted as made from what Bossuet called "a supernumerary bone" of Adam.

Thus humanity is male and man defines woman not in herself but as relative to him; she is not regarded as an autonomous being. Michelet writes: "Woman, the relative being . . ." And Benda is most positive in his *Rapport d' Uriel*: "The body of man makes sense in itself quite apart from that of woman, whereas the latter seems wanting in significance by itself . . . Man can think of himself without woman. She cannot think of herself without man." And she is simply what man decrees; thus she is called "the sex," by which is meant that she appears essentially to the male as a sexual being. For him she is sex—absolute sex, no less. She is defined and differentiated with reference to man and not he with reference to her; she is the incidental, the inessential as opposed to the essential. He is the Subject, he is the Absolute—she is the Other.[8]

The category of the *Other* is as primordial as consciousness itself. In the most primitive societies, in the most ancient mythologies, one finds the expression of a duality—that of the Self and the Other. This duality was not originally attached to the division of the sexes; it was not dependent upon any empirical facts. It is revealed in such works as that of Granet on Chinese thought and those of Dumézil on the East Indies and Rome. The feminine element was at first no more involved in such pairs as Varuna-Mitra, Uranus-Zeus, Sun-Moon, and Day-Night than it was in the contrasts between Good and Evil, lucky and unlucky auspices, right and left, God and Lucifer. Otherness is a fundamental category of human thought.

Thus it is that no group ever sets itself up as the One without at once setting up the Other over against itself. If three travelers chance to occupy the same compartment, that is enough to make vaguely hostile "others" out of all the rest of the passengers on the train. In small-town eyes all persons not belonging to the village are "strangers" and suspect; to the native of a country all who inhabit other countries are "foreigners"; Jews are "different" for the anti-Semite, Negroes are "inferior" for American racists, aborigines are "natives" for colonists, proletarians are the "lower class" for the privileged.

Lévi-Strauss, at the end of a profound work on the various forms of primitive societies, reaches the following conclusion: "Passage from the state of Nature to the state of Culture is marked by man's ability to view biological relations as a series of contrasts; duality, alternation, opposition, and symmetry, whether under definite or vague forms, constitute not so much phenomena to be explained as fundamental and immediately given data of social reality."[4] These phenomena would be incomprehensible if in fact human society were simply a *Mitsein* or fellowship based on solidarity and friendliness. Things become clear, on the contrary, if, following Hegel, we find in consciousness itself a fundamental hostility toward every other consciousness; the subject can be posed only in being opposed—he sets himself up as the essential, as opposed to the other, the inessential, the object.

But the other consciousness, the other ego, sets up a reciprocal claim. The native traveling abroad is shocked to find himself in turn regarded as a "stranger" by the natives of neighboring countries. As a matter of fact, wars, festivals, trading, treaties, and contests among tribes, nations, and classes tend to deprive the concept *Other* of its absolute sense and to make manifest its relativity; willy-nilly, individuals and groups are forced to realize the reciprocity of their relations. How is it, then, that this reciprocity has not been recognized between the sexes, that one of the contrasting terms is set up as the sole essential, denying any relativity in regard to its correlative and defining the latter as pure otherness? Why is it that women do not dispute male sovereignty? No subject will readily volunteer to become the object, the inessential; it is not the Other who, in defining himself as the Other, establishes the One. The Other is posed as such by the One in defining himself as the One. But if the Other is not to regain the status of being the One, he must be submissive enough to accept this alien point of view. Whence comes this submission in the case of woman?

There are, to be sure, other cases in which a certain category has been able to dominate another completely for a time. Very often this privilege depends upon inequality of numbers—the majority imposes its rule upon the minority or persecutes it. But women are not a minority, like the American Negroes or the Jews; there are as many women as men on earth. Again, the two groups concerned have often been originally independent; they may have been formerly unaware of each other's existence, or perhaps they recognized each other's autonomy. But a historical event has resulted in the subjugation of the weaker by the stronger. The scattering of the Jews, the introduction of slavery into America, the conquests of imperialism are examples in point. In these cases the oppressed retained at least the memory of former days; they possessed in common a past, a tradition, sometimes a religion or a culture.

The parallel drawn by Bebel between women and the proletariat is valid in that neither ever formed a minority or a separate collective unit of mankind. And instead of a single historical event it is in both cases a historical development that explains their status as a class and accounts for the membership of *particular individuals* in that class. But proletarians have not always existed, whereas there have always been women. They are women in virtue of their anatomy and physiology. Throughout history they have always been subordinated to men,[5] and hence their dependency is not the result of a historical event or a social change—it was not something that *occurred*. The reason why otherness in this case seems to be an absolute is in part that it lacks the contingent or incidental nature of historical facts. A condition brought about at a certain time can be abolished at some other time, as the Negroes of Haiti and others have proved; but it might seem that a natural condition is beyond the possibility of change. In truth, however, the nature of things is no more immutably given, once for all, than is historical reality. If woman seems to be the inessential which never becomes the essential, it is because she herself fails to bring about this change. Proletarians say "We"; Negroes also. Regarding themselves as subjects, they transform the bourgeois, the whites, into "others." But women do not say "We," except at some congress of feminists or similar formal demonstration; men say "women," and women use the same word in referring to themselves. They do not authentically assume a subjective attitude. The proletarians have accomplished the revolution in Russia, the Negroes in Haiti, the Indo-Chinese are battling for it in Indo-China; but the women's effort has never been anything more than a symbolic agitation. They have gained only what men have been willing to grant; they have taken nothing, they have only received.[6]

The reason for this is that women lack concrete means for organizing themselves into a unit which can stand face to face with the correlative unit. They have no past, no history, no religion of their own; and they have no such solidarity of work and interest as that of the proletariat. They are not even promiscuously herded together in the way that creates community feeling among the American Negroes, the ghetto Jews, the workers of Saint-Denis, or the factory bands of Renault. They live dispersed among the males, attached through residence, housework, economic condition, and social standing to certain men—fathers or husbands—more firmly than they are to other women. If they belong to the bourgeoisie, they feel solidarity with men of that class, not with proletarian women; if they are white, their allegiance is to white men, not to Negro women. The proletariat can propose to massacre the ruling class, and a sufficiently fanatical Jew or Negro might dream of getting sole possession of the atomic bomb and making humanity wholly Jewish or black; but woman cannot even dream of exterminating the males. The bond that unites her to her oppressors is not comparable to any other. The division of the sexes is a biological fact, not an event in human history. Male and female stand opposed within a primordial *Mitsein*, and woman has not broken it. The couple is a fundamental unity with its two halves riveted together, and the cleavage of society along the line of sex is impossible. Here is to be found the basic trait of woman: she is the Other in a totality of which the two components are necessary to one another.

One could suppose that this reciprocity might have facilitated the liberation of woman. When Hercules sat at the feet of Omphale and helped with her spinning, his desire for her held him captive; but why did she fail to gain a lasting power? To revenge herself on Jason, Medea killed their children; and this grim legend would seem to suggest that she might have obtained a formidable influence over him through his love for his offsprings. In *Lysistrata* Aristophanes gaily depicts a band of women who joined forces to gain social ends through the sexual needs of their men; but this is only a play. In the legend of the Sabine women, the latter soon abandoned their plan of remaining sterile to punish their ravishers. In truth woman has not been socially emancipated through man's need—sexual desire and the desire for offspring—which makes the male dependent for satisfaction upon the female.

Master and slave, also, are united by a reciprocal need, in this case economic, which does not liberate the slave. In the relation of master to slave the master does not make a point of the need that he has for the other; he has in his grasp the power of satisfying this need through his own action; whereas the slave, in his dependent condition, his hope and fear, is quite conscious of the need he has for his master. Even if the need is at botton equally urgent for both, it always works in favor of the oppressor and against the oppressed. That is why the liberation of the working class, for example, has been slow.

Now, woman has always been man's dependent, if not his slave; the two sexes have never shared the world in equality. And even today woman is heavily handicapped, though her situation is beginning to change. Almost nowhere is her legal status the same as man's,[7] and frequently it is much to her disadvantage. Even when her rights are legally recognized in the abstract, long-standing custom prevents their full expression in the mores. In the economic sphere men and women can almost be said to make up two castes; other things being equal, the former hold the better jobs, get higher wages, and have more opportunity for success than their new competitors. In industry and politics men have a great many more positions and they monopolize the most important posts. In addition to all this, they enjoy a traditional prestige that the education of children tends in every way to support, for the present enshrines the past—and in the past all history has been made by men. At the present time, when women are beginning to take part in the affairs of the world, it is still a world that belongs to men—they have no doubt of it all and women have scarcely any. To decline to be the Other, to refuse to be a party to the deal—this would be for women to renounce all the advantages conferred upon them by their alliance with the superior caste. Man-the-sovereign will provide woman-the-liege with material protection and will undertake the moral justification of her existence; thus she can evade at once both economic risk and the metaphysical risk of a liberty in which ends and aims must be contrived without assistance. Indeed, along with the ethical urge of each individual to affirm his subjective existence, there is also the temptation to forgo liberty and become a thing. This is an inauspicious road, for he who takes it—passive, lost, ruined—becomes henceforth the creature of another's will, frustrated in his transcendence and deprived of every value.

But it is an easy road; on it one avoids the strain involved in undertaking an authentic existence. When man makes of woman the *Other*, he may, then, expect her to manifest deep-seated tendencies toward complicity. Thus, woman may fail to lay claim to the status of subject because she lacks definite resources, because she feels the necessary bond that ties her to man regardless of reciprocity, and because she is often very well pleased with her role as the *Other*.

But it will be asked at once: how did all this begin? It is easy to see that the duality of the sexes, like any duality, gives rise to conflict. And doubtless the winner will assume the status of absolute. But why should man have won from the start? It seems possible that women could have won the victory; or that the outcome of the conflict might never have been decided. How is it that this world has always belonged to the men and that things have begun to change only recently? Is this change a good thing? Will it bring about an equal sharing of the world between men and women?

These questions are not new, and they have often been answered. But the very fact that women *is the Other* tends to cast suspicion upon all the justifications that men have ever been able to provide for it. These have all too evidently been dictated by men's interest.

In particular those who condemned to stagnation are often pronounced happy on the pretext that happiness consists in being at rest. This notion we reject, for our perspective is that of existentialist ethics. Every subject plays his part as such specifically through exploits or projects that serve as a mode of transcendence; he achieves liberty only through a continual reaching out toward other liberties. There is no justification for present existence other than its expansion into an indefinitely open future. Every time transcendence falls back into immanence, stagnation, there is a degradation of existence into the *"en-soi"*—the brutish life of subjection to given conditions—and of liberty into constraint and contingence. This downfall represents a moral fault if the subject consents to it; if it is inflicted upon him, it spells frustration and oppression. In both cases it is an absolute evil. Every individual concerned to justify his existence feels that his existence involves an undefined need to transcend himself, to engage in freely chosen projects.

Now, what peculiarly signalizes the situation of woman is that she—a free and autonomous being like all human creatures—nevertheless finds herself living in a world where men compel her to assume the status of the Other. They propose to stabilize her as object and to doom her to immanence since her transcendence is to be overshadowed and forever transcended by another ego (*conscience*) which is essential and sovereign. The drama of woman lies in this conflict between the fundamental aspirations of every subject (ego)—who always regards the self as the essential—and the compulsions of a situation in which she is the inessential. How can a human being in woman's situation attain fulfillment? What roads are open to her? Which are blocked? How can independence be recovered in a state of dependency? What circumstances limit woman's liberty and how can they be overcome? These are the fundamental questions on which I would fain throw some light. This means that I am interested in the fortunes of the individual as defined not in terms of happiness but in terms of liberty.

Quite evidently this problem would be without significance if we were to believe that woman's destiny is inevitably determined by physiological, psychological, or economic forces. Hence I shall discuss first of all the light in which woman is viewed by biology, psychoanalysis, and historical materialism. Next I shall try to show exactly how the concept of the "truly feminine" has been fashioned—why woman has been defined as the Other—and what have been the consequences from man's point of view. Then from woman's point of view I shall describe the world in which women must live; and thus we shall be able to envisage the difficulties in their way as, endeavoring to make their escape from the sphere hitherto assigned them, they aspire to full membership in the human race.

NOTES

1. *Franchise*, dead today.
2. The Kinsey Report [Alfred C. Kinsey and others: *Sexual Behavior in the Human Male* (W. B. Saunders Co., 1948)] is no exception, for it is limited to describing the sexual characteristics of American men, which is quite a different matter.
3. E. Lévinas does not forget this idea explicitly in his essay *Temps et l'Autre*. "Is there not a case in which otherness, alterity *[altérité]*, unquestionably marks the nature of a being, as its essence, an instance of otherness not consisting purely and simply in the opposition of two species of the same genus? I think that the feminine represents the contrary in its absolute sense, this contrariness being in no wise affected by any relation between it and its correlative and thus remaining absolutely other. Sex is not a certain specific difference . . . no more is the sexual difference a mere contradiction. . . . Nor does this difference lie in the duality of two complementary terms, for two complementary terms imply a pre-existing whole. . . . Otherness reaches its full flowering in the feminine, a term of the same rank as consciousness but of opposite meaning."

   I suppose that Lévinas does not forget that woman, too, is aware of her own consciousness, or ego. But it is striking that he deliberately takes a man's point of view, disregarding the reciprocity of subject and object. When he writes that woman is mystery, he implies that she is mystery for man. Thus his description, which is intended to be objective, is in fact an assertion of masculine privilege.
4. See *C. Lévi-Strauss: Les Structures élementaires de la parenté*. My thanks are due to C. Lévi-Strauss for his kindness in furnishing me with the proofs of his work, which, among others, I have used liberally in Part II.
5. With rare exceptions, perhaps, like certain matriarchal rulers, queens, and the like—Tr.
6. See Part II, ch. viii.
7. At the moment an "equal rights" amendment to the Constitution of the United States is before Congress.

2

SHULAMITH FIRESTONE

The Dialectic of Sex

Sex class is so deep as to be invisible. Or it may appear as a superficial inequality, one that can be solved by merely a few reforms, or perhaps by the full integration of women into the labor force. But the reaction of the common man, woman, and child—"*That? Why you can't change that!* You must be out of your mind!"—is the closest to the truth. We are talking about something every bit as deep as that. This gut reaction—the assumption that, even when they don't know it, feminists are talking about changing a fundamental biological condition—is an honest one. That so profound a change cannot be easily fit into traditional categories of thought, e.g., "political," is not because these categories do not apply but because they are not big enough: radical feminism bursts through them. If there were another word more all-embracing than *revolution* we would use it.

Until a certain level of evolution had been reached and technology had achieved its present sophistication, to question fundamental biological conditions was insanity. Why should a woman give up her precious seat in the cattle car for a bloody struggle she could not hope to win? But, for the first time in some countries, the preconditions for feminist revolution exist—indeed, the situation is beginning to *demand* such a revolution.

The first women are fleeing the massacre, and, shaking, and tottering, are beginning to find each other. Their first move is a careful joint observation, to resensitize a fractured consciousness. This is painful: No matter how many levels of consciousness one reaches, the problem always goes deeper. It is everywhere. The division yin and yang pervades all culture, history, economics, nature itself; modern Western versions of sex discrimination are only the most recent layer. To so heighten one's sensitivity to sexism presents problems far worse than the black militant's new awareness of racism: Feminists have to question, not just all of *Western* culture, but the organization of culture itself, and further, even the very organization of nature. Many women give up in despair: if *that's* how deep it goes they don't want to know. Others continue strengthening and enlarging the movement, their painful sensitivity to female oppression existing for a purpose: eventually to eliminate it.

Before we can act to change a situation, however, we must know how it has arisen and evolved, and through what institutions it now operates. Engels' "[We must] examine the historic succession of events from which the antagonism has sprung in order to discover in the conditions thus created the means of ending the conflict." For feminist revolution we shall need an analysis of the dynamics of sex war as comprehensive as the Marx-Engels analysis of class antagonism was for the economic revolution. More comprehensive. For we are dealing with a larger problem, with an oppression that goes back beyond recorded history to the animal kingdom itself.

In creating such an analysis we can learn a lot from Marx and Engels: Not their literal opinions about women —about the condition of women as an oppressed class they know next to nothing, recognizing it only where it overlaps with economics—but rather their analytic *method*.

Marx and Engels outdid their socialist forerunners in that they developed a method of analysis which was both *dialectical* and *materialist*. The first in centuries to view history dialectically, they saw the world as process, a natural flux of action and reaction, of opposites yet inseparable and interpenetrating. Because they were able to perceive history as movie rather than as snapshot, they attempted to avoid falling into the stagnant "metaphysical" view that had trapped so many other great minds. (This sort of analysis itself may be a product of the sex division, as discussed in Chapter 9.) They combined this view of the dynamic interplay of historical forces with a materialist one, that is, they attempted for the first time to put historical and cultural change on a real basis, to trace the development of economic classes to organic causes. By understanding thoroughly the mechanics of history, they hoped to show men how to master it.

Socialist thinkers prior to Marx and Engels, such as Fourier, Owen, and Bebel, had been able to do no more than moralize about existing social inequalities, positing an ideal world where class privilege and exploitation should not exist—in the same way that early feminist thinkers posited a world where male privilege and exploitation ought not exist—by mere virtue of good will. In both cases, because the early thinkers did not really understand how the social injustice had evolved, maintained itself, or could be eliminated, their ideas existed in a cultural vacuum, utopian. Marx and Engels, on the other hand, attempted a scientific approach to history. They traced the class conflict to its real economic origins, projecting an economic solution based on objective economic preconditions already present: the seizure by the proletariat of the means of production would lead to a communism in which government had withered away, no longer needed to repress the lower class for the sake of the higher. In the classless society the interests of every individual would be synonymous with those of the larger society.

But the doctrine of historical materialism, much as it was a brilliant advance over previous historical analysis, was not the complete answer, as later events bore out. For though Marx and Engels grounded their theory in reality, it was only a *partial* reality. Here is Engels' strictly economic definition of historical materialism from *Socialism: Utopian or Scientific:*

> Historical materialism is that view of the course of history which seeks the *ultimate* cause and the great moving power of all historical events in the economic development of society, in the changes of the modes of production and exchange, in the consequent division of society into distinct classes, and in the struggles of these classes against one another. (Italics mine)

Further, he claims:

> ... that all past history with the exception of the primitive stages was the history of class struggles; that these warring classes of society are always the products of the modes of production and exchange—in a word, of the economic conditions of their time; that the *economic* structure of society always furnishes the real basis, starting from which we can alone work out the *ultimate* explanation of the whole superstructure of juridical and political institutions as well as of the religious, philosophical, and other ideas of a given historical period. (Italics mine)

It would be a mistake to attempt to explain the oppression of women according to this strictly economic interpretation. The class analysis is a beautiful piece of work, but limited: although correct in a linear sense, it does not go deep enough. There is a whole sexual substratum of the historical dialectic that Engels at times dimly perceives, but because he can see sexuality only through an economic filter, reducing everything to that, he is unable to evaluate in its own right.

Engels did observe that the original division of labor was between man and woman for the purposes of child-breeding; that within the family the husband was the owner, the wife the means of production, the children the labor; and that reproduction of the human species was an important economic system distinct from the means of production.

But Engels has been given too much credit for these scattered recognitions of the oppression of women as a class. In fact he acknowledged the sexual class system only where it overlapped and illuminated his economic construct. Engels didn't do so well even in this respect. But Marx was worse: There is a growing recognition of Marx's bias against women (a cultural bias shared by Freud as well as all men of culture), dangerous if one attempts to squeeze feminism into an orthodox Marxist framework— freezing what were only incidental insights of Marx and Engels about sex class into dogma. Instead, we must enlarge historical materialism to *include* the strictly Marxian, in the same way that the physics of relativity did not invalidate Newtonian physics so much as it drew a circle around it, limiting its application—but only through comparison—to a smaller sphere. For an economic diagnosis traced to ownership of the means of production, even of the means of *re*production, does not explain everything. There is a level of reality that does not stem directly from economics.

The assumption that, beneath economics, reality is psychosexual is often rejected as ahistorical by those who accept a dialectical materialist view of history because it seems to land us back where Marx began: groping through a fog of utopian hypotheses, philosophical systems that might be right, that might be wrong (there is no way to tell), systems that explain concrete historical developments by *a priori* categories of thought; historical materialism, however, attempted to explain "knowing" by "being" and not vice versa.

But there is still an untried third alternative: We can attempt to develop a materialist view of history based on sex itself.

The early feminist theorists were to a materialist view of sex what Fourier, Bebel, and Owen were to a materialist view of class. By and large, feminist theory has been as inadequate as were the early feminist attempts to correct sexism. This was to be expected. The problem is so immense that, at first try, only the surface could be skimmed, the most blatant inequalities described. Simone de Beauvoir was the only one who came close to—who perhaps has done—the definitive analysis. Her profound work *The Second Sex*—which appeared as recently as the early fifties to a world convinced that feminism was dead—for the first time attempted to ground feminism in its historical base. Of all feminist theorists De Beauvoir is the most comprehensive and far-reaching, relating feminism to the best ideas in our culture.

It may be this virtue is also her one failing: she is almost too sophisticated, too knowledgeable. Where this becomes a weakness—and this is still certainly debatable—is in her rigidly existentialist interpretation of feminism (one wonders how much Sartre had to do with this). This in view of the fact that all cultural systems, including existentialism, are themselves determined by the sex dualism. She says:

> Man never thinks of himself without thinking of the Other; he views the world under the sign of duality *which is not in the first place sexual in character*. But being different from man, who sets himself up as the Same, it is naturally to the category of the Other that woman is consigned; the Other includes woman. (Italics mine.)

Perhaps she has overshot her mark: Why postulate a fundamental Hegelian concept of Otherness as the final explanation—and then carefully document the biological and historical circumstances that have pushed the class "women" into such a category—when one has never seriously considered the much simpler and more likely possibility that this fundamental dualism sprang from the sexual division itself? To posit *a priori* categories of thought and existence—"Otherness," "Transcendence," "Immanence"—into which history then falls may not be necessary. Marx and Engels had discovered that these philosophical categories themselves grew out of history.

Before assuming such categories, let us first try to develop an analysis in which biology itself—procreation—is at the origin of the dualism. The immediate assumption of the layman that the unequal division of the sexes is "natural" may be well-founded. We need not immediately look beyond this. Unlike economic class, sex class sprang directly from a biological reality: men and women were created different, and not equally privileged. Although, as De Beauvoir points out, this difference of itself did not necessitate the development of a class system—the domination of one group by another—the reproductive *functions* of these differences did. The biological family is an inherently unequal power distribution. The need for power leading to the development of classes arises from the psychosexual formation of each individual according to this basic imbalance, rather than, as Freud, Norman O. Brown and others have, once again overshooting their mark, postulated, some irreducible conflict of Life against Death, Eros vs. Thanatos.

The *biological family*—the basic reproductive unit of male/female/infant, in whatever form of social organization—is characterized by these fundamental—if not immutable—facts:

1) That women throughout history before the advent of birth control were at the continual mercy of their biology—menstruation, menopause, and "female ills," constant painful childbirth, wetnursing and care of infants, all of which made them dependent on males (whether brother, father, husband, lover, or clan, government, community-at-large) for physical survival.
2) That human infants take an even longer time to grow up than animals, and thus are helpless and, for some short period at least, dependent on adults for physical survival.
3) That a basic mother/child interdependency has existed in some form in every society, past or present, and thus has shaped the psychology of every mature female and every infant.
4) That the natural reproductive difference between the sexes led directly to the first division of labor at the origins of class, as well as furnishing the paradigm of caste (discrimination based on biological characteristics).

These biological contingencies of the human family cannot be covered over with anthropological sophistries. Anyone observing animals mating, reproducing, and caring for their young will have a hard time accepting the "cultural relativity" line. For no matter how many tribes in Oceania you can find where the connection of the father to fertility is not known, no matter how many matrilineages, no matter how many cases of sex-role reversal, male housewifery, or even empathic labor pains, these facts prove only one thing: the amazing *flexibility* of human nature. But human nature is adaptable to something, it is, yes, determined by its environmental conditions. And the biological family that we have described has existed everywhere throughout time. Even in matriachies where woman's fertility is worshipped, and the father's role is unknown or unimportant, if perhaps not on the genetic father, there is still some dependence of the female and the infant on the male. And though it is true that the nuclear family is only a recent development, one which, as I shall attempt to show, only intensifies the psychological penalties of the biological family, though it is true that throughout history there have been many variations on this biological family, the contingencies I have described existed in all of them, causing specific psychosexual distortions in the human personality.

But to grant that the sexual imbalance of power is biologically based is not to lose our case. We are no longer just animals. And the Kingdom of Nature does not reign absolute. As Simone de Beauvior herself admits:

> The theory of historical materialism has brought to light some important truths. Humanity is not an animal species, it is a historical reality. Human society is an antiphysis—in a sense it is against nature; it does not passively submit to the presence of nature but rather takes over the control of nature on its own behalf. This arrogation is not an inward, subjective operation; it is accomplished objectively in practical action.

Thus, the "natural" is not necessarily a "human" value. Humanity has begun to outgrow nature: we can no longer justify the maintenance of a discriminatory sex class system on grounds of its origins in Nature. Indeed, for pragmatic reasons alone it is beginning to look as if we *must* get rid of it (see Chapter 10).

The problem becomes political, demanding more than a comprehensive historical analysis, when one realizes that, though man is increasingly capable of freeing himself from the biological conditions that created his tyranny over women and children, he has little reason to want to give this tyranny up. As Engels said, in the context of economic revolution:

> It is the law of division of labor that lies at the basis of the division into classes [Note that this division itself grew out of a fundamental biological division]. But this does not prevent the ruling class, once having the upper hand, from consolidating its power at the expense of the working class, from turning its social leadership into an intensified exploitation of the masses.

Though the sex class system may have originated in fundamental biological conditions, this does not guarantee once the biological basis of their oppression has been swept away that women and children will be freed. On the contrary, the new technology, especially fertility control, may be used against them to reinforce the entrenched system of exploitation.

So that just as to assure elimination of economic classes requires the revolt of the underclass (the proletariat) and, in a temporary dictatorship, their seizure of the means of *production*, so to assure the elimination of sexual classes requires the revolt of the underclass (women) and the seizure of control of *reproduction*: not only the full restoration to women of ownership of their own bodies, but also their (temporary) seizure of control of human fertility—the new population biology as well as all the social institutions of childbearing and childrearing: And just as the end goal of socialist revolution was not only the elimination of the economic class *privilege* but of the economic class *distinction* itself, so the end goal of feminist revolution must be, unlike that of the first feminist movement, not just the elimination of male *privilege* but of the sex *distinction* itself: genital differences between human beings would no longer matter culturally. (A reversion to an unobstructed *pansexuality*—Freud's "polymorphous perversity"—would probably supersede hetero/homo/bi-sexuality.) The reproduction of the species by one sex for the benefit of both would be replaced by (at least the option of) artificial reproduction: children would be born to both sexes equally, or independently of either, however one chooses to look at it; the dependence of the child on the mother (and vice versa) would give way to a greatly shortened dependence on a small group of others in general, and any remaining inferiority to adults in physical strength would be compensated for culturally. The division of labor would be ended by the elimination of labor altogether (cybernation). The tyranny of the biological family would be broken.

And with it the psychology of power. As Engels claimed for strictly socialist revolution:

> The existence of not simply this or that ruling class but of any ruling class at all [will have] become an obsolete anachronism.

That socialism has never come near achieving this predicated goal is not only the result of unfulfilled or misfired economic preconditions, but also because the Marxian analysis itself was insufficient: it did not dig deep enough to the psychosexual roots of class. Marx was onto something more profound than he knew when he observed that the family contained within itself in embryo all the antagonisms that later develop on a wide scale within the society and the state. For unless revolution uproots the basic social organization, the biological family—the vinculum through which the psychology of power can always be smuggled—the tapeworm of exploitation will never be annihilated. We shall need a sexual revolution much larger than—inclusive of—a socialist one to truly eradicate all class systems.

* * *

I have attempted to take the class analysis one step further to its roots in the biological division of the sexes. We have not thrown out the insights of the socialists; on the contrary, radical feminism can enlarge their analysis, granting it an even deeper basis in objective conditions and thereby explaining many of its insolubles. As a first step in this direction, and as the groundwork for our own analysis we shall expand Engels' definition of historical materialism. Here is the same definition quoted above now rephrased to include the biological division of the sexes for the purpose of reproduction, which lies at the origins of class:

> Historical materialism is that view of the course of history which seeks the ultimate cause and the great moving power of all historic events in the dialectic of sex: the division of society into two distinct biological classes for procreative reproduction, and the struggles of these classes with one another; in the changes in the modes of marriage, reproduction and childcare created by these struggles; in the connected development of other physically-differentiated classes [castes]; and in the

first division of labor based on sex which developed into the [economic-cultural] class system.

And here is the cultural superstructure, as well as the economic one, traced not just back to (economic) class, but all the way back to sex:

> All past history [note that we can now eliminate "with the exception of primitive stages"] was the history of class struggle. These warring classes of society are always the product of the modes of organization of the biological family unit for reproduction of the species, as well as of the strictly economic modes of production and exchange of goods and services. The sexual-reproductive organization of society always furnishes the real basis, starting from which we can alone work out the ultimate explanation of the whole superstructure of economic, juridical and political institutions as well as of the religious, philosophical and other ideas of a given historical period.

And now Engels' projection of the results of a materialist approach to history is more realistic:

> The whole sphere of the conditions of life which environ man and have hitherto ruled him now comes under the dominion and control of man who for the first time becomes the real conscious Lord of Nature, master of his own social organization.

In the following chapters we shall assume this definition of historical materialism, examining the cultural institutions that maintain and reinforce the biological family (especially its present manifestation, the nuclear family) and its result, the power psychology, an aggressive chauvinism now developed enough to destroy us. We shall integrate this with a feminist analysis of Freudianism: for Freud's cultural bias, like that of Marx and Engels, does not invalidate his perception entirely. In fact, Freud had insights of even greater value than those of the socialist theorists for the building of a new dialectical materialism based on sex. We shall attempt, then, to correlate the best of Engels and Marx (the historical materialist approach) with the best of Freud (the understanding of the inner man and woman and what shapes them) to arrive at a solution both political and personal yet grounded in real conditions. We shall see that Freud observed the dynamics of psychology correctly in their immediate social context, but because the fundamental structure of that social context was basic to all humanity— to different degrees—it appeared to be nothing less than an absolute existential condition which it would be insane to question—forcing Freud and many of his followers to postulate a *priori* constructs like the Death Wish to explain the origins of these universal psychological drives. This in turn made the sicknesses of humanity irreducible and uncurable—which is why his proposed solution (psychoanalytic therapy), a contradiction in terms, was so weak compared to the rest of his work, and such a resounding failure in practice—causing those of social/political sensibility to reject not only his therapeutic solution, but his most profound discoveries as well.

3

GAYLE RUBIN

The Traffic in Women

Notes on the "Political Economy" of Sex

The literature on women—both feminist and anti-feminist—is a long rumination on the question of the nature and genesis of women's oppression and social subordination. The question is not a trivial one, since the answers given it determine our visions of the future, and our evaluation of whether or not it is realistic to hope for a sexually egalitarian society. More importantly, the analysis of the causes of women's oppression forms the basis for any assessment of just what would have to be changed in order to achieve a society without gender hierarchy. Thus, if innate male aggression and dominance are at the root of female oppression, then the feminist program would logically require either the extermination of the offending sex, or else a eugenics project to modify its character. If sexism is a by-product of capitalism's relentless appetite for profit, then sexism would wither away in the advent of a successful socialist revolution. If the world historical defeat of women occurred at the hands of an armed patriarchal revolt, then it is time for Amazon guerrillas to start training in the Adirondacks.

It lies outside the scope of this paper to conduct a sustained critique of some of the currently popular explanations of the genesis of sexual inequality—theories such as the popular evolution exemplified by *The Imperial Animal*, the alleged overthrow of prehistoric matriarchies, or the attempt to extract all of the phenomena of social subordination from the first volume of *Capital*. Instead, I want to sketch some elements of an alternate explanation of the problem.

Marx once asked: "What is a Negro slave? A man of the black race. The one explanation is as good as the other. A Negro is a Negro. He only becomes a slave in certain relations. A cotton spinning jenny is a machine for spinning cotton. It becomes *capital* only in certain relations. Torn from these relationships it is no more capital than gold in itself is money or sugar is the price of sugar" (Marx, 1971b:28). One might paraphrase: What is a domesticated woman? A female of the species. The one explanation is as good as the other. A woman is a woman. She only becomes a domestic, a wife, a chattel, a playboy bunny, a prostitute, or a human dictaphone in certain relations. Torn from these relationships, she is no more the helpmate of man than gold in itself is money . . . etc. What then are these relationships by which a female becomes an oppressed woman? The place to begin to unravel the system of relationships by which women become the prey of men is in the overlapping works of Claude Lévi-Strauss and Sigmund Freud. The domestication of women, under other names, is discussed at length in both of their *oeuvres*. In reading through these works, one begins to have a sense of a systematic social apparatus which takes up females as raw materials and fashions domesticated women as products. Neither Freud nor Lévi-Strauss sees his work in this light, and certainly neither turns a critical glance upon the processes he describes. Their analyses and descriptions must be read, therefore, in something like the way in which Marx read the classical political economists who preceded him (on this, see Althusser and Balibar, 1970:11–69). Freud and Lévi-Strauss are in some sense analogous to Ricardo and Smith: They see neither the implications of what they are saying, nor the implicit critique which their work can generate when subjected to a feminist eye. Nevertheless, they provide conceptual tools with which one can build descriptions of the part of social life which is the locus of the oppression of women, of sexual minorities, and of certain aspects of human personality within individuals. I call that part of social life the "sex/gender system," for lack of a more elegant term. As a preliminary definition, a "sex/gender system" is the set of arrangements by which a society transforms biological sexuality into products of human activity, and in which these transformed sexual needs are satisfied.

The purpose of this essay is to arrive at a more fully developed definition of the sex/gender system, by way of a somewhat idiosyncratic and exegetical reading of Lévi-Strauss and Freud. I use the word "exegetical" deliberately. The dictionary defines "exegesis" as a "critical explanation or analysis; especially, interpretation of the Scriptures." At times, my reading of Lévi-Strauss and Freud is freely interpretive, moving from the explicit content of a text to its presuppositions and implications. My reading of certain psychoanalytic texts is filtered through a lens provided by Jacques Lacan, whose own interpretation of the Freudian scripture has been heavily influenced by Lévi-Strauss.[1]

I will return later to a refinement of the definition of a sex/gender system. First, however, I will try to demonstrate the need for such a concept by discussing the failure of classical Marxism to fully express or conceptualize sex oppression. This failure results from the fact that Marxism, as a theory of social life, is relatively unconcerned with sex. In Marx's map of the social world, human beings are workers, peasants, or capitalists; that they are also men and women is not seen as very significant. By con trast, in the maps of social reality drawn by Freud and Lévi-Strauss, there is a deep recognition of the place of sexuality in society, and of the profound differences between the social experience of man and women.

MARX

There is no theory which accounts for the oppression of women—in its endless variety and monotonous similarity, cross-culturally and throughout history—with anything like the explanatory power of the Marxist theory of class oppression. Therefore, it is not surprising that there have been numerous attempts to apply Marxist analysis to the question of women. There are many ways of doing this. It has been argued that women are a reserve labor force for capitalism, that women's generally lower wages provide extra surplus to a capitalist employer, that women serve the ends of capitalist consumerism in their roles as administrators of family consumption, and so forth.

However, a number of articles have tried to do something much more ambitious—to locate the oppression of women in the heart of the capitalist dynamic by pointing to the relationship between housework and the reproduction of labor (see Benston, 1969; Dalla Costa, 1972; Larguia and Dumoulin, 1972; Gerstein, 1973; Vogel, 1973; Secombe, 1974; Gardiner, 1974; Rowntree, M. & J., 1970). To do this is to place women squarely in the definition of capitalism, the process in which capital is produced by the extraction of surplus value from labor by capital.

Briefly, Marx argued that capitalism is distinguished from all other modes of production by its unique aim: the creation and expansion of capital. Whereas other modes of production might find their purpose in making useful things to satisfy human needs, or in producing a surplus for a ruling nobility, or in producing to insure sufficient sacrifice for the edification of the gods, capitalism produces capital. Capitalism is a set of social relations—forms of property, and so forth—in which production takes the form of turning money, things, and people into capital. And capital is a quantity of goods or money which, when exchanged for labor, reproduces and augments itself by extracting unpaid labor, or surplus value, from labor and into itself.

> The result of the capitalist production process is neither a mere product (use-value) nor a *commodity*, that is, a use-value which has exchange value. Its result, its product, is the creation of *surplus-value* for capital, and consequently the actual *transformation* of money or commodity into capital. . . ." (Marx, 1969:399; italics in the original)

The exchange between capital and labor which produces surplus value, and hence capital, is highly specific. The worker gets a wage; the capitalist gets the things the worker has made during his or her time of employment. If the total value of the things the worker has made exceeds the value of his or her wage, the aim of capitalism has been achieved. The capitalist gets back the cost of the wage, plus an increment—surplus value. This can occur because the wage is determined not by the value of what the laborer makes, but by the value of what it takes to keep him or her going—to reproduce him or her form day to day, and to reproduce the entire work force from one generation to the next. Thus, surplus value is the difference between what the laboring class produces as a whole, and the amount of that total which is recycled into maintaining the laboring class.

> The capital given in exchange for labour power is converted into necessaries, by the consumption of which the muscles, nerves, bones, and brains of existing labourers are reproduced, and new labourers are begotten . . . the individual consumption of the labourer, whether it proceed within the workshop or outside it, whether it be part of the process of production or not, forms therefore a factor of the production and reproduction of capital; just as cleaning machinery does. . . . (Marx, 1972:572)

> Given the individual, the production of labour-power consists in his reproduction of himself or his maintenance. For his maintenance he requires a given quantity of the means of subsistence. . . . Labour-power sets itself in action only by working. But thereby a definite quantity of human muscle, brain, nerve, etc., is wasted, and these require to be restored. . . . (ibid.:171)

The amount of the difference between the reproduction of labor power and its products depends, therefore, on the determination of what it takes to reproduce that labor power. Marx tends to make that determination on the basis of the quantity of commodities—food, clothing, housing, fuel—which would be necessary to maintain the health, life, and strength of a worker. But these commodities must be consumed before they can be sustenance, and they are not immediately in consumable form when they are purchased by the wage. Additional labor must be performed upon these things before they can be turned into people. Food must be cooked, clothes cleaned, beds made, wood chopped, etc. Housework is therefore a key element in the process of the reproduction of the laborer from whom surplus value is taken. Since it is usually women who do housework, it has been observed that it is through the reproduction of labor power that women are articulated into the surplus value nexus which is the *sine qua non* of capitalism.[2] It can be further argued that since no wage is paid for housework, the labor of women in the home contributes to the ultimate quantity of surplus value realized by the capitalist. But to explain women's usefulness to capitalism is one thing. To argue that this usefulness explains the genesis of the oppression of women is quite another. It is precisely at this point that the analysis of capitalism ceases to explain very much about women and the oppression of women.

Women are oppressed in societies which can by no stretch of the imagination be described as capitalist. In the Amazon valley and the New Guinea highlands, women are frequently kept in their place by gang rape when the ordinary mechanisms of masculine intimidation prove insufficient. "We tame our women with the banana," said one Mundurucu man (Murphy, 1959:195). The ethnographic record is littered with practices whose effect is to keep women "in their place"—men's cults, secret initiations, arcane male knowledge, etc. And pre-capitalist, feudal Europe was hardly a society in which there was no sexism. Capitalism has taken over, and rewired, notions of male and female which predate it by centuries. No analysis of the reproduction of labor power under capitalism can explain foot-binding, chastity belts, or any of the incredible array of Byzantine, fetishized indignities, let alone the more ordinary ones, which have been inflicted upon women in various times and places. The analysis of the reproduction of labor power does not even explain why it is usually women who do domestic work in the home, rather than men.

In this light it is interesting to return to Marx's discussion of the reproduction of labor. What is necessary to reproduce the worker is determined in part by the biological needs of the human organism, in part by the physical conditions of the place in which it lives, and in part by cultural tradition. Marx observed that beer is necessary for the reproduction of the English working class, and wine necessary for the French.

> ... *the number and extent of his [the worker's] so-called necessary wants, as also the modes of satisfying them, are themselves the product of historical development*, and depend therefore to a great extent on the degree of civilization of a country, more particularly on the conditions under which, and consequently on the habits and degree of comfort in which, the class of free labourers has been formed. *In contradistinction therefore to the case of other commodities, there enters into the determination of the value of labour-power a historical and moral element....* (Marx, 1972:171, my italics)

It is precisely this "historical and moral element" which determines that a "wife" is among the necessities of a worker, that women rather than men do housework, and that capitalism is heir to a long tradition in which women do not inherit, in which women do not lead, and in which women do not talk to god. It is this "historical and moral element" which presented capitalism with a cultural heritage of forms of masculinity and femininity. It is within this "historical and moral element" that the entire domain of sex, sexuality, and sex oppression is subsumed. And the briefness of Marx's comment only serves to emphasize the vast area of social life which it covers and leaves unexamined. Only by subjecting this "historical and moral element" to analysis can the structure of sex oppression be delineated.

ENGELS

In *The Origin of the Family, Private Property, and the State,* Engels sees sex oppression as part of capitalism's heritage from prior social forms. Moreover, Engles integrates sex and sexuality into his theory of society. *Origin* is a frustrating book. Like the nineteenth-century tomes on the history of marriage and the family which it echoes, the state of the evidence in *Origin* renders it quaint to a reader familiar with more recent developments in anthropology. Nevertheless, it is a book whose considerable insight should not be over-shadowed by its limitations. The idea that the "relations of sexuality" can and should be distinguished from the "relations of production" is not the least of Engels' intuitions:

> According to the materialistic conception, the determining factor in history is, in the final instance, the production and reproduction of immediate life. *This again, is of a*

twofold character: on the one hand, the production of the means of existence, of food, clothing, and shelter and the tools necessary for that production; on the other side, the production of human beings themselves, the propagation of the species. The social organization under which the people of a particular historical epoch and a particular country live is determined by both kinds of production: by the stage of development of labor on the one hand, and of the family on the other . . . (Engels, 1972: 71–72; my italics)

This passage indicates an important recognition—that a human group must do more than apply its activity to reshaping the natural world in order to clothe, feed, and warm itself. We usually call the system by which elements of the natural world are transformed into objects of human consumption the "economy." But the needs which are satisfied by economic activity even in the richest, Marxian sense, do not exhaust fundamental human requirements. A human group must also reproduce itself from generation to generation. The needs of sexuality and procreation must be satisfied as much as the need to eat, and one of the most obvious deductions which can be made from the data of anthropology is that these needs are hardly ever satisfied in any "natural" form, any more than are the needs for food. Hunger is hunger, but what counts as food is culturally determined and obtained. Every society has some form of organized economic activity. Sex is sex, but what counts as sex is equally culturally determined and obtained. Every society also has a sex/gender system—a set of arrangements by which the biological raw material of human sex and procreation is shaped by human, social intervention and satisfied in a conventional manner, no matter how bizarre some of the conventions may be.[3]

The realm of human sex, gender, and procreation has been subjected to, and changed by, relentless social activity for millennia. Sex as we know it—gender identity, sexual desire and fantasy, concepts of childhood—is itself a social product. We need to understand the relations of its production, and forget, for awhile, about food, clothing, automobiles, and transistor radios. In most Marxist tradition, and even in Engels' book, the concept of the "second aspect of material life" has tended to fade into the background, or to be incorporated into the usual notions of "material life." Engels' suggestion has never been followed up and subjected to the refinement which it needs. But he does indicate the existence and importance of the domain of social life which I want to call the sex/gender system.

Other names have been proposed for the sex/gender system. The most common alternatives are "mode of reproduction" and "patriarchy." It may be foolish to quibble about terms, but both of these can lead to confusion. All three proposals have been made in order to introduce a distinction between "economic" systems and "sexual" systems, and to indicate that sexual systems have a certain autonomy and cannot always be explained in terms of economic forces. "Mode of reproduction," for instance, has been proposed in opposition to the more familiar "mode of production." But this terminology links the "economy" to production, and the sexual system to "reproduction." It reduces the richness of either system, since "productions" and "reproductions" take place in both. Every mode of production involves reproduction—of tools, labor, and social relations. We cannot relegate all of the multi-faceted aspects of social reproduction to the sex system. Replacement of machinery is an example of reproduction in the economy. On the other hand, we cannot limit the sex system to "reproduction" in either the social or biological sense of the term. A sex/gender system is not simply the reproductive moment of a "mode of production." The formation of gender identity is an example of production in the realm of the sexual system. And a sex/gender system involves more than the "relations of procreation," reproduction in the biological sense.

The term "patriarchy" was introduced to distinguish the forces maintaining sexism from other social forces, such as capitalism. But the use of "patriarchy" obscures other distinctions. Its use is analogous to using capitalism to refer to all modes of production, whereas the usefulness of the term "capitalism" lies precisely in that it distinguishes between the different systems by which societies are provisioned and organized. Any society will have some system of "political economy." Such a system may be egalitarian or socialist. It may be class stratified, in which case the oppressed class may consist of serfs, peasants, or slaves. The oppressed class may consist of wage laborers, in which case the system is properly labeled "capitalist." The power of the term lies in its implication that, in fact, there are alternatives to capitalism.

Similarly, any society will have some systematic ways to deal with sex, gender, and babies. Such a system may be sexually egalitarian, at least in theory, or it may be "gender stratified," as seems to be the case for most or all of the known examples. But it is important—even in the face of a depressing history—to maintain a distinction between the human capacity and necessity to create a sexual world, and the empirically oppressive ways in which sexual worlds have been organized. Patriarchy subsumes both meanings into the same term. Sex/gender system, on the other hand, is a neutral term which refers to the domain and indicates that oppression is not inevitable in that domain, but is the product of the specific social relations which organize it.

Finally, there are gender-stratified systems which are not adequately described as patriarchal. Many New Guinea societies (Enga, Maring, Bena Bena, Huli, Melpa, Kuma, Gahuku-Gama, Fore, Marind Anim, ad nauseum; see Berndt, 1962; Langness, 1967; Rappaport, 1975; Read, 1952; Meggitt, 1970; Glasse, 1971; Strathern, 1972; Reay, 1959; Van Baal, 1966; Lindenbaum, 1973) are viciously oppressive to women. But the power of males in these groups is not founded on their roles as fathers or patriarchs, but on their collective adult maleness, embodied in secret cults, men's houses, warfare, exchange networks, ritual knowledge, and various initiation procedures. Patriarchy is a specific form of male dominance, and the use of the term ought to be confined to the Old Testament-type pastoral nomads from whom the term comes, or groups like them. Abraham was a Patriarch—one old man whose absolute power over wives, children, herds, and dependents was an aspect of the institution of fatherhood, as defined in the social group in which he lived.

Whichever term we use, what is important is to develop concepts to adequately describe the social organization of sexuality and the reproduction of the conventions of sex and gender. We need to pursue the project Engels abandoned when he located the subordination of women in a development within the mode of production.[4] To do this, we can imitate Engels in his method rather than in his results. Engels approached the task of analyzing the "second aspect of material life" by way of an examination of a theory of kinship systems. Kinship systems are and do many things. But they are made up of, and reproduce, concrete forms of socially organized sexuality. Kinship systems are observable and empirical forms of sex/gender systems.

KINSHIP

(On the part played by sexuality
 in the transition from ape to "man")

To an anthropologist, a kinship system is not a list of biological relatives. It is a system of categories and statuses which often contradict actual genetic relationships. There are dozens of examples in which socially defined kinship statuses take precedence over biology. The Nuer custom of "woman marriage" is a case in point. The Nuer define the status of fatherhood as belonging to the person in whose name cattle bridewealth is given for the mother. Thus, a woman can be married to another woman, and be husband to the wife and father of her children, despite the fact that she is not the inseminator (Evans-Pritchard, 1951:107–09).

In pre-state societies, kinship is the idiom of social interaction, organizing economic, political, and ceremonial, as well as sexual, activity. One's duties, responsibilities, and privileges vis-à-vis others are defined in terms of mutual kinship or lack thereof. The exchange of goods and services, production and distribution, hostility and solidarity, ritual and ceremony, all take place within the organizational structure of kinship. The ubiquity and adaptive effectiveness of kinship has led many anthropologists to consider its invention, along with the invention of language, to have been the developments which decisively marked the discontinuity between semi-human hominids and human beings (Sahlins, 1960; Livingstone, 1969; Lévi-Strauss, 1969).

While the idea of the importance of kinship enjoys the status of a first principle in anthropology, the internal workings of kinship systems have long been a focus for intense controversy. Kinship systems vary wildly from one culture to the next. They contain all sorts of bewildering rules which govern whom one may or may not marry. Their internal complexity is dazzling. Kinship systems have for decades provoked the anthropological imagination into trying to explain incest taboos, cross-cousin marriage, terms of descent, relationships of avoidance or forced intimacy, clans and sections, taboos on names—the diverse array of items found in descriptions of actual kinship systems. In the nineteenth century, several thinkers attempted to write comprehensive accounts of the nature and history of human sexual systems (see Fee, 1973). One of these was *Ancient Society*, by Lewis Henry Morgan. It was this book which inspired Engels to write *The Origin of the Family, Private Property, and the State*. Engels' theory is based upon Morgan's account of kinship and marriage.

In taking up Engels' project of extracting a theory of sex oppression from the study of kinship, we have the advantage of the maturation of ethnology since the nineteenth century. We also have the advantage of a peculiar and particularly appropriate book, Lévi-Strauss' *The Elementary Structures of Kinship*. This is the boldest twentieth-century version of the nineteenth-century project to understand human marriage. It is a book in which kinship is explicitly conceived of as an imposition of cultural organization upon the facts of biological procreation. It is permeated with an awareness of the importance of sexuality in human society. It is a description of society which does not assume an abstract, genderless human subject. On the contrary, the human subject in Lévi-Strauss's work is always either male or female, and the divergent social destinies of the two sexes can therefore be traced. Since Lévi-Strauss sees the essence of kinship systems to lie in an exchange of women between men, he constructs an implicit theory of sex oppression. Aptly, the book is dedicated to the memory of Lewis Henry Morgan.

> "Vile and precious merchandise"
> —Monique Wittig

The Elementary Structures of Kinship is a grand statement on the origin and nature of human society. It is a treatise on the kinship systems of approximately one-third of the ethnographic globe. Most fundamentally, it is an attempt to discern the structural principles of kinship. Lévi-Strauss argues that the application of these principles (summarized in the last chapter of *Elementary Structures*) to kinship data reveals an intelligible logic to the taboos and marriage rules which have perplexed and mystified Western anthropologists. He constructs a chess game of such complexity that it cannot be recapitulated here. But two of his chess pieces are particularly relevant to women—the "gift" and the incest taboo, whose dual articulation adds up to his concept of the exchange of women.

The Elementary Structures is in part a radical gloss on another famous theory of primitive social organization, Mauss' *Essay on the Gift* (See also Sahlins, 1972: Chap. 4). It was Mauss who first theorized as to the significance of one of the most striking features of primitive societies: the extent to which giving, receiving, and reciprocating gifts dominates social intercourse. In such societies, all sorts of things circulate in exchange—food, spells, rituals, words, names, ornaments, tools, and powers.

> Your own mother, your own sister, your own pigs, your own yams that you have piled up, you may not eat. Other people's mothers, other people's sisters, other people's pigs, other people's yams that they have piled up, you may eat. (Arapesh, cited in Lévi-Strauss, 1969:27)

In a typical gift transaction, neither party gains anything. In the Trobriand Islands, each household maintains a garden of yams and each household eats yams. But the yams a household grows and the yams it eats are not the same. At harvest time, a man sends the yams he has cultivated to the household of his sister; the household in which he lives is provisioned by his wife's brother (Malinowski, 1929). Since such a procedure appears to be a useless one from the point of view of accumulation or trade, its logic has been sought elsewhere. Mauss proposed that the significance of gift giving is that it expresses, affirms, or creates a social link between the partners of an exchange. Gift giving confers upon its participants a special relationship of trust, solidarity, and mutual aid. One can solicit a friendly relationship in the offer of a gift; acceptance implies a willingness to return a gift and a confirmation of the relationship. Gift exchange may also be the idiom of competition and rivalry. There are many examples in which one person humiliates another by giving more than can be reciprocated. Some political systems, such as the Big Man systems of highland New Guinea, are based on exchange which is unequal on the material plane. An aspiring Big Man wants to give away more goods than can be reciprocated. He gets his return in political prestige.

Although both Mauss and Lévi-Strauss emphasize the solidary aspects of gift exchange, the other purposes served by gift giving only strengthen the point that it is an ubiquitous means of social commerce. Mauss proposed that gifts were the threads of social discourse, the means by which such societies were held together in the absence of specialized governmental institutions. "The gift is the primitive way of achieving the peace that in civil society is secured by the state. . . . Composing society, the gift was the liberation of culture" (Sahlins, 1972:169, 175).

Lévi-Strauss adds to the theory of primitive reciprocity the idea that marriages are a most basic form of gift exchange, in which it is women who are the most precious of gifts. He argues that the incest taboo should best be understood as a mechanism to insure that such exchanges take place between families and between groups. Since the existence of incest taboos is universal, but the content of their prohibitions variable, they cannot be explained as having the aim of preventing the occurrence of genetically close matings. Rather, the incest taboo imposes the social aim of exogamy and alliance upon the biological events of sex and procreation. The incest taboo divides the universe of sexual choice into categories of permitted and prohibited sexual partners. Specifically, by forbidding unions within a group it enjoins marital exchange between groups.

> The prohibition on the sexual use of a daughter or a sister compels them to be given in marriage to another man, and at the same time it establishes a right to the daughter or sister of this other man. . . . The woman whom one does not take is, for that very reason, offered up. (Lévi-Strauss, 1969:51)

> The prohibition of incest is less a rule prohibiting marriage with the mother, sister, or daughter, than a rule obliging the mother, sister, or daughter to be given to others. It is the supreme rule of the gift. . . . (Ibid.:481)

The result of a gift of women is more profound than the result of other gift transactions, because the relationship thus established is not just one of reciprocity, but one of kinship. The exchange partners have become affines, and their descendents will be related by blood: "Two people may meet in friendship and exchange gifts and yet quarrel and fight in later times, but intermarriage connects them in a permanent manner" (Best, cited in Lévi-Strauss, 1969:481). As is the case with other gift giving, marriages are not always so simply activities to make peace. Marriages may be highly competitive, and there are plenty of affines who fight each other. Nevertheless, in a general sense the argument is that the taboo on incest results in a wide network of relations, a set of people whose connections with one another are a kinship structure. All other levels, amounts, and directions of exchange—including hostile ones—are ordered by this structure. The marriage ceremonies recorded in the ethnographic literature are moments in a ceaseless and ordered procession in which women, children, shells, words, cattle names, fish, ancestors, whale's teeth, pigs, yams, spells, dances, mats, etc., pass from hand to hand, leaving as their tracks the ties that bind. Kinship is organization, and organization gives power. But who is organized?

If it is women who are being transacted, then it is the men who give and take them who are linked, the woman being a conduit of a relationship rather than a partner to it.[5] The exchange of women does not necessarily imply that women are objectified, in the modern sense, since objects in the primitive world are imbued with highly personal qualities. But it does imply a distinction between gift and giver. If women are the gifts, then it is men who are the exchange partners. And it is the partners, not the presents, upon whom reciprocal exchange confers its quasi-mystical power of social linkage. The relations of such a system are such that women are in no position to realize the benefits of their own circulation. As long as the relations specify that men exchange women, it is men who are the beneficiaries of the product of such exchanges—social organization.

> The total relationship of exchange which constitutes marriage is not established between a man and a woman, but between two groups of men, and the woman figures only as one of the objects in the exchange, not as one of the partners. . . . This remains true even when the girl's feelings are taken into consideration, as, moreover, is usually the case. In acquiescing to the proposed union, she precipitates or allows the exchange to take place, she cannot alter its nature. . . . (Lévi-Strauss in ibid.:115)[6]

To enter into a gift exchange as a partner, one must have something to give. If women are for men to dispose of, they are in no position to give themselves away.

> "What woman," mused a young Northern Melpa man, "is ever strong enough to get up and say, 'Let us make *moka*, let us find wives and pigs, let us give our daughters to men, let us wage war, let us kill our enemies!' No indeed not! . . .they are little rubbish things who stay at home simply, don't you see?" (Strathern, 1972:161)

What women indeed! The Melpa women of whom the young man spoke can't get wives, they are wives, and what they get are husbands, an entirely different matter. The Melpa women can't give their daughters to men, because they do not have the same rights in their daughters that their male kin have, rights of bestowal (although *not* of ownership).

The "exchange of women" is a seductive and powerful concept. It is attractive in that it places the oppression of women within social systems, rather than in biology. Moreover, it suggests that we look for the ultimate locus of women's oppression within the traffic in women, rather than within the traffic in merchandise. It is certainly not difficult to find ethnographic and historical examples of trafficking in women. Women are given in marriage, taken in battle, exchanged for favors, sent as tribute, traded, bought, and sold. Far from being confined to the "primitive" world, these practices seem only to become more pronounced and commercialized in more "civilized" societies. Men are of course also trafficked—but as slaves, hustlers, athletic stars, serfs, or as some other catastrophic social status, rather than as men. Women are transacted as slaves, serfs, and prostitutes, but also simply as women. And if men have been sexual subjects—exchangers—and women sexual semi-objects—gifts—for much of human history, then many customs, clichés, and personality traits seem to make a great deal of sense (among others, the curious custom by which a father gives away the bride).

The "exchange of women" is also a problematic concept. Since Lévi-Strauss argues that the incest taboo and the results of its application constitute the origin of culture, it can be deduced that the world historical defeat of women occurred with the origin of culture, and is a prerequisite of culture. If his analysis is adopted in its pure form, the feminist program must include a task even more onerous than the extermination of men; it must attempt to get rid of culture and substitute some entirely new phenomena on the face of the earth. However, it would be a dubious proposition at best to argue that if there were no exchange of women there would be no culture, if for no other reason than that culture is, by definition, inventive. It is even debatable that "exchange of women" adequately describes all of the empirical evidence of kinship systems. Some cultures, such as the Lele and the Luma, exchange women explicitly and overtly. In other cultures, the exchange of women can be inferred. In some—particularly those hunters and gatherers excluded from Lévi-Strauss's sample—the efficacy of the concept becomes altogether questionable. What are we to make of a concept which seems so useful and yet so difficult?

The "exchange of women" is neither a definition of culture nor a system in and of itself. The concept is an acute, but condensed, apprehension of certain aspects of the social relations of sex and gender. A kinship system is an imposition of social ends upon a part of the natural world. It is therefore "production" in the most general sense of the term: a molding, a transformation of objects (in this case, people) to and by a subjective purpose (for this sense of production, see Marx, 1971a:80–99). It has its own relations of production, distribution, and exchange, which include certain "property" forms in people. These forms are not exclusive, private property rights, but rather different sorts of rights that various people have in other people. Marriage transactions—the gifts and material which circulate in the ceremonies marking a marriage—are a rich source of data for determining exactly who has which rights in whom. It is not difficult to deduce from such transactions that in most cases women's rights are considerably more residual than those of men.

Kinship systems do not merely exchange women. They exchange sexual access, genealogical statuses, lineage names and ancestors, rights and *people*—men, women, and children—in concrete systems of social relationships. These relationships always include certain rights for men, others for women. "Exchange of women" is a shorthand for expressing that the social relations of a kinship system specify that men have certain rights in their female kin, and that women do not have the same rights either to themselves or to their male kin. In this sense, the exchange of women is a profound perception of a system in which women do not have full rights to themselves. The exchange of women becomes an obfuscation if it is seen as a cultural necessity, and when it is used as the single tool with which an analysis of a particular kinship system is approached.

If Lévi-Strauss is correct in seeing the exchange of women as a fundamental principle of kinship, the subordination of women can be seen as a product of the relationships by which sex and gender are organized and produced. The economic oppression of women is derivative and secondary. But there is an "economics" of sex and gender, and what we need is a political economy of sexual systems. We need to study each society to determine the exact mechanisms by which particular conventions of sexuality are produced and maintained. The "exchange of women" is an initial step toward building an arsenal of concepts with which sexual systems can be described.

DEEPER INTO THE LABYRINTH

More concepts can be derived from an essay by Lévi-Strauss, "The Family," in which he introduces other considerations into his analysis of kinship. In *The Elementary Structures of Kinship*, he describes rules and systems of sexual combination. In "The Family," he raises the issue of the preconditions necessary for marriage systems to operate. He asks what sort of "people" are required by kinship systems, by way of an analysis of the sexual division of labor.

Although every society has some sort of division of tasks by sex, the assignment of any particular task to one sex or the other varies enormously. In some groups, agriculture is the work of women, in others, the work of men. Women carry the heavy burdens in some societies, men in others. There are even examples of female hunters and warriors, and of men performing child-care tasks. Lévi-Strauss concludes from a survey of the division of labor by sex that it is not a biological specialization, but must have some other purpose. This purpose, he argues, is to insure the union of men and women by making the smallest viable economic unit contain at least one man and one woman.

> The very fact that it [the sexual division of labor] varies endlessly according to the society selected for consideration shows that . . . it is the mere fact of its existence which is mysteriously required, the form under which it comes to exist being utterly irrelevant, at least from the point of view of any natural necessity . . . the sexual division of labor is nothing else than a device to institute a reciprocal state of dependency between the sexes. (Lévi-Strauss, 1971:347–48)

The division of labor by sex can therefore be seen as a "taboo": a taboo against the sameness of men and women, a taboo dividing the sexes into two mutually exclusive categories, a taboo which exacerbates the biological differences between the sexes and thereby *creates* gender. The division of labor can also be seen as a taboo against sexual arrangements other than those containing at least one man and one woman, thereby enjoining heterosexual marriage.

The argument in "The Family" displays a radical questioning of all human sexual arrangements, in which no aspect of sexuality is taken for granted as "natural" (Hertz, 1960, constructs a similar argument for a thoroughly cultural explanation of the denigration of left-handedness). Rather, all manifest forms of sex and gender are seen as being constituted by the imperatives of social systems. From such a perspective, even *The Elementary Structures of Kinship* can be seen to assume certain preconditions. In purely logical terms, a rule forbidding some marriages and commanding others presupposes a rule enjoining marriage. And marriage presupposes individuals who are disposed to marry.

It is of interest to carry this kind of deductive enterprise even further than Lévi-Strauss does, and to explicate the logical structure which underlies his entire analysis of kinship. At the most general level, the social organization of sex rests upon gender, obligatory heterosexuality, and the constraint of female sexuality.

Gender is a socially imposed division of the sexes. It is a product of the social relations of sexuality. Kinship systems rest upon marriage. They therefore transform males and females into "men" and "women," each an incomplete half which can only find wholeness when united with the other. Men and women are, of course, different. But they are not as different as day and night, earth and sky, yin and yang, life and death. In fact, from the standpoint of nature, men and women are closer to each other than either is to anything else—for instance, mountains, kangaroos, or coconut palms. The idea that men and women are more different from one another than either is from anything else must come from somewhere other than nature. Furthermore, although there is an average difference between males and females on a variety of traits, the range of variation of those traits shows considerable overlap. There will always be some women who are taller than some men, for instance, even though men are on the average taller than women. But the idea that men and women are two mutually exclusive categories must arise out of something other than a nonexistent "natural" opposition.[7] Far from being an expression of natural differences, exclusive gender identity is the suppression of natural similarities. It requires repression: in men, of whatever is the local version of "feminine" traits; in women, of the local definition of "masculine" traits. The division of the sexes has the effect of repressing some of the personality characteristics of virtually everyone, men and women. The same social system which oppresses women in its relations of exchange, oppresses everyone in its insistence upon a rigid division of personality.

Furthermore, individuals are engendered in order that marriage be guaranteed. Lévi-Strauss comes dangerously close to saying that heterosexuality is an instituted process. If biological and hormonal imperatives were as overwhelming as popular mythology would have them, it would hardly be necessary to insure heterosexual unions by means of economic interdependency. Moreover, the incest taboo presupposes a prior, less articulate taboo on homosexuality. A prohibition against *some* heterosexual unions assumes a taboo against *non*-heterosexual unions. Gender is not only an identification with one sex; it also entails that sexual desire be directed toward the other sex. The sexual division of labor is implicated in both aspects of gender—male and female it creates them, and it creates them heterosexual. The suppression of the homosexual component of human sexuality, and by corollary, the oppression of homosexuals, is therefore a product of the same system whose rules and relations oppress women.

In fact, the situation is not so simple, as is obvious when we move from the level of generalities to the analysis of specific sexual systems. Kinship systems do not merely encourage heterosexuality to the detriment of homosexuality. In the first place, specific forms of heterosexuality may be required. For instance, some marriage systems have a rule of obligatory cross-cousin marriage. A person in such a system is not only heterosexual, but "cross-cousin-sexual." If the rule of marriage further specifies matrilateral cross-cousin marriage, then a man will be "mother's-brother's-daughter-sexual" and a woman will be "father's-sister's-son-sexual."

On the other hand, the very complexities of a kinship system may result in particular forms of institutionalized homosexuality. In many New Guinea groups, men and women are considered to be so inimical to one another that the period spent by a male child *in utero* negates his maleness. Since male life force is thought to reside in semen, the boy can overcome the malevolent effects of his fetal history by obtaining and consuming semen. He does so through a homosexual partnership with an older male kinsman (Kelly, 1974; see also Van Baal, 1966; Williams, 1936).

In kinship systems where bridewealth determines the statuses of husband and wife, the simple prerequisites of marriage and gender may be overridden. Among the Azande, women are monopolized by older men. A young man of means may, however, take a boy as wife while he waits to come of age. He simply pays a bridewealth (in spears) for the boy, who is thereby turned into a wife (Evans-Pritchard, 1970). In Dahomey, a woman could turn herself into a husband if she possessed the necessary bridewealth (Herskovitz, 1937).

The institutionalized "transvesticism" of the Mohave permitted a person to change from one sex to the other. An anatomical man could become a woman by means of a special ceremony, and an anatomical woman could in the same way become a man. The transvestite then took a wife or husband of her/his own anatomical sex and opposite social sex. These marriages, which we would label homosexual, were heterosexual ones by Mohave standards, unions of opposite socially defined sexes. By comparison with our society, this whole arrangement permitted a great deal of freedom. However, a person was not permitted to be some of both genders—he/she could be either male or female, but not a little of each (Deveraux, 1937; see also McMurtrie, 1914; Sonenschein, 1966).

In all of the above examples, the rules of gender division and obligatory heterosexuality are present even in their transformations. These two rules apply equally to the constraint of both male and female behavior and personality. Kinship systems dictate some sculpting of the sexuality of both sexes. But it can be duduced from *The Elementary Structures of Kinship* that more constraint is applied to females when they are pressed into the service of kinship than to males. If women are exchanged, in whatever sense we take the term, marital debts are reckoned in female flesh. A woman must become the sexual partner of some man to whom she is owed as return on a previous marriage. If a girl is promised in infancy, her refusal to participate as an adult would disrupt the flow of debts and promises. It would be in the interests of the smooth and continuous operation of such a system if the woman in question did not have too many ideas of her own about whom she might want to sleep with. From the standpoint of the system, the preferred female sexuality would be one which responded to the desire of others, rather than one which actively desired and sought a response.

This generality, like the ones about gender and heterosexuality, is also subject to considerable variation and free play in actual systems. The Lele and the Kuma provide two of the clearest ethnographic examples of the exchange of women. Men in both cultures are perpetually engaged in schemes which necessitate that they have full control over the sexual destinies of their female kinswomen. Much of the drama in both societies consists in female attempts to evade the sexual control of their kinsmen. Nevertheless, female resistance in both cases is severely circumscribed (Douglas, 1963; Reay, 1959).

One last generality could be predicted as a consequence of the exchange of women under a system in which rights to women are held by men. What would happen if our hypothetical woman not only refused the man to whom she was promised, but asked for a woman instead? If a single refusal were disruptive, a double refusal would be insurrectionary. If each woman is promised to some man, neither has a right to dispose of herself. If two women managed to extricate themselves from the debt nexus, two other women would have to be found to replace them. As long as men have rights in women which women do not have in themselves, it would be sensible to expect that homosexuality in women would be subject to more suppression than in men.

In summary, some basic generalities about the organization of human sexuality can be derived from an exegesis of Lévi-Strauss's theories of kinship. These are the incest taboo, obligatory heterosexuality, and an asymmetric division of the sexes. The asymmetry of gender—the difference between exchanger and exchanged—entails the constraint of female sexuality. Concrete kinship systems will have more specific conventions, and these conventions vary a great deal. While particular socio-sexual systems vary, each one is specific, and individuals within it will have to conform to a finite set of possibilities. Each new generation must learn and become its sexual destiny, each person must be encoded with its appropriate status within the system. It would be extraordinary for one of us to calmly assume that we would conventionally marry a mother's brother's daughter, or a father's sister's son. Yet there are groups in which such a marital future is taken for granted.

Anthropology, and descriptions of kinship systems, do not explain the mechanisms by which children are engraved with the conventions of sex and gender. Psychoanalysis, on the other hand, is a theory about the reproduction of kinship. Psychoanalysis describes the residue left within individuals by their confrontation with the rules and regulations of sexuality of the societies to which they are born.

PSYCHOANALYSIS AND ITS DISCONTENTS

The battle between psychoanalysis and the women's and gay movements has become legendary. In part, this confrontation between sexual revolutionaries and the clinical establishment has been due to the evolution of psychoanalysis in the United States, where clinical tradition has fetishized anatomy. The child is thought to travel through its organismic stages until it reaches its anatomical destiny and the missionary position. Clinical practice has often seen its mission as the repair of individuals who somehow have become derailed en route to their "biological" aim. Transforming moral law into scientific law, clinical practice has acted to enforce sexual convention upon unruly participants. In this sense, psychoanalysis has often become more than a theory of the mechanisms of the reproduction of sexual arrangements; it has been one of those mechanisms. Since the aim of the feminist and gay revolts is to dismantle the apparatus of sexual enforcement, a critique of psychoanalysis has been in order.

But the rejection of Freud by the women's and gay movements has deeper roots in the rejection by psychoanalysis of its own insights. Nowhere are the effects on women of male-dominated social systems better documented than within the clinical literature. According to the Freudian orthodoxy, the attainment of "normal" femininity extracts severe costs from women. The theory of gender acquisition could have been the basis of a critique of sex roles. Instead, the radical implications of Freud's theory have been radically repressed. This tendency is evident even in the original formulations of the theory, but it has been exacerbated over time until the potential for a critical psychoanalytic theory of gender is visible only in the symptomatology of its denial-an intricate rationalization of sex roles as they are. It is not the purpose of this paper to conduct a psychoanalysis of the psychoanalytic unconscious; but I do hope to demonstrate that it exists. Moreover, the salvage of psychoanalysis from its own motivated repression is not for the sake of Freud's good name. Psychoanalysis contains a unique set of concepts for understanding men, women, and sexuality. It is a theory of sexuality in human society. Most importantly, psychoanalysis provides a description of the mechanisms by which the sexes are divided and deformed, of how bisexual, androgynous infants are transformed into boys and girls.[8] Psychoanalysis is a feminist thoery *manqué*.

THE OEDIPUS HEX

Until the late 1920s, the psychoanalytic movement did not have a distinctive theory of feminine development. Instead, variants of an "Electra" complex in women had been proposed, in which female experience was thought to be a mirror image of the Oedipal complex described for males. The boy loved his mother, but gave her up out of fear of the father's threat of castration. The girl, it was thought, loved her father, and gave him up out of fear of maternal vengeance. This formulation assumed that both children were subject to a biological imperative toward heterosexuality. It also assumed that the children were already, before the Oedipal phase, "little" men and women.

Freud had voiced reservations about jumping to conclusions about women on the basis of data gathered from men. But his objections remained general until the discovery of the pre-Oedipal phase in women. The concept of the pre-Oedipal phase enabled both Freud and Jeanne Lampl de Groot to articulate the classic psychoanalytic theory of femininity.[9] The idea of the pre-Oedipal phase in women produced a dislocation of the biologically derived presuppositions which underlay notions of an "Electra" complex. In the pre-Oedipal phase, children of both sexes were psychically indistinguishable, which meant that their differentiation into masculine and feminine children had to be explained, rather than assumed. Pre-Oedipal children were described as bisexual. Both sexes exhibited the full range of libidinal attitudes, active and passive. And for children of both sexes, the mother was the object of desire.

In particular, the characteristics of the pre-Oedipal female challenged the ideas of a primordial heterosexuality and gender identity. Since the girl's libidinal activity was directed toward the mother, her adult heterosexuality had to be explained:

> It would be a solution of ideal simplicity if we could suppose that from a particular age onwards the elementary influences of the mutual attraction between the sexes makes itself felt and impels the small woman towards men. . . . But we are not going to find things so easy; we scarcely know whether we are to believe seriously in the power of which poets talk so much and with such enthusiasm but which cannot be further dissected analytically. (Freud, 1965:119)

Moreoever, the girl did not manifest a "feminine" libidinal attitude. Since her desire for the mother was active and aggressive, her ultimate accession to "femininity" had also to be explained:

> In conformity with its peculiar nature, psychoanalysis does not try to describe what a woman is . . . but sets about enquiring how she comes into being, how a woman develops out of a child with a bisexual disposition. (Ibid.: 116)

In short, feminine development could no longer be taken for granted as a reflex of biology. Rather, it had become immensely problematic. It is in explaining the acquisition of "femininity" that Freud employs the concepts of penis envy and castration which have infuriated feminists since he first introduced them. The girl turns from the mother and represses the "masculine" elements of her libido as a result of her recognition that she is castrated. She compares her tiny clitoris to the larger penis, and in the face of its evident superior ability to satisfy the mother, falls prey to penis envy and a sense of inferiority. She gives up her struggle for the mother and assumes a passive feminine position vis-à-vis the father. Freud's account can be read as claiming that femininity is a consequence of the anatomical differences between the sexes. He has therefore been accused of biological determinism. Nevertheless, even in his most anatomically stated versions of the female castration complex, the "inferiority" of the woman's genitals is a product of the situational context: the girl feels less "equipped" to possess and satisfy the mother. If the pre-Oedipal lesbian were not confronted by the heterosexuality of the other, she might draw different conclusion about the relative status of her genitals.

Freud was never as much of a biological determinist as some would have him. He repeatedly stressed that all adult sexuality resulted from psychic, not biologic, development. But his writing is often ambiguous, and his wording leaves plenty of room for the biological interpretations which have been so popular in American psycho-analysis. In France, on the other hand, the trend in psychoanalytic theory has been to de-biologize Freud, and to conceive of psychoanalysis as a theory of information rather than organs. Jacques Lacan, the instigator of this line of thinking, insists that Freud never meant to say anything about anatomy, and that Freud's theory was instead about language and the cultural meanings imposed upon anatomy. The debate over the "real" Freud is extremely interesting, but it is not my purpose here to contribute to it. Rather, I want to rephrase the classic theory of femininity in Lacan's terminology, after introducing some of the pieces on Lacan's conceptual chessboard.

KINSHIP, LACAN, AND THE PHALLUS

Lacan suggests that psychoanalysis is the study of the traces left in the psyches of individuals as a result of their conscription into systems of kinship.

> Isn't it striking that Lévi-Strauss, in suggesting that implication of the structures of language with that part of the social laws which regulate marriage ties and kinship, is already conquering the very terrain in which Freud situates the unconscious? (Lacan, 1968:48)

> For where on earth would one situate the determinations of the unconsciousness if it is not in those nominal cadres in which marriage ties and kinship are always grounded. . . . And how would one apprehend the analytical conflicts and their Oedipean prototype outside the engagements which have fixed, long before the subject came into the world, not only his destiny, but his identity itself? (Ibid.:126)

> This is precisely where the Oedipus complex. . .may be said, in this connection, to mark the limits which our discipline assigns to subjectivity: that is to say, what the subject can know of his unconscious participation in the movement of the complex structures of marriage ties, by verifying the symbolic effects in his individual existence of the tangential movement towards incest. . . . (Ibid.:40)

Kinship is the culturalization of biological sexuality on the societal level; psycho-analysis describes the transformation of the biological sexuality of individuals as they are enculturated.

Kinship terminology contains information about the system. Kin terms demarcate statuses, and indicate some of the attributes of those statuses. For instance, in the Trobriand Islands a man calls the women of his clan by the term for "sister." He calls the women of clans into which he can marry by a term indicating their marriageability. When the young Trobriand male learns these terms, he learns which women he can safely desire. In Lacan's scheme, the Oedipal crisis occurs when a child learns of the sexual rules embedded in the terms for family and relatives. The crisis begins when the child comprehends the system and his or her place in it; the crisis is resolved when the child accepts that place and accedes to it. Even if the child refuses its place, he or she cannot escape knowledge of it. Before the Oedipal phase, the sexuality of the child is labile and relatively unstructured. Each child contains all of the sexual possibilities available to human expression. But in any given society, only some of these possibilities will be expressed, while others will be constrained. When the child leaves the Oedipal phase, its libido and gender identity have been organized in conformity with the rules of the culture which is domesticating it.

The Oedipal complex is an apparatus for the production of sexual personality. It is a truism to say that societies will inculcate in their young the character traits appropriate to carrying on the business of society. For instance, E. P. Thompson (1963) speaks of the transformation of the personality structure of the English working class, as artisans were changed into good industrial workers. Just as the social forms of labor demand certain kinds of personality, the social forms of sex and gender demand certain kinds of people. In the most general terms, the Oedipal complex is a machine which fashions the appropriate forms of sexual individuals (see also the discussion of different forms of "historical individuality" in Althusser and Balibar, 1970:112, 251–53).

In the Lacanian theory of psychoanalysis, it is the kin terms that indicate a structure of relationships which will determine the role of any individual or object within the Oedipal drama. For instance, Lacan makes a distinction between the "function of the father" and a particular father who embodies this function. In the same way, he makes a radical distinction between the penis and the "phallus," between organ and information. The phallus is a set of meanings conferred upon the penis. The differentiation between phallus and penis in contemporary French psychoanalytic terminology emphasizes the idea that the penis could not and does not play the role attributed to it in the classical terminology of the castration complex.[10]

In Freud's terminology, the Oedipal complex presents two alternatives to a child: to have a penis or to be castrated. In contrast, the Lacanian theory of the castration complex leaves behind all reference to anatomical reality:

> The theory of the castration complex amounts to having the male organ play a dominant role—this time as a symbol—*to the extent that its absence or presence transforms an anatomical difference into a major classification of humans, and to the extent that, for each subject, this presence or absence is not taken for granted, is not reduced purely and simply to a given, but is the problematical result of an intra- and intersubjective process* (the subject's assumption of his own sex). (Laplanche and Pontalis, in Mehlman, 1972:198–99; my italics)

The alternative presented to the child may be rephrased as an alternative between having, or not having, the phallus. Castration is not having the (symbolic) phallus. Castration is not a real "lack," but a meaning conferred upon the genitals of a woman:

> Castration may derive support from . . . the apprehension in the Real of the absence of the penis in women—but even this supposes a symbolization of the object, since the Real is full, and "lacks" nothing. Insofar as one finds castration in the genesis of neurosis, it is never real but symbolic. . . .(Lacan, 1968:271)

The phallus is, as it were, a distinctive feature differentiating "castrated" and "noncastrated." The presence or absence of the phallus carries the differences between two sexual statuses, "man" and "woman" (see Jakobson and Halle, 1971, on distinctive features). Since these are not equal, the phallus also carries a meaning of the dominance of men over women, and it may be inferred that "penis envy" is a recognition thereof. Moreover, as long as men have rights in women which women do not have in themselves, the phallus also carries the meaning of the difference between "exchanger" and "exchanged," gift and giver. Ultimately, neither the classical Freudian nor the rephrased Lacanian theories of the Oedipal process make sense unless at least this much of the paleolithic relations of sexuality are still with us. We still live in a "phallic" culture.

Lacan also speaks of the phallus as a symbolic object which is exchanged within and between families (see also Wilden, 1968:303–305). It is interesting to think about this observation in terms of primitive marriage transactions and exchange networks. In those transactions, the exchange of women is usually one of many cycles of exchange. Usually, there are other objects circulating as well as women. Women move in one direction, cattle, shells, or mats in the other. In one sense, the Oedipal complex is an expression of the circulation of the phallus in intrafamily exchange, an inversion of the circulation of women in interfamily exchange. In the cycle of exchange manifested by the Oedipal complex, the phallus passes through the medium of women from one man to another—from father to son, from mother's brother to sister's son, and so forth. In this family *Kula* ring, women go one way, the phallus the other. It is where we aren't. In this sense, the phallus is more than a feature which distinguishes the sexes: it is the embodiment of the male status, to which men accede, and in which certain rights inhere—among them, the right to a woman. It is an expression of the transmission of male dominance. It passes through women and settles upon men.[11] The tracks which it leaves include gender identity, the division of the sexes. But it leaves more than this. It leaves "penis envy," which acquires a rich meaning of the disquietude of women in a phallic culture.

OEDIPUS REVISITED

We return now to the two pre-Oedipal androgynes, sitting on the border between biology and culture. Lévi-Strauss places the incest taboo on that border, arguing that its initiation of the exchange of women constitutes the origin of society. In this sense, the incest taboo and the exchange of women are the content of the original social contract (see Sahlins, 1972: Chap. 4). For individuals, the Oedipal crisis occurs at the same divide, when the incest taboo initiates the exchange of the phallus.

The Oedipal crisis is precipitated by certain items of information. The children discover the differences between the sexes, and that each child must become one or the other gender. They also discover the incest taboo, and that some sexuality is prohibited—in this case, the mother is unavailable to either child because she "belongs" to the father. Lastly, they discover that the two genders do not have the same sexual "rights" or futures.

In the normal course of events, the boy renounces his mother for fear that otherwise his father would castrate him (refuse to give him the phallus and make him a girl). But by this act of renunciation, the boy affirms the relationships which have given mother to father and which will give him, if he becomes a man, a woman of his own. In exchange for the boy's affirmation of his father's right to his mother, the father affirms the phallus in his son (does not castrate him). The boy exchanges his mother for the phallus, the symbolic token which can later be exchanged for a woman. The only thing required of him is a little patience. He retains his initial libidinal organization and the sex of his original love object. The social contract to which he has agreed will eventually recognize his own rights and provide him with a woman of his own.

What happens to the girl is more complex. She, like the boy, discovers the taboo against incest and the division of the sexes. She also discovers some unpleasant information about the gender to which she is being assigned. For the boy, the taboo on incest is a taboo on certain women. For the girl, it is a taboo on all women. Since she is in a homosexual position vis-à-vis the mother, the rule of heterosexuality which dominates the scenario makes her position excruciatingly untenable. The mother, and all women by extension, can only be properly beloved by someone "with a penis" (phallus). Since the girl has no "phallus," she has no "right" to love her mother or another woman, since she is herself destined to some man. She does not have the symbolic token which can be exchanged for a woman.

If Freud's wording of this moment of the female Oedipal crisis is ambiguous, Lampl de Groot's formulation makes the context which confers meaning upon the genitals explicit:

> ... *if the little girl comes to the conclusion that such an organ is really indispensable to the possession of the mother, she experiences* in addition to the narcissistic insults common to both sexes still another blow, namely *a feeling of inferiority about her genitals.* (Lampl de Groot, 1933:497; my italics)

The girl concludes that the "penis" is indispensable for the possession of the mother because only those who possess the phallus have a "right" to be a woman and the token of exchange. She does not come to her conclusion because of the natural superiority of the penis either in and of itself, or as an instrument for making love. The hierarchical arrangement of the male and female genitals is a result of the definitions of the situation—the rule of obligatory heterosexuality and the relegation of women (those without the phallus, castrated) to men (those with the phallus).

The girl then begins to turn away from the mother, and to the father.

> To the girl, it [castration] is an accomplished fact, which is irrevocable, but the recognition of which compels her finally to renounce her first love object and to taste to the full the bitterness of its loss ... the father is chosen as a love-object, the enemy becomes the beloved.... (Lampl de Groot, 1948:213)

This recognition of "castration" forces the girl to redefine her relationship to herself, her mother, and her father.

She turns from the mother because she does not have the phallus to give her. She turns from the mother also in anger and disappointment, because the mother did not give her a "penis" (phallus). But the mother, a woman in a phallic culture, does not have the phallus to give away (having gone through the Oedipal crisis herself a generation earlier). The girl then turns to the father because only he can "give her the phallus," and it is only through him that she can enter into the symbolic exchange system in which the phallus circulates. But the father does not give her the phallus in the same way that he gives it to the boy. The phallus is affirmed in the boy, who then has it to give away. The girl never gets the phallus. It passes through her, and in its passage is transformed into a child. When she "recognizes her castration" she accedes to the place of a woman in a phallic exchange network. She can "get" the phallus—in intercourse, or as a child—but only as a gift from a man. She never gets to give it away.

When she turns to the father, she also represses the "active" portions of her libido:

> The turning away from her mother is an extremely important step in the course of a little girl's development. It is more than a mere change of object . . . hand in hand with it there is to be observed a marked lowering of the active sexual impulses and a rise of the passive ones. . . . The transition to the father object is accomplished with the help of the passive trends in so far as they have escaped the catastrophe. The path to the development of femininity now lies open to the girl. (Freud, 1961b:239)

The ascendance of passivity in the girl is due to her recognition of the futility of realizing her active desire, and of the unequal terms of the struggle. Freud locates active desire in the clitoris and passive desire in the vagina, and thus describes the repression of active desire as the repression of clitoral eroticism in favor of passive vaginal eroticism. In this scheme, cultural stereotypes have been mapped onto the genitals. Since the work of Masters and Johnson, it is evident that this genital division is a false one. Any organ—penis, clitoris, vagina—can be the locus of either active or passive eroticism. What is important in Freud's scheme, however, is not the geography of desire, but its self-confidence. It is not an organ which is repressed, but a segment of erotic possibility. Freud notes that "More constraint has been applied to the libido when it is pressed into the service of the feminine function . . ." (Freud, 1965:131). The girl has been robbed.

If the Oedipal phase proceeds normally and the girl "accepts her castration," her libidinal structure and object choice are now congruent with the female gender role. She has become a little woman—feminine, passive, heterosexual. Actually, Freud suggests that there are three alternate routes out of the Oedipal catastrophe. The girl may simply freak out, repress sexuality altogether, and become asexual. She may protest, cling to her narcissism and desire, and become either "masculine" or homosexual. Or she may accept the situation, sign the social contract, and attain "normality."

Karen Horney is critical of the entire Freud/Lampl de Groot scheme. But in the course of her critique she articulates its implications:

> . . . when she [the girl] first turns to a man (the father), it is in the main only by way of the narrow bridge of resentment . . . we should feel it a contradiction if the relation of woman to man did not retain throughout life some tinge of this enforced substitute for that which was really desired. . . . The same character of something remote from instinct, secondary and substitutive, would, even in normal women, adhere to the wish for motherhood. . . . The special point about Freud's viewpoint is rather that it sees the wish for motherhood not as an innate formation, but as something that can be reduced psychologically to its ontogenetic elements and draws its energy originally from homosexual or phallic instinctual elements. . . . It would allow, finally, that women's whole reaction to life would be based on a strong subterranean resentment. (Horney, 1973:148–49)

Horney considers these implications to be so far-fetched that they challenge the validity of Freud's entire scheme. But it is certainly plausible to argue instead that the creation of "femininity" in women in the course of socialization is an act of psychic brutality, and that it leaves in women an immense resentment of the suppression to which they were subjected. It is also possible to argue that women have few means for realizing and expressing their residual anger. One can read Freud's essays on femininity as descriptions of how a group is prepared psychologically, at a tender age, to live with its oppression.

There is an additional element in the classic discussions of the attainment of womanhood. The girl first turns to the father because she must, because she is "castrated" (a woman, helpless, etc.). She then discovers that "castration" is a prerequisite to the father's love, that she must be a woman for him to love her. She therefore begins to desire "castration," and what had previously been a disaster becomes a wish.

> Analytic experience leaves no room for doubt that the little girl's first libidinal relation to her father is masochistic, and the masochistic wish in its earliest distinctively feminine phase is: "I want to be castrated by my father." (Deutsch, 1948a:228)

Deutsch argues that such masochism may conflict with the ego, causing some women to flee the entire situation in defense of their self-regard. Those women to whom the choice is "between finding bliss in suffering or peace in renunciation" (ibid.: 231) will have difficulty in attaining a healthy attitude to intercourse and motherhood. Why Deutsch appears to consider such women to be special cases, rather than the norm, is not clear from her discussion.

The psychoanalytic theory of femininity is one that sees female development based largely on pain and humiliation, and it takes some fancy footwork to explain why anyone ought to enjoy being a woman. At this point in the classic discussions biology makes a triumphant return. The fancy footwork consists in arguing that finding joy in pain is adaptive to the role of women in reproduction, since childbirth and defloration are "painful." Would it not make more sense to question the entire procedure? If women, in finding their place in a sexual system, are robbed of libido and forced into a masochistic eroticism, why did the analysts not argue for novel arrangements, instead of rationalizing the old ones?

Freud's theory of femininity has been subjected to feminist critique since it was first published. To the extent that it is a rationalization of female subordination, this critique has been justified. To the extent that it is a description of a process which subordinates women, this critique is a mistake. As a description of how phallic culture domesticates women, and the effects in women of their domestication, psychoanalytic theory has no parallel (see also Mitchell, 1971 and 1974; Lasch, 1974). And since psychoanalysis is a theory of gender, dismissing it would be suicidal for a political movement dedicated to eradicating gender hierarchy (or gender itself). We cannot dismantle something that we underestimate or do not understand. The oppression of women is deep; equal pay, equal work, and all of the female politicians in the world will not extirpate the roots of sexism. Lévi-Strauss and Freud elucidate what would otherwise be poorly perceived parts of the deep structures of sex oppression. They serve as reminders of the intractability and magnitude of what we fight, and their analyses provide preliminary charts of the social machinery we must rearrange.

WOMEN UNITE TO OFF THE OEDIPAL RESIDUE OF CULTURE

The precision of the fit between Freud and Lévi-Strauss is striking. Kinship systems require a division of the sexes. The Oedipal phase divides the sexes. Kinship systems include sets of rules governing sexuality. The Oedipal crisis is the assimilation of these rules and taboos. Compulsory heterosexuality is the product of kinship. The Oedipal phase constitutes heterosexual desire. Kinship rests on a radical difference between the rights of men and women. The Oedipal complex confers male rights upon the boy, and forces the girl to accommodate herself to her lesser rights.

This fit between Lévi-Strauss and Freud is by implication an argument that our sex/gender system is still organized by the principles outlined by Lévi-Strauss, despite the entirely nonmodern character of his data base. The more recent data on which Freud bases his theories testifies to the endurance of these sexual structures. If my reading of Freud and Lévi-Strauss is accurate, it suggests that the feminist movement must attempt to resolve the Oedipal crisis of culture by reorganizing the domain of sex and gender in such a way that each individual's Oedipal experience would be less destructive. The dimensions of such a task are difficult to imagine, but at least certain conditions would have to be met.

Several elements of the Oedipal crisis would have to be altered in order that the phase not have such disastrous effects on the young female ego. The Oedipal phase institutes a contradiction in the girl by placing irreconcilable demands upon her. On the one hand, the girl's love for the mother is induced by the mother's job of child care. The girl is then forced to abandon this love because of the female sex role—to belong to a man. If the sexual division of labor were such that adults of both sexes cared for children equally, primary object choice would be bisexual. If heterosexuality were not obligatory, this early love would not have to be suppressed, and the penis would not be overvalued. If the sexual property system were reorganized in such a way that men did not have overriding rights in women (if there was no exchange of women) and if there were no gender, the entire Oedipal drama would be a relic. In short, feminism must call for a revolution in kinship.

The organization of sex and gender once had functions other than itself—it organized society. Now, it only organizes and reproduces itself. The kinds of relationships of sexuality established in the dim human past still dominate our sexual lives, our ideas about men and women, and the ways we raise our children. But they lack the functional load they once carried. One of the most conspicuous features of kinship is that it has been systematically stripped of its functions—political, economic, educational, and organizational. It has been reduced to its barest bones—*sex and gender*.

Human sexual life will always be subject to convention and human intervention. It will never be completely "natural," if only because our species is social, cultural, and articulate. The wild profusion of infantile sexuality will always be tamed. The confrontation between immature and helpless infants and the developed social life of their elders will probably always leave some residue of disturbance. But the mechanisms and aims of this process need not be largely independent of conscious choice. Cultural evolution provides us with the opportunity to seize control of the means of sexuality, reproduction, and socialization, and to make conscious decisions to liberate human sexual life from the archaic relationships which deform it. Ultimately, a thoroughgoing feminist revolution would liberate more than women. It would liberate forms of sexual expression, and it would liberate human personality from the straightjacket of gender.

"Daddy, daddy, you bastard, I'm through."
—Sylvia Plath

In the course of this essay I have tried to construct a theory of women's oppression by borrowing concepts from anthropology and psychoanalysis. But Lévi-Strauss and Freud write within an intellectual tradition produced by a culture in which women are oppressed. The danger in my enterprise is that the sexism in the tradition of which they are a part tends to be dragged in with each borrowing. "We cannot utter a single destructive proposition which has not already slipped into the form, the logic, and the implicit postulations of precisely what it seeks to contest" (Derrida, 1972:250). And what slips in is formidable. Both psychoanalysis and structural anthropology are, in one sense, the most sophisticated ideologies of sexism around.[12]

For instance, Lévi-Strauss sees women as being like words, which are misused when they are not "communicated" and exchanged. On the last page of a very long book, he observes that this creates something of a contradiction in women since women are at the same time "speakers" and "spoken." His only comment on this contradiction is this:

But woman could never become just a sign and nothing more, since even in a man's world she is still a person, and since insofar as she is defined as a sign she must be recognized as a generator of signs. In the matrimonial dialogue of men, woman is never purely what is spoken about; for if women in general represent a certain category of signs, destined to a certain kind of communication, each woman preserves a particular value arising from her talent, before and after marriage, for taking her part in a duet. In contrast to words, which have wholly become signs, woman has remained at once a sign and a value. *This explains why the relations between the sexes have preserved that affective richness, ardour and mystery which doubtless originally permeated the entire universe of human communications.* (Lévi-Strauss, 1969:496; my italics)

This is an extraordinary statement. Why is he not, at this point, denouncing what kinship systems do to women, instead of presenting one of the greatest rip-offs of all time as the root of romance?

A similar insensitivity is revealed within psychoanalysis by the inconsistency with which it assimilates the critical implications of its own theory. For instance, Freud did not hesitate to recognize that his findings posed a challenge to conventional morality:

> We cannot avoid observing with critical eyes, and we have found that it is impossible to give our support to conventional sexual morality or to approve highly of the means by which society attempts to arrange the practical problems of sexuality in life. *We can demonstrate with ease that what the world calls its code of morals demands more sacrifices than it is worth*, and that its behavior is neither dictated by honesty nor instituted with wisdom. (Freud, 1943:376–77; my emphasis)

Nevertheless, when psychoanalysis demonstrates with equal facility that the ordinary components of feminine personality are masochism, self-hatred, and passivity,[13] a similar judgment is *not* made. Instead, a double standard of interpretation is employed. Masochism is bad for men, essential to women. Adequate narcissism is necessary for men, impossible for women. Passivity is tragic in man, while lack of passivity is tragic in a woman.

It is this double standard which enables clinicians to try to accommodate women to a role whose destructiveness is so lucidly detailed in their own theories. It is the same inconsistent attitude which permits therapists to consider lesbianism as a problem to be cured, rather than as the resistance to a bad situation that their own theory suggests.[14]

There are points within the analytic discussions of femininity where one might say, "This is oppression of women," or "We can demonstrate with ease that what the world calls femininity demands more sacrifices than it is worth." It is precisely at such points that the implications of the theory are ignored, and are replaced with formulations whose purpose is to keep those implications firmly lodged in the theoretical unconscious. It is at these points that all sorts of mysterious chemical substances, joys in pain, and biological aims are substituted for a critical assessment of the costs of femininity. These substitutions are the symptoms of theoretical repression, in that they are not consistent with the usual canons of psychoanalytic argument. The extent to which these rationalizations of femininity go against the grain of psychoanalytic logic is strong evidence for the extent of the need to suppress the radical and feminist implications of the theory of femininity (Deutsch's discussions are excellent examples of this process of substitution and repression).

The argument which must be woven in order to assimilate Lévi-Strauss and Freud into feminist theory is somewhat tortuous. I have engaged it for several reasons. First, while neither Lévi-Strauss nor Freud questions the undoubted sexism endemic to the systems they describe, the questions which ought to be posed are blindingly obvious. Secondly, their work enables us to isolate sex and gender from "mode of production," and to counter a certain tendency to explain sex oppression as a reflex of economic forces. Their work provides a framework in which the full weight of sexuality and marriage can be incorporated into an analysis of sex oppression. It suggests a conception of the women's movement as analogous to, rather than isomorphic with, the working-class movement, each addressing a different source of human discontent. In Marx's vision, the working-class movement would do more than throw off the burden of its own exploitation. It also had the potential to change society, to liberate humanity, to create a classless society. Perhaps the women's movement has the task of effecting the same kind of social change for a system of which Marx had only an imperfect apperception. Something of this sort is implicit in Wittig (1973)—the dictatorship of the Amazon *guérillères* is a temporary means for achieving a genderless society.

The sex/gender system is not immutably oppressive and has lost much of its traditional function. Nevertheless, it will not wither away in the absence of opposition. It still carries the social burden of sex and gender, of socializing the young, and of providing ultimate propositions about the nature of human beings themselves. And it serves economic and political ends other than those it was originally designed to further (cf. Scott, 1965). The sex/gender system must be reorganized through political action.

Finally, the exegesis of Lévi-Strauss and Freud suggests a certain vision of feminist politics and the feminist utopia. It suggests that we should not aim for the elimination of men, but for the elimination of the social system which creates sexism and gender. I personally find a vision of an Amazon matriarchate, in which men are reduced to servitude or oblivion (depending on the possibilities for parthenogenetic reproduction), distasteful and inadequate. Such a vision maintains gender and the division of the sexes. It is a vision which simply inverts the arguments of those who base their case for inevitable male dominance on ineradicable and *significant* biological differences between the sexes. But we are not only oppressed *as* women, we are oppressed by having to be women, or men as the case may be. I personally feel that the feminist movement must dream of even more than the elimination of the oppression of women. It must dream of the elimination of obligatory sexualities and sex roles. The dream I find most compelling is one of an androgynous and genderless (though not sexless) society, in which one's sexual anatomy is irrelevant to who one is, what one does, and with whom one makes love.

THE POLITICAL ECONOMY OF SEX

It would be nice to be able to conclude here with the implications for feminism and gay liberation of the overlap between Freud and Lévi-Strauss. But I must suggest, tentatively, a next step on the agenda: a Marxian analysis of sex/gender systems. Sex/gender systems are not ahistorical emanations of the human mind; they are products of historical human activity.

We need, for instance, an analysis of the evolution of sexual exchange along the lines of Marx's discussion in *Capital* of the evolution of money and commodities. There is an economics and a politics to sex/gender systems which is obscured by the concept of "exchange of women." For instance, a system in which women are exchangeable only for one another has different effects on women than one in which there is a commodity equivalent for women.

> That marriage in simple societies involves an "exchange" is a somewhat vague notion that has often confused the analysis of social systems. The extreme case is the exchange of "sisters," formerly practiced in parts of Australia and Africa. Here the term has the precise dictionary meaning of "to be received as an equivalent for," "to give and receive reciprocally." From quite a different standpoint the virtually universal incest prohibition means that marriage systems necessarily involve "exchanging" siblings for spouses, giving rise to a reciprocity that is purely notational. But in most societies marriage is mediated by a set of intermediary transactions. If we see these transactions as simply implying immediate or long-term reciprocity, then the analysis is likely to be blurred. . . . The analysis is further limited if one regards the passage of property simply as a symbol of the transfer of rights, for then the nature of the objects handed over . . . is of little importance. . . . Neither of these approaches is wrong; both are inadequate. (Goody, 1973:2)

There are systems in which there is no equivalent for a woman. To get a wife, a man must have a daughter, a sister, or other female kinswoman in whom he has a right of bestowal. He must have control over some female flesh. The Lele and Kuma are cases in point. Lele men scheme constantly in order to stake claims in some as yet unborn girl, and scheme further to make good their claims (Douglas, 1963). A Kuma girl's marriage is determined by an intricate web of debts, and she has little say in choosing her husband. A girl is usually married against her will, and her groom shoots an arrow into her thigh to symbolically prevent her from running away. The young wives almost always do run away, only to be returned to their new husbands by an elaborate conspiracy enacted by their kin and affines (Reay, 1959).

In other societies, there is an equivalent for women. A woman can be converted into bridewealth, and bridewealth can be in turn converted into a woman. The dynamics of such systems vary accordingly, as does the specific kind of pressure exerted upon women. The marriage of a Melpa woman is not a return for a previous debt. Each transaction is self-contained, in that the payment of a bridewealth in pigs and shells will cancel the debt. The Melpa woman therefore has more latitude in choosing her husband than does her Kuma counterpart. On the other hand, her destiny is linked to bridewealth. If her husband's kin are slow to pay, her kin may encourage her to leave him. On the other hand, if her consanguineal kin are satisfied with the balance of payments, they may refuse to back her in the event that she wants to leave her husband. Moreover, her male kinsmen use the bridewealth for their own purposes, in *moka* exchange and for their own marriages. If a woman leaves her husband, some or all of the bridewealth will have to be returned. If, as is usually the case, the pigs and shells have been distributed or promised, her kin will be reluctant to back her in the event of marital discord. And each time a woman divorces and remarries, her value in bridewealth tends to depreciate. On the whole, her male consanguines will lose in the event of a divorce, unless the groom has been deliquent in his payments. While the Melpa woman is freer as a new bride than a Kuma woman, the bridewealth system makes divorce difficult or impossible (Strathern, 1972).

In some societies, like the Nuer, bridewealth can only be converted into brides. In others, bridewealth can be converted into something else, like political prestige. In this case, a woman's marriage is implicated in a political system. In the Big Man systems of Highland New Guinea, the material which circulates for women also circulates in the exchanges on which political power is based. Within the political system, men are in constant need of valuables to disburse, and they are dependent upon input. They depend not only upon their immediate partners, but upon the partners of their partners, to several degrees of remove. If a man has to return some bridewealth he may not be able to give it to someone who planned to give it to someone else who intended to use it to give a feast upon which his status depends. Big men are therefore concerned with the domestic affairs of others, whose relationship with them may be extremely indirect. There are cases in which headmen intervene in marital disputes involving indirect trading partners in order that *moka* exchanges not be disrupted (Bulmer, 1969:11). The weight of this entire system may come to rest upon one woman kept in a miserable marriage.

In short, there are other questions to ask of a marriage system than whether or not it exchanges women. Is the woman traded for a woman, or is there an equivalent? Is this equivalent only for women, or can it be turned into something else? If it can be turned into something else, is it turned into political power or wealth? On the other hand, can bridewealth be obtained only in marital exchange, or can it be obtained from elsewhere? Can women be accumulated through amassing wealth? Can wealth be accumulated by disposing of women? Is a marriage system part of a system of stratification?[15]

These last questions point to another task for a political economy of sex. Kinship and marriage are always parts of total social systems, and are always tied into economic and political arrangements.

Lévi-Strauss . . . rightly argues that the structural implications of a marriage can only be understood if we think of it as one item in a whole series of transactions between kin groups. So far, so good. But in none of the examples which he provides in his book does he carry this principle far enough. The reciprocities of kinship obligation are not merely symbols of alliance, they are also economic transactions, political transactions, charters to rights of domicile and land use. No useful picture of "how a kinship system works" can be provided unless these several aspects or implications of the kinship organization are considered simultaneously. (Leach, 1971:90)

Among the Kachin, the relationship of a tenant to a landlord is also a relationship between a son-in-law and a father-in-law. "The procedure for acquiring land rights of any kind is in almost all cases tantamount to marrying a woman from the lineage of the lord" (ibid.:88). In the Kachin system, bridewealth moves from commoners to aristocrats, women moving in the opposite direction.

From an economic aspect the effect of matrilateral cross-cousin marriage is that, on balance, the headman's lineage constantly pays wealth to the chief's lineage in the form of bridewealth. The payment can also, from an analytical point of view, be regarded as a rent paid to the senior landlord by the tenant. The most important part of this payment is in the form of consumer goods—namely cattle. The chief converts this perishable wealth into imperishable prestige through the medium of spectacular feasting. The ultimate consumers of the goods are in this way the original producers, namely, the commoners who attend the feast. (Ibid.:89)

In another example, it is traditional in the Trobriands for a man to send a harvest gift—urigubu—of yams to his sister's household. For the commoners, this amounts to a simple circulation of yams. But the chief is polygamous, and marries a woman from each subdistrict within his domain. Each of these subdistricts therefore sends urigubu to the chief, providing him with a bulging storehouse out of which he finances feasts, craft production, and kula expeditions. This "fund of power" underwrites the political system and forms the basis for chiefly power (Malinowski, 1970).

In some systems, position in a political hierarchy and position in a marriage system are intimately linked. In traditional Tonga, women married up in rank. Thus, low-ranking lineages would send women to higher ranking lineages. Women of the highest lineage were married into the "house of Fiji," a lineage defined as outside the political system. If the highest ranking chief gave his sister to a lineage other than one which had no part in the ranking system, he would no longer be the highest ranking chief. Rather, the lineage of his sister's son would outrank his own. In times of political rearrangement, the demotion of the previous high-ranking lineage was formalized when it gave a wife to a lineage which it had formerly outranked. In traditional Hawaii, the situation was the reverse. Women married down, and the dominant lineage gave wives to junior lines. A paramount would either marry a sister or obtain a wife from Tonga. When a junior lineage usurped rank, it formalized its position by giving a wife to its former senior line.

There is even some tantalizing data suggesting that marriage systems may be implicated in the evolution of social strata, and perhaps in the development of early states. The first round of the political consolidation which resulted in the formation of a state in Madagascar occurred when one chief obtained title to several autonomous districts through the vagaries of marriage and inheritance (Henry Wright, personal communication). In Samoa, legends place the origin of the paramount title—the *Tafa'ifa*—as a result of intermarriage between ranking members of four major lineages. My thoughts are too speculative, my data too sketchy, to say much on this subject. But a search ought to be undertaken for data which might demonstrate how marriage systems intersect with large-scale political processes like state-making. Marriage systems might be implicated in a number of ways: in the accumulation of wealth and the maintenance of differential access to political and economic resources; in the building of alliances; in the consolidation of high-ranking persons into a single closed strata of endogamous kin.

These examples—like the Kachin and the Trobriand ones—indicate that sexual systems cannot, in the final analysis, be understood in complete isolation. A full-bodied analysis of women in a single society, or throughout history, must take *everything* into account: the evolution of commodity forms in women, systems of land tenure, political arrangements, subsistence technology, etc. Equally important, economic and political analyses are incomplete if they do not consider women, marriage, and sexuality. Traditional concerns of anthropology and social science—such as the evolution of social stratification and the origin of the state—must be reworked to include the implications of matrilateral cross-cousin marriage, surplus extracted in the form of daughters, the conversion of female labor into male wealth, the conversion of female lives into marriage alliances, the contribution of marriage to political power, and the transformations which all of these varied aspects of society have undergone in the course of time.

This sort of endeavor is, in the final analysis, exactly what Engels tried to do in his effort to weave a coherent analysis of so many of the diverse aspects of social life. He tried to relate men and women, town and country, kinship and state, forms of property, systems of land tenure, convertibility of wealth, forms of exchange, the technology of food production, and forms of trade, to name a few, into a systematic historical account. Eventually, someone will have to write a new version of *The Origin of the Family, Private Property, and the State*, recognizing the mutual interdependence of sexuality, economics, and politics without underestimating the full significance of each in human society.

ACKNOWLEDGMENTS

Acknowledgements are an inadequate expression of how much this paper, like most, is the product of many minds. They are also necessary to free others of the responsibility for what is ultimately a personal vision of a collective conversation. I want to free and thank the following persons: Tom Anderson and Arlene Gorelick, with whom I co-authored the paper from which this one evolved; Rayna Reiter, Larry Shields, Ray Kelly, Peggy White, Norma Diamond, Randy Reiter, Frederick Wyatt, Anne Locksley, Juliet Mitchell, and Susan Harding, for countless conversations and ideas; Marshall Sahlins, for the revelation of anthropology; Lynn Eden, for sardonic editing; the members of Women's Studies 340/004, for my initiation into teaching; Sally Brenner, for heroic typing; Susan Lowes, for incredible patience; and Emma Goldman, for the title.

NOTES

1. Moving between Marxism, structuralism, and psychoanalysis produces a certain clash of epistemologies. In particular, structuralism is a can from which worms crawl out all over the epistemological map. Rather than trying to cope with this problem, I have more or less ignored the fact that Lacan and Lévi-Strauss are among the foremost living ancestors of the contemporary French intellectual revolution (see Foucault, 1970). It would be fun, interesting, and, if this were France, essential, to start my argument from the center of the structuralist maze and work my way out from there, along the lines of a "dialectical theory of signifying practices" (see Hefner, 1974).

2. A lot of the debate on women and housework has centered around the question of whether or not housework is "productive" labor. Strictly speaking, housework is not ordinarily "productive" in the technical sense of the term (I. Gough, 1972; Marx, 1969:387–413). But this distinction is irrelevant to the main line of the argument. Housework may not be "productive," in the sense of directly producing surplus value and capital, and yet be a crucial element in the production of surplus value and capital.

3. That some of them are pretty bizarre, from our point of view, only demonstrates the point that sexuality is expressed through the intervention of culture (see Ford and Beach, 1972). Some examples may be chosen from among the exotica in which anthropologists delight. Among the Banaro, marriage involves several socially sanctioned sexual partnerships. When a woman is married, she is initiated into intercourse by the sib-friend of her groom's father. After bearing a child by this man, she begins to have intercourse with her husband. She also has an institutionalized partnership with the sib-friend of her husband. A man's partners include his wife, the wife of his sib-friend, and the wife of his sib-friend's son (Thurnwald 1916). Multiple intercourse is a more pronounced custom among the Marind Anim. At the time of marriage, the bride has intercourse with all of the members of the groom's clan, the groom coming last. Every major festival is accompanied by a practice known as *otiv-bombari*, in which semen is collected for ritual purposes. A few women have intercourse with many men, and the resulting semen is collected in coconut-shell buckets. A Marind male is subjected to multiple homosexual intercourse during initiation (Van Baal, 1966). Among the Etoro, heterosexual intercourse is taboo for between 205 and 260 days a year (Kelly, 1974). In much of New Guinea, men fear copulation and think that it will kill them if they engage in it without magical precautions (Glasse, 1971; Meggitt, 1970). Usually, such ideas of feminine pollution express the subordination of women. But symbolic systems contain internal contradictions, whose logical extensions sometimes lead to inversions of

the propositions on which a system is based. In New Britain, men's fear of sex is extreme that rape appears to be feared by men rather than women. Women run after the men, who flee from them, women are the sexual aggressors, and it is bridegrooms who are reluctant (Goodale and Chowning, 1971). Other interesting sexual variations can be found in Yalmon (1963) and K. Gough (1959).

4. Engels thought that men acquired wealth in the form of herds and, wanting to pass this wealth to their own children, overthrew "mother right" in favor of patrilineal inheritance. "The overthrow of mother right was the *world historical defeat of the female sex*. The man took command in the home also; the woman was degraded and reduced to servitude; she became the slave of his lust and a mere instrument for the production of children" (Engels, 1972:120–21; italics in original). As has been often pointed out, women do not necessarily have significant social authority in societies practicing matrilineal inheritance (Schneider and Gough, 1962).

5. "What, would you like to marry your sister? What is the matter with you? Don't you want a brother-in-law? Don't you realize that if you marry another man's sister and another man marries your sister, you will have at least two brothers-in-law, while if you marry your own sister you will have none? With whom will you hunt, with whom will you garden, whom will you go visit?" (Arapesh, cited in Lévi-Strauss, 1969:485).

6. This analysis of society as based on bonds between men by means of women makes the separatist responses of the women's movement thoroughly intelligible. Separatism can be seen as a mutation in social structure, as an attempt to form social groups based on unmediated bonds between women. It can also be seen as a radical denial of men's "rights" in women, and as a claim by women of rights in themselves.

7. "The woman shall not wear that which pertaineth unto a man, neither shall a man put on a woman's garment: for all that do so *are* abomination unto the LORD thy God" (Deuteronomy, 22:5; emphasis not mine).

8. "In studying women we cannot neglect the methods of a science of the mind, a theory that attempts to explain how women become women and men, men. The borderline between the biological and the social which finds expression in the family is the land psychoanalysis sets out to chart, the land where sexual distinction originates." (Mitchell, 1971:167)

   What is the *object* of psychoanalysis? . . . but the *'effects,'* prolonged into the surviving adult, of the extraordinary adventure which from birth the liquidation of the Oedipal phase transforms a small animal conceived by a man and a woman into a small human child . . . the 'effects' still present in the survivors of the forced 'humanization' of the small human animal into a *man* or a *woman*. . . ." (Althusser, 1969:57,59; italics in original)

9. The psychoanalytic theories of femininity were articulated in the context of a debate which took place largely in the International Journal of Psychoanalysis and The Psychoanalytic Quarterly in the late 1920s and early 1930s. Articles representing the range of discussion include: Freud, 1961a, 1961b, 1965; Lampl

de Groot, 1933, 1948; Deutsch, 1948a, 1948b; Horney, 1973; Jones, 1933. Some of my dates are of reprints; for the original chronology, see Chasseguet-Smirgel (1970: introduction). The debate was complex, and I have simplified it. Freud, Lampl de Groot, and Deutsch argued that femininity developed out of a bisexual, "phallic" girl-child; Horney and Jones argued for an innate femininity. The debate was not without its ironies. Horney defended women against penis envy by postulating that women are born and not made; Deutsch, who considered women to be made and not born, developed a theory of feminine masochism whose best rival is Story of O. I have attributed the core of the "Freudian" version of female development equally to Freud and to Lampl de Groot. In reading through the articles, it has seemed to me that the theory is as much (or more) hers as it is his.

10. I have taken my position on Freud somewhere between the French structuralist interpretations and American biologistic ones, because I think that Freud's wording is similarly somewhere in the middle. He does talk about penises, about the "inferiority" of the clitoris, about the psychic consequences of anatomy. The Lacanians, on the other hand, argue from Freud's text that he is unintelligible if his words are taken literally, and that a thoroughly nonanatomical theory can be deduced as Freud's intention (see Althusser, 1969). I think that they are right; the penis is walking around too much for its role to be taken literally. The detachability of the penis, and its transformation in fantasy (e.g., penis = feces = child = gift), argue strongly for a symbolic interpretation. Nevertheless, I don't think that Freud was as consistent as either I or Lacan would like him to have been, and some gesture must be made to what he said, even as we play with what he must have meant.

11. The pre-Oedipal mother is the "phallic mother," e.g., she is believed to possess the phallus. The Oedipal-inducing information is that the mother does not possess the phallus. In other words, the crisis is precipitated by the "castration" of the mother, by the recognition that the phallus only passes through her, but does not settle on her. The "phallus" must pass through her, since the relationship of a male to every other male is defined through a woman. A man is linked to a son by a mother, to his nephew by virtue of a sister, etc. Every relationship between male kin is defined by the woman between them. If power is a male prerogative, and must be passed on, it must go through the woman-in-between. Marshall Sahlins (personal communication) once suggested that the reason women are so often defined as stupid, polluting, disorderly, silly, profane, or whatever, is that such categorizations define women as "incapable" of possessing the power which must be transferred through them.

12. Parts of Wittig's Les Guêrillêres (1973) appear to be tirades against Lévi-Strauss and Lacan. For instance:

> Has he not indeed written, power and the possession of women, leisure and the enjoyment of women? He writes that you are currency, an item of exchange. He writes, barter, barter, possession and acquisition of women and merchandise. Better for you to see your guts in the sun and utter the death rattle than

to live a life that anyone can appropriate. What belongs to you on this earth? Only death. No power on earth can take that away from you. And—consider explain tell yourself—if happiness consists in the possession of something, then hold fast to this sovereign happiness—to die. (Wittig, 1973: 115–16; see also 106–107; 113–14; 134)

The awareness of French feminists of Lévi-Strauss and Lacan is most clearly evident in a group called "Psychoanalyse et Politique" which defined its task as a feminist use and critique of Lacanian psychoanalysis.

13. "Every woman adores a facist."—Sylvia Plath

14. One clinician, Charlotte Wolff (1971) has taken the psychoanalytic theory of womanhood to its logical extreme and proposed that lesbianism is a healthy response to female socialization.

> Women who do not rebel against the status of object have declared themselves defeated as persons in their own right. (Wolff, 1971:65)

> The lesbian girl is the one who, by all means at her disposal, will try to find a place of safety inside and outside the family, through her fight for equality with the male. She will not, like other women, play up to him: indeed, she despises the very idea of it. (Ibid.:59)

> The lesbian was and is unquestionably in the avant-garde of the fight for equality of the sexes, and for the psychical liberation of women. (Ibid.: 66)

It is revealing to compare Wolff's discussion with the articles on lesbianism in Marmor, 1965.

15. Another line of inquiry would compare bridewealth systems to dowry systems. Many of these questions are treated in Goody and Tambiah, 1973.

4

THE COMBAHEE RIVER COLLECTIVE

A Black Feminist Statement

We are a collective of black feminists who have been meeting together since 1974.[1] During that time we have been involved in the process of defining and clarifying our politics, while at the same time doing political work within our own group and in coalition with other progressive organizations and movements. The most general statement of our politics at the present time would be that we are actively committed to struggling against racial, sexual, heterosexual, and class oppression and see as our particular task the development of integrated analysis and practice based upon the fact that the major systems of oppression are interlocking. The synthesis of these oppressions creates the conditions of our lives. As black women we see black feminism as the logical political movement to combat the manifold and simultaneous oppressions that all women of color face.

We will discuss four major topics in the paper that follows: (1) The genesis of contemporary black feminism; (2) what we believe, i.e., the specific province of our politics; (3) the problems in organizing black feminists, including a brief herstory of our collective; and (4) black feminist issues and practice.

1. THE GENESIS OF CONTEMPORARY BLACK FEMINISM

Before looking at the recent development of black feminism, we would like to affirm that we find our origins in the historical reality of Afro-American women's continuous life-and-death struggle for survival and liberation. Black women's extremely negative relationship to the American political system (a system of white male rule) has always been determined by our membership in two oppressed racial and sexual castes. As Angela Davis points out in "Reflections on the Black Woman's Role in the Community of Slaves," black women have always embodied, if only in their physical manifestation, an adversary stance to white male rule and have actively resisted its inroads upon them and their communities in both dramatic and subtle ways. There have always been black women activists—some known, like Sojourner Truth, Harriet Tubman, Frances E. W. Harper, Ida B. Wells Barnett, and Mary Church Terrell, and thousands upon thousands unknown—who had a shared awareness of how their sexual identity combined with their racial identity to make their whole life situation and the focus of their political struggles unique. Contemporary black feminism is the outgrowth of countless generations of personal sacrifice, militancy, and work by our mothers and sisters.

A black feminist presence has evolved most obviously in connection with the second wave of the American women's movement beginning in the late 1960s. Black, other Third World, and working women have been involved in the feminist movement from its start, but both outside reactionary forces and racism and elitism within the movement itself have served to obscure our participation. In 1973 black feminists, primarily located in New York, felt the necessity of forming a separate black feminist group. This became the National Black Feminist Organization (NBFO).

Black feminist politics also have an obvious connection to movements for black liberation, particularly those of the 1960s and 1970s. Many of us were active in those movements (civil rights, black nationalism, the Black Panthers), and all of our lives were greatly affected and changed by their ideology, their goals, and the tactics used to achieve their goals. It was our experience and disillusionment within these liberation movements, as well as experience on the periphery of the white male left, that led to the need to develop a politics that was antiracist, unlike those of white women, and antisexist, unlike those of black and white men.

There is also undeniably a personal genesis for black feminism, that is, the political realization that comes from the seemingly personal experiences of individual black women's lives. Black feminists and many more black women who do not define themselves as feminists have all experienced sexual oppression as a constant factor in our day-to-day existence.

Black feminists often talk about their feelings of craziness before becoming conscious of the concepts of sexual politics, patriarchal rule, and, most importantly, feminism, the political analysis and practice that we women use to struggle against our oppression. The fact that racial politics and indeed racism are pervasive factors in our lives did not allow us, and still does not allow most black women, to look more deeply into our own experiences and define those things that make our lives what they are and our oppression specific to us. In the process of consciousness-raising, actually life-sharing, we began to recognize the commonality of our experiences and, from that sharing and growing consciousness, to build a politics that will change our lives and inevitably end our oppression.

Our development also must be tied to the contemporary economic and political position of black people. The post-World War II generation of black youth was the first to be able to minimally partake of certain educational and employment options, previously closed completely to black people. Although our economic position is still at the very bottom of the American capitalist economy, a handful of us have been able to gain certain tools as a result of tokenism in education and employment which potentially enable us to more effectively fight our oppression.

A combined antiracist and antisexist position drew us together initially, and as we developed politically we addressed ourselves to heterosexism and economic oppression under capitalism.

2. WHAT WE BELIEVE

Above all else, our politics initially sprang from the shared belief that black women are inherently valuable, that our liberation is a necessity not as an adjunct to somebody else's but because of our need as human persons for autonomy. This may seem so obvious as to sound simplistic, but it is apparent that no other ostensibly progressive movement has ever considered our specific oppression a priority or worked seriously for the ending of that oppression. Merely naming the pejorative stereotypes attributed to black women (e.g., mammy, matriarch, Sapphire, whore, bulldagger), let alone cataloguing the cruel, often murderous, treatment we receive, indicates how little value has been placed upon our lives during four centuries of bondage in the Western hemisphere. We realize that the only people who care enough about us to work consistently for our liberation is us. Our politics evolve from a healthy love for ourselves, our sisters, and our community which allows us to continue our struggle and work.

This focusing upon our own oppression is embodied in the concept of identity politics. We believe that the most profound and potentially the most radical politics come directly out of our own identity, as opposed to working to end somebody else's oppression. In the case of black women this is a particularly repugnant, dangerous, threatening, and therefore revolutionary concept because it is obvious from looking at all the political movements that have preceded us that anyone is more worthy of liberation than ourselves. We reject pedestals, queenhood, and walking ten paces behind. To be recognized as human, levelly human, is enough.

We believe that sexual politics under patriarchy is as pervasive in black women's lives as are the politics of class and race. We also often find it difficult to separate race from class from sex oppression because in our lives they are most often experienced simultaneously. We know that there is such a thing as racial-sexual oppression which is neither solely racial nor solely sexual, e.g., the history of rape of black women by white men as a weapon of political repression.

Although we are feminists and lesbians, we feel solidarity with progressive black men and do not advocate the fractionalization that white women who are separatists demand. Our situation as black people necessitates that we have solidarity around the fact of race, which white women of course do not need to have with white men, unless it is their negative solidarity as racial oppressors. We struggle together with black men against racism, while we also struggle with black men about sexism.

We realize that the liberation of all oppressed peoples necessitates the destruction of the political-economic systems of capitalism and imperialism as well as patriarchy. We are socialists because we believe the work must be organized for the collective benefit of those who do the work and create the products and not for the profit of the bosses. Material resources must be equally distributed among those who create these resources. We are not convinved, however, that a socialist revolution that is not also a feminist and antiracist revolution will guarantee our liberation. We have arrived at the necessity for developing an understanding of class relationships that takes into account the specific class position of black women who are generally marginal in the labor force, while at this particular time some of us are temporarily viewed as doubly desirable tokens at white-collar and professional levels. We need to articulate the real class situation of persons who are not merely raceless, sexless workers, but for whom racial and sexual oppression are significant determinants in their working/economic lives. Although we are in essential agreement with Marx's theory as it applied to the very specific economic relationships he analyzed, we know that this analysis must be extended further in order for us to understand our specific economic situation as black women.

A political contribution which we feel we have already made is the expansion of the feminist principle that the personal is political. In our consciousness-raising sessions, for example, we have in many ways gone beyond white women's revelations because we are dealing with the implications of race and class as well as sex. Even our black women's style of talking/testifying in black language about what we have experienced has a resonance that is both cultural and political. We have spent a great deal of energy delving into the cultural and experiential nature of our oppression out of necessity because none of these matters have ever been looked at before. No one before has ever examined the multilayered texture of black women's lives.

As we have already stated, we reject the stance of lesbian separatism because it is not a viable political analysis or strategy for us. It leaves out far too much and far too many people, particularly black men, women, and children. We have a great deal of criticism and loathing for what men have been socialized to be in this society: what they support, how they act, and how they oppress. But we do not have the misguided notion that it is their maleness, per se—i.e., their biological maleness—that makes them what they are. As black women we find any type of biological determinism a particularly dangerous and reactionary basis upon which to build a politic. We must also question whether lesbian separatism is an adequate and progressive political analysis and strategy, even for those who practice it, since it so completely denies any but the sexual sources of women's oppression, negating the facts of class and race.

3. PROBLEMS IN ORGANIZING BLACK FEMINISTS

During our years together as a black feminist collective we have experienced success and defeat, joy and pain, victory and failure. We have found that it is very difficult to organize around black feminist issues, difficult even to announce in certain contexts that we are black feminists. We have tried to think about the reasons for our difficulties, particularly since the white women's movement continues to be strong and to grow in many directions. In this section we will discuss some of the general reasons for the organizing problems we face and also talk specifically about the stages in organizing our own collective.

The major source of difficulty in our political work is that we are not just trying to fight oppression on one front or even two, but instead to address a whole range of oppressions. We do not have racial, sexual, heterosexual or class privilege to rely upon, nor do we have even the minimal access to resources and power that groups who possess any one of these types of privilege have.

The psychological toll of being a black woman and the difficulties this presents in reaching political consciousness and doing political work can never be underestimated. There is a very low value placed upon black women's psyches in this society, which is both racist and sexist. As an early group member once said, "We are all damaged people merely by virtue of being black women." We are dispossessed psychologically and on every other level, and yet we feel the necessity to struggle to change our condition and the condition of all black women. In "A Black Feminist's Search for Sisterhood," Michele Wallace arrives at this conclusion:

> We exist as women who are black who are feminists, each stranded for the moment, working independently because there is not yet an environment in this society remotely congenial to our struggle—because, being on the bottom, we would have to do what no one else has done: we would have to fight the world.[2]

Wallace is not pessimistic but realistic in her assessment of black feminists' position, particularly in her allusion to the nearly classic isolation most of us face. We might use our position at the bottom, however, to make a clear leap into revolutionary action. If black women were free, it would mean that everyone else would have to be free since our freedom would necessitate the destruction of all the systems of oppression.

Feminism is, nevertheless, very threatening to the majority of black people because it calls into question some of the most basic assumptions about our existence, i.e., that gender should be a determinant of power relationships. Here is the way male and female roles were defined in a black nationalist pamphlet from the early 1970s.

> We understand that it is and has been traditional that the man is the head of the house. He is the leader of the house/nation because his knowledge of the world is broader, his awareness is greater, his understanding is fuller and his application of this information is wiser. . . . After all, it is only reasonable that the man be the head of the house because he is able to defend and protect the development of his home. . . . Women cannot do the same things as men—they are made by nature to function differently. Equality of men and women is something that cannot happen even in the abstract world. Men are not equal to other men, i.e., ability, experience, or even understanding. The value of men and women can be seen as in the value of gold and silver—they are not equal but both have great value. We must realize

that men and women are a complement to each other because there is no house/family without a man and his wife. Both are essential to the development of any life.[3]

The material conditions of most black women would hardly lead them to upset both economic and sexual arrangements that seem to represent some stability in their lives. Many black women have a good understanding of both sexism and racism, but because of the everyday constrictions of their lives cannot risk struggling against them both.

The reaction of black men to feminism has been notoriously negative. They are, of course, even more threatened than black women by the possibility that black feminists might organize around our own needs. They realize that they might not only lose valuable and hard-working allies in their struggles but that they might also be forced to change their habitually sexist ways of interacting with and oppressing black women. Accusations that black feminism divides the black struggle are powerful deterrents to the growth of an autonomous black women's movement.

Still, hundreds of women have been active at different times during the three-year existence of our group. And every black women who came, came out of a strongly felt need for some level of possibility that did not previously exist in her life.

When we first started meeting early in 1974 after the NBFO first eastern regional conference, we did not have a strategy for organizing, or even a focus. We just wanted to see what we had. After a period of months of not meeting, we began to meet again late in the year and started doing an intense variety of consciousness-raising. The overwhelming feeling that we had is that after years and years we had finally found each other. Although we were not doing political work as a group, individuals continued their involvement in lesbian politics, sterilization abuse and abortion rights work. Third World Women's International Women's Day activities, and support activity for the trials of Dr. Kenneth Edelin, Joan Little, and Inez Garcia. During our first summer, when membership had dropped off considerably, those of us remaining devoted serious discussion to the possibility of opening a refuge for battered women in a black community. (There was no refuge in Boston at that time.) We also decided around that time to become an independent collective since we had serious disagreements with NBFOs bourgeois-feminist stance and their lack of a clear political focus.

We also were contacted at that time by socialist feminists, with whom we had worked on abortion rights activities, who wanted to encourage us to attend the National Socialist Feminist Conference in Yellow Springs. One of our members did attend and despite the narrowness of the ideology that was promoted at that particular conference, we became more aware of the need for us to understand our own economic situation and to make our own economic analysis.

In the fall, when some members returned, we experienced several months of comparative inactivity and internal disagreements which were first conceptualized as a lesbian-straight split but which were also the result of class and political differences. During the summer those of us who were still meeting had determined the need to do political work and to move beyond consciousness-raising and serving exclusively as an emotional support group. At the beginning of 1976, when some of the women who had not wanted to do political work and who also had voiced disagreements stopped attending of their own accord, we again looked for a focus. We decided at that time, with the addition of new members, to become a study group. We had always shared our reading with each other, and some of us had written papers on black feminism for group discussion a few months before this decision was made. We began functioning as a study group and also began discussing the possibility of starting a black feminist publication. We had a retreat in the late spring which provided a time for both political discussion and working out interpersonal issues. Currently we are planning to gather together a collection of black feminist writing. We feel that it is absolutely essential to demonstrate the reality of our politics to other black women and believe that we can do this through writing and distributing our work. The fact that individual black feminists are living in isolation all over the country, that our own numbers are small, and that we have some skills in writing, printing, and publishing makes us want to carry out these kinds of projects as a means of organizing black feminists as we continue to do political work in coalition with other groups.

4. BLACK FEMINIST ISSUES AND PRACTICE

During our time together we have identified and worked on many issues of particular relevance to black women. The inclusiveness of our politics makes us concerned with any situation that impinges upon the lives of women, Third World, and working people. We are of course particularly committed to working on those struggles in which race, sex, and class are simultaneous factors in oppression. We might, for example, become involved in workplace organizing at a factory that employs Third World women or picket a hospital that is cutting back on already inadequate health care to a Third World community, or set up a rape crisis center in a black neighborhood. Organizing around welfare or daycare concerns might also be a focus. The work to be done and the countless issues that this work represents merely reflect the pervasiveness of our oppression.

Issues and projects that collective members have actually worked on are sterilization abuse, abortion rights, battered women, rape, and health care. We have also done many workshops and educationals on black feminism on college campuses, at women's conferences, and most recently for high school women.

One issue that is of major concern to us and that we have begun to publicly address is racism in the white women's movement. As black feminists we are made constantly and painfully aware of how little effort white women have made to understand and combat their racism, which requires among other things that they have a more than superficial comprehension of race, color, and black history and culture. Eliminating racism in the white women's movement is by definition work for white women to do, but we will continue to speak to and demand accountability on this issue. \\

In the practice of our politics we do not believe that the end always justifies the means. Many reactionary and destructive acts have been done in the name of achieving "correct" political goals. As feminists we do not want to mess over people in the name of politics. We believe in collective process and a nonhierarchical distribution of power within our own group and in our vision of a revolutionary society. We are committed to a continual examination of our politics as they develop through criticism and self-criticism as an essential aspect of our practice. As black feminists and lesbians we know that we have a very definite revolutionary task to perform and we are ready for the lifetime of work and struggle before us.

NOTES

1. This statement is dated April 1977.
2. Michele Wallace, "A Black Feminist's Search for Sisterhood," *The Village Voice*. 28 July 1975, pp. 6–7.
3. Mumininas of Committee for Unified Newark, *Mwanamke Mwananchi* (*The Nationalist Woman*), Newark, N.J., c. 1971, pp. 4–5.

5

WENDY W. WILLIAMS

The Equality Crisis

Some Reflections on Culture, Courts, and Feminism

INTRODUCTION

To say that courts are not and never have been the source of radical social change is an understatement. They reflect, by and large, mainstream views, mostly after those views are well established, although very occasionally (as in *Brown v. Board of Education*, the great school desegregation case) the Court moves temporarily out ahead of public opinion. What women can get from the courts—what we have gotten in the past decade—is a qualified guarantee of equal treatment. We can now expect, for the most part, that courts will rule that the privileges the law explicitly bestows on men must also be made available to women.

Because courts, as institutions of circumscribed authority, can only review in limited and specific ways the laws enacted by elected representatives, their role in promoting gender equality is pretty much confined to telling legislators what they cannot do, or extending the benefit of what they have done, to women. In an important sense, then, courts will do no more than measure women's claim to equality against legal benefits and burdens that are an expression of white male middle-class interests and values.[1] This means, to rephrase the point, that women's equality as delivered by the courts can only be an integration into a pre-existing, predominantly male world. To the extent that women share those predominant values or aspire to share that world on its own terms, resort to the courts has, since the early 1970s, been the most efficient, accessible, and reliable mode of redress. But to the extent that the law of the public world must be reconstructed to reflect the needs and values of both sexes, change must be sought from legislatures rather than the courts. And women, whose separate experience has not been adequately registered in the political process, are the ones who must seek the change.

Nonetheless, I am going to talk about courts because what they do—what the Supreme Court does—is extremely important, for a number of reasons. (1) The way courts define equality, within the limits of their sphere, does indeed matter in the real world (2) Legal cases have been and continue to be a focal point of debate about the meaning of equality; our participation in that debate and reflection upon it has enabled us to begin to form coherent overall theories of gender equality that inform our judgments about what we should seek from legislatures as well as courts. (3) The cases themselves, the participation they attract and the debate they engender, tell us important things about societal norms, cultural tensions, indeed, cultural limits concerning gender and sexual roles.

My thesis is that we (feminists) are at a crisis point in our evaluation of equality and women and that perhaps one of the reasons for the crisis is that, having dealt with the easy cases, we (feminists and courts) are now trying to cope with issues that touch the hidden nerves of our most profoundly embedded cultural values. . . .

I. A BRIEF HISTORY OF GENDER EQUALITY AND THE SUPREME COURT

Just before the American Revolution, Blackstone, in the course of his comprehensive commentary on the common law, set forth the fiction that informed and guided the treatment of married women in the English law courts. When a woman married, her legal identity merged into that of her husband; she was civilly dead.[2] She couldn't sue, be sued,[3] enter into contracts,[4] make wills,[5] keep her own earnings,[6] control her own property.[7] She could not even protect her own physical integrity—her husband had the right to chastise her (although only with a switch no bigger than his thumb),[8] restrain her freedom,[9] and impose sexual intercourse upon her against her will.[10]

Beginning in the middle of the nineteenth century, the most severe civil disabilities were removed in this country by state married women's property acts.[11] Blackstone's unities fiction was for the most part replaced by a theory that recognized women's legal personhood but which assigned her a place before the law different and distinct from that of her husband. This was the theory of the separate spheres of men and women, under which the husband was the couple's representative in the public world and its breadwinner; the wife was the center of the private world of the family.[12] Because it endowed women with a place, role, and importance of their own, the doctrine of the separate spheres was an advance over the spousal unities doctrine. At the same time, however, it preserved and promoted the dominance of male over female.[13] The public world of men was governed by law while the private world of women was outside the law, and man was free to exercise his prerogatives as he chose.

Perhaps the best-known expression of the separate spheres ideology is Justice Bradley's concurring opinion in an 1873 Supreme Court case, *Bradwell v. Illinois*, which begins with the observation that "Civil law, as well as nature herself, has always recognized a wide difference in the respective spheres and destinies of man and woman"[14] and concludes, in ringing tones, that the "paramount destiny and mission of woman are to fulfill the noble and benign offices of wife and mother."[15] The separate spheres ideology was used in Bradwell to uphold the exclusion of women from legal practice. Thirty-five years later, in *Muller v. Oregon*,[16] it became the basis for upholding legislation governing the hours women were permitted to work in the paid labor force. Women's special maternal role, said the Court, justified special protections in the workplace.[17] As late as 1961, in a challenge by a criminal defendant, the Court upheld a statute creating an automatic exemption from jury duty for all women who failed to volunteer their names for the jury pool, saying, "[W]oman is still regarded as the center of home and family life. We cannot say that it is constitutionally impermissible for a State. . .to conclude that a woman should be relieved from the civil duty of jury service unless she herself determines that such service is consistent with her own special responsibilities."[18]

The separate spheres ideology was repudiated by the Supreme Court only in the last twelve years. The engine of destruction was, as a technical matter, the more rigorous standard of review that the Court began applying to sex discrimination cases beginning in 1971.[19] By 1976 the Court was requiring that sex-based classifications bear a "substantial" relationship to an "important" governmental purpose.[20] This standard, announced in *Craig v. Boren*, was not as strong as that used in race cases,[21] but it was certainly a far cry from the rational basis standard that had traditionally been applied to sex-based classifications.

As a practical matter, what the Court did was strike down sex-based classifications that were premised on the old breadwinner-homemaker, master-dependent dichotomy inherent in the separate spheres ideology. Thus, the Supreme Court insisted that women wage earners receive the same benefits for their families under military,[22] social security,[23] welfare,[24] and workers compensation[25] programs as did male wage earners; that men receive the same child care allowance when their spouses died as women did;[26] that the female children of divorce be entitled to support for the same length of time as male children, so that they too could get the education necessary for life in the public world;[27] that the duty of support through alimony not be visited exclusively on husbands;[28] that wives as well as husbands participate in the management of the community property;[29] and that wives as well as husbands be eligible to administer their deceased relatives' estates.[30]

All this happened in the little more than a decade that has elapsed since 1971. The achievement is not an insubstantial one. Yet it also seems to me that in part what the Supreme Court did was simply to recognize that the real world outside the courtroom had already changed. [Women] were in fact no longer chiefly housewife-dependents. The family wage no longer existed; for a vast number of two-parent families, two wage earners were an economic necessity. In addition, many families were headed by a single parent. It behooved the Court to account for this new reality and it did so by recognizing that the breadwinner-homemaker dichotomy was an outmoded stereotype.

II. MEN'S CULTURE: AGGRESSOR IN WAR AND SEX

Of course, not all of the Supreme Court cases involved the breadwinner-homemaker stereotype. The other cases can be grouped in several ways; for my purposes I will place them in two groups. One group is composed of the remedial or compensatory discrimination cases—the cases in which a statute treats women differently and better than men for the purpose of redressing past unequal treatment.[31] The other group, the focus of this paper, consists of the cases that don't really seem to fit into any neat category but share a common quality. Unlike the cases discussed above, they do not deal with laws that rest on an economic model of the family that no longer predominates; rather, they concern themselves with other, perhaps more basic, sex-role arrangements. They are what I would call, simply, the "hard" cases, and for the most part, they are cases in which a sex-based classification was upheld by the Court.[32] There are a number of ways one could characterize and analyze them. I want to view them from one of those possible perspectives, namely, what they tell us about the state of our culture with respect to the equality of men and women. What do they say about the cultural limits of the equality principle?

In the 1980–81 Term the Supreme Court decided three sex-discrimination cases. One was *Kirshberg v. Feenstra*,[33] a case which struck down the Louisiana statute that gave husbands total control over the couple's property. That, to my mind, was an easy case. It falls within the line of cases I have already described which dismantle the old separate spheres ideology. The other two cases were *Rostker v. Goldberg*,[34] the case which upheld the male-only draft registration law, and *Michael M. v. Superior Court*,[35] the case upholding the California statutory rape law. They are prime candidates for my hard-cases category.

Justice Rehnquist wrote the opinion of the Court in both *Rostker* and *Michael M*. In *Rostker*, the draft registration case, his reasoning was a simple syllogism. The purpose of the registration, he said, is to identify the draft pool.[36] The purpose of the draft is to provide combat troops.[37] Women are excluded from combat.[38] Thus, men and women are not similarly situated with respect to the draft,[39] and it is therefore constitutional to register males only.[40] Of course, the problem with his syllogism was that one of the premises—that the purpose of the draft is exclusively to raise combat troops—was and is demonstrably false,[41] but the manipulation of the facts of that case is not what I mean to focus on here.

In *Michael M.*, 17 1/2-year-old man and a 16 1/2-year-old woman had sexual intercourse. The 17 1/2-year-old man was prosecuted under California's statutory rape law, which made such intercourse criminal for the man but not the woman.[42] Rehnquist, for a plurality of the Court, accepted the utterly dubious proposition put forward by the State of California that the purpose of the statutory rape statute was to prevent teenage pregnancies. The difference in treatment under the statute is justified, he said, because men and women are not similarly situated with respect to this purpose.[43] Because the young woman is exposed to the risk of pregnancy, she is deterred from sexual intercourse by that risk. The young man, lacking such a natural deterrent, needs a legal deterrent, which the criminal statute provides.[44]

I think that perhaps the outcomes of these two cases—in which the sex-based statutes were upheld—were foregone conclusions and that the only question, before they were decided, was *how* the court would rationalize the outcome. This is perhaps more obvious in the draft case than the statutory rape case, but applies, I think, to both. Let me explain.

Suppose you could step outside our culture, rise above its minutiae, and look at its great contours. Having done so, speculate for a moment about where society might draw the line and refuse to proceed further with gender equality. What does our culture identify as quintessentially masculine? Where is the locus of traditional masculine pride and self-identity? What can we identify in men's cultural experience that most divides it from women's cultural experience? Surely, one rather indisputable answer to that question is "war": physical combat and its modern equivalents. (One could also answer that preoccupation with contact sports is such a difference, but that is, perhaps, just a subset of physical combat).

Not surprisingly, the Court in *Rostker* didn't come right out and say "We've reached our cultural limits." Yet I [find] it significant that even the Justices who dissented on the constitutionality of the draft registration law seemed to concede the constitutionality of excluding women from combat.[45] When Congress considered whether women should be drafted, it was much more forthright about its reasons and those reasons support my thesis. The Senate Armed Services Committee Report states:

> [T]he starting point for any discussion of the appropriateness of registering women for the draft is the question of the proper role of women in combat. The principle that women should not intentionally and routinely engage in combat *is fundamental, and enjoys wide support among our people.*[46]

In addition, the committee expressed three specific reasons for excluding women from combat. First, registering women for assignment to combat "would leave the actual performance of sexually mixed units as an experiment to be conducted in war with unknown risk—a risk that the committee finds militarily unwarranted and dangerous."[47] Second, any attempt to assign women to combat could "affect the national resolve at the time of mobilization."[48] Third, drafting women would "place unprecedented strains on family life."[49] The committee envisioned a young mother being drafted leaving a young father home to care for the family and concluded. "The committee is strongly of the view that such a result. . .is unwise and unacceptable to a large majority of our people."[50] To translate. Congress was worried that (1) sexually mixed units would not be able to function—perhaps because of sex in the foxhole? (2) if women were assigned to combat, the nation might be reluctant to go to war, presumably because the specter of women fighting would deter a protective and chivalrous populace; and (3) the idea that mom could go into battle and dad keep the home fires burning is simply beyond the cultural pale. In short, current notions of acceptable limits on sex-role behavior would be surpassed by putting women into combat.

But what about statutory rape? Not such a clear case, you say. I disagree. Buried perhaps a bit deeper in our collective psyches but no less powerful and perhaps even more fundamental than our definition of man as aggressor in war is man as aggressor in sex. The original statutory rape laws were quite explicitly based on this view. Then, as is true even today, men were considered the natural and proper initiators of sex. In the face of male sexual initiative, women could do one of two things, yield or veto, "consent" or decline. What normal women did not, *should* not, do was to initiate sexual contact, to be the sexual aggressor. The premise underlying statutory rape laws was that young women's chastity was precious and their naivete enormous. Their inability knowingly to consent to sexual intercourse meant that they required protection by laws which made their consent irrelevant but punished and deterred the "aggressive" male.

The Court's opinion, I believe, is implicitly based on stereotypes concerning male sexual aggression and female sexual passivity, despite Justice Rehnquist's express denial of that possibility.[51] His recitation of the facts of the case sets the stage for the sexual gender-role pigeon-holing that follows: "After being struck in the face for rebuffing petitioner's advances, Sharon," we are told, "*submitted* to sexual intercourse with petitioner."[52] Although, in theory, coercion and consent are relevant only to the crime of rape, not to statutory rape, we are thus provided with the details of this particular statutory rape case, details which cast Michael and Sharon as prototypes of the sexually aggressive male and the passive female.

But it is Rehnquist's description of the lower court opinion that most clearly reveals sex role assumptions that lead first the California high court and then the United States Supreme Court to uphold the legislation. He says, "Because *males alone* can 'physiologically cause the result which the law properly seeks to avoid [pregnancy], the California Supreme Court further held that the gender classification was readily justified as a means of identifying *offender* and *victim*."[53] The statement is remarkable for two (related) reasons. The first and most dramatic is the strangeness of the biological concept upon which it is based. Do the justices still believe that each sperm carries a homunculus—a tiny person—who need only be planted in the woman in order to grow? Are they ignorant of ova? Or has sex-role ideology simply outweighed scientific fact? Since no one has believed in homunculi for at least a century, it must be the latter. Driven by the stereotype of male as aggressor/offender and woman as passive victim, even the facts of conception are transformed to fit the image.

The second is the characterization of man and woman as "offender" and "victim." Statutory rape is, in criminal law terms, a clear instance of a victimless crime, since all parties are, by definition, voluntary participants. In what sense, then, can Rehnquist assert that the woman is victim and the man offender? One begins to get an inkling when, later, the Justice explains that the statutory rape law is "protective" legislation: "The statute here protects women from sexual intercourse at an age when those consequences are particularly severe."[54] His preconceptions become manifest when, finally, Rehnquist on one occasion calls the statute a "rape" statute[55]—by omitting the word "statutory" inadvertently exposing his hidden assumptions and underlining the belief structure which the very title of the crime, "statutory rape," lays bare.

What is even more interesting to me than the Court's resolution of these cases is the problem they cause for feminist analysis. The notion that men are frequently the sexual aggressors and that the law ought to be able to take that reality into account in very concrete ways is hardly one that feminists could reject out of hand (I'm thinking here of sexual harassment and forcible rape, among other things); it is therefore an area, like the others I'm about to discuss, in which we need to pay special attention to our impulses lest we inadvertently support and give credence to the very social constructs and behaviors we so earnestly mean to oppose. Should we, for example, defend traditional rape laws on the ground that rape, defined by law as penetration by the penis of the vagina, is a sexual offense the psychological and social consequences of which are so unique, severe, and rooted in age-old power relationships between the sexes that a gender-neutral law would fail in important ways to deal with the world as it really is? Or should we insist that equality theory requires that we reorganize our understanding of sexual crime, that unwanted sexual intrusion of types other than male-female sexual intercourse can similarly violate and humiliate the victim, and that legislation which defines sexual offenses in gender-neutral terms, because it resists our segregationist urges, and affirms our common humanity, is therefore what feminists should support? These are not easy questions, but they must be answered if feminist lawyers are to press a coherent theory of equality upon the courts in these hard cases.

As for *Rostker v. Goldberg*, the conflicts among feminists were overtly expressed. Some of us felt it essential that we support the notion that a single-sex draft was unconstitutional; others felt that feminists should not take such a position. These latter groups explicitly contrasted the female ethic of nurturance and life-giving with a male ethic of aggression and militarism and asserted that if we argued to the Court that single-sex registration is unconstitutional we would be betraying ourselves and supporting what we find least acceptable about the male world.

To me, this latter argument quite overtly taps qualities that the culture has ascribed to woman-as-childrearer and converts them to a normative value statement, one with which it is easy for us to sympathize. This is one of the circumstances in which the feeling that "I want what he's got but I don't want to be what he's had to be in order to get it" comes quickly to the surface. But I also believe that the reflexive response based on these deeper cultural senses leads us to untenable positions.

The single-sex laws upheld in *Michael M.* and *Rostker* ultimately do damage to women. For one thing, they absolve women of personal responsibility in the name of protection. There is a sense in which women have been victims of physical aggression in part because they have not been permitted to act as anything but victims.[56] For another, do we not acquire a greater right to claim our share from society if we too share its ultimate jeopardies? To me, *Rostker* never posed the question of whether women should be forced as men now are to fight wars, but whether we, like them, must take the responsibility for deciding whether or not to fight, whether or not to bear the cost of risking our lives, on the one hand, or resisting in the name of peace, on the other. And do we not, by insisting upon our differences at these crucial junctures, promote and reinforce the us-them dichotomy that permits the Rehnquists and the Stewarts to resolve matters of great importance and complexity by the simplistic, reflexive assertion that men and women "are simply not similarly situated?"

III. WOMEN'S CULTURE: MOTHER OF HUMANITY

We have looked briefly at the male side of the cultural equation. What are the cultural limits on women's side? Step outside the culture again and speculate. If we find limits and conflicts surrounding the male role as aggressor in war and sex, what will be the trouble spots at the opposite pole? What does the culture identify as quintessentially female? Where does our pride and self-identity lie? Most probably, I think, some-where in the realm of behaviors and concerns surrounding maternity.

I would expect the following areas to be the places where the move toward equal-ity of the sexes might come into collision with cultural limits, both in judicial opin-ions and in ourselves: treatment of maternity in the workplace, the tender years presumption, and joint custody of children upon divorce. The issues surrounding pregnancy and maternity are the most difficult from a theoretical point of view and for that reason may be the best illustration of the conflict I am trying to explore.

Let me start again with a Supreme Court case. As discussed earlier, before 1971, the ideology of the separate spheres informed Supreme Court opinions; it allowed the courts to view men and women as basically on different life tracks and therefore never really similarly situated. That fundamentally dichotomous view which characterized man as breadwinner, woman as homemaker-childrearer, foreclosed the possibility that the courts could successfully apply an equality model to the sexes.

Once the Supreme Court took on the task of dismantling the statutory structure build upon the separate spheres ideology, it had to face the question of how to treat pregnancy itself. Pregnancy was, after all, the centerpiece, the linchpin, the essential feature of women's separate sphere.[57] The stereotypes, the generalizations, the role expectations were at their zenith when a woman became pregnant. Gender equality would not be possible, one would think, unless the Court was willing to examine, at least as closely as other gender-related rulemaking, those prescriptions concerning pregnancy itself. On the other hand, the capacity to bear a child is a crucial, indeed definitional, difference between women and men. While it is obvious that the sexes can be treated equally with respect to characteristics that they share, how would it be possible to apply the equality principle to a characteristic unique to women?

So what did the Court do? It drew the line at pregnancy. Of *course* it would take a more critical look at sex discrimination than it had in the past—but, it said, discrimi-nation on the basis of pregnancy is not sex discrimination.[58] Now here was a simple but decisive strategy for avoiding the doctrinal discomfort that inclusion of preg-nancy within the magic circle of stricter review would bring with it. By placing preg-nancy altogether outside that class of phenomena labeled sex discrimination, the Court need not apply to classifications related to pregnancy the level of scrutiny it had already reserved, in cases such as *Reed v. Reed* and *Frontiero v. Richardson*, for gender classifications.[59] Pregnancy classifications would henceforth be subject only to the most casual review.

The position was revealed for the first time in 1974 in *Geduldig v. Aiello*,[60] a case challenging under the equal protection clause exclusion of pregnancy-related dis-abilities from coverage by an otherwise comprehensive state disability insurance program. The Court explained, in a footnote, that pregnancy classifications were not sex-based but were, instead, classifications based upon a physical condition and should be treated accordingly:

> The California insurance program does not exclude anyone from benefit eligibility because of gender *but merely removes one physical condition- pregnancy—from the list of compensable disabilities.* While it is true that only women can become pregnant, it does not follow that every legislative classification concerning pregnancy is a sex-based classification . . . Normal pregnancy is an objectively identifiable physical condition with unique characteristics . . .[L]awmakers are constitutionally free to include or exclude pregnancy from the coverage of legislation such as this on any reasonable basis, *just as with respect to any other physical condition.*[61]

The second time the Supreme Court said pregnancy discrimination is not sex discrimination was in *General Electric Company v. Gilbert*,[62] decided in 1976. *Gilbert* presented the same basic facts—exclusion of pregnancy-related disabilities from a comprehensive disability program—but this case was brought under Title VII rather than the equal protection clause. The Court nonetheless relied on *Geduldig*, saying that when Congress prohibited "sex discrimination," it didn't mean to include within the definition of that term pregnancy discrimination.[63]

There was, however, an additional theory available in *Gilbert* because it was a Title VII case that was not available in the equal protection case. That theory was that if an employer's rule has a disparate effect on women, even though there is no intent to discriminate, it might also violate Title VII. And did the Court find that the exclusion of pregnancy-related disabilities had a disparate effect on women? It did not.[64] Men and women, said Justice Rehnquist, received coverage for the disabilities they had in common. Pregnancy was an *extra* disability, since only women suffered it. To compensate women for it would give them more than men got. So here there was no disparate effect—the exclusion of pregnancy merely insured the basic equality of the program.[65]

The remarkable thing about this statement, like Rehnquist's later assertion in *Michael M.* that only men can "cause" pregnancy, is its peculiarly blinkered male vision. After all, men received coverage under General Electric's disability program for disabilities they did not have in common with women, including disabilities linked to exclusively male aspects of the human anatomy.[66] Thus, the only sense in which one can understand pregnancy to be "extra" is in some reverse-Freudian psychological fashion. Under Freud's interpretation, women were viewed by both sexes as inadequate men (men *minus*) because they lacked penises.[67] In Rehnquist's view, woman is now man *plus*, because she shares all his physical characteristics except that she also gets pregnant. Under either of these extravagantly skewed views of the sexes, however, man is the measure against which the anatomical features of woman are counted and assigned value, and when the addition or subtraction is complete, woman comes out behind.

The corollary to *Gilbert* appeared in *Nashville Gas Co. v. Satty*,[68] decided in 1977. There the Court finally found a pregnancy rule that violated Title VII. The role's chief characteristic was its gratuitously punitive effect. It provided that a woman returning from maternity leave lost all of the seniority she acquired *prior* to her leave.[69] Here, said Rehnquist, we have a case where women are not seeking extra benefits for pregnancy. Here's a case where a woman, now back at work and no longer pregnant, has actually had something taken away from her—her pre-pregnancy seniority—and she therefore suffers a burden that men don't have to bear.[70] This rule therefore has a disproportionate impact on women.

Roughly translated, *Gilbert* and *Satty* read together seemed to stand for the proposition that insofar as a rule deprives a woman of benefits for actual pregnancy, that rule is lawful under Title VII. If, on the other hand, it denies her benefits she had earned while not pregnant (and hence like a man) and now seeks to use upon return to her non-pregnant (male-like) status, it has a disproportionate effect on women and is not lawful.

In summary, then, the Court seems to be of the view that discrimination on the basis of pregnancy isn't sex discrimination. The Court achieves this by, on the one hand, disregarding the "ineluctible link" between gender and pregnancy, treating pregnancy as just another physical condition that the employer or state can manipulate on any arguably rational basis, and on the other hand, using women's special place in "the scheme of human existence"[71] as a basis for treating her claim to benefits available to other disabled workers as a claim not to equal benefits but to special treatment. The equality principle, according to the Court, cannot be bent to such ends.

In reaction to *Gilbert* and, to a lesser extent, to *Satty*, Congress amended the definitions section of Title VII to provide that discrimination on the basis of pregnancy, childbirth, and related medical conditions was, for purposes of the Act, sex discrimination. The amendment, called the Pregnancy Discrimination Act (PDA),[72] required a rather radical change in approach to the pregnancy issue from that adopted by the Court. In effect, Title VII creates a general presumption that men and women are alike in all relevant respects and casts the burden on the employer to show otherwise in any particular case.[73] The PDA, likewise, rejects the presumption that pregnancy is so unique that special rules concerning it are to be treated as prima facie reasonable. It substitutes the contrary presumption that pregnancy, at least in the workplace context, is like other physical conditions which may affect workers. As with gender classifications in general, it places the burden of establishing pregnancy's uniqueness in any given instance on the employer. The amendment itself specifies how this is to be done:

> [W]omen affected by pregnancy, childbirth, or related medical conditions shall be treated the same for all employment-related purposes, including receipt of benefits under fringe benefit programs, as other persons not so affected but similar in their ability or inability to work. . . .[74]

Under the PDA, employers cannot treat pregnancy less favorably than other potentially disabling conditions, but neither can they treat it more favorably. And therein lies the crisis.

At the time the PDA was passed, all feminist groups supported it. Special treatment of pregnancy in the workplace had always been synonymous with unfavorable treatment; the rules generally had the effect of forcing women out of the work force and back into the home when they became pregnant. By treating pregnancy discrimination as sex discrimination, the PDA required that pregnant women be treated as well as other wage earners who became disabled. The degree to which this assisted women depended on the generosity of their particular employers' sick leave or disability policy, but anything at all was better than what most pregnant women had had before.

The conflict within the feminist community arose because some states had passed legislation which, instead of placing pregnant women at a disadvantage, gave them certain positive protections. Montana, for example, passed a law forbidding employers to fire women who became pregnant and requiring them to give such women reasonable maternity leave.[75] The Miller-Wohl Company, an employer in that state, had a particularly ungenerous sick leave policy. Employees were entitled to no sick leave in their first year of employment and five days per year thereafter.[76] On August 1, 1979, the company hired a pregnant woman who missed four or five days over the course of the following three weeks because of morning sickness. The company fired her. She asserted her rights under the Montana statute. The company sought declaratory relief in federal court, claiming that Montana's special treatment statute was contrary to the equality principle mandated by the PDA and was therefore invalid under the supremacy clause of the constitution.[77]

Feminists split over the validity of the Montana statute. Some of us felt that the statute was, indeed, incompatible with the philosophy of the PDA.[78] Others of us argued that the PDA was passed to *help* pregnant women, which was also the objective of the Montana statute.[79] Underneath are very different views of what women's equality means; the dispute is therefore one of great significance for feminists.

The Montana statute *was* meant to help pregnant women. It was passed with the best of intentions. The philosophy underlying it is that pregnancy is central to a woman's family role and that the law should take special account of pregnancy to protect that role for the working wife. And those who supported the statute can assert with great plausibility that pregnancy is a problem that men don't have, an extra source of workplace disability, and that women workers cannot adequately be protected if pregnancy is not taken into account in special ways. They might also add that procreation plays a special role in human life, is viewed as a fundamental right by our society, and therefore is appropriately singled out on social policy grounds. The instinct to treat pregnancy as a special case is deeply imbedded in our culture, indeed in every culture. It seems natural, and *right*, to treat it that way.

Yet, at a deeper level, the Supreme Court in cases like *Gilbert*, and the feminists who seek special recognition for pregnancy, are starting from the same basic assumption, namely, that women have a special place in the scheme of human existence when it comes to maternity. Of course, one's view of how that basic assumption cuts is shaped by one's perspective. What businessmen, Supreme Court Justices, and feminists make of it is predictably quite different. But the same doctrinal approach that permits pregnancy to be treated *worse* than other disabilities is the same one that will allow the state constitutional freedom to create special *benefits* for pregnant women. The equality approach to pregnancy (such as that embodied in the PDA) necessarily creates not only the desired floor under the pregnant women's rights but also the ceiling which the *Miller-Wohl* case threw into relief. It we can't have it both ways, we need to think carefully about which way we want to have it.

My own feeling is that, for all its problems, the equality approach is the better one. The special treatment model has great costs. First, as discussed above, is the reality that conceptualizing pregnancy as a special case permits unfavorable as well as favorable treatment of pregnancy. Our history provides too many illustrations of the former to allow us to be sanguine about the wisdom of urging special treatment.

Second, treating pregnancy as a special case divides us in ways that I believe are destructive in a particular political sense as well as a more general sense. On what basis can we fairly assert, for example, that the pregnant woman fired by Miller-Wohl deserved to keep her job when any other worker who got sick for any other reason did not? Creating special privileges of the Montana type has, as one consequence, the effect of shifting attention away from the employer's inadequate sick leave policy or the state's failure to provide important protections to all workers and focusing it upon the unfairness of protecting one class of worker and not others.

Third, as our experience with single-sex protective legislation earlier in this century demonstrated, what appear to be special "protections" for women often turn out to be, at best, a double-edged sword. It seems likely, for example, that the employer who wants to avoid the inconveniences and costs of special protective measures will find reasons not to hire women of childbearing age in the first place.[80]

Fourth, to the extent the state (or employers as proxies for the state) can lay claim to an interest in women's special procreational capacity for "the future well-being of the race," as *Muller v. Oregon* put it in 1908,[81] our freedom of choice about the direction of our lives is more limited than that of men in significant ways. This danger is hardly a theoretical one today. The Supreme Court has [shown a willingness] to permit restrictions on abortion in deference to the state's interest in the "potential life" of the fetus,[82] and private employers are adopting policies of exclusion of women of childbearing capacity in order to protect fetuses from exposure to possibly hazardous substances in the workplace.[83]

More fundamentally, though, this issue, like the others I discussed earlier, has everything to do with how, in the long run, we want to define women's and men's places and roles in society.

Implicit in the PDA approach to maternity issues is a stance toward parenthood and work that is decidedly different from that embodied in the special-treatment approach to pregnancy. For many years, the prototype of the enlightened employer maternity policy was one which provided for a mandatory unpaid leave of absence for the woman employee commencing four or five months before and extending for as long as six months after childbirth.[84] Such maternity leaves were firmly premised on that aspect of the separate spheres ideology which assigned motherhood as woman's special duty and prerogative; employers believed that women should be treated as severed from the labor force from the time their pregnancies became apparent until their children emerged from infancy.[85] Maternity leave was always based upon cultural constructs and ideologies rather than upon biological necessity, upon role expectations rather than irreducible differences between the sexes.

The PDA also has significant ideological content. It makes the prototypical maternity leave policy just described illegal. In its stead, as discussed above, is a requirement that the employer extend to women disabled by pregnancy the same disability or sick leave available to other workers. If the employer chooses to extend the leave time beyond the disability period, it must make such leaves available to male as well as to female parents. Title VII requires sex neutrality with respect to employment practices directed at parents.[86] It does not permit the employer to base policies on the separate spheres ideology. Accordingly, the employer must devise its policies in such a way that women and men can, if they choose, structure the allocation of family responsibilities in a more egalitarian fashion. It forecloses the assumption that women are necessarily and inevitably destined to carry the dual burden of homemaker and wage earner.

Statutes such as the Montana statute challenged in the *Miller-Wohl* case are rooted in the philosophy that women have a special and different role and deserve special and different treatment. Feminists can plausibly and forcibly claim that such laws are desirable and appropriate because they reflect the material reality of women's lives. We can lay claim to such accommodations based on the different pattern of our lives, our commitment to children, our cultural destiny. We can even resort to arguments based on biological imperatives and expect that at least some members of the Supreme Court might lend a sympathetic ear. Justice Stevens suggested one such approach in a footnote to his dissent in *Caban v. Mohammed*,[87] a case invalidating a law that granted to unwed mothers but denied to unwed fathers the right to withhold consent to adoption of their children. He observed:

> [T]here is some sociological and anthropological research indicating that by virtue of the symbiotic relationship between mother and child during pregnancy and the initial contact between mother and child directly after birth a physical and psychological bond immediately develops between the two that is not then present between the infant and the father or any other person. [Citations omitted.][88] [Brackets in original.]

Justice Stevens' seductive bit of science is useful for making my point, although other illustrations might do as well. Many women who have gone through childbirth have experienced the extraordinary sense of connection to their newborn that the literature calls "bonding."[89] It may be, as some have contended, that the monolithic role women have so long played has been triggered and sustained by this phenomenon, that the effect of this bonding has made it emotionally possible for women to submit to the stringent limitations imposed by law and culture upon the scope and nature of their aspirations and endeavors.[90] On the other hand, it seems entirely possible that the concept of exclusive mother-infant bonding—the latest variation on "maternal instinct"—is a social construct designed to serve ideological ends.[91]

Less than a century ago, doctors and scientists were generally of the view that a woman's intellect, her capacity for education, for reasoning, for public undertakings, was biologically limited.[92] While men were governed by their intellect, women were controlled by their uteruses.[93] No reputable scientist or doctor would make such claims today. But if women are now understood to share with men a capacity for intellectual development, is it not also possible that mother-infant bonding is, likewise, only half the story? What Justice Stevens overlooks is the evidence of the capacity of fathers (the exploration of whose nurturing potential is as new as their opportunity actively to participate in the birth of their children) to "bond" as well.

Again, the question is, are we clinging, without really reflecting upon it, to culturally dictated notions that underestimate the flexibility and potential of human beings of both sexes and which limit us as a class and as individuals?

CONCLUSION: CONFRONTING YIN AND YANG

The human creature seems to be constructed in such a way as to be largely culture bound. We should not, therefore, be surprised that the creaky old justices on the Supreme Court and we somewhat less creaky feminists sometimes—perhaps often—respond to the same basic characterizations of male and female—although, unquestionably, the justices tend sometimes to do different things with those basic characterizations than feminists would do. At this point, we need to think as deeply as we can about what we want the future of women and men to be. Do we want equality of the sexes—or do we want justice for two kinds of human beings who are fundamentally different? If we gain equality, will we lose the special sense of kinship that grows out of experiences central to our lives and not shared by the other sex? Are feminists defending a separate women's culture while trying to break down the barriers created by men's separate culture? Could we, even if we wanted to, maintain the one while claiming our place within the other? *Michael M.*, which yokes assumptions about male sexual aggression with the conclusion that the sexes are not similarly situated because of women's pregnancy, and the Senate report on the all-male draft, which suggests that what sends men to war and leaves women at home is a fundamental trade-off by which men are assigned to battle and women to child rearing, should give us pause. I for one suspect a deep but sometimes nearly invisible set of complementarities, a yin-yang of sex-role assumptions and assignments so complex and interrelated that we cannot successfully dismantle any of it without seriously exploring the possibility of dismantling it all. The "hard cases"—cases like *Michael M., Rostker, Gilbert, Geduldig, Caban*—give us an opportunity to rethink our basic assumptions about women and men, assumptions sometimes buried beneath our consciousness. They allow us to ask afresh who we are, what we want, and if we are willing to begin to create a new order of things.

NOTES

1. This point is probably an obvious one. Until very recently, women were not rep-
    resented among the lawmakers. S. Tolchin & M. Tolchin, Clout: Womanpower
    and Politics 17 (1973) (in 1973, women constituted 52 percent of the population
    and 53 percent of the voting population, but only 3 percent of the country's
    elected officials). A deliberative body made up exclusively of men—or whites,
    the rich, or Catholics—no matter how strong their desire to represent "all of
    the people," will, at least sometimes, inadequately discern, much less build into
    their laws, provisions that reflect the needs and interests of women—or non-
    whites, the poor, or Protestants. This is not to say that there is a monolithic
    "women's viewpoint" any more than there is a monolithic "men's viewpoint."
    Plainly there is not. Rather, it is to suggest that women's life experiences still
    differ sufficiently from men's that a diverse group of women would bring a
    somewhat different set of perceptions and insights to certain issues than would
    a similarly diverse group of men. . . .
2. 2 *Blackstone's Commentaries* [444] (St. George Tucker ed. 1803).
3. *Id.* at 442 43. The common law disability was not honored in the equity courts,
    where married women could sue and be sued in their own right. See, e.g., 2 J.
    Story, *Commentaries on Equity Jurisprudence* 597–98 (1836) [hereinafter cited as
    Story, Equity].
4. At common law marriage destroyed the general contracrual capacity of a
    woman. Because marriage deprived her of ownership of her personal property
    and control over her real property, she possessed nothing which could be bound
    by her contracts. R. Morris, *Studies in the History of American Law* 173 (1959)
    [hereinafter cited as Morris, Studies]. . . . As was the case with other disabilities,
    the contractual incapacity of married women was somewhat mitigated under
    equitable principles. . . . 2 Bishop, *Commentaries on the Law* at 418–20 528–32
    (1875); . . . Story, Equity, *supra* note 4, at 626–28. . . .
5. At common law, the wife could not make a will with respect to her real property,
    2 Bishop, *Commentaries on the Law of Married Women* 535, at 422 (1875),
    although equity would compel the heir of the wife to make a conveyance to the
    party to whom she sought by will to leaver her real property, Story, Equity, *supra*
    note 4, at 615–16. . . .
6. . . . . Morris, *Studies, supra* note 5, at 166–67; Story, Equity, supra note 4, at 630.
    The wife's earnings, as personalty, became the husband's. Since the wife had a
    common law duty to provide services to her husband, see I J. Bishop, *Marriage,
    Divorce and Separation* 1183–84, at 510 (1891), the fruits of her labors, including
    earned income, were his. *Id.* at 1202, at 579.
7. 1 Bishop, *Marriage, Divorce and Separation* 1202, at 579. Her husband acquired
    an estate in her real property by virtue of marriage, which entitled him to con-
    trol the property as well as receive the profits from it. C. Moynahan, *Introduction
    to the Law of Real Property* 52–54 (1962). Again, equity modified the harshness of

the common law by permitting the creation of an equitable estate under certain circumstances. Story, *Equity, supra* note 4, at 608 14.

8. *See, e.g.*, 2 Blackstone, *Commentaries*, 444–45 (St. George Tucker ed. 1803.

9. 1 Blackstone, *Commentaries*, 444 (St. George Tucker ed. 1803)...

10. The history of the common law rule that marriage was a defense to a charge of rape is traced in *State v. Smith*, 148 N. J. Super. 219, 372 A.2d 386 (Essex County Ct. 1977). Several states have abrogated this doctrine by statute. See generally Barry, *Spousal Rape: The Uncommon Law*, 66 A. B. A. J. 1088 (1980).

11. ... These early separate estate acts were limited measures; they did not grant women a right to their own earnings nor a general contractual capacity. Those developments emerged in the final third of the century. New York, for example, created such rights in an 1860 amendment to the 1848 act. [Johnston, *Sex and Property: The Common Law Tradition, The Law School Curriculum, and Developments Toward Equality*, 47 N. Y. U. L. Rev. 1033, 1066 (1972)].

12. See, *e.g.*, N. Cott, *The Bonds of Womanhood: "Woman's Sphere" in New England*, 1780–1835, at 197.200 (1977).

13. Separate spheres ideology was used, for example, to justify denial of the vote to women, E Flexner, *Century of Struggle: The Women's Rights Movement in The United States* 306 (rev. ed. 1975); to exclude them from the practice of law. Bradwell v. Illinois, 83 U. S. 130 (1873); and to excuse them from participation in jury service, *Hoyt v. Florida*, 368 U. S. 57 (1961).

The Court in Muller v. Oregon, 208 U. S. 412, 421 22, a case upholding limitations on the hours women were permitted to work, was quite explicit on the subject: "Still again, history disclosed the fact that woman has always been dependent upon man. He established his control at the outset by superior physical strength, and this control in various forms, with diminishing intensity, has continued to the present... Though limitations upon personal and contractual rights may be removed by legislation, there is that in her disposition and habits of life which will operate against full assertion of those rights. She will still be where some legislation to protect her seems necessary to secure real equality of right."

14. 83 U. S. 130, 141 (1873).

15. *Id.*

16. 208 U. S. 412 (1908).

17. "[H]er physical structure and the proper discharge of her maternal functions—having in view not merely her own health, but the well-being of the race -justify legislation to protect her from the greed as well as the passion of man...." Id. at 422.

18. *Hoyt v. Florida*, 368 U. S. 57, 62 (1961).

19. *Reed v. Reed*, 404 U. S. 71, 75 (1971)...

20. *Craig v. Boren*, 429 U. S. 190, 197 (1976). "[C]lassifications by gender must serve important governmental objectives and must be substantially related to the achievement of those objectives."

21. *Reed* had required that the gender-based classification bear "fair and substantial relationship to the object of the legislation." 404 U. S. at 76. The typical articulation of the standard applicable to racial classifications was that the classification must be "necessary" to a "compelling state purpose." The effect of *Craig*, then, was to maintain the "substantial relationship" requirement of *Reed* and to add to it a heavier burden upon the state with respect to the state's purpose. The result was a standard consciously parallel in its elements to, but less stringent than, the racial classification standard.

22. *Frontiero v. Richardson*, 411 U. S. 677 (1973).

23. *Califano v. Goldfarb*, 430 U. S. 199 (1977).

24. *Califano v. Westcott*, 443 U. S. 76 (1979).

25. *Wengler v. Druggists Mutual Insurance Co.*, 446 U. S. 142 (1980).

26. *Weinberger v. Wiesenfeld*, 420 U. S. 636 (1975).

27. *Stanton v. Stanton*, 421 U. S. 7 (1975).

28. *Orr v. Orr*, 440 U. S. 268 (1979).

29. *Kirschberg v. Feenstra*, 450 U. S. 455 (1981).

30. *Reed v. Reed*, 404 U. S. 71 (1971).

31. See, e.g., *Kahn v. Shevin*, 416 U. S. 351 (1974) (Florida statute granting widows but not widowers property tax exemption constitutional because intended to assist sex financially most affected by spousal loss) and *Califano v. Webster.* 430 U. S. 313 (1977) (Social Security Act section creating benefit calculation formula more favorable to women than men held constitutional because intended to compensate women for wage discrimination). . . .

32. See, e.g., *Schlesinger v. Ballard*, 419 U. S. 498 (1975) (Court upheld (5–4) law that results in discharge of male officers if twice passed over for promotion, but guarantees female officers 13-year tenure before discharge for lack of promotion); *Rostker v. Goldberg*, 453 U. S. 57 (1981); *Michael M. v. Superior Court*, 450 U. S. 464 (1981); *Dothard v. Rawlinson*, 443 U. S. 321 (1977); *Geduldig v. Aiello*, 417 U. S. 484 (1974): *General Electric Corp. v. Gilbert*, 429 U. S. 125 (1976); *Nashville Gas Co. v. Satty*, 434 U. S. 136 (1977). All of these cases were authored either by Justice Stewart or by Justice Rehnquist.

33. 450 U. S. 455 (1981).

34. 453 U. S. 57 (1981).

35. 450 U. S. 464 (1981).

36. 453 U. S. at 75.

37. *Id.* at 75.

38. *Id.* The Court pointed out that the Navy and Air Force combat exclusions are statutory; the Army and Marine Corps "precludes the use of women in combat as a matter of established policy." *Id.*

39. *Id.* at 78–79.

40. *Id.*

41. See dissent of Justice White, joined by Justice Brennan, *id.* at 85.

42. 450 U. S. at 466, California's statute, which renamed the crime "il intercourse"

in 1970, proscribed the act of sexual intercourse "accomplished with female not the wife of the perpetrator, where the female is under the age of 18 years." Cal. Penal Code 261.5 (West Supp. 1982).

43. 450 U. S. at 471.

44. *Id.* at 473. . . .

45. 453 U. S. at 83 (White J. dissenting, joined by Brennan, J.: "I assume what has not been challenged in this case—that excluding women from combat positions does not offend the Constitution"). *Id.* at 93 (Marshall, J., dissenting, joined by Brennan, J.: "Had appellees raised a constitutional challenge to the prohibition against assignment of women to combat, this discussion in the Senate Report might well provide persuasive reasons for upholding the restrictions. But the validity of the combat restrictions is not an issue we need decide in this case").

46. Department of Defense Authorization Act of 1981. S. Rep. No. 826, 96th Cong., 2d Sess., *reprinted in* U. S. Code Cong. & Ad. News 2646, 2647 (emphasis added).

47. *Id.*

48. *Id.*

49. *Id.* at 2649.

50. *Id.*

51. "Contrary to [defendant's] assertions, the statute does not rest on the assumption that males are generally the aggressors." 450 U. S. at 475.

52. *Id.* at 467, Justice Blackmun, concurring, for some unknown reason graced posterity with extensive quotations from the transcript of the preliminary hearing (the actual details of the sexual liaison were not relevant to the constitutional issue presented to the court). The facts are a marvelous illustration of the cultural phenomenon of male initiator, female responder. But Justice Blackmun chose to delete (and Justice Rehnquist failed to mention) the young woman's specific response to the defendant's rather forceful request for sexual intercourse. Justice Mosk, of the California Supreme Court, supplies the detail: "In due course Michael told sharon to remove her pants, and when at first she demurred he allegedly struck her twice. *Sharon testified she then said to herself, 'Forget it,' and decided to let him do as he wished.* The couple then had intercourse." *Id.* at 484 85; 25 Cal. 3d at 616, 159 Cal. Rptr, at 345, 601 P.2d at 577 (emphasis added). Sharon was not entirely in a passive-responsive mode, however. After Sharon and the defendant, Michael, had spent some time hugging and kissing in the bushes. Sharon's sister and two other young men approached them. Sharon declined to go home with her sister, who then left with one of the two. Sharon thereupon approached and began kissing Bruce, the other young man. When Bruce left, Sharon then rejoined Michael, whereupon the events giving rise to his prosecution transpired. 450 U. S. at 486 87; 25 Cal. 3d at 616, 159 Cal. Rptr. at 345, 601 P.2d at 577.

53. 450 U. S. at 467 (emphasis added).

54. 450 U. S. at 471–72. . . .

55. *Id.* at 475.

56. Susan Brownmiller observes that "Women are trained to be rape victims. . . . Rape seeps into our childhood consciousness by imperceptible degrees. Even before we learn to read we have become indoctrinated into a victim mentality." S. Brownmiller, *Against Our Will: Men, Women and Rape*, 309 (1975).

57. See, *e.g.*, *General Electric Co. v. Gilbert*, 429 U. S. 125, 161–62 (1976) (Stevens, J., dissenting).

58. *Geduldig v. Aiello*, 417 U. S. 484, 496 n.20 (1974).

59. In *Reed v. Reed*, 404 U. S. 17 (1971), the Court said that sex classifications were "subject to scrutiny," *id.* at 75, and that such classifications must bear a "fair and substantial relation to the object of the legislation." *Id.* at 76 (quoting *Royster Guano Co. v. Virginia*, 253 U. S. 412, 415 (1920)). In *Frontiero v. Richardson*, 411 U. S. 677 (1973), the Court came within one vote of deciding that sex classifications were "suspect" and that the state must prove that such classifications were necessary to a compelling state interest, the standard it applied in race cases. In *Geduldig*, the Court said, "The dissenting opinion to the contrary, this case is thus a far cry from cases like Reed . . . and Frontiero . . . involving discrimination based upon gender as such." 417 U. S. at 496 n.20.

60. 417 U. S. 484.

61. *Id.* at 496–97 n.20 (emphasis added).

62. 429 U. S. 125.

63. *Id.* 135.

64. *Id.* at 136–40.

65. *Id.*

66. *Id.* at 152 (Brennan. J., dissenting).

67. See, *e.g.*, Whitbeck, "Theories of Sexual Difference," in *Women and Philosophy* 68 (Gould & Wattofsky eds. 1976). . . .

68. 434 U. S. 136 (1977).

69. *Id.* at 137.

70. *Id.* at 142.

71. *Gilbert*, 429 U. S. at 139 n. 17 See also *Satty*, 434 U. S. at 142. . . .

72. 42 U. S. C. 2000e(k) (Supp. IV 1980).

73. Thus, Title VII makes it an unlawful employment practice for an employer to classify on the basis of sex, 42 U. S. C. 2000e-2(a), unless the employer can establish that sex is a "bona fide occupational qualification reasonably necessary to the normal operation of [the] particular business or enterprise," 42 U. S. C. 2000c-2(c). The exception has been narrowly interpreted. See *Dorhard v. Rawlinson*, 433 U. S. 321, 334 (1977) ("We are persuaded . . . that the bfoq exception was in fact meant to be an extremely narrow exception to the general prohibition of discrimination on the basis of sex.") Once the plaintiff establishes the existence of a sex-based classification, the burden of persuasion shifts to the employer to establish that sex is a bfoq. See, *e.g.*, *Weeks v. Southern Bell Tel. and Tel. Co.*, 408 F.2d 228, 235 (5th Cir. 1969).

74. 42 U. S. C. 2000c(k) (Supp IV 1980).

75. Mont. Code Ann 39-7-201 to 209 (1981). The law also provided that an

employee disabled as a result of pregnancy was entitled to her accrued disability or leave benefits. *Id.* at 39–7-203(3). . . .

76. *Miller-Wohl Co. v. Comm'r of Labor & Industry, State of Montana,* 414 E Supp. 1264, 1265 (D. Mont. 1981), *rev'd on procedural grounds.* 685 E2d 1088 (9th Cir. 1982).

77. *Id.* The trial court held that the statute did not conflict with the PDA because employers could comply with the state act and avoid discrimination by extending to persons disabled for other reasons the protections the act guarantees to pregnant women.

78. I did, for example.

79. See brief amicus curiae submitted on behalf of Equal Rights Advocates, Inc., Employment Law Center, and California Fair Employment Practice Commission in *Miller-Wohl.*

80. Title VII does not permit such practices. As a practical matter, however, proof of such motivations is difficult. Actions based on a class sufficiently large to illuminate the hidden motivation are prohibitively expensive and complex.

81. 208 U. S. 412, 422. . . .

82. See, *e.g., Harris v. McRae,* 448 U. S. 297, 325 (1980) . . .; *Maher v. Roe,* 432 U. S. 464, 478–79 (1977). . . . See also *Poelker v. Doe,* 432 U. S. 519, 520–21 (1977).

83. See generally Williams, *Firing the Woman to Protect the Fetus: The Reconciliation of Fetal Protection with Employment Opportunity Goals Under Title VII.* 69 Geo. L. J. 641, 647–50 (1981).

84. . . . National Industrial Conference Board, *Maternity Leaves of Absence,* 21 Management Record 232 34, 250–63 (1959). . . .

85. See, *e.g., Meyer, Women and Employee Benefits* 2, 4 (1978) (The reason many employers resist paying disability benefits for pregnancy-related disabilities is that "a specific group—mothers-to-be- . . . is widely regarded as being made up of terminal employees whose loyalty will be to their homes and children rather than to the corporation.")

86. See *Phillips v. Martin Marietta Corp.,* 400 U. S. 542 (1971) (company policy prohibiting the hiring of mothers but not fathers of preschool-aged children violates section 703(a) of Title VII). . .

87. 441 U. S. 380 (1979).

88. *Id.* at 405 n.10 (Stevens, J., dissenting).

89. I certainly number myself among those who have experienced this magical feeling and know, from many conversations with other mothers, that my experience is hardly unique. It seems apparent, however, that my reaction is not universal. See J. Bernard, *The Future of Motherhood* 35 (1974). More importantly, falling in love with a child is apparently not limited to mothers or even to biological parents. . . .

90. See, e.g., Rossi, "A Biosocial Perspective on Parenting," *Daedalus,* Spring 1977, at 3–5.

91. See, e.g., Arnay, "Maternal-Infant Bonding: The Politics of Falling in Love With Your Child," 6 *Feminist Studies* 546 (1980). Arnay reviews the bonding lit-

erature and concludes that its claims have not been adequately established. *Id.* at 548–56. He warns that "Bonding theory lends legitimacy to the notion that women are the only appropriate attendants for children." *Id.* at 564. . . .

92. Both blacks and caucasian women were believed to have smaller and less convoluted brains and therefore restricted intellects. See, e.g., J. Haller & R. Haller, *The Physician and Sexuality in Victorian America* 53–61 (1978); S. Gould, *The Mismeasure of Man* 103–107 (1981). Women who did exert their intellects were thought to endanger their reproductive organs and even, if they pursued careers, to desex themselves and become "mannish" women. See Smith-Rosenberg and Rosenberg, *The Female Animal: Medical and Biological Views of Women and Her Role in Nineteenth-Century America*, 60 J. Am. Hist. 332 (1973): Haller & Haller, supra, at 60–61; B. Ehrenreich & D. English, *For Her Own Good: 150 Years of the Experts' Advice to Women* 125–31 (1979).

Ehrenreich and English point out that men, too, were faced with a competition between their brains and their reproductive organs for their bodies' limited energy supply, but in the case of men, doctors recommended that they enhance their intellects by preserving their male fluids: "Since the mission of the male (the middle-class male, anyway) was to be a businessman, professor, lawyer, or gynecologist- he had to be careful to conserve all his energy for the 'higher functions.' Doctors warned men not to 'spend their seed' (the material essence of their energy) recklessly in marital relations, and of course not to let it dribble away in secret vice or prurient dreams." *Id.* at 126.

93. B. Ehrenreich & D. English, *supra* note 129, at 120 25. . . .

With and Against Marx

While writers such as Firestone and Rubin saw the need to establish some relation between their theories and Marxism, others saw the need to address the relationship between Marxism and feminism in more elaborate ways. At the end of her essay, Rubin pointed to the need for feminists to relate changes in "the sex-gender system" to changes in the political and economic spheres of society. The question remained: how were these relationships to be understood?

Included here are three different types of answers to this question: 1) a "two-system" model reflected in the essay by Heidi Hartmann, 2) a "one-system" model reflected in the chapter by Michèle Barrett and, 3) an "anti-systems" model reflected in my own essay.

One problem with thinking about "the sex-gender" system as distinct from the system of politics or economics is that women's oppression occurs in all domains. Women are oppressed not only sexually but also as domestic laborers, as wage workers, and through exclusion from political participation. The question arises: how can we understand women's oppression in *all* domains. Hartmann and Barrett propose materialist theories to do so, while recognizing the limitations of Marxism's elaboration of "materialism." Both of these theorists want to explain women's oppression through appeal to "the social relations of production," understanding this phrase more broadly than Marxists had.

For Hartmann, the major problem with traditional Marxism is that it focused too exclusively on only one aspect of "the social relations of production," that concerned with the production of things. But as Engels himself was aware, "the social relations of production" also include the production of people. Hartmann's essay can be described as reflecting a type of "dual systems" materialism. She argues that while traditional Marxism had supplied a historical analysis of social relationships concerned with the production of things, it lacked a historical analysis of those social relationships concerned with the production of people. Rejecting many radical feminist understanding of "patriarchy" as too ahistorical, she retains the term to refer to a historically specific set of social relationships concerned with the production of people. This latter set of social relationships evolved parallel to that historical evolution of the social production of things that resulted in capitalism.

According to Hartmann, while there have been some tensions between the two sets of social relationships that constitute patriarchy and capitalism, for the most part, and contingently, they have been mutually supporting. The partnership that evolved between these two sets of social relationships was solidified through the creation of the idea of "the family wage." This concept enabled capitalism to pay women less for wage labor and use women as a reserve labor army while also exploiting women's domestic labor in the production of a qualified male labor force. By necessitating women's economic dependence on men, it also guaranteed that women married and that men retained control over women in the domestic sphere. The devaluation of women's domestic labor both reinforced patriarchy's devaluation of women while also devaluing those human needs for nurturance and care, which capitalism has never been able to adequately acknowledge or value.

Barrett's analysis primarily differs from Hartmann's in that Barrett locates women's oppression not in a separate and parallel set of social relations to capitalism but within the relations of production of capitalism itself. While Barrett describes women's oppression as operating at the level of ideology, she also describes this ideology as grounded within a particular division of labor entrenched within capitalism. Constituting part of the very structure of capitalism is a historically inherited division of labor between both domestic and wage labor and male and female labor in the wage labor sphere. Thus, without looking to capitalism as the source of women's oppression, Barrett is able to retain not only the materialism of Marxism, but even the idea that materialism's historical evolution can be depicted through a unified narrative.

From my perspective, the strength of Barrett's analysis lies in its appeal to history to explain women's oppression today. But, unlike Barrett, I see no need to position this appeal within the unified analytic framework of "materialism." As I argue in my essay included here, the problem with Marxism's appeal to "mode of production," was not only that it left out domestic labor or the social relations of sexuality, but that this phrase functioned in Marxist analyses ambiguously. On the one hand, when understood narrowly to include only "the production of things"—an understanding employed by many traditional Marxists—it did leave women's oppression unexplained. However, to the extent it is broadened to include also "the production of people," it becomes too vague to be genuinely explanatory.

Thus, as I argue, it is not Marx's analytic framework that is helpful in explaining women's oppression as well as other forms of oppression. However, this is not to say there is nothing of use in Marx's writings for feminists. Marx contributed to a way of thinking of social structures as not naturally given but as the products of historical evolution. In conjunction, he provided certain powerful historical analyses: of the economic structures of some societies at particular periods of time, of the relationship of such structures to other aspects of human life within those societies, and of the origins of such structures out of previous arrangements. From the perspective of understanding women's oppression, Marxism offers a powerful historical narrative about the growing separation and dominance of the sphere of the economy out of earlier social orders dominated by kinship. This narrative contributes to an understanding of women's oppression both as workers and as sexual beings. In short, I suggest, in an early "postmodern" move, that feminists look to Marx not for an analytic metanarrative, but for what he has to offer in his more specific historical analyses.

6

HEIDI HARTMANN

The Unhappy Marriage
of Marxism and Feminism

Towards a More Progressive Union

The "marriage" of marxism and feminism has been like the marriage of husband and wife depicted in English common law: marxism and feminism are one, and that one is marxism.[1] Recent attempts to integrate marxism and feminism are unsatisfactory to us as feminists because they subsume the feminist struggle into the "larger" struggle against capital. To continue our simile further, either we need a healthier marriage or we need a divorce.

The inequalities in this marriage, like most social phenomena, are no accident. Many marxists typically argue that feminism is at best less important than class conflict and at worst divisive of the working class. This political stance produces an analysis that absorbs feminism into the class struggle. Moreover, the analytic power of marxism with respect to capital has obscured its limitations with respect to sexism. We will argue here that while marxist analysis provides essential insight into the laws of historical development, and those of capital in particular, the categories of marxism are sex-blind. Only a specifically feminist analysis reveals the systemic character of relations between men and women. Yet feminist analysis by itself is inadequate because it has been blind to history and insufficiently materialist. Both marxist analysis, particularly its historical and materialist method, and feminist analysis, especially the identification of patriarchy as a social and historical structure, must be drawn upon if we are to understand the development of western capitalist societies and the predicament of women within them. In this essay we suggest a new direction for marxist feminist analysis.

Part I of our discussion examines several marxist approaches to the "woman question." We then turn, in Part II, to the work of radical feminists. After noting the limitations of radical feminist definitions of patriarchy, we offer our own. In Part III we try to use the strengths of both marxism and feminism to make suggestion both about the development of capitalist societies and about the present situation of women. We attempt to use marxist methodology to analyze feminist objectives, correcting the imbalance in recent socialist feminist work, and suggesting a more complete analysis of our present socioeconomic formation. We argue that a materialist analysis demonstrates that patriarchy is not simply a psychic, but also a social and economic structure. We suggest that our society can best be understood once it is recognized that it is organized both in capitalistic and in patriarchal ways. While pointing out tensions between patriarchal and capitalist interests, we argue that the accumulation of capital both accommodates itself to patriarchal social structure and helps to perpetuate it. We suggest in this context that sexist ideology has assumed a peculiarly capitalist form in the present, illustrating one way that patriarchal relations tend to bolster capitalism. We argue, in short, that a partnership of patriarchy and capitalism has evolved.

In the concluding section, Part IV, we argue that the *political* relations of marxism and feminism account for the dominance of marxism over feminism in the left's understanding of the woman question. A more progressive union of marxism and feminism, then, requires not only improved intellectual understanding of relations of class and sex, but also that alliance replace dominance and subordination in left politics.

I. MARXISM AND THE WOMAN QUESTION

The woman question has never been the "feminist question." The feminist question is directed at the causes of sexual inequality between women and men, of male dominance over women. Most marxist analyses of women's position take as their question the relationship of women to the economic system, rather than that of women to men, apparently assuming the latter will be explained in their discussion of the former. Marxist analysis of the woman question has taken three main forms. All see women's oppression in our connection (or lack of it) to production. Defining women as part of the working class, these analyses consistently subsume women's relation to men under workers' relation to capital. First, early marxists, including Marx, Engels, Kautsky, and Lenin, saw capitalism drawing all women into the wage labor force, and saw this process destroying the sexual division of labor. Second, contemporary marxists have incorporated women into an analysis of everyday life in capitalism. In this view, all aspects of our lives are seen to reproduce the capitalist system and we are all workers in the system. And third, marxist feminists have focussed on housework and its relation to capital, some arguing that housework produces surplus value and that houseworkers work directly for capitalists.

While the approach of the early marxists ignored housework and stressed women's labor force participation, the two more recent approaches emphasize housework to such an extent they ignore women's current role in the labor market. Nevertheless, all three attempt to include women in the category working class and to understand women's oppression as another aspect of class oppression. In doing so all give short shrift to the object of feminist analysis, the relations between women and men. While our "problems" have been elegantly analyzed, they have been misunderstood. The focus of marxist analysis has been class relations: the object of marxist analysis has been understanding the laws of motion of capitalist society. While we believe marxist methodology *can* be used to formulate feminist strategy, these marxist feminist approaches discussed above clearly do not do so; their marxism clearly dominates their feminism.

As we have already suggested, this is due in part to the analytical power of marxism itself. Marxism is a theory of the development of class society, of the accumulation process in capitalist societies, of the reproduction of class dominance, and of the development of contradictions and class struggle. Capitalist societies are driven by the demands of the accumulation process, most succinctly summarized by the fact that production is oriented to exchange, not use. In a capitalist system production is important only insofar as it contributes to the making of profits, and the use value of products is only an incidental consideration. Profits derive from the capitalists' ability to exploit labor power, to pay laborers less than the value of what they produce. The accumulation of profits systematically transforms social structure as it transforms the relations of production. The reserve army of labor, the poverty of great numbers of people and the near-poverty of still more, these human reproaches to capital are by-products of the accumulation process itself. From the capitalist's point of view, the reproduction of the working class may "safely be left to itself."[14] At the same time, capital creates an ideology, which grows up along side it, of individualism, competitiveness, domination, and in our time, consumption of a particular kind. Whatever one's theory of the genesis of ideology one must recognize these as the dominant values of capitalist societies.

Marxism enables us to understand many aspects of capitalist societies: the structure of production, the generation of a particular occupational structure, and the nature of the dominant ideology. Marx's theory of the development of capitalism is a theory of the development of "empty places." Marx predicted, for example, the growth of the proletariat and the demise of the petit bourgeoisie. More precisely and in more detail, Braverman among others has explained the creation of the "places" clerical worker and service worker in advanced capitalist societies.[15] Just as capital creates these places indifferent to the individuals who fill them, the categories of marxist analysis, class, reserve army of labor, wage-laborer, do not explain why particular people fill particular places. They give no clues about why *women* are subordinate to *men* inside and outside the family and why it is not the other way around. *Marxist categories, like capital itself, are sex-blind.* The categories of marxism cannot tell us who will fill the empty places. Marxist analysis of the woman question has suffered from this basic problem.

II. RADICAL FEMINISM AND PATRIARCHY

The great thrust of radical feminist writing has been directed to the documentation of the slogan "the personal is political." Women's discontent, radical feminists argued, is not the neurotic lament of the maladjusted, but a response to a social structure in which women are systematically dominated, exploited, and oppressed. Women's inferior position in the labor market, the male-centered emotional structure of middle class marriage, the use of women in advertising, the so-called understanding of women's psyche as neurotic—popularized by academic and clinical psychology—aspect after aspect of women's lives in advanced capitalist society was researched and analyzed. The radical feminist literature is enormous and defies easy summary. At the same time, its focus on psychology is consistent. The New York Radical Feminists' organizing document was "The Politics of the Ego." "The personal is political" means for radical feminists, that the original and basic class division is between the sexes, and that the motive force of history is the striving of men for power and domination over women, the dialectic of sex.[22]

Radical feminist analysis has greatest strength in its insights into the present. Its greatest weakness is a focus on the psychological which blinds it to history.

The reason for this lies not only in radical feminist method, but also in the nature of patriarchy itself, for patriarchy is a strikingly resilient form of social organization. Radical feminists use patriarchy to refer to a social system characterized by male domination over women. Kate Millett's definition is classic:

> our society . . . is a patriarchy. The fact is evident at once if one recalls that the military, industry, technology, universities, science, political offices, finances—in short, every avenue of power within the society, including the coercive force of the police, is entirely in male hands.[24]

This radical feminist definition of patriarchy applies to most societies we know of and cannot distinguish among them. The use of history by radical feminists is typically limited to providing examples of the existence of patriarchy in all times and places.[25] For both marxist and mainstream social scientists before the women's movement, patriarchy referred to a system of relations between men, which formed the political and economic outlines of feudal and some pre-feudal societies, in which hierarchy followed ascribed characteristics. Capitalist societies are understood as meritocratic, bureaucratic, and impersonal by bourgeois social scientists; marxists see capitalist societies as systems of class domination.[26] For both kinds of social scientists neither the historical patriarchal societies nor today's western capitalist societies are understood as systems of relations between men that enable them to dominate women.

Towards a Definition of Patriarchy

We can usefully define patriarchy as a set of social relations between men, which have a material base, and which, though hierarchical, establish or create interdependence and solidarity among men that enable them to dominate women. Though patriarchy is hierarchical and men of different classes, races, or ethnic groups have different places in the patriarchy, they also are united in their shared relationship of dominance over their women; they are dependent on each other to maintain that domination. Hierarchies "work" at least in part because they create vested interests in the status quo. Those at the higher levels can "buy off" those at the lower levels by offering them power over those still lower. In the hierarchy of patriarchy, all men, whatever their rank in the patriarchy, are bought off by being able to control at least some women. There is some evidence to suggest that when patriarchy was first institutionalized in state societies, the ascending rulers literally made men the heads of their families (enforcing their control over their wives and children) in exchange for the men's ceding some of their tribal resources to the new rulers.[27] Men are dependent on one another (despite their hierarchical ordering) to maintain their control over women.

The material base upon which patriarchy rests lies most fundamentally in men's control over women's labor power. Men maintain this control by excluding women from access to some essential productive resources (in capitalist societies, for example, jobs that pay living wages) and by restricting women's sexuality.[28] Monogamous heterosexual marriage is one relatively recent and efficient form that seems to allow men to control both these areas. Controlling women's access to resources and their sexuality, in turn, allows men to control women's labor power, both for the purpose of serving men in many personal and sexual ways and for the purpose of rearing children. The services women render men, and which exonerate men from having to perform many unpleasant tasks (like cleaning toilets) occur outside as well as inside the family setting. Examples outside the family include the harrassment of women workers and students by male bosses and professors as well as the common use of secretaries to run personal errands, make coffee, and provide "sexy" surroundings. Rearing children, whether or not the children's labor power is of immediate benefit to their fathers, is nevertheless a crucial task in perpetuating patriarchy as a system. Just as class society must be reproduced by schools, work places, consumption norms, etc., so must patriarchal social relations. In our society children are generally reared by women at home, women socially defined and recognized as inferior to men, while men appear in the domestic picture only rarely. Children raised in this way generally learn their places in the gender hierarchy well. Central to this process, however, are the areas outside the home where patriarchal behaviors are taught and the inferior position of women enforced and reinforced: churches, schools, sports, clubs, unions, armies, factories, offices, health centers, the media, etc.

The material base of patriarchy, then, does not rest solely on childrearing in the family, but on all the social structures that enable men to control women's labor. The aspects of social structures that perpetuate patriarchy are theoretically identifiable, hence separable from their other aspects. Gayle Rubin has increased our ability to identify the patriarchal element of these social structures enormously by identifying "sex/gender systems":

> a "sex/gender system" is the set of arrangements by which a society transforms biological sexuality into products of human activity, and in which these transformed sexual needs are satisfied.[29]

We are born female and male, biological sexes, but we are created woman and man, socially recognized genders. *How* we are so created is that second aspect of the *mode* of production of which Engels spoke, "the production of human beings themselves, the propagation of the species."

How people propagate the species is socially determined. If, biologically, people are sexually polymorphous, and society were organized in such a way that all forms of sexual expression were equally permissible, reproduction would result only from some sexual encounters, the heterosexual ones. The strict division of labor by sex, a social invention common to all known societies, creates two very separate genders and a need for men and women to get together for economic reasons. It thus helps to direct their sexual needs toward heterosexual fulfillment, and helps to ensure biological reproduction. In more imaginative societies, biological reproduction might be ensured by other techniques, but the division of labor by sex appears to be the universal solution to date. Although it is theoretically possible that a sexual division of labor not imply inequality between the sexes, in most known societies, the socially acceptable division of labor by sex is one which accords lower status to women's work. The sexual division of labor is also the underpinning of sexual subcultures in which men and women experience life differently; it is the material base of male power which is exercised (in our society) not just in not doing housework and in securing superior employment, but psychologically as well.

How people meet their sexual needs, how they reproduce, how they inculcate social norms in new generations, how they learn gender, how it feels to be a man or a woman—all occur in the realm Rubin labels the sex/gender system. Rubin emphasizes the influence of kinship (which tells you with whom you can satisfy sexual needs) and the development of gender specific personalities via childrearing and the "oedipal machine." In addition, however, we can use the concept of the sex/gender system to examine all other social institutions for the roles they play in defining and reinforcing gender hierarchies. Rubin notes that theoretically a sex/gender system could be female dominant, male dominant, or egalitarian, but declines to label various known sex/gender systems or to periodize history accordingly. We choose to label our present sex/gender system patriarchy, because it appropriately captures the notion of hierarchy and male dominance which we see as central to the present system.

Economic production (what marxists are used to referring to as *the* mode of production) and the production of people in the sex/gender sphere both determine "the social organization under which the people of a particular historical epoch and a particular country live," according to Engels. The whole of society, then, can be understood by looking at both these types of production and reproduction, people and things.[30] There is no such thing as "pure capitalism," nor does "pure patriarchy" exist, for they must of necessity coexist. What exists is patriarchal capitalism, or patriarchal feudalism, or egalitarian hunting/gathering societies, or matriarchal horticultural societies, or patriarchal horticultural societies, and so on. There appears to be no necessary connection between *changes* in the one aspect of production and changes in the other. A society could undergo transition from capitalism to socialism, for example, and remain patriarchal.[31] Common sense, history, and our experience tell us, however, that these two aspects of production are so closely intertwined, that change in one ordinarily creates movement, tension, or contradiction in the other.

Racial hierarchies can also be understood in this context. Further elaboration may be possible along the lines of defining color/race systems, arenas of social life that take biological color and turn it into a social category, race. Racial hierarchies, like gender hierarchies, are aspects of our social organization, of how people are produced and reproduced. They are not fundamentally ideological; they constitute that second aspect of our mode of production, the production and reproduction of people. It might be most accurate then to refer to our societies not as, for example, simply capitalist, but as patriarchal capitalist white supremacist. In Part III below, we illustrate one case of capitalism adapting to and making use of racial orders and several examples of the interrelations between capitalism and patriarchy.

Capitalist development creates the places for a hierarchy of workers, but traditional marxist categories cannot tell us who will fill which places. Gender and racial hierarchies determine who fills the empty places. *Patriarchy is not simply hierarchical organization*, but hierarchy in which *particular* people fill *particular* places. It is in studying patriarchy that we learn why it is women who are dominated and how. While we believe that most known societies have been patriarchal, we do not view patriarchy as a universal, unchanging phenomenon. Rather patriarchy, the set of interrelations among men that allow men to dominate women, has changed in form and intensity over time. It is crucial that the hierarchy among men, and their differential access to patriarchal benefits, be examined. Surely, class, race, nationality, and even marital status and sexual orientation, as well as the obvious age, come into play here. And women of different class, race, national, marital status, or sexual orientation groups are subjected to different degrees of patriarchal power. Women may themselves exercise class, race, or national power, or even patriarchal power (through their family connections) over men lower in the patriarchal hierarchy than their own male kin.

To recapitulate, we define patriarchy as a set of social relations which has a material base and in which there are hierarchical relations between men and solidarity among them which enable them in turn to dominate women. The material base of patriarchy is men's control over women's labor power. That control is maintained by excluding women from access to necessary economically productive resources and by restricting women's sexuality. Men exercise their control in receiving personal service work from women, in not having to do housework or rear children, in having access to women's bodies for sex, and in feeling powerful and being powerful. The crucial elements of patriarchy as we *currently* experience them are: heterosexual marriage (and consequent homophobia), female childrearing and housework, women's economic dependence on men (enforced by arrangements in the labor market), the state, and numerous institutions based on social relations among men—clubs, sports, unions, professions, universities, churches, corporations, and armies. All of these elements need to be examined if we are to understand patriarchal capitalism.

Both hierarchy and interdependence among men and the subordination of women are *integral* to the functioning of our society; that is, these relationships are *systemic*. We leave aside the question of the creation of these relations and ask, can we recognize patriarchal relations in capitalist societies? Within capitalist societies we must discover those same bonds between men which both bourgeois and marxist social scientists claim no longer exist or are, at the most, unimportant leftovers. Can we understand how these relations among men are perpetuated in capitalist societies? Can we identify ways in which patriarchy has shaped the course of capitalist development?

III. THE PARTNERSHIP OF PATRIARCHY AND CAPITAL

How are we to recognize patriarchal social relations in capitalist societies? It appears as if each woman is oppressed by her own man alone; her oppression seems a private affair. Relationships among men and among families seem equally fragmented. It is hard to recognize relationships among men, and between men and women, as *systematically* patriarchal. We argue, however, that patriarchy as a system of relations between men and women exists in capitalism, and that in capitalist societies a healthy and strong partnership exists between patriarchy and capital. Yet if one begins with the concept of patriarchy and an understanding of the capitalist mode of production, one recognizes immediately that the partnership of patriarchy and capital was not inevitable; men and capitalists often have conflicting interests, particularly over the use of women's labor power. Here is one way in which this conflict might manifest itself: the vast majority of men might want their women at home to personally service them. A smaller number of men, who are capitalists, might want most women (not their own) to work in the wage labor market. In examining the tensions of this conflict over women's labor power historically, we will be able to identify the material base of patriarchal relations in capitalist societies, as well as the basis for the partnership between capital and patriarchy.

Industrialization and the Development of Family Wages

Marxists made quite logical inferences from a selection of the social phenomena they witnessed in the nineteenth century. But marxists ultimately underestimated the strength of the preexisting patriarchal social forces with which fledgling capital had to contend and the need for capital to adjust to these forces. The industrial revolution was drawing all people into the labor force, including women and children; in fact the first factories used child and female labor almost exclusively.[32] That women and children could earn wages separately from men both undermined authority relations (as discussed in Part I above) and kept wages low for everyone.

Male workers resisted the wholesale entrance of women and children into the labor force, and sought to exclude them from union membership and the labor force as well. In 1846 the *Ten-Hours' Advocate* stated:

> It is needless for us to say, that all attempts to improve the morals and physical condition of female factory workers will be abortive, unless their hours are materially reduced. Indeed we may go so far as to say, that married females would be much better occupied in performing the domestic duties of the household, than following the never-tiring motion of machinery. We therefore hope the day is not distant, when the husband will be able to provide for his wife and family, without sending the former to endure the drudgery of a cotton mill.

In the United States in 1954 the National Typographical Union resolved not to "encourage by its act the employment of female compositors." Male unionists did not want to afford union protection to women workers; they tried to exclude them instead. In 1879 Adolph Strasser, president of the Cigarmakers International Union, said: "We cannot drive the females out of the trade, but we can restrict their daily quota of labor through factory laws."[36]

While the problem of cheap competition could have been solved by organizing the wage earning women and youths, the problem of disrupted family life could not be. Men reserved union protection for men and argued for protective labor laws for women and children.[37] Protective labor laws, while they may have ameliorated some of the worst abuses of female and child labor, also limited the participation of adult women in many "male" jobs.[38] Men sought to keep high wage jobs for themselves and to raise male wages generally. They argued for wages sufficient for their wage labor alone to support their families. This "family wage" system gradually came to be the norm for stable working class families at the end of the nineteenth century and the beginning of the twentieth.[39] Several observers have declared the non wage-working wife to be part of the standard of living of male workers.[40] Instead of fighting for equal wages for men and women, male workers sought the family wage, wanting to retain their wives' services at home. In the absence of patriarchy a unified working class might have confronted capitalism, but patriarchal social relations divided the working class, allowing one part (men) to be bought off at the expense of the other (women). Both the hierarchy between men and the solidarity among them were crucial in this process of resolution. Family wages may be understood as a resolution of the conflict over women's labor power which was occurring between patriarchal and capitalist interests at that time.

Family wages for most adult men imply men's acceptance, and collusion in, lower wages for others, young people, women and socially defined inferior men as well (Irish, blacks, etc., the lowest groups in the patriarchal hierarchy who are denied many of the patriarchal benefits). Lower wages for women and children and inferior men are enforced by job segregation in the labor market, in turn maintained by unions and management as well as by auxiliary institutions like schools, training programs, and even families. Job segregation by sex, by insuring that women have the lower paid jobs, both assures women's economic dependence on men and reinforces notions of appropriate spheres for women and men. For most men, then, the development of family wages secured the material base of male domination in two ways. First, men have the better jobs in the labor market and earn higher wages than women. The lower pay women receive in the labor market both perpetuates men's material advantage over women and encourages women to choose wifery as a career. Second, then, women do housework, childcare, and perform other services at home which benefit men directly.[41] Women's home responsibilities in turn reinforce their inferior labor market position.[42]

The resolution that developed in the early twentieth century can be seen to benefit capitalist interests as well as patriarchal interests. Capitalists, it is often argued, recognized that in the extreme conditions which prevailed in the early nineteenth century industrialization, working class families could not adequately reproduce themselves. They realized that housewives produced and maintained healthier workers than wage-working wives and that educated children became better workers than noneducated ones. The bargain, paying family wages to men and keeping women home, suited the capitalists at the time as well as the male workers. Although the terms of the bargain have altered over time, it is still true that the family and women's work in the family serve capital by providing a labor force and serve men as the space in which they exercise their privilege. Women, working to serve men and their families, also serve capital as consumers.[43] The family is also the place where dominance and submission are learned, as Firestone, the Frankfurt School, and many others have explained.[44] Obedient children become obedient workers; girls and boys each learn their proper roles.

While the family wage shows that capitalism adjusts to patriarchy, the changing status of children shows that patriarchy adjusts to capital. Children, like women, came to be excluded from wage labor. As children's ability to earn money declined, their legal relationship to their parents changed. At the beginning of the industrial era in the United States, fulfilling children's need for their fathers was thought to be crucial, even primary, to their happy development; fathers had legal priority in cases of contested custody. As children's ability to contribute to the economic well-being of the family declined, mothers came increasingly to be viewed as crucial to the happy development of their children, and gained legal priority in cases of contested custody.[45] Here patriarchy adapted to the changing economic role of children: when children were productive, men claimed them; as children became unproductive, they were given to women.

The Partnership in the Twentieth Century

The prediction of nineteenth century marxists that patriarchy would wither away in the face of capitalism's need to proletarianize everyone has not come true. Not only did marxists underestimate the strength and flexibility of patriarchy, they also overestimated the strength of capital. They envisioned the new social force of capitalism, which had torn feudal relations apart, as virtually all powerful. Contemporary observers are in a better position to see the difference between the tendencies of "pure" capitalism and those of "actual" capitalism as it confronts historical forces in everyday practice. Discussions of the partnership between capital and racial orders and of labor market segmentation provide additional examples of how "pure" capitalist forces meet up with historical reality. Great flexibility has been displayed by capitalism in this process.

Marxists who have studied South Africa argue that although racial orders may not allow the equal proletarianization of everyone, this does not mean that racial barriers prevent capital accumulation.[46] In the abstract, analysts could argue about which arrangements would allow capitalists to extract the most surplus value. Yet in a particular historical situation, capitalists must be concerned with social control, the resistance of groups of workers, and the intervention of the state. The state might intervene in order to reproduce society as a whole; it might be necessary to police some capitalists, to overcome the worst tendencies of capital. Taking these factors into account, capital*ists* maximize greatest *practicable* profits. If for purposes of social control, capitalists organize work in a particular way, nothing about capital itself determines who (that is, which individuals with which ascriptive characteristics) shall occupy the higher, and who the lower rungs of the wage labor force. It helps, of course, that capitalists themselves are likely to be the dominant social group and hence racist (and sexist). Capitalism inherits the ascribed characteristics of the dominant groups as well as of the subordinate ones.

Recent arguments about the tendency of monopoly capital to create labor market segmentation are consistent with this understanding.[47] Where capitalists purposely segment the labor force, using ascriptive characteristics to divide the working class, this clearly derives from the need for social control rather than accumulation needs in the narrow sense.[48] And over time, not all such divisive attempts are either successful (in dividing) or profitable. The ability of capital to shape the workforce depends both on the particular imperatives of accumulation in a narrow sense (for example, is production organized in a way that requires communication among a large number of workers? If so, they had better all speak the same language)[49] and on social forces within a society which may encourage/force capital to adapt (the maintenance of separate washroom facilities in South Africa for whites and blacks can only be understood as an economic cost to capitalists, but one less than the social cost of trying to force South African whites to wash up with blacks).

If the first element of our argument about the course of capitalist development is that capital is not all-powerful, the second is that capital is tremendously flexible. Capital accumulation encounters preexisting social forms, and both destroys them and adapts to them. The adaptation of capital can be seen as a reflection of the *strength* of these preexisting forms to persevere in new environments. Yet even as they perseve, they are not unchanged. The ideology with which race and sex are understood today, for example, is strongly shaped by the particular ways racial and sexual divisions are reinforced in the accumulation process.

The Family and the Family Wage Today

We argued above, that, with respect to capitalism and patriarchy, the adaptation, or mutual accommodation, took the form of the development of the family wage in the early twentieth century. The family wage cemented the partnership between patriarchy and capital. Despite women's increased labor force participation, particularly rapid since World War II, the family wage is still, we argue, the cornerstone of the present sexual division of labor—in which women are primarily responsible for housework and men primarily for wage work. Women's lower wages in the labor market (combined with the need for children to be reared by someone) assure the continued existence of the family as a necessary income pooling unit. The family, supported by the family wage, thus allows the control of women's labor by men both within and without the family.

Though women's increased wage work may cause stress for the family (similar to the stress Kautsky and Engels noted in the nineteenth century), it would be wrong to think that as a consequence, the concepts and the realities of the family and of the sexual division of labor will soon disappear. The sexual division of labor reappears in the labor market, where women work at women's jobs, often the very jobs they used to do only at home—food preparation and service, cleaning of all kinds, caring for people, and so on. As these jobs are low-status and low-paying patriarchal relations remain intact, though their material base shifts somewhat from the family to the wage differential, from family-based to industrially-based patriarchy.[50]

Industrially based patriarchal relations are enforced in a variety of ways. Union contracts which specify lower wages, lesser benefits, and fewer advancement opportunities for women are not just atavistic hangovers—a case of sexist attitudes or male supremacist ideology—they maintain the material base of the patriarchal system. While some would go so far as to argue that patriarchy is already absent from the family (see, for example, Stewart Ewen, *Captains of Consciousness*),[51] we would not. Although the terms of the compromise between capital and patriarchy are changing as additional tasks formerly located in the family are capitalized, and the location of the deployment of women's labor power shifts,[52] it is nevertheless true, as we have argued above, that the wage differential caused by extreme job segregation in the labor market reinforces the family, and, with it, the domestic division of labor, by encouraging women to marry. The "ideal" of the family wage—that a man can earn enough to support an entire family—may be giving way to a new ideal that both men and women contribute through wage earning to the cash income of the family. The wage differential, then, will become increasingly necessary in perpetuating patriarchy, the male control of women's labor power. The wage differential will aid in *defining* women's work as secondary to men's at the same time it necessitates women's actual continued economic dependence on men. The sexual division of labor in the labor market and elsewhere should be understood as a manifestation of patriarchy which serves to perpetuate it.

Many people have argued that though the partnership between capital and patriarchy exists now, it may *in the long run* prove intolerable to capitalism; capital may eventually destroy both familial relations and patriarchy. The argument proceeds logically that capitalist social relations (of which the family is not an example) tend to become universalized, that women will become increasingly able to earn money and will increasingly refuse to submit to subordination in the family, and that since the family is oppressive particularly to women and children, it will collapse as soon as people can support themselves outside it.

We do not think that the patriarchal relations embodied in the family can be destroyed so easily by capital, and we see little evidence that the family system is presently disintegrating. Although the increasing labor force participation of women has made divorce more feasible, the incentives to divorce are not overwhelming for women. Women's wages allow very few women to support themselves and their children independently and adequately. The evidence for the decay of the traditional family is weak at best. The divorce rate has not so much increased, as it has evened out among classes; moreover, the remarriage rate is also very high. Up until the 1970 census, the first-marriage age was continuing its historic decline. Since 1970 people seem to have been delaying marriage and childbearing, but most recently, the birth rate has begun to increase again. It is true that larger proportions of the population are now living outside traditional families. Young people, especially, are leaving their parents' homes and establishing their own households before they marry and start traditional families. Older people, especially women, are finding themselves alone in their own households, after their children are grown and they experience separation or death of a spouse. Nevertheless, trends indicate that the new generations of young people will form nuclear families at some time in their adult lives in higher proportions than ever before. The cohorts, or groups of people, born since 1930 have much higher rates of eventual marriage and childrearing than previous cohorts. The duration of marriage and childrearing may be shortening, but its incidence is still spreading.[53]

The argument that capital destroys the family also overlooks the social forces which make family life appealing. Despite critiques of nuclear families as psychologically destructive, in a competitive society the family still meets real needs for many people. This is true not only of long-term monogamy, but even more so for raising children. Single parents bear both financial and psychic burdens. For working class women, in particular, these burdens make the "independence" of labor force participation illusory. Single parent families have recently been seen by policy analysts as transitional family formations which become two-parent families upon remarriage.[54]

It could be that the effects of women's increasing labor force participation are found in a declining sexual division of labor within the family, rather than in more frequent divorce, but evidence for this is also lacking. Statistics on who does house-work, even in families with wage-earning wives, show little change in recent years; women still do most of it.[55] The double day is a reality for wage-working women. This is hardly surprising since the sexual division of labor outside the family, in the labor market, keeps women financially dependent on men—even when they earn a wage themselves. The future of patriarchy does not, however, rest solely on the future of familial relations. For patriarchy, like capital, can be surprisingly flexible and adaptable.

Whether or not the patriarchal division of labor, inside the family and elsewhere, is "ultimately" intolerable to capital, it is shaping capitalism now. As we illustrate below, patriarchy both legitimates capitalist control and delegitimates certain forms of struggle against capital.

Ideology in the Twentieth Century

Patriarchy, by establishing and legitimating hierarchy among men (by allowing men of all groups to control at least some women), reinforces capitalist control, and cap-italist values shape the definition of patriarchal good.

The psychological phenomena Shulamith Firestone identifies are particular examples of what happens in relationships of dependence and domination. They follow from the realities of men's social power—which women are denied—but they are shaped by the fact that they happen in the context of a capitalist society.[56] If we examine the characteristics of men as radical feminists describe them—competi-tive, rationalistic, dominating—they are much like our description of the dominant values of capitalist society.

This "coincidence" may be explained in two ways. In the first instance, men, as wage laborers, are absorbed in capitalist social relations at work, driven into the competition these relations prescribe, and absorb the corresponding values.[57] The radical feminist description of men was not altogether out of line for capitalist soci-eties. Secondly, even when men and women do not actually behave in the way sexual norms prescribe, men *claim for themselves* those characteristics which are valued in the dominant ideology. So, for example, the authors of *Crestwood Heights* found that while the men, who were professionals, spent their days manipulating subordinates (often using techniques that appeal to fundamentally irrational motives to elicit the preferred behavior), men and women characterized men as "rational and pragmatic." And while the women devoted great energies to studying scientific methods of child-rearing and child development, men and women in Crestwood Heights char-acterized women as "irrational and emotional."[58]

This helps to account not only for "male" and "female" characteristics in capitalist societies, but for the particular form sexist ideology takes in capitalist soci-eties. Just as women's work serves the dual purpose of perpetuating male domination and capitalist production, so sexist ideology serves the dual purpose of glorifying male characteristics/capitalist values, and denigrating female characteristics/social need. If women were degraded or powerless in other societies, the reasons (rationalizations) men had for this were different. Only in a capitalist society does it make sense to look down on women as emotional or irrational. As epithets, they would not have made sense in the renaissance. Only in a capitalist society does it make sense to look down on women as "dependent." "Dependent" as an epithet would not make sense in feudal societies. Since the division of labor ensures that women as wives and mothers in the family are largely concerned with the production of use values, the denigration of these activities obscures capital's inability to meet socially determined need at the same time that it degrades women in the eyes of men, providing a rationale for male dominance. An example of this may be seen in the peculiar ambivalence of television commercials. On one hand, they address themselves to the real obstacles to providing for socially determined needs: detergents that destroy clothes and irritate skin, shoddily made goods of all sorts. On the other hand, concern with these problems must be denigrated; this is accomplished by mocking women, the workers who must deal with these problems.

A parallel argument demonstrating the partnership of patriarchy and capitalism may be made about the sexual division of labor in the work force. The sexual division of labor places women in low-paying jobs, and in tasks thought to be appropriate to women's role. Women are teachers, welfare workers, and the great majority of workers in the health fields. The nurturant roles that women play in these jobs are of low status because capitalism emphasizes personal independence and the ability of private enterprise to meet social needs, emphases contradicted by the need for collectively provided social services. As long as the social importance of nurturant tasks can be denigrated because women perform them, the confrontation of capital's priority on exchange value by a demand for use values can be avoided. In this way, it is not feminism, but sexism that divides and debilitates the working class.

IV. TOWARDS A MORE PROGRESSIVE UNION

Many problems remain for us to explore. Patriarchy as we have used it here remains more a descriptive term than an analytic one. If we think marxism alone inadequate, and radical feminism itself insufficient, then we need to develop new categories. What makes our task a difficult one is that the same features, such as the division of labor, often reinforce both patriarchy and capitalism, and in a thoroughly patriarchal capitalist society, it is hard to isolate the mechanisms of patriarchy. Nevertheless, this is what we must do. We have pointed to some starting places: looking at who benefits from women's labor power, uncovering the material base of patriarchy, investigating the mechanisms of hierarchy and solidarity among men. The questions we must ask are endless.

Can we speak of the laws of motion of a patriarchal system? How does patriarchy generate feminist struggle? What kinds of sexual politics and struggle between the sexes can we see in societies other than advanced capitalist ones? What are the contradictions of the patriarchal system and what is their relation to the contradictions of capitalism? We know that patriarchal relations gave rise to the feminist movement, and that capital generates class struggle—but how has the relation of feminism to class struggle been played out in historical contexts? In this section we attempt to provide an answer to this last question.

Feminism and the Class Struggle

Historically and in the present, the relation of feminism and class struggle has been either that of fully separate paths ("bourgeois" feminism on one hand, class struggle on the other), or, within the left, the dominance of feminism by marxism. With respect to the latter, this has been a consequence both of the analytic power of marxism, and of the power of men within the left. These have produced both open struggles on the left, and a contradictory position for marxist feminists.

Most feminists who also see themselves as radicals (antisystem, anti-capitalist, anti-imperialist, socialist, communist, marxist, whatever) agree that the radical wing of the women's movement has lost momentum while the liberal sector seems to have seized the time and forged ahead. Our movement is no longer in that exciting, energetic period when no matter what we did, it worked—to raise consciousness, to bring more women (more even than could be easily incorporated) into the movement, to increase the visibility of women's issues in the society, often in ways fundamentally challenging to both the capitalist and patriarchal relations in society. Now we sense parts of the movement are being coopted and "feminism" is being used against women—for example, in court cases when judges argue that women coming out of long-term marriages in which they were housewives don't need alimony because we all know women are liberated now. The failure to date to secure the passage of the Equal Rights Amendment in the United States indicates the presence of legitimate fears among many women that feminism will continue to be used against women, and it indicates a real need for us to reassess our movement, to analyze why it has been coopted in this way. It is logical for us to turn to marxism for help in that reassessment because it is a developed theory of social change. Marxist theory is well developed compared to feminist theory, and in our attempt to use it, we have sometimes been sidetracked from feminist objectives.

The left has always been ambivalent about the women's movement, often viewing it as dangerous to the cause of socialist revolution. When left women espouse feminism, it may be personally threatening to left men. And of course many left organizations benefit from the labor of women. Therefore, many left analyses (both in progressive and traditional forms) are self-serving, both theoretically and politically. They seek to influence women to abandon attempts to develop an independent understanding of women's situation and to adopt the "left's" analyses of the situation. As for our response to this pressure, it is natural that, as we ourselves have turned to marxist analysis, we would try to join the "fraternity" using this paradigm, and we may end up trying to justify our struggle to the fraternity rather than trying to analyze the situation of women to improve our political practice. Finally, many marxists are satisfied with the traditional marxist analysis of the women question. They see class as the correct framework with which to understand women's position. Women should be understood as part of the working class; the working class's struggle against capitalism should take precedence over any conflict between men and women. Sex conflict must not be allowed to interfere with class solidarity.

As the economic situation in the United States has worsened in the last few years, traditional marxist analysis has reasserted itself. In the sixties the civil rights movement, the student free speech movement, the antiwar movement, the women's movement, the environmental movement, and the increased militancy of professional and white collar groups all raised new questions for marxists. But now the return of obvious economic problems such as inflation and unemployment had eclipsed the importance of these demands and the left has returned to the "fundamentals"— working class (narrowly defined) politics. The growing "marxist-leninist preparty" sects are committed antifeminists, in both doctrine and practice. And there are signs that the presence of feminist issues in the academic left is declining as well. Day care is disappearing from left conferences. As marxism or political economy become intellectually acceptable, the "old boys" network of liberal academia is replicated in a sidekick "young boys" network of marxists and radicals, nonetheless male in membership and outlook despite its youth and radicalism.

The pressures on radical women to abandon this silly stuff and become "serious" revolutionaries have increased. Our work seems a waste of time compared to inflation and unemployment. It is symptomatic of male dominance that *our* unemployment was never considered in a crisis. In the last major economic crisis, the 1930s, the vast unemployment was partially dealt with by excluding women from many kinds of jobs—one wage job per family, and that job was the man's. Capitalism and patriarchy recovered—strengthened from the crisis. Just as economic crises serve a restorative function for capitalism by correcting imbalances, so they might serve patriarchy. The thirties put women back in their place.

The struggle against capital and patriarchy cannot be successful if the study and practice of the issues of feminism is abandoned. A struggle aimed only at capitalist relations of oppression will fail, since their underlying supports in patriarchal relations of oppression will be overlooked. And the analysis of patriarchy is essential to a definition of the kind of socialism useful to women. While men and women share a need to overthrow capitalism they retain interests particular to their gender group. It is not clear—from our sketch, from history, or from male socialists—that the socialism being struggled for is the same for both men and women. For a humane socialism would require not only consensus on what the new society should look like and what a healthy person should look like, but more concretely, it would require that men relinquish their privilege.

As women we must not allow ourselves to be talked out of the urgency and importance of our tasks, as we have so many times in the past. We must fight the attempted coercion, both subtle and not so subtle, to abandon feminist objectives.

This suggests two strategic considerations. First, a struggle to establish socialism must be a struggle in which groups with different interests form an alliance. Women should not trust men to liberate them after the revolution, in part, because there is no reason to think they would know how; in part, because there is no necessity for them to do so. In fact their immediate self-interest lies in our continued oppression.

Instead we must have our own organizations and our own power base. Second, we think the sexual division of labor within capitalism has given women a practice in which we have learned to understand what human interdependence and needs are. While men have long struggled *against* capital, women know what to struggle *for*.[59] As a general rule, men's position in patriarchy and capitalism prevents them from recognizing both human needs for nurturance, sharing, and growth, and the potential for meeting those needs in a nonhierarchical, nonpatriarchial society. But even if we raise their consciousness, men might assess the potential gains against the potential losses and choose the status quo. Men have more to lose than their chains.

As feminist socialists, we must organize a practice which addresses both the struggle against patriarchy and the struggle against capitalism. We must insist that the society we want to create is a society in which recognition of interdependence is liberation rather than shame, nurturance is a universal, not an oppressive practice, and in which women do not continue to support the false as well as the concrete freedoms of men.

NOTES

Earlier drafts of this essay appeared in 1975 and 1977 coauthored with Amy B. Bridges. Unfortunately, because of the press of current commitments, Amy was unable to continue with this project, joint from its inception and throughout most of its long and controversial history. Over the years many individuals and groups offered us comments, debate, and support. Among them I would like to thank Marxist Feminist Group I, the Women's Studies College at SUNY Buffalo, the Women's Studies Program at the University of Michigan, various groups of the Union for Radical Political Economics, and Temma Kaplan, Anne Markusen, and Jane Flax for particularly careful, recent readings. A version substantially similar to the current one was published in *Capital and Class* in the summer of 1979. I would like to thank the editors of *Capital and Class*, Lydia Sargent, and other members of South End Press for their interest in this essay.

1. Often paraphrased as "the husband and wife are one and that one is the husband," English law held that "by marriage, the husband and wife are one person in law: that is, the very being or legal existence of the women is suspended during the marriage, or at least is incorporated and consolidated into that of the Husband," I. Blackstone, *Commentaries*, 1965, pp. 442–445, cited in Kenneth M. Davidson, Ruth B. Ginsburg, and Herma H. Kay, *Sex Based Discrimination* (St. Paul, Minn.: West Publishing Co., 1974), p. 117.

2. Frederick Engels, *The Origin of the Family, Private Property and the State*, edited, with an introduction by Eleanor Burke Leacock (New York: International Publishers, 1972).

3. Frederick Engels, *The Condition of the Working Class in England* (Stanford, Calif.: Stanford University Press, 1958). See esp. pp. 162–66 and p. 296.

4. Eli Zaretsky, "Capitalism, the Family, and Personal Life," *Socialist Revolution*,

Part I in No. 13–14 (January-April 1973), pp. 66–125, and Part II in No. 15 (May-June 1973), pp. 19–70. Also Zaretsky, "Socialist Politics and the Family," *Socialist Revolution* (now *Socialist Review*). No. 19 (January-March 1974), pp. 83–98, and *Capitalism, the Family and Personal Life* (New York: Harper & Row, 1976). Insofar as they claim their analyses are relevant to women, Bruce Brown's *Marx, Freud, and the Critique of Everyday Life* (New York: Monthly Review Press, 1973) and Henri Lefebvre's *Everyday Life in the Modern World* (New York: Harper & Row, 1971) may be grouped with Zaretsky.

5. In this Zaretsky is following Margaret Benston ("The Political Economy of Women's Liberation," *Monthly Review*, Vol. 21, No. 4 [September 1961], pp. 13–27), who made the cornerstone of her analysis that women have a different relation to capitalism than men. She argued that women at home produce use values, and that men in the labor market produce exchange values. She labeled women's work precapitalist (and found in women's common work the basis for their political unity.) Zaretsky builds on this essential difference in men's and women's work, but labels them both capitalist.

6. Zaretsky, "Personal Life," Part I, p. 114.

7. Mariarosa Dalla Costa, "Women and the Subversion of the Community," in *The Power of Women and the Subversion of the Community* by Mariatosa Dalla Costa and Selma James (Bristol, England: Falling Wall Press, 1973; second edition) pamphlet, 78 pps.

8. It is interesting to note that in the original article (cited in n. 7 above) Dalla Costa suggests that wages for housework would only further institutionalize woman's housewife role (pp. 32,34) but in a note (n. 16,pp. 52–52) she explains the demand's popularity and its use as a consciousness raising tool. Since then she has actively supported the demand. See Dalla Costa, "A General Strike," in *All Work and No Pay: Women, Housework, and the Wages Due*, ed. Wendy Edmond and Suzie Fleming (Bristol, England: Falling Wall Press, 1975).

9. The text of the article reads: "We have to make clear that, within the wage, domestic work produces not merely use values, but is essential to the production of surplus value" (p. 31). Note 12 reads: "What we mean precisely is that housework as work is *productive* in the Marxian sense, that is, producing surplus value" (p. 52, original emphasis). To our knowledge this claim has never been made more rigorously by the wages for housework group. Nevertheless marxists have responded to the claim copiously.

10. The literature of the debate includes Lise Vogel. "The Earthly Family," *Radical America*, Vol. 7, no. 4–5 (July-October 1973), pp. 9–50; Ira Gerstein, "Domestic Work and Capitalism," *Radical America*, Vol. 7, no. 4–5 (July-October 1973, pp. 101–128; John Harrison, "Political Economy of Housework," *Bulletin of the Conference of Socialist Economists*, Vol. 3, no. 1 (1973); Wally Seccombe, "The Housewife and her Labour under Capitalism," *New Left Review*, no. 83 (January-February 1974), pp. 3–24; Margaret Coulson, Branka Magas, and Hilary Wainwright, "The Housewife and her Labour under Capitalism,' A Critique," *New Left Review*, no. 89 (January-February 1975), pp. 59–71; Jean Gardiner,

"Women's Domestic Labour," *New Left Review*, no. 89 (January-February 1975), pp. 47–58; Ian Gough and John Harrison, "Unproductive Labour and Housework Again," *Bulletin of the Conference of Socialist Economists*, Vol. 4, no. 1 (1975); Jean Gardiner, Susan Himmelweit and Maureen Mackintosh, "Women's Domestic Labour," *Bulletin of the Conference of Socialist Economists*, Vol. 4, no. 2 (1975); Wally Seccombe, "Domestic Labour: Reply to Critics," *New Left Review*, no. 94 (November-December 1975), pp. 85–96; Terry Fee, "Domestic Labor: An Analysis of Housework and its Relation to the Production Process," *Review of Radical Political Economics*, Vol. 8, no. 1 (Spring 1976), pp. 1–8; Susan Himmelweit and Simon Mohun, "Domestic Labour and Capital," *Cambridge Journal of Economics*, Vol. 1, no. 1 (March 1977), pp. 15–31.

11. In the U. S., the most often heard political criticism of the wages for housework group has been its opportunism.

12. Laura Oren documents this for the working class in "Welfare of Women in Laboring Families: England, 1860–1950," *Feminist Studies*, Vol. 1, no. 3–4 (Winter-Spring 1973), pp. 107–25.

13. The late Stephen Hymer pointed out to us a basic weakness in Engels' analysis in *Origins*, a weakness that occurs because Engels fails to analyze the labor process within the family. Engels argues that men enforced monogamy because they wanted to leave their property to their own children. Hymer argued that far from being a 'gift,' among the petit bourgeoisie, possible inheritance is used as a club to get children to work for their fathers. One must look at the labor process and who benefits from the labor of which others.

14. This is a paraphrase. Karl Marx wrote: "The maintenance and reproduction of the working class is, and must ever be, a necessary condition to the reproduction of capital. But the capitalist may safely leave its fulfillment to the labourer's instincts of self-preservation and propagation." [*Capital* (New York: International Publishers, 1967), Vol. 1, p. 572.]

15. Harry Braverman, *Labor and Monopoly Capital* (New York: Monthly Review Press. 1975).

16. Juliet Mitchell, *Women's Estate* (New York: Vintage Books, 1973). p. 92.

17. Engels, *Origins*, "Preface to the First Edition," pp. 71–72. The continuation of this quotation reads, ". . . by the stage of development of labor on the one hand and of the family on the other." It is interesting that, by implication, labor is excluded from occurring within the family; this is precisely the blind spot we want to overcome in this essay.

18. Juliet Mitchell, "Women: The Longest Revolution," *New Left Review*, No. 40 (November-December 1966), pp. 11–37, also reprinted by the New England Free Press.

19. Juliet Mitchell, *Psychoanalysis and Feminism* (New York: Pantheon Books, 1974), 20.

20. Mitchell, *Psychoanalysis*, p. 412.

21. Shulamith Firestone, *The Dialectic of Sex* (New York; Bantam Books, 1971).

22. "Politics of Ego: A Manifesto for New York Radical Feminists," can be found

in *Rebirth of Feminism*, ed. Judith Hole and Ellen Levine (New York: Quadrangle Books, 1971), pp. 440–443. "Radical feminists" are those feminists who argue that the most fundamental dynamic of history is men's striving to dominate women. 'Radical' in this context does *not* mean anti-capitalist, socialist, counter-cultural, etc., but has the specific meaning of this particular set of feminist beliefs or group of feminists. Additional writings of radical feminists, of whom the New York Radical Feminists are probably the most influential, can be found in *Radical Feminism*, ed. Ann Koedt (New York: Quadrangle Press, 1972).

23. Focusing on power was an important step forward in the feminist critique of Freud. Firestone argues, for example, that if little girls "envied" penises it was because they recognized that little boys grew up to be members of a powerful class and little girls grew up to be dominated by them. Powerlessness, not neurosis, was the heart of women's situation. More recently, feminists have criticized Firestone for rejecting the usefulness of the concept of the unconscious. In seeking to explain the strength and continuation of male dominance, recent feminist writing has emphasized the fundamental nature of gender-based personality differences, their origins in the unconscious, and the consequent difficulty of their eradication. See Dorothy Dinnerstein, *The Mermaid and the Minotaur* (New York: Harper Colophon Books, 1977), Nancy Chodorow, *The Reproduction of Mothering* (Berkeley: University of California Press, 1978), and Jane Flax, "The Conflict Between Nurturance and Autonomy in Mother-Daughter Relationships and Within Feminism," *Feminist Studies*, Vol. 4, no. 2 (June 1978), pp. 141–189.

24. Kate Millett, *Sexual Politics* (New York: Avon Books, 1971), p. 25.

25. One example of this type of radical feminist history is Susan Brownmiller's *Against Our Will, Men, Women, and Rape* (New York: Simon & Shuster, 1975).

26. For the bourgeois social science view of patriarchy, see, for example, Weber's distinction between traditional and legal authority, *Max Weber: The Theories of Social and Economic Organization*, ed. Talcott Parson (New York: The Free Press, 1964), pp. 328–357. These views are also discussed in Elizabeth Fee, "The Sexual Politics of Victorian Social Anthropology," *Feminist Studies*, Vol. 1, nos. 3–4 (Winter-Spring 1973), pp. 23–29, and in Robert A. Nisbet, *The Sociological Tradition* (New York: Basic Books, 1966), especially Chapter 3, "Community."

27. See Viana Muller, "The Formation of the State and the Oppression of Women: Some Theoretical Considerations and a Case Study in England and Wales," *Review of Radical Political Economics*, Vol. 9, no. 3 (Fall 1977), pp. 7–21.

28. The particular ways in which men control women's access to important economic resources and restrict their sexuality vary enormously, both from society to society, from subgroup to subgroup, and across time. The examples we use to illustrate patriarchy in this section, however, are drawn primarily from the experience of whites in western capitalist countries. The diversity is shown in *Toward on Anthropology of Women*, ed. Rayna Rapp Reiter (New York:

Monthly Review Press, 1975), *Woman, Culture and Society*, ed. Michelle Rosaldo and Louise Lamphere (Stanford, California: Stanford University Press, 1974), and *Females, Males, Families*: A *Biosocial Approach*, by Liba Leibowitz (North Scituate, Massachusetts: Duxbury Press, 1978). The control of women's sexuality is tightly linked to the place of children. An understanding of the demand (by men and capitalists) for children is crucial to understanding changes in women's subordination.

Where children are needed for their present or future labor power, women's sexuality will tend to be directed toward reproduction and childrearing. When children are seen as superfluous, women's sexuality for other than reproductive purposes is encouraged, but men will attempt to direct it towards satisfying male needs. The Cosmo girl is a good example of a woman "liberated" from childrearing only to find herself turning all her energies toward attracting and satisfying men. Capitalists can also use female sexuality to their own ends, as the success of Cosmo in advertising consumer products shows.

29. Gayle Rubin, "The Traffic in Women," in *Anthropology of Women*, ed. Reiter, p. 159.

30. Himmelweit and Mohun point out that both aspects of production (people and things) are logically necessary to describe a mode of production because by definition a mode of production must be capable of reproducing itself. Either aspect alone is not self-sufficient. To put it simply the production of things requires people, and the production of people requires things. Marx, though recognizing capitalism's need for people did not concern himself with how they were produced or what the connections between the two aspects of production were. See Himmelweit and Mohun, "Domestic Labour and Capital" (note 10 above).

31. For an excellent discussion of one such transition to socialism, *see* Batya Weinbaum, "Women in Transition to Socialism: Perspectives on the Chinese Case," *Review of Radical Political Economics*, Vol. 8, no. 1 (Spring 1976), pp. 34–58.

32. It is important to remember that in the preindustrial period, women contributed a large share to their families' subsistence—either by participating in a family craft or by agricultural activities. The initiation of wage work for women both allowed and required this contribution to take place independently from the men in the family. The new departure, then, was not that women earned income, but that they did so beyond their husbands' or fathers' control. Alice Clark, *The Working Life of Women in the Seventeenth Century* (New York: Kelly, 1969) describes women's preindustrial economic roles and the changes that occurred as capitalism progressed. It seems to be the case that Marx, Engels, and Kautsky were not fully aware of women's economic role before capitalism.

33. Karl Kautsky, *The Class Struggle* (New York: Norton, 1971), pp. 25–26.

34. We might add, "outside the household," Kautsky, *Class Struggle*, p. 26, our emphasis.

35. Cited in Neil Smelser, *Social Change and the Industrial Revolution* (Chicago: University of Chicago Press, 1959), p. 301.

36. These examples are from Heidi I. Hartmann, "Capitalism, Patriarchy, and Job Segregation by Sex," *Signs: Journal of Women in Culture and Society*, Vol. 1, no. 3, pt. 2 (Spring 1976), pp. 162–163.

37. Just as the factory laws were enacted for the benefit of all capitalists against the protest of some, so too, protective legislation for women and children may have been enacted by the state with a view toward the reproduction of the working class. Only a completely instrumentalist view of the state would deny that the factory laws and protective legislation legitimate the state by providing concessions and are responses to the demands of the working class itself.

38. For a more complete discussion of protective labor legislation and women, see Ann C. Hill, "Protective Labor Legislation for Women: Its Origin and Effect," mimeographed (New Haven, Conn.: Yale Law School, 1970) parts of which have been published in Barbara A. Babcock, Ann E. Freedman, Eleanor H. Norton, and Susan C. Ross, *Sex Discrimination and the Law: Causes and Remedies* (Boston: Little, Brown & Co., 1975), an excellent law text. Also see Hartmann, "Job Segregation by Sex," pp. 164–166.

39. A reading of Alice Clark, *The Working Life of Women*, and Ivy Pinchbeck, *Women Workers*, suggests that the expropriation of production from the home was followed by a social adjustment process creating the social norm of the family wage. Heidi Hartmann, in *Capitalism and Women's Work in the Home, 1900–1930* (Unpublished Ph. D. dissertation. Yale University, 1974; forthcoming Temple University Press) argues, based on qualitative data, that this process occurred in the U. S. in the early twentieth century. One should be able to test this hypothesis quantitatively by examining family budget studies for different years and noting the trend of the proportion of the family income for different income groups, provided by the husband. However, this data is not available in comparable form for our period. The family wage resolution has probably been undermined in the post World War II period. Carolyn Shaw Bell, in "Working Women's Contribution to Family Income," *Eastern Economic Journal*, Vol. 1, no. 3 (July 1974), pp. 185–201, presents current data and argues that it is now incorrect to assume that the man is the primary earner of the family. Yet whatever the *actual* situation today or earlier in the century, we would argue that the social norm *was* and *is* that men should earn enough to support their families. To say it has been the norm is not to say it has been universally achieved. In fact, it is precisely the failure to achieve the norm that is noteworthy. Hence the observation that in the absence of sufficiently high wages, "normative" family patterns disappear, as for example, among immigrants in the nineteenth century and third world Americans today. Oscar Handlin, *Boston's Immigrants* (New York: Atheneum, 1968) discusses mid-nineteenth century Boston, where Irish women were employed in textiles; women constituted more than half of all wage laborers and often supported

unemployed husbands. The debate about family structure among Black Americans today still rages; see Carol B. Stack, *All Our Kin: Strategies for Survival in a Black Community* (New York: Harper and Row, 1974), esp. Chap. 1. We would also argue (see below) that for most families the norm is upheld by the relative places men and women hold in the labor market.

40. Hartmann, *Women's Work*, argues that the non-working wife was generally regarded as part of the male standard of living in the early twentieth century (see p. 136, n. 6) and Gerstein, "Domestic Work," suggests that the norm of the working wife enters into the determination of the value of male labor power (see p. 121).

41. The importance of the fact that women perform labor services for men in the home cannot be overemphasized. As Pat Mainardi said in "The Politics of Housework," "[t]he measure of your oppression is his resistance" (in *Sisterhood is Powerful*, ed. Robin Morgan [New York: Vintage Books, 1970], p. 451). Her article, perhaps as important for us as Firestone on love, is an analysis of power relations between women and men as exemplified by housework.

42. Libby Zimmerman has explored the relation of membership in the primary and secondary labor markets to family patterns in New England. See her *Women in the Economy: A Case study of Lynn, Massachusetts, 1760–1974* (Unpublished Ph. D dissertation, Heller School, Brandeis, 1977). Batya Weinbaum is currently exploring the relationship between family roles and places in the labor market. See her "Redefining the Question of Revolution," *Review of Radical Political Economics*, Vol, 9, no. 3 (Fall 1977), pp. 54, 78, and *The Curious Courtship of Women's Liberation and Socialism* (Boston: South End Press, 1978). Additional studies of the interaction of capitalism and patriarchy can be found in Zillah Eisenstein, ed., *Capitalist Patriarchy and the case for Socialist Feminism* (New York: Monthly Review Press, 1978).

43. See Batya Weinbaum and Amy Bridges, "The Other Side of the Paycheck: Monopoly Capital and the Structure of Consumption," *Monthly Review*, Vol. 28, no. 3 (July-August 1976), pp. 88–103, for a discussion of women's consumption work.

44. For the view of the Frankfurt School, see Max Horkheimer, "Authority and the Family," in *Critical Theory* (New York: Herder & Herder, 1972) and Frankfurt Institute of Social Research, "The Family," in *Aspects of Sociology* (Boston: Beacon, 1972).

45. Carol Brown, "Patriarchial Capitalism and the Female-Headed Family," *Social Scientist* (India); no. 40–41 (November-December 1975), pp. 28–39.

46. For more on racial orders, see Stanley Greenberg, "Business Enterprise in a Racial Order," *Politics and Society*, Vol. 6, no. 2 (1976), pp. 213–240, and Michael Burroway, *The Color of Class in the Copper Mines: From African Advancement to Zambianization* (Manchester, England: Manchester University Press, Zambia Papers No. 7, 1972).

47. See Michael Reich, David Gordon, and Richard Edwards, "A Theory of Labor Market Segmentation," *American Economic Review*, Vol. 63, no. 2 (May 1973),

pp. 359–365, and the book they edited, *Labor Market Segmentation* (Lexington, Mass: D. C. Heath, 1975) for a discussion of labor market segmentation.

48. See David M. Gordon, "Capitalist Efficiency and Socialist Efficiency," *Monthly Review*, Vol. 28, no. 3 (July-August 1976), pp. 19–39, for a discussion of qualitative efficiency (social control needs) and quantitative efficiency (accumulation needs).

49. For example, Milwaukee manufacturers organized workers in production first according to ethnic groups, but later taught all workers to speak English, as technology and appropriate social control needs changed. See Gerd Korman, *Industrialization, Immigrants, and Americanizers, the View from Milwaukee, 1866–1921* (Madison: The State Historical Society of Wisconsin, 1967).

50. Carol Brown, in "Patriarchal Capitalism," argues, for example, that we are moving from "family based" to "industrially-based" patriarchy within capitalism.

51. Stewart Ewen, *Captains of Consciousness* (New York: Random House, 1976).

52. Jean Gardiner, in "Women's Domestic Labour" (see n. 10), clarifies the cause for the shift in location of women's labor, from capital's point of view. She examines what capital needs (in terms of the level of real wages, the supply of labor, and the size of markets) at various stages of growth and of the business cycle. She argues that in times of boom or rapid growth it is likely that socializing housework (or more accurately capitalizing it) would be the dominant tendency, and that in times of recession, housework will be maintained in its traditional form. In attempting to assess the likely direction of the British economy, however, Gardiner does not assess the economic needs of patriarchy. We argue in this essay that unless one takes patriarchy as well as capital into account one cannot adequately assess the likely direction of the economic system.

53. For the proportion of people in nuclear families, see Peter Uhlenberg, "Cohort Variations in Family Life Cycle Experiences of U. S. Females," *Journal of Marriage and the Family*, Vol. 36, no. 5 (May 1974), pp. 284–92. For remarriage rates see Paul C. Glick and Arthur J. Norton, "Perspectives on the Recent Upturn in Divorce and Remarriage," *Demography*, Vol. 10 (1974), pp. 301–14. For divorce and income levels see Arthur J. Norton and Paul C. Glick, "Marital Instability: Past, Present, and Future," *Journal of Social Issues*, Vol. 32, no. 1 (1976), pp. 5–20. Also see Mary Jo Bane, *Here to Stay: American Families in the Twentieth Century* (New York: Basic Books, 1976).

54. Heather L. Ross and Isabel B. Sawhill, *Time of Transition: The Growth of Families Headed by Women* (Washington, D. C.: The Urban Institute, 1975).

55. See Kathryn E. Walker and Margaret E. Woods *Time Use: A Measure of Household Production of Family Goods and Services* (Washington D. C.: American Home Economics Association, 1976; and Heidi I. Hartmann, "The Family as the Locus of Gender, Class, and Political Struggle: The Example of Housework," *Signs: Journal of Women in Culture and Society*, Vol. 6, no. 3 (Spring 1981).

56. Richard Sennett's and Jonathan Cobb's *The Hidden Injuries of Class* (New York: Random House, 1973) examines similar kinds of psychological phenomena within hierarchical relationships between men at work.

57. This should provide some clues to class differences in sexism, which we cannot explore here.

58. See John R. Seeley, et al., *Crestwood Heights* (Toronto: University of Toronto Press, 1956), pp. 382–94. While men's place may be characterized as "in production" this does not mean that women's place is simply "not in production"—her tasks, too, are shaped by capital. Her non-wage work is the resolution, on a day-to-day basis, of production for exchange with socially determined need, the provision of use values in a capitalist society (this is the context of consumption). See Weinbaum and Bridges, "The Other Side of the Paycheck," for a more complete discussion of this argument. The fact that women provide "merely" use values in a society dominated by exchange values can be used to denigrate women.

59. Lise Vogel, "The Earthly Family" (see n. 10).

7

MICHÈLE BARRETT

Capitalism and Women's Liberation

. . . In conclusion I want briefly to return to the conceptual problems raised in the first chapter and the political issues mentioned in the preface. What light has this discussion thrown on the usefulness of the concept of patriarchy or the attempt to analyse women's oppression in terms of the reproduction of capitalism? To what extent are we justified in regarding the oppression of women as an ideological process? What are the possibilities for achieving women's liberation in capitalism and what relationship does or should the political mobilization of women have with a revolutionary socialist movement?

I have argued that it is inadequate to attempt to grasp the character of women's oppression in contemporary capitalism in terms of the supposed needs of capitalism itself. The reasoning in favour of this analysis has tended to be couched in terms of capital's support for a system of the reproduction of labour power, through domestic labour in the household, that operates at the lowest possible cost and provides a cheap and flexible reserve army of married women workers to lower the price of wages in general. Although these are undoubtedly important points in any explanation of capital's support for a household in which a wife and children are assumed to be dependent upon a male breadwinner, the argument leaves unexplained many aspects of women's oppression. The charge that this argument is a functionalist one is not in my view as important as the fact that it tends towards a reductionist account of women's oppression and denies specific aspects of women's subordination to men in the pre-capitalist period, in socialist societies and within the different classes of contemporary capitalism.

I have argued that this particular form of household, and its accompanying ideology of women's dependence, is not the only possible form for an efficient reproduction of labour-power in capitalist relations of production. It is the product of historical struggles between men and women, both within the working class and the bourgeoisie. Furthermore, the 'reproduction' thesis can deal only in a very mechanistic way with the complexity of the ideological construction of gender as it has developed in capitalism. A consideration of the areas of sexuality and the cultural representation of gender demonstrates a need to understand the force of ideology in the production and reproduction of the categories of masculinity and femininity on which such an analysis implicitly depends, but tends not to explore.

These arguments need not be ruled out altogether, but it is necessary to historicize them. A model of women's dependence has become entrenched in the relations of production of capitalism, in the divisions of labour in wage work and between wage labour and domestic labour. As such, an oppression of women that is not in any essentialist sense pre-given by the logic of capitalist development has become necessary for the ongoing reproduction of the mode of production in its present form. Hence, the oppression of women, although not a functional prerequisite of capitalism, has acquired a material basis in the relations of production and reproduction of capitalism today.

It follows that although important dimensions of women's oppression cannot be accounted for with reference to the categories of Marxism, it is equally impossible to establish the analytic independence of a system of oppression such as the category of 'patriarchy' suggests. The resonance of this concept lies in its recognition of the trans-historical character of women's oppression, but in this very appeal to longevity it deprives us of an adequate grasp of historical change. How useful is it to collapse widow-burning in India with 'the coercion of privacy' in Western Europe, into a concept of such generality? What we need to analyse are precisely the mechanisms by which women's oppression is secured in different contexts, since only then can we confront the problem of how to change it.

Feminists who employ the concept of patriarchy vary in the extent to which they ground it in biological differences between the sexes or in inevitable power structures stemming from these differences. A number of writers have inquired into the historical origins of patriarchy and, related to this, the question of whether these origins are biologically determined. No one would want to deny that there are physiological differences between the sexes, but what is at issue is how these natural differences are constructed as divisions by human social agency. Racists who attempt to provide 'scientific' apologias for the oppression of blacks are treated with the contempt they deserve and we should be equally wary of apologias for gender division, including those emanating from feminist quarters. The valorization of the female principle that a biologistic use of the concept of patriarchy encourages should be rejected at all levels.

I would not, however, want to argue that the concept of patriarchy should be jettisoned. I would favour retaining it for use in contexts where male domination is expressed through the power of the father over women and over younger men. Clearly some societies have been organized around this principle, although not capitalist ones. Insofar as feminist appropriations of psychoanalytic theory have attempted to cast this principle as a primary psychic dynamic of contemporary gender construction, I have dissented from their conclusions. Nevertheless, there remain elements of what might properly be called patriarchal power in the recent history of women's oppression and these can usefully be identified, for instance in some aspects of fascist ideology and the relations of the bourgeois family in the nineteenth century. Hence I would argue for a more precise and specific use of the concept of patriarchy, rather than one which expands it to cover all expressions of male domination and thereby attempts to construe a descriptive term as a systematic explanatory theory.

The discussion throughout this book has emphasized the importance of ideology in the construction and reproduction of women's oppression. A particular household organization and an ideology of familialism are central dimensions of women's oppression in capitalism and it is only through an analysis of ideology that we can grasp the oppressive myth of an idealized natural 'family' to which all women must conform. It is only through an analysis of ideology and its role in the construction of gendered subjectivity that we can account for the desires of women as well as men to reproduce the very familial structures by which we are oppressed. To argue this is not to suggest that needs for intimacy, sexual relations, emotional fulfilment, parenthood and so on are in themselves oppressive. What is oppressive is the assumption that the present form of such needs is the only possible form, and that the manner in which they should be met is through the family as it is today. We can have little knowledge of the form such personal needs have taken in the past, and still less of what form they might take in a future society. What feminism requires, however, in order to reach out to a wider group of women, is a more perceptive and sympathetic account not only of how or why a dominant meaning of femininity has been constructed, but how or why women have sought, consciously and unconsciously, to embrace and desire it. This requires not simply an analysis of collusion or false consciousness, but a much deeper analysis of subjectivity and identity, which presents us with the task of carrying on where earlier feminists such as Simone de Beauvoir have begun.

If we accept the importance of ideology in an analysis of women's oppression the question arises whether we should see that oppression as located solely at the ideological level. Some feminists, and many socialists, have arrived at this conclusion and I have tried to differentiate my position from theirs. To argue that women's oppression rests exclusively on ideological processes would involve one or other of two alternative assumptions. Either you need to hold that ideology is absolutely autonomous of the economic relations of capitalism, in which case it is plausible that a completely dissociated ideology of gender could exist independently of those relations; or you need to hold that ideology is always grounded in material relations but that gender ideology is grounded in economic relations between men and women that exist independently of capitalism. The first view is idealist, divorcing ideology entirely from material conditions; the second view is materialist but poses a different set of material determinants from those specified by Marxism. (A third possibility, that the ideology of gender is necessarily determined by the material relations of capitalist production, appears to me to be untenable and I have argued against it in several contexts.)

It is, perhaps, possible to resolve this problem without recourse to the analytically paralysing thesis of 'absolute autonomy', or to a form of materialism that displaces the labour/capital contradiction from its centrality in the analysis of capitalist society. First, we can note that the ideology of gender—the meaning of masculinity and feminity—has varied historically and should not be treated as static or unified, but should be examined in the different historical and class contexts in which it occurs. Second, we can note that the meaning of gender in capitalism today is tied to a household structure and division of labour that occupy a particular place in the relations of production, and that, therefore, this ideology does, concretely and historically, have some material basis. Third, we can recognize the difficulty of posing economic and ideological categories as exclusive and distinct. The relations of production and reproduction of contemporary capitalism may operate in general according to exploitative capital accumulation processes that are technically 'sex blind', but they take the form of a division of labour in which ideology is deeply embedded.

Thus I would want to argue that ideology is an extremely important site for the construction and reproduction of women's oppression, but I would resist the suggestion that this ideological level can be dissociated from economic relations. Here I would take some distance from the feminist appropriation of post-Althusserian theories that seek to locate all aspects of women's oppression in terms of a theory of discourse. Although I have drawn on a modified form of some of these ideas, notably in order to analyse the changing definition of 'the family', I would not be prepared to argue that men and women themselves represent discursive categories in which differences are produced. Masculinity and femininity obviously are categories of meaning in one sense, but men and women occupy positions in the division of labour and class structure which, although not pre-given, are historically concrete and identifiable. The general claim that women's oppression is to be located at the level of ideological production alone is either unduly restricting in our analysis, or rests on an unacceptably expansionist definition of the scope of 'ideology'.

These arguments come together around the question of historical analysis. A major problem in the development of Marxist feminist work has been a tendency to try to resolve questions such as the independence or otherwise of women's oppression from the capitalist mode of production, or the degree to which women's oppression is to be seen as ideological, by posing them as strictly theoretical issues to which a correct formulation can provide an answer. It is, however, unlikely that such a formulation will materialize, since the questions themselves are historical rather than exclusively theoretical.

One way of illustrating this point would be to pose the question: was capitalism progressive for women or not? Marxists and feminists have attempted to answer this question by a process of theoretical deduction and within both approaches the answer has varied extremely. If we pose the question historically, the issues become clearer. Feudal households were not, in any class, egalitarian as between men and women, but the development of capitalism brought an exacerbation of these divisions, a far greater degree of dependence of women on men within the household, and constructed a wage-labour system in which the relationship of women to the class structure came to be partially mediated by an assumed or actual dependence on a male wage. These developments, however, are only partly attributable to forces internal to capitalist production and also reflect a struggle within the working class.

Once the problem is posed in this way, it becomes clear that there is no programmatic answer to the question of whether women's liberation might be achieved within capitalism. We can, however, come to some conclusions. The liberation of women would require, first, a redivision of the labour and responsibilities of childcare. Whether privatized or collectivized, it would be mandatory that this be shared between men and women. Second, the actual or assumed dependence of women on a male wage (or capital) would need to be done away with. Third, the ideology of gender would need to be transformed. None of these seem to me to be compatible with capitalism as it exists in Britain and comparable societies today. The widespread and profound job-segregation characterizing the social division of labour will prove intractable. Male employment is predicated upon the assumption that domestic and childcare responsibilities are unimportant for them, and this holds true in all classes. State provisions, although not entirely inflexible, constitute at present a leaden weight of support for the male-breadwinner system of household maintenance. The ideology of gender and sexuality is deeply engrained in our consciousness.

These divisions are systematically embedded in the structure and texture of capitalist social relations in Britain and they play an important part in the political and ideological stability of this society. They are constitutive of our subjectivity as well as, in part, of capitalist political and cultural hegemony. They are interwoven into a fundamental relationship between the wage-labour system and the organization of domestic life and it is impossible to imagine that they could be extracted from the relations of production and reproduction of capitalism without a massive transformation of those relations taking place. Hence, the slogan 'No women's liberation without socialism; no socialism without women's liberation' is more than a pious hope. Although both parts of this slogan properly call for an active political intention and commitment to achieve these objectives, both also indicate the reality of the situation in which we now struggle.

At the same time, it must be emphasized that the conditions affecting improvements in women's position vary with changes in capitalism. It is more plausible to look for a lifting of the burden of domestic labour from women in times of high female employment and capitalist expansion. It is not altogether impossible that capital might wake up to the 'wastage of talent' involved in the present educational system and attempt to reduce the channelling of girls away from useful technological subjects. The effects of new technology may create a situation where the relationship between the household and wage labour is less crucial for social production, and hence create the conditions for a more equal distribution of childcare. These developments are possible, even if we may deem them unlikely, but in any case the situation would be analogous to that in socialist societies where, for instance, policy on abortion and contraception is influenced by projected labour needs.

It would be a foolish and doctrinaire stance to deny the possibility of improvement and reform under capitalism. Bourgeois women have already effected a dramatic change in respect of their civil rights—to own property, to vote, stand for public office and enter the professions. These are sweeping changes, and a restructuring of the ideological and political parameters of women's situation is not inconceivable. It is perhaps less clear what changes we could expect in the case of working-class women. The 'double shift' of domestic labour and poorly paid wage labour is also affected by variations in the strength of the capitalist economy, and the present recession is likely to lower women's standard of living generally and force many women into particularly exploited jobs in order to maintain some contribution to the household budget. These issues bite deeply on the political project of socialist feminism. By generations of socialists we stand accused of bourgeois, diversionary, individualist reformism. By our sisters we are charged with betraying feminism in favour of a sexist, male class struggle. The rhetoric on both sides may have shifted a bit, but the questions still are: does the women's liberation movement have a 'middle-class' basis? Do existing forms of class struggle represent feminist demands? The accusation that the women's movement is 'middle class' in fact robs it of a justified recognition of the unique achievements in forging common objectives across the boundaries of class. The movement is by no means restricted to women of one class. Although class divisions may cause problems that need to be worked on internally, the concept of sisterhood does have some political reality within the movement. More accurately, though, it is undoubtedly the case that—certainly in the early years of the present movement—feminist political struggle was disproportionately engaged in by women who were highly educated, many of them university graduates. Although education is sharply divided by class, it is not completely reducible to it. This problem has not gone unnoticed in the movement, particularly in Britain. Rather, it has posed the question of how to make feminism relevant to women across a range of different experiences and situations. In particular, it means that without losing our vital emphasis on sexual politics we need to engage as much as possible in struggles over the conditions, hours, pay, security of women workers. These are areas which the labour movement has in the past severely neglected and we need to ensure that women's interests are fought for and feminist demands made.

What, then, might we conclude as to the relationship between women's liberation and the left? A politically autonomous women's liberation movement does not require elaborate justification, and indeed we have correctly assumed a right to organize independently of men, however sympathetic male supporters may be to our general objectives. The political and ideological processes that contribute so massively to women's oppression must be fought by those affected by them, and there has been little justification for the view that existing programmes for socialism will automatically bring about women's liberation. In addition to this, the battle within the trade-union movement—for instance, for equal pay and a shorter working day in opposition to men's demands for a family wage and a shorter working week—needs to be fought by a strong feminist presence with a base in an autonomous women's movement.

There are, however, fundamental political imperatives directing us not only towards a strong feminist presence on the left but towards some kind of alliance between the women's liberation movement and the left. This certainly does not mean that the women's movement should be subsumed under the left, nor that its function should be to radicalize and renovate an ailing organizational structure. In this respect I would tend to be somewhat critical of the view expressed by the authors of *Beyond the Fragments* that the libertarian, grass-roots style of the women's movement could be taken as a model for a new socialist organizational form.[1] Important though questions of organization are, I would not see the potential benefits of some kind of alliance as consisting in what each movement could learn from the other in these respects. The more urgent question to be asked is whether there are *political objectives* in common that might constitute a basis for a relationship.

At present there are, I think, some major areas of at best a difference of political emphasis, and at worst outright conflict. An obvious thorny example is that of biological reproduction. As Sue Himmelweit has pointed out, there is surely some conflict between a feminist insistence on the right of each individual woman to decide when and whether she will have a child and a socialist notion of collective responsibility in relation to reproduction.[2] Problems such as these cannot be evaded. There are, however, many issues where objective interests might coincide and provide a basis for greater unity. One such example would be the question of women's wages and working conditions. As I suggested in Chapter 5, the labour movement has in the past used exclusionary practices to define women workers as less skilled than men, thereby confirming women in low paid and insecure jobs and facilitating capital's use of cheap and flexible female labour as a means of keeping general wages down. This has strengthened the divisions between men and women within the working class, and it is a major task of feminists and the left to challenge these practices and assumptions and offer an alternative strategy. Such a strategy could be grounded in shared objectives of both socialism and feminism.

There are more general reasons underlying a drive towards an alliance. Feminism seeks to change not simply men or women, or both, as they exist at present, but seeks to change the relations between them. Although the basis for this will be provided by an autonomous women's liberation movement the strategy must involve political engagement with men rather than a policy of absolute separatism. Socialist men, like other men, stand to lose political power and social privilege from the liberation of women but, more than other men, they have shown now and in the past some political intention to support feminist struggle. This is not a question of benevolence on their part. For if women's oppression is entrenched in the structure of capitalism then the struggle for women's liberation and the struggle for socialism cannot wholly be disengaged. Just as we cannot conceive of women's liberation under the oppression of capitalism so we cannot conceive of a socialism whose principles of equality, freedom and dignity are vitiated by the familiar iniquities of gender.

NOTES

1. Sheila Rowbotham, Lynne Segal and Hilary Wainwright, *Beyond the Fragments: Feminism and the Making of Socialism*, Landun 1980.
2. Sue Himmelwett, "Abortion: Individual Choice and Social Control," *Feminist Review*, no. 5, 1980.

8

LINDA NICHOLSON

Feminism and Marx

Integrating Kinship with the Economic

As liberal theory in the seventeenth century began to reflect the separation of kinship and state taking place in that period, so also in the eighteenth and nineteenth centuries a new branch of study arose, economic theory, which similarly reflected a comparable separation of the economy from both the state and kinship taking place in these centuries. While nascent versions of an "economy" can be traced back at least to the middle ages, it was only by the eighteenth century that this sphere became independent enough to generate its own body of theory, constructed in the writings of such figures as Smith, Ricardo and Marx.

Distinguishing Karl Marx in this list, not only from Smith and Ricardo, but even more strongly from economic theorists who were to come later, was his recognition that the seemingly autonomous operation of the economy belied its interdependence with other aspects of social life. Marx, more than most economic theorists, had a strong sense of history and in consequence was aware of the origins of contemporary economic relations in older political and familial relations and the continuous interaction of state, family and economy even in the context of their historical separation. However, while Marx more than most economic theorists was aware of the interconnection of family, state and economy, his theory did not consistently abide by this awareness. Most importantly, the assumption common to much economic theory, that there is cross-culturally an economic component of human existence which can be studied independently from other aspects of human life, exists as a significant strand within his writings, and most prominently in what might be called his philosophical anthropology or cross-cultural theory on the nature of human life and social organization. Indeed, Marx, by building a philosophical anthropology on the basis of this assumption, developed and made more explicit that very perspective in much other economic theory which he in other contexts criticized.

This inconsistency makes Marx a crucial figure for feminist theory. As feminist theory has challenged that assumption of the necessary and analytic distinctiveness of the family and state predominant in a liberal worldwide, so also must it challenge the assumption of the analytic distinctiveness of the economic present in both a liberal and marxist worldview. The irony here is that in furthering this project, feminist theory has in Marx both a strong ally and a serious opponent. As we shall see in the following, feminists can employ much of the historical work of Marx and many marxists in comprehending the separation of family, state and economy as an historical and not natural phenomenon, and in comprehending the interaction of these spheres even in the context of their separation. On the other hand, Marx's philosophical anthropology, by continuing and indeed reinforcing our modern assumptions of the autonomy of the economic, raises serious obstacles for marxism's understanding of gender. To make this case requires that we now examine the content of this anthropology.

A. MARX AND PRODUCTION

Basic to Marx's views on human life and social organization is his concept of production. But from a feminist perspective, this concept is fundamentally ambiguous: focusing either on all human activities necessary to the reproduction of the species (including such activities as nursing and childrearing) or focusing exclusively on those activities concerned with the making of food and physical objects. This ambiguity in focus is illustrated in the following passage (emphasis added):

> The production of life, both of one's own in labour and of fresh life in procreation now appears as a double relationship: on the one hand as a natural, and on the other as a social relationship. By social we understand the co-operation of several individuals, no matter under what conditions, in what manner and to what end. It follows from this that a certain mode of production, *or industrial stage*, is always combined with a certain mode of cooperation, or social stage, and this mode of cooperation is itself a "productive force." Further, that the multitude of productive forces accessible to men determines the nature of society, hence, that the "history of humanity" must always be studied and treated in relation to the *history of industry and exchange*.[1]

In the first sentence "production" refers to all activities necessary for species survival; by the middle of the passage its meaning has become restricted to those activities which are geared to the creation of material objects (industrial). While from the meaning of "production" in the first sentence, Marx could include family forms under the "modes of cooperation" he describes, by the middle of the paragraph its meaning has become such to now include only those "modes of cooperation" found within the "history of industry and exchange." In effect, Marx has eliminated from his theoretical focus all activities basic to human survival which fall outside of a capitalist "economy." Those activities he has eliminated include not only those iden- tified by feminists as "reproductive" (childcare, nursing) but also those concerned with social organization, i.e. those regulating kinship relations or in modern societies those we would classify as "political".[2] Marx's ability to do this was made possible by his moving from a broad to a narrow meaning of "production."

This ambiguity in Marx's use of "production" can be further understood in terms of the variety of meanings the word possesses. Firstly, in its broadest meaning it can refer to any activity that has consequences. More narrowly, "production" refers to those activities that result in objects. Finally, in an even more specific sense, it refers to those activities that result in objects that are bought and sold, i.e. commodities. Similarly, if we look at such related words as "labor" and "product" we can find a con- fusion between respectively 1) activity requiring any effort and the result of such activity, 2) activity resulting in an object and that object and 3) activity resulting in a commodity and that commodity.

Marx and many of his later followers often do not make clear which of these meanings they are employing when they use these and related words. For example, when Marx claims that labor is the motor of historical change, does he mean all human effort which changes the natural and/or social environment, only that effort which results in objects, or effort which results in commodities? Similarly, Marx's con- cept of the "economy" often becomes confusing, in part as a consequence of ambi- guities in his use of "production." To illustrate this point it is helpful to refer to the preface to the *Contribution to the Critique of Political Economy*:

> In the social production of their existence, men inevitably enter into definite rela- tions, which are independent of their will, namely relations of production appro- priate to a given stage in the development of their material forces of production. The totality of these relations of production constitutes the economic structure of society, the real foundation, on which arises a legal and political superstructure and to which correspond definite forms of social consciousness. The mode of pro- duction of material life conditions the general process of social, political and intel- lectual life.[3]

In the above, Marx equates the "economic structure of society" with its "relations of production." Since a reasonable interpretation of "mode of production of mate- rial life" would be all activities conducive to the creation and re-creation of a soci- ety's physical existence, the "relations of production" should reasonably include all social interaction having this object as its end. Thus the family should count as a com- ponent of the "economy." Even if we interpret the phrase "mode of production of material life" to refer only to activities concerned with the gathering, hunting or growing of food and the making of objects, the family, in many societies, would still be included as a component of the economy. Neither of these two meanings of "economy," however, is the same as its meaning in post-industrial capitalism where the "economy" comes to refer principally to the activities of those engaged in the creation and exchange of commodities. Thus Marx's concept of "economy" in the above is ambiguous as a consequence of the ambiguity in his concept of production.

Such ambiguities in the meaning of key words in Marx's theory in turn make possible certain serious problems within the theory. In particular, they enable Marx to falsely project features of capitalist society onto all societies, and with most relevance for the purposes of this essay, to cross-culturally project the autonomization and primacy of the economic in capitalist societies. This point is illustrated by examining Marx's claim that "the changes in the economic foundation lead sooner or later to the transformation of the whole immense superstructure." This claim is intended as a universal claim of social theory, i.e. it is meant to state that in all societies there is a certain relation between the "economy" and the "superstructure." If we interpret "economy" here to refer to "all activities necessary to meet the conditions of human survival," the claim is non-problematic but trivial. More frequently, "economy" is interpreted by Marx and marxists to refer to "those activities concerned with the production of food and objects." Here, while the claim ceases being trivial, it now contains certain problems as a cross-cultural claim. While all societies have some means of organizing the production of food and objects as well as some means of organizing sexuality and childcare, it is only in capitalist society that the former set of activities becomes differentiated from the latter under the concept of the "economic" and takes on a certain priority. Thus by employing the more specific meaning of "economic" in his cross-cultural claims, Marx projects the separation and primacy of the "economic" found in capitalist society onto all human societies.

Thus, let us look more closely at this projection of the primacy of the "economic." Marx, by giving primacy to the "economic" cannot merely be arguing that the production of food and objects is a necessary condition for human life to continue. That certainly is true but the same can be said about many other aspects and activities of human beings: that we breathe, communicate with each other through language and other means, engage in heterosexual activity which results in childbearing, create forms of social organization, raise children, etc. Rather Marx appears to be making the stronger and more interesting claim that the ways in which we produce food and objects in turn structures the manner in which other necessary human activities are performed. But the force of this latter claim, I would argue, rests upon a feature true only for capitalist society: that here the mode in which food and object production is organized to a significant extent does structure other necessary human activities. This is because in capitalist society, the production of food and objects takes on an importance going beyond its importance as a necessary life activity.

To express the same point in another way: in so far as capitalist society organizes the production and distribution of food and objects according to the profit motive, those activities concerned with the making and exchanging of food and goods assume a value and importance relatively *independent* of their role in satisfying human needs. The ability of such activities to generate a profit gives to them a priority which can be mistakenly associated with their function in satisfying such needs. As Marshall Sahlins has noted, this priority makes credible a kind of reflectionist or economic determinist theory where the system of production and exchange appears basic:

> Since the objectives and relations of each subsystem are distinct, each has a certain internal logic and a relative autonomy. But since all are subordinated to the requirements of the economy, this gives credibility to the kind of reflectionist theory which perceives in the superstructure the differentiations (notably of class) established in production and exchange.[4]

Thus, if in capitalist society such activities as raising children, or nursing the sick had been as easily conductive to making a profit, as did become activities concerned with the production of food and objects, we might in turn believe that the manner in which human societies raise children or nurse their sick structures all other life activities in which they engage.

More significant for the purposes of this essay than even Marx's projection of the primacy of the economic found in capitalist societies into his cross-cultural theory, is his projection of the *autonomy* of the economic into that theory. To illustrate how that projection is a function of certain unique features of his time, I would like now to look more closely at the historical context in which Marx wrote.

B. THE HISTORICAL CONTEXT OF MARXISM

One theorist whose work can provide us with useful tools for understanding the historical context of marxism is Karl Polanyi. One of the major theses of his book *The Great Transformation* is similar to a point stressed here: that while it is true that all societies must satisfy the needs of biology to stay alive, it is only true of modern society that the satisfaction of some of these needs in ever increasing amounts becomes a central motive of action. This transformation Polanyi identifies with the establishment of a market economy whose full development, he argues, does not occur until the nineteenth century. Polanyi acknowledges the existence of markets, both external and local, prior to this century. However, he makes a distinction between what he describes as external, local and internal trade. External and local trade are complementary to the economies in which they exist. They involve the transfer of goods from a geographical area where they are available to an area where they are not available. The trading that goes on between town and countryside or between areas different in climate represent such types of trading. Internal trade differs from both of the above in that it is essentially competitive, involving "a very much larger number of exchanges in which similar goods from different sources are offered in competition with one another."[5] Polanyi claims that these different forms of trade have different origins; in particular, internal trade arose neither from external or local trade, as common sense might suggest, but rather from the deliberate intervention on the part of the state.[6] The mercantile system of the fifteenth and sixteenth centuries established its initial conditions, making possible the beginnings of a national market.

While state intervention was necessary to establish the initial conditions for a national market, the true flourishing of such a market required the absence of at least some of the kinds of state regulation found under mercantilism.[7] A market economy is one where the movement of the elements of the economy—goods, labor, land, money—is governed by the actions of the market. Under feudalism and the guild system, non-market mechanisms controlled two of these elements, land and labor. This non-market control over labor and land did not disappear under mercantilism; it merely changed its form. The principles of statute and ordinance became employed over that of custom and tradition.[8] Indeed, as Polanyi claims, it is not until after 1834 in England, with the repeal of the Speenhamland law, which had provided government subsidies for the unemployed and underemployed, that the last of these elements, labor, becomes freed to become a commodity. Thus it was not until the nineteenth century in England that a market economy could be said to be fully functioning.

The above discussion of the emergence of a market economy may help us understand its distinctive features. Of key importance is the dominance of the principle of price as the mechanism for organizing the production and distribution of goods. This means that not until all of the elements necessary to the production and distribution of goods are controlled by price, can a market economy be said to be functioning. A market economy demands the freeing of the elements comprising the economy from the governance of other social institutions, such as the state or the family. Polanyi does not discuss the decline of the family in governing such elements. He does, however, stress the separation of the political and the economic as a necessary condition of a market economy:

> A self-regulating market demands nothing less than the institutionalized separation of society into an economic and political sphere. Such a dichotomy is, in effect, merely the restatement, from the point of view of society as a whole, of the existence of a self-regulating market. It might be argued that the separateness of the two spheres obtains in every type of society at all times. Such an inference, however, would be based on a fallacy. True, no society can exist without a system of some kind which ensures order in the production and distribution of goods. But that does not imply the existence of separate economic institutions; normally, the economic order is merely a function of the social, in which it is contained. Neither under tribal, nor feudal, nor mercantile conditions was there, as we have shown, a separate economic system in society. Nineteenth century society, in which economic activity was isolated and imputed to a distinctive economic motive was, indeed, a singular departure.[9]

Polanyi goes on to argue that not only does a market economy require the separation of the elements of the economy from other spheres of social life, but that this means in effect the dominance of the principle of the market over other social principles. Since two of the elements of the economy, land and labor, are basic features of social life, to subordinate them to market mechanisms is in effect to subordinate society to the market:

> But labor and land are not other than the human beings themselves of which every society consists and the natural surrounding in which it exists. To include them in the market mechanism means to subordinate the substance of society itself to the laws of the market.[10]

We might qualify Polanyi's argument by saying that it is not all labor which becomes subordinate to the laws of the market when the economy becomes a market economy; domestic labor does not, at least in any simple sense. Since, however, *some* of the labor essential to human survival does become subordinated to the market, we can still accede to this point of the growing dominance of the market. Moreover, we might also agree with his further claim that the organization of the economic system under a market mechanism means also the dominance of the economic. He argues that this occurs because "the vital importance of the economic factor to the existence of society precludes any other result. For once the economic system is organized in separate institutions, based on specific motives and conferring a special status, society must be shaped in such a manner as to allow that system to function according to its own laws. This is the meaning of the familiar assertion that a market economy can function only in a market society.[11] Such an argument can be supplemented by the claim that the alliance of the production of goods with the acquisitive motive means the rise in importance of the production of goods over other life activities. The acquisitive motive is such so that to allow it as a motive means to allow it as a dominant motive.

Thus, a thesis often thought of as central to marxism, the separation and dominance of the economic, is in effect a defining condition of a market economy. Moreover, as follows from Polanyi's analysis, it is just this condition which only becomes true within the nineteenth century. Thus one can conclude that marxism as social theory is very much a product of its time, insightful as an exposition of that which was becoming true, and false to the extent that the limited historical applicability of its claims was not recognized.

As noted, Polanyi claims that a defining condition of a market economy is a separation of the economic and political. Not noted by him, but also essential, is the separation of the economic from the domestic and familial. Indeed, when we think of what is pivotal about industralization it is that the production of goods ceases being organized by kinship relations and an activity of the household. The creation of goods by members of the household for the purpose of use by the household and organized primarily in accordance with family roles becomes replaced by the creation of goods by members of many different households for the purpose of exchange and organized in accordance with the profit motive. The commodization of the elements of production means not only, as Polanyi notes, a withdrawal of control on the part of the state over these elements but also a withdrawal on the part of the family.

When labor remained at home, its content and organization was primarily a family matter; when it left only its consequences, wages, remained such.

Thus from the above analysis we can comprehend the emergence of the "economic" as separate from both the family and the state as the outcome of an historical process. This kind of analysis is one which I shall show is most in sympathy with the requirements of feminism. It is also one which might be used to both challenge and explain the tendency amongst Marx and his followers to employ the category of the "economic" cross-culturally. The irony, however, is that such an historical analysis could itself be described as "marxist." Polanyi's work builds on the kinds of historical investigations Marx himself carried out in studying the emergence of capitalism out of earlier social forms. This irony reinforces a point suggested earlier—that while in Marx's concrete historical analysis there is much from which feminism can draw in comprehending the changing relation of family, state and economy, it is most strongly in Marx's cross-cultural claims that the theory becomes unhelpful to feminism. To elaborate this point, that is to show that it is precisely Marx's ahistoricity which accounts for the theory's weaknesses in analyzing gender, I would now like to focus specifically on the consequences of these problems for marxism's analysis of gender.

C. MARX ON WOMEN, GENDER RELATIONS AND THE FAMILY

In comprehending marxism on gender it is important to note that Marx's concept of class relies on the narrow translation of "production" and "economic"—i.e. as incorporating only those activities concerned with the making of food and objects. Thus the criterion which Marx employs to demarcate class position, "relation to the means of production," is understood as relation to the means of producing food and objects. For Marx, the first class division arose over the struggle for appropriation of the first social surplus, meaning the first social surplus of food and objects. A consequence of such a definition of class is to eliminate from consideration historical conflicts over other socially necessary activities such as childbearing and childrearing. A second consequence is to eliminate from consideration changes in the organization of such activities as components of historical change. The theory thus eliminates from consideration activities which historically have been at least one important component in gender relations. But here we can ask of the theory certain questions: why ought we to eliminate or to count as less important in our theory of history changes in reproduction or childrearing practices than changes involved in food or object producing activities? Firstly, does it even make sense to attempt to separate the changes involved, prior to the time when these activities were themselves differentiated, i.e. prior to the time when the "economy" became differentiated from the "family"? Furthermore, is not the assumption of the greater importance of changes in production itself a product of a society which gives priority to food and object creation over other life activities?

Many feminist theorists have noted the consequences for Marx of leaving out reproductive activities from his theory of history. Mary O'Brien, for example, argues that one effect is to separate historical continuity from biological continuity, which one might note is particularly ironic for a "materialist":

> Thus Marx talks continuously of the need for men to "reproduce" themselves, and by this he almost always means reproduction of the self on a daily basis by the continual and necessary restoking of the organism with fuel for its biological needs. Man makes himself materially, and this is of course true. Man, however, is also "made" reproductively by the parturitive labour of women, but Marx ultimately combines these two processes. This has the effect of negating biological continuity which is mediated by women's reproductive labour, and replacing this with productive continuity in which men, in making themselves, also make history. Marx never observes that men are in fact separated *materially* from both nature and biological continuity by the alienation of the male seed in copulation.[12]

Similarly, though from a different perspective, Marx's lack of consideration of "reproductive" activities enables him to ignore, to the extent that he does, the component of socialization in human history. In other words, the failures in Marx's theory which result from his attraction to a narrow interpretation of "materialism" might have been alleviated had he paid more attention to the activity of child-rearing.

As O'Brien points out, there is a tendency for Marx to negate the sociability and historicity of reproductive activities, to see such activities as natural and thus ahistorical.[13] Alternatively, he occasionally treats changes in the organization of such activities as historical effects of changes in productive relations. Thus she notes that in *The Communist Manifesto*, Marx treats the family as a superstructural effect of the economy.[14] This is evidenced also in a letter to P. V. Annenkov of December 28, 1846, where Marx states: "Assume particular stages of development of production, commerce and consumption and you will have a corresponding social constitution, a corresponding organization of the family, of orders and classes, in a word, a corresponding civil society. . . ."[15] Here again, such tendencies in Marx can be explained by looking to the role and ideology of the family in an industrial society. When "productive" activities leave the household and in turn come to constitute the world of change and dynamism, then activities of "reproduction" become viewed as either the brute, physiological and non-historical aspects of human existence or as byproducts of changes in the economy.

One important problem which specifically follows from seeing "reproductive" activities as universally the consequence of "productive" activities, is that we are thereby prevented from comprehending the integration of "production" and "reproduction" in pre-capitalist societies. A consequence is that we fail to see how women and men in such societies occupy very distinctive relations to those activities concerned with the making of food and objects *in connection with* those rules regulating marriage and sexuality. Morover, this distinctive relation to "productive" activities cannot be described solely in terms of a "division of labor." While there appears some consistent gender division of labor throughout history in relation even to the making of food and objects, women have also had less control over the means and results of such activity than men, again, *in connection with* those very rules which organize marriage and sexuality in kinship organized societies.

The conclusion, however, of this recognition is that gender, certainly in kinship organized societies, and perhaps to varying extents in societies following, should be viewed as a significant class division even following a traditional understanding of class. In other words, even if we subscribe to the traditional marxist translation of production to refer to activities concerned with the making of food and objects, then gender relations, since historically involving different access to control over these activities, constitute class relations. This point takes us beyond the traditional feminist castigation of marxism for its sole focus on production. Part of the limitation of that castigation was that it shared with marxists the belief in the separability of "productive" and "reproductive" activities. But if we recognize this separability as historically tied to a form of social organization where the principle of exchange has to a certain extent replaced the principle of kinship as a means of organizing the production and distribution of goods, then our comprehension of the limitations of marxism on gender is deepened.

Another means of explicating this point is by noting that when Marx and marxists use the category of "class," they have most paradigmatically in mind the examples of such societies as capitalism or feudalism. In feudal society kinship relations to a significant extent still organize production relations, but gender here may be less fundamental in some instances in indicating relation to the "means of production" than connection with a specific parental lineage. In capitalist societies, connection with a specific parental lineage remains a component in constituting class, but only also in conjunction with the actions of the market. Neither society, however, illuminates the case of more "egalitarian" societies where differences in parental lineages amongst men may be less important an indicator of differences in control over production than gender. In other words, whether gender is or is not an important class indicator must be empirically determined in every instance and we cannot assume, as do many marxists, that gender and class are inherently distinct. Rather the evidence seems to be that in many early societies gender is a very fundamental class indicator, a fact resonating throughout subsequent history, though also in conjunction with, and at times in subordination to, other factors.

This last point brings us finally to the issue of marxism's ability to analyze gender in capitalist society. Much of my criticism of Marx has rested on the claim that he falsely generalizes features of capitalist society onto societies where such features do not hold and that it is this failure which accounts for the theory's weaknesses in analyzing gender. The implication of this argument would be that the theory is adequate as an account of capitalism and as an account of gender relations within capitalist society. One problem, however, with this conclusion is that it ignores the fact that capitalist socety contains aspects of pre-capitalist societies within it which are highly relevant to gender. For example, it is true that in capitalist society the economy does become more autonomous of other realms than has been true of any earlier society. But in so far as marxism as theory treats the "economic" as autonomous, it loses sight of the ways in which even capitalist economies grew out of and continue to be affected by "non-economic" aspects of human existence. Indeed, marxism, by attributing autonomy to the "economic" comes close to that liberal position which would deny the influence over the market of such factors as gender, religion, politics, etc. Of course, in specific contexts and in specific disagreements with liberals and conservatives, marxists often argue for the determinacy of such non-economic factors. Again, however, marxism as historical analysis appears incompatible with marxism as cross-cultural theory.

The way out of this dilemma for marxists would be to eliminate the cross-cultural theory and more consistently follow the historical analysis. This would mean describing the progressive domination of the state and later the market over kinship as an historical process.[16] This type of approach could enable marxism to correct two failures which are linked within the theory: its failure in explaining gender and the history of gender relations, and its failure to be adequately cognizant of the historical limitedness of certain of its claims. By recognizing that the progressive domination of the market has been an historical process, it might avoid the latter failure. By recognizing both the centrality of kinship in structuring early societies and its centuries long interaction with such other institutions as the state and the market, it could provide itself with a means for analyzing gender. It is ironic to note here that marxists have occasionally described radical feminism as ahistorical. Whereas radical feminism pointed to the universality of the family, marxists argued that this institution is always the changing effect of developments in the economy. However, it may be a function of marxism's failure to pay sufficient enough attention to the fundamentality of kinship and its changing relation to other social institutions and practices that has caused the theory to become falsely ahistorical itself.

D. MARXISM AND FEMINISM

From the above analysis of the failures of marxism in explaining gender, we can resolve certain disputes amongst contemporary marxist feminists. As noted, marxist feminists have recognized that Marx's category of "production" leaves out of account many traditional female activities. In response, some have argued that we need to augment this category with the category of "reproduction." This, for example, is the position of Mary O'Brien:

> What does have to be done is a modification of Marx's socio-historical model, which must now account for two opposing substructures, that of production and that of reproduction. This in fact improves the model.[17]

Other marxist feminists offer similar or somewhat revised models. Ann Ferguson and Nancy Folbre, for example, prefer to label the augmented category "sex-affective production" rather than "reproduction." They note that the term "reproduction" is used by Marx to describe the "economic process over time." To employ it to refer to activities such as childbearing and childrearing might result in some confusion. Moreover, they argue, by including those traditionally female identified tasks under the category of "production," we are reminded of the social usefulness of such tasks.[18]

Such proposals have been described by Iris Young as constituting variants of what she labels "dual systems theory." Young also recognizes the narrowness of Marx's category of production:

> Such traditional women's tasks as bearing and rearing children, caring for the sick, cleaning, cooking, etc. fall under the category of labor as much as the making of objects in a factory. Using the category of production or labor to designate only the making of concrete material objects in a modern factory has been one of the unnecessary tragedies of Marxian theory.[19]

Young, however, does not approve of focusing on those activities which have fallen outside of this category to make marxism more explanatory of gender. One weakness in such a solution is that it fails to account for gender relations which occur within "production."[20] In other words, Young is making the point stated earlier in this essay: that gender has been a significant variable even amongst those activities concerned with the making of food and objects. Thus any analysis of gender must do more than enlarge the traditional category.

The basic problem of dual systems theory, according to Young, is that it does not seriously enough challenge the very framework of marxism.[21] That this framework is gender blind must indicate a serious deficiency, whose remedy cannot merely be supplementation. Moreover, dual systems theory, by making the issue of women's oppression separate and distinct from that which is covered by marxism, reinforces the idea that women's oppression is merely a supplemental topic to the major concerns of marxism.

The analysis put forth in the preceding enables us both to understand the attractiveness of dual systems theory and to meet the above challenge of Young. Dual systems theorists are correct in recognizing that an important source of marxism's inability to analyze gender is the narrowness of its category of production. Where they go wrong, however, is in not seeing this problem as in turn a function of marxism's engulfment within the categories of its time. Marx's exclusion of certain activities from "production" is not sufficiently appreciated as a symptom of the particular period the theory is reflecting. Within industrial society many of those activities the category leaves out do become identified with women and become viewed as outside of production. This very exclusion is reflected within Marx's categories.

This assessment of the failure of Marx's category provides us with a different remedy than that proposed by dual systems theorists. While we might agree with such theorists that the addition of the category of "reproduction" to the category of "production" might be necessary for understanding gender relations within industrial society, neither category is necessarily useful for analyzing earlier societies. Indeed, since there is no reason to believe that the kinds of social divisions expressed by these categories played a significant role in structuring gender relations within such societies, there would be no reason for employing them. This is not to say, of course, that gender did not play a significant role in earlier societies. It is rather that the categories through which we need to grasp it have to be understood as historically changing, reflecting the changing emergence, dominance and decline of different institutions. Thus in early societies it appears that the key institution in structuring gender, as well as those activities we would label political or economic, is kinship. Social theory must focus on the differential power relations expressed within this institution to explain relations between men and women as well as amongst men as a group and women as a group. For later periods, we need to focus on the transformation of kinship into family, and the emergence of the economy and the state as separated spheres. Thus for the modern period we need to focus on that very *historical* separation of spheres which led liberals to differentiate the family and the state and marxists to differentiate production and reproduction.

E. CONCLUSION

In sum, the marxist tendency to employ categories rooted in capitalist social relations and its failure in comprehending gender are deeply related. In so far as marxists interpret "production" as necessarily distinct from "reproduction," then aspects of capitalist society are falsely universalized and gender relations in both pre-capitalist and capitalist societies are obscured. In pre-capitalist societies, childrearing practices, sexual relations and what we call "productive" activities are organized conjointly through the medium of kinship. Thus in these societies, issues of gender and issues of class are inseparable. Moreover, within capitalist society, this integration of gender and class continues both in so far as the progressively separating sphere of the economic bears traces of its origins in its continued functioning, and also in so far as the separation of the economic from the family and household remains incomplete. Thus understanding gender, both in its pre-capitalist and capitalist manifestations, requires an awareness of the historical nature of the separation of the economic rather than its presupposition in the categories employed.

The complication of course, is that marxism both does and does not maintain such an awareness. Certainly, both Marx and most of his followers are at one level aware of the autonomization of the economic as an historical process. The problem, however, is that this awareness is conjoined with a theoretical framework which presupposes the separation of the economic as a cross-cultural phenomenon. Of note for the purposes of this collection, is that it is those theorists associated with critical theory who have tended to distinguish marxism as historical analysis from marxism as cross-cultural theory and who have tended to support the former over the latter. Thus Georg Lukacs, in *History and Class Consciousness* first raised the question of the cross-cultural applicability of Marx's concept of class and Jürgen Habermas in *Knowledge and Human Interests* distinguished Marx's empirical analyses and his philosophical self-understanding.[22]

Not noted, however, by these theorists or by others who have raised similar questions about marxism as cross-cultural theory, is the power of gender to serve as a concrete and fundamental example of the problem. As argued, it is in the very ambiguities of Marx's concept of "production," that the theory's failures in understanding gender and its tendency to falsely universalize capitalist social relations come together. Thus the feminist critique of marxism goes beyond what is often perceived as a relatively superficial call to incorporate gender to become a powerful voice in the analysis of its basic weaknesses and a necessary means in the task of its reconstruction.

NOTES

1. Karl Marx and Frederick Engels, *The German Ideology* (Moscow: Progress Publishers, 1968), p. 39.
2. Jürgen Habermas has made a similar objection to Marx's work. Habermas notes that while Marx does claim to incorporate the aspect of symbolic interaction, understood under the concept of "relations of production," within his theory, this aspect is ultimately eliminated within Marx's basic frame of reference. This point replicates the criticism of feminists in that in both cases Marx is cited for an ambiguity in his concept of "production." In the problems pointed to by Habermas there is an ambiguity in Marx's inclusion under "production" of either both "the forces and the relations of production" or more narrowly of only "the forces of production." In the problems pointed to by feminists, there is an ambiguity concerning even what "forces of production" might include. In all cases, such ambiguity is made possible by Marx's moving from broader to more narrow meanings of "production." For Habermas's critique see, *Knowledge and Human Interests*, trans. Jeremy Shapiro (Boston: Beacon Press, 1972), pp. 25–63.
3. Karl Marx, *A Contribution to the Critique of Political Economy*, ed. and intro. by Maurice Dobb (New York: International Publishers, 1920), pp. 20–21.
4. Marshall Sahlins, *Culture and Practical Reason* (Chicago: The University of Chicago Press, 1976), p. 212.
5. Karl Polanyi, *The Great Transformation* (Boston: Beacon Press, 1957), p. 60.
6. *Ibid.*, p. 66.
7. As Polanyi argues, the absence of some regulation does not mean the absence of all regulation. On the contrary he claims that markets and regulation grew up together.
8. Polanyi, p. 20.
9. *Ibid.*, p. 71.
10. *Idem.*
11. *Ibid.*, p. 57.
12. Mary O'Brien, "Reproducing Marxist Man," in *The Sexism of Social and Political Theory*, eds. Lorenne M. G. Clark and Lynda Lange (Toronto: University of Toronto Press, 1979), p. 107.
13. *Ibid.*, p. 102 and p. 111.
14. *Ibid.*, p. 105.

15. Karl Marx, *The Poverty of Philosophy* (New York: International Publishers, 1963), p. 180.

16. This point of the progression of kinship to state to market has been made often in the marxist literature. See, for example, Frederick Engels, *The Origin of the Family, Private Property and the State*, ed. and with an intro. by Eleanor Burke Leacock (New York: International Publishers, 1972), pp. 72–73.

17. O'Brien, p. 114.

18. Ann Ferguson and Nancy Folbre, "The Unhappy Marriage of Patriarchy and Capitalism" in Lydia Sargent, ed., *Women and Revolution* (Boston: South End Press, 1981), p. 318.

19. Iris Young, "Beyond the Unhappy Marriage: A Critique of Dual Systems Theory," in *Women and Revolution*, p. 52.

20. *Ibid.*, p. 49.

21. *Idem.*

22. Georg Lukacs, *History and Class Consciousness*, trans. Rodney Livingstone (Cambridge, Mass.: MIT, 1971), Jürgen Habermas, *Knowledge and Human Interests*, p. 42.

Gynocentrism

Women's Oppression, Women's Identity, and Women's Standpoint

In the early 1970s, second wave feminists began to focus more extensively than previously on the differences between women and men. I describe this move as an intensity of focus rather than a complete change of direction, because a focus on the differences between women and men was a crucial element of the radical feminism of the late 1960s. In many respects, the "difference" or "gynocentric" feminism that began to emerge in the early 1970s can be seen as the logical extension of the growing recognition by many feminists of the importance of gender as an organizing principle of individual identity and social organization. Taking that recognition and applying it to analyses of the psyches of women and men led to theories that emphasized differences between women and men. To be sure, within this overall theoretical move, there were major variations as diverse feminists thought about the importance of gender in distinctive ways.

A focus on the differences between women and men, combined with the radical feminist sense of the magnitude of women's oppression, led first to an elaboration of women's minds as deeply shaped by the experience of oppression. An essay that expressed this orientation was "The Woman Identified Woman." The writers argued that women are socialized to internalize a conception of themselves as lesser beings. To counter such socialization, women need to contruct their own conceptions of what being a woman is about and to begin prizing and loving themselves *as* women. Women need to become "woman identified."

And building on the early second wave insight that "The Personal is Political," the essay directly linked women's oppression to their emotional and sexual connections with men. The writers focused on the idea that women are connected with their oppressors in ways other groups are not so connected, through the physical and emotional ties of sex and love. They argued that, for women to be in a position where they can learn to love themselves and become "woman identified," women need to break such ties. In one of the most powerful early statements of this position, lesbianism became described as a central element of the very politics of women's liberation.

This idea that women's oppression was linked to women's sexual relationships with men was beginning to surface in much thinking and writing of the time. The idea received its most theoretically sophisticated articulation in the writings of Catharine MacKinnon. A central claim of MacKinnon's is that sexuality defines gender and represents the key arena of men's domination over women. For MacKinnon, sexuality as we know it, *is* domination.

What does it mean to say that sexuality *is* domination? MacKinnon is arguing against a widely held view that sexuality is a neutral domain of pleasure. The feminist appropriation of this latter view claims that this arena of pleasure has often been denied to women and in such denial has existed one source of women's oppression. MacKinnon argues that sexuality, rather than existing as a neutral domain of pleasure, is infused with power. Moreover, this power that constitutes the very dynamic of sexual desire is defined in terms of the masculine/feminine distinction. Thus the very content of masculinity is to sexually desire/have power over women as the content of femininity is to be sexually desired by/subordinated to men. The content of gender and the content of sexuality are identical as expressed in the linkage of the two in the word "sex." As MacKinnon argues, it is only by understanding gender, sexuality, and their relationship in such terms that we can make sense of so many aspects of present and many previous societies: the pervasiveness and content of pornography, the similarities in content between what is understood as "normal" male sexual initiation and sexual harassment, and the similarities in content between what is understood as "normal" heterosexuality and rape.

In this view, women's identity is constituted by women's position as victim. This does not mean that being a woman entails passivity. Women can negotiate, strategize against, and fight their oppression. But all such actions represent responses to the condition of powerlessnesss that defines what it means to be a woman. Even lesbianism must be understood within such terms because women's sexuality, like all other aspects of women's existence, is constructed, according to MacKinnon, under conditions of male supremacy.

Other theorists took seriously the idea of women's differences from men's but their accounts of such differences depended less on the idea of woman as victim. These latter theorists described at least some of women's differences from men in positive terms. Nancy Chodorow's work stood in the forefront of this turn. Chodorow constructed a theory whose description of certain differences between women and men not only struck a receptive chord with many, but also seemed to make sense of many important patterns of social life: of difficulties in heterosexual relationships, of why women as opposed to men are psychologically oriented towards mothering, and of why men are disposed towards dominating women. The chapter included here describes such differences primarily in the context of explaining some of the problems of heterosexual relationships.

Chodorow draws on many of the premises of object relations theory to argue that the cross-cultural tendency for women to bear primary responsibility for early parenting generates important differences between boys' and girls' experiences in the pre-oedipal and oedipal period. The consequences are deep seated differences in the psyches of male and female adults. In societies marked by primary female parenting, boys, to resolve the oedipal complex and become heterosexual, need only transfer their early affective bonds with mothers to someone of the same sex as their mothers. Girls, on the other hand, need to transfer, at least partially, such early affective bonds from mothers to fathers to accomplish the same goals. On the other hand, to achieve gender identity, boys must repress their early identification with mothers; girls do not need to suppress as fully as do boys their early identification with mothers, an identification itself more intensified by their mothers' identification with them.

Because girls' attachment to fathers represents an addition rather than replacement to an earlier attachment to mothers, and because girls do not need to repress as extensively as do boys their early identification with mothers, girls grow up with a sense of self that is highly relational, sexually oriented to men but also open to and requiring affective relationships with women and children. The more ambivalent and curtailed identification of boys with their mothers, combined with their more straightforward transfer of affection from mothers to a sexual partner of the same sex, leads to a sense of self as more separate and distinct from others and more endangered by relationships in general.

As feminists were focusing on women's differences from men, many, particularly in the academy, were beginning to view existing knowledges as ignoring not only women's contributions but also those kinds of perspectives women might bring. Chodorow's theory provided an important resource for this project: a convincing explanation and description of the cognitive and affective dimensions of those differences that highlighted what a woman's perspective might add.

One feminist researcher who employed Chodorow's theory as a means to reveal male bias in academic work was Carol Gilligan, whose initial focus was the moral development theory of Lawrence Kohlberg. Arguing that the theory began from a problematic listening to the stories of boys only, she claimed that the developmental model Kohlberg constructed had a masculine bias. That girls and women tended to score relatively lower than boys and men on Kohlberg's tests of moral development attested not to their moral developmental inferiority but to the biases of the tests.

The problem, according to Gilligan, was that the model did not take into account women's greater tendency to define themselves in relation to others and to judge themselves by their ability to care. These tendencies stand in contrast to those tendencies of men to understand adult maturity in terms of individuation and to view morality in terms of abstract principles and norms. From Gilligan's perspective, neither tendency is inherently superior to the other and each expresses itself in terms of different stages of psychological development. The problem lay only in trying to evaluate women's moral maturity through a model based on male development.

The work of Chodorow and Gilligan began to express the idea that women see the world differently from men. This idea was elaborated in sophisticated ways by the work of standpoint theorists, represented here in the essays by Nancy Hartsock and Patricia Hill Collins. For Hartsock, a sexual division of labor, to a certain degree common to all western, class societies, entails that women's work possesses certain characteristic features. While some of these features, such as an emphasis on change, a direct relation with nature, a need to integrate mind and body, and a greater concern for quality rather than quantity, also characterize the work of male manual laborers, other features of female work are unique to women. Women's work, according to Hartsock, tends to be more structured by total immersion and repetition. As mothers, or as those who have been been socialized to become such, women are heavily involved in processes of change and growth and of learning how to let others grow. Women's bodily experiences of menstruation, coitus, pregnancy, and childbirth challenge the boundaries between body and external world. Drawing on the work of Chodorow, Hartsock points to the emphasis on relationality in women's lives as opposed to the greater tendencies of men to draw boundaries between themselves, others, and the world around them.

While Chodorow and Gilligan tend to depict the differences between women and men in somewhat neutral terms, emphasizing the positive and negative aspects of both, Hartsock sees women's experiences as providing the basis for a liberatory vision. She places such a vision in contrast to the life destroying vision which she views as emerging from the experiences of men. Labelling the latter "abstract masculinity," she sees it expressed in the dominant worldview of class societies. It is only from the life experiences of women that there lies the potential for a perspective that can challenge such a worldview. Such a perspective, while based on the life experiences of women, does not emerge directly from women's lives but must be struggled to be achieved, and can be done so only when historical circumstances permit.

The position of Patricia Hill Collins is similar to that of Hartsock insofar as Collins believes that the life experiences of a particular group—in Collins' case, African American women—provide the basis for a distinctive vantage point on the world. Recognizing diversity in the lives of black women, Collins, nevertheless claims there are certain core themes that are common to all such lives, such as a legacy of struggle against racism and sexism. Also like Hartsock, Collins believes that such experiences do not directly lead to such a vantage point, but must be interpreted, in Collins' case, through the work of African American women intellectuals. And like Hartsock, Collins believes that the vision generated provides a distinctive and positive liberatory perspective.

However, there are some important differences. Whereas Hartsock sees a feminist standpoint as representing an encompassing vision to change the world for all, Collins sees a black feminist standpoint in different terms. While she sees black feminist thought as a needed perspective to articulate the distinctive experiences of black women, she does not view it as providing the sole perspective upon which to base a new world order. Rather she sees it contributing to and interacting with the visions generated from the experiences of other groups. While she believes that being a black woman does create the potential for certain positive and liberatory ways of viewing the world, Collins rejects a separatist or exclusionary understanding of such a standpoint. As she claims, the primary guiding principle of black feminism is a humanist vision of community.

9

RADICALESBIANS

The Woman Identified Woman

Our awareness is due to all women who have struggled and learned in consciousness raising groups, but particularly to gay women whose path has delineated and focused the women's movement on the nature and underlying causes of our oppression.

What is a lesbian? A lesbian is the rage of all women condensed to the point of explosion. She is the woman who, often beginning at an extremely early age, acts in accordance with her inner compulsion to be a more complete and freer human being than her society—perhaps then, but certainly later—cares to allow her. These needs and actions, over a period of years, bring her into painful conflict with people, situations, the accepted ways of thinking, feeling and behaving, until she is in a state of continual war with everything around her, and usually with her self. She may not be fully conscious of the political implications of what for her began as personal necessity, but on some level she has not been able to accept the limitations and oppression laid on her by the most basic role of her society—the female role. The turmoil she experiences tends to induce guilt proportional to the degree to which she feels she is not meeting social expectations, and/or eventually drives her to question and analyze what the rest of her society more or less accepts. She is forced to evolve her own life pattern, often living much of her life alone, learning usually much earlier than her "straight" (heterosexual) sisters about the essential aloneness of life (which the myth of marriage obscures) and about the reality of illusions. To the extent that she cannot expel the heavy socialization that goes with being female, she can never truly find peace with herself. For she is caught somewhere between accepting society's view of her—in which case she cannot accept herself—and coming to understand what this sexist society has done to her and why it is functional and necessary for it to do so. Those of us who work that through find ourselves on the other side of a tortuous journey through a night that may have been decades long. The perspective gained from that journey, the liberation of self, the inner peace, the real love of self and of all women, is something to be shared with all women—because we are all women.

It should first be understood that lesbianism, like male homosexuality, is a category of behavior possible only in a sexist society characterized by rigid sex roles and dominated by male supremacy. Those sex roles dehumanize women by defining us as a supportive/serving caste *in relation to* the master caste of men, and emotionally cripple men by demanding that they be alienated from their own bodies and emotions in order to perform their economic/political/military functions effectively. Homosexuality is a by-product of a particular way of setting up roles (or approved patterns of behavior) on the basis of sex; as such it is an inauthentic (not consonant with "reality") category. In a society in which men do not oppress women, and sexual expression is allowed to follow feelings, the categories of homosexuality and heterosexuality would disappear.

But lesbianism is also different from male homosexuality, and serves a different function in the society. "Dyke" is a different kind of put-down from "faggot," although both imply you are not playing your socially assigned sex role. . .are not therefore a "real woman" or a "real man." The grudging admiration felt for the tomboy, and the queasiness felt around a sissy boy point to the same thing: the contempt in which women —or those who play a female role—are held. And the investment in keeping women in that contemptuous role is very great. Lesbian is the word, the label, the condition that holds women in line. When a woman hears this word tossed her way, she knows she is stepping out of line. She knows that she has crossed the terrible boundary of her sex role. She recoils, she protests, she reshapes her actions to gain approval. Lesbian is a label invented by the Man to throw at any woman who dares to be his equal, who dares to challenge his prerogatives (including that of all women as part of the exchange medium among men), who dares to assert the primacy of her own needs. To have the label applied to people active in women's liberation is just the most recent instance of a long history; older women will recall that not so long ago, any woman who was successful, independent, not orienting her whole life about a man, would hear this word. For in this sexist society, for a woman to be independent means she *can't be* a woman—she must be a dyke. That in itself should tell us where women are at. It says as clearly as can be said: women and person are contradictory terms. For a lesbian is not considered a "real woman." And yet, in popular thinking, there is really only one essential difference between a lesbian and other women: that of sexual orientation—which is to say, when you strip off all the packaging, you must finally realize that the essence of being a "woman" is to get fucked by men.

"Lesbian" is one of the sexual categories by which men have divided up humanity. While all women are dehumanized as sex objects, as the objects of men they are given certain compensations: identification with his power, his ego, his status, his protection (from other males), feeling like a "real woman," finding social acceptance by adhering to her role, etc. Should a woman confront herself by confronting another woman, there are fewer rationalizations, fewer buffers by which to avoid the stark horror of her dehumanized condition. Herein we find the overriding fear of many women toward being used as a sexual object by a woman, which not only will bring her no male-connected compensations, but also will reveal the void which is woman's real situation. This dehumanization is expressed when a straight woman learns that a sister is a lesbian; she begins to relate to her lesbian sister as her potential sex object, laying a surrogate male role on the lesbian. This reveals her heterosexual conditioning to make herself into an object when sex is potentially involved in a relationship, and it denies the lesbian her full humanity. For women, especially those in the movement, to perceive their lesbian sisters through this male grid of role definitions is to accept this male cultural conditioning and to oppress their sisters much as they themselves have been oppressed by men. Are we going to continue the male classification system of defining all females in sexual relation to some other category of people? Affixing the label lesbian not only to a woman who aspires to be a person, but also to any situation of real love, real solidarity, real primacy among women, is a primary form of divisiveness among women: it is the condition which keeps women within the confines of the feminine role, and it is the debunking/scare term that keeps women from forming any primary attachments, groups, or associations among ourselves.

Women in the movement have in most cases gone to great lengths to avoid discussion and confrontation with the issue of lesbianism. It puts people up-tight. They are hostile, evasive, or try to incorporate it into some "broader issue." They would rather not talk about it. If they have to, they try to dismiss it as a "lavender herring." But it is no side issue. It is absolutely essential to the success and fulfillment of the women's liberation movement that this issue be dealt with. As long as the label "dyke" can be used to frighten a woman into a less militant stand, keep her separate from her sisters, keep her from giving primacy to anything other than men and family—then to that extent she is controlled by the male culture. Until women see in each other the possibility of a primal commitment which includes sexual love, they will be denying themselves the love and value they readily accord to men, thus affirming their second class status. As long as male acceptability is primary—both to individual women and to the movement as a whole—the term lesbian will be used effectively against women. Insofar as women want only more privileges within the system, they do not want to antagonize male power. They instead seek acceptability for women's liberation, and the most crucial aspect of the acceptability is to deny lesbianism—i.e., to deny any fundamental challenge to the basis of the female. It should also be said that some younger, more radical women have honestly begun to discuss lesbianism, but so far it has been primarily as a sexual "alternative" to men. This, however, is still giving primacy to men, both because the idea of relating more completely to women occurs as a negative reaction to men, and because the lesbian relationship is being characterized simply by sex, which is divisive and sexist. On one level, which is both personal and political, women may withdraw emotional and sexual energies from men, and work out various alternatives for those energies in their own lives. On a different political/psychological level, it must be understood that what is crucial is that women begin disengaging from male-defined response patterns. In the privacy of our own psyches, we must cut those cords to the core. For irrespective of where our love and sexual energies flow, if we are male-identified in our heads, we cannot realize our autonomy as human beings.

But why is it that women have related to and through men? By virtue of having been brought up in a male society, we have internalized the male culture's definition of ourselves. That definition consigns us to sexual and family functions, and excludes us from defining and shaping the terms of our lives. In exchange for our psychic servicing and for performing society's non-profitmaking functions, the man confers on us just one thing: the slave status which makes us legitimate in the eyes of the society in which we live. This is called "femininity" or "being a real woman" in our cultural lingo. We are authentic, legitimate, real to the extent that we are the property of some man whose name we bear. To be a woman who belongs to no man is to be invisible, pathetic, inauthentic, unreal. He confirms his image of us—of what we have to be in order to be acceptable by him—but not our real selves; he confirms our womanhood—as he defines it, in relation to him—but cannot confirm our personhood, our own selves as absolutes. As long as we are dependent on the male culture for this definition, for this approval, we cannot be free.

The consequence of internalizing this role is an enormous reservoir of self-hate. This is not to say the self-hate is recognized or accepted as such; indeed most women would deny it. It may be experienced as discomfort with her role, as feeling empty, as numbness, as restlessness, as a paralyzing anxiety at the center. Alternatively, it may be expressed in shrill defensiveness of the glory and destiny of her role. But it does exist, often beneath the edge of her consciousness, poisoning her existence, keeping her alienated from herself, her own needs, and rendering her a stranger to other women. They try to escape by identifying with the oppressor, living through him, gaining status and identity from his ego, his power, his accomplishments. And by not identifying with other "empty vessels" like themselves. Women resist relating on all levels to other women who will reflect their own oppression, their own secondary status, their own self-hate. For to confront another woman is finally to confront oneself—the self we have gone to such lengths to avoid. And in the mirror we know we cannot really respect and love that which we have been made to be.

As the source of self-hate and the lack of real self are rooted in our male-given identity, we must create a new sense of self. As long as we cling to the idea of "being a woman," we will sense some conflict with that incipient self, that sense of I, that sense of a whole person. It is very difficult to realize and accept that being "feminine" and being a whole person are irreconcilable. Only women can give to each other a new sense of self. That identity we have to develop with reference to ourselves, and not in relation to men. This consciousness is the revolutionary force from which all else will follow, for ours is an organic revolution. For this we must be available and supportive to one another, give our commitment and our love, give the emotional support necessary to sustain this movement. Our energies must flow toward our sisters, not backward toward our oppressors. As long as woman's liberation tries to free women without facing the basic heterosexual structure that binds us in one-to-one-relationship with our oppressors, tremendous energies will continue to flow into trying to straighten up each particular relationship with a man, into finding how to get better sex, how to turn his head around—into trying to make the "new man" out of him, in the delusion that this will allow us to be the "new woman." This obviously splits our energies and commitments, leaving us unable to be committed to the construction of the new patterns which will liberate us.

It is the primacy of women relating to women, of women creating a new consciousness of and with each other, which is at the heart of women's liberation, and the basis for the cultural revolution. Together we must find, reinforce, and validate our authentic selves. As we do this, we confirm in each other that struggling, incipient sense of pride and strength, the divisive barriers begin to melt, we feel this growing solidarity with our sisters. We see ourselves as prime, find our centers inside of ourselves. We find receding the sense of alienation, of being cut off, of being behind a locked window, of being unable to get out what we know is inside. We feel a real-ness, feel at last we are coinciding with ourselves. With that real self, with that consciousness, we begin a revolution to end the imposition of all coercive identifications, and to achieve maximum autonomy in human expression.

10

CATHARINE A. MACKINNON

Sexuality

What is it about women's experience that produces a distinctive perspective on social reality? How is an angle of vision and an interpretive hermeneutics of social life created in the group, women? What happens to women to give them a particular interest in social arrangements, something to have a consciousness of? How are the qualities we know as male and female socially created and enforced on an everyday level? Sexual objectification of women—first in the world, then in the head, first in visual appropriation, then in forced sex, finally in sexual murder[1]—provides answers.

Male dominance is sexual. Meaning: men in particular, if not men alone, sexualize hierarchy; gender is one. As much a sexual theory of gender as a gendered theory of sex, this is the theory of sexuality that has grown out of consciousness raising. Recent feminist work, both interpretive and empirical, on rape, battery, sexual harassment, sexual abuse of children, prostitution and pornography, support it.[2] These practices, taken together, express and actualize the distinctive power of men over women in society; their effective permissibility confirms and extends it. If one believes women's accounts of sexual use and abuse by men;[3] if the pervasiveness of male sexual violence against women substantiated in these studies is not denied, minimized, or excepted as deviant or episodic;[4] if the fact that only 7.8 percent of women in the United States are not sexually assaulted or harassed in their lifetimes is considered not ignorable or inconsequential;[5] if the women to whom it happens are not considered expendable; if violation of women is understood as sexualized on some level—then sexuality itself can no longer be regarded as unimplicated. Nor can the meaning of practices of sexual violence be categorized away as violence not sex. The male sexual role, this information and analysis taken together suggest, centers on aggressive intrusion on those with less power. Such acts of dominance are experienced as sexually arousing, as sex itself.[6] They therefore are. The new knowledge on the sexual violation of women by men thus frames an inquiry into the place of sexuality in gender and of gender in sexuality.

A feminist theory of sexuality based on these data locates sexuality within a theory of gender inequality, meaning the social hierarchy of men over women. To make a theory feminist, it is not enough that it be authored by a biological female, nor that it describe female sexuality as different from (if equal to) male sexuality, or as if sexuality in women ineluctably exists in some realm beyond, beneath, above, behind—in any event, fundamentally untouched and unmoved by—an unequal social order. A theory of sexuality becomes feminist methodologically, meaning feminist in the post-marxist sense, to the extent it treats sexuality as a social construct of male power: defined by men, forced on women, and constitutive of the meaning of gender. Such an approach centers feminism on the perspective of the subordination of women to men as it identifies sex—that is, the sexuality of dominance and submission—as crucial, as a fundamental, as on some level definitive, in that process. Feminist theory becomes a project of analyzing that situation in order to face it for what it is, in order to change it.

Focusing on gender inequality without a sexual account of its dynamics, as most work has, one could criticize the sexism of existing theories of sexuality and emerge knowing that men author scripts to their own advantage, women and men act them out; that men set conditions, women and men have their behavior conditioned; that men develop developmental categories through which men develop, and women develop or not; that men are socially allowed selves hence identities with personalities into which sexuality is or is not well integrated, women being that which is or is not integrated, that through the alterity of which a self experiences itself as having an identity; that men have object relations, women are the objects of those relations; and so on. Following such critique, one could attempt to invert or correct the premises or applications of these theories to make them gender neutral, even if the reality to which they refer looks more like the theories—once their gender specificity is revealed—than it looks gender neutral. Or, one could attempt to enshrine a distinctive "women's reality" as if it really were permitted to exist as something more than one dimension of women's response to a condition of powerlessness. Such exercises would be revealing and instructive, even deconstructive, but to limit feminism to correcting sex bias by acting in theory as if male power did not exist in fact, including by valorizing in writing what women have had little choice but to be limited to becoming in life, is to limit feminist theory the way sexism limits women's lives: to a response to terms men set.

A distinctively feminist theory conceptualizes social reality, including sexual reality, on its own terms. The question is, what are they? If women have been substantially deprived not only of their own experience but of terms of their own in which to view it, then a feminist theory of sexuality which seeks to understand women's situation in order to change it must first identify and criticize the construct "sexuality" as a construct that has circumscribed and defined experience as well as theory. This requires capturing it in the world, in its situated social meanings, as it is being constructed in life on a daily basis. It must be studied in its experienced empirical existence, not just in the texts of history (as Foucault does), in the social psyche (as Lacan does), or in language (as Derrida does). Sexual meaning is not made only, or even primarily, by words and in texts. It is made in social relations of power in the world, through which process gender is also produced. In feminist terms, the fact that male power has power means that the interests of male sexuality construct what sexuality as such means, including the standard way it is allowed and recognized to be felt and expressed and experienced, in a way that determines women's biographies, including sexual ones. Existing theories, until they grasp this, will not only misattribute what they call female sexuality to women as such, as if it were not imposed on women daily; they will also participate in enforcing the hegemony of the social construct "desire," hence its product, "sexuality," hence its construct "woman," on the world.

The gender issue, in this analysis, becomes the issue of what is taken to be "sexuality"; what sex means and what is meant by sex, when, how, with whom, and with what consequences to whom. Such questions are almost never systematically confronted, even in discourses that purport feminist awareness. What sex is—how it comes to be attached and attributed to what it is, embodied and practiced as it is, contextualized in the ways it is, signifying and referring to what it does—is taken as a baseline, a given, except in explanations of what happened when it is thought to have gone wrong. It is as if "erotic," for example, can be taken as having an understood referent, although it is never defined, except to imply that it is universal yet individual, ultimately variable and plastic, essentially indefinable but overwhelmingly positive. "Desire," the vicissitudes of which are endlessly extolled and philosophized in culture high and low, is not seen as fundamentally problematic or as calling for explanation on the concrete, interpersonal operative level, unless (again) it is supposed to be there and is not. To list and analyze what seem to be the essential elements for male sexual arousal, what has to be there for the penis to work, seems faintly blasphemous, like a pornographer doing market research. Sex is supposed both too individual and too universally transcendent for that. To suggest that the sexual might be continuous with something other than sex itself—something like politics—is seldom done, is treated as detumescent, even by feminists. It is as if sexuality comes from the stork.

Sexuality, in feminist light, is not a discrete sphere of interaction or feeling or sensation or behavior in which preexisting social divisions may or may not be played out. It is a pervasive dimension of social life, one that permeates the whole, a dimension along which gender occurs and through which gender is socially constituted; it is a dimension along which other social divisions, like race and class, partly play themselves out. Dominance eroticized defines the imperatives of its masculinity, submission eroticized defines its femininity. So many distinctive features of women's status as second class—the restriction and constraint and contortion, the servility and the display, the self-mutilation and requisite presentation of self as a beautiful thing, the enforced passivity, the humiliation—are made into the content of sex for women. Being a thing for sexual use is fundamental to it. This approach identifies not just a sexuality that is shaped under conditions of gender inequality but reveals this sexuality itself to be the dynamic of the inequality of the sexes. It is to argue that the excitement at reduction of a person to a thing, to less than a human being, as socially defined, is its fundamental motive force. It is to argue that sexual difference is a function of sexual dominance. It is to argue a sexual theory of the distribution of social power by gender, in which this sexuality that is sexuality is substantially what makes the gender division be what it is, which is male dominant, wherever it is, which is nearly everywhere.

Across cultures, in this perspective, sexuality is whatever a given culture or subculture defines it as. The next question concerns its relation to gender as a division of power. Male dominance appears to exist cross-culturally, if in locally particular forms. Across cultures, is whatever defines women as "different" the same as whatever defines women as "inferior" the same as whatever defines women's "sexuality"? Is that which defines gender inequality as merely the sex difference also the content of the erotic, cross-culturally? In this view, the feminist theory of sexuality is its theory of politics, its distinctive contribution to social and political explanation. To explain gender inequality in terms of "sexual politics"[7] is to advance not only a political theory of the sexual that defines gender but also a sexual theory of the political to which gender is fundamental.

In this approach, male power takes the social form of what men as a gender want sexually, which centers on power itself, as socially defined. In capitalist countries, it includes wealth. Masculinity is having it; femininity is not having it. [Masculinity precedes male as femininity precedes female, and male sexual desire defines both.] Specifically, "woman" is defined by what male desire requires for arousal and satisfaction and is socially tautologous with "female sexuality" and "the female sex." In the permissible ways a woman can be treated, the ways that are socially considered not violations but appropriate to her nature, one finds the particulars of male sexual interests and requirements. [In the concomitant sexual paradigm, the ruling norms of sexual attraction and expression are fused with gender identity formation and affirmation, such that sexuality equals heterosexuality equals the sexuality of (male) dominance and (female) submission.]

Post-Lacan, actually post-Foucault, it has become customary to affirm that sexuality is socially constructed.[8] Seldom specified is what, socially, it is constructed of, far less who does the constructing or how, when, or where.[9] When capitalism is the favored social construct, sexuality is shaped and controlled and exploited and repressed by capitalism; not, capitalism creates sexuality as we know it. When sexuality is a construct of discourses of power, gender is never one of them; force is central to its deployment but through repressing it, not through constituting it; speech is not concretely investigated for its participation in this construction process. Power is everywhere therefore nowhere, diffuse rather than pervasively hegemonic. "Constructed" seems to mean influenced by, directed, channeled, as a highway constructs traffic patterns. Not: Why cars? Who's driving? Where's everybody going? What makes mobility matter? Who can own a car? Are all these accidents not very accidental? Although there are partial exceptions (but disclaimers notwithstanding) the typical model of sexuality which is tacitly accepted remains deeply Freudian[10] and essentialist: sexuality is an innate sui genetis primary natural prepolitical uncondi-tioned[11] drive divided along the biological gender line, centering on heterosexual intercourse, that is, penile intromission, full actualization of which is repressed by civ-ilization. Even if the sublimation aspect of this theory is rejected, or the reasons for the repression are seen to vary (for the survival of civilization or to maintain fascist control or to keep capitalism moving), sexual expression is implicitly seen as the expression of something that is to a significant extent pre-social and is socially denied its full force. Sexuality remains largely pre-cultural and universally invariant, social only in that it needs society to take socially specific forms. The impetus itself is a hunger, an appetite founded on a need; what it is specifically hungry for and how it is satisfied is then open to endless cultural and individual variance, like cuisine, like cooking.

Allowed/not allowed is this sexuality's basic ideological axis. The fact that sexuality is ideologically bounded is known. That these are its axes, central to the way its "drive" is driven, and that this is fundamental to gender and gender is fundamental to it, is not.[12] Its basic normative assumption is that whatever is considered sexuality should be allowed to be "expressed." Whatever is called sex is attributed a normatively positive valence, an affirmative valuation. This *ex cathedra* assumption, affirmation of which appears indispensable to one's credibility on any subject that gets near the sexual, means that sex as such (whatever it is) is good—natural, healthy, positive, appropriate, pleasurable, wholesome, fine, one's own, and to be approved and expressed. This, sometimes characterized as "sex-positive," is, rather obviously, a value judgment.

Kinsey and his followers, for example, clearly thought (and think) the more sex the better. Accordingly, they trivialize even most of those cases of rape and child sexual abuse they discern as such, decry women's sexual refusal as sexual inhibition, and repeatedly interpret women's sexual disinclination as "restrictions" on men's natural sexual activity, which left alone would emulate (some) animals.[13] Followers of the neo-Freudian derepression imperative have similarly identified the frontier of sexual free-dom with transgression of social restraints on access, with making the sexually disallowed allowed, especially male sexual access to anything. The struggle to have everything sexual allowed in a society we are told would collapse if it were, creates a sense of resistance to, and an aura of danger around, violating the powerless. If we knew the boundaries were phony, existed only to eroticize the targeted transgressable, would penetrating them feel less sexy? Taboo and crime may serve to eroticize what would otherwise feel about as much like dominance as taking candy from a baby. Assimilating actual powerlessness to male prohibition, to male power, provides the appearance of resistance, which makes overcoming possible, while never undermining the reality of power, or its dignity, by giving the powerless actual power. The point is, allowed/not allowed becomes the ideological axis along which sexuality is experienced when and because sex—gender and sexuality—is about power.

One version of the derepression hypothesis that purports feminism is: civilization having been male dominated, female sexuality has been repressed, not allowed. Sexu-ality as such still centers on what would otherwise be considered the reproductive act, on intercourse: penetration of the erect penis into the vagina (or appropriate substitute orifices), followed by thrusting to male ejaculation. If reproduction actually had anything to do with what sex was for, it would not happen every night (or even twice a week) for forty or fifty years, nor would prostitutes exist. "We had sex three times" typically means the man entered the woman three times and orgasmed three times. Female sexuality in this model refers to the presence of this theory's "sexuality," or the desire to be so treated, in biological females; "female" is somewhere between an adjective and a noun, half possessive and half biological ascription. Sexual freedom means women are allowed to behave as freely as men to express this sexuality, to have it allowed, that is (hopefully) shamelessly and without social constraints to initiate genital drive satisfaction through heterosexual intercourse.[14] Hence, the liberated woman. Hence, the sexual revolution.

The pervasiveness of such assumptions about sexuality throughout otherwise diverse methodological traditions is suggested by the following comment by a scholar of violence against women:

> If women were to escape the culturally stereotyped role of disinterest in and resistance to sex and to take on an assertive role in expressing their own sexuality, rather than leaving it to the assertiveness of men, it would contribute to the reduction of rape . . . First, and most obviously, voluntary sex would be available to more men, thus reducing the "need" for rape. Second, and probably more important, it would help to reduce the confounding of sex and aggression.[15]

In this view, somebody must be assertive for sex to happen. Voluntary sex—sexual equality—means equal sexual aggression. If women freely expressed "their own sexuality," more heterosexual intercourse would be initiated. Women's "resistance" to sex is an imposed cultural stereotype, not a form of political struggle. Rape is occasioned by women's resistance, not by men's force; or, male force, hence rape, is created by women's resistance to sex. Men would rape less if they got more voluntarily compliant sex from women. Corollary: the force in rape is not sexual to men.

Underlying this quotation lurks the view, as common as it is tacit, that if women would just accept the contact men now have to rape to get—if women would stop resisting or (in one of the pornographers' favorite scenarios) become sexual aggressors—rape would wither away. On one level, this is a definitionally obvious truth. When a woman accepts what would be rape if she did not accept it, what happens is sex. If women were to accept forced sex as sex, "voluntary sex would be available to more men." If such a view is not implicit in this text, it is a mystery how women equally aggressing against men sexually would eliminate, rather than double, the confounding of sex and aggression. Without such an assumption, only the confounding of sexual aggression with gender would be eliminated. If women no longer resisted male sexual aggression, the confounding of sex with aggression would, indeed, be so epistemologically complete that it would be eliminated. No woman would ever be sexuality violated, because sexual violation would be sex. The situation might resemble the one evoked by a society categorized as "rape-free" in part because the men assert there is no rape there: "our women never resist."[16] Such pacification also occurs in "rape-prone" societies like the United States, where some force may be perceived as force, but only above certain threshold standards.[17]

While intending the opposite, some feminists have encouraged and participated in this type of analysis by conceiving rape as violence, not sex.[18] While this approach gave needed emphasis to rape's previously effaced elements of power and dominance, it obscured its elements of sex. Aside from failing to answer the rather obvious question, if it is violence not sex, why didn't he just hit her? this approach made it impossible to see that violence is sex when it is practiced as sex.[19] This is obvious once what sexuality is, is understood as a matter of what it means and how it is interpreted. To say rape is violence not sex preserves the "sex is good" norm by simply distinguishing forced sex as "not sex," whether it means sex to the perpetrator or even, later, to the victim, who has difficulty experiencing sex without reexperiencing the rape. Whatever is sex cannot be violent; whatever is violent cannot be sex. This analytic wish-fulfillment makes it possible for rape to be opposed by those who would save sexuality from the rapists while leaving the sexual fundamentals of male dominance intact.

While much previous work on rape has analyzed it as a problem of inequality between the sexes but not as a problem of unequal sexuality on the basis of gender,[20] other contemporary explorations of sexuality that purport to be feminist lack comprehension either of gender as a form of social power or of the realities of sexual violence. For instance, the editors of *Powers of Desire* take sex "as a central form of expression, one that defines identity and is seen as a primary source of energy and pleasure."[21] This may be how it "is seen," but it is also how the editors, operatively, see it. As if women choose sexuality as definitive of identity. As if it is as much a form of women's "expression" as it is men's. As if violation and abuse are not equally central to sexuality as women live it.

The *Diary* of the Barnard conference on sexuality pervasively equates sexuality with "pleasure." "Perhaps the overall question we need to ask is: how do women . . . negotiate sexual pleasure?"[22] As if women under male supremacy have power to. As if "negotiation" is a form of freedom. As if pleasure and how to get it, rather than dominance and how to end it, is the "overall" issue sexuality presents feminism. As if women do just need a good fuck. In these texts, taboos are treated as real restrictions—as things that really are not allowed—instead of as guises under which hierarchy is eroticized. The domain of the sexual is divided into "restriction, repression, and danger" on the one hand and "exploration, pleasure, and agency" on the other.[23] This division parallels the ideological forms through which dominance and submission are eroticized, variously socially coded as heterosexuality's male/female, lesbian culture's butch/femme, and sadomasochism's top/bottom.[24] Speaking in role terms, the one who pleasures in the illusion of freedom and security within the reality of danger is the "girl"; the one who pleasures in the reality of freedom and security within the illusion of danger is the "boy". That is, the *Diary* uncritically adopts as an analytic tool the central dynamic of the phenomenon it purports to be analyzing. Presumably, one is to have a sexual experience of the text.

The terms of these discourses preclude or evade crucial feminist questions. What do sexuality and gender inequality have to do with each other? How do dominance and submission become sexualized, or, why is hierarchy sexy? How does it get attached to male and female? Why does sexuality center on intercourse, the reproductive act by physical design? Is masculinity the enjoyment of violation, femininity the enjoyment of being violated? Is that the social meaning of intercourse? Do "men love death"?[25] Why? What is the etiology of heterosexuality in women? Is its pleasure women's stake in subordination?

Taken together and taken seriously, feminist inquiries into the realities of rape, battery, sexual harassment, incest, child sexual abuse, prostitution, and pornography answer these questions by suggesting a theory of the sexual mechanism. Its script, learning, conditioning, developmental logos, imprinting of the microdot, its deus ex machina, whatever sexual process term defines sexual arousal itself, is force, power's expression. Force is sex, not just sexualized; force is the desire dynamic, not just a response to the desired object when desire's expression is frustrated. Pressure, gender socialization, withholding benefits, extending indulgences, the how-to books, the sex therapy are the soft end; the fuck, the fist, the street, the chains, the poverty are the hard end. Hostility and contempt, or arousal of master to slave, together with awe and vulnerability, or arousal of slave to master—these are the emotions of this sexuality's excitement. "Sadomasochism is to sex what war is to civil life: the magnificent experience," wrote Susan Sontag.[26] "[I]t is hostility—the desire, overt or hidden, to harm another person—that generates and enhances sexual excitement," wrote Robert Stoller.[27] Harriet Jacobs a slave, speaking of her systematic rape by her master, wrote, "It seems less demeaning to give one's self, than to submit to compulsion."[25] It is clear from the data that the force in sex and the sex in force is a matter of simple empirical description—unless one accepts that force in sex is not force anymore, it is just sex; or, if whenever a woman is forced it is what she really wants, or it or she does not matter; or, unless prior aversion or sentimentality substitutes what one wants sex to be, or will condone or countenance as sex, for what is actually happening.

To be clear: what is sexual is what gives a man an erection. Whatever it takes to make a penis shudder and stiffen with the experience of its potency is what sexuality means culturally. Whatever else does this, fear does, hostility does, hatred does, the helplessness of a child or a student or an infantilized or restrained or vulnerable woman does, revulsion does, death does. Hierarchy, a constant creation of person/thing, top/bottom, dominance/subordination relations, does. What is understood as violation, conventionally penetration and intercourse, defines the paradigmatic sexual encounter. The scenario of sexual abuse is: you do what I say. These textualities and these relations, situated within as well as creating a context of power in which they can be lived out, become sexuality. All this suggests that what is called sexuality is the dynamic of control by which male dominance—in forms that range from intimate to institutional, from a look to a rape—eroticizes and thus defines man and woman, gender identity and sexual pleasure. It is also that which maintains and defines male supremacy as a political system. Male sexual desire is thereby simultaneously created and serviced, never satisfied once and for all, while male force is romanticized, even sacralized, potentiated and naturalized, by being submerged into sex itself.

In contemporary philosophical terms, nothing is "indeterminate" in the post-structuralist sense here; it is all too determinate.[29] Nor does its reality provide just one perspective on a relativistic interpersonal world that could mean anything or its opposite.[30] The reality of pervasive sexual abuse and its erotization does not shift relative to perspective, although whether or not one will see it or accord it significance may. Interpretation varies relative to place in sexual abuse, certainly; but the fact that women are sexually abused as women, located in a social matrix of sexualized subordination, does not go away because it is often ignored or authoritatively disbelieved or interpreted out of existence. Indeed, some ideological supports for its persistence rely precisely upon techniques of social indeterminancy: no language but the obscene to describe the unspeakable, denial by the powerful casting doubt on the facticity of the injuries, actually driving its victims insane. Indeterminacy, in this light, is a neo-Cartesian mind game that raises acontextualized interpretive possibilities that have no real social meaning or real possibility of any, thus dissolving the ability to criticize the oppressiveness of actual meanings without making space for new ones. The feminist point is simple. Men are women's material conditions. If it happens to women, it happens.

Women often find ways to resist male supremacy and to expand their spheres of action. But they are never free of it. Women also embrace the standards of women's place in this regime as "our own" to varying degrees and in varying voices—as affirmation of identity and right to pleasure, in order to be loved and approved and paid, in order just to make it through another day. This, not inert passivity, is the meaning of being a victim.[31] The term is not moral: who is to blame or to be pitied or condemned or held responsible. It is not prescriptive: what we should do next. It is not strategic: how to construe the situation so it can be changed. It is not emotional: what one feels better thinking. It is descriptive: who does what to whom and gets away with it.

Thus the question Freud never asked is the question that defines sexuality in a feminist perspective: what do men want? Pornography provides an answer. Pornography permits men to have whatever they want sexuality. It is their "truth about sex."[32] It connects the centrality of visual objectification to both male sexual arousal, and male models of knowledge and verification, objectivity with objectification. It shows how men see the world, how in seeing it they access and possess it, and how this is an act of dominance over it. It shows what men want and gives it to them. From the testimony of the pornography, what men want is: women bound, women battered, women tortured, women humiliated, women degraded and defiled, women killed. Or, to be fair to the soft core, women sexually accessible, have-able, there for them, wanting to be taken and used, with perhaps just a little light bondage. Each violation of women—rape, battery, prostitution, child sexual abuse, sexual harassment—is made sexuality, made sexy, fun, and liberating of women's true nature in the pornography. Each specifically victimized and vulnerable group of women, each tabooed target group—Black women, Asian women, Latin women, Jewish women, pregnant women, disabled women, retarded women, poor women, old women, fat women, women in women's jobs, prostitutes, little girls—distinguishes pornographic genres and subthemes, classified according to diverse customers' favorite degradation. Women are made into and coupled with anything considered lower than human: animals, objects, children, and (yes) other women. Anything women have claimed as their own—motherhood, athletics, traditional men's jobs, lesbianism, feminism—is made specifically sexy, dangerous, provocative, punished, made men's in pornography.

Pornography is a means through which sexuality is socially constructed, a site of construction, a domain of exercise. It constructs women as things for sexual use and constructs its consumers to desperately want women, to desperately want possession and cruelty and dehumanization. Inequality itself, subjection itself, hierarchy itself, objectification itself, with self-determination ecstatically relinquished, is the apparent consent of women's sexual desire and desirability. "The major theme of pornography as a genre," writes Andrea Dworkin, "is male power."[33] Women are in pornography to be violated and taken, men to violate and take them, either on screen or by camera or pen, on behalf of the viewer. Not that sexuality in life or in media never expresses love and affection; only that love and affection are not what is sexualized in this society's actual sexual paradigm, as pornography testifies to it. Violation of the powerless, intrusion on women, is. The milder forms, possession and use, the mildest of which is visual objectification, are. This sexuality of observation, visual intrusion and access, of entertainment, makes sex largely a spectator sport for its participants.

If pornography has not become sex to and from the male point of view, it is hard to explain why the pornography industry makes a known ten billion dollars a year selling it as sex mostly to men; why it is used to teach sex to child prostitutes, to recalcitrant wives and girlfriends and daughters, to medical students, and to sex offenders; why it is nearly universally classified as a subdivision of "erotic literature"; why it is protected and defended as if it were sex itself.[34] And why a prominent sexologist fears that enforcing the views of feminists against pornography in society would make men "erotically inert wimps."[35] No pornography, no male sexuality.

A feminist critique of sexuality in this sense is advanced in Andrea Dworkin's *Pornography: Men Possessing Women*. Building on her earlier identification of gender inequality as a system of social meaning,[36] an ideology lacking basis in anything other than the social reality its power constructs and maintains, she argues that sexuality is a construct of that power, given meaning by, through, and in pornography. In this perspective, pornography is not harmless fantasy or a corrupt and confused misrepresentation of otherwise natural healthy sex, nor is it fundamentally a distortion, reflection, projection, expression, representation, fantasy, or symbol of it.[37] Through pornography, among other practices, gender inequality becomes both sexual and socially real. Pornography "reveals that male pleasure is inextricably tied to victimizing, hurting, exploiting." "Dominance in the male system is pleasure." Rape is "the defining paradigm of sexuality," to avoid which boys choose manhood and homophobia.[38]

Women, who are not given a choice, are objectified; or, rather, "the object is allowed to desire, if she desires to be an object."[39] Psychology sets the proper bounds of this objectification by terming its improper excesses "fetishism," distinguishing the uses from the abuses of women.[40] Dworkin shows how the process and content of women's definition as women, as an under-class, are the process and content of their sexualization as objects for male sexual use. The mechanism is (again) force, imbued with meaning because it is the means to death;[41] and death is the ultimate sexual act, the ultimate making of a person into a thing.

Why, one wonders at this point, is intercourse "sex" at all? In pornography, conventional intercourse is one act among many; penetration is crucial but can be done with anything; penis is crucial but not necessarily in the vagina. Actual pregnancy is a minor subgenetic theme, about as important in pornography as reproduction is in rape. Thematically, intercourse is incidental in pornography, especially when compared with force, which is primary. From pornography one learns that forcible violation of women is the essence of sex. Whatever is that and does that is sex. Everything else is secondary. Perhaps the reproductive act is considered sexual because it is considered an act of forcible violation and defilement of the female distinctively as such, not because it "is" sex a priori.

To be sexually objectified means having a social meaning imposed on your being that defines you as to be sexually used, according to your desired uses, and then using you that way. Doing this is sex in the male system. Pornography is a sexual practice of this because it exists in a social system in which sex in life is no less mediated than it is in representation. There is no irreducible essence, no "just sex." If sex is a social construct of sexism, men have sex with their image of a woman. Pornography creates an accessible sexual object, the possession and consumption of which is male sexuality, to be possessed and consumed as which is female sexuality. This is not because pornography depicts objectified sex, but because it creates the experience of a sexuality which is itself objectified. The appearance of choice or consent, with their attribution to inherent nature, is crucial in concealing the reality of force. Love of violation, variously termed female masochism and consent, comes to define female sexuality,[42] legitimating this political system by concealing the force on which it is based.

In this system, a victim, usually female, always feminized, is "never forced, only actualized."[43] Women whose attributes particularly fixate men—such as women with large breasts—are seen as full of sexual desire. Women men want, want men. Women fake vaginal orgasms, the only "mature" sexuality, because men demand that women enjoy vaginal penetration.[44] Raped women are seen as asking for it: if a man wanted her, she must have wanted him. Men force women to become sexual objects, "that thing which causes erection, then hold themselves helpless and powerless when aroused by her."[45] Men who sexually harass say women sexually harass them. They mean they are aroused by women who turn them down. This elaborate projective system of demand characteristics—taken to pinnacles like fantasizing a clitoris in a woman's throat[46] so that men can enjoy forced fellario in real life, assured that women do too—is surely a delusional structure deserving of serious psychological study. Instead, it is women who resist it who are studied, seen as in need of explanation and adjustment, stigmatized as inhibited and repressed and asexual. The assumption that in matters sexual women really want what men want from women, makes male force against women in sex invisible. It makes rape sex. Women's sexual "reluctance, dislike, and frigidity," women's puritanism and prudery in the face of this sex, is "the silent rebellion of women against the force of the penis . . . an ineffective rebellion, but a rebellion nonetheless."[42]

Nor is homosexuality without stake in this gendered sexual system. Putting to one side the obviously gendered content of expressly adopted roles, clothing, and sexual mimicry, to the extent the gender of a sexual object is crucial to arousal, the structure of social power which stands behind and defines gender is hardly irrelevant, even if it is rearranged. Some have argued that lesbian sexuality—meaning here simply women having sex with women, not with men—solves the problem of gender by eliminating men from women's voluntary sexual encounters.[48] Yet women's sexuality remains constructed under conditions of male supremacy; women remain socially defined as women in relation to men; the definition of women as men's inferiors remains sexual even if not heterosexual, whether men are present at the time or not. To the extent gay men choose men because they are men, the meaning of masculinity is affirmed as well as undermined. It may also be that sexuality is so gender marked that it carries dominance and submission with it, whatever the gender of its participants.

Each structural requirement of this sexuality as revealed in pornography is professed in recent defenses of sadomasochism, described by proponents as that sexuality in which "the basic dynamic . . . is the power dichotomy."[49] Exposing the prohibitory underpinnings on which this violation model of the sexual depends, one advocate says: "We select the most frightening, disgusting or unacceptable activities and transmute them into pleasure." The relational dynamics of sadomasochism do not even negate the paradigm of male dominance, but conform precisely to it: the ecstasy in domination ("I like to hear someone ask for mercy or protection"); the enjoyment of inflicting psychological as well as physical torture ("I want to see the confusion, the anger, the turn-on, the helplessness"); the expression of belief in the inferior's superiority belied by the absolute contempt ("the bottom must be my superior . . . playing a bottom who did not demand my respect and admiration would be like eating rotten fruit"); the degradation and consumption of women through sex ("she feeds me the energy I need to dominate and abuse her"); the health and personal growth rationale ("it's a healing process"); the anti-puritan radical therapy justification ("I was taught to dread sex . . . It is shocking and profoundly satisfying to commit this piece of rebellion, to take pleasure exactly as I want it, to exact it like tribute"); the bipolar doublethink in which the top enjoys "sexual service" while "the will to please is the bottom's source of pleasure." And the same bottom line of all top-down sex: "I want to be in control." The statements are from a female sadist. The good news is, it is not biological.

As pornography connects sexuality with gender in social reality, the feminist critique of pornography connects feminist work on violence against women with its inquiry into women's consciousness and gender roles. It is not only that women are the principal targets of rape, which by conservative definition happens to almost half of all women at least once in their lives. It is not only that over one-third of all women are sexually molested by older trusted male family members or friends or authority figures as an early, perhaps initiatory, interpersonal sexual encounter. It is not only that at least the same percentage, as adult women, are battered in homes by male intimates. It is not only that about one-fifth of American women have been or are known to be prostitutes, and most cannot get out of it. It is not only that 85 percent of working women will be sexually harassed on the job, many physically, at some point in their working lives.[30] All this documents the extent and terrain of abuse and the effectively unrestrained and systematic sexual aggression by less than one-half of the population against the other more than half. It suggests that it is basically allowed.

It does not by itself show that availability for this treatment defines the identity attributed to that other half of the population; or, that such treatment, all this torment and debasement, is socially considered not only rightful but enjoyable, and is in fact enjoyed by the dominant half; or, that the ability to engage in such behaviors defines the identity of that half. And not only of that half. Now consider the content of gender roles. All the social requirements for male sexual arousal and satisfaction are identical with the gender definition of "female." All the essentials of the male gender role are also the qualities sexualized as "male" in male dominant sexuality. If gender is a social construct, and sexuality is a social construct, and the question is, of what is each constructed, the fact that their contents are identical—not to mention that the word *sex* refers to both—might be more than a coincidence.

As to gender, what is sexual about pornography is what is unequal about social life. To say that pornography sexualizes gender and genders sexuality means that it provides a concrete social process through which gender and sexuality become functions of each other. Gender and sexuality, in this view, become two different shapes taken by the single social equation of male with dominance and female with submission. Feeling this as identity, acting it as role, inhabiting and presenting it as self, is the domain of gender. Enjoying it as the erotic, centering upon when it elicits genital arousal, is the domain of sexuality. Inequality is what is sexualized through pornography; it is what is sexual about it. The more unequal, the more sexual. The violence against women in pornography is an expression of gender hierarchy, the extremity of the hierarchy expressed and created through the extremity of the abuse, producing the extremity of the male sexual response. Pornography's multiple variations on and departures from the male dominant/female submissive sexual/gender theme are not exceptions to these gender regularities. They affirm them. The capacity of gender reversals (dominatrixes) and inversions (homosexuality) to stimulate sexual excitement is derived precisely from their mimicry or parody or negation or reversal of the standard arrangement. This affirms rather than undermines or qualifies the standard sexual arrangement as the standard sexual arrangement, the definition of sex, the standard from which all else is defined, that in which sexuality as such inheres.

Male sexuality is apparently activated by violence against women and expresses itself in violence against women to a significant extent. If violence is seen as occupying the most fully achieved end of a dehumanization continuum on which objectification occupies the least express end, one question that is raised is whether some form of hierarchy—the dynamic of the continuum—is currently essential for male sexuality to experience itself. If so, and if gender is understood to be a hierarchy, perhaps the sexes are unequal so that men can be sexually aroused. To put it another way, perhaps gender must be maintained as a social hierarchy so that men will be able to get erections; or, part of the male interest in keeping women down lies in the fact that it gets men up. Maybe feminists are considered castrating because equality is not sexy.

Recent inquiries into rape support such suspicions. Men often rape women, it turns out, because they want to and enjoy it. The act, including the dominance, is sexually arousing, sexually affirming, and supportive of the perpetrator's masculinity.

Add this to rape's pervasiveness and permissibility, together with the belief that it is both rare and impermissible. Combine this with the similarity between the patterns, rhythms, roles, and emotions, not to mention acts, which make up rape (and battery) on the one hand and intercourse on the other. All this makes it difficult to sustain the customary distinctions between pathology and normalcy, parophilia and nomophilia, violence and sex, in this area. Some researchers have previously noticed the centrality of force to the excitement value of pornography but have tended to put it down to perversion. Robert Stoller, for example, observes that pornography today depends upon hostility, voyeurism, and sadomasochism and calls perversion "the erotic form of hatred."[66] If the perverse in this context is seen not as the other side of a bright normal/abnormal line but as an undiluted expression of a norm that permeates many ordinary interactions, hatred of women—that is, misogyny—becomes a dynamic of sexual excitement itself.

All women live in sexual objectification the way fish live in water. With no alternatives, the strategy to acquire self-respect and pride is: I chose it.

Consider the conditions under which this is done. This is a culture in which women are socially expected—and themselves necessarily expect and want—to be able to distinguish the socially, epistemologically, indistinguishable. Rape and intercourse are not authoritatively separated by any difference between the physical acts or amount of force involved but only legally, by a standard that centers on the man's interpretation of the encounter. Thus, although raped women, that is, most women, are supposed to be able to feel every day and every night that they have some meaningful determining part in having their sex life—their life, period—not be a series of rapes, the most they provide is the raw data for the man to see as he sees it. And he has been seeing pornography. Similarly, "consent" is supposed to be the crucial line between rape and intercourse, but the legal standard for it is so passive, so acquiescent, that a woman can be dead and have consented under it. The mind fuck of all of this makes liberalism's complicitous collapse into "I chose it" feel like a strategy for sanity. It certainly makes a woman at one with the world.

The general theory of sexuality emerging from this feminist critique does not consider sexuality to be an inborn force inherent in individuals, nor cultural in the Freudian sense, in which sexuality exists in a cultural context but in universally invariant stages and psychic representations. It appears instead to be culturally specific, even if so far largely invariant because male supremacy is largely universal, if always in specific forms. Although some of its abuses (like prostitution) are accentuated by poverty, it does not vary by class, although class is one hierarchy it sexualizes. Sexuality becomes, in this view, social and relational, constructing and constructed of power. Infants, though sensory, cannot be said to possess sexuality in this sense because they have not had the experiences (and do not speak the language) that give it social meaning. Since sexuality is its social meaning, infant erections, for example, are clearly sexual in the sense that this society centers its sexuality on them, but to relate to a child as though his erections mean what adult erections have been conditioned to mean is a form of child abuse. Such erections have the meaning they acquire in social life only to observing adults.

At risk of further complicating the issues, perhaps it would help to think of women's sexuality as women's like Black culture is Blacks': it is, and it is not. The parallel cannot be precise in part because, owing to segregation, Black culture developed under more autonomous conditions than women, intimately integrated with men by force, have had. Still, both can be experienced as a source of strength, joy, expression, and as an affirmative badge of pride.[82] Both remain nonetheless stigmatic in the sense of a brand, a restriction, a definition as less. This is not because of any intrinsic content or value, but because the social reality is that their shape, qualities, texture, imperative, and very existence are a response to powerlessness. They exist as they do because of lack of choice. They are created out of social conditions of oppression and exclusion. They may be part of a strategy for survival or even of change. But, as is, they are not the whole world, and it is the whole world that one is entitled to. This is why interpreting female sexuality as an expression of women's agency and autonomy, as if sexism did not exist, is always denigrating and bizarre and reductive, as it would be to interpret Black culture as if racism did not exist. As if Black culture just arose freely and spontaneously on the plantations and in the ghettos of North America, adding diversity to American pluralism.

So long as sexual inequality remains unequal and sexual, attempts to value sexuality as women's, possessive as if women possess it, will remain part of limiting women to it, to what women are now defined as being. Outside of truly rare and contrapuntal glimpses (which most people think they live almost their entire sex life within), to seek an equal sexuality without political transformation is to seek equality under conditions of inequality. Rejecting this, and rejecting the glorification of settling for the best that inequality has to offer or has stimulated the resourceful to invent, are what Ti-Grace Atkinson meant to reject when she said: "I do not know any feminist: worthy of that name who, if forced to choose between freedom and sex, would choose sex. She'd choose freedom every time."[83]

NOTES

1. See Jane Caputi, *The Age of Sex Crime* (Bowling Green, Ohio: Bowling Green State University Popular Press, 1987); Deborah Cameron and Elizabeth Frazer, *The Lust to Kill: A Feminist Investigation of Sexual Murder* (New York: New York University Press, 1987).

2. A few basic citations from the massive body of work on which this chapter draws are:

    On Rape: Diana E. H. Russell and Nancy Howell, "The Prevalence of Rape in the United States Revisited," *Signs: Journal of Women in Culture and Society* 8 (Summer 1983): 668–695; D. Russell, *Rape in Marriage* (New York: Macmillan,

1982); Lorenne M. G. Clark and Debra Lewis, *The Politics of Rape: The Victim's Perspective* (New York: Stein & Day, 1975); Andrea Medea and Kathleen Thompson, *Against Rape* (New York: Farrar, Straus and Giroux, 1974); Susan Brownmiller, *Against Our Will: Men, Women, and Rape* (New York: Simon and Schuster, 1975); Irene Frieze, "Investigating the Causes and Consequences of Marital Rape," *Signs: Journal of Women in Culture and Society* 8 (Spring 1983): 532–553; Nancy Gager and Cathleen Schurr, *Sexual Assault: Confronting Rape in America* (New York: Grosset & Dunlap, 1976); Gary LaFree, "Male Power and Female Victimization: Towards a Theory of Interracial Rape," *American Journal of Sociology* 88 (1982): 311–328; Martha Butt, "Cultural Myths and Supports for Rape," *Journal of Personality and Social Psychology* 38 (1980): 217–230; Kalamu ya Salaam, "Rape: A Radical Analysis from the African-American Perspective," in *Our Women Keep Our Skies from Falling* (New Orleans: Nkombo, 1980); J. Check and N. Malamuth, "An Empirical Assessment of Some Feminist Hypotheses about Rape," *International Journal of Women's Studies* 8 (1985): 414–423.

On battery: D. Martin, *Battered Wives* (San Francisco: Glide Productions, 1976); S. Steinmerz, *The Cycle of Violence: Assertive, Aggressive, and Abusive Family Interaction* (New York: Praeger, 1977); R. Emerson Dobash and Russell Dobash, *Violence against Wives: A Case against the Patriarchy* (New York: Free Press, 1979); R. Langley and R. Levy, *Wife Beating: The Silent Crisis* (New York: E. P. Dutton, 1977); Evan Stark, Anne Flitcraft, and William Frazier, "Medicine and Patriarchal Violence: The Social Construction of a 'Private' Event," *International Journal of Health Services* 9 (1979): 461–493; Lenore Walker, *The Battered Woman* (New York: Harper & Row, 1979).

On sexual harassment: Merit Systems Protection Board, *Sexual Harassment in the Federal Workplace: Is it a Problem?* (Washington, D. C.: U. S. Government Printing Office, 1981); C. A. MacKinnon, *Sexual Harassment of Working Women* (New Haven: Yale University Press, 1979); Donna Benson and Gregg Thomson, "Sexual Harassment on a University Campus: The Confluence of Authority Relations, Sexual Interest, and Gender Stratification," *Social Problems* 29 (1982): 236–251; Phyllis Crocker and Anne E. Simon, "Sexual Harassment in Education," 10 *Capital University Law Review* 541 (1981).

On incest and child sexual abuse: D. Finkelhor, *Sexually Victimized Children* (New York: Free Press, 1979); J. Herman, *Father-Daughter Incest* (Cambridge, Mass.: Harvard University Press, 1981); D. Finkelhor, *Child Sexual Abuse: Theory and Research* (New York: Free Press, 1984); A. Jaffe, L. Dynneson, and R. Ten-Bensel, "Sexual Abuse of Children. An Epidemologic Study," *American Journal of Diseases of Children* 129 (1975): 689–695; K. Brady, *Father's Days: A True Story of Incest* (New York: Seaview Books, 1979); L. Armstrong, *Kiss Daddy Goodnight* (New York: Hawthorn Press, 1978); S. Burler, *Conspiracy of Silence: The Trauma of Incest* (San Francisco: New Glide Publications, 1978); A. Burgess, N. Groth, L. Homstrom, and S. Sgroi, *Sexual Assault of Children and Adolescents* (Lexington, Mass.: Lexington Books, 1978); F. Rush, *The Best-Kept Secret: Sexual Abuse of Children* (Englewood Cliffs, N. J.: Prentice-Hall, 1980); Diana E. H. Russell,

"The Prevalence and Seriousness of Incestuous Abuse: Stepfathers v. Biological Fathers," *Child Abuse and Neglect: The International Journal* 8 (1984): 15–22; idem, "The Incidence and Prevalence of Intrafamilial and Extrafamilial Sexual Abuse of Female Children," ibid. 7 (1983): 133—146; idem, *The Secret Trauma: Incestuous Abuse of Women and Girls* (New York: Basic Books, 1986).

On prostitution: Kathleen Barry, *Female Sexual Slavery* (Englewood Cliffs, N. J.: Prentice Hall, 1979); M. Griffin, "Wives, Hookers and the Law," 10 *Student Lawyer* 18—21 (January 1982); J. James and J. Meyerding, "Early Sexual Experience as a Factor in Prostitution," *Archives of Sexual Behavior* 7 (1978): 31—42; United Nations Economic and Social Council, Commission on Human Rights, Sub-Commission on Prevention of Discrimination and Protection of Minorities, Working Group on Slavery, *Suppression of the Traffic in Persons and of the Exploitation of the Prostitution of Others*, E/Cn.4/AC.2/5 (New York, 1976); Jennifer James, *The Politics of Prostitution* (Seattle: Social Research Associates, 1975); Kate Millett, *The Prostitution Papers* (New York: Avon Books, 1973).

On pornography: L. Lederer, ed., *Take Back the Night: Women on Pornography* (New York: William Morrow, 1980): Andrea Dworkin, *Pornography: Men Possessing Women* (New York: Perigee, 1981); Linda Lovelace and Michael McGrady, *Ordeal* (Secaucus, N. J.: Citadel Press, 1980); P. Bogdanovich, *The Killing of the Unicorn: Dorothy Stratten, 1960—1980* (New York: William Morrow, 1984); M. Langelan, "The Political Economy of Pornography," *Aegis: Magazine on Ending Violence against Women* 32 (August 1981): 5–7. D. Leidholdr, "Where Pornography Meets Fascism," *WIN New.* March 15, 1983, pp. 18–22; E. Donnerstein. "Erotica and Human Aggression," in *Aggression: Theoretical and Empirical Review*, ed. R. Green and E. Donnerstein (New York: Academic Press, 1983); idem, "Pornography: It's Effects on Violence Against Women," in *Pornography and Sexual Aggression*, ed. N. Malamuth and E. Donnerstein (Orlando. Fla.: Academic Press, 1984); Geraldine Finn. "Against Sexual Imagery, Alternative or Otherwise" (Paper presented at Symposium on Images of Sexuality in Art and Media, Ottawa, March 13–16, 1985); Diana E. H. Russell. "Pornography and Rape: A Causal Model," *Political Psychology* 9 (1988): 41–74; M. McManus, ed., *Final Report of the Attorney General's Commission on Pornography* (Nashville: Rutledge Hill Press, 1986).

See generally: Diana E. H. Russell, *Sexual Exploitation: Rape, Child Sexual Abuse, and Workplace Sexual Harassment* (Beverly Hills: Russell Sage, 1984); D. Russell and N. Van de Ven, *Crimes Against Women: Proceedings of the International Tribunal* (Millbrae, Calif.: Les Femmes, 1976); E. Stanko, *Intimate Intrusions: Women's Experience of Male Violence* (London: Routledge & Kegan Paul, 1985); Ellen Morgan, *The Erotization of Male Dominance/Female Submission* (Pittsburgh: Know, 1975): Adrienne Rich, "Compulsory Heterosexuality and Lesbian Existence," *Signs: Journal of Women in Culture and Society* 5 (Summer 1980): 631–660; J. Long Laws and P. Schwartz, *Sexual Scripts: The Social Construction of Female Sexuality* (Hinsdale. III.: Dryden Press, 1977), L. Phelps, "Female Sexual Alienation," in *Women: A Feminist Perspective*, ed. J. Freeman (Palo Alto, Calif.:

Mayfield, 1979); Shere Hite, *The Hite Report: A Nationwide Survey of Female Sexuality* (New York: Macmillan, 1976); Andrea Dworkin, *Intercourse* (New York: Free Press, 1987). Recent comparative work provides confirmation and contrasts: Pat Caplan, ed., *The Cultural Construction of Sexuality* (New York: Tavistock, 1987); Marjorie Shostak, *Nisa: The Life and Words of a !Kung Woman* (New York: Vinrage Books, 1983).

3. Freud's decision to disbelieve women's accounts of being sexually abused as children was apparently central in the construction of the theories of fantasy and possibly also of the unconscious. That is, to some degree, his belief that the sexual abuse in his patients' accounts did not occur created the need for a theory like fantasy, like unconscious, to explain the reports. See Rush, *The Best-Kept Secret*; Jeffrey M. Masson, *The Assault on Truth: Freud's Suppression of the Seduction Theory* (New York: Farrar, Straus and Giroux, 1984). One can only speculate on the course of the modern psyche (not to mention modern history) had the women been believed.

4. E. Schur, *Labeling Women Deviant: Gender, Stigma, and Social Control* (Philadelphia: Temple University Press, 1984) (a superb review of studies which urges a "continuum" rather than a "deviance" approach to issues of sex inequality).

5. This figure was calculated at my request by Diana E. H. Russell on the random-sample data base of 930 San Francisco households discussed in *The Secret Trauma*, pp. 20–37, and *Rape in Marriage*, pp. 27–41. The figure includes all the forms of rape or other sexual abuse or harassment surveyed, noncontact as well as contact, from gang rape by strangers and marital rape to obscene phone calls, unwanted sexual advances on the street, unwelcome requests to pose for pornography, and subjection to peeping toms and sexual exhibitionists (flashers).

6. S. D. Smithyman, "The Undetected Rapist" (Ph. D. diss., Claremont Graduate School, 1978); N. Groth, *Men Who Rape: The Psychology of the Offender* (New York: Plenum Press, 1979); D. Scully and J. Marolla, "'Riding the Bull at Gilley's': Convicted Rapists Describe the Rewards of Rape," *Social Problems* 32 (1985): 251. (The manuscript subtitle was "Convicted Rapists Describe the Pleasure of Raping.")

7. Kate Millett, *Sexual Politics* (Garden City, N. Y.: Doubleday, 1970).

8. Jacques Lacan, *Feminine Sexuality*, trans. Jacqueline Rose, ed. Juliet Mitchell and Jacqueline Rose (New York: Norton, 1982); Michel Foucault. *The History of Sexuality*, vol. 1: An Introduction (New York: Random House, 1980); idem, *Power/Knowledge*, ed. C. Gordon (New York: Pantheon, 1980).

   See generally (including materials reviewed in) R. Padgug, "Sexual Matters; On Conceptualizing Sexuality in History," *Radical History Review* 70 (Spring/Summer 1979), e.g., p. 9; M. Vicinus, "Sexuality and Power: A Review of Current Work in the History of Sexuality," *Feminist Studies* 8 (Spring 1982): 133–155; S. Ortner and H. Whitehead, *Sexual Meanings: The Cultural Construction of Gender and Sexuality* (Cambridge: Cambridge University Press, 1981); Red Collective, *The Politics of Sexuality in Capitalism* (London: Black Rose Press, 1978; J. Weeks, *Sex, Politics, and Society: The Regulation of Sexuality since 1800*

(New York: Longman, 1981); J. D'Emilio, *Sexual Politics, Sexual Communities: The Making of a Homosexual Minority in the United States 1940–1970* (Chicago: University of Chicago Press, 1983); A. Snitow, C. Stansell, and S. Thompson, eds., Introduction to *Powers of Desire: The Politics of Sexuality* (New York: Monthly Review Press, 1983); E. Dubois and L. Gordon, "Seeking Ecstasy on the Battlefield: Danger and Pleasure in Nineteenth-Century Feminist Social Thought," *Feminist Studies* 9 (Spring 1983): 7:25.

9. An example is Jeffrey Weeks, *Sexuality and Its Discontents* (London: Routledge & Kegan Paul, 1985).

10. Luce Irigaray's critique of Freud in *Speculum of the Other Women* (Ithaca; Cornell University Press, 1974) acutely shows how Freud constructs sexuality from the male point of view, with woman as deviation from the norm. But she, too, sees female sexuality not as constructed by male dominance but only repressed under it.

11. For those who think that such notions are atavisms left behind by modern scientists, see one entirely typical conceptualization of "sexual pleasure, a powerful unconditioned stimulus and reinforcer" in N. Malamuth and B. Spinner, "A Longitudinal Content Analysis of Sexual Violence in the Best-Selling Erotic Magazines," *Journal of Sex Research* 16 (August 1980): 226. See also B. Ollman's discussion of Wilhelm Reich in *Social and Sexual Revolution* (Boston: South End Press, 1979), eps. pp. 186–187.

12. Foucault's contributions to such an analysis and his limitations are discussed illuminatingly in Frigga Haug, ed., *Female Sexualization*, trans, Erica Carter (London: Verso, 1987), pp. 190–198.

13. A. Kinsey, W. Pomeroy, C. Martin, and P. Gebhard, *Sexual Behavior in the Human Female* (Philadelphia: W. B. Saunders, 1953); A. Kinsey, W. Pomeroy, and C. Martin, *Sexual Behavior in the Human Male* (Philadelphia: W. B. Saunders, 1948). See the critique of Kinsey in Dworkin, *Pornography*, pp. 179–198.

14. Examples include: D. English, "The Politics of Porn: Can Feminists Walk the Line?" *Mother Jones*, April 1980, pp. 20–23, 43–44, 48–50; D. English, A. Hollibaugh, and G. Rubin, "Talking Sex: A Conversation on Sexuality and Feminism," *Socialist Review* 58 (July-August) 1981); J. B. Elshtain, "The Victim Syndrome: A Troubling Turn in Feminism," *The Progressive*, June 1982, pp. 40–47; Ellen Willis, *Village Voice*, November 12, 1979. This approach also tends to characterize the basic ideology of "human sexuality courses" as analyzed by C. Vance in Snitow, Stansell, and Thompson, *Powers of Desire*, pp. 371–384. The view of sex so promulgated is distilled in the following quotation, coming after an alliterative list, probably intended to be humorous, headed "determinants of sexuality" (on which "power" does not appear, although every other word begins with p): "Persistent puritanical pressures promoting propriety, purity, and prudery are opposed by a powerful, primeval, procreative passion to plunge his pecker into her pussy"; "Materials from Course on Human Sexuality," College of Medicine and Dentistry of New Jersey, Rurgers Medical School, January 29 February 2, 1979, p. 39.

15. A third reason is also given: "to the extent that sexism in societal and family structure is responsible for the phenomena of 'compulsive masculinity' and structured antagonism between the sexes, the elimination of sexual inequality would reduce the number of 'power trip' and 'degradation ceremony' motivated rapes," M. Straus, "Sexual Inequality, Cultural Norms, and Wife-Beating," *Victimology: An International Journal* 1 (1976): 54–76. Note that these structural factors seem to be considered nonsexual, in the sense that "power trip" and "degradation ceremony" motivated rapes are treated as not erotic to the perpetrators *because* of the elements of dominance and degradation, nor is "structured antagonism" seen as an erotic element of rape or sex (or family).

16. P. R. Sanday, "The Socio-Cultural Context of Rape: A Cross-Cultural Study," *Journal of Social Issues* 87, no. 4 (1981): 16. See also M. Lewin, "Unwanted Intercourse: The Difficulty of Saying 'No,'" *Psychology of Women Quarterly* 9 (1985): 184–192.

17. See Chapter 9 for discussion.

18. Susan Brownmiller, *Aganist Our Will*, originated this approach, which has since become ubiquitous.

19. Annie McCombs helped me express this thought; letter to *Off Our Backs* (Washington, D. C., October 1984), p. 34.

20. Brownmiller, *Against Our Will*, did analyze rape as something men do to women, hence as a problem of gender, even though her concept of gender is biologically based. See, e.g., her pp. 4. 6, and discussion in chap. 3. An exception is Clark and Lewis, *Rape*.

21. Snitow, Stansell, and Thompson, Introduction to *Powers of Desire*, p. 9.

22. C. Vance, "Concept Paper: Toward a Politics of Sexuality," in *Diary of a Conference on Sexuality*, ed. H. Alderfer, B. Jaker, and M. Nelson (Record of the planning committee of the conference "The Scholar and the Feminist IX: Toward a Politics of Sexuality," April 24, 1982), p. 27: to address "women's sexual pleasure, choice, and autonomy, acknowledging that sexuality is simultaneously a domain of restriction, repression and danger as well as a domain of exploration, pleasure and agency." Parts of the *Diary*, with the conference papers, were later published in C. Vance, ed., *Pleasure and Danger: Exploring Female Sexuality* (London: Routledge & Kegan Paul, 1984).

23. Vance, "Concept Paper," p. 38.

24. For example see A. Hollibaugh and C. Moraga. "What We're Rollin' Around in Bed With: Sexual Silences in Feminism," in Snitow, Stansell, and Thompson, *Powers of Desire*, pp. 394–405, esp, 398; Samois, *Coming to Power* (Berkeley, Calif.: Alyson Publications, 1983).

25. Andrea Dworkin, "Why So-called Radical Men Love and Need Pornography," in Lederer, *Take Back the Night*, p. 148.

26. Susan Sontag, "Fascinating Fascism," in *Under the Sign of Saturn* (New York: Farrar, Straus and Giroux, 1980), p. 103

27. Robert Stoller, *Sexual Excitement: Dynamics of Erotic Life* (New York: Pantheon Books, 1979). p. 6.

28. Harriet Jacobs, quoted in Rennie Simson, "The Afro-American Female: The Historical Context of the Construction of Sexual Identity," in Snitow, Stansell, and Thompson, *Powers of Desire*, p. 231. Jacobs subsequently resisted by hiding in an attic cubbyhole "almost deprived of light and air, and with no space to move my limbs, for nearly seven years" to avoid him.

29. A similar rejection of indeterminacy can be found in Linda Alcoff, "Cultural Feminism versus Post-Structuralism: The Identity Crisis in Feminist Theory," *Signs: Journal of Women in Culture and Society* 13 (Spring 1988): 419–420. The article otherwise misdiagnoses the division in feminism as that between so-called cultural feminists and post-structuralism, when the division is between those who take sexual misogyny seriously as a mainspring to gender hiearchy and those who wish, liberal-fashion, to affirm "differences" without seeing that sameness/difference is a dichotomy of exactly the sort that post-structuralism purports to deconstruct.

30. See Sandra Harding, "Introduction: Is There a Feminist Method?" in *Feminism and Methodology* (Bloomington: Indiana University Press, 1987), pp. 1–14.

31. One of the most compelling accounts of active victim behavior is provided in *Give Sorrow Words: Maryse Holder's Letters from Mexico*, intro. Kate Millett (New York: Grove Press, 1980). Ms. Holder wrote a woman friend of her daily, frantic, and always failing pursuit of men, sex, beauty, and feeling good about herself: "Fuck fucking, will *feel* self-respect" (p. 94). She was murdered soon after by an unknown assailant.

32. This phrase comes from Michel Foucault, "The West and the Truth of Sex," *Sub-stance* 5 (1978): 20. Foucault does not criticize pornography in these terms.

33. Dworkin, *Pornography*, p. 24.

34. J. Cook, "The X-Rated Economy," *Forbes*, September 18, 1978, p. 18; Langelan, "The Political Economy of Pornography," p. 5; *Public Hearings on Ordinances to Add Pornography as Discrimination Against Women* (Minneapolis, December 12–13, 1983); F. Schauer, "Response: Pornography and the First Amendment," 40 *University of Pittsburgh Law Review*, 605, 616 (1979).

35. John Money, professor of medical psychology and pediatrics, John Hopkins Medical Institutions, letter to Clive M. Davis, April 18, 1948. The same view is expressed by Al Goldstein, editor of *Screw*, a pornographic newspaper, concerning antipornography feminists, termed "nattering nabobs of sexual negativism": "We must repeat to ourselves like a mantra: sex is good; nakedness is a joy; an erection is beautiful. . . Don't let the bastards get you limp"; "Dear Playboy," *Playboy*, June 1985, p. 12.

36. Andrea Dworkin, "The Root Cause," in *Our Blood: Prophesies and Discourses on Sexual Politics* (New York: Harper & Row, 1976), pp. 96–111.

37. See Chapter 12 for further discussion.

38. Dworkin, *Pornography* pp. 69, 136, and chap. 2 "Men and Boys." "In practice, fucking is an act of possession—simultaneously an act of ownership, taking, force, it is conquering; it expresses in intimacy power over and against, body to body, person to thing. 'The sex act' means penile intromission followed by

penile thrusting, or fucking. The woman is acted on, the man acts and through action expresses sexual power, the power of masculinity. Fucking requires that the male act on one who has less power and this valuation is so deep, so completely implicit in the act, that the one who is fucked is stigmatized as feminine during the act even when not anatomically female. In the male system, sex is the penis, the penis is sexual power, its use in fucking is manhood"; p. 23.

39. Ibid., p. 109.
40. Ibid., pp. 113–128.
41. Ibid., p. 174.
42. Freud believed that the female nature was inherently masochistic; Sigmund Freud, Lecture XXXlll, "The Psychology of Women," in *New Introductory Lectures on Psychoanalysis* (London: Hogarth Prwess. 1933). Helene Deutsch, Marie Bonaparte, Sandor Rado, Adolf Grunberger, Melanie Klein, Helle Thorning, Georges Bataille. Theodore Reik, Jean-Paul Sartre, and Simone de Beauvoir all described some version of female masochism in their work, each with a different theoretical account for virtually identical observations. See Helene Deutsch, "The Significance of Masochism in the Mental Life of Women," *International Journal of Psychoanalysis* 11 (1930); 48–60; idem in *The Psychology of Women* (New York: Grune & Stratton, 1944). Several are summarized by Janine Chasseguet-Smirgel, ed., in her Introduction to *Female Sexuality: New Psychoanalystic Views* (Ann Arbot: University of Michigan Press, 1970); Theodore Reik, *Masochism in Sex and Society* (New York: Grove Press, 1962), p. 217; Helle Thorning, "The Mother-Daughter Relationship and Sexual Ambivalence," *Heresies* 12 (1979): 3–6; Georges Bataille, *Death and Sensuality* (New York: Walker and Co., 1962); Jean-Paul Sartre, "Concrete Relations with Others," in *Being and Nothingness: An Essay on Phenomenological Ontology*, trans, Hazel E. Barnes (New York: Philosophical Library, (1956), pp. 361–430. Betsey Belote stated: "masochistic and hysterical behavior is so similar to the concept of 'femininity' that the three are not clearly distinguishable"; "Masochistic Syndrome, Hysterical Personality, and the Illusion of the Healthy Woman," in *Female Psychology: The Emerging Self*, ed. Sue Cox (Chicago; Science Research Associates, 1976), p. 347. See also S. Bartky, "Feminine Masochism and the Politics of Personal Transformation," *Women's Studies International Forum* 7 (1984): 327–328. Andrea Dworkin writes: "I belive that freedom for women must begin in the repudiation of our own masochism. . . I believe that ridding ourselves of our own deeply entrenched masochism, which takes so many tortured forms, is the first priority; it is the first deadly blow that we can strike against systematized male dominance," *Our Blood.* p. 111.
43. Dworkin, *Pornography*, p. 146.
44. Anne Koedt, "The Myth of the Vaginal Organism," in *Notes from the Second Year: Women's Liberation* (New York: Radical Feminism, 1970); Ti-Grace Atkinson, *Amazon Odyssey: The First Collection of Writing by the Political Pioneer of the Women's Movement* (New York: Links Books, 1974); Phelps, "Female Sexual Alienation."

45. Dworkin, *Pornography*, p. 22.

46. This is the plot of *Deep Throat*, the pornographic film Linda "Lovelace" was forced to make. It may be the largest-grossing pornography film in the history of the world (McManus, *Final Report*, p. 345). That this plot is apparently enjoyed to such a prevalent extent suggests that it appeals to something extant in the male psyche.

47. Dworkin, "The Root Cause," p. 56.

48. A prominent if dated example is Jill Johnston, *Lesbian Nation: The Feminist Solution* (New York: Simon and Schuster, 1973).

49. This and the following quotations in this paragraph are from P. Califia, "A Secret Side of Lesbian Sexuality," *The Advocate* (San Francisco), December 27, 1979, pp. 19–21, 27–28.

50. The statistics in this paragraph are drawn from the sources referenced in note 2, above, as categorized by topic. Kathleen Barry defines "female sexual slavery" as a condition of prostitution which one cannot get out of.

51. Robert Stoller, *Perversion: The Erotic Form of Hatred* (New York: Pantheon, 1975), p. 87.

52. This is also true of Foucault, *The History of Sexuality*. Foucault understands that sexuality must be discussed with method, power, class, and the law. Gender, however, eludes him. So he cannot distinguish between the silence about sexuality that Victorianism has made into a noisy discourse and the silence that has *been* women's sexuality under conditions of subordination by and to men. Although he purports to grasp sexuality, including desire itself, as social, he does not see the content of its determination as a sexist social order that eroticizes potency as male and victimization as female. Women are simply beneath significant notice.

53. On sexuality, see, e.g., A. Lorde, *Uses of the Erotic: The Erotic as Power* (Brooklyn, N. Y.: Out and Out Books, 1978); and Haunani-Kay Trask, *Eros and Power: The Promise of Feminist Theory* (Philadelphia: University of Pennsylvania Press, 1986). Both creatively attempt such a reconstitution. Trask's work suffers from an underlying essentialism in which the realities of sexual abuse are not examined or seen as constituting women's sexuality as such. Thus, a return to mother and body can be urged as social bases for reclaiming a feminist eros. Another reason the parallel cannot be at all precise is that Black women and their sexuality make up both Black culture and women's sexuality, inhabiting both sides of the comparison. In other words, parallels which converge and interact are not parallels. The comparison may nonetheless be heuristically useful both for those who understand one experience but not the other and for those who can compare two dimensions of life which overlap and resonate together at some moments and diverge sharply in dissonance at others.

54. Ti-Grace Atkinson, "Why I'm against S/M Liberation," in *Against Sadomasochism: A Radical Feminist Analysis*, ed. F. Linden, D. Pagano, D. Russell, and S. Star (Palo Alto, Calif.: Frog in the Well, 1982), p. 91.

11

NANCY CHODOROW

The Psychodynamics of the Family

Let us recall that we left the pubescent girl in a triangular situation and expressed the hope that later she would dissolve the sexually mixed triangle. . . . in favor of heterosexuality. This formulation was made for the sake of simplification. Actually, whether a constitutional bisexual factor contributes to the creation of such a triangle or not, this triangle can never be given up completely. The deepest and most ineradicable emotional relations with both parents share in its formation. It succeeds another relation, even older and more enduring-the relationship between mother and child, which every man or woman preserves from his birth to his death. It is erroneous to say that the little girl gives up her first mother relation in favor of the father. She only gradually draws him into the alliance, develops from the mother-child exclusiveness toward the triangular parent-child relation and continues the latter, just as she does the former, although in a weaker and less elemental form, all her life. Only the principal part changes; now the mother, now the father plays it. The ineradicability of affective constellations manifests itself in later repetitions.

—Helene Deutsch,
The Psychology of Women

A woman *is* her mother
That's the main thing

—Ann Sexton,
"Housewife"

OEDIPAL ASYMMETRIES AND HETEROSEXUAL KNOTS[1]

The same oedipally produced ideology and psychology of male dominance, repression, and denial of dependence that propel men into the nonfamilial competitive work world place structural strains on marriage and family life. Because women mother, the development and meaning of heterosexual object-choice differ for men and women. The traditional psychoanalytic account of femininity and masculinity begins from this perception. In our society, marriage has assumed a larger and larger emotional weight, supposedly offsetting the strains of increasingly alienated and bureaucratized work in the paid economy. It no longer has the economic and political basis it once had, and the family has collapsed in upon its psychological and personal functions as production, education, religion, and care for the sick and aged have left the home. In this context, the contradictions between women's and men's heterosexuality that result from women's performing mothering functions stand out clearly.

According to psychoanalytic theory, heterosexual erotic orientation is a primary outcome of the oedipus complex for both sexes. Boys and girls differ in this, however. Boys retain one primary love object throughout their boyhood. For this reason, the development of masculine heterosexual object choice is relatively continuous: "In males the path of this development is straightforward, and the advance from the 'phallic' phase does not take place in consequence of a complicated 'wave of repression' but is based upon a ratification of that which already exists. . ."[2] In theory, a boy resolves his oedipus complex by repressing his attachment to his mother. He is therefore ready in adulthood to find a primary relationship with someone *like* his mother. When he does, the relationship is given meaning from its psychological reactivation of what was originally an intense and exclusive relationship—first an identity, then a "dual-unity," finally a two-person relationship.

Things are not so simple for girls: "Psychoanalytic research discovered at the very outset that the development of the infantile libido to the normal heterosexual object-choice is in women rendered difficult by certain peculiar circumstances."[3] These "peculiar circumstances" are universal facts of family organization. Because her first love object is a woman, a girl, in order to attain her proper heterosexual orientation, must transfer her primary object choice to her father and men. This creates asymmetry in the feminine and masculine oedipus complex, and difficulties in the development of female sexuality, given heterosexuality as a developmental goal.

For girls, just as for boys, mothers are primary love objects. As a result, the structural inner object setting of female heterosexuality differs from that of males. When a girl's father does become an important primary person, it is in the context of a bisexual relational triangle. A girl's relation to him is emotionally in reaction to, interwoven and competing for primacy with, her relation to her mother. A girl usually turns to her father as an object of primary interest from the exclusivity of the relationship to her mother, but this libidinal turning to her father does not substitute for her attachment to her mother. Instead, a girl retains her preoedipal tie to her mother (an intense tie involved with issues of primary identification, primary love, dependence, and separation) and builds oedipal attachments to both her mother and her father upon it. These attachments are characterized by eroticized demands for exclusivity, feelings of competition, and jealousy. She retains the internalized early relationship, including its implications for the nature of her definition of self, and internalizes these other relationships in addition to and not as replacements for it.

For girls, then, there is no absolute change of object, nor exclusive attachment to their fathers. Moreover, a father's behavior and family role, and a girl's relationship to him, are crucial to the development of heterosexual orientation in her. But fathers are comparatively unavailable physically and emotionally. They are not present as much and are not primary caretakers, and their own training for masculinity may have led them to deny emotionality. Because of the father's lack of availability to his daughter, and because of the intensity of the mother-daughter relationship in which she participates, girls tend not to make a total transfer of affection to their fathers but to remain also involved with their mothers, and to oscillate emotionally between mother and father.

The implications of this are twofold. First, the nature of the heterosexual relationship differs for boys and girls. Most women emerge from their oedipus complex oriented to their father and men as primary *erotic* objects, but it is clear that men tend to remain *emotionally* secondary, or at most emotionally equal, compared to the primacy and exclusivity of an oedipal boy's emotional tie to his mother and women. Second, because the father is an additional important love object, who becomes important in the context of a relational triangle, the feminine inner object world is more complex than the masculine. This internal situation continues into adulthood and affects adult women's participation in relationships. Women, according to Deutsch, experience heterosexual relationships in a triangular context, in which men are not exclusive objects for them. The implication of her statement is confirmed by cross-cultural examination of family structure and relations between the sexes, which suggests that conjugal closeness is the exception and not the rule.[4]

Because mother and father are not the same *kind* of parent, the nature and intensity of a child's relationship to them differ as does the relationship's degree of exclusiveness. Because children first experience the social and cognitive world as continuous with themselves and do not differentiate objects, their mother, as first caretaking figure, is not a separate person and has no separate interests. In addition, this lack of separateness is in the context of the infant's total dependence on its mother for physical and psychological survival. The internalized experience of self in the original mother-relation remains seductive and frightening: Unity was bliss, yet meant the loss of self and absolute dependence. By contrast, a child has always differentiated itself from its father and known him as a separate person with separate interests. And the child has never been totally dependent on him. Her father has not posed the original narcissistic threat (the threat to basic ego integrity and boundaries) nor provided the original narcissistic unity (the original experience of oneness) to a girl. Oedipal love for the mother, then, contains both a threat to selfhood and a promise of primal unity which love for the father never does. A girl's love for her father and women's attachment to men reflect all aspects of these asymmetries.

Men cannot provide the kind of return to oneness that women can. Michael Balint argues that the return to the experience of primary love—the possibility of regressing to the infantile stage of a sense of oneness, no reality testing, and a tranquil sense of well-being in which all needs are satisfied—is a main goal of adult sexual relationships: "This primary tendency, I shall be loved always, everywhere, in every way, my whole body, my whole being—without any criticism, without the slightest effort on my part—is the final aim of all erotic striving."[5] He implies, though, that women can fulfill this need better than men, because a sexual relationship with a woman reproduces the early situation more completely and is more completely a return to the mother. Thus, males in coitus come nearest to the experience of refusion with the mother—"The male comes nearest to achieving this regression during coitus: with his semen in reality, with his penis symbolically, with his whole self in phantasy."[6]

Women's participation here is dual. (Balint is presuming women's heterosexuality.) First, a woman identifies with the man penetrating her and thus experiences through identification refusion with a woman (mother). Second, she *becomes* the mother (phylogenetically the all-embracing sea, ontogenetically the womb). Thus, a woman in a heterosexual relationship cannot, like a man, recapture as *herself* her own experience of merging. She can do so only by identifying with someone who can, on the one hand, and by identifying with the person with whom she was merged on the other. The "regressive restitution" (Balint's term) which coitus brings, then, is not complete for a woman in the way that it is for a man.

Freud speaks to the way that women seek to recapture their relationship with their mother in heterosexual relationships.[7] He suggests that as women "change object" from mother to father, the mother remains their primary internal object, so that they often impose on their relation to their father, and later to men, the issues which preoccupy them in their internal relation to their mother. They look in relations to men for gratifications that they want from a woman. Freud points to the common clinical discovery of a woman who has apparently taken her father as a model for her choice of husband, but whose marriage in fact repeats the conflicts and feelings of her relationship with her mother. For instance, a woman who remains ambivalently dependent on her mother, or preoccupied internally with the question of whether she is separate or not, is likely to transfer this stance and sense of self to a relationship with her husband.[8] Or she may identify herself as a part-object of her male partner, as an extension of her father and men, rather than an extension of her mother and women.*

But children seek to escape from their mother as well as return to her. Fathers serve in part to break a daughter's primary unity with and dependence on her mother. For this and a number of other reasons, fathers and men are idealized.[9] A girl's father provides a last ditch escape from maternal omnipotence, so a girl cannot risk driving him away. At the same time, occupying a position of distance and ideological authority in the family, a father may be a remote figure understood to a large extent through her

---

*   This is obviously only one side of the psychological matter. Chasseguet-Smirgel, who points this out, notes that men also gain satisfaction and security from turning their all-powerful mother into a part-object attachment.

mother's interpretation of his role. This makes the development of a relationship based on his real strengths and weaknesses difficult. Finally, the girl herself has not received the same kind of love from her mother as a boy has. Mothers experience daughters as one with themselves; their relationships to daughters are "narcissistic," while those with their sons are more "anaclitic."

Thus, a daughter looks to her father for a sense of separateness and for the same confirmation of her specialness that her brother receives from her mother. She (and the woman she becomes) is willing to deny her father's limitations (and those of her lover or husband) as long as she feels loved.[10] She is more able to do this because his distance means that she does not really know him. The relationship, then, because of the father's distance and importance to her, occurs largely as fantasy and idealization, and lacks the grounded reality which a boy's relation to his mother has.

These differences in the experience of self in relation to father and mother are reinforced by the different stages at which boys and girls are likely to enter the oedipal situation. Girls remain longer in the preoedipal relationship, enter the oedipus situation later than boys, and their modes of oedipal resolution differ. Bibring, Slater, and John Whiting have suggested that in the absence of men, a mother sexualizes her relationship with her son early, so that "oedipal" issues of sexual attraction and connection, competition and jealousy, become fused with "preoedipal" issues of primary love and oneness. By contrast, since the girl's relationship to her father develops later, her sense of self is more firmly established. If oedipal and preoedipal issues are fused for her, this fusion is more likely to occur in relation to her mother, and not to her father. Because her sense of self is firmer, and because oedipal love for her father is not so threatening, a girl does not "resolve" her oedipus complex to the same extent as a boy. This means that she grows up more concerned with both internalized and external object-relationships, while men tend to repress their oedipal needs for love and relationship. At the same time, men often become intolerant and disparaging of those who can express needs for love, as they attempt to deny their own needs.*[11]

Men defend themselves against the threat posed by love, but needs for love do not disappear through repression. Their training for masculinity and repression of affective relational needs, and their primarily nonemotional and impersonal relationships in the public world make deep primary relationships with other men hard to come by.[12] Given this, it is not surprising that men tend to find themselves in heterosexual relationships.

These relationships to women derive a large part of their meaning and dynamics from the men's relation to their mothers. But the maternal treatment described by Bibring, Slater, and Whiting creates relational problems in sons. When a boy's mother has treated him as an extension of herself and at the same time as a sexual object, he learns to use his masculinity and possession of a penis as a narcissistic defense. In

---

*   Chasseguet-Smirgel argues that what Freud and Brunswick call the boy's "normal contempt" for women, and consider a standard outcome of the oedipus complex, is a pathological and defensive reaction to the sense of inescapable maternal omnipotence rather than a direct outcome of genital differences.

adulthood, he will look to relationships with women for narcissistic-phallic reassurance rather than for mutual affirmation and love. Because their sexualized preoedipal attachment was encouraged, while their oedipal-genital wishes were thwarted and threatened with punishment, men may defensively invest more exclusively in the instinctual gratifications to be gained in a sexual relationship in order to avoid risking rejection of love.

Women have not repressed affective needs. They still want love and narcissistic confirmation and may be willing to put up with limitations in their masculine lover or husband in exchange for evidence of caring and love. This can lead to the denial of more immediately felt aggressive and erotic drives. Chasseguet-Smirgel suggests that a strong sexuality requires the expression of aggressive, demanding impulses fused with erotic love impulses and idealization. To the extent that women feel conflict and fear punishment especially over all impulses they define as aggressive, their sexuality suffers.*

As a result of the social organization of parenting, then, men operate on two levels in women's psyche. On one level, they are emotionally secondary and not exclusively loved—are not primary love objects like mothers. On another, they are idealized and experienced as needed, but are unable either to express their own emotional needs or respond to those of women. As Grunberger puts it, "The tragedy of this situation is that the person who could give [a woman] this confirmation, her sexual partner, is precisely the one who, as we have just seen, has come to despise narcissistic needs in an effort to disengage himself from them."[13]

This situation is illuminated by sociological and clinical findings. Conventional wisdom has it, and much of our everyday observation confirms, that women are the romantic ones in our society, the ones for whom love, marriage, and relationships matter. However, several studies point out that men love and fall in love romantically, women sensibly and rationally.[14] Most of these studies argue that in the current situation, where women are economically dependent on men, women must make rational calculations for the provision of themselves and their (future) children. This view suggests that women's apparent romanticism is an emotional and ideological response to their very real economic dependence. On the societal level, especially given economic inequity, men are exceedingly important to women. The recent tendency for women to initiate divorce and separation more than men as income becomes more available to them (and as the feminist movement begins to remove the stigma of "divorce") further confirms this.

Adult women are objectively dependent on men economically, just as in childhood girls are objectively dependent on their fathers to escape from maternal domination.

---

*   She suggests that this reaction, in which aggressive and erotic drives opposed to idealization are counter-cathected and repressed, better explains feminine frigidity and what Marie Bonaparte and Deutsch consider to be the "normal" feminine spiritualization of sex. Bonaparte explains these in terms of women's lesser libidinal energy, and Deutsch explains them as constitutional inhibition.

Their developed ability to romanticize rational decisions (to ignore or even idealize the failings of their father and men because of their dependence) stands women in good stead in this adult situation.

There is another side to this situation, however. Women have acquired a real capacity for rationality and distance in heterosexual relationships, qualities built into their earliest relationship with a man. Direct evidence for the psychological primacy of this latter stance comes from findings about the experience of loss itself. George Goethals reports the clinical finding that men's loss of at least the first adult relationship "throws them into a turmoil and a depression of the most extreme kind"[15]—a melancholic reaction to object-loss of the type Freud describes in "Mourning and Melancholia"—in which they withdraw and are unable to look elsewhere for new relationships. He implies, by contrast, that first adult loss may not result in as severe a depression for a woman, and claims that his women patients did not withdraw to the same extent and were more able to look elsewhere for new relationships. Zick Rubin reports similar findings.[16] The women he studied more frequently broke up relationships, and the men, whether or not they initiated the break-up, were more depressed and lonely afterward. Jessie Bernard, discussing older people, reports that the frequency of psychological distress, death, and suicide is much higher among recently widowed men than women, and indicates that the same difference can be found in a comparison of divorced men and women.[17]

These studies imply that women have other resources and a certain distance from their relationships to men. My account stresses that women have a richer, ongoing inner world to fall back on, and that the men in their lives do not represent the intensity and exclusivity that women represent to men. Externally, they also retain and develop more relationships. It seems that, developmentally, men do not become as emotionally important to women as women do to men.

Because women care for children, then, heterosexual symbiosis has a different "meaning" for men and women. Freud originally noted that "a man's love and a woman's are a phase apart psychologically."[18] He and psychoanalytic thinkers after him point to ways in which women and men, though usually looking for intimacy with each other, do not fulfill each other's needs because of the social organization of parenting. Differences in female and male oedipal experiences, all growing out of women's mothering, create this situation. Girls enter adulthood with a complex layering of affective ties and a rich, ongoing inner object world. Boys have a simpler oedipal situation and more direct affective relationships, and this situation is repressed in a way that the girl's is not. The mother remains a primary internal object to the girl, so that heterosexual relationships are on the model of a nonexclusive, second relationship for her, whereas for the boy they recreate an exclusive, primary relationship.

As a result of being parented by a woman, both sexes look for a return to this emotional and physical union. A man achieves this directly through the heterosexual bond, which replicates the early mother-infant exclusivity. He is supported in this endeavor by women, who, through their own development, have remained open to relational needs, have retained an ongoing inner affective life, and have learned to deny the limitations of masculine lovers for both psychological and practical reasons.

Men both look for and fear exclusivity. Throughout their development, they have tended to repress their affective relational needs, and to develop ties based more on categorical and abstract role expectations, particularly with other males. They are likely to participate in an intimate heterosexual relationship with the ambivalence created by an intensity which one both wants and fears—demanding from women what men are at the same time afraid of receiving.

As a result of being parented by a woman and growing up heterosexual, women have different and more complex relational needs in which an exclusive relationship to a man is not enough. As noted previously, this is because women situate themselves psychologically as part of a relational triangle in which their father and men are emotionally secondary or, at most, equal to their mother and women. In addition, the relation to the man itself has difficulties. Idealization, growing out of a girl's relation to her father, involves denial of real feelings and to a certain extent an unreal relationship to men. The contradictions in women's heterosexual relationships, though, are due as much to men's problems with intimacy as to outcomes of early childhood relationships. Men grow up rejecting their own needs for love, and therefore find it difficult and threatening to meet women's emotional needs. As a result, they collude in maintaining distance from women.

THE CYCLE COMPLETED: MOTHERS AND CHILDREN

Families create children gendered, heterosexual, and ready to marry. But families organized around women's mothering and male dominance create incompatibilities in women's and men's relational needs. In particular, relationships to men are unlikely to provide for women satisfaction of the relational needs that their mothering by women and the social organization of gender have produced. The less men participate in the domestic sphere, and especially in parenting, the more this will be the case.

Women try to fulfill their need to be loved, try to complete the relational triangle, and try to reexperience the sense of dual unity they had with their mother, which the heterosexual relationship tends to fulfill for men. This situation daily reinforces what women first experienced developmentally and intrapsychically in relation to men. While they are likely to become and remain erotically heterosexual, they are encouraged both by men's difficulties with love and by their own relational history with their mothers to look elsewhere for love and emotional gratification.

One way that women fulfill these needs is through the creation and maintenance of important personal relations with other women. Cross-culturally, segregation by gender is the rule: Women tend to have closer personal ties with each other than men have, and to spend more time in the company of women than they do with men. In our society, there is some sociological evidence that women's friendships are affectively richer than men's.[19] In other societies, and in most subcultures of our own, women remain involved with female relatives in adulthood.[20] Deutsch suggests further that adult female relationships sometimes express a woman's psychological participation in the relational triangle. Some women, she suggests, always need a woman rival in their relationship to a man; others need a best friend with whom they share all confidences about their heterosexual relationships. These relationships are one way of resolving and recreating the mother-daughter bond and are an expression of women's general relational capacities and definition of self in relationship.

However, deep affective relationships to women are hard to come by on a routine, daily, ongoing basis for many women. Lesbian relationships do tend to recreate mother-daughter emotions and connections,[21] but most women are heterosexual. This heterosexual preference and taboos against homosexuality, in addition to objective economic dependence on men, make the option of primary sexual bonds with other women unlikely—though more prevalent in recent years. In an earlier period, women tended to remain physically close to their own mother and sisters after marriage, and could find relationships with other women in their daily work and community. The development of industrial capitalism, however—and the increasingly physically iso-lated nuclear family it has produced—has made these primary relationships more rare and has turned women (and men) increasingly and exclusively to conjugal family rela-tionships for emotional support and love.[22]

There is a second alternative, made all the more significant by the elimination of the first, which also builds both upon the nature of women's self-definition in a het-erosexual relationship and upon the primary mother-child bond. As Deutsch makes clear, women's psyche consists in a layering of relational constellations. The preoedi-pal mother-child relation and the oedipal triangle have lasted until late in a woman's childhood, in fact throughout her development. To the extent that relations with a man gain significance for a woman, this experience is incomplete. Given the triangu-lar situation and emotional asymmetry of her own parenting, a woman's relation to a man *requires* on the level of psychic structure a third person, since it was originally established in a triangle. A man's relation to women does not. His relation to his mother was originally established first as an identity, then as a dual unity, then as a two-person relationship, before his father ever entered the picture.

On the level of psychic structure, then, a child completes the relational triangle for a woman. Having a child, and experiencing her relation to a man in this context, enables her to reimpose intrapsychic relational structure on the social world, while at the same time resolving the generational component of her oedipus complex as she takes a new place in the triangle—a maternal place in relation to her own child.

The mother-child relationship also recreates an even more basic relational constel-lation. The exclusive symbiotic mother-child relationship of a mother's own infancy reappears, a relationship which all people who have been mothered want basically to recreate. This contrasts to the situation of a man. A man often wants a child through his role-based, positional identification with his father, or his primary or personal identification with his mother. Similarly, a woman has been involved in relational identification processes with her mother, which include identifying with a mother who has come to stand to both sexes as someone with unique capacities for mothering. Yet on a less conscious, object-relational level, having a child recreates the desired mother-child exclusivity for a woman and interrupts it for a man, just as the man's father intruded into his relation to his mother. Accordingly, as Benedek, Zilboorg, and

Bakan suggest, men often feel extremely jealous toward children.* These differences hold also on the level of sexual and biological fantasy and symbolism. A woman, as I have suggested, cannot return to the mother in coitus as directly as can a man. Symbolically her identification with the man can help. However, a much more straightforward symbolic return occurs through her identification with the child who is in her womb: "Ferenczi's 'maternal regression' is realized for the woman in equating coitus with the situation of sucking. The last act of this regression (return into the uterus) which the man accomplishes by the act of introjection in coitus, is realized by the woman in pregnancy in the complete identification between mother and child."[23]

For all these reasons, it seems psychologically logical to a woman to turn her marriage into a family, and to be more involved with these children (this child) than her husband. By doing so, she recreates for herself the exclusive intense primary unit which a heterosexual relationship tends to recreate for men. She recreates also her internalized asymmetrical relational triangle. These relational issues and needs predate and underlie her identifications, and come out of normal family structure regardless of explicit role training. Usually, however, this training intensifies their effects. In mothering, a woman acts also on her personal identification with a mother who parents and her own training for women's role.

This account indicates a larger structural issue regarding the way in which a woman's relation to her children recreates the psychic situation of the relationship to her mother. This relationship is recreated on two levels: most deeply and unconsciously, that of the primary mother-infant tie; and upon this, the relationship of the bisexual triangle. Because the primary mother-infant unit is exclusive, and because oscillation in the bisexual triangle includes a constant pull back to the mother attachment, there may be a psychological contradiction for a woman between interest in and commitment to children and that to men. Insofar as a woman experiences her relationship to her child on the level of intrapsychic structure as exclusive, her relationship to a man may therefore be superfluous.

Freud points tentatively to this (to him, unwelcome) situation, in contrasting men's and women's object-love. In his essay "On Narcissism," he claims that "complete object-love of the attachment type is, properly speaking, characteristic of the male."[24] Women, by contrast, tend to love narcissistically—on one level, to want to be loved or to be largely self-sufficient; on another, to love someone as an extension of their self rather than a differentiated object. He implies here that the necessary mode of relating to infants is the normal way women love. Yet he also claims that women do attain true object love, but only in relation to their children—who are both part of them and separate. Freud's stance here seems to be that of the excluded man viewing women's potential psychological self-sufficiency vis-à-vis *men*. This situation may be the basis of the early psychoanalytic claim that women are more narcissistic than men, since clinically it is clear that men have just as many and as serious problems of fundamental object-relatedness as do women.[25]

Clinical accounts reveal this contradiction between male-female and mother-child love. Fliess and Deutsch point to the extreme case where children are an exclusively

---

*   This is not to deny the conflicts and resentments which women may feel about their children.

mother-daughter affair.[26] Some women fantasize giving their mother a baby, or even having one from her. These are often teenage girls with extreme problems of attachment and separation in relation to their mothers, whose fathers were more or less irrelevant in the home. Often a girl expresses this fantasy through either not knowing who the father of her baby is, or knowing and not caring. Her main object is to take her baby home to her mother.

Deutsch points out that in women's fantasies and dreams, sexuality and eroticism are often opposed to motherhood and reproduction.[27] She reports clinical and literary cases of women who choose either sexuality or motherhood exclusively, mothers for whom sexual satisfactions become insignificant, women with parthenogenic fantasies. Benedek and Winnicott observe that the experience of pregnancy, and the anticipation of motherhood, often entail a withdrawal of a woman's interest from other primary commitments to her own body and developing child. As Benedek puts it, "The woman's interest shifts from extraverted activities to her body and its welfare. Expressed in psychodynamic terms: the libido is withdrawn from external, heterosexual objects, becomes concentrated upon the self."[28]

This libidinal shift may continue after birth. Psychological and libidinal gratifications from the nursing relationship may substitute for psychological and libidinal gratifications formerly found in heterosexual involvements.[29] The clinical findings and theoretical claims of Bakan, Benedek, and Zilboorg concerning men's jealousy of their children confirm this as a possibility.

On the level of the relational triangle also, there can be a contradiction between women's interest in children and in men. This is evident in Freud's suggestion that women oscillate psychologically between a preoedipal and oedipal stance (he says between periods of "masculinity" and "femininity") and that women's and men's love is a phase apart psychologically (that a woman is more likely to love her son than her husband). Deutsch points out that a man may or may not be psychologically necessary or desirable to the mother-child exclusivity. When she is oriented to the man, a woman's fantasy of having children is "I want a child by him, *with him*"; when men are emotionally in the background, it is "I want a *child*."[30]

Women come to want and need primary relationships to children. These wants and needs result from wanting intense primary relationships, which men tend not to provide both because of their place in women's oedipal constellation and because of their difficulties with intimacy. Women's desires for intense primary relationships tend not to be with other women, both because of internal and external taboos on homosexuality, and because of women's isolation from their primary female kin (especially mothers) and other women.

As they develop these wants and needs, women also develop the capacities for participating in parent-child relationships. They develop capacities for mothering. Because of the structural situation of parenting, women remain in a primary, preoedipal relationship with their mother longer than men. They do not feel the need to repress or cut off the capacity for experiencing the primary identification and primary love which are the basis of parental empathy. Also, their development and oedipal resolution do not require the ego defense against either regression or relation which characterizes masculine development. Women also tend to remain bound up in preoedipal issues in relation to their own mother, so that they in fact have some unconscious investment in reactivating them. When they have a child, they are more liable than a man to do so. In each critical period of their child's development, the parent's own development conflicts and experiences of that period affect their attitudes and behavior.[31] The preoedipal relational stance, latent in women's normal relationship to the world and experience of self, is activated in their coming to care for an infant, encouraging their empathic identification with this infant which is the basis of maternal care.

Mothering, moreover, involves a double identification for women, both as mother *and* as child. The whole preoedipal relationship has been internalized and perpetuated in a more ongoing way for women than for men. Women take both parts in it. Women have capacities for primary identification with their child through regression to primary love and empathy. Through their mother identification, they have ego capacities and the sense of responsibility which go into caring for children. In addition, women have an investment in mothering in order to make reparation to their own mother (or to get back at her). Throughout their development, moreover, women have been building layers of identification with their mothers upon the primary internalized mother-child relationship.[32]

Women develop capacities for mothering from their object-relational stance. This stance grows out of the special nature and length of their preoedipal relationship to their mother; the nonabsolute repression of oedipal relationships; and their general ongoing mother-daughter preoccupation as they are growing up. It also develops because they have not formed the same defenses against relationships as men. Related to this, they develop wants and needs to be mothers from their oedipal experience and the contradictions in heterosexual love that result.

The *wants and needs* which lead women to become mothers put them in situations where their mothering *capacities* can be expressed. At the same time, women remain in conflict with their internal mother and often their real mother as well. The preoccupation with issues of separation and primary identification, the ability to recall their early relationship to their mother—precisely those capacities which enable mothering—are also those which may lead to over-identification and pseudoempathy based on maternal projection rather than any real perception or understanding of their infant's needs.[33] Similarly, the need for primary relationships becomes more prominent and weighted as relationships to other women become less possible and as father/husband absence grows. Though women come to mother, and to be mothers, the very capacities and commitments for mothering can be in contradiction one with the other and within themselves. Capacities which enable mothering are also precisely those which can make mothering problematic.

GENDER PERSONALITY AND THE REPRODUCTION OF MOTHERING

In spite of the apparently close tie between women's capacities for childbearing and lactation on the one hand and their responsibilities for child care on the other, and in spite of the probable prehistoric convenience (and perhaps survival necessity) of a sexual division of labor in which women mothered, biology and instinct do not provide adequate explanations for how women come to mother. Women's mothering as a feature of social structure requires an explanation in terms of social structure. Conventional feminist and social psychological explanations for the genesis of gender roles—girls and boys are "taught" appropriate behaviors and "learn" appropriate feelings—are insufficient both empirically and methodologically to account for how women become mothers.

Methodologically, socialization theories rely inappropriately on individual intention. Ongoing social structures include the means for their own reproduction—in the regularized repetition of social processes, in the perpetuation of conditions which require members' participation, in the genesis of legitimating ideologies and institutions, and in the psychological as well as physical reproduction of people to perform necessary roles. Accounts of socialization help to explain the perpetuation of ideologies about gender roles. However, notions of appropriate behavior, like coercion, cannot in themselves produce parenting. Psychological capacities and a particular object-relational stance are central and definitional to parenting in a way that they are not to many other roles and activities.

Women's mothering includes the capacities for its own reproduction. This reproduction consists in the production of women with, and men without, the particular psychological capacities and stance which go into primary parenting. Psychoanalytic theory provides us with a theory of social reproduction that explains major features of personality development and the development of psychic structure, and the differential development of gender personality in particular. Psychoanalysts argue that personality both results from and consists in the ways a child appropriates, internalizes, and organizes early experiences in their family—from the fantasies they have, the defenses they use, the ways they channel and redirect drives in this object-relational context. A person subsequently imposes this intrapsychic structure, and the fantasies, defenses, and relational modes and preoccupations which go with it, onto external social situations. This reexternalization (or mutual reexternalization) is a major constituting feature of social and interpersonal situations themselves.

Psychoanalysis, however, has not had an adequate theory of the reproduction of mothering. Because of the teleological assumption that anatomy is destiny, and that women's destiny includes primary parenting, the ontogenesis of women's mothering has been largely ignored, even while the genesis of a wide variety of related disturbances and problems has been accorded widespread clinical attention. Most psychoanalysts agree that the basis for parenting is laid for both genders in the early relationship to a primary caretaker. Beyond that, in order to explain why *women* mother, they tend to rely on vague notions of a girl's subsequent identification with her mother, which makes her and not her brother a primary parent, or on an unspecified and uninvestigated innate femaleness in girls, or on logical leaps from lactation or early vaginal sensations to caretaking abilities and commitments.

The psychoanalytic account of male and female development, when reinterpreted, gives us a developmental theory of the reproduction of women's mothering. Women's mothering reproduces itself through differing object-relational experiences and differing psychic outcomes in women and men. As a result of having been parented by a woman, women are more likely than men to seek to be mothers, that is, to relocate themselves in a primary mother-child relationship, to get gratification from the mothering relationship, and to have psychological and relational capacities for mothering.

The early relation to a primary caretaker provides in children of both genders both the basic capacity to participate in a relationship with the features of the early parent-child one, and the desire to create this intimacy. However, because women mother, the early experience and preoedipal relationship differ for boys and girls. Girls retain more concern with early childhood issues in relation to their mother, and a sense of self involved with these issues. Their attachments therefore retain more preoedipal aspects. The greater length and different nature of their preoedipal experience, and their continuing preoccupation with the issues of this period, mean that women's sense of self is continuous with others and that they retain capacities for primary identification, both of which enable them to experience the empathy and lack of reality sense needed by a cared-for infant. In men, these qualities have been curtailed, both because they are early treated as an opposite by their mother and because their later attachment to her must be repressed. The relational basis for mothering is thus extended in women, and inhibited in men, who experience themselves as more separate and distinct from others.

The different structure of the feminine and masculine oedipal triangle and process of oedipal experience that results from women's mothering contributes further to gender personality differentiation and the reproduction of women's mothering. As a result of this experience, women's inner object world, and the affects and issues associated with it, are more actively sustained and more complex than men's. This means that women define and experience themselves relationally. Their heterosexual orientation is always in internal dialogue with both oedipal and preoedipal mother-child relational issues. Thus, women's heterosexuality is triangular and requires a third person—a child—for its structural and emotional completion. For men, by contrast, the heterosexual relationship alone recreates the early bond to their mother; a child interrupts it. Men, moreover, do not define themselves in relationship and have come to suppress relational capacities and repress relational needs. This prepares them to participate in the affect-denying world of alienated work, but not to fulfill women's needs for intimacy and primary relationships.

The oedipus complex, as it emerges from the asymmetrical organization of parenting, secures a psychological taboo on parent-child incest and pushes boys and girls in the direction of extrafamilial heterosexual relationships. This is one step toward the reproduction of parenting. The creation and maintenance of the incest taboo and of heterosexuality in girls and boys are different, however. For boys, superego formation and identification with their father, rewarded by the superiority of masculinity, maintain the taboo on incest with their mother, while heterosexual orientation continues from their earliest love relation with her. For girls, creating them as heterosexual in the first place maintains the taboo. However, women's heterosexuality is not so exclusive as men's. This makes it easier for them to accept or seek a male substitute for their fathers. At the same time, in a male-dominant society, women's exclusive emotional heterosexuality is not so necessary, nor is her repression of love for her father. Men are more likely to initiate relationships, and women's economic dependence on men pushes them anyway into heterosexual marriage.

Male dominance in heterosexual couples and marriage solves the problem of women's lack of heterosexual commitment and lack of satisfaction by making women more reactive in the sexual bonding process. At the same time, contradictions in heterosexuality help to perpetuate families and parenting by ensuring that women will seek relations to children and will not find heterosexual relationships alone satisfactory. Thus, men's lack of emotional availability and women's less exclusive heterosexual commitment help ensure women's mothering.

Women's mothering, then, produces psychological self-definition and capacities appropriate to mothering in women, and curtails and inhibits these capacities and this self-definition in men. The early experience of being cared for by a woman produces a fundamental structure of expectations in women and men concerning mothers' lack of separate interests from their infants and total concern for their infants' welfare. Daughters grow up identifying with these mothers, about whom they have such expectations. This set of expectations is generalized to the assumption that women naturally take care of children of all ages and the belief that women's "maternal" qualities can and should be extended to the nonmothering work that they do. All these results of women's mothering have ensured that women will mother infants and will take continuing responsibility for children.

The reproduction of women's mothering is the basis for the reproduction of women's location and responsibilities in the domestic sphere. This mothering, and its generalization to women's structural location in the domestic sphere, links the contemporary social organization of gender and social organization of production and contributes to the reproduction of each. That women mother as a fundamental organizational feature of the sex-gender system: It is basic to the sexual division of labor and generates a psychology and ideology of male dominance as well as an ideology about women's capacities and nature. Women, as wives and mothers, contribute as well to the daily and generational reproduction, both physical and psychological, of male workers and thus to the reproduction of capitalist production.

Women's mothering also reproduces the family as it is constituted in male-dominant society. The sexual and familial division of labor in which women mother creates a sexual division of psychic organization and orientation. It produces socially gendered women and men who enter into asymmetrical heterosexual relationships; it produces men who react to, fear, and act superior to women, and who put most of their energies into the nonfamilial work world and do not parent. Finally, it produces women who turn their energies toward nurturing and caring for children—in turn reproducing the sexual and familial division of labor in which women mother.

Social reproduction is thus asymmetrical. Women in their domestic role reproduce men and children physically, psychologically, and emotionally. Women in their domestic role as houseworkers reconstitute themselves physically on a daily basis and reproduce themselves as mothers, emotionally and psychologically, in the next generation. They thus contribute to the perpetuation of their own social roles and position in the hierarchy of gender.

Institutionalized features of family structure and the social relations of reproduction reproduce themselves. A psychoanalytic investigation shows that women's mothering capacities and commitments, and the general psychological capacities and wants which are the basis of women's emotion work, are built developmentally into feminine personality. Because women are themselves mothered by women, they grow up with the relational capacities and needs, and psychological definition of self-in-relationship, which commits them to mothering. Men, because they are mothered by women, do not. Women mother daughters who, when they become women, mother.

NOTES

1. Some of the material in this section appeared previously in Nancy Chodorow, 1976, "Oedipal Asymmetries and Heterosexual Knots," *Social Problems* 23, # 4. pp. 454–468.
2. Deutsch, 1925, "The Psychology of Woman," p. 165.
3. Ibid.
4. This claim comes from my reading of ethnographic literature and is confirmed by anthropologist Michelle Z. Rosaldo (personal communication).
5. Michael Balint, 1935, "Critical Notes on the Theory," p. 50.
6. Michael Balint, 1956a, "Perversions and Genitality," in *Primary Love and Psycho-Analytic Technique*, p. 141. Balint follows Sandor Ferenczi here (1924, *Thalassa: A Theory of Genitality*.
7. Freud, 1931, "Female Sexuality."
8. See Freedman, 1961, "On Women Who Hate," for an excellent clinical account of this.
9. See Chasseguet-Smirgel, 1964, "Feminine Guilt," and Grunberger, 1964, "Outline for a Study."
10. For sociological confirmation of this, see William M. Kephart, 1967, "Some Correlates of Romantic Love." *Journal of Marriage and the Family*, 29, pp. 479–474, and Zick Rubin, 1970. "Measurement of Romantic Love," *Journal of Personality and Social Psychology*, 6, pp. 265–273.
11. Chasseguet-Smirgel, 1964, "Feminine Guilt," and Grunberger, 1964, "Outline for a Study."
12. Alan Booth (1972, "Sex and Social Participation," *American Sociological Review*, 37, pp. 183–193) reports that women's friendships in our society are affectively richer than men's. Along the same lines, Mirra Komarovsky (1974, "Patterns of Self-Disclosure of Male Undergraduates," *Journal of Marriage and the Family*, 36, # 4, pp. 677–686) found that men students confided more in a special woman friend and that they maintained a front of strength with men. Moreover, these men felt at a disadvantage vis-à-vis their woman confidante, because she tended to have a number of other persons in whom she could confide.
13. Grunberger, 1964, "Outline for a Study," p. 74.
14. See Martha Baum, 1971, "Love, Marriage and the Division of Labor," *Sociological Inquiry* 41, #1, pp. 107–117; Arlie Russell Hochschild, 1975a, "Attending to,

being rediscovered in the social sciences. This discovery occurs when theories formerly considered to be sexually neutral in their scientific objectivity are found instead to reflect a consistent observational and evaluative bias. Then the presumed neutrality of science, like that of language itself, gives way to the recognition that the categories of knowledge are human constructions. The fascination with point of view that has informed the fiction of the twentieth century and the corresponding recognition of the relativity of judgment infuse our scientific understanding as well when we begin to notice how accustomed we have become to seeing life through men's eyes.

A recent discovery of this sort pertains to the apparently innocent classic *The Elements of Style* by William Strunk and E. B. White. The Supreme Court ruling on the subject of discrimination in classroom texts led one teacher of English to notice that the elementary rules of English usage were being taught through examples which counterposed the birth of Napoleon, the writings of Coleridge, and statements such as "He was an interesting talker. A man who had traveled all over the world and lived in half a dozen countries," with "Well, Susan, this is a fine mess you are in" or, less drastically, "He saw a woman, accompanied by two children, walking slowly down the road."

Psychological theorists have fallen as innocently as Strunk and White into the same observational bias. Implicitly adopting the male life as the norm, they have tried to fashion women out of a masculine cloth. It all goes back, of course, to Adam and Eve—a story which shows, among other things, that if you make a woman out of a man, you are bound to get into trouble. In the life cycle, as in the Garden of Eden, the woman has been the deviant.

The penchant of developmental theorists to project a masculine image, and one that appears frightening to women, goes back at least to Freud (1905), who built his theory of psychosexual development around the experiences of the male child that culminate in the Oedipus complex. In the 1920s, Freud struggled to resolve the contradictions posed for his theory by the differences in female anatomy and the different configuration of the young girl's early family relationships. After trying to fit women into his masculine conception, seeing them as envying that which they missed, he came instead to acknowledge, in the strength and persistence of women's pre-Oedipal attachments to their mothers, a developmental difference. He considered this difference in women's development to be responsible for what he saw as women's developmental failure.

Having tied the formation of the superego or conscience to castration anxiety, Freud considered women to be deprived by nature of the impetus for a clear-cut Oedipal resolution. Consequently, women's superego—the heir to the Oedipus complex—was compromised: it was never "so inexorable, so impersonal, so independent of its emotional origins as we require it to be in men." From this observation of difference, that "for women the level of what is ethically normal is different from what it is in men," Freud concluded that women "show less sense of justice than men, that they are less ready to submit to the great exigencies of life, that they are more often influenced in their judgments by feelings of affection or hostility" (1925, pp. 257–258).

Thus a problem in theory became cast as a problem in women's development, and the problem in women's development was located in their experience of relationships. Nancy Chodorow (1974), attempting to account for "the reproduction within each generation of certain general and nearly universal differences that characterize masculine and feminine personality and roles," attributes these differences between the sexes not to anatomy but rather to "the fact that women, universally, are largely responsible for early child care." Because this early social environment differs for and is experienced differently by male and female children, basic sex differences recur in personality development. As a result, "in any given society, feminine personality comes to define itself in relation and connection to other people more than masculine personality does" (pp. 43–44).

In her analysis, Chodorow relies primarily on Robert Stoller's studies which indicate that gender identity, the unchanging core of personality formation, is "with rare exception firmly and irreversibly established for both sexes by the time a child is around three." Given that for both sexes the primary caretaker in the first three years of life is typically female, the interpersonal dynamics of gender identity formation are different for boys and girls. Female identity formation takes place in a context of ongoing relationship since "mothers tend to experience their daughters as more like, and continuous with, themselves." Correspondingly, girls, in identifying themselves as female, experience themselves as like their mothers, thus fusing the experience of attachment with the process of identity formation. In contrast, "mothers experience their sons as a male opposite," and boys, in defining themselves as masculine, separate their mothers from themselves, thus curtailing "their primary love and sense of empathic tie." Consequently, male development entails a "more emphatic individuation and a more defensive firming of experienced ego boundaries." For boys, but not girls, "issues of differentiation have become intertwined with sexual issues" (1978, pp. 150, 166–167).

Writing against the masculine bias of psychoanalytic theory, Chodorow argues that the existence of sex differences in the early experiences of individuation and relationship "does not mean that women have 'weaker' ego boundaries than men or are more prone to psychosis." It means instead that "girls emerge from this period with a basis for 'empathy' built into their primary definition of self in a way that boys do not." Chodorow thus replaces Freud's negative and derivative description of female psychology with a positive and direct account of her own: "Girls emerge with a stronger basis for experiencing another's needs or feelings as one's own (or of thinking that one is so experiencing another's needs and feelings). Furthermore, girls do not define themselves in terms of the denial of preoedipal relational modes to the same extent as do boys. Therefore, regression to these modes tends not to feel as much a basic threat to their ego. From very early, then, because they are parented by a person of the same gender . . . girls come to experience themselves as less differentiated than boys, as more continuous with and related to the external object-world, and as differently oriented to their inner object-world as well" (p. 167).

Consequently, relationships, and particularly issues of dependency, are experienced differently by women and men. For boys and men, separation and individuation are critically tied to gender identity since separation from the mother is essential for the development of masculinity. For girls and women, issues of femininity or feminine identity do not depend on the achievement of separation from the mother or on the progress of individuation. Since masculinity is defined through separation while femininity is defined through attachment, male gender identity is threatened by intimacy while female gender identity is threatened by separation. Thus males tend to have difficulty with relationships, while females tend to have problems with individuation. The quality of embeddedness in social interaction and personal relationships that characterizes women's lives in contrast to men's, however, becomes not only a descriptive difference but also a developmental liability when the milestones of childhood and adolescent development in the psychological literature are markers of increasing separation. Women's failure to separate then becomes by definition a failure to develop.

The sex differences in personality formation that Chodorow describes in early childhood appear during the middle childhood years in studies of children's games. Children's games are considered by George Herbert Mead (1934) and Jean Piaget (1932) as the crucible of social development during the school years. In games, children learn to take the role of the other and come to see themselves through another's eyes. In games, they learn respect for rules and come to understand the ways rules can be made and changed.

Janet Lever (1976), considering the peer group to be the agent of socialization during the elementary school years and play to be a major activity of socialization at that time, set out to discover whether there are sex differences in the games that children play. Studying 181 fifth-grade, white, middle-class children, ages ten and eleven, she observed the organization and structure of their play-time activities. She watched the children as they played at school during recess and in physical education class, and in addition kept diaries of their accounts as to how they spent their out-of-school time. From this study, Lever reports sex differences: boys play out of doors more often than girls do; boys play more often in large and age-heterogeneous groups; they play competitive games more often, and their games last longer than girls' games. The last is in some ways the most interesting finding. Boys' games appeared to last longer not only because they required a higher level of skill and were thus less likely to become boring, but also because, when disputes arose in the course of a game, boys were able to resolve the disputes more effectively than girls: "During the course of this study, boys were seen quarrelling all the time, but not once was a game terminated because of a quarrel and no game was interrupted for more than seven minutes. In the gravest debates, the final word was always, to 'repeat the play,' generally followed by a chorus of 'cheater's proof'" (p. 482). In fact, it seemed that the boys enjoyed the legal debates as much as they did the game itself, and even marginal players of lesser size or skill participated equally in these recurrent squabbles. In contrast, the eruption of disputes among girls tended to end the game.

Thus Lever extends and corroborates the observations of Piaget in his study of the rules of the game, where he finds boys becoming through childhood increasingly fascinated with the legal elaboration of rules and the development of fair procedures for adjudicating conflicts, a fascination that, he notes, does not hold for girls. Girls, Piaget observes, have a more "pragmatic" attitude toward rules, "regarding a rule as good as long as the game repaid it" (p. 83). Girls are more tolerant in their attitudes toward rules, more willing to make exceptions, and more easily reconciled to innovations. As a result, the legal sense, which Piaget considers essential to moral development, "is far less developed in little girls than in boys" (p. 77).

The bias that leads Piaget to equate male development with child development also colors Lever's work. The assumption that shapes her discussion of results is that the male model is the better one since it fits the requirements for modern corporate success. In contrast, the sensitivity and care for the feelings of others that girls develop through their play have little market value and can even impede professional success. Lever implies that, given the realities of adult life, if a girl does not want to be left dependent on men, she will have to learn to play like a boy.

To Piaget's argument that children learn the respect for rules necessary for moral development by playing rule-bound games, Lawrence Kohlberg (1969) adds that these lessons are most effectively learned through the opportunities for role-taking that arise in the course of resolving disputes. Consequently, the moral lessons inherent in girls' play appear to be fewer than in boys'. Traditional girls' games like jump rope and hopscotch are turn-taking games, where competition is indirect since one person's success does not necessarily signify another's failure. Consequently, disputes requiring adjudication are less likely to occur. In fact, most of the girls whom Lever interviewed claimed that when a quarrel broke out, they ended the game. Rather than elaborating a system of rules for resolving disputes, girls subordinated the continuation of the game to the continuation of relationships.

Lever concludes that from the games they play, boys learn both the independence and the organizational skills necessary for coordinating the activities of large and diverse groups of people. By participating in controlled and socially approved competitive situations, they learn to deal with competition in a relatively forthright manner—to play with their enemies and to compete with their friends—all in accordance with the rules of the game. In contrast, girls' play tends to occur in smaller, more intimate groups, often the best-friend dyad, and in private places. This play replicates the social pattern of primary human relationships in that its organization is more cooperative. Thus, it points less, in Mead's terms, toward learning to take the role of "the generalized other," less toward the abstraction of human relationships. But it fosters the development of the empathy and sensitivity necessary for taking the role of "the particular other" and points more toward knowing the other as different from the self.

The sex differences in personality formation in early childhood that Chodorow derives from her analysis of the mother-child relationship are thus extended by Lever's observations of sex differences in the play activities of middle childhood. Together these accounts suggest that boys and girls arrive at puberty with a different interpersonal orientation and a different range of social experiences. Yet, since adolescence is considered a crucial time for separation, the period of "the second individuation process" (Blos, 1967), female development has appeared most divergent and thus most problematic at this time.

"Puberty," Freud says, "which brings about so great an accession of libido in boys, is marked in girls by a fresh wave of *repression*," necessary for the transformation of the young girl's "masculine sexuality" into the specifically feminine sexuality of her adulthood (1905, pp. 220–221). Freud posits this transformation on the girl's acknowledgment and acceptance of "the fact of her castration" (1931, p. 229). To the girl, Freud explains, puberty brings a new awareness of "the wound to her narcissism" and leads her to develop, "like a scar, a sense of inferiority" (1925, p. 253). Since in Erik Erikson's expansion of Freud's psychoanalytic account, adolescence is the time when development hinges on identity, the girl arrives at this juncture either psychologically at risk or with a different agenda.

The problem that female adolescence presents for theorists of human development is apparent in Erikson's scheme. Erikson (1950) charts eight stages of psychosocial development, of which adolescence is the fifth. The task at this stage is to forge a coherent sense of self, to verify an identity that can span the discontinuity of puberty and make possible the adult capacity to love and work. The preparation for the successful resolution of the adolescent identity crisis is delineated in Erikson's description of the crises that characterize the preceding four stages. Although the initial crisis in infancy of "trust versus mistrust" anchors development in the experience of relationship, the task then clearly becomes one of individuation. Erikson's second stage centers on the crisis of "autonomy versus shame and doubt," which marks the walking child's emerging sense of separateness and agency. From there, development goes on through the crisis of "initiative versus guilt," successful resolution of which represents a further move in the direction of autonomy. Next, following the inevitable disappointment of the magical wishes of the Oedipal period, children realize that to compete with their parents, they must first join them and learn to do what they do so well. Thus in the middle childhood years, development turns on the crisis of "industry versus inferiority," as the demonstration of competence becomes critical to the child's developing self-esteem. This is the time when children strive to learn and master the technology of their culture, in order to recognize themselves and to be recognized by others as capable of becoming adults. Next comes adolescence, the celebration of the autonomous, initiating, industrious self through the forging of an identity based on an ideology that can support and justify adult commitments. But about whom is Erikson talking?

Once again it turns out to be the male child. For the female, Erikson (1968) says, the sequence is a bit different. She holds her identity in abeyance as she prepares to attract the man by whose name she will be known, by whose status she will be defined, the man who will rescue her from emptiness and loneliness by filling "the inner space." While for men, identity precedes intimacy and generativity in the optimal cycle of human separation and attachment, for women these tasks seem instead to be fused. Intimacy goes along with identity, as the female comes to know herself as she is known, through her relationships with others.

Yet despite Erikson's observation of sex differences, his chart of life-cycle stages remains unchanged: identity continues to precede intimacy as male experience continues to define his life-cycle conception. But in this male life cycle there is little preparation for the intimacy of the first adult stage. Only the initial stage of trust versus mistrust suggests the type of mutuality that Erikson means by intimacy and generativity and Freud means by genitality. The rest is separateness, with the result that development itself comes to be identified with separation, and attachments appear to be developmental impediments, as is repeatedly the case in the assessment of women.

Erikson's description of male identity as forged in relation to the world and of female identity as awakened in a relationship of intimacy with another person is hardly new. In the fairy tales that Bruno Bettleheim (1976) describes an identical portrayal appears. The dynamics of male adolescence are illustrated archetypically by the conflict between father and son in "The Three Languages." Here a son, considered hopelessly stupid by his father, is given one last chance at education and sent for a year to study with a master. But when he returns, all he has learned is "what the dogs bark." After two further attempts of this sort, the father gives up in disgust and orders his servants to take the child into the forest and kill him. But the servants, those perpetual rescuers of disowned and abandoned children, take pity on the child and decide simply to leave him in the forest. From there, his wanderings take him to a land beset by furious dogs whose barking permits nobody to rest and who periodically devour one of the inhabitants. Now it turns out that our hero has learned just the right thing: he can talk with the dogs and is able to quiet them, thus restoring peace to the land. Since the other knowledge he acquires serves him equally well, he emerges triumphant from his adolescent confrontation with his father, a giant of the life-cycle conception.

In contrast, the dynamics of female adolescence are depicted through the telling of a very different story. In the world of the fairy tale, the girl's first bleeding is followed by a period of intense passivity in which nothing seems to be happening. Yet in the deep sleeps of Snow White and Sleeping Beauty, Bettelheim sees that inner concentration which he considers to be the necessary counterpart to the activity of adventure. Since the adolescent heroines awake from their sleep, not to conquer the world, but to marry the prince, their identity is inwardly and interpersonally defined. For women, in Bettelheim's as in Erikson's account, identity and intimacy are intricately conjoined. The sex differences depicted in the world of fairy tales, like the fantasy of the woman warrior in Maxine Hong Kingston's (1977) recent autobiographical novel which echoes the old stories of Troilus and Cressida and Tancred and Chlorinda, indicate repeatedly that active adventure is a male activity, and that if a woman is to embark on such endeavors, she must at least dress like a man.

These observations about sex difference support the conclusion reached by David McClelland (1975) that "sex role turns out to be one of the most important determinants of human behavior; psychologists have found sex differences in their studies from the moment they started doing empirical research." But since it is difficult to say "different" without saying "better" or "worse," since there is a tendency to construct a single scale of measurement, and since that scale has generally been derived from and standardized on the basis of men's interpretations of research data drawn predominantly or exclusively from studies of males, psychologists "have tended to regard male behavior as the 'norm' and female behavior as some kind of deviation from that norm" (p. 81). Thus, when women do not conform to the standards of psychological expectation, the conclusion has generally been that something is wrong with the women.

What Matina Horner (1972) found to be wrong with women was the anxiety they showed about competitive achievement. From the beginning, research on human motivation using the Thematic Apperception Test (TAT) was plagued by evidence of sex differences which appeared to confuse and complicate data analysis. The TAT presents for interpretation an ambiguous cue—a picture about which a story is to be written or a segment of a story that is to be completed. Such stories, in reflecting projective imagination, are considered by psychologists to reveal the ways in which people construe what they perceive, that is, the concepts and interpretations they bring to their experience and thus presumably the kind of sense that they make of their lives. Prior to Horner's work it was clear that women made a different kind of sense than men of situations of competitive achievement, that in some way they saw the situations differently or the situations aroused in them some different response.

On the basis of his studies of men, McClelland divided the concept of achievement motivation into what appeared to be its two logical components, a motive to approach success ("hope success") and a motive to avoid failure ("fear failure"). From her studies of women, Horner identified as a third category the unlikely motivation to avoid success ("fear success"). Women appeared to have a problem with competitive achievement, and that problem seemed to emanate from a perceived conflict between femininity and success, the dilemma of the female adolescent who struggles to integrate her feminine aspirations and the identifications of her early childhood with the more masculine competence she has acquired at school. From her analysis of women's completions of a story that began, "after first term finals, Anne finds herself at the top of her medical school class," and from her observation of women's performance in competitive achievement situations, Hornor reports that, "when success is likely or possible, threatened by the negative consequences they expect to follow success, young women become anxious and their positive achievement strivings become thwarted" (p. 171). She concludes that this fear "exists because for most women, the anticipation of success in competitive achievement activity, especially against men, produces anticipation of certain negative consequences, for example, threat of social rejection and loss of femininity" (1968, p. 125).

Such conflicts about success, however, may be viewed in a different light. Georgia Sassen (1980) suggests that the conflicts expressed by the women might instead indicate "a heightened perception of the 'other side' of competitive success, that is, the great emotional costs at which success achieved through competition is often gained—an understanding which, though confused, indicates some underlying sense that something is rotten in the state in which success is defined as having better grades than everyone else" (p. 15). Sassen points out that Horner found success anxiety to be present in women only when achievement was directly competitive, that is, when one person's success was at the expense of another's failure.

In his elaboration of the identity crisis, Erikson (1968) cites the life of George

Bernard Shaw to illustrate the young person's sense of being co-opted prematurely by success in a career he cannot wholeheartedly endorse. Shaw at seventy, reflecting upon his life, described his crisis at the age of twenty as having been caused not by the lack of success or the absence of recognition, but by too much of both: "I made good in spite of myself, and found, to my dismay, that Business, instead of expelling me as the worthless imposter I was, was fastening upon me with no intention of letting me go. Behold me, therefore, in my twentieth year, with a business training, in an occupation which I detested as cordially as any sane person lets himself detest anything he cannot escape from. In March 1876 I broke loose" (p. 143). At this point Shaw settled down to study and write as he pleased. Hardly interpreted as evidence of neurotic anxiety about achievement and competition, Shaw's refusal suggests to Erikson "the extraordinary workings of an extraordinary personality [coming] to the fore" (p. 144).

We might on these grounds begin to ask, not why women have conflicts about competitive success, but why men show such readiness to adopt and celebrate a rather narrow vision of success. Remembering Piaget's observation, corroborated by Lever, that boys in their games are more concerned with rules while girls are more concerned with relationships, often at the expense of the game itself—and given Chodorow's conclusion that men's social orientation is positional while women's is personal—we begin to understand why, when "Anne" becomes "John" in Horner's tale of competitive success and the story is completed by men, fear of success tends to disappear. John is considered to have played by the rules and won. He has the *right* to feel good about his success. Confirmed in the sense of his own identity as separate from those who, compared to him, are less competent, his positional sense of self is affirmed. For Anne, it is possible that the position she could obtain by being at the top of her medical school class may not, in fact, be what she wants.

"It is obvious," Virginia Woolf says, "that the values of women differ very often from the values which have been made by the other sex" (1929, p. 76). Yet, she adds, "it is the masculine values that prevail." As a result, women come to question the normality of their feelings and to alter their judgments in deference to the opinion of others. In the nineteenth century novels written by women, Woolf sees at work "a mind which was slightly pulled from the straight and made to alter its clear vision in deference to external authority." The same deference to the values and opinions of others can be seen in the judgments of twentieth century women. The difficulty women experience in finding or speaking publicly in their own voices emerges repeatedly in the form of qualification and self-doubt, but also in intimations of a divided judgment, a public assessment and private assessment which are fundamentally at odds.

Yet the deference and confusion that Woolf criticizes in women derive from the values she sees as their strength. Women's deference is rooted not only in their social subordination but also in the substance of their moral concern. Sensitivity to the needs of others and the assumption of responsibility for taking care lead women to attend to voices other than their own and to include in their judgment other points of view. Women's moral weakness, manifest in an apparent diffusion and confusion of judgment, is thus inseparable from women's moral strength, an overriding concern with relationships and responsibilities. The reluctance to judge may itself be indicative of the care and concern for others that infuse the psychology of women's development and are responsible for what is generally seen as problematic in its nature.

Thus women not only define themselves in a context of human relationship but also judge themselves in terms of their ability to care. Women's place in man's life cycle has been that of nurturer, caretaker, and helpmate, the weaver of those networks of relationships on which she in turn relies. But while women have thus taken care of men, men have, in their theories of psychological development, as in their economic arrangements, tended to assume or devalue that care. When the focus on individuation and individual achievement extends into adulthood and maturity is equated with personal autonomy, concern with relationships appears as a weakness of women rather than as a human strength (Miller, 1976).

The discrepancy between womanhood and adulthood is nowhere more evident than in the studies on sex-role stereotypes reported by Broverman, Vogel, Broverman, Clarkson, and Rosenkrantz (1972). The repeated finding of these studies is that the qualities deemed necessary for adulthood—the capacity for autonomous thinking, clear decision-making, and responsible action—are those associated with masculinity and considered undesirable as attributes of the feminine self. The stereotypes suggest a splitting of love and work that relegates expressive capacities to women while placing instrumental abilities in the masculine domain. Yet looked at from a different perspective, these stereotypes reflect a conception of adulthood that is itself out of balance, favoring the separateness of the individual self over connection to others, and leaning more toward an autonomous life of work than toward the interdependence of love and care.

The discovery now being celebrated by men in mid-life of the importance of intimacy, relationships, and care is something that women have known from the beginning. However, because that knowledge in women has been considered "intuitive" or "instinctive," a function of anatomy coupled with destiny, psychologists have neglected to describe its development. In my research, I have found that women's moral development centers on the elaboration of that knowledge and thus delineates a critical line of psychological development in the lives of both of the sexes. The subject of moral development not only provides the final illustration of the reiterative pattern in the observation and assessment of sex differences in the literature on human development, but also indicates more particularly why the nature and significance of women's development has been for so long obscured and shrouded in mystery.

The criticism that Freud makes of women's sense of justice, seeing it as compromised in its refusal of blind impartiality, reappears not only in the work of Piaget but also in that of Kohlberg. While in Piaget's account (1932) of the moral judgment of the child, girls are an aside, a curiosity to whom he devotes four brief entries in an index that omits "boys" altogether because "the child" is assumed to be male, in the research from which Kohlberg derives his theory, females simply do not exist. Kohlberg's (1958, 1981) six stages that describe the development of moral judgment from childhood to adulthood are based empirically on a study of eighty-four boys whose development Kohlberg has followed for a period of over twenty years.

Although Kohlberg claims universality for his stage sequence, those groups not included in his original sample rarely reach his higher stages (Edwards, 1975; Holstein, 1976; Simpson, 1974). Prominent among those who thus appear to be deficient in moral development when measured by Kohlberg's scale are women, whose judgments seem to exemplify the third stage of his six-stage sequence. At this stage morality is conceived in interpersonal terms and goodness is equated with helping and pleasing others. This conception of goodness is considered by Kohlberg and Kramer (1969) to be functional in the lives of mature women insofar as their lives take place in the home. Kohlberg and Kramer imply that only if women enter the traditional arena of male activity will they recognize the inadequacy of this moral perspective and progress like men toward higher stages where relationships are subordinated to rules (stage four) and rules to universal principles of justice (stages five and six).

Yet herein lies a paradox, for the very traits that traditionally have defined the "goodness" of women, their care for and sensitivity to the needs of others, are those that mark them as deficient in moral development. In this version of moral development, however, the conception of maturity is derived from the study of men's lives and reflects the importance of individuation in their development. Piaget (1970), challenging the common impression that a developmental theory is built like a pyramid from its base in infancy, points out that a conception of development instead hangs from its vertex of maturity, the point toward which progress is traced. Thus, a change in the definition of maturity does not simply alter the description of the highest stage but recasts the understanding of development, changing the entire account.

When one begins with the study of women and derives developmental constructs from their lives, the outline of a moral conception different from that described by Freud, Piaget, or Kohlberg begins to emerge and informs a different description of development. In this conception, the moral problem arises from conflicting responsibilities rather than from competing rights and requires for its resolution a mode of thinking that is contextual and narrative rather than formal and abstract. This conception of morality as concerned with the activity of care centers moral development around the understanding of responsibility and relationships, just as the conception of morality as fairness ties moral development to the understanding of rights and rules.

This different construction of the moral problem by women may be seen as the critical reason for their failure to develop within the constraints of Kohlberg's system. Regarding all constructions of responsibility as evidence of a conventional moral understanding, Kohlberg defines the highest stages of moral development as deriving from a reflective understanding of human rights. That the morality of rights differs from the morality of responsibility in its emphasis on separation rather than connection, in its consideration of the individual rather than the relationship as primary, is illustrated by two responses to interview questions about the nature of morality. The first comes from a twenty-five-year-old man, one of the participants in Kohlberg's study:

[*What does the word morality mean to you?*] Nobody in the world knows the answer. I think it is recognizing the right of the individual, the rights of other individuals, not interfering with those rights. Act as fairly as you would have them treat you. I think it is basically to preserve the human being's right to existence. I think that is the most important. Secondly, the human being's right to do as he pleases, again without interfering with somebody else's rights.

[*How have your views on morality changed since the last interview?*] I think I am more aware of an individual's rights now. I used to be looking at it strictly from my point of view, just for me. Now I think I am more aware of what the individual has a right to.

Kohlberg (1973) cites this man's response as illustrative of the principled conception of human rights that exemplifies his fifth and sixth stages. Commenting on the response, Kohlberg says: "Moving to a perspective outside of that of his society, he identifies morality with justice (fairness, rights, the Golden Rule), with recognition of the rights of others as these are defined naturally or intrinsically. The human being's right to do as he pleases without interfering with somebody else's rights is a formula defining rights prior to social legislation" (pp. 29–30).

The second response comes from a woman who participated in the rights and responsibilities study. She also was twenty-five and, at the time, a third-year law student:

[*Is there really some correct solution to moral problems, or is everybody's opinion equally right?*] No, I don't think everybody's opinion is equally right. I think that in some situations there may be opinions that are equally valid, and one could conscientiously adopt one of several courses of action. But there are other situations in which I think there are right and wrong answers, that sort of inhere in the nature of existence, of all individuals here who need to live with each other to live. We need to depend on each other, and hopefully it is not only a physical need but a need of fulfilment in ourselves, that a person's life is enriched by cooperating with other people and striving to live in harmony with everybody else, and to that end, there are right and wrong, there are things which promote that end and that move away from it, and in that way it is possible to choose in certain cases among different courses of action that obviously promote or harm that goal.

[*Is there a time in the past when you would have thought about these things differently?*] Oh, yeah, I think that I went through a time when I thought that things were pretty relative, that I can't tell you what to do and you can't tell me what to do, because you've got your conscience and I've got mine.

[*When was that?*] When I was in high school. I guess that it just sort of dawned on me that my own ideas changed, and because my own judgment changed, I felt I couldn't judge another person's judgment. But now I think even when it is only the person himself who is going to be affected, I say it is wrong to the extent it doesn't cohere with what I know about human nature and what I know about you, and just from what I think is true about the operation of the universe, I could say I think you are making a mistake.

[*What led you to change, do you think?*] Just seeing more of life, just recognizing that there are an awful lot of things that are common among people. There are certain things that you come to learn promote a better life and better relationships and more personal fulfillment than other things that in general tend to do the opposite, and the things that promote these things, you would call morally right.

This response also represents a personal reconstruction of morality following a period of questioning and doubt, but the reconstruction of moral understanding is based not on the primacy and universality of individual rights, but rather on what she describes as a "very strong sense of being responsible to the world." Within this construction, the moral dilemma changes from how to exercise one's rights without interfering with the rights of others to how "to lead a moral life which includes obligations to myself and my family and people in general." The problem then becames one of limiting responsibilities without abandoning moral concern. When asked to describe herself, this women says that she values "having other people that I am tied to, and also having people that I am responsible to. I have a very strong sense of being responsible to the world, that I can't just live for my enjoyment, but just the fact of being in the world gives me an obligation to do what I can to make the world a better place to live in, no matter how small a scale that may be on." Thus while Kohlberg's subject worries about people interfering with each other's rights, this woman worries about "the possibility of omission, of your not helping others when you could help them."

The issue that this women raises is addressed by Jane Loevinger's fifth "autonomous" stage of ego development, where autonomy, placed in a context of relationships, is defined as modulating an excessive sense of responsibility through the recognition that other people have responsibility for their own destiny. The autonomous stage in Loevinger's account (1970) witnesses a relinquishing of moral dichotomies and their replacement with "a feeling for the complexity and multifaceted character of real people and real situations" (p. 6). Whereas the rights conception of morality that informs Kohlberg's principled level (stages five and six) is geared to arriving at an objectively fair or just resolution to moral dilemmas upon which all rational persons could agree, the responsibility conception focuses instead on the limitations of any particular resolution and describes the conflicts that remain.

Thus it becomes clear why a morality of rights and noninterference may appear frightening to women in its potential justification of indifference and unconcern. At the same time, it becomes clear why, from a male perspective, a mortality of responsibility appears inconclusive and diffuse, given its insistent contextual relativism. Women's moral judgments thus elucidate the pattern observed in the description of the developmental differences between the sexes, but they also provide an alternative conception of maturity by which these differences can be assessed and their implications traced. The psychology of women that has consistently been described as distinctive in its greater orientation toward relationships and interdependence implies a more contextual mode of judgment and a different moral understanding. Given the differences in women's conceptions of self and morality, women bring to the life cycle a different point of view and order human experience in terms of different priorities.

The myth of Demeter and Persephone, which McClelland (1975) cites as exemplifying the feminine attitude toward power, was associated with the Eleusinian Mysteries celebrated in ancient Greece for over two thousand years. As told in the Homeric *Hymn to Demeter*, the story of Persephone indicates the strengths of interdependence, building up resources and giving, that McClelland found in his research on power motivation to characterize the mature feminine style. Although, McClelland says, "it is fashionable to conclude that no one knows what went on in the Mysteries, it is known that they were probably the most important religious ceremonies, even partly on the historical record, which were organized by and for women, especially at the onset before men by means of the cult of Dionysos began to take them over." Thus McClelland regards the myth as "a special presentation of feminine psychology" (p. 96). It is, as well, a life-cycle story par excellence.

Persephone, the daughter of Demeter, while playing in a meadow with her girlfriends, sees a beautiful narcissus which she runs to pick. As she does so, the earth opens and she is snatched away by Hades, who takes her to his underworld kingdom. Demeter, goddess of the earth, so mourns the loss of her daughter that she refuses to allow anything to grow. The crops that sustain life on earth shrivel up, killing men and animals alike, until Zeus takes pity on man's suffering and persuades his brother to return Persephone to her mother. But before she leaves, Persephone eats some pomegranate seeds, which ensures that she will spend part of every year with Hades in the underworld.

The elusive mystery of women's development lies in its recognition of the continuing importance of attachment in the human life cycle. Woman's place in man's life cycle is to protect this recognition while the developmental litany intones the celebration of separation, autonomy, individuation, and natural rights. The myth of Persephone speaks directly to the distortion in this view by reminding us that narcissism leads to death, that the fertility of the earth is in some mysterious way tied to the continuation of the mother-daughter relationship, and that the life cycle itself arises from an alternation between the world of women and that of men. Only when life-cycle theorists divide their attention and begin to live with women as they have lived with men will their vision encompass the experience of both sexes and their theories become correspondingly more fertile.

REFERENCES

Belenky, Mary F. "Conflict and Development: A Longitudinal Study of the Impact of Abortion Decisions on Moral Judgments of Adolescent and Adult Women." PhD. Diss., Harvard University, 1978.

Bergling, Kurt. *Moral Development: The Validity of Kohlberg's Theory*. Stockholm Studies in Educational Psychology 23. Stockholm, Sweden: Almqvist and Wiksell International, 1981.

Bergman, Ingmar. *Wild Strawberries* (1957). In *Four Screen Plays of Ingmar Bergman*, trans. Lars Malmstrom and David Kushner. New York: Simon and Schuster, 1960.

Bettelheim, Bruno. "The Problem of Generations." In E. Erikson, ed., *The Challenge of Youth*. New York: Doubleday, 1965.

———. *The Uses of Enchantment*. New York: Alfred A. Knopf, 1976.

Blos, Peter. "The Second Individuation Process of Adolescence." In A. Freud, ed., *The Psychoanalytic Study of the Child*, vol. 22. New York: International Universities Press, 1967.

Broverman, I., Vogel, S., Broverman, D., Clarkson, F., and Rosenkrantz, P. "Sex-role Stereotypes: A Current Appraisal." *Journal of Social Issues* 28 (1972): 59–78.

Chekhov, Anton. *The Cherry Orchard* (1904). In *Best Plays by Chekhov*, trans. Stark Young. New York: The Modern Library, 1956.

Chodorow, Nancy. "Family Structure and Feminine Personality." In M. Z. Rosaldo and L. Lamphere, eds., *Woman, Culture and Society*. Stanford; Stanford University Press, 1974.

———. *The Reproduction of Mothering*, Berkeley: University of California Press, 1978.

Coles. Robert. *Children of Crisis*. Boston: Little, Brown, 1964.

Didion, Joan. "The Women's Movement." *New York Times Book Review*, July 30, 1972, pp. 1–2, 14.

Douvan, Elizabeth, and Adelson, Joseph. *The Adolescent Experience*. New York: John Wiley and Sons, 1966.

Drabble, Margaret. *The Waterfall*. Hammondsworth, Eng.: Pengum Books, 1969.

Edwards, Carolyn P. "Societal Complexity and Moral Development: A Kenyan Study." *Ethos* 3 (1975): 505–527.

Eliot, George. *The Mill on the Floss* (1860). New York: New American Library, 1965.

Erikson, Erik H. *Childhood and Society*. New York: W. W. Norton, 1950.

———. *Young Man Luther*. New York: W. W. Norton. 1958.

———. *Insight and Responsibility*. New York: W. W. Norton, 1964.

———. *Identity; Youth and Crisis*. New York: W. W. Norton, 1968

———. *Gandhi's Truth*. New York: W. W. Norton, 1969.

———. "Reflections on Dr. Borg's Life Cycle." Daedalus 105 (1976): 1 29. (Also in Erikson, ed., *Adulthood*. New York: W. W. Norton, 1978.)

Freud, Sigmund, *The Standard Edition of the Complete Psychological Works of Sigmund Freud*, trans. and ed. James Strachey. London: The Hogarth Press, 1961.

———. *Three Essays on the Theory of Sexuality* (1905). Vol. VII.

———. "Civilized Sexual Morality and Modern Nervous Illness" (1908). Vol. IX.

———. "On Narcissism: An Introduction" (1914). Vol. XIV.

———. "Some Psychical Consequences of the Anatomical Distinction Between the Sexes" (1925). Vol. XIX.

———. *The Question of Lay Analysis* (1926). Vol. XX.

———. *Civilization and Its Discontents* (1930/1929). Vol. XXI.

———. "Female Sexuality" (1931). Vol. XXI.

———. *New Introductory Lectures on Psycho-analysis*. (*1933/1932*). Vol. XXII.

Gilligan, Carol, "Moral Development in the College Years." In A. Chickering, ed., *The Modern American College*. San Francisco: Jossey-Bass, 1981.

Gilligan, Carol, and Belenky, Mary F. "A Naturalistic Study of Abortion Decisions." In R. Selman and R. Yando, eds., *Clinical-Developmental Psychology*. New Directions for Child Development, no. 7. San Francisco: Jossey-Bass, 1980.

Gilligan, Carol, and Murphy, John Michael, "Development from Adolescence to Adulthood: The Philosopher and the 'Dilemma of the Fact.'" In D. Kuhn, ed., *Intellectual Development Beyond Childhood*. New Directions for Child Development, no. 5. San Francisco: Jossey-Bass, 1979.

Haan, Norma. "Hypothetical and Actual Moral Reasoning in a Situation of Civil Disobedience." *Journal of Personality and Social Psychology* 32 (1975): 255–270.

Holstein, Constance. "Development of Moral Judgment. A Longitudinal Study of Males and Females." *Child Development* 47 (1976): 51–61.

Horner, Matina S. "Sex Differences in Achievement Motivation and Performance in Competitive and Noncompetitive Situations." Ph. D. Diss., University of Michigan, 1968. University Microfilms #6912135.

"Toward an Understanding of Achievement-Related Conflicts in Women." *Journal of Social Issues* 28 (1972): 157–175.

Ibsen, Henrik. *A Doll's House* (1879). In *Ibsen Plays*, trans. Peter Watts. Hammondsworth. Eng.: Penguin Books, 1965.

Joyce, James. *A Portrait of the Artist as a Young Man* (1916) New York: The Viking Press. 1956.

Kingston, Maxine Hong. *The Woman Warrior*. New York: Alfred A. Knopf, 1977.

Kohlberg, Lawrence. "The Development of Modes of Thinking and Choices in Years 10 to 16." Ph. D. Diss., University of Chicago, 1958.

———. "Stage and Sequence: The Cognitive-Development Approach to Socialization." In D. A. Goslin, ed., *Handbook of Socialization Theory and Research*. Chicago: Rand McNally, 1969.

———. "Continuities and Discontinuities in Childhood and Adult Moral Development Revisited." In *Collected Papers on Moral Development and Moral Education*. Moral Education Research Foundation, Harvard University, 1973.

———. "Moral Stages and Moralization: The Cognitive-Developmental Approach." In T. Lickona, ed., *Moral Development and Behavior: Theory, Research and Social Issues*, New York: Holt, Rinehart and Winston, 1976.

———. *The Philosophy of Moral Development*. San Francisco: Harper and Row, 1981.

Kohlberg, L., and Gilligan, C. "The Adolescent as a Philosopher: The Discovery of the Self in a Post-Conventional World." *Daedalus* 100 (1971): 1051–1086.

Kohlberg, L., and Kramer, R. "Continuities and Discontinuities in Child and Adult Moral Development." *Human Development* 12 (1969): 93–120.

Langdale, Sharry, and Gilligan, Carol. Interim Report to the National Institute of Education, 1980.

Lever, Janet. "Sex Differences in the Games Children Play." *Social Problems* 23 (1976): 478–487.

———. "Sex Differences in the Complexity of Children's Play and Games." *American Sociological Review* 43 (1978): 471–483.

Levinson, Daniel J. *The Seasons of a Man's Life*. New York: Alfred A. Knopf, 1978.

Loevinger, Jane, and Wessler, Ruth. *Measuring Ego Development*. San Francisco: Jossey Bass, 1970.

Lyons, Nona. "Seeing the Consequences: The Dialectic of Choice and Reflectivity in Human Development." Qualifying Paper, Graduate School of Education, Harvard University, 1980.

Maccoby, Eleanor, and Jacklin, Carol. *The Psychology of Sex Differences*. Stanford: Stanford University Press, 1974.

May, Robert. *Sex and Fantasy*. New York: W. W. Norton, 1980.

McCarthy, Mary. *Memories of a Catholic Girlhood*. New York: Harcourt Brace Jovanovich, 1946.

McClelland, David C. *Power: The Inner Experience*. New York: Irvington, 1975.

McClelland, D. C., Atkinson, J. W., Clark, R. A., and Lowell, E. I. *The Achievement Motive*. New York: Irvington, 1953.

Mead, George Herbert. *Mind, Self, and Society*. Chicago: University of Chicago Press, 1934.

Miller, Jean Baker. *Toward a New Psychology of Women*. Boston: Beacon Press, 1976.

Murphy, J. M., and Gilligan, C. "Moral Development in Late Adolescence and Adulthood: A Critique and Reconstruction of Kohlberg's Theory." *Human Development* 23 (1980): 77–104.

Perry, William. *Forms of Intellectual and Ethical Development in the College Years*. New York: Holt, Rinehart and Winston, 1968.

Piaget, Jean. *The Moral Judgment of the Child* (1932). New York: The Free Press, 1965.

———. *Six Psychological Studies*. New York: Viking Books, 1968.

———. *Structuralism*. New York: Basic Books, 1970.

Pollak, Susan, and Gilligan, Carol. "Images of Violence in Thematic Apperception Test Stories." *Journal of Personality and Social Psychology* 42, no. 1 (1982): 159–167.

Rubin, Lillian. *Worlds of Pain*. New York: Basic Books, 1976.

Sassen, Georgia. "Success Anxiety in Women: a Constructivist Interpretation of Its Sources and Its Significance." *Harvard Educational Review* 50 (1980): 13–25.

Schneir, Miriam, ed., *Feminism: The Essential Historical Writings*. New York: Vintage Books, 1972.

Simpson, Elizabeth L. "Moral Development Research: A Case Study of Scientific Cultural Bias." *Human Development* 17 (1974): 81–106.

Stack, Carol B. *All Our Kin*. New York: Harper and Row, 1974.

Stoller, Robert, J. "A Contribution to the Study of Gender Identity." *International Journal of Psycho-Analysis* 45 (1964): 220–226.

Strunk, William Jr., and White, E. B. *The Elements of Style* (1918). New York: Macmillan, 1958.

Terman, L., and Tyler, L. "Psychological Sex Differences." In L. Carmichael, ed., *Manual of Child Psychology*. 2nd ed. New York: John Wiley and Sons, 1954.

Tolstoy, Sophie A. *The Diary of Tolstoy's Wife, 1860–1891*, trans. Alexander Werth,

London: Victor Gollanez, 1928. (Also in M. J. Moffat and C. Painter, eds., *Revelations*. New York: Vintage Books, 1975.)

Vaillant, George E. *Adaptation to Life*. Boston: Little, Brown, 1977.

Whiting, Beatrice, and Pope, Carolyn. "A Cross-Cultural Analysis of Sex Difference in the Behavior of Children Age Three to Eleven." *Journal of Social Psychology* 91 (1973): 171–188.

Woolf, Virginia. *A Room of One's Own*. New York: Harcourt, Brace and World, 1929.

13

NANCY C. M. HARTSOCK

The Feminist Standpoint

Developing the Ground
for a Specifically Feminist Historical Materialism

The power of the Marxian critique of class domination stands as an implicit suggestion that feminists should consider the advantages of adopting a historical materialist approach to understanding phallocratic domination. A specifically feminist historical materialism might enable us to lay bare the laws of tendency which constitute the structure of patriarchy over time and to follow its development in and through the Western class societies on which Marx's interest centered. A feminist materialism might in addition enable us to expand the Marxian account to include all human activity rather than focussing on activity more characteristic of males in capitalism. The development of such a historical and materialist account is a very large task, one which requires the political and theoretical contributions of many feminists. Here I will address only the question of the epistemological underpinnings such a materialism would require. Most specifically, I will attempt to develop, on the methodological base provided by Marxian theory, an important epistemological tool for understanding and opposing all forms of domination—a feminist standpoint.

Despite the difficulties feminists have correctly pointed to in Marxian theory, there are several reasons to take over much of Marx's approach. First, I have argued elsewhere that Marx's method and the method developed by the contemporary women's movement recapitulate each other in important ways.[1] This makes it possible for feminists to take over a number of aspects of Marx's method. Here, I will adopt his distinction between appearance and essence, circulation and production, abstract and concrete, and use these distinctions between dual levels of reality to work out the theoretical forms appropriate to each level when viewed not from the standpoint of the proletariat but from a specifically feminist standpoint. In this process I will explore and expand the Marxian argument that socially mediated interaction with nature in the process of production shapes both human beings and theories of knowledge. The Marxian category of labor, including as it does both interaction with other humans and with the natural world can help to cut through the dichotomy of nature and culture, and, for feminists, can help to avoid the false choice of characterizing the situation of women as either "purely natural" or "purely social". As embodied humans we are of course inextricably both natural and social, though feminist theory to date has, for important strategic reasons, concentrated attention on the social aspect.

I set off from Marx's proposal that a correct vision of class society is available from only one of the two major class positions in capitalist society. On the basis of this meta-theoretical claim, he was able to develop a powerful critique of class domination. The power of Marx's critique depended on the epistemology and ontology supporting this meta-theoretical claim. Feminist Marxists and materialist feminists more generally have argued that the position of women is structurally different from that of men, and that the lived realities of women's lives are profoundly different from those of men.[2] They have not yet, however, given sustained attention to the epistemological consequences of such a claim. Faced with the depth of Marx's critique of capitalism, feminist analysis, as Iris Young has correctly pointed out, often

> accepts the traditional Marxian theory of production relations, historical change, and analysis of the structure of capitalism in basically unchanged form. It rightly criticizes that theory for being essentially gender-blind, and hence seeks to supplement Marxist theory of capitalism with feminist theory of a system of male domination. Taking this route, however, tacitly endorses the traditional Marxian position that "the woman question" is auxiliary to the central questions of a Marxian theory of society.[3]

By setting off from the Marxian meta-theory I am implicitly suggesting that this, rather than his critique of capitalism, can be most helpful to feminists. I will explore some of the epistemological consequences of claiming that women's lives differ structurally from those of men. In particular, I will suggest that like the lives of proletarians according to Marxian theory, women's lives make available a particular and privileged vantage point on male supremacy, a vantage point which can ground a powerful critique of the phallocratic institutions and ideology which constitute the capitalist form of patriarchy. After a summary of the nature of a standpoint as an epistemological device, I will address the question of whether one can discover a feminist standpoint on which to ground a specifically feminist historical materialism. I will suggest that the sexual division of labor forms the basis for such a standpoint and will argue that on the basis of the structures which define women's activity as contributors to subsistence and as mothers one could begin, though not complete, the construction of such an epistemological tool. I hope to show how just as Marx's understanding of the world from the standpoint of the proletariat enabled him to go beneath bourgeois ideology, so a feminist standpoint can allow us to understand patriarchal institutions and ideologies as perverse inversions of more humane social relations.

THE NATURE OF A STANDPOINT

A standpoint is not simply an interested position (interpreted as bias) but is interested in the sense of being engaged. It is true that a desire to conceal real social relations can contribute to an obscurantist account, and it is also true that the ruling gender and class have material interests in deception. A standpoint, however, carries with it the contention that there are some perspectives on society from which, however well-intentioned one may be, the real relations of humans with each other and with the natural world are not visible. This contention should be sorted into a number of distinct epistemological and political claims: (1) Material life (class position in Marxist theory) not only structures but sets limits on the understanding of social relations. (2) If material life is structured in fundamentally opposing ways for two different groups, one can expect that the vision of each will represent an inversion of the other, and in systems of domination the vision available to the rulers will be both partial and perverse. (3) The vision of the ruling class (or gender) structures the material relations in which all parties are forced to participate, and therefore cannot be dismissed as simply false. (4) In consequence, the vision available to the oppressed group must be struggled for and represents an achievement which requires both science to see beneath the surface of the social relations in which all are forced to participate, and the education which can only grow from struggle to change those relations. (5) As an engaged vision, the understanding of the oppressed, the adoption of a standpoint exposes the real relations among human beings as inhuman, points beyond the present, and carries a historically liberatory role.

The concept of a standpoint structures epistemology in a particular way. Rather than a simple dualism, it posits a duality of levels of reality, of which the deeper level or essence both includes and explains the "surface" or appearance, and indicates the logic by means of which the appearance inverts and distorts the deeper reality. In addition, the concept of a standpoint depends on the assumption that epistemology grows in a complex and contradictory way from material life. Any effort to develop a standpoint must take seriously Marx's injunction that "all mysteries which lead theory to mysticism find their rational solution in human practice and in the comprehension of this practice."[4] Marx held that the source both for the proletarian standpoint and the critique of capitalism it makes possible is to be found in practical activity itself. The epistemological (and even ontological) significance of human activity is made clear in Marx's argument not only that persons are active but that reality itself consists of "sensuous human activity, practice."[5] Thus Marx can speak of products as crystallized or congealed human activity or work, of products as conscious human activity in another form. He can state that even plants, animals, light, etc. constitute theoretically a part of human consciousness, and a part of human life and activity.[6] As Marx and Engels summarize their position,

> As individuals express their life, so they are. What they are, therefore, coincides with their production, both with *what* they produce and with *how* they produce. The nature of individuals thus depends on the material conditions determining their production.[7]

This starting point has definite consequences for Marx's theory of knowledge. If humans are not what they eat but what they do, especially what they do in the course of production of subsistence, each means of producing subsistence should be expected to carry with it *both* social relations *and* relations to the world of nature which express the social understanding contained in that mode of production. And in any society with systematically divergent practical activities, one should expect the growth of logically divergent world views. That is, each division of labor, whether by gender or class, can be expected to have consequences for knowledge. Class society, according to Marx, does produce this dual vision in the form of the ruling class vision and the understanding available to the ruled.

On the basis of Marx's description of the activity of commodity exchange in capitalism, the ways in which the dominant categories of thought simply express the mystery of the commodity form have been pointed out. These include a dependence on quantity, duality and opposition of nature to culture, a rigid separation of mind and body, intention and behavior.[8] From the perspective of exchange, where commodities differ from each other only quantitatively, it seems absurd to suggest that labor power differs from all other commodities. The sale and purchase of labor power from the perspective of capital is simply a contract between free agents, in which "the agreement [the parties] come to is but the form in which they give legal expression of their common will." It is a relation of equality.

> because each enters into relation with the other, as with a simple owner of commodities, and they exchange equivalent for equivalent. . . The only force that brings them together and puts them in relation with each other, is the selfishness, the gain and the private interests of each. Each looks to himself only, and no one troubles himself about the rest, and just because they do so, do they all, in accordance with the pre-established harmony of things, or under the auspices of an all shrewd providence, work together to their mutual advantage, for the common weal and in the interest of all.

This is the only description available within the sphere of circulation or exchange of commodities, or as Marx might put it, at the level of appearance. But at the level of production, the world looks far different. As Marx puts it,

> On leaving this sphere of simple circulation or of exchange of commodities. . .we can perceive a change in the physiognomy of our *dramatis personae*. He who before

was the money-owner, now strides in front as capitalist; the possessor of labor-power follows as his laborer. The one with an air of importance, smirking intent on business; the other timid and holding back, like one who is bringing his own hide to market and has nothing to expect but—a hiding.

This is a vastly different account of the social relations of the buyer and seller of labor power.[9] Only by following the two into the realm of production and adopting the point of view available to the worker could Marx uncover what is really involved in the purchase and sale of labor power, i.e. uncover the process by which surplus value is produced and appropriated by the capitalist, and the means by which the worker is systematically disadvantaged.[10]

If one examines Marx's account of the production and extraction of surplus value, one can see in it the elaboration of each of the claims contained in the concept of a standpoint. First, the contention that material life structures understanding points to the importance of the epistemological consequences of the opposed models of exchange and production. It is apparent that the former results in a dualism based on both the separation of exchange from use, and on the positing of exchange as the only important side of the dichotomy. The epistemological result if one follows through the implications of exchange is a series of opposed and hierarchical dualities—mind/body, ideal/material, social/natural, self/other—even a kind of solipsism—replicating the devaluation of use relative to exchange. The proletarian and Marxian valuation of use over exchange on the basis of involvement in production, in labor, results in a dialectical rather than dualist epistemology: the dialectical and interactive unity (distinction within a unity) of human and natural worlds, mind and body, ideal and material, and the cooperation of self and other (community).

As to the second claim of a standpoint, a Marxian account of exchange vs. production indicates that the epistemology growing from exchange not only inverts that present in the process of production but in addition is both partial and fundamentally perverse. The real point of the production of goods and services is, after all, the continuation of the species, a possibility dependent on their use. The epistemology embodied in exchange then, along with the social relations it expresses, not only occupies only one side of the dualities it constructs, but also reverses the proper ordering of any hierarchy in the dualisms: use is primary, not exchange.

The third claim for a standpoint indicates a recognition of the power realities operative in a community, and points to the ways the ruling group's vision may be *both* perverse *and* made real by means of that group's power to define the terms for the community as a whole. In the Marxian analysis, this power is exercised in both control of ideological production, and in the real participation of the worker in exchange. The dichotomous epistemology which grows from exchange cannot be dismissed either as simply false or as an epistemology relevant to only a few: the worker as well as the capitalist engages in the purchase and sale of commodities, and if material life structures consciousness, this cannot fail to have an effect. This leads into the fourth claim for a standpoint—that it is achieved rather than obvious, a mediated rather than immediate understanding. Because the ruling group controls the means of mental as well as physical production, the production of ideals as well as goods, the standpoint of the oppressed represents an achievement both of science (analysis) and of political struggle on the basis of which this analysis can be conducted.

Finally, because it provides the basis for revealing the perversion of both life and thought, the inhumanity of human relations, a standpoint can be the basis for moving beyond these relations. In the historical context of Marx's theory, the engaged vision available to the producers, by drawing out the potentiality available in the actuality, that is, by following up the possibility of abundance capitalism creates, leads towards transcendence. Thus, the proletariat is the only class which has the possibility of creating a classless society. It can do this simply (!) by generalizing its own condition, that is, by making society itself a propertyless producer.[11]

These are the general characteristics of the standpoint of the proletariat. What guidance can feminists take from this discussion? I hold that the powerful vision of both the perverseness and reality of class domination made possible by Marx's adoption of the standpoint of the proletariat suggests that a specifically feminist standpoint could allow for a much more profound critique of phallocratic ideologies and institutions than has yet been achieved. The effectiveness of Marx's critique grew from its uncompromising focus on material life activity, and I propose here to set out from the Marxian contention that not only are persons active, but that reality itself consists of "sensuous human activity, practice". But rather than beginning with men's labor, I will focus on women's life activity and on the institutions which structure that activity in order to raise the question of whether this activity can form the ground for a distinctive standpoint, that is, to determine whether it meets the requirements for a feminist standpoint. (I use the term feminist" rather than "female" here to indicate both the achieved character of a standpoint and that a standpoint by definition carries a liberatory potential.)

Women's work in every society differs systematically from men's. I intend to pursue the suggestion that this division of labor is the first and in some societies the only division of labor, and moreover, that it is central to the organization of social labor more generally. On the basis of an account of the sexual division of labor, one should be able to begin to explore the oppositions and differences between women's and men's activity and their consequences for epistemology. While I cannot attempt a complete account, I will put forward a schematic and simplified account of the sexual division of labor and its consequences for epistemology. I will sketch out a kind of ideal type of the social relations and world view characteristic of male and female activity in order to explore the epistemology contained in the institutionalized sexual division of labor. In so doing, I do not mean to attribute this vision to individual women or men any more than Marx (or Lukacs) meant their theory of class consciousness to apply to any particular worker or group of workers. My focus is instead on institutionalized social practices and on the specific epistemology and ontology manifested by the institutionalized sexual division of labor. Individuals, as individuals, may change their activity in ways which move them outside the outlook embodied in these institutions, but such a move can be significant only when it occurs at the level of society as a whole.

I will discuss the "sexual division of labor" rather than the "gender division of labor" to stress, first my belief that the division of labor between women and men cannot be reduced to purely social dimensions. One must distinguish between what Sara Ruddick has termed "invariant and *nearly* unchangeable" features of human life, and those which despite being "*nearly* universal" are "certainly changeable."[12] Thus, the fact that women and not men *bear* children is not (yet) a social choice, but that women and not men rear children in a society structured by compulsory heterosexuality and male dominance is clearly a societal choice. A second reason to use the term "sexual division of labor" is to keep hold of the bodily aspect of existence—perhaps to grasp it over-firmly in an effort to keep it from evaporating altogether. There is some biological, bodily component to human existence. But its size and substantive content will remain unknown until at least the certainly changeable aspects of the sexual division of labor are altered.

On a strict reading of Marx, of course, my enterprise here is illegitimate. While on the one hand, Marx remarked that the very first division of labor occurred in sexual intercourse, he argues that the division of labor only becomes "truly such" when the division of mental and manual labor appears. Thus, he dismisses the sexual division of labor as of no analytic importance. At the same time, a reading of other remarks— such as his claim that the mental/manual division of labor is based on the "natural" division of labor in the family—would seem to support the legitimacy of any attention to the sexual division of labor and even add weight to the radical feminist argument that capitalism is an outgrowth of male dominance, rather than vice versa.

On the basis of a schematic account of the sexual division of labor, I will begin to fill in the specific content of the feminist standpoint and begin to specify how women's lives structure an understanding of social relations, that is, begin to follow out the epistemological consequences of the sexual division of labor. In addressing the institutionalized sexual division of labor, I propose to lay aside the important differences among women across race and class boundaries and instead search for central commonalities. I take some justification from the fruitfulness of Marx's similar strategy in constructing a simplified, two class, two man model in which everything was exchanged at its value. Marx's schematic account in Volume I of *Capital* left out of account such factors as imperialism, the differential wages, work, and working conditions of the Irish, the differences between women, men, and children, and so on. While all of these factors are important to the analysis of contemporary capitalism, none changes either Marx's theories of surplus value or alienation, two of the most fundamental features of the Marxian analysis of capitalism. My effort here takes a similar form in an attempt to move toward a theory of the extraction and appropriation of women's activity and women themselves. Still, I adopt this strategy with some reluctance, since it contains the danger of making invisible the experience of lesbians or women of color.[13] At the same time, I recognize that the effort to uncover a feminist standpoint assumes that there are some things common to all women's lives in Western class societies.

The feminist standpoint which emerges through an examination of women's activities is related to the proletarian standpoint, but deeper going. Women and workers inhabit a world in which the emphasis is on change rather than stasis, a world characterized by interaction with natural substances rather than separation from nature, a world in which quality is more important than quantity, a world in which the unification of mind and body is inherent in the activities performed. Yet, there are some important differences, differences marked by the fact that the proletarian (if male) is immersed in this world only during the time his labor power is being used by the capitalist. If, to paraphrase Marx, we follow the worker home from the factory, we can once again perceive a change in the *dramatis personae*. He who before followed behind as the worker, timid and holding back, with nothing to expect but a hiding, now strides in front while a third person, not specifically present in Marx's account of the transaction between capitalist and worker (both of whom are male) follows timidly behind, carrying groceries, baby and diapers.

THE SEXUAL DIVISION OF LABOR

Women's activity as institutionalized has a double aspect—their contribution to subsistence, and their contribution to childrearing. Whether or not all of us do both, women as a sex are institutionally responsible for producing both goods and human beings and all women are forced to become the kinds of people who can do both. Although the nature of women's contribution to subsistence varies immensely over time and space, my primary focus here is on capitalism, with a secondary focus on the Western class societies which preceded it.[14] In capitalism, women contribute both production for wages and production of goods in the home, that is, they like men sell their labor power and produce both commodities and surplus value, and produce use-values in the home. Unlike men, however, women's lives are institutionally defined by their production of use-values in the home.[15] And here we begin to encounter the narrowness of the Marxian concept of production. Women's production of use-values in the home has not been well understood by socialists. It is no surprise to feminists that Engels, for example, simply asks how women can continue to do the work in the home and also work in production outside the home. Marx too takes for granted women's responsibility for household labor. He repeats, as if it were his own, the question of a Belgian factory inspector: If a mother works for wages, "how will [the household's] internal economy be cared for; who will look after the young children; who will get ready the meals, do the washing and mending?"[16]

Let us trace both the outlines and the consequences of woman's dual contribution to subsistence in capitalism. Women's labor, like that of the male worker, is contact with material necessity. Their contribution to subsistence, like that of the male worker, involves them in a world in which the relation to nature and to concrete human requirements is central, both in the form of interaction with natural substances whose quality, rather than quantity is important to the production of meals, clothing, etc., and in the form of close attention to the natural changes in these substances. Women's labor both for wages and even more in household production involves a unification of mind and body for the purpose of transforming natural substances into socially defined goods. This too is true of the labor of the male worker.

There are, however, important differences. First, women as a group work more than men. We are all familiar with the phenomenon of the "double day," and with indications that women work many more hours per week than men.[17] Second, a larger proportion of women's labor time is devoted to the production of use-values than men's. Only some of the goods women produce are commodities (however much they live in a society structured by commodity production and exchange). Third, women's production is structured by repetition in a different way than men's. While repetition for both the woman and the male worker may take the form of production of the same object, over and over—whether apple pies or brake linings—women's work in housekeeping involves a repetitious cleaning.[18]

Thus, the male worker in the process of production, is involved in contact with necessity, and interchange with nature as well as with other human beings but the process of production or work does not consume his whole life. The activity of a woman in the home as well as the work she does for wages keeps her continually in contact with a world of qualities and change. Her immersion in the world of use—in concrete, many-qualitied, changing material processes—is more complete than his. And if life itself consists of sensuous activity, the vantage point available to women on the basis of their contribution to subsistence represents an intensification and deepening of the materialist world view and consciousness available to the producers of commodities in capitalism, an intensification of class consciousness. The availability of this outlook to even non-working-class women has been strikingly formulated by Marilyn French in *The Women's Room*.

> Washing the toilet used by three males, and the floor and walls around it, is, Mira thought, coming face to face with necessity. And that is why women were saner than men, did not come up with the mad, absurd schemes men developed; they were in touch with necessity, they had to wash the toilet bowl and floor.[19]

The focus on women's subsistence activity rather than men's leads to a model in which the capitalist (male) lives a life structured completely by commodity exchange and not at all by production, and at the furthest distance from contact with concrete material life. The male worker marks a way station on the path to the other extreme of the constant contact with material necessity in women's contribution to subsistence. There are of course important differences along the lines of race and class. For example, working class men seem to do more domestic labor than men higher up in the class structure—car repairs, carpentry, etc. And until very recently, the wage work done by most women of color replicated the housework required by their own households. Still, there are commonalities present in the institutionalized sexual division of labor which make women responsible for both housework and wage work.

The female contribution to subsistence, however, represents only a part of women's labor. Women also produce/reproduce men (and other women) on both a daily and a long-term basis. This aspect of women's "production" exposes the deep inadequacies of the concept of production as a description of women's activity. One does not (cannot) produce another human being in anything like the way one produces an object such as a chair. Much more is involved, activity which cannot easily be dichotomized into play or work. Helping another to develop, the gradual relinquishing of control, the experience of the human limits of one's action—all these are important features of women's activity as mothers. Women as mothers even more than as workers, are institutionally involved in processes of change and growth, and more than workers, must understand the importance of avoiding excessive control in order to help others grow.[20] The activity involved is far more complex than the instrumental working with others to transform objects. (Interestingly, much of women's wage work—nursing, social work, and some secretarial jobs in particular—requires and depends on the relational and interpersonal skills women learned by being mothered by someone of the same sex.)

This aspect of women's activity too is not without consequences. Indeed, it is in the production of men by women and the appropriation of this labor and women themselves by men that the opposition between feminist and masculinist experience and outlook is rooted, and it is here that features of the proletarian vision are enhanced and modified for the woman and diluted for the man. The female experience in reproduction represents a unity with nature which goes beyond the proletarian experience of interchange with nature. As another theorist has put it," reproductive labor might be said to combine the functions of the arthitect and the bee; like the architect, parturitive woman knows what she is doing; like the bee, she cannot help what she is doing." And just as the worker's acting on the external world changes both the world and the worker's nature, so too "a new life changes the world and the consciousness of the woman."[21] In addition, in the process of producing human beings, relations with others may take a variety of forms with deeper significance than simple cooperation with others for common goals—forms which range from a deep unity with another through the many-leveled and changing connections mothers experience with growing children. Finally, the female experience in bearing and rearing children involves a unity of mind and body more profound than is possible in the worker's instrumental activity.

Motherhood in the large sense, i.e., motherhood as an institution rather than experience, including pregnancy and the preparation for motherhood almost all female children receive as socialization, results in the construction of female existence as centered with a complex relational nexus.[22] One aspect of this relational existence is centered on the experience of living in a female rather than male body. There are a series of boundary challenges inherent in the female physiology—challenges which make it impossible to maintain rigid separation from the object world. Menstruation, coitus, pregnancy, childbirth, lactation—all represent challenges to bodily boundaries.[23] Adrienne Rich has described the experience of pregnancy as one in which the embryo was both inside and

> daily more separate, on its way to becoming separate from me and of itself. In early pregnancy the stirring of the fetus felt like ghostly tremors of my own body, later like the movements of a being imprisoned in me; but both sensations were *my* sensations, contributing to my own sense of physical and psychic space.[24]

In turn, the fact that women but not men are primarily responsible for young children means that the infant first experiences itself as not fully differentiated from the mother, and then as an I in relation to an It that it later comes to know as female.[25]

Jane Flax and Nancy Chodorow have argued that the object relations school of psychoanalytic theory puts forward a materialist psychology, one which I propose to treat as a kind of empirical hypothesis. If the account of human development provided by object relations is correct, one ought to expect to find consequences—both psychic, and social. According to object relations theory, the process of differentiation from a woman by both male and female children reinforces boundary confusion in female egos and boundary strengthening in males. Individuation is far more conflictual for male than for female children, in part because both mother and son experience the other as a definite "other." The experience of oneness on the part of both mother and infant seems to last longer with girls.[26]

The complex relational world inhabited by women has its start in the experience and resolution of the oedipal crisis, cleanly resolved for the boy, whereas the girl is much more likely to retain both parents as love objects. The nature of the crisis itself differs by sex: the boy's love for the mother is an extension of mother-infant unity and thus essentially threatening to his ego and independence. Male ego-formation necessarily requires repressing this first relation and negating the mother.[27] In contrast, the girls' love for the father is less threatening both because it occurs outside this unity and because it occurs at a later stage of development. For boys, the central issue to be resolved concerns gender identification; for girls the issue is psycho-sexual development.[28] Chodorow concludes that girls' gradual emergence from the oedipal period takes place in such a way that empathy is built into their primary definition of self, and they have a variety of capacities for experiencing another's needs or feelings as their own. Put another way girls, because of female parenting, are less differentiated from others than boys, more continuous with and related to the external object world. They are differently oriented to their inner object world as well.[29]

The more complex female relational world is reinforced by the process of socialization. Girls learn roles from watching their mothers; boys must learn roles from rules which structure the life of an absent male figure. Girls can identify with a concrete example present in daily life; boys must identify with an abstract set of maxims only occasionally concretely present in the form of the father. Thus, not only do girls learn roles with more interpersonal and relational skills, but the process of role learning itself is embodied in the concrete relation with the mother. The male, in contrast, must identify with an abstract, cultural stereotype and learn abstract behaviors not attached to a well-known person. Masculinity is idealized by boys whereas femininity is concrete for girls.[30]

Women and men, then, grow up with personalities affected by different boundary experiences, differently constructed and experienced inner and outer worlds, and preoccupations with different relational issues. This early experience forms an important ground for the female sense of self as connected to the world and the male sense of self as separate, distinct, and even disconnected. By retaining the preoedipal attachment to the mother, girls come to define and experience themselves as continuous with others. In sum, girls enter adulthood with a more complex layering of affective ties and a rich, ongoing inner set of object relations. Boys, with a simpler oedipal situation and a clear and early resolution, have repressed ties to another. As a result, women define and experience themselves relationally and men do not.[31]

ABSTRACT MASCULINITY AND THE FEMINIST STANDPOINT

This excursion into psychoanalytic theory has served to point to the differences in the male and female experience of self due to the sexual division of labor in childrearing. These different (psychic) experiences both structure and are reinforced by the differing patterns of male and female activity required by the sexual division of labor, and are thereby replicated as epistemology and ontology. The differential male and female life activity in class society leads on the one hand toward a feminist standpoint and on the other toward an abstract masculinity.

Because the problem for the boy is to distinguish himself from the mother and to protect himself against the real threat she poses for his identity, his conflictual and oppositional efforts lead to the formation of rigid ego boundaries. The way Freud takes for granted the rigid distinction between the "me and not-me" makes the point well: "Normally, there is nothing of which we are more certain than the feeling of ourself, of our own ego. This ego appears to us as something autonomous and unitary, marked off distinctly from everything else." At least toward the outside, "the ego seems to maintain clear and sharp lines of demarcation."[32] Thus, the boy's construction of self in opposition to unity with the mother, his construction of identity as differentiation from the other, sets a hostile and combative dualism at the heart of both the community men construct and the masculinist world view by means of which they understand their lives.

I do not mean to suggest that the totality of human relations can be explained by psychoanalysis. Rather I want to point to the ways male rather than female experience and activity replicates itself in both the hierarchical and dualist institutions of class society and in the frameworks of thought generated by this experience. It is interesting to read Hegel's account of the relation of self and other as a statement of male experience: the relation of the two consciousnesses takes the form of a trial by death. As Hegel describes it, "each seeks the death of the other."

> Thus, the relation of the two self-conscious individuals is such that they provide themselves and each other through a life-and-death struggle. They must engage in this struggle, for they must raise their certainty for *themselves* to truth, both in the case of the other and in their own case.[33]

The construction of the self in opposition to another who threatens one's very being reverberates throughout the construction of both class society and the masculinist world view and results in a deepgoing and hierarchical dualism. First, the male experience is characterized by the duality of concrete versus abstract. Material reality as experienced by the boy in the family provides no model, and is unimportant in the attainment of masculinity. Nothing of value to the boy occurs with the family, and masculinity becomes an abstract ideal to be achieved over the opposition of daily life.[34] Masculinity must be attained by means of opposition to the concrete world of daily life, by escaping from contact with the female world of the household into the masculine world of public life. This experience of two worlds, one valuable, if abstract and deeply unattainable, the other useless and demeaning, if concrete and necessary, lies at the heart of a series of dualisms—abstract/concrete, mind/body, culture/nature, ideal/real, stasis/change. And these dualisms are overlaid by gender: only the first of each pair is associated with the male.

Dualism, along with the dominance of one side of the dichotomy over the other, marks phallocentric society and social theory. These dualisms appear in a variety of forms—in philosophy, technology, political theory, and the organization of class society itself. One can, for example, see them very clearly worked out in Plato, although they appear in many other forms.[35] There, the concrete/ abstract duality takes the form of an opposition of material to ideal, and a denial of the relevance of the material world to the attainment of what is of fundamental importance: love of knowledge, or philosophy (masculinity). The duality between nature and culture takes the form of a devaluation of work or necessity, and the primacy instead of purely social interaction for the attainment of undying fame. Philosophy itself is separate from nature, and indeed, exists only on the basis of the domination of (at least some) of the philosopher's own nature.[36] Abstract masculinity, then, can be seen to have structured Western social relations and the modes of thought to which these relations give rise at least since the founding of the *polis*.

The oedipal roots of these hierarchical dualisms are memorialized in the overlay of female and male connotations: it is not accidental that women are associated with quasi-human and non-human nature, that the female is associated with the body and material life, that the lives of women are systematically used as examples to characterize the lives of those ruled by their bodies rather than their minds.[37]

Both the fragility and fundamental falseness of the masculinist ideology and the deeply problematic nature of the social relations from which it grows are apparent in its reliance on a series of counterfactual assumptions and contentions. Consider how the following contentions are contrary to lived experience: the body is both irrelevant and in opposition to the (real) self, an impediment to be overcome by the mind; the female mind either does not exist (Do women have souls?) or works in such incomprehensible ways as to be unintelligible (the "enigma of woman"); what is real and primary is imperceptible to the senses and impervious to nature and natural change. What is remarkable is not only that these contentions have absorbed a great deal of philosophical energy, but, along with a series of other counterfactuals, have structured social relations for centuries.

Interestingly enough the epistemology and society constructed by men suffering from the effects of abstract masculinity have a great deal in common with that imposed by commodity exchange. The separation and opposition of social and natural worlds, of abstract and concrete, of permanence and change, the effort to define only the former of each pair as important, the reliance on a series of counter factual assumptions—all this is shared with the exchange abstraction. Abstract masculinity shares still another of its aspects with the exchange abstraction: it forms the basis for an even more problematic social synthesis. Hegel's analysis makes clear the problematic social relations available to the self which maintains itself by opposition: each of the two subjects struggling for recognition risks its own death in the struggle to kill the other, but if the other is killed the subject is once again alone.[38] In sum, then, the male experience when replicated as epistemology leads to a world conceived as, and (in fact) inhabited by, a number of fundamentally hostile others whom one comes to know by means of opposition (even death struggle) and yet with whom one must construct a social relation in order to survive.

The female construction of self in relation to others leads in an opposite direction—toward opposition to dualisms of any sort, valuation of concrete, everyday life, sense of a variety of connectednesses and continuities both with other persons and with the natural world. If material life structures consciousness, women's relationally defined existence, bodily experience of boundary challenges, and activity of transforming both physical objects and human beings must be expected to result in a world view to which dichotomies are foreign. Women experience others and themselves along a continuum whose dimensions are evidenced in Adrienne Rich's argument that the child carried for nine months can be defined "*neither* as me or as not-me," and she argues that inner and outer are not polar opposites but a continuum.[39] What the sexual division of labor defines as women's work turns on issues of change rather than stasis, the changes involved in producing both use-values and commodities, but more profoundly in the activity of rearing human beings who change in both more subtle and more autonomous ways than any inanimate object. Not only the qualities of things but also the qualities of people are important in women's work: quantity becomes peripheral. In addition, far more than the instrumental cooperation of the workplace is required; the mother-child relation and the maintenance of the family, while it has instrumental aspects, is not defined by them. Finally, the unity of mental and manual labor, and the directly sensuous nature of much of women's work leads to a more profound unity of mental and manual labor, social and natural worlds, than is experienced by the male worker in capitalism. The unity grows from the fact that women's bodies, unlike men's, can be themselves instruments of production: in pregnancy, giving birth or lactation, arguments about a division of mental from manual labor are fundamentally foreign.

That this is indeed women's experience is documented in both the theory and practice of the contemporary women's movement and needs no further development here.[40] The more important question here is whether female experience and the world view constructed by female activity can meet the criteria for a standpoint. If we return to the five claims carried by the concept of a standpoint, it seems clear that women's material life activity has important epistemological and ontological consequences for both the understanding and construction of social relations. Women's activity, then, does satisfy the first requirement of a standpoint.

I can now take up the second claim made by a standpoint: that the female experience not only inverts that of the male, but forms a basis on which to expose abstract masculinity as both partial and fundamentally perverse, as not only occupying only one side of the dualities it has constructed, but reversing the proper valuation of human activity. The partiality of the masculinist vision and of the societies which support this understanding is evidenced by its confinement of activity proper to the male to only one side of the dualisms. Its perverseness, however, lies elsewhere. Perhaps the most dramatic (though not the only) reversal of the proper order of things characteristic of the male experience is the substitution of death for life.

The substitution of death for life results at least in part from the sexual division of labor in childrearing. The self-surrounded by rigid ego-boundaries, certain of what is inner and what is outer, the self experienced as walled city, is discontinuous with others. Georges Bataille has made brilliantly clear the ways in which death emerges as the only possible solution to this discontinuity and has followed the logic through to argue that reproduction itself must be understood not as the creation of life, but as death. The core experience to be understood is that of discontinuity and its consequences. As a consequence of this experience of discontinuity and aloneness, penetration of ego-boundaries, or fusion with another is experienced as violent. Thus, the desire for fusion with another can take the form of domination of the other. In this form, it leads to the only possible fusion with a threatening other: when the other ceases to exist as a separate, and for that reason, threatening being. Insisting that another submit to one's will is simply a milder form of the destruction of discontinuity in the death of the other since in this case one is no longer confronting a discontinuous and opposed will, despite its discontinuous embodiment. This is perhaps one source of the links between sexual activity, domination, and death.

Bataille suggests that killing and sexual activity share both prohibitions and religious significance. Their unity is demonstrated by religious sacrifice since the latter:

> is intentional like the act of the man who lays bare, desires and wants to penetrate his victim. The lover strips the beloved of her identity no less than the blood-stained priest his human or animal victim. The woman in the hands of her assailant is despoiled of her being . . . loses the firm barrier that once separated her from others . . . is brusquely laid open to the violence of the sexual urges set loose in the organs of reproduction; she is laid open to the impersonal violence that overwhelms her from without.[41]

Note the use of the term "lover" and "assailant" as synonyms and the presence of the female as victim.

The importance of Bataille's analysis lies in the fact that it can help to make clear the links between violence, death, and sexual fusion with another, links which are not simply theoretical but actualized in rape and pornography. Images of women in chains, being beaten, or threatened with attack carry clear social messages, among them that "the normal male is sexually aggressive in a brutal and demeaning way."[42] Bataille's analysis can help to understand why "men advertise, even brag, that their movie is the 'bloodiest thing that ever happened in front of a camera'."[43] The analysis is supported by the psychoanalyst who suggested that although one of the important dynamics of pornography is hostility, "one can raise the possibly controversial question whether in humans (especially males) powerful sexual excitement can ever exist without brutality also being present."[44]

Bataille's analysis can help to explain what is erotic about "snuff" films, which not only depict the torture and dismemberment of a woman, but claim that the actress is *in* fact killed. His analysis suggests that perhaps she is a sacrificial victim whose discontinuous existence has been succeeded in her death by "the organic continuity of life drawn into the common life of the beholders."[45] Thus, the pair "lover-assailant" is not accidental. Nor is the connection of reproduction and death.

"Reproduction," Bataille argues, "implies the existence of *discontinuous* beings." This is so because, "Beings which reproduce themselves are distinct from one another, and those reproduced are likewise distinct from each other, just as they are distinct from their parents. Each being is distinct from all others. His birth, his death, the events of his life may have an interest for others, but he alone is directly concerned in them. He is born alone. He dies alone. Between one being and another, there is a *gulf*, a discontinuity."[46] (Clearly it is not just a gulf, but is better understood as a chasm.) In reproduction sperm and ovum unite to form a new entity, but they do so from the death and disappearance of two separate beings. Thus, the new entity bears within itself "the transition to continuity, the fusion, fatal to both, of two separate beings."[47] Thus, death and reproduction are intimately linked, yet Bataille stresses that "it is only death which is to be identified with continuity." Thus, despite the unity of birth and death in this analysis, Bataille gives greater weight to a "tormenting fact: the urge towards love, pushed to its limit, is an urge toward death."[48] Bataille holds to this position despite his recognition that reproduction is a form of growth. The growth, however, he dismisses as not being "ours," as being only "impersonal."[49] This is not the female experience, in which reproduction is hardly impersonal, nor experienced as death. It is, of course, in a literal sense, the sperm which is cut off from its source, and lost. No wonder, then, at the masculinist occupation with death, and the feeling that growth is "impersonal," not of fundamental concern to oneself. But this complete dismissal of the experience of another bespeaks a profound lack of empathy and refusal to recognize the very being of another. It is a manifestation of the chasm which separates each man from every other being and from the natural world, the chasm which both marks and defines the problem of community.

The preoccupation with death instead of life appears as well in the argument that it is the ability to kill (and for centuries, the practice) which sets humans above animals. Even Simone de Beauvoir has accepted that "it is not in giving life but in risking life that man is raised above the animal: that is why superiority has been accorded in humanity not to the sex that brings forth but to that which kills."[50] That superiority has been accorded to the sex which kills is beyond doubt. But what kind of experience and vision can take reproduction, the creation of new life, and the force of life in sexuality, and turn it into death—not just in theory but in the practice of rape, pornography, and sexual murder? Any why give pride of place to killing? This is not only an inversion of the proper order of things, but also a refusal to recognize the real activities in which men as well as women are engaged. The producing of goods and the reproducing of human beings are certainly life-sustaining activities. And even the deaths of the ancient heroes in search of undying fame were pursuits of life, and represented the attempt to avoid death by attaining immortality. The search for life, then, represents the deeper reality which lies beneath the glorification of death and destruction.

Yet one cannot dismiss the substitution of death for life as simply false. Men's power to structure social relations in their own image means that women too must participate in social relations which manifest and express abstract masculinity. The most important life activities have consistently been held by the powers that be to be unworthy of those who are fully human most centrally because of their close connections with necessity and life: motherwork (the rearing of children), housework, and until the rise of capitalism in the West, any work necessary to subsistence. In addition, these activities in contemporary capitalism are all constructed in ways which systematically degrade and destroy the minds and bodies of those who perform them.[51] The organization of motherhood as an institution in which a woman is alone with her children, the isolation of women from each other in domestic labor, the female pathology of loss of self in service to others— all mark the transformation of life into death, the distortion of what could have been creative and communal activity into oppressive toil, and the destruction of the possibility of community present in women's relational self-definition. The ruling gender's and class's interest in maintaining social relations such as these is evidenced by the fact that when women set up other structures in which the mother is not alone with her children, isolated from others—as is frequently the case in working class communities or communities of people of color—these arrangements are categorized as pathological deviations.

The real destructiveness of the social relations characteristic of abstract masculinity, however, is now concealed beneath layers of ideology. Marxian theory needed to go beneath the surface to discover the different levels of determination which defined the relation of capitalist and (male) worker. These levels of determination and laws of motion or tendency of phallocratic society must be worked out on the basis of female experience. This brings me to the fourth claim for a standpoint—its character as an achievement of both analysis and political struggle occurring in a particular historical space. The fact that class divisions should have proven so resistant to analysis and required such a prolonged political struggle before Marx was able to formulate the theory of surplus value indicates the difficulty of this accomplishment. And the rational control of production has certainly not been achieved.

Feminists have only begun the process of revaluing female experience, searching for common threads which connect the diverse experiences of women, and searching for the structural determinants of the experiences. The difficulty of the problem faced by feminist theory can be illustrated by the fact that it required a struggle even to define household labor, if not done for wages, as work, to argue that what are held to be acts of love instead must be recognized as work whether or not wages are paid.[52] Both the valuation of women's experience, and the use of this experience as a ground for critique are required. A feminist standpoint may be present on the basis of the common threads of female experience, but it is neither self-evident nor obvious.

Finally, because it provides a way to reveal the perverseness and inhumanity of human relations, a standpoint forms the basis for moving beyond these relations. Just as the proletarian standpoint emerges out of the contradiction between appearance and essence in capitalism, understood as essentially historical and constituted by the relation of capitalist and worker, the feminist standpoint emerges both out of the contradiction between the systematically differing structure of male and female life activity in Western cultures. It expresses female experience at a particular time and place, located within a particular set of social relations. Capitalism, Marx noted, could not develop fully until the notion of human equality achieved the status of universal truth.[53] Despite women's exploitation both as unpaid reproducers of the labor force and as a sex-segregated labor force available for low wages, then, capitalism poses problems for the continued oppression of women. Just as capitalism enables the proletariat to raise the possibility of a society free from class domination, so too, it provides space to raise the possibility of a society free from all forms of domination. The articulation of a feminist standpoint based on women's relational self-definition and activity exposes the world men have constructed and the self-understanding which manifests these relations as partial and perverse. More importantly, by drawing out the potentiality available in the actuality and thereby exposing the inhumanity of human relations, it embodies a distress which requires a solution. The experience of continuity and relation—with others, with the natural world, of mind with body—provides on ontological base for developing a non-problematic social synthesis, a social synthesis which need not operate through the denial of the body, the attack on nature, or the death struggle between the self and other, a social synthesis which does not depend on any of the forms taken by abstract masculinity.

What is necessary is the generalization of the potentiality made available by the activity of women—the defining of society as a whole as propertyless producer both of use-values and of human beings. To understand what such a transformation would require we should consider what is involved in the partial transformation represented by making the whole of society into propertyless producers of use-values—i.e. socialist revolution. The abolition of the division between mental and manual labor cannot take place simply by means of adopting worker-self-management techniques, but instead requires the abolition of provate property, the seizure of state power, and lengthy post-revolutionary class struggle. Thus, I am not suggesting that shared parenting arrangements can abolish the sexual division of labor. Doing away with this division of labor would of course require institutionalizing the participation of both women and men in childrearing; but just as the rational and conscious control of the production of goods and services requires a vast and far-reaching social transformation, so the rational and conscious organization of reproduction would entail the transformation both of *every* human relation, and of human relations to the natural world. The magnitude of the task is apparent if one asks what a society without institutionalized gender differences might look like.

CONCLUSION

An analysis which begins from the sexual division of labor—understood not as taboo, but as the real, material activity of concrete human beings—could form the basis for an analysis of the real structures of women's oppression, an analysis which would not require that one sever biology from society, nature from culture, an analysis which would expose the ways women both participate in and oppose their own subordination. The elaboration of such an analysis cannot but be difficult. Women's lives, like men's, are structured by social relations which manifest the experience of the dominant gender and class. The ability to go beneath the surface of appearances to reveal the real but concealed social relations requires both theoretical and political activity. Feminist theorists must demand that feminist theorizing be grounded in women's material activity and must as well be a part of the political struggle necessary to develop areas of social life modeled on this activity. The outcome could be the development of a political economy which included women's activity as well as men's, and could as well be a step toward the redefining and restructuring of society as a whole on the basis of women's activity.

Generalizing the activity of women to the social system as a whole would raise, for the first time in human history, the possibility of a fully human community, a community structured by connection rather than separation and opposition. One can conclude then that women's life activity does form the basis of a specifically feminist materialism, a materialism which can provide a point from which both to critique and to work against phallocratic ideology and institutions.

My argument here opens a number of avenues for future work. Clearly, a systematic critique of Marx on the basis of a more fully developed understanding of the sexual division of labor is in order. And this is indeed being undertaken by a number of feminists. A second avenue for further investigation is the relation between exchange and abstract masculinity. An exploration of Mauss's *The Gift* would play an important part in this project, since he presents the solipsism of exchange as an overlay on and substitution for a deeper going hostility, the exchange of gifts as an alternative to war. We have seen that the necessity for recognizing and receiving recognition from another to take the form of a death struggle memorializes the male rather than female experience of emerging as a person in opposition to a woman in the context of a deeply phallocratic world. If the community of exchangers (capitalists) rests on the more overtly and directly hostile death struggle of self and other, one might be able to argue that what underlies the exchange abstraction is abstract masculinity. One might then turn to the question of whether capitalism rests on and is a consequence of patriarchy. Perhaps then feminists can produce the analysis which could amend Marx to read: "Though class society appears to be the source, the cause of the oppression of women, it is rather its consequence." Thus, it is "only at the last culmination of the development of class society [that] this, its secret, appear[s] again, namely, that on the one hand it is the *product* of the oppression of women, and that on the other it is the *means* by which women participate in and create their own oppression".[55]

NOTES

I take my title from Iris Young's call for the development of a specifically feminist historical materialism. See "Socialist Feminism and the Limits of Dual Systems Theory," in *Socialist Review* 10, 2/3 (March-June, 1980). My work on this paper is deeply indebted to a number of women whose ideas are incorporated here, although not always used in the ways they might wish. My discussions with Donna Haraway and Sandra Harding have been intense and ongoing over a period of years. I have also had a number of important and useful conversations with Jane Flax, and my project here has benefitted both from these contacts, and from the opportunity to read her paper, "Political Philosophy and the Patriarchal Unconscious: A Psychoanalytic Perspective on Epistemology and Metaphysics." In addition I have been helped immensely by collective discussions with Annette Bickel, Sarah Begus, and Alexa Freeman. All of these people (along with Iris Young and Irene Diamond) have read and commented on drafts of this paper. I would also like to thank Alison Jaggar for continuing to question me about the basis on which one could claim the superiority of a feminist standpoint and for giving me the opportunity to deliver the paper at the University of Cincinnati Philosophy Department Colloquium; and Stephen Rose for taking the time to read and comment on a rough draft of the paper at a critical point in its development.

1. See my "Feminist Theory and the Development of Revolutionary Strategy," in Zillah Eisenstein, ed., *Capitalist Patriarchy and the Case for Socialist Feminism* (New York: Monthly Review, 1978).

2. The recent literature on mothering is perhaps the most detailed on this point. See Dorothy Dinnerstein, *The Mermaid and the Minotaur* (New York: Harper and Row, 1976); Nancy Chodorow, The *Reproduction of Mothering* (Berkeley: University of California Press, 1978).

3. Iris Young, "Socialist Feminism and the Limits of Dual Systems Theory," in *Socialist Review* 10, 2/3 (March-June, 1980), p. 180.

4. Eighth Thesis on Feuerbach, in Karl Marx, "Theses on Feuerbach," in *The German Ideology*, C. J. Arthur, ed. (New York: International Publishers, 1970), p. 121.

5. *Ibid.* Conscious human practice, then, is at once both an epistemological category and the basis for Marx's conception of the nature of humanity itself. To put the case even more strongly, Marx argues that human activity has both an ontological and epistemological status, that human feelings are not "merely anthropological phenomena," but are "truly ontological affirmations of being." See Karl Marx, *Economic and Philosophic Manuscripts of 1844*, Dirk Struik, ed. (New York: International Publishers, 1964). pp. 113, 165, 188.

6. Marx, *1844*, p. 112. Nature itself, for Marx, appears as a form of human work, since he argues that humans duplicate themselves actively and come to contemplate themselves in a world of their own making. (*Ibid.*, p. 114). On the more general issue of the relation of natural to human worlds see the very interesting account by Alfred Schmidt, *The Concept of Nature in Marx*, tr. Ben Foukes (London: New Left Books, 1971).

7. Marx and Engels, *The German Ideology*, pp. 42.

8. See Alfred Sohn-Rethel, *Intellectual and Manual Labor: A Critique of Epistemology* (London: MacMillan, 1978). I should note that my analysis both depends on and is in tension with Sohn-Rethel's. Sohn-Rethel argues that commodity exchange is a characteristic of all class societies—one which comes to a head in capitalism

or takes its most advanced form in capitalism. His project, which is not mine, is to argue that (a) commodity exchange, a characteristic of all class societies, is an original source of abstraction, (b) that this abstraction contains the formal element essential for the cognitive faculty of conceptual thinking and (c) that the abstraction operating in exchange, an abstraction in practice, is the source of the ideal abstraction basic to Greek philosophy and to modern science. (See *Ibid.*, p. 28). In addition to a different purpose, I should indicate several major differences with Sohn-Rethel. First, he treats the productive forces as separate from the productive relations of society and ascribes far too much autonomy to them. (See, for example, his discussions on pp. 84–86, 95.) I take the position that the distinction between the two is simply a device used for purposes of analysis rather than a feature of the real world. Second, Sohn-Rethel characterizes the period preceding generalized commodity production as primitive communism. (See p. 98.) This is however an inadequate characterization of tribal societies.

9. Karl Marx, *Capital*, Vol. I (New York: International Publishers 1967), p. 176.

10. I have done this elsewhere in a systematic way. For the analysis, see my discussion of the exchange abstraction in *Money, Sex, and Power: An Essay on Domination and Community* (New York: Longman, Inc., 1983).

11. This is Iris Young's point. I am indebted to her persuasive arguments for taking what she terms the "gender differentiation of labor" as a central category of analysis (Young, "Dual Systems Theory," p. 185). My use of this category, however, differs to some extent from hers. Young's analysis of women in capitalism does not seem to include marriage as a part of the division of labor. She is more concerned with the division of labor in the productive sector.

12. See Sara Ruddick, "Maternal Thinking," *Feminist Studies* (Summer, 1980), p. 364.

13. See, for discussions of this danger, Adrienne Rich, "Disloyal to Civilization: Feminism, Racism, Gynephobia, "in *On Lies, Secrets, and Silence* (New York: W. W. Norton & Co., 1979), pp. 275–310; Elly Bulkin, "Racism and Writing: Some Implications for White Lesbian Critics," in *Sinister Wisdom*, No. 6 (Spring, 1980).

14. Some cross-cultural evidence indicates that the status of women varies with the work they do. To the extent that women and men contribute equally to subsistence, women's status is higher than it would be if their subsistence-work differed profoundly from that of men; that is, if they do none or almost all of the work of subsistence, their status remains low. See Peggy Sanday, "Female Status in the Public Domain," in Michelle Rosaldo and Louise Lamphere, eds., *Women, Culture, and Society* (Stanford: Stanford University Press, 1974), p. 199. See also Iris Young's account of the sexual division of labor in capitalism, mentioned above.

15. It is irrelevant to my argument here that women's wage labor takes place under different circumstances than men's—that is, their lower wages, their confinement to only a few occupational categories, etc. I am concentrating instead on the formal, structural features of women's work. There has been much effort to

argue that women's domestic labor is a source of surplus value, that is, to include it within the scope of Marx's value theory as productive labor, or to argue that since it does not produce surplus value it belongs to an entirely different mode of production, variously characterized as domestic or patriarchal. My strategy here is quite different from this. See, for the British debate, Mariarosa Dalla Costa and Selma James, *The Power of Women and the Subversion of the Community* (Falling Wall Press, Bristol, 1975); Wally Secombe, "The Housewife and Her Labor Under Capitalism," *New Left Review* 83 (January-February, 1974); Jean Gardiner, "Women's Domestic Labour," *New Left Review* 89 (March, 1975); and Paul Smith, "Domestic Labour and Marx's Theory of Value," in Annette Kuhn and Ann Marie Wolpe, eds., *Feminism and Materialism* (Boston: Routledge and Kegal Paul, 1978). A portion of the American debate can be found in Ira Gerstein, "Domestic Work and Capitalism," and Lisa Vogel, "The Earthly Family," *Radical America* 7, 4/5 (July-October, 1973); Ann Ferguson, "Women as a New Revolutionary Class," in Pat Walker, ed., *Between Labor and Capital* (Boston: South End Press, 1979).

16. Frederick Engels, *Origins of the Family, Private Property and the State* (New York: International Publishers, 1942); Karl Marx, *Capital*, Vol. I, p. 671. Marx and Engels have also described the sexual division of labor as natural or spontaneous. See Mary O'Brien, "Reproducing Marxist Man," in Lorenne Clark and Lynda Lange, eds., *The Sexism of Social and Political Theory: Women and Reproduction from Plato to Nietzsche* (Toronto: University of Toronto Press, 1979).

17. For a discussion of women's work, see Elise Boulding, "Familial Constraints on Women's Work Roles," in Martha Blaxall and B. Reagan, eds., *Women and the Workplace* (Chicago, University of Chicago Press, 1976), esp. the charts on pp. 111, 113.

    An interesting historical note is provided by the fact that even Nausicaa, the daughter of a Homeric king, did the household laundry. (See M. I. Finley, *The World of Odysseus* (Middlesex, England: Penguin, 1979), p. 73.) While aristocratic women were less involved in actual labor, the difference was one of degree. And as Aristotle remarked in *The Politics*, supervising slaves is not a particularly uplifting activity. The life of leisure and philosophy, so much the goal for aristocratic Athenian men, then, was almost unthinkable for any woman.

18. Simone de Beauvoir holds that repetition has a deeper significance and that women's biological destiny itself is repetition. (See *The Second Sex*, tr. H. M. Parshley (New York: Knopf, 1953), p. 59.) But see also her discussion of housework in *Ibid.*, pp. 434ff. There her treatment of housework is strikingly negative. For de Beauvoir, transcendence is provided in the historical struggle of self with other and with the natural world. The oppositions she sees are not really stasis vs. change, but rather transcendence, escape from the muddy concreteness of daily life, from the static, biological, concrete repetition of "placid femininity."

19. Marilyn French, *The Women's Room* (New York: Jove, 1978), p. 214.

20. Sara Ruddick, "Maternal Thinking," presents an interesting discussion of these and other aspects of the thought which emerges from the activity of mothering.

Although I find it difficult to speak the language of interests and demands she uses, she brings out several valuable points. Her distinction between maternal and scientific thought is very intriguing and potentially useful (see esp. pp. 350–353).

21. O'Brien, "Reproducing Marxist Man," p. 115, n. 11.

22. It should be understood that I am concentrating here on the experience of women in Western culture. There are a number of cross-cultural differences which can be expected to have some effect. See, for example, the differences which emerge from a comparison of childrearing in ancient Greek society with that of the contemporary Mbuti in central Africa. See Phillip Slater, *The Glory of Hera* (Boston: Beacon, 1968) and Colin Turnbull, "The Politics of Non-Aggression," in Ashley Montagu, ed., *Learning Non-Aggression* (New York: Oxford University Press, 1978).

23. See Nancy Chodorow, "Family Structure and Feminine Personality," in Michelle Rosaldo and Louise Lamphere, *Woman, Culture, and Society* (Stanford: Stanford University Press, 1974), p. 59.

24. *Of Woman Born* (New York: Norton, 1976), p. 63.

25. See Chodorow, "The Reproduction of Mothering," and Flax, "The Conflict Between Nurturance and Autonomy in Mother-Daughter Relations and in Feminism," *Feminist Studies* 4, 2 (June, 1978). I rely on the analyses of Dinnerstein and Chodorow but there are difficulties in that they are attempting to explain why humans, both male and female, fear and hate the female. My purpose here is to invert their arguments and to attempt to put forward a positive account of the epistemological consequences of this situation. What follows is a summary of Chodorow, "The Reproduction of Mothering."

26. Chodorow, *Reproduction*, pp. 105–109.

27. This is Jane Flax's point.

28. Chodorow, *Reproduction*, pp. 127–131, 163.

29. *Ibid.*, p. 166.

30. *Ibid.*, pp. 174–178. Chodorow suggests a correlation between father absence and fear of women (p. 213), and one should, treating this as an empirical hypothesis, expect a series of cultural differences based on the degree of father absence. Here the ancient Greeks and the Mbuti provide a fascinating contrast. (See above, note 22.)

31. *Ibid.*, p. 198. The flexible and diffuse female ego boundaries can of course result in the pathology of loss of self in responsibility for and dependence on others. (The obverse of the male pathology of experiencing the self as walled city.)

32. Sigmund Freud, *Civilization and Its Discontents* (New York: Norton, 1961), pp. 12–13.

33. Hegel, *Phenomenology of Spirit* (New York: Oxford University Press, 1979), trans. A. V. Miller, p. 114. See also Jessica Benjamin's very interesting use of this discussion in "The Bonds of Love: Rational Violence and Erotic Domination," *Feminist Studies* 6, 1 (June, 1980).

34. Alvin Gouldner has made a similar argument in his contention that the Platonic

stress on hierarchy and order resulted from a similarly learned opposition to daily life which was rooted in the young aristocrat's experience of being taught proper behavior by slaves who could not themselves engage in this behavior. See *Enter Plato* (New York: Basic Books, 1965), pp. 351–355.

35. One can argue, as Chodorow's analysis suggests, that their extreme form in his philosophy represents an extreme father-absent (father-deprived?) situation. A more general critique of phallocentric dualism occurs in Susan Griffin, *Woman and Nature* (New York: Harper & Row, 1978).

36. More recently, of course, the opposition to the natural world has taken the form of destructive technology. See Evelyn Fox Keller, "Gender and Science," *Psychoanalysis and Contemporary Thought* 1, 3 (1978), reprinted in this volume.

37. See Elizabeth Spelman, "Metaphysics and Misogyny: The Soul and Body in Plato's Dialogues," mimeo. One analyst has argued that its basis lies in the fact that "the early mother, monolithic representative of nature, is a source, like nature, of ultimate distress as well as ultimate joy. Like nature, she is both nourishing and disappointing, both alluring and threatening . . . The infant loves her . . . and it hates her because, like nature, she does not perfectly protect and provide for it . . . The mother, then like nature, which sends blizzards and locusts as well as sunshine and strawberries—is perceived as capricious, sometimes actively malevolent." Dinnerstein, p. 95.

38. See Benjamin, p. 152. The rest of her analysis goes in a different direction than mine, though her account of *The Story of O* can be read as making clear the problems for any social synthesis based on the Hegelian model.

39. *Of Woman Born*, p. 64, p. 167. For a similar descriptive account, but a dissimilar analysis, see David Bakan, *The Duality of Human Existence* (Boston: Beacon, 1966).

40. My arguments are supported with remarkable force by both the theory and practice of the contemporary women's movement. In theory, this appears in different forms in the work of Dorothy Riddle, "New Visions of Spiritual Power," *Quest: A Feminist Quarterly* 1, 3 (Spring, 1975): Susan Griffin, *Women and Nature*, esp. Book IV: "The Separate Rejoined'; Adrienne Rich, *Of Woman Born*, esp. pp. 62–68; Linda Thurston, "On Male and Female Principle," *The Second Wave* 1, 2 (Summer, 1971). In feminist political organizing, this vision has been expressed as an opposition of leadership and hierarchy, as an effort to prevent the development of organizations divided into leaders and followers. It has also taken the form of an insistence on the unity of the personal and the political, a stress on the concrete rather than on abstract principles (an opposition to theory), and a stress on the politics of everyday life. For a fascinating and early example, see Pat Mainardi, "The Politics of Housework," in Leslie Tanner, ed., *Voices of Women's Liberation* (New York: New American Library, 1970).

41. George Bataille, *Death and Sensuality* (New York: Arno Press, 1977), p. 90.

42. Women Against Violence Against Women Newsletter, June, 1976, p. 1.

43. *Aegis: A Magazine on Ending Violence Against Women*, November/December, 1978, p. 3.

44. Robert Stoller, *Perversion: The Erotic Form of Hatred* (New York: Pantheon, 1975), p. 88.

45. Bataille, p. 91. See pp. 91ff for a more complete account of the commonalities of sexual activity and ritual sacrifice.

46. *Death and Sensuality*, p. 12 (italics mine). See also de Beauvoir's discussion in *The Second Sex*, pp. 135, 151.

47. Bataille, p. 14.

48. *Ibid.*, p. 42. While Adrienne Rich acknowledges the violent feelings between mothers and children, she quite clearly does not put these at the heart of the relation (*Of Women Born*).

49. Bataille, pp. 95–96.

50. *The Second Sex*, p. 58. It should be noted that killing and risking life are ways of indicating one's contempt for one's body, and as such are of a piece with the Platonic search for disembodiment.

51. Consider, for example, Rich's discussion of pregnancy and childbirth, Ch. VI and VII, *Of Women Born*. And see also Charlotte Perkins Gilman's discussion of domestic labor in *The Home* (Urbana, Ill.: The University of Illinois Press, 1972).

52. The Marxist-feminist efforts to determine whether housework produces surplus value and the feminist political strategy of demanding wages for housework represent two (mistaken) efforts to recognize women's non-wage activity at work. Perhaps domestic labor's non-status as work is one of the reasons why its wages—disproportionately paid to women of color—are so low, and working conditions so poor.

53. *Capital*, Vol. I, p. 60.

54. The phrase is O'Brien's, p. 113.

55. See Marx, *1844*, p. 117.

14

PATRICIA HILL COLLINS

Defining Black Feminist Thought

Widely used yet rarely defined, Black feminist thought encompasses diverse and contradictory meanings. Two interrelated tensions highlight issues in defining Black feminist thought. The first concerns the thorny question of who can be a Black feminist. One current response, explicit in Patricia Bell Scott's (1982b) "Selected Bibliography on Black Feminism," classifies all African-American women, regardless of the content of our ideas, as Black feminists. From this perspective, living as Black women provides experiences to stimulate a Black feminist consciousness. Yet indiscriminately labeling all Black women in this way simultaneously conflates the terms *woman* and *feminist* and identifies being of African descent—a questionable biological category—as being the sole determinant of a Black feminist consciousness. As Cheryl Clarke points out, "I criticized Scott. Some of the women she cited as 'black feminists' were clearly not feminist at the time they wrote their books and still are not to this day" (1983, 94).

The term *Black feminist* has also been used to apply to selected African-Americans—primarily women—who possess some version of a feminist consciousness. Beverly Guy-Sheftall (1986) contends that both men and women can be "Black feminists" and names Frederick Douglass and William E. B. DuBois as prominent examples of Black male feminists. Guy-Sheftall also identifies some distinguishing features of Black feminist ideas: namely, that Black women's experiences with both racial and gender oppression that result in needs and problems distinct from white women and Black men, and that Black women must struggle for equality both as women and as African-Americans. Guy-Sheftall's definition is helpful in that its use of ideological criteria fosters a definition of Black feminist thought that encompasses both experiences and ideas. In other words, she suggests that experiences gained from living as African-American women stimulate a Black feminist sensibility. But her definition is simultaneously troublesome because it makes the biological category of Blackness the prerequisite for possessing such thought. Furthermore, it does not explain why these particular ideological criteria and not others are the distinguishing ones.

The term Black feminist has also been used to describe selected African-American women who possess some version of a feminist consciousness (Beale 1970; Hooks 1981; Barbara Smith 1983; White 1984). This usage of the term yields the most restrictive notion of who can be a Black feminist. The ground-breaking Combahee River Collective (1982) document, "A Black Feminist Statement," implicitly relies on this definition. The Collective claims that "as Black women we find any type of biological determinism a particularly dangerous and reactionary basis upon which to build a politic" (p.17). But in spite of this statement, by implying that only African-American women can be Black feminists, they require a biological prerequisite for race and gender consciousness. The Collective also offers its own ideological criteria for identifying Black feminist ideas. In contrast to Beverly Guy-Sheftall, the Collective places a stronger emphasis on capitalism as a source of Black women's oppression and on political activism as a distinguishing feature of Black feminism.

Biologically deterministic criteria for the term *black* and the accompanying assumption that being of African desccent somehow produces a certain consciousness or perspective are inherent in these definitions. By presenting race as being fixed and immutable—something rooted in nature—these approaches mask the historical construction of racial categories, the shifting meaning of race, and the crucial role of politics and ideology in shaping conceptions of race (Gould 11981; Omi and Winant 1986). In contrast, much greater variation is afforded the term feminist. Feminists are seen as ranging from biologically determined—as is the case in radical feminist thought, which argues that only women can be feminists—to notions of feminists as individuals who have undergone some type of political transformation theoretically achievable by anyone.

Though the term Black feminist could also be used to describe any individual who embraces Black feminist ideas, the separation of biology from ideology required for this usage is rarely seen in the works of Black women intellectuals. Sometimes the contradictions among these competing definitions can be so great that Black women writers use all simultaneously.

Consider the following passage from Deborah McDowell's essay "New Directions for Black Feminist Criticism":

> I use the term here simply to refer to Black female critics who analyze the works of Black female writers from a feminist political perspective. But the term can also apply to any criticism written by a Black woman regardless of her subject or perspective—a book written by a male from a feminist or political perspective, a

book written by a Black woman or about Black women authors in general, or any writings by women. (1985, 191)

While McDowell implies that elite white men could be "black feminists," she is clearly unwilling to state so categorically. From McDowell's perspective, whites and Black men who embrace a specific political perspective, and Black women regardless of political perspective, could all potentially be deemed Black feminist critics.

The ambiguity surrounding current perspectives on who can be a Black feminist is directly tied to a second definitional tension in Black feminist thought: the question of what constitutes Black feminism. The range of assumptions concerning the relationship between ideas and their advocates as illustrated in the works of Patricia Bell Scott, Beverly Guy-Sheftall, the Combahee River Collective, and Deborah McDowell leads to problems in defining Black feminist theory itself. Once a person is labeled a "Black feminist," then ideas forwarded by that individual often become defined as Black feminist thought. This practice accounts for neither changes in the thinking of an individual nor differences among Black feminist theorists.

A definition of Black feminist thought is needed that avoids the materialist position that being Black and/or female generates certain experiences that automatically determine variants of a Black and/or feminist consciousness. Claims that Black feminist thought is the exclusive province of African-American women, regardless of the experiences and worldview of such women, typify this position. But a definition of Black feminist thought must also avoid the idealist position that ideas can be evaluated in isolation from the groups that create them. Definitions claiming that anyone can produce and develop Black feminist thought risk obscuring the special angle of vision that Black women bring to the knowledge production process.

THE DIMENSIONS OF A BLACK WOMEN'S STANDPOINT

Developing adequate definitions of Black feminist thought involves facing this complex nexus of relationships among biological classification, the social construction of race and gender as categories of analysis, the material conditions accompanying these changing social constructions, and Black women's consciousness about these themes. One way of addressing the definitional tensions in Black feminist thought is to specify the relationship between a Black women's standpoint—those experiences and ideas shared by African-American women that provide a unique angle of vision on self, community, and society—and theories that interpret these experiences.[1] I suggest that Black feminist thought consists of specialized knowledge created by African-American women which clarifies a standpoint of and for Black women. In other words, Black feminist thought encompasses theoretical interpretations of Black women's reality by those who live it.

This definition does not mean that all African-American women generate such thought or that other groups do not play a critical role in its production. Before exploring the contours and implications of this working definition, understanding five key dimension of a Black women's standpoint is essential.

The Core Themes of a Black Women's Standpoint

All African-American women share the common experience of being Black women in a society that denigrates women of African descent. This commonality of experience suggests that certain characteristic themes will be prominent in a Black women's standpoint. For example, one core theme is a legacy of struggle. Katie Cannon observes, "throughout the history of the United States, the interrelationship of white supremacy and male superiority has characterized the Black woman's reality as a situation of struggle—a struggle to survive in two contradictory worlds simultaneously, one white, privileged, and oppressive, the other black, exploited, and oppressed" (1985, 30). Black women's vulnerability to assaults in the workplace, on the street, and at home has stimulated Black women's independence and self-reliance.

In spite of differences created by historical era, age, social class, sexual orientation, or ethnicity, the legacy of struggle against racism and sexism is a common thread binding African-American women. Anna Julia Cooper, a ninteenth-century Black woman intellectual, describes Black women's vulnerability to sexual violence:

> I would beg . . . to add my plea for the *Colored Girls* of the South:—that large, bright, promising fatally beautiful class . . . so full of promise and possibilities, yet so sure of destruction; often without a father to whom they dare apply the loving term, often without a stronger brother to espouse their cause and defend their honor with his life's blood; in the midst of pitfalls and snares, waylaid by the lower classes of white men, with no shelter, no protection. (Cooper 1892, 240)

Yet during this period Black women struggled and built a powerful club movement and numerous community organizations (Giddings 1984, 1988; Gilkes 1985).

Age offers little protection from this legacy of struggle. Far too many young Black girls inhabit hazardous and hostile environments. In 1975 I received an essay entitled "My World" from Sandra, a sixth-grade student who was a resident of one of the most dangerous public housing projects in Boston. Sandra wrote, "My world is full of people getting rape. People shooting on another. Kids and grownups fighting over girlsfriends. And people without jobs who can't afford to get a education so they can get a job . . . winos on the streets raping and killing little girls." Her words poignantly express a growing Black feminist sensibility that she may be victimized by racism and poverty. They also reveal her awareness that she is vulnerable to rape as a gender-specific form of sexual violence. In spite of her feelings about her community, Sandra not only walked the streets daily but managed safely to deliver three younger siblings to school. In doing so she participated in a Black women's legacy of struggle.

This legacy of struggle constitutes one of several core themes of a Black women's standpoint. Efforts to reclaim the Black feminist intellectual tradition are revealing Black women's longstanding attention to a series of core themes first recorded by Maria W. Stewart (Richardson 1987). Stewart's treatment of the interlocking nature of race, gender, and class oppression, her call for replacing denigrated images of Black womanhood with self-defined images, her belief in Black women's activism as mothers, teachers, and Black community leaders, and her sensitivity to sexual politics are all core themes advanced by a variety of Black feminist intellectuals.

Variation of Responses to Core Themes

The existence of core themes does not mean that African-American women respond to these themes in the same way. Diversity among Black women produces different concrete experiences that in turn shape various reactions to the core themes. For example, when faced with stereotypical, controlling images of Black women, some women—such as Sojourner Truth—demand, "ain't I a woman?" By deconstructing the conceptual apparatus of the dominant group, they invoke a Black women's legacy of struggle. In contrast, other women internalize the controlling images and come to believe that they are the stereotypes (Brown-Collins and Sussewell 1986).

A variety of factors explain the diversity of responses. For example, although all African-American women encounter racism, social class differences among African-American women influence how racism is experienced. A young manager who graduated with honors from the University of Maryland describes the specific form racism can take for middle-class Blacks. Before flying to Cleveland to explain a marketing plan for her company, her manager made her go over it three or four times in front of him so that she would not forget *her* marketing plan. Then he explained how to check luggage at an airport and how to reclaim it. "I just sat at lunch listening to this man talking to me like I was a monkey who could remember but couldn't think," the Black female manager recalled. When she had had enough, she responded, "I asked him if he wanted to tie my money up in a handkerchief and put a note on me saying that I was an employee of this company. In case I got lost I would be picked up by Traveler's Aid, and Traveler's Aid would send me back" (Davis and Watson 1985, 86). Most middle-class Black women do not encounter such blatant incidents, but many working-class Blacks do. For both groups the racist belief that African-Americans are less intelligent than whites remains strong.

Sexual orientation provides another key factor. Black lesbians have identified homophobia in general and the issues they face living as Black lesbians in homophobic communities as being a major influence on their angle of vision on everyday events (Shockley 1974; Lorde 1982, 1984; Clarke et al. 1983; Barbara Smith 1983). Beverly Smith describes how being a lesbian affected her perceptions of the wedding of one of her closest friends: "God, I wish I had one friend here. Someone who knew me and would understand how I feel. I am masquerading as a nice, straight, middle-class Black 'girl'" (1983, 172). While the majority of those attending the wedding saw only a festive event, Beverly Smith felt that her friend was being sent into a form of bondage.

Other factors such as ethnicity, region of the country, urbanization, and age combine to produce a web of experiences shaping diversity among African-American women. As a result, it is more accurate to discuss a Black *women's* standpoint than a Black *woman's* standpoint.

The Interdependence of Experience and Consciousness

Black women's work and family experiences and grounding in traditional African-American culture suggest that African-American women as a group experience a world different from that of those who are not Black and female. Moreover, these concrete experiences can stimulate a distinctive Black feminist consciousness concerning that material reality.[2] Being Black and female may expose African-American women to certain common experiences, which in turn may predispose us to a distinctive group consciousness, but it in no way guarantees that such a consciousness will develop among all women or that it will be articulated as such by the group.

Many African-American women have grasped this connection between what one does and how one thinks. Hannah Nelson, an elderly Black domestic worker, discusses how work shapes the perspectives of African-American and white women: "Since I have to work, I don't really have to worry about most of the things that most of the white women I have worked for are worrying about. And if these women did their own work, they would think just like I do—about this, anyway" (Gwaltney 1980, 4). Ruth Shays, a Black inner-city resident, points out how variations in men's and women's experiences lead to differences in perspective. "The mind of the man and the mind of the woman is the same" she notes, "but this business of living makes women use their minds in ways that men don' even have to think about" (Gwaltney 1980, 33).

This connection between experience and consciousness that shapes the everyday lives of all African-American women pervades the works of Black women activists and scholars. In her autobiography, Ida B. Wells describes how the lynching of her friends had such an impact on her worldview that she subsequently devoted much of her life to the antilynching cause (Duster 1970). Sociologist Joyce Ladner's (1972) *Tomorrow's Tomorrow*, a ground-breaking study of Black female adolescence, emerged from her discomfort with the disparity between the teachings of mainstream scholarship and her experiences as a young Black woman in the South. Similarly, the transformed consciousness experienced by Janie, the light-skinned heroine of Zora Neale Hurston's (1937) classic *Their Eyes Were Watching God*, from obedient granddaughter and wife to a self-defined African-American woman, can be directly traced to her experiences with each of her three husbands. In one scene Janie's second husband, angry because she served him a dinner of scorched rice, underdone fish, and soggy bread, hits her. That incident stimulates Janie to stand "where he left her for unmeasured time" and think. Her thinking leads to the recognition that "her image of Jody tumbled down and shattered . . . she had an inside and an outside now and suddenly she knew how not to mix them" (p.63).

Consciousness and the Struggle for a Self-Defined Standpoint

African-American women as a group may have experiences that provide us with a unique angle of vision. But expressing a collective, self-defined Black feminist consciousness is problematic precisely because dominant groups have a vested interest in suppressing such thought.[3] As Hannah Nelson notes, "I have grown to womanhood in a world where the saner you are, the madder you are made to appear" (Gwaltney 1980, 7). Ms. Nelson realizes that those who control the schools, media, and other cultural institutions of society prevail in establishing their viewpoint as superior to others.

An oppressed group's experiences may put its members in a position to see things differently, but their lack of control over the ideological apparatuses of society makes expressing a self-defined standpoint more difficult. Elderly domestic worker Rosa Wakefield assesses how the standpoints of the powerful and those who serve them diverge:

> If you eats these dinners and don't cook 'em, if you wears these clothes and don't buy or iron them, then you might start thinking that the good fairy or some spirit did all that.... Black folks don't have no time to be thinking like that.... But when you don't have anything else to do, you can think like that. It's bad for your mind, though. (Gwaltney 1980, 88)

Ms. Wakefield has a self-defined perspective growing from her experiences that enables her to reject the standpoint of more powerful groups. And yet ideas like hers are typically suppressed by dominant groups. Groups unequal in power are correspondingly unequal in their ability to make their standpoint known to themselves and others.

Individual African-American women have long displayed varying types of consciousness regarding our shared angle of vision. By aggregating and articulating these individual expressions of consciousness, a collective, focused group consciousness becomes possible. Black women's ability to forge these individual, unarticulated, yet potentially powerful expressions of everyday consciousness into an articulated, self-defined, collective standpoint is key to Black women's survival. As Audre Lorde points out, "it is axiomatic that if we do not define ourselves for ourselves, we will be defined by others—for their use and to our detriment" (1984, 45).

One fundamental feature of this struggle for a self-defined standpoint involves tapping sources of everyday, unarticulated consciousness that have traditionally been denigrated in white, male-controlled institutions. For Black women, the struggle involves embracing a consciousness that is simultaneously Afrocentric and feminist. What does this mean?

Research in African-American Studies suggests that an Afrocentric worldview exists which is distinct from and in many ways opposed to a Eurocentric worldview (Okanlawon 1972; Asante 1987; Myers 1988). Standard scholarly social constructions of blackness and race define these concepts as being either reflections of quantifiable, biological differences among humans or residual categories that emerged in response to institutionalized racism (Lyman 1972; Bash 1979; Gould 1981; Omi and Winant 1986). In contrast, even though it often relies on biological notions of the "race," Afrocentric scholarship suggests that "blackness" and Afrocentricity reflect longstanding belief systems among African peoples (Diop 1974; Richards 1980; Asante 1987). While Black people were forced to adapt these Afrocentric belief systems in the face of different institutional arrangements of white domination, the continuation of an

Afrocentric worldview has been fundamental to African-Americans' resistance to racial oppression (Smitherman 1977; Webber 1978; Sobel 1979; Thompson 1983). In other words, being Black encompasses *both* experiencing white domination *and* individual and group valuation of an independent, long-standing Afrocentric consciousness.

African-American women draw on this Afrocentric worldview to cope with racial oppression. But far too often Black women's Afrocentric consciousness remains unarticulated and not fully developed into a self-defined standpoint. In societies that denigrate African ideas and peoples, the process of valuing an Afrocentric worldview is the result of self-conscious struggle.

Similar concerns can be raised about the issue of what constitutes feminist ideas (Eisenstein 1983; Jaggar 1983). Being a biological female does not mean that one's ideas are automatically feminist. Self-conscious struggle is needed in order to reject patriarchal perceptions of women and to value women's ideas and actions. The fact that more women than men identify themselves as feminists reflects women's greater experience with the negative consequences of gender oppression. Becoming a feminist is routinely described by women (and men) as a process of transformation, of struggling to develop new interpretations of familiar realities.

The struggles of women from different racial/ethnic groups and those of women and men within African-American communities to articulate self-defined standpoints represent similar yet distinct processes. While race and gender are both socially constructed categories, constructions of gender rest on clearer biological criteria than do constructions of race. Classifying African-Americans into specious racial categories is considerably more difficult than noting the clear biological differences distinguishing females from males (Patterson 1982). But though united by biological sex, women do not form the same type of group as do African-Americans, Jews, native Americans, Vietnamese, or other groups with distinct histories, geographic origins, cultures, and social institutions. The absence of an identifiable tradition uniting women does not mean that women are characterized more by differences than by similarities. Women do share common experiences, but the experiences are not generally the same type as those affecting racial and ethnic groups (King 1988). Thus while expressions of race and gender are both socially constructed, they are not constructed in the same way. The struggle for an Afrocentric feminist consciousness requires embracing both an Afrocentric worldview and a feminist sensibility and using both to forge a self-defined standpoint.[4]

The Interdependence of Thought and Action

One key reason that standpoints of oppressed groups are suppressed is that self-defined standpoints can stimulate resistance. Annie Adams, a Southern Black woman, describes how she became involved in civil rights activities:

> When I first went into the mill we had segregated water fountains. . . Same thing about the toilets. I had to clean the toilets for the inspection room and then, when I got ready to go to the bathroom, I had to go all the way to the bottom of the stairs to the cellar. So I asked my boss man, "what's the difference? If I can go in there and

clean them toilets, why can't I use them?" Finally, I started to use that toilet. I decided I wasn't going to walk a mile to go to the bathroom. (Byerly 1986, 134)

In this case Ms. Adams found the standpoint of the "boss man" inadequate, developed one of her own, and acted on it. Her actions illustrate the connections among concrete experiences with oppression, developing a self-defined standpoint concerning those experiences, and the acts of resistance that can follow.

This interdependence of thought and action suggests that changes in thinking may be accompanied by changed actions and that altered experiences may in turn stimulate a changed consciousness. The significance of this connection is succinctly expressed by Patrice L. Dickerson, an astute Black feminist college student, who writes, "it is a fundamental contention of mine that in a social context which denies and deforms a person's capacity to realize herself, the problem of self-consciousness is not simply a problem of thought, but also a problem of practice, . . . the demand to end a deficient consciousness must be joined to a demand to eliminate the conditions which caused it" (personal communication, 1988). The struggle for a self-defined Afrocentric feminist consciousness occurs through a merger of thought and action.

This dimension of a Black women's standpoint rejects either/or dichotomous thinking that claims that *either* thought *or* concrete action is desirable and that merging the two limits the efficacy of both. Such approaches generate deep divisions among theorists and activists which are more often fabricated than real. Instead, by espousing a both/and orientation that views thought and action as part of the same process, possibilities for new relationships between thought and action emerge. That Black women should embrace a both/and conceptual orientation grows from Black women's experiences living as both African-Americans and women and, in many cases, in poverty.

Very different kinds of "thought" and "theories" emerge when abstract thought is joined with concrete action. Denied positions as scholars and writers which allow us to emphasize purely theoretical concerns, the work of most Black women intellectuals is influenced by the merger of action and theory. The activities of nineteenth-century Black women intellectuals such as Anna J. Cooper, Frances Ellen Watkins Harper, Ida B. Wells, and Mary Church Terrell exemplify this tradition of merging intellectual work and activism. These women both produced analyses of Black women's oppression and worked to eliminate that oppression. The Black women's club movement they created was both an activist and an intellectual endeavor.

Contemporary Black women intellectuals continue to draw on this tradition of using everyday actions and experiences in our theoretical work.[5] bell hooks describes the impact working as an operator at the telephone company had on her efforts to write *Ain't I A Woman: Black Women and Feminism* (1981). The women she worked with wanted her to "write a book that would make our lives better, one that would make other people understand the hardships of being black and female" (1989, 152). To hooks, "it was different to be writing in a context where my ideas were not seen as separate from real people and real lives" (p. 152). Similarly, Black feminist historian Elsa Barkley Brown describes the importance her mother's ideas played in the scholarship she eventually produced on African-American washerwomen. Initially Brown used the lens provided by her training as a historian and assessed her sample group as devalued service workers. But over time she came to understand washerwomen as entrepreneurs. By taking the laundry to whoever had the largest kitchen, they created a community and a culture among themselves. In explaining the shift of vision that enabled her to reassess this portion of Black women's history, Brown notes, "it was my mother who taught me how to ask the right questions—and all of us who try to do this thing called scholarship on a regular basis are fully aware that asking the right questions is the most important part of the process" (1986, 14).

REARTICULATING A BLACK WOMEN'S STANDPOINT

The existence of a Black women's standpoint does not mean that African-American women appreciate its content, see its significance, or recognize the potential that a fully articulated Afrocentric feminist standpoint has as a catalyst for social change. One key role for Black women intellectuals is to ask the right questions and investigate all dimensions of a Black women's standpoint with and for African-American women.[6] Black women intellectuals thus stand in a special relationship to the community of African-American women of which we are a part, and this special relationship frames the contours of Black feminist thought.

This special relationship of Black women intellectuals to the community of African-American women parallels the existence of two interrelated levels of knowledge (Berger and Luckmann 1966). The commonplace, taken-for-granted knowledge shared by African-American women growing from our everyday thoughts and actions constitutes a first and most fundamental level of knowledge. The ideas that Black women share with one another on an informal, daily basis about topics such as how to style our hair, characteristics of "good" Black men, strategies for dealing with white folks, and skills of how to "get over" provide the foundations for this taken-for-granted knowledge.

Experts or specialists who participate in and emerge from a group produce a second, more specialized type of knowledge. The range of Black women intellectuals discussed in Chapter 1 are these specialists, and their theories clarifying a Black women's standpoint form the specialized knowledge of Black feminist thought. The two types of knowledge are interdependent. While Black feminist thought articulates the taken-for-granted knowledge shared by African-American women as a group, the consciousness of Black women may be transformed by such thought. The actions of educated Black women within the Black women's club movement typify this special relationship between Black women intellectuals and the wider community of African-American women:

> It is important to recognize that black women like Frances Harper, Anna Julia Cooper, and Ida B. Wells were not isolated figures of intellectual genius; they were shaped by and helped to shape a wider movement of Afro-American women. This is not to claim that they were representative of all black women; they and their coun-

terparts formed an educated, intellectual elite, but an elite that tried to develop a cultural and historical perspective that was organic to the wider condition of black womanhood. (Carby 1987, 115).

The work of these women is important because it illustrates a tradition of joining scholarship and activism, and thus it taps the both/and conceptual orientation of a Black women's standpoint.

The suppression of Black feminist thought in mainstream scholarship and within its Afrocentric and feminist critiques has meant that Black women intellectuals have traditionally relied on alternative institutional locations to produce specialized knowledge about a Black women's standpoint. Many Black women scholars, writers, and artists have worked either alone, as was the case with Maria W. Stewart, or within African-American community organizations, the case for Black women in the club movement. The emergence of Black women's studies in colleges and universities during the 1980s, and the creation of a community of African-American women writers such as Toni Morrison, Alice Walker, and Gloria Naylor, have created new institutional locations where Black women intellectuals can produce specialized thought. Black women's history and Black feminist literary criticism constitute two focal points of this renaissance in Black women's intellectual work (Carby 1987). These are parallel movements: the former aimed at documenting social structural influences on Black women's consciousness; the latter, at exploring Black women's consciousness (self-definitions) through the freedom that art provides.

One danger facing African-American women intellectuals working in these new locations concerns the potential isolation from the types of experiences that stimulate an Afrocentric feminist consciousness—lack of access to other Black women and to a Black women's community. Another is the pressure to separate thought from action—particularly political activism—that typically accompanies training in standard academic disciplines. In spite of these hazards, contemporary Afrocentric feminist thought represents the creative energy flowing between these two focal points of history and literature, an unresolved tension that both emerges from and informs the experiences of African-American women.

The potential significance of Black feminist thought as specialized thought goes far beyond demonstrating that African-American women can be theorists. Like the Black women's activist tradition from which it grows and which it seeks to foster, Black feminist thought can create collective identity among African-American women about the dimensions of a Black women's standpoint. Through the process of rearticulation. Black women intellectuals offer African-American women a different view of themselves and their world from that forwarded by the dominant group (Omi and Winant 1986, 93). By taking the core themes of a Black women's standpoint and infusing them with new meaning. Black women intellectuals can stimulate a new consciousness that utilizes Black women's everyday, taken-for-granted knowledge. Rather than raising consciousness. Black feminist thought affirms and rearticulates a consciousness that already exists. More important, this rearticulated consciousness empowers African-American women and stimulates resistance.

Sheila Radford-Hill stresses the importance of rearticulation as an essential ingre-dient of an empowering Black feminist theory in her essay "Considering Feminism as a Model for Social Change." In evaluating whether Black women should espouse fem-inist programs, Radford-Hill suggests, "the essential issue that black women must confront when assessing a feminist position is as follows: If I, as a black woman, 'become a feminist,' what basic tools will I gain to resist my individual and group oppression" (1986, 160)? For Radford-Hill, the relevance of feminism as a vehicle for social change must be assessed in terms of its "ability to factor black women and other women of color into alternative conceptions of power and the consequences of its use" (p. 160). Thus Black feminist thought aims to develop a theory that is emancipa-tory and reflective and which can aid African-American women's struggles against oppression.

The earlier definition of Black feminist thought can now be reformulated to encompass the expanded definition of standpoint, the relationship between everyday and specialized thought, and the importance of rearticulation as one key dimension of Black feminist thought. Restated, Black feminist thought consists of theories or spe-cialized thought produced by African-American women intellectuals designed to express a Black women's standpoint. The dimensions of this standpoint include the presence of characteristic core themes, the diversity of Black women's experiences in encountering these core themes, the varying expressions of Black women's Afrocentric feminist consciousness regarding the core themes and their experiences with them, and the interdependence of Black women's experiences, consciousness, and actions. This specialized thought should aim to infuse Black women's experiences and everyday thought with new meaning by rearticulating the interdependence of Black women's experiences and consciousness. Black feminist thought is *of* African-American women in that it taps the multiple relationships among Black women needed to produce a self-defined Black women's standpoint. Black feminist thought is *for* Black women in that it empowers Black women for political activism.

At first glance, this expanded definition could be read to mean that only African-American women can participate in the production of Black feminist thought and that only Black women's experiences can form the content of that thought. But this model of Black feminism is undermined as a critical perspective by being dependent on those who are biologically Black and female. Given that I reject exclusionary definitions of Black feminism which confine "black feminist criticism to black women critics of black women artists depicting black women" (Carby 1987, 9), how does the expanded definition of Black feminist thought address the two original definitional tensions?

WHO CAN BE A BLACK FEMINIST?: THE CENTRALITY OF BLACK WOMEN INTELLECTUALS TO THE PRODUCTION OF BLACK FEMINIST THOUGHT

I aim to develop a definition of Black feminist thought that relies exclusively neither on a materialist analysis—one whereby all African-American women by virtue of biology become automatically registered as "authentic Black feminists"—nor on an idealist analysis whereby the background, worldview, and interests of the thinker are deemed irrelevant in assessing his or her ideas. Resolving the tension between these two extremes involves reassessing the centrality Black women intellectuals assume in producing Black feminist thought. It also requires examining the importance of coalitions with Black men, white women, people of color, and other groups with distinctive standpoints. Such coalitions are essential in order to foster other groups' contributions as critics, teachers, advocates, and disseminators of a self-defined Afrocentric feminist standpoint.

Black women's concrete experiences as members of specific race, class, and gender groups as well as our concrete historical situations necessarily play significant roles in our perspectives on the world. No standpoint is neutral because no individual or group exists unembedded in the world. Knowledge is gained not by solitary individuals but by Black women as socially constituted members of a group (Narayan 1989). These factors all frame the definitional tensions in Black feminist thought.

Black women intellectuals are central to Black feminist thought for several reasons. First, our experiences as African-American women provide us with a unique standpoint on Black womanhood unavailable to other groups. It is more likely for Black women as members of an oppressed group to have critical insights into the condition of our own oppression than it is for those who live outside those structures. One of the characters in Frances Ellen Watkins Harper's 1892 novel, *Iola Leroy*, expresses this belief in the special vision of those who have experienced oppression:

> Miss Leroy, out of the race must come its own thinkers and writers. Authors belonging to the white race have written good books, for which I am deeply grateful, but it seems to be almost impossible for a white man to put himself completely in our place. No man can feel the iron which enters another man's soul. (Carby 1987, 62)

Only African-American women occupy this center and can "feel the iron" that enters Black women's souls, because we are the only group that has experienced race, gender, and class oppression as Black women experience them. The importance of Black women's leadership in producing Black feminist thought does not mean that others cannot participate. It does mean that the primary responsibility for defining one's own reality lies with the people who live that reality, who actually have those experiences.

Second, Black women intellectuals provide unique leadership for Black women's empowerment and resistance. In discussing Black women's involvement in the feminist movement, Sheila Radford-Hill points out the connections among self-definition, empowerment, and taking actions in one's own behalf:

> Black women now realize that part of the problem within the movement was our insistence that white women do for/with us what we must do for/with ourselves: namely, frame our own social action around our own agenda for change. . . . Critical to this discussion is the right to organize on one's own behalf. . . . Criticism by black feminists must reaffirm this principle. (1986, 162)

Black feminist thought cannot challenge race, gender, and class oppression without empowering African-American women. "Oppressed people resist by identifying themselves as subjects, by defining their reality, shaping their new identity, naming their history, telling their story," notes bell hooks (1989, 43). Because self-definition is key to individual and group empowerment, using an epistemology that cedes the power of self-definition to other groups, no matter how well-meaning, in essence perpetuates Black women's subordination. As Black feminist sociologist Deborah K. King succinctly states, "Black feminism asserts self-determination as essential" (1988, 72).

Stressing the importance of Black women's centrality to Black feminist thought does not mean that all African-American women exert this leadership. While being an African-American women generally provides the experiential base for an Afrocentric feminist consciousness, these same conditions suppress its articulation. It is not acquired as a finished product but must continually develop in relation to changing conditions.

Bonnie Johnson emphasizes the importance of self-definition. In her critique of Patricia Bell Scott's bibliography on Black feminism, she challenges both Scott's categorization of all works by Black women as being Black feminist and Scott's identification of a wide range of African-American women as Black feminists: "Whether I think they're feminists is irrelevant. *They* would not call themselves feminist" (Clarke et al. 1983, 94). As Patrice L. Dickerson contends, "a person comes into being and knows herself by her achievements, and through her efforts to become and know herself, she achieves" (personal correspondence 1988). Here is the heart of the matter. An Afrocentric feminist consciousness constantly emerges and is part of a self-conscious struggle to merge thought and action.

Third, Black women intellectuals are central in the production of Black feminist thought because we alone can create the group autonomy that must precede effective coalitions with other groups. This autonomy is quite distinct from separatist positions whereby Black women withdraw from other groups and engage in exclusionary politics. In her introduction to *Home Girls, A Black Feminist Anthology*, Barbara Smith describes this difference: "Autonomy and separatism are fundamentally different. Whereas autonomy comes from a position of strength, separatism comes from a position of fear. When we're truly autonomous we can deal with other kinds of people, a multiplicity of issues, and with difference, because we have formed a solid base of strength" (1983, xl). Black women intellectuals who articulate an autonomous, self-defined standpoint are in a position to examine the usefulness of coalitions with other groups, both scholarly and activist, in order to develop new models for social change. However, autonomy to develop a self-defined, independent analysis does not mean that Black feminist thought has relevance only for African-American women or that we must confine ourselves to analyzing our own experiences. As Sonia Sanchez points out, "I've always known that if you write from a black experience, you're writing from a universal experience as well. . . . I know you don't have to whitewash yourself to be universal" (in Tate 1983, 142).

While Black feminist thought may originate with Black feminist intellectuals, it cannot flourish isolated from the experiences and ideas of other groups. The dilemma is that Black women intellectuals must place our own experiences and consciousness at the center of any serious efforts to develop Black feminist thought yet not have that thought become separatist and exclusionary. bell hooks offers a solution to this problem by suggesting that we shift from statements such as "I am a feminist" to those such as "I advocate feminism." Such an approach could "serve as a way women who are concerned about feminism as well as other political movements could express their support while avoiding linguistic structures that give primacy to one particular group" (1984, 30).

By advocating, refining, and disseminating Black feminist thought, other groups—such as Black men, white women, white men, and other people of color—further its development. Black women can produce an attenuated version of Black feminist thought separated from other groups. Other groups cannot produce Black feminist thought without African-American women. Such groups can, however, develop self-defined knowledge reflecting their own standpoints. But the full actualization of Black feminist thought requires a collaborative enterprise with Black women at the center of a community based on coalitions among autonomous groups.

Coalitions such as these require dialogues among Black women intellectuals and within the larger African-American women's community. Exploring the common themes of a Black women's standpoint is an important first step. Moreover, finding ways of handling internal dissent is especially important for the Black women's intellectual community. Evelynn Hammond describes how maintaining a united front for whites stifles her thinking: "What I need to do is challenge my thinking, to grow. On white publications sometimes I feel like I'm holding up the banner of black womanhood. And that doesn't allow me to be as critical as I would like to be" (in Clarke et al. 1983, 104). Cheryl Clarke observes that she has two dialogues: one with the public and the private ones in which she feels free to criticize the work of other Black women. Clarke states that the private dialogues are the ones that "have changed my life, have shaped the way I feel . . . have mattered to me" (p. 103).

Coalitions also require dialogues with other groups. Rather than rejecting our marginality, Black women intellectuals can use our outsider-within stance as a position of strength in building effective coalitions and stimulating dialogue. Barbara Smith suggests that Black women develop dialogues based on a "commitment to principled coalitions, based not upon expediency, but upon our actual need for each other" (1983, xxxiii). Dialogues among and coalitions with a range of groups, each with its own distinctive set of experiences and specialized thought embedded in those experiences, form the larger, more general terrain of intellectual and political discourse necessary for furthering Black feminism. Through dialogues exploring how relations of domination and subordination are maintained and changed, parallels between Black women's experiences and those of other groups become the focus of investigation.

Dialogue and principled coalition create possibilities for new versions of truth. Alice Walker's answer to the question of what she felt were the major differences between the literature of African-Americans and whites offers a provocative glimpse of the types of truths that might emerge through an epistemology based on dialogue and coalition. Walker did not spend much time considering this question, since it was not the difference between them that interested her, but, rather, the way Black writers and white writers seemed to be writing one immense story, with different parts of the story coming from a multitude of different perspectives. In a conversation with her mother, Walker refines this epistemological vision: "I believe that the truth about any subject only comes when all sides of the story are put together, and all their different meanings make one new one. Each writer writes the missing parts to the other writer's story. And the whole story is what I'm after" (1983, 49). Her mother's response to Walker's vision of the possibilities of dialogues and coalitions hints at the difficulty of sustaining such dialogues under oppressive conditions: "'Well, I doubt if you can ever get the *true* missing parts of anything away from the white folks,' my mother says softly, so as not to offend the waitress who is mopping up a nearby table; 'they've sat on the truth so long by now they've mashed the life out of it'" (1983, 49).

WHAT CONSTITUTES BLACK FEMINISM?
THE RECURRING HUMANIST VISION

A wide range of African-American women intellectuals have advanced the view that Black women's struggles are part of a wider struggle for human dignity and empowerment. In an 1893 speech to women, Anna Julia Cooper cogently expressed this alternative worldview:

> We take our stand on the solidarity of humanity, the oneness of life, and the unnaturalness and injustice of all special favoritisms, whether of sex, race, country, or condition. . . . The colored woman feels that woman's cause is one and universal; and that . . . not till race, color, sex, and condition are seen as accidents, and not the substance of life; not till the universal title of humanity to life, liberty, and the pursuit of happiness is conceded to be inalienable to all; not till then is woman's lesson taught and woman's cause won—not the white woman's nor the black woman's, not the red woman's but the cause of every man and of every woman who has writhed silently under a mighty wrong. (Loewenberg and Bogin 1976, 330–31)

Like Cooper, many African-American women intellectuals embrace this perspective regardless of particular political solutions we propose, our fields of study, or our historical periods. Whether we advocate working through separate Black women's organizations, becoming part of women's organizations, working within existing political structures, or supporting Black community institutions, African-American women intellectuals repeatedly identify political actions such as these as a *means* for human empowerment rather than ends in and of themselves. Thus the primary guiding principle of Black feminism is a recurring humanist vision (Steady 1981, 1987).[7]

Alice Walker's preference for the term *womanist*, a term she describes as "womanist is to feminist as purple is to lavender," addresses this notion of the solidarity of humanity. To Walker, one is "womanist" when one is "committed to the survival and wholeness of entire people, male and female." A womanist is "not a separatist, except periodically for health" and is "traditionally universalist, as is 'Mama, why are we brown, pink, and yellow, and our cousins are white, beige, and black?' Ans.: 'Well, you know the colored race is just like a flower garden, with every color flower represented'" (1983, xi). By redefining all people as "people of color," Walker universalizes what are typically seen as individual struggles while simultaneously allowing space for autonomous movements of self-determination.

In assessing the sexism of the Black nationalist movement of the 1960s, Black feminist lawyer Pauli Murray identifies the dangers inherent in separatism as opposed to autonomy, and also echoes Cooper's concern with the solidarity of humanity:

> The lesson of history that all human rights are indivisible and that the failure to adhere to this principle jeopardizes the rights of all is particularly applicable here. A built-in hazard of an aggressive ethnocentric movement which disregards the interests of other disadvantaged groups is that it will become parochial and ultimately self-defeating in the face of hostile reactions, dwindling allies, and mounting frustrations. . . . Only a broad movement for human rights can prevent the Black Revolution from becoming isolated and can insure ultimate success. (Murray 1970, 102)

Without a commitment to human solidarity, suggests Murray, any political movement—whether nationalist, feminist or antielitist—may be doomed to ultimate failure.

bell hook's analysis of feminism adds another critical dimension that must be considered: namely, the necessity of self-conscious struggle against a more generalized ideology of domination:

> To me feminism is not simply a struggle to end male chauvinism or a movement to ensure that women will have equal rights with men; it is a commitment to eradicating the ideology of domination that permeates Western culture on various levels— sex, race, and class, to name a few—and a commitment to reorganizing U. S. society so that the self-development of people can take precedence over imperialism, economic expansion, and material desires. (hooks 1981, 194)

Former assemblywoman Shirley Chisholm also points to the need for self-conscious struggle against the stereotypes buttressing ideologies of domination. In "working toward our own freedom, we can help others work free from the traps of their stereotypes," she notes. "In the end, antiblack, antifemale, and all forms of discrimination are equivalent to the same thing—antihumanism. . . We must reject not only the stereotypes that others have of us but also those we have of ourselves and others" (1970, 181).

This humanist vision is also reflected in the growing prominence of international issues and global concerns in the works of contemporary African-American women intellectuals (Lindsay 1980; Steady 1981, 1987). Economists Margaret Simms and Julianne Malveaux's 1986 edited volume, *Slipping Through the Cracks: The Status of Black Women*, contains articles on Black women in Tanzania, Jamaica, and South Africa.

Angela Davis devotes an entire section of her 1989 book, *Women, Culture and Politics*, to international affairs and includes essays on Winnie Mandela and on women in Egypt. June Jordan's 1985 volume, *On Call*, includes essays on South Africa, Nicaragua, and the Bahamas. Alice Walker writes compellingly of the types of links these and other Black women intellectuals see between African-American women's issues and those of other groups: "To me, Central America is one large plantation; and I see the people's struggle to be free as a slave revolt" (1988, 177).

The words and actions of Black women intellectuals from different historical times and addressing markedly different audiences resonate with a strikingly similar theme of the oneness of all human life. Perhaps the most succinct version of the humanist vision in Black feminist thought is offered by Fannie Lou Hamer, the daughter of sharecroppers, and a Mississippi civil rights activist. While sitting on her porch, Ms. Hamer observed, "Ain't no such thing as I can hate anybody and hope to see God's face" (Jordan 1981, xi).

Taken together, the ideas of Anna Julia Cooper, Pauli Murray, bell hooks, Alice Walker, Fannie Lou Hamer, and other Black women intellectuals too numerous to mention suggest a powerful answer to the question "What is Black feminism?" Inherent in their words and deeds is a definition of Black feminism as a process of self-conscious struggle that empowers women and men to actualize a humanist vision of community.

NOTES

1. For discussions of the concept of standpoint, see Hartsock (1983a, 1983b), Jaggar (1983), and Smith (1987). Even though I use standpoint epistemologies as an organizing concept in this volume, they remain controversial. For a helpful critique of standpoint epistemologies, see Harding (1986). Haraway's (1988) reformulation of standpoint epistemologies approximates my use here.

2. Scott (1985) defines consciousness as the symbols, norms, and ideological forms people create to give meaning to their acts For de Lauretis (1986), consciousness is a process, a "particular configuration of subjectivity,.. produced at the intersection of meaning with experience. . . . Consciousness is grounded in personal history, and self and identity are understood within particular cultural contexts. Consciousness . . . is never fixed, never attained once and for all, because discursive boundaries change with historical conditions" (p. 8).

3. The presence of a Black women's culture of resistance (Terborg-Penn 1986; Dodson and Gilkes 1987) that is both Afrocentric and feminist challenges two prevailing interpretations of the consciousness of oppressed groups. One approach claims that subordinate groups identify with the powerful and have no valid independent interpretation of their own oppression. The second assumes the oppressed are less human than their rulers, and are therefore less capable of interpreting their own experiences (Rollins 1985: Scott 1985). Both approaches see any independent consciousness expressed by oppressed groups as being either not of their own making or inferior to that of the dominant group. More

important, both explanations suggest that the alleged lack of political activism on the part of oppressed groups stems from their flawed consciousness of their own subordination.

4. Even though I will continue to use the term *Afrocentric feminist thought* interchangeably with the phrase *Black feminist thought*, I think they are conceptually distinct.

5. Canadian sociologist Dorothy Smith (1987) also views women's concrete, everyday world as stimulating theory. But the everyday she examines is individual, a situation reflecting in part the isolation of white, middle-class women. In contrast, I contend that the collective values in Afrocentric communities, when combined with the working-class experiences of the majority of Black women, provide a collective as well as an individual concrete.

6. See Harold Cruse's (1967) analysis of the Black intellectual tradition and John Child's (1984) discussion of the desired relationship of Black intellectuals to African-American culture. Childs argues against a relationship wherein "the people recede. They become merely the raw energy which the intellectuals must reshape, refine, and give voice to. A temptation for these intellectuals is to see themselves as the core formative force through which cultures come into conscious existence and through which it is returned, now complete, to the people" (p. 69). Like Childs, I suggest that the role of Black women intellectuals is to "illuminate the very intricacy and strength of the peoples' thought" (p. 87).

7. My use of the term *humanist* grows from an Afrocentric historical context distinct from that criticized by Western feminists. I use the term to tap an Afrocentric humanism as cited by West (1977–78), Asante (1987) and Turner (1984) and as part of the Black theological tradition (Mitchell and Lewter 1986; Cannon 1988). See Harris (1981) for a discussion of the humanist tradition in the works of three Black women writers. See Richards (1990) for a discussion of African-American spirituality, a key dimension of Afrocentric humanism. Novelist Margaret Walker offers one of the clearest discussions of Black humanism. Walker claims: "I think it is more important now to emphasize humanism in a technological age than ever before, because it is only in terms of humanism that society can redeem itself. I believe that mankind is only one race—the human race. There are many strands in the family of man—many races. The world has yet to learn to appreciate the deep reservoirs of humanism in all races, and particularly in the Black race" (Rowell 1975, 12).

Theorizing Difference/ PART
Deconstructing Identity 4

The issue of differences among women was recognized from the early days of second wave theorizing. Statements such as the one by The Combahee River Collective as well as other writings by women of color spoke to the necessity of acknowledging race. Lesbians early protested against assuming heterosexuality in describing women's lives. And the influence of Marxism meant that many feminists in the late 1960s and early 1970s brought to their theorizing an awareness of historical change and class position. The problem, however, was that in the growing tendency to document the seriousness of women's oppression and the fundamentality of gender as an organizing principle of social life, many feminists began to create encompassing generalizations about "woman" and "patriarchy." Differences among women were acknowledged, but minimally incorporated into the basic threads of the theory. And since those who were creating the theory tended to be those of privileged social position, not surprisingly, the theory tended to reflect the patterns most visible to them.

One early voice against such tendencies was that of Monique Wittig. In her influential essay, "One is Not Born a Woman," Wittig distinguishes between "woman" and "women." Whereas "women" depicts the content of specific social relationships, "woman" is a political concept. While the content of "woman" is often taken to be based on biology, Wittig argues that it is a normative category, used in the service of compulsory heterosexuality. Thus she claims that the refusal to become or remain heterosexual always entails the refusal to be a man or woman. And, following from these claims, feminism becomes the political movement that fights for the disappearance of the category of "woman."

While Wittig focuses on the disciplinary uses of the concept of "woman" in the service of compulsory heterosexuality, Elsa Barkley Brown and Norma Alarcón focus on the disciplinary uses of this concept in the service of feminism. Barkley Brown claims that within as well as outside of feminism, history and politics are often thought about in linear, symmetrical ways. She suggests that they are better understood in a manner suggested by jazz, where multiple rhythms are played simultaneously and in dialogue with each other. The point here is that women's lives are not just different, but the differences are relational. Thus, the lives of middle class white women are the way they are because of the kind of lives lived by working class people and people of color. While sometimes relationships among women's lives are acknowledged, it is mostly the less privileged who are seen as having their lives affected by the more privileged. Thus, people tend to see black women's lives as shaped by the lives of white women but not vice versa. This tendency reinforces the idea that the lives of white women represent the norm. However, Barkley Brown argues that to understand the experiences of white women in the United States *in any context*, we need to see how race has shaped their lives in relation to black women. In other words, instead of seeing white women as without race and black women as similar to white women except for having a race, we need to see race as that which constructs the lives of black and white women in relation to each other. This way of thinking about race might have prevented the tendency among some white feminists to see Anita Hill's experiences as explainable in the same terms as those of a white woman. This move deracialized Hill and made her vulnerable to the manipulative use of race by Clarence Thomas and his supporters.

Alarcón links the use of a unitary conception of womanhood to a view of the subject of feminism as an autonomous, self-determining entity. She argues that this type of understanding of feminism is presupposed by any form of standpoint theory. In accord with Barkley Brown, she notes that one of its problems is that it makes the content of feminism the common denominater among women, ignoring differences that transcend such "commonness" but that may be important to any specific determination of womanhood. Moreover, some of those specific determinations of womanhood involve opposition to other women.

Such a view of the subject of consciousness as unitary is, therefore, according to Alarcón, always made from a posture of domination. To assume that consciousness is unitary is to necessarily privilege one aspect of identity and to erase all others. It represents a denial of the recognition of the need for struggle, among the diverse aspects of ourselves as well as with others. Such an assumption cannot grasp the subjectivity of women of color who must situtate themselves within multiple antagonisms. But, the alternative, she argues, is not merely a view of the subject as multiple. Even those women of color who are able to depict the multiplicity of their lives have obtained the privilege necessary to describe one's situation. For Alarcón, this suggests that "to privilege the subject, even if multiple voiced, is not enough."

The theme of the deprivileging of the subject is taken up by Judith Butler. Butler does not argue against the idea of the subject per se so much as against the idea of it as prior to rather than the effect of our actions. When we act *as* a woman or *as* a lesbian we constitute as an effect the very subjectivity our action is taken to be the effect of. The psyche, for Butler, always exceeds the subjectivity we aim to display. Thus, our gender identity is never simple; as it is constituted by differently gendered others, so it is not internally self-identical. Yet, in acting *as* a woman we seek, unsuccessfully, to portray ourselves as possessing such a unitary gender. The same can be said for acting *as* a gay or a lesbian. To act "as a lesbian" always goes beyond the simple injunction to act as one already is; rather, it involves the demand to performatively enact some stipulated idea of what a gay or lesbian "really is."

While Butler sees identity categories as regulatory, she does not advocate their abolition. Rather, she argues for their use as means to destabilize the regimes they are intended to support. Using identity categories in this way means, however, opening up their meanings, making them "sites of necessary trouble." Butler talks about parodic imitation as a means of illuminating the constructed and derivative nature of so called "original" or biologically based forms of identity, such as "heterosexual" or "male" or "female." Within the regime of compulsory heterosexuality, it is often presumed that there is first a sex that is expressed in a gender and then in a sexuality. Subversion of such a regime would mean showing the derivative nature of gender and sex *from* sexuality, that is of employing sexuality against the idea of fixed conceptions of gender and sexual identity.

15

MONIQUE WITTIG

One is Not Born a Woman

A materialist feminist[1] approach to women's oppression destroys the idea that women are a "natural group"; "a racial group of a special kind, a group perceived *as natural*, a group of men considered as materially specific in their bodies."[2] What the analysis accomplishes on the level of ideas, practice makes actual at the level of facts: by its very existence, lesbian society destroys the artificial (social) fact constituting women as a "natural group." A lesbian society[3] pragmatically reveals that the division from men of which women have been the object is a political one and shows how we have been ideologically rebuilt into a "natural group." In the case of women, ideology goes far since our bodies as well as our minds are the product of this manipulation. We have been compelled in our bodies and in our minds to correspond, feature by feature, with the *idea* of nature that has been established for us. Distorted to such an extent that our deformed body is what they call "natural," what is supposed to exist as such before oppression. Distorted to such an extent that in the end oppression seems to be a consequence of this "nature" within ourselves (a nature which is only an *idea*. What a materialist analysis does by reasoning, a lesbian society accomplishes practically: not only is there no natural group "women" (we lesbians are a living proof of it), but as individuals as well we question "woman," which for us, as for Simone de Beauvoir thirty years ago, is only a myth. She said: "One is not born, but becomes a woman. No biological, psychological, or economic fate determines the figure that the human female presents in society: it is civilization as a whole that produces this creature, intermediate between male and eunuch, which is described as feminine."[4]

However, most of the feminists and lesbian-feminists in America and elsewhere still believe that the basis of women's oppression *is biological as well as* historical. Some of them even claim to find their sources in Simone de Beauvoir.[5] The belief in mother right and in a "prehistory" when women created civilization (because of a biological predisposition) while the coarse and brutal men hunted (because of a biological predisposition), is symmetrical with the biologizing interpretation of history produced up to now by the class of men. It is still the same method of finding in women and men a biological explanation of their division, outside of social facts. For me this could never constitute a lesbian approach to women's oppression, since it assumes that the basis of society or the beginning of society lies in heterosexuality. Matriarchy is no less heterosexual than patriarchy: it is only the sex of the oppressor that changes. Furthermore, not only is this conception still imprisoned in the categories of sex (woman and man), but it holds onto the idea that the capacity to give birth (biology) is what defines a woman. Although practical facts and ways of living contradict this theory in lesbian society, there are lesbians who affirm that "women and men are different species or races (the words are used interchangeably): men are biologically inferior to women; male violence is a biological inevitability . . ."[6] By doing this, by admitting that there is a "natural" division between women and men, we naturalize history, we assume that men and women have always existed and will always exist. Not only do we naturalize history, but also consequently we naturalize the social phenomena which express our oppression, making change impossible. For example, instead of seeing giving birth as a forced production, we see it as a "natural," "biological" process, forgetting that in our societies births are planned (demography), forgetting that we ourselves are programmed to produce children, while this is the only social activity "short of war"[7] that presents such a great danger of death. Thus, as long as we will be "unable to abandon by will or impulse a lifelong and centuries-old commitment to childbearing as the female creative act,"[8] gaining control of the production of children will mean much more than the mere control of the material means of this production; women will have to abstract themselves from the definition "woman" which is imposed upon them.

A materialist feminist approach shows that what we take for the cause or origin of oppression is in fact only the *mark*[9] imposed by the oppressor: the "myth of woman,"[10] plus its material effects and manifestations in the appropriated consciousness and bodies of women. Thus, this mark does not preexist oppression: Colette Guillaumin has shown that before the socioeconomic reality of black slavery, the concept of race did not exist, at least not in its modern meaning, since it was applied to the lineage of families. However, now, race, exactly like sex, is taken as an "immediate given," a "sensible given," "physical features," belonging to a natural order. But what we believe to be a physical and direct perception is only a sophisticated and mythic construction, an "imaginary formation,"[11] which reinterprets physical features (in themselves as neutral as any others but marked by the social system) through the network of relationships in which they are perceived. (They are seen *black*, therefore they *are* black; they are seen as *women*, therefore, they *are* women. But before being *seen* that way, they first had to be *made* that way.) A lesbian consciousness should always remember and acknowledge how "unnatural," compelling, totally oppressive, and destructive being "woman" was for us in the old days before the women's liberation movement. It was a political constraint and those who resisted it were accused of not being "real" women. But then we were proud of it, since in the accusation there was already something like a shadow of victory: the avowal by the oppressor that "woman" is not something that goes without saying, since to be one, one has to be a "real" one. We were at the same time accused of wanting to be men. Today this double accusation has been taken up again with enthusiasm in the context of the women's liberation movement by some feminists and also, alas, by some lesbians whose political goal seems somehow to be becoming more and more "feminine." To refuse to be a woman, however, does not mean that one has to become a man. Besides, if we take as an example the perfect "butch," the classic example which provokes the most horror, whom Proust would have called a woman/man, how is her alienation different from that of someone who wants to become a woman? Tweedledum and Tweedledee. At least for a woman, wanting to become a man proves that she escapes her initial programming. But even if she would like to, with all her strength, she cannot become a man. For becoming a man would demand from a woman not only the external appearance of a man but his consciousness as well, that is, the consciousness of one who disposes by right of at least two "natural" slaves during his life span. This is impossible and one feature of lesbian oppression consists precisely of making women out of reach for us, since women belong to men. Thus a lesbian *has to* be something else, a not-woman, a not-man, a product of society, not a product of nature, for there is no nature in society.

The refusal to become (or to remain) heterosexual always meant to refuse to become a man or a woman, consciously or not. For a lesbian this goes further than the refusal of the *role* "woman." It is the refusal of the economic, ideological, and political power of a man. This, we lesbians, and nonlesbians as well, knew before the beginning of the lesbian and feminist movement. However, as Andrea Dworkin emphasizes, many lesbians recently "have increasingly tried to transform the very ideology that has enslaved us into a dynamic, religious, psychologically compelling celebration of female biological potential."[12] Thus, some avenues of the feminist and lesbian movement lead us back to the myth of woman which was created by men especially for us, and with it we sink back into a natural group. Thirty years ago we stood up to fight for a sexless society.[13] Now we find ourselves entrapped in the familiar deadlock of "woman is wonderful." Thirty years ago Simone de Beauvoir underlined particularly the false consciousness which consists of selecting among the features of the myth (that women are different from men) those which look good and using them as a definition for women. What the concept of "woman is wonderful" accomplishes is that it retains for defining women the best features (best according to whom?) which oppression has granted us, and it does not radically question the categories "man" and "woman," which are political categories and not natural givens. It puts us in a position of fighting within the class "women" not as the other classes do, for the disappearance of our class, but for the defense of "woman" and its reenforcement. It leads us to develop with complacency "new" theories about our specificity: thus, we call our passivity "nonviolence," when the main and emergent point for us is to fight our passivity (our fear, rather, a justified one). The ambiguity of the term "feminist" sums up the whole situation. What does "feminist" mean? Feminist is formed with the word "femme," "woman," and means: someone who fights for women. For many of us it means someone who fights for women as a class and for the disappearance of this class. For many others it means someone who fights for woman and her defense—for the myth, then, and its reinforcement. But why was the word "feminist" chosen if it retains the least ambiguity? We chose to call ourselves "feminists" ten years ago, not in order to support or reinforce the myth of woman nor to identify ourselves with the oppressor's definition of us, but rather to affirm that our movement had a history and to emphasize the political link with the old feminist movement.

It is then this movement that we can put in question for the meaning that it gave to feminism. It so happens that feminism in the last century could never resolve its contradictions on the subject of nature/culture, woman/society. Women started to fight for themselves as a group and rightly considered that they shared common features of oppression. But for them these features were natural and biological rather than social. They went so far as to adopt the Darwinist theory of evolution. They did not belive like Darwin, however, "that women were less evolved than men, but they did belive that male and female natures had diverged in the course of evolutionary development and that society at large reflected this polarization."[14] "The failure of early feminism was that it only attacked the Darwinist charge of female inferiority, while accepting the foundations of this charge—namely, the view of woman as 'unique.'"[15] And finally it was women scholars—and not feminists—who scientifically destroyed this theory. But the early feminists had failed to regard history as a dynamic process which develops from conflicts of interests. Furthermore, they still believed as men do that the cause (origin) of their oppression lay within themselves. And therefore the feminists of this first front after some astonishing victories found themselves at an impasse out of a lack of reasons for fighting. They upheld the illogical principle of "equality in difference," an idea now being born again. They fell back into the trap which threatens us once again: the myth of woman.

Thus it is our historical task, and only ours, to define what we call oppression in materialist terms, to make it evident that women are a class, which is to say that the category "woman" as well as the category "man" are political and economic categories not eternal ones. Our fight aims to suppress men as a class, not through a genocidal, but a political struggle. Once the class "men" disappears, "women" as a class will disappear as well, for there are no slaves without masters. Our first task, it seems, is to always thoroughly dissociate "women" (the class within which we fight) and "woman," the myth. For "woman" does not exist for us: it is only an imaginary formation, while "women" is the product of a social relationship. We felt this strongly when everywhere we refused to be called a "*woman's* liberation movement." Furthermore, we have to destroy the myth inside and outside ourselves. "Woman" is not each one of us, but the political and ideological formation which negates "women" (the product of a relation of exploitation). "Woman" is there to confuse us, to hide the reality "women." In order to be aware of being a class and to become a class we have to first kill the myth of "woman" including its most seductive aspects (I think about Virginia

Woolf when she said the first task of a woman writer is to kill "the angel in the house.") But to become a class we do not have to suppress our individual selves, and since no individual can be reduced to her/his oppression we are also confronted with the historical necessity of constituting ourselves as the individual subjects of our history as well. I believe this is the reason why all these attempts at "new" definitions of woman are blossoming now. What is at stake (and of course not only for women) is an individual definition as well as a class definition. For once one has acknowledged oppression, one needs to know and experience the fact that one can constitute oneself as a subject (as opposed to an object of oppression), that one can become *someone* in spite of oppression, that one has one's own identity. There is no possible fight for someone deprived of an identity, no internal motivation for fighting, since although I can fight only with others, first I fight for myself.

The question of the individual subject is historically a difficult one for everybody. Marxism, the last avatar of materialism, the science which has politically formed us, does not want to hear anything about a "subject." Marxism has rejected the transcendental subject, the subject as constitutive of knowledge, the "pure" consciousness. All that thinks per se, before all experience, has ended up in the garbage can of history, because it claimed to exist outside matter, prior to matter, and needed God, spirit, or soul to exist in such a way. This is what is called "idealism." As for individuals, they are only the product of social relations, therefore their consciousness can only be "alienated." (Marx, in *The German Ideology*, says precisely that individuals of the dominating class are also alienated although they are the direct producers of the ideas that alienate the classes oppressed by them. But since they draw visible advantages from their own alienation they can bear it, without too much suffering.) There exists such a thing as class consciousness, but a consciousness which does not refer to a particular subject, except as participating in general conditions of exploitation at the same time as the other subjects of their class, all sharing the same consciousness. As for the practical class problems—outside of the class problems as traditionally defined—that one could encounter (for example, sexual problems), they were considered as "bourgeois" problems that would disappear with the final victory of the class struggle. "Individualistic," "subjectivist," "petit bourgeois," these were the labels given to any person who had shown problems which could not be reduced to the "class struggle" itself.

Thus Marxism has refused the attribute of being a subject to the members of oppressed classes. In doing this, Marxism, because of the ideological and political power this "revolutionary science" immediately exercised upon the workers' movement and all other political groups, has prevented all categories of oppressed peoples from constituting themselves historically as subjects (subjects of their struggle, for example). This means that the "masses" did not fight for themselves but for the party or its organizations. And when an economic transformation took place (end of private property, constitution of the socialist state), no revolutionary change took place within the new society, because the people themselves did not change.

For women, Marxism had two results. It prevented them from being aware that they are a class and therefore from constituting themselves as a class for a very long time, by leaving the relation "women/men" outside of the social order, by turning it into a natural relation, doubtlessly for Marxists the only one along with the relation of mothers to children to be seen this way, and by hiding the class conflict between men and women behind a natural division of labor (*The German Ideology*). This concerns the theoretical (ideological) level. On the practical level, Lenin, the party, all the communist parties up to now, including all the most radical political groups, have always reacted to any attempt on the part of women to reflect and form groups based on their own class problem with an accusation of divisiveness. By uniting, we women, are dividing the strength of the people. This means that for the Marxists women *belong* either to the bourgeois class, or to the proletariat class, in other words, to the men of these classes. In addition, Marxist theory does not allow women any more than other classes of oppressed people to constitute themselves as historical subjects, because marxism does not take into account the fact that a class also consists of individuals one by one. Class consciousness is not enough. We must try to understand philosophically (politically) these concepts of "subject" and "class consciousness" and how they work in relation to our history. When we discover that women are the objects of oppression and appropriation, at the very moment that we become able to perceive this, we become subjects in the sense of cognitive subjects, through an operation of abstraction. Consciousness of oppression is not only a reaction to (fight against) oppression. It is also the whole conceptual reevaluation of the social world, its whole reorganization with new concepts, from the point of view of oppression. It is what I would call the science of oppression created by the oppressed. This operation of understanding reality has to be undertaken by every one of us: call it a subjective, cognitive practice. The movement back and forth between the levels of reality (the conceptual reality and the material reality of oppression, which are both social realities) is accomplished through language.

It is we who historically must undertake the task of defining the individual subject in materialist terms. This certainly seems to be an impossibility since materialism and subjectivity have always been mutually exclusive. Nevertheless, and rather than despairing of ever understanding, we must recognize the *need* to reach subjectivity in the abandonment by many of us to the myth "woman" (the myth of woman being only a snare that holds us up). This real necessity for everyone to exist as an individual, as well as a member of a class, is perhaps the first condition for the accomplishment of a revolution, without which there can be no real fight or transformation. But the opposite is also true; without class and class consciousness there are no real subjects, only alienated individuals. For women to answer the question of the individual subject in materialist terms is first to show, as the lesbians and feminists did, that supposedly "subjective," "individual," "private" problems are in fact social problems, class problems; that sexuality is not for women an individual and subjective expression, but a social institution of violence. But once we have shown that all so-called personal problems are in fact class problems, we will still be left with the question of the subject of each singular woman—not the myth, but each one of us. At this point, let us say that a new personal and subjective definition for all humankind can only be found beyond the categories of sex (woman and man) and that the advent of individual subjects demands first destroying the categories of sex, ending the use of them, and rejecting all sciences which still use these categories as their fundamentals (practically all social sciences).

To destroy "woman," does not mean that we aim, short of physical destruction, to destroy lesbianism simultaneously with the categories of sex, because lesbianism provides for the moment the only social form in which we can live freely. Lesbian is the only concept I know of which is beyond the categories of sex (woman and man), because the designated subject (lesbian) is *not* a woman, either economically, or politically, or ideologically. For what makes a woman is a specific social relation to a man, a relation that we have previously called servitude,[16] a relation which implies personal and physical obligation as well as economic obligation ("forced residence,"[17] domestic corvée, conjugal duties, unlimited production of children, etc.), a relation which lesbians escape by refusing to become or to stay heterosexual. We are escapees from our class in the same way as the American runaway slaves were when escaping slavery and becoming free. For us this is an absolute necessity; our survival demands that we contribute all our strength to the destruction of the class of women within which men appropriate women. This can be accomplished only by the destruction of heterosexuality as a social system which is based on the oppression of women by men and which produces the doctrine of the difference between the sexes to justify this oppression.

NOTES

1. Christine Delphy. "For a Feminist Materialism," in this number of *Feminist Issues*.
2. Colette Guillaumin. "Race et nature: Systeme des marques groupe naturel et rapport sociaux, *Pluriel* 11 (1977).
3. I use the word society with an extended anthropological meaning, since strictly speaking it does not refer to societies in the sense that lesbian societies do not exist completely autonomously from heterosexual social systems. Nevertheless, they are more than simply communities.
4. Simone de Beauvoir, *The Second Sex* (New York: Bantam House), p. 249.
5. Redstockings. *Feminist Revolution* (New York: Random House. 1978), p. 18.
6. Andrea Dworkin, "Biological Superiority, the World's Most Dangerous and Deadly Idea," *Heresies* 6: 46.
7. Ti-Grace Atkinson, *Amazon Odyssey* (New York: Links Books. 1974), p. 15.
8. Andrea Dworkin, op cit., p. 55.
9. Colette Guillaumin, op. cit.
10. Simone de Beauvoir, op. cit.
11. Colette Guillaumin, op. cit.
12. Andrea Dworkin, op. cit.
13. Ti-Grace Atkinson, op. cit., p. 6: "If feminism has any logic at all, it must be working for a sexless society."
14. Rosalind Rosenberg, "In Search of Woman's Nature," *Feminist Studies* 3, no. 1/2 (1975), 144.
15. Ibid. p. 146.
16. In an article published by *L'Idiot International* (Mai 1970) whose original title was "Pour un mouvement de liberation des femmes."
17. Christiane Rochefort, *Les Stances à Sophie* (Paris: Grasset, 1963).

16

ELSA BARKLEY BROWN

"What Has Happened Here"

The Politics of Difference in Women's History and Feminist Politics

My work is not traditional. I like it that way. If people tell me to turn my ends under, I'll leave them raggedy. If they tell me to make my stitches small and tight, I'll leave them loose. Sometimes you can trip over my stitches they're so big. You can always recognize the traditional quilters who come by and see my quilts. They sort of cringe. They fold their hands in front of them as if to protect themselves from the cold. When they come up to my work they think to themselves, "God, what has happened here—all these big crooked stitches." I appreciate these quilters. I admire their craft. But that's not my kind of work. I would like them to appreciate what I'm doing. They are quilters. But I am an artist. And I tell stories.

—Yvonne Wells, quoted in *Stitching Memories: African American Story Quilts*

Questions of difference loom large in contemporary intellectual and political discussions. Although many women's historians and political activists understand the intellectual and political necessity, dare I say moral, intellectual, and political correctness of recognizing the diversity of women's experiences, this recognition is often accompanied with the sad (or angry) lament that too much attention to difference disrupts the relatively successful struggle to produce and defend women's history and women's politics, necessary corollaries of a women's movement. Like the traditionalists who view Yvonne Wells's quilts,[1] many women's historians and feminist activists cringe at the big and loose rather than small and tight stitches that now seem to bind women's experiences. They seek a way to protect themselves and what they have created as women's history and women's politics, and they wonder despairingly, "'God, what has happened here.'" I do not say this facetiously; the fear that all this attention to the differences among women will leave us with only a void, a vacuum, or chaos is a serious concern. Such despair, I believe, is unnecessary, the product of having accepted the challenge to the specifics of our historical knowledge and political organizing while continuing to privilege a linear, symmetrical (some would say Western) way of thinking about history and politics themselves.

I am an optimist. It is an optimism born of reflecting on particular historical and cultural experiences. If I offer some elements of the cultural understandings underpinning those experiences as instructive at this juncture of our intellectual and political journey, it is because "culture, in the largest sense is, after all, a resource that provides the context in which [we] perceive [our] social world. Perceptions of alternatives in the social structure [can] take place only within a framework defined by the patterns and rhythms" of our particular cultural understandings. A rethinking of the cultural aesthetics that underlie women's history and women's politics is essential to what I perceive as the necessary rethinking of the intellectual and political aesthetics.[2]

And it is here that I think African-American culture is instructive as a way of rethinking, of reshaping our thinking processes, our understandings of history and politics themselves. Like Yvonne Wells, Zora Neale Hurston—anthropologist, folklorist, playwright, and novelist—also addressed questions of cultural difference and, in the process, suggested ways of thinking about difference itself:

> Asymmetry is a definite feature of Negro art. . . . The sculpture and the carvings are full of this beauty and lack of symmetry. It is present in the literature, both prose and verse. . . . It is the lack of symmetry which makes Negro dancing so difficult for white dancers to learn. The abrupt and unexpected changes. The frequent change of key and time are evidences of this quality in music. . . . The presence of rhythm and lack of symmetry are paradoxical, but there they are. Both are present to a marked degree. There is always rhythm, but it is the rhythm of segments. Each unit has a rhythm of its own, but when the whole is assembled it is lacking in symmetry. But easily workable to a Negro who is accustomed to the break in going from one part to another, so that he adjusts himself to the new tempo.[3]

Wells and Hurston point to nonlinear ways of thinking about the world, of hearing multiple rhythms and thinking music not chaos, ways that challenge the notion that sufficient attention to difference leads to intellectual chaos, to political vacuum, or to intellectual and political void. Considering Wells's and Hurston's reflections on cultural difference might show us that it is precisely differences which are the path to a community of intellectual and political struggle.[4]

Also instructive is the work of Luisah Teish. In *Jambalaya: The Natural Woman's Book of Personal Charms and Practical Rituals*, she writes about going home to New

Orleans for a visit and being met by her family at the airport: "Before I can get a good look in my mother's face, people begin arranging themselves in the car. They begin to talk gumbo ya ya, and it goes on for 12 days. . . . Gumbo ya ya is a creole term that means 'Everybody talks at once.'" It is through gumbo ya ya that Teish learns everything that has happened in her family and community and she conveys the essential information about herself in the group.[5] That is, it is through gumbo ya ya that Teish tells the history of her sojourn to her family and they tell theirs to her. They do this simultaneously because, in fact, their histories are joined—occurring simultaneously, in connection, in dialogue with each other. To relate their tales separately would be to obliterate that connection.

To some people listening to such a conversation, gumbo ya ya may sound like chaos. We may better be able to understand it as something other than confusion if we overlay it with jazz, for gumbo ya ya is the essence of a musical tradition where "the various voices in a piece of music may go their own ways but still be held together by their relationship to each other."[6] In jazz, for example, each member has to listen to what the other is doing and know how to respond while each is, at the same time, intent upon her own improvisation. It is in this context that jazz pianist Ojeda Penn has called jazz an expression of true democracy, for each person is allowed, in fact required, to be an individual, to go her or his own way, and yet to do so in concert with the group.[7]

History also is everybody talking at once, multiple rhythms being played simultaneously. The events and people we write about did not occur in isolation but in dialogue with a myriad of other people and events. In fact, at any given moment millions of people are all talking at once. As historians we try to isolate one conversation and to explore it, but the trick is then how to put that conversation in a context which makes evident its dialogue with so many others—how to make this one lyric stand alone and at the same time be in connection with all the other lyrics being sung.

Unfortunately, it seems to me, few historians are good jazz musicians; most of us write as if our training were in classical music. We require surrounding silence—of the audience, of all the instruments not singled out as the performers in this section, even often of any alternative visions than the composer's. That then makes it particularly problematic for historians when faced with trying to understand difference while holding on to an old score that has in many ways assumed that despite race, class, ethnicity, sexuality, and other differences, at core all women do have the same gender; that is, the rhythm is the same and the conductor can point out when it is time for each of us to play it. Those who would alter the score or insist on being able to keep their own beat simultaneously with the orchestrated one are not merely presenting a problem of the difficulty of constructing a framework that will allow for understanding the experiences of a variety of women but as importantly the problem of confronting the political implications of such a framework, not only for the women under study but also for the historians writing those studies.

I think we still operate at some basic levels here. This is an opinion which may not be widely shared among women's historians. For I am aware that there is a school of thought within women's history that believes that it, more than any other field of history, has incorporated that notable triumvirate—race, class, and gender—and has addressed difference. But my point is that recognizing and even including difference is, in and of itself, not enough. If fact, such recognition and inclusion may be precisely the way to avoid the challenges, to reaffirm the very traditional stances women's history sees itself as challenging, and to write a good classical score—silencing everyone else until the spotlight is on them but allowing them no interplay throughout the composition. We need to recognize not only differences but also the relational nature of those differences. Middle-class white women's lives are not just different from working-class white, Black, and Latina women's lives. It is important to recognize that middle-class women live the lives they do precisely because working-class women live the lives they do. White women and women of color not only live different lives but white women live the lives they do in large part because women of color live the ones they do.

Let me here grossly simplify two hundred years of Black and white women's history in the United States. Among the major changes we have seen has been the greater labor force participation of white middle-class women; the increasing movement of white middle-class women from the home to voluntary associations within the larger society to formal public political roles; the shift among Black women from agricultural labor to industrial, service, and clerical work; the emergence of Black working-class women from the kitchens of white women to jobs in the private sector; and the shift of middle-class Black women to jobs in the public sector. We could, and often do, set these experiences side by side, thus acknowledging the differences in the experiences of different women. And most often, whether stated or not, our acknowledgement of these differences leads us to recognize how Black women's life choices have been constrained by race—how race has shaped their lives. What we are less apt to acknowledge (that is, to make explicit and to analyze) is how white women's lives are also shaped by race.[8] Even less do I see any real recognition of the relational nature of these differences.

But white middle-class women moved from a primary concern with home and children to involvement in voluntary associations when they were able to have their homes and children cared for by the services—be they direct or indirect—of other women. White middle-class women have been able to move into the labor force in increasing numbers not just differently from other women but precisely because of the different experience of other women and men. The growth in white women's participation in the labor force over the last two decades and the increased opportunities for managerial and professional positions for white women have accompanied the U.S. transition from an industrial to a technological economy. This transition is grounded in the very deindustrialization and decentralization which has meant the export of capital to other parts of the world, where primarily people of color—many of them female—face overwhelming exploitation from multinational corporations' industrial activities and the flight of business from urban (particularly inner-city) areas within the United States and thus the tremendous rise in unemployment and underemployment among African American women and men.[9] It is precisely the connection between global industrial exploitation, rising unemployment and under-

employment in inner-city, largely minority communities, and the growth in opportunities for the middle-class (and especially white middle-class women) which are likely
to go unexplored. The change in the economy has meant not only the growth of the
highly publicized "high-technology" jobs but also the tremendous growth in distinctly
"low-tech" service jobs. The increased labor force participation of white middle-class
women has been accompanied, indeed made possible, by the increased availability outside the home of services formerly provided inside the home—cleaning, food, health,
and personal services. These jobs are disproportionately filled by women of color—
African American, Latina, Asian American.[10] Middle-class Black women were hired to
perform social service functions in the public sector at the same time that white
middle-class women were moving from performing these functions, often as volunteer work, to better paid and higher status positions in the private sector.[11]

We are likely to acknowledge that white middle-class women have had a different
experience from African American, Latina, Asian American, and Native American
women; but the relation, the fact that these histories exist simultaneously, in dialogue
with each other, is seldom apparent in the studies we do, not even in those studies that
perceive themselves as dealing with the diverse experiences of women. The overwhelming tendency now, it appears to me, is to acknowledge and then ignore differences among women. Or, if we acknowledge a relationship between Black and white
women's lives, it is likely to be only that African American women's lives are shaped by
white women's but not the reverse. The effect of this is that acknowledging difference
becomes a way of reinforcing the notion that the experiences of white middle-class
women are the norm; all others become deviant—different from.

This reflects the fact that we have still to recognize that being a woman is, in fact,
not extractable from the context in which one is a woman—that is, race, class, time, and
place. We have still to recognize that all women do not have the same gender. In other
words, we have yet to accept the fact that one cannot write adequately about the lives
of white women in the United States *in any context* without acknowledging the way in
which race shaped their lives. One important dimension of this would involve understanding the relationship between white women and white men as shaped by race.
This speaks not just to the history we write but to the way we understand our own
lives. And I believe it challenges women's history at its core, for it suggests that until
women's historians adequately address difference and the causes for it, they have not
and cannot adequately tell the history of even white middle-class women.

The objections to all of this take many forms but I would like to address two of
them. First, the oft-repeated lament of the problems of too many identities; some
raise this as a conceptual difficulty, others as a stylistic one. In either case, such a discussion reinforces the notion that women of color, ethnic women, and lesbians are
deviant, not the norm. And it reinforces not just the way in which some histories are
privileged but also the way in which some historians are privileged. In fact, in women's
history difference means "not white middle-class heterosexual," thus renormalizing
white middle-class heterosexual women's experiences. One result of this is that white
middle-class heterosexual women do not often have to think about difference or to see
themselves as "other."[12] Not only do people of color not have the luxury in this soci-

ety of deciding whether to identify racially but historians writing about people of color also do not have the privilege of deciding whether to acknowledge, at least at some basic level, their multiple identities. No editor or publisher allows a piece on Black or Latina women to represent itself as being about "women." On the other hand, people who want to acknowledge that their pieces are about "white" women often have to struggle with editors to get that in their titles and consistently used throughout their pieces—the objection being it is unnecessary, superfluous, too wordy, awkward. Historians writing about heterosexual women seldom feel compelled to consistently establish that as part of their subjects' identity whereas historians writing about lesbian women must address sexuality. Does this imply that sexuality is a factor only in the lives of lesbian women, that is, that they are not only different from but deviant? These seem to me to be issues that historians cannot address separately from questions of the privilege some people have in this society and the way in which some historians have a vested interest in duplicating that privilege within historical constructions.

Another objection to the attention to difference is the fear, expressed in many ways, that we will in the process lose the "voice of gender."[13] This reifies the notion that all women have the same gender and requires that most women's voices be silenced and some privileged voice be given center stage. But that is not the only problem with this assumption for it also ignores the fact that gender does not have a voice; women and men do. They raise those voices constantly and simultaneously in concert, in dialogue with each other. Sometimes the effect may seem chaotic because they respond to each other in such ways; sometimes it may seem harmonic. But always it is polyrhythmic; never is it a solo or single composition.

Yet there is in the academy and society at large a continuing effort to uphold some old and presumably well-established literary and historical canon. Those bent on protecting such seem well trained in classical music; they stand on the stage and proudly proclaim: "We have written the score; we are conducting it; we will choose those who will play it without changing a chord; and everyone else should be silent." Unfortunately, much of the current lament among women's historians about the dangers, disruptiveness, and chaos of difference sounds much like this—reifying a classical score, composed and conducted this time by women.

This is not merely a question of whether one prefers jazz to classical music. Like most intellectual issues, this one, too, has real political consequences. We have merely to think about the events surrounding Anita Hill's fall 1991 testimony before the Senate Judiciary Committee. When Professor Hill testified, a number of women, individually and collectively, rallied to her support and to advance awareness of the issue of sexual harassment. Many of Hill's most visible supporters, however, ignored the fact that she is a Black woman, thirteenth child of Oklahoma farmers, or treated these as merely descriptive or incidental matters.[14] The National Organization for Women, feminist legal scholar Catharine MacKinnon, and others spoke forcefully and eloquently about the reality of sexual harassment in women's lives but in doing so often persisted in perpetuating a deracialized notion of women's experiences.[15] One wonders if many white feminists, especially, were not elated to have found an issue and a Black woman who could become a universal symbol, evidence of the common bonds of womanhood. Elevating Hill to such a status, however, required ignoring the racialized and class-specific histories of women's sexuality and stereotypes and our different histories of sexual harassment and sexual violence.[16]

In the end, I would argue, the ignoring of these racialized and class-specific histories became a political liability. Having constructed Anita Hill as a generic or universal woman with no race or class, and having developed an analysis of sexual harassment in which race and class were not central issues, many of Hill's supporters were unable to deal with the racialized and class-specific discussion when it emerged. This suggests how little our scholarship and politics have taught us about the construction of race in the United States, and I think this is connected to the failure to construct race as a significant factor in white women's experiences.[17] Once Clarence Thomas played the race card and a string of his female supporters raised the class issue, they had much of the public discussion to themselves.[18] Thomas and his supporters did not create a race and class context. They exploited it.

Thomas's analysis of Hill's charges and the committee hearings as "a modern day lynching based in white men's sexual stereotypes of black men hinge[d] on assuming that race should be considered only when thinking about his situation."[19] He, therefore, constructed himself as a Black man confronting a generic (read, for many people, "white" or "whitened") woman assisted by white men. "Thomas outrageously manipulated the legacy of lynching in order to shelter himself from Anita Hill's allegations"; by "trivializ[ing] and misrepresent[ing] this painful part of African American people's history," Thomas was able "to deflect attention away from the reality of sexual abuse in African American women's lives."[20] Such a strategy could only have been countered effectively by putting the experience of sexual harassment for Anita Hill in the context of her being a Black woman in the United States.[21]

Eleven years prior, Anita Hill embarked on her legal career. This was a woman who began her formal education before the Morris, Oklahoma, schools were integrated and who had gone on to graduate from one of the country's most elite law schools. When she confronted the sexual harassment, so painfully described in her testimony, the weight of how to handle these advances lay on Anita Hill not merely as "a woman or a Yale Law School graduate," but as "a young black woman, the daughter of Oklahoma farmers, whose family and community expected her to do well. It is essential to understand how this may have shaped both her experiences and her responses."[22] Hill's friend, Ellen Wells, herself the victim of sexual harassment on the job, explained much in her succinct statement before the committee: "You don't walk around carrying your burdens so that everyone can see them. You're supposed to carry that burden and try to make the best of it."[23]

Few Black women of Anita Hill's age and older grew up unaware of the frequency of sexual abuse as part of Black women's employment history. Many of us were painfully aware that one reason our families worked so hard to shield us from domestic and factory work was to shield us from sexual abuse. And we were aware that the choices many of our mothers made (or our fathers insisted upon) to forego employment were in fact efforts to avoid abusive employment situations. Sexual harassment as a legal theory and a public discussion in white middle-class communities may be a late 1970s' phenomenon, but sexual harassment has been not only a widespread phenomenon of Black women's labor history but also the subject of widespread public and private discussion within Black communities.[24] From the late nineteenth century on, Black women and men spoke out about the frequency of sexual abuse of Black women laborers, the majority of whom were employed in domestic service.

In fact, it is hard to read the politics of Black communities, especially Black women's organizations, in the late nineteenth and early twentieth centuries without recognizing this awareness of the reality of sexual harassment.[25] By the mid-twentieth century this was no longer as public a discussion in our communities as it had been in the late nineteenth and early twentieth centuries, but it was still a significant part of the private discussion and necessary socialization to being a Black female living in a racial and racist society.[26] A collective memory of sexual harassment runs deep in African American communities and many Black women, especially those born before the 1960s' civil rights movement, would likely recognize sexual harassment not as a singular experience but as part of a collective and common history.

Given the economic and racial circumstances, Black women understand from an early age that figuring out how to endure, survive, and move forward is an essential responsibility. As a newly minted, young, Black professional, the pride of one's family and community, the responsibility to do so would be even greater. You think, "they endured and so should I." You think you are expected to represent success. How can you dash your family's and community's joy at your achievements and their hopes that education, mobility, and a good job would protect you?[27]

Analyses which offered as explanation of Hill's long silence only that it was representative of the common tendency of women to individualize the experience, to feel isolated, and therefore not to report such incidents assume in fact a lack of socialization around these issues or a socialization which leads women to see themselves as alone, unique in these experiences; and they miss the complexity of such experiences for differing women.[28] By complicating the discussion past singular explanations or in ways that truly explored the differential dimensions and expressions of power, one might have expanded the base of support—support not based on a commonality of experience but on a mobilization that precisely spoke to particularities and differences.

Anita Hill experienced sexual harassment not as a woman who had been harassed by a man but as a Black woman harassed by a Black man. Race is a factor in all cases of sexual abuse—inter- or intraracial—although it is usually only explored in the former. When white middle-class and upper-class men harass and abuse white women they are generally protected by white male privilege; when Black men harass and abuse white women they may be protected by male privilege, but they are as likely to be subject to racial hysteria; when Black men harass and abuse Black women they are often supported by racist stereotypes which assume different sexual norms and different female value among Black people.[29] I think we understand this only if we recognize that race is operative even when all the parties involved are white.

But, recognizing race as a factor in sexual harassment and sexual abuse requires us particularly to consider the consequences of the sexual history and sexual stereotypes of African Americans, especially African American women. "Throughout U. S. history Black women have been sexually stereotyped as immoral, insatiable, perverse; the initiators in all sexual contacts—abusive or otherwise." A result of such stereotyping as well as of the political, economic, and social privileges that resulted to white people (especially white men but also white women) from such stereotyping is that "the common assumption in legal proceedings as well as in the larger society has been that black women cannot be raped or otherwise sexually abused."[30] This has several effects. One is that Black women are most likely not to be believed if they speak of unwarranted sexual advances or are believed to have been willing or to have been the initiator. Both white and Black women have struggled throughout the nineteenth and twentieth centuries to gain control of their sexual selves. But while white elite women's sexual history has included the long effort to break down Victorian assumptions of sexuality and respectability in order to gain control of their sexual selves, Black women's sexual history has required the struggle to be accepted as respectable in an effort to gain control of their sexual selves.[31] Importantly, this has resulted in what Darlene Clark Hine has described as a culture of dissemblance—Black women's sexuality is often concealed, that is, Black women have had to learn to cover up all public suggestions of sexuality, even of sexual abuse. Black women, especially middle-class women, have learned to present a public image that never reveals their sexuality.[32]

Further, given the sexual stereotyping of Black men, a young Anita Hill may also have recognized that speaking of the particularities of Thomas's harassment of her had the potential to restigmatize the whole Black community—male and female. This is not merely, as some have suggested, about protecting Black men or being "dutiful daughters." Black women sought their own as well as the larger community's protection through the development of a politics of respectability.[33] Respectable behavior would not guarantee one's protection from sexual assault, but the absence of such was certain to reinforce racist notions of Black women's greater sexuality, availability, or immorality, as well as the racist notions of Black men's bestiality which were linked to that.

Thomas exploited these issues. Only a discussion which explored the differences and linkages in Black and white women's and working-class and middle-class women's struggles for control of their sexual selves could have effectively addressed his manipulation of race and class and addressed the fears that many Black people, especially women, had at the public discussion of what they perceived as an intraracial sexual issue. Dismissing or ignoring these concerns or imposing a universal feminist standard which ignores the differential consequences of public discourse will not help us build a political community around these issues.

Attending to the questions of race and class surrounding the Thomas hearings would have meant that we would not have had a linear story to tell. The story we did have would not have made good quick sound bites or simple slogans for it would have been far more complicated. But, in the end, I think, it would have spoken to more people's experiences and created a much broader base of understanding and support for issues of sexual harassment. Complicating it certainly would have allowed a fuller confrontation of the manipulation and exploitation of race and class on the part of Thomas and his supporters. The political liability here and the threat to creating a community of struggle came from *not* focusing on differences among women and *not* seriously addressing the race and class dimensions of power and sexual harassment. It would, of course, have been harder to argue that things would have been different if there were a woman on the committee.[34] But then many Black working-class women, having spent their days toiling in the homes of white elite women, understood that femaleness was no guarantee of support and mutuality. Uncomplicated discussions of universal women's experiences cannot address these realities. Race (and yes gender, too) is at once too simple an answer and at the same time a more complex answer than we have yet begun to make it.

The difficulty we have constructing this more complicated story is not merely a failure to deal with the specifics of race and class; the difficulty is also, I believe, in how we see history and politics—in an underlying focus on linear order and symmetry which makes us wary, fearing that layering multiple and asymmetrical stories will only result in chaos with no women's history or women's story to tell, that political community is a product of homogeneity, and that exploring too fully our differences will leave us void of any common ground on which to build a collective struggle. These are the ideas/assumptions which I want to encourage us to think past.

I suggest African American culture as a means to learning to think differently about history and politics. I do this not merely because these are cultural forms with which I am familiar and comfortable. Rather, I do this because there is a lot that those who are just confronting the necessity to be aware of differences can learn from those who have had always to be aware of such. Learning to think nonlinearly, asymmetrically, is I believe essential to our intellectual and political developments. A linear history will lead us to a linear politics and neither will serve us well in an asymmetrical world.

NOTES

This is a revised and expanded version of a paper that was presented at the American Historical Association in New York in December 1990 and published as "Polyrhythms and Improvisation: Lessons for Women's History," *History Workshop Journal* 31 (Spring 1991): 85–90. For thinking through the original paper and/or this expanded version with me, I thank Deborah Britzman, Carol Boyce Davies, Marilynn Desmond, Evelyn Nakano Glenn, Tera Hunter, Robin D. G. Kelley, Deborah K. King, Jerma Jackson, Leslie S. Rowland, Susan Sterrett, and the editors of *Feminist Studies*.

1. See *Stitching Memories: African American Story Quilts*, Gallery Guide, Eva Grudin, curator (Williamstown, Mass.: Williams College Museum of Art, 1989), 1.

2. Elsa Barkley Brown, "African American Women's Quilting: A Framework for Conceptualizing and Teaching African American Women's History," *Signs* 14 (Summer 1989): 925–26.

3. Zora Neale Hurston, "Characteristics of Negro Expression," in *Negro: An Anthology*, ed. Nancy Cunard (London: Wishart, 1934); reprinted in Zora Neale Hurston, *The Sanctified Church* (Berkeley, Calif.: Turtle Island Press, 1983), 54–55.

4. My thinking that communities of struggle are created out of and sustained by difference as much as similarity is, in part, the product of my research on southern urban African American communities in the late nineteenth and early twentieth centuries. See Elsa Barkley Brown, "Weaving Threads of Community: The Richmond Example" (Paper presented at the Southern Historical Association, Fifty-fourth Annual Meeting, Norfolk, Virginia, 12 Nov. 1988); and 'Not Alone to Build This Pile of Brick': Institution Building and Community in Richmond, Virginia" (Paper presented at The Age of Booker T. Washington: Conference in Honor of Louis Harlan, University of Maryland, College Park, May 1990).

5. Luisah Teish, *Jambalaya: The Natural Woman's Book of Personal Charms and Practical Rituals* (San Francisco: Harper & Row, 1985), 139–40.

6. Lawrence Levine, *Black Culture and Black Consciousness: Afro-American Folk Thought from Slavery to Freedom* (New York: Oxford University Press, 1977), 133.

7. Ojeda Penn, "Jazz: American Classical Music as a Philosophic and Symbolic Entity" (Faculty lecture series, Fifteenth Anniversary of African and African-American Studies Program, Emory University, Atlanta, Georgia, March 1986).

8. We need historical studies of white women in the United States comparable to the work begun by Alexander Saxton, David Roediger, Vron Ware, and Ann Laura Stoler—work which takes seriously the study of the racial identity of white U. S. men and white European women and men. Sec, Alexander Saxton, *The Rise and Fall of the White Republic: Class Politics and Mass Culture in Nineteenth-Century America* (New York: Verso, 1990); David R. Roediger, *The Wages of Whiteness: Race and the Making of the American Working Class* (New York: Verso, 1991); Vron Ware, *Beyond the Pale: White Women, Racism, and History* (London: Verso, 1992); Ann Laura Stoler, "Carnal Knowledge and Imperial Power: Gender, Race, and Morality in Colonial Asia," in *Gender at the Crossroads of Knowledge: Feminist Anthropology in the Postmodern Era*, ed. Micaela di Leonardo (Berkeley: University of California Press, 1991), 51–101.

9. Linda Burnham, "Struggling to Make the Turn: Black Women and the Transition to a Post-Industrial Society" (Paper presented at "Survival and Resistance: Black Women in the Americas Symposium," Schomburg Center for Research in Black Culture, New York City, 9 June 1989).

10. Evelyn Nakano Glenn, "From Servitude to Service Work: Historical Continuities in the Racial Division of Reproductive Labor," *Signs* (Autumn 1992).

11. Social service work in the late nineteenth and early twentieth centuries was often performed as volunteer work by Black and white women. With the development of the welfare state, white middle-class women increasingly were able to perform these functions as paid employees of the state and social service agencies. After World War II, as white middle-class women increasingly moved into private sector jobs, Black women were able, for the first time in large numbers, to move out of domestic and industrial work into clerical and professional positions. But they did so principally through their employment in the public sector providing social service functions for Black clients under the pay and scrutiny of local, state, and federal governments. See Teresa L. Amott and Julie A. Matthaei,

Race, Gender, and Work: A Multicultural Economic History of Women in the United States (Boston: South End Press, 1991); Linda Gordon, "Black and White Visions of Welfare: Women's Welfare Activism, 1890–1945," *Journal of American History* 78 (September 1991): 559–90; Elizabeth Higginbotham, "Employment for Professional Black Women in the Twentieth Century," Research Paper No. 3, Memphis State University Center for Research on Women, 1985.

12. One result of this is that women of color often come to stand for the "messiness" and "chaos" of history and politics much as an "aesthetic of uniformity" led the Radio City Music Hall Rockettes to perceive the addition of Black dancers to their chorus line as making "it ugly ('unaesthetic'), imbalanced ('nonuniform'), and sloppy ('imprecise')." See Patricia J. Williams's wonderful discussion in *The Alchemy of Race and Rights* (Cambridge: Harvard University Press, 1991), 116–18.

13. See, for example, "Editor's Notes," *Journal of Women's History* 1 (Winter 1990): 7.

14. The discussion which follows should not be read as a critique of Hill's testimony but rather of those who set themselves out as political and intellectual experts able to speak with authority on "women's issues." It is concerned with public discussion in mainstream media by those identifying themselves as feminist activists, primarily white. My focus on such is a reflection of the scope of this essay and is not intended to hold white women solely or even primarily responsible for the state of public discussion. For my analysis that addresses and critiques developments within the Black community and among Black organizations, see "Imaging Lynching: African American Communities, Collective Memory, and the Politics of Respectability," in *Reflections on Anita Hill: Race, Gender, and Power in the United States*, ed. Geneva Smitherman (Detroit: Wayne State University Press, forthcoming). Finally, I am not naive enough to think the conclusion of the Thomas confirmation process would have been different if these issues had been effectively addressed. I do believe public discussion and political mobilization then and in the future could have been shaped differently by these discussions. Given that for two decades Black women have, according to almost all polls, supported feminist objectives in larger numbers than white women, I think we have to look to something other than Black women's reported antifeminism or privileging of race over gender for the answer to why an effective cross-race, cross-class political mobilization and discussion did not develop.

15. This is not to say that they did not acknowledge that Hill was Black or even, in Catharine MacKinnon's case, that "most of the women who have brought forward claims that have advanced the laws of sexual harassment have been black. Because racism is often sexualized, black women have been particularly clear in identifying this behavior as a violation of their civil rights." See *People*, 28 Oct. 1991, 49. It is to say that having acknowledged this, race is not a significant factor in the analysis of women's experience of sexual harassment. For a more extensive analysis of this and other issues raised in this essay, see "Imaging Lynching," and Elsa Barkley Brown, "Can We Get There from Here? The Contemporary Political Challenge to a Decade of Feminist Research and Politics" (Paper prepared for "What Difference Does Difference Make? The Politics of

Race, Class, and Gender Conference," Duke University-University of North Carolina Center for Research on Women, Chapel Hill, 31 May 1992).

16. For an analysis fully attuned to questions of race and class, see Kimberlé Crenshaw's participation in "Roundtable: Sexuality after Thomas/Hill," *Tikkun*, January/February 1992, 25–30. See also Crenshaw's analysis of Thomas's nomination pre-Anita Hill in "Roundtable: Doubting Thomas," *Tikkun*, September/October 1991, 23–30. It is useful to compare Crenshaw's analysis in the first with Ellen Willis's and in the latter with Catharine MacKinnon's.

17. In fact, race has been methodologically and theoretically written out of many analyses of sexual harassment. See, for example, the pioneering historical work of Mary Bularzik and the pioneering legal theory of Catharine MacKinnon. Bularzik is, quite appropriately, writing on white women and developing a discussion of the class dimension of sexual harassment; in the process, however, she offhandedly dismisses many Black women's understandings as false consciousness since they "often interpreted sexual harassment as racism, not sexism." See "Sexual Harassment at the Workplace: Historical Notes," *Radical America* 12 (July-August 1978), reprinted in *Workers' Struggles, Past and Present: A "Radical America" Reader*, ed. James Green (Philadelphia: Temple University Press, 1983), 117–35. MacKinnon acknowledges race as a factor only in cases involving persons of different races. See, for example, *Sexual Harassment of Working Women: A Case of Sex Discrimination* (New Haven: Yale University Press, 1979), 30–31. More importantly, her legal theory is built upon a notion of universal women and generic men which assumes that "men" are white and heterosexual.

> Over time, women have been economically exploited, relegated to domestic slavery, used in denigrating entertainment, deprived of a voice and authentic culture, and disenfranchised and excluded from public life. Women, by contrast with comparable men, have systematically been subjected to physical insecurity; targeted for sexual denigration and violation; depersonalized and denigrated; deprived of respect, credibility, and resources; and silenced—and denied public presence, voice, and representation of their interests. *Men as men have generally not had these things done to them; that is, men have had to be Black or gay (for instance) to have these things done to them as men.*

See *Toward a Feminist Theory of the State* (Cambridge: Harvard University Press, 1989), 160 (emphasis mine).

18. Thomas did this most significantly in his dramatic calling up of the lynching issue and situating himself, for the first time in the hearings, as a Black man, and also in his efforts to portray Hill as a Black woman who felt inferior to and threatened by lighter skinned and white women. The following analysis, for reasons of space, addresses the manipulation of issues of race; for a more extensive analysis of the class issue, see my "Imaging Lynching," and "Can We Get There from Here?"

19. Letter to The Honorable Senators of the United States from African American Academic and Professional Women Who Oppose the Clarence Thomas Nomination, 15 Oct. 1991; "Official Statement to All Members of the United States

Senate from African American Academic and Professional Women: A Petition to Reject the Clarence Thomas Nomination," 15 Oct. 1991; see also, "Official Statement to All Members of the United States Senate—A Petition of African-American Professors of Social Science and Law," 12 Oct. 1991; all in my possession.

20. "African American Women in Defense of Ourselves," Guest Editorial *New York Amsterdam News*, 26 Oct. 1991 and Advertisement in *New York Times*, 17 Nov. 1991; San Francisco *Sun Reporter*, 20 Nov. 1991; *Capital Spotlight* (Washington, D. C.), 21 Nov. 1991; *Los Angeles Sentinel*, 21 Nov. 1991; *Chicago Defender*, 23 Nov. 1991; *Atlanta Inquirer*, 23 Nov. 1991; *Carolinian* (Raleigh, N. C.), 28 Nov. 1991.

21. The following discussion is not meant to speak for or analyze specifically Anita Hill's personal experience but to suggest the ways in which complicating the issues was essential to a discussion which would engage women from differing racial and class backgrounds.

22. "Official Statement to All Members of the United States Senate from African American Academic and Professional Women."

23. Ellen Wells, testimony before Senate Judiciary Committee, 13 Oct. 1991.

24. Mary Bularzik documents the longstanding recognition and discussion of sexual harassment of white working-class women but argues that white middle-class women were initially more reluctant to make public the sexual harassment that accompanied their employment. See "Sexual Harassment in the Workplace."

25. For public discussions of the connections between Black women's employment conditions and sexual abuse, see, for example, Maggie Lena Walker, "Traps for Women," Bethel A. M. E. Church, Richmond, Virginia, 15 Mar. 1925:

> Poverty is a trap for *women*, and especially for our women. . . . When I walk along the avenue of our city and I see our own girls employed in the households of the whites, my heart aches with pain. Not that I cast a slur, or say one word against any kind of honest employment, yet when I see the good, pure, honest colored girl who is compelled to be a domestic in a white man's family—while I applaud the girl for her willingness to do honest work in order to be self supporting, and to help the mother and father who have toiled for her, yet, I tremble lest she should slip and fall a victim to some white man's lust.

See Maggie Lena Walker Papers, Maggie Lena Walker National Historical Site, Richmond, Virginia. See Black female domestic workers' own public accounts. For example:

> I lost my place because I refused to let the madam's husband kiss me. . . . I believe nearly all white men take, and expect to take, undue liberties with their colored female servants—not only the fathers, but in many cases the sons also. Those servants who rebel against such familiarity must either leave or expect a mighty hard time, if they stay.

See A Negro Nurse, "More Slavery at the South," *Independent* 72 (25 Jan. 1912): 197–98. Black club women such as Fannie Barrier Williams talked publicly of the letters they received from Black parents urging them to work to secure employment opportunities that would save their daughters from "going into the [white] homes of the South as servants." See "A Northern Negro's Autobiography," *Independent* 57 (14 July 1904): 96.

26.   The primary persons continuing these discussions were, of course, domestic workers themselves. See, for example, "When maids would get together, they'd talk of it. . . . They always had to fight off the woman's husband," in Florence Rice's interview with Gerda Lerner, quoted in *Black Women in White America: A Documentary History*, ed. Gerda Lerner (New York: Vintage Books, 1972), 275; or "nobody was sent out before you was told to be careful of the white man or his sons" in Elizabeth Clark-Lewis," 'This Work had a' End': The Transition from Live-In to Day Work," *Southern Women: The Intersection of Race, Class, and Gender*, Working Paper No. 2, Center for Research on Women, Memphis State University, 15. It was common practice for domestic workers to gather together to socialize and/or to provide support and advice regarding working conditions, survival strategies, and so on. Because many of these gatherings occurred in the workers' homes, they were often overheard if not participated in by the young people in the homes. See, for example, Bonnie Thornton Dill, "Making Your Job Good Yourself': Domestic Service and the Construction of Personal Dignity," in *Women and the Politics of Empowerment*, ed. Ann Bookman and Sandra Morgen (Philadelphia: Temple University Press, 1988), 33–52; Paule Marshall, "From the Poets in the Kitchen," *New Your Times Book Review*, 9 Jan. 1983. Because the majority of Black women in the labor force up to 1960 were employed as domestic workers, a substantial number of African American women grew up with one or more family members who did domestic work and therefore were in frequent earshot of such conversations. In my own family a majority of my aunts and great-aunts were employed in either domestic or factory work; my mother, even though she had a college degree, when she took on paid employment to supplement the family income worked as a domestic or in a factory. For discussions of sexual abuse among Black women factory workers, see, for example, Beverly W. Jones, "Race, Sex, and Class: Black Female Tobacco Workers in Durham, North Carolina, 1920–1940, and the Development of Female Consciousness," *Feminist Studies* 10(Fall 1984): 443–50. Robin D. G. Kelley suggests that the strategies adopted by Black female factory operatives to resist sexual harassment may have been passed down and developed out of domestic workers' experiences. "'We Are Not What We Seem': Towards a Black Working-Class Infrapolitics in the Twentieth Century South" (unpublished paper cited by permission of the author).

27.   These are obviously not just questions exclusive to Africa Americam women but suggest what may happen to any group of people when so few are able to succeed and what may happen when you see yourself, and are seen, as representing your community and not just yourself. I think of Chinua Achebe's protagonist in *A Man of the People*, of Alice Dunbar-Nelson's diary entries which reveal her awareness of her responsibility to maintain a particular image even when she had not the money to do so, and of Black male professionals employed in Rich-

mond in the early twentieth century who told me of the difficulty they had making ends meet financially when their professional positions paid very little but their obligation to represent the potential for African American people's success meant that the Black community did not want them taking on second jobs as hotel waiters or janitors. All expressed an awareness that many people depended—not just financially but psychological—on their success and a belief that they needed to portray success and hide all traces that mobility had not allowed them to escape the traps of any of the others.

28. See, for example, Catharine MacKinnon in "Hill's Accusations Ring True to a Legal Trailblazer," *Detroit Free Press*, 13 Oct. 1991, 6F.

29. One of the most egregious examples of the latter as related to this particular case can be seen in Orlando Patterson's argument that if Thomas said the things Hill charged he was merely engaging in a "down-home style of courting" which would have been "immediately recognizable" to Hill "and most women of Southern working-class backgrounds, white or black, especially the latter" but which would have been "completely out of the cultural frame of [the] white upper-middle-class work world" of the senators who would vote on his confirmation. See, "Race, Gender, and Liberal Fallacies," *New York Times*, 20 Oct. 1991, and the even more obnoxious defense of his position in *Reconstruction* 1,4 (1992): 68–71, 75–77.

30. "African American Women in Defense of Ourselves." For a good discussion of the sexual stereotypes of African American women in the late nineteenth and early twentieth centuries, see Beverly Guy-Sheftall, Daughters of Sorrow: Attitudes toward Black Women, 1880–1920 (Brooklyn: Carlson Publishing, 1990), esp. chaps. 3 and 4. See also Patricia Morton, *Disfigured Images: The Historical Assault on Afro-American Women* (New York: Praeger, 1991).

31. Crenshaw, "Roundtable: Sexuality after Thomas/Hill," 29.

32. Darlene Clark Hine, "Rape and the Culture of Dissemblance: Preliminary Thoughts on the Inner Lives of Black Midwestern Women," *Signs* 14 (Summer 1989): 912–20.

33. The implications of this are explored in my "Imaging Lynching."

34. This became a common argument during and in the days following the hearings; see, for example, Barbara Ehrenreich, "Women Would Have Known," *Times*, 21 Oct. 1991, 104.

17

NORMA ALARCÓN

The Theoretical Subject(s) of *This Bridge Called My Back* and Anglo-American Feminism

This Bridge Called My Back: *Writings by Radical Women of Color*, edited by Chicana writers Cherríe Moraga and Gloria Anzaldúa,* was intended as a collection of essays, poems, tales and testimonials that would give voice to the contradictory experiences of "women of color." In fact, the editors state:

> We are the colored in a white feminist movement.
> We are the feminists among the people of our culture.
> We are often the lesbians among the straight.[1]

By giving voice to such experiences, each according to her style, the editors and contributors believed they were developing a theory of subjectivity and culture that would demonstrate the considerable differences between them and Anglo-American women, as well as between them and Anglo-European men and men of their own

---

* Hereafter cited as *Bridge*, the book has two editions. I use the second edition published by Kitchen Table Press, 1983. The first edition was published by Persephone Press, 1981.

culture. As speaking subjects of a new discursive formation, many of *Bridge's* writers were aware of the displacement of their subjectivity across a multiplicity of discourses: feminist/lesbian, nationalist, racial, socioeconomic, historical, etc. The peculiarity of their displacement implies a multiplicity of positions from which they are driven to grasp or understand themselves and their relations with the real, in the Althusserian sense of the word.[2] *Bridge* writers, in part, were aware that these positions are often incompatible or contradictory, and others did not have access to the maze of discourses competing for their body and voice. The self-conscious effort to reflect on their "flesh and blood experiences to concretize a vision that can begin to heal our 'wounded knee'"[3] led many *Bridge* speakers to take a position in conflict with multiple intercultural and intracultural discursive interpretations in an effort to come to grips with "the many-headed demon of oppression."[4]

Since its publication in 1981, *Bridge* has had a diverse impact on Anglo American feminist writings in the United States. Teresa de Lauretis, for example, claims that *Bridge* has contributed to a "shift in feminist consciousness,"[5] yet her explanation fails to clarify what the shift consists of and for whom. There is little doubt, however, that *Bridge*, along with the 1980s writings by many women of color in the United States, has problematized many a version of Anglo-American feminism, and has helped open the way for alternative feminist discourses and theories. Presently, however the impact among most Anglo American theorists appears to be more cosmetic than not because, as Jane Flax has recently noted, "The modal 'person' in feminist theory still appears to be a self-sufficient individual adult."[6] This particular "modal person" corresponds to the female subject most admired in literature which Gayatri Chakravorty Spivak had characterized as one who "articulates herself in shifting relationship to. . .the constitution and 'interpellation' of the subject not only as individual but as 'individualist.'"[7] Consequently, the "native female" or "woman of color" can be excluded from the discourse of feminist theory. The "native female"—object of colonialism and racism—is excluded because, in Flax's terms, white feminists have not "explored how our understanding of gender relations, self, and theory are partially constituted in and through experiences of living in a culture in which asymmetric race relations are a central organizing principle of society."[8] Thus, the most popular subject of Anglo American feminist is an autonomous, self-making, self determining subject who first proceeds according to the *logic of identification* with regard to the subject of consciousness, a notion usually viewed as the purview of man, but now claimed for women." Believing that in this respect she is the same as man, she now claims the right to pursue her own identity, to name herself, to pursue self-knowledge, and, in the words of Adrienne Rich, to effect "a change in the concept of sexual identity."[10]

Though feminism has problematized gender relations, indeed, as Flax observes, gender is "the single most important advance in feminist theory,"[11] it has not problematized the subject of knowledge and her complicity with the notion of consciousness as "synthetic unificatory power, the centre and active point of organization of representations determining their concatenation."[12] The subject (and object) of knowledge is now a woman, but the inherited view of consciousness has not been questioned at all. As a result, some Anglo-American feminist subjects of consciousness have tended to become a parody of the masculine subject of consciousness, thus revealing their ethnocentric liberal underpinnings. In 1982, Jean Bethke Elshtain had noted the "masculine cast" of radical feminist language, for example, noting the terms of "raw power, brute force, martial discipline, law and order with a feminist face—and voice."[13] Also in critiquing liberal feminism and its language, she notes that "no vision of the political community that might serve as the ground work of a life in common is possible within a political life dominated by a self-interested, predatory individualism."[14] Althusser argues that this tradition "has privileged the category of the 'subject' as Origin, Essence and Cause, responsible in its internality for all determinations of the external object. In other words, this tradition has promoted Man, in his ideas and experience, as the source of knowledge, morals and history."[15] By identifying in this way with this tradition standpoint epistemologists have substituted, ironically, woman for man. This 'logic of identification' as a first step in constructing the theoretical subject of feminism is often veiled from standpoint epistemologists because greater attention is given to naming female identity, and describing women's ways of knowing as being considerably different than men's.[16] By emphasizing 'sexual difference,' the second step takes place, often called oppositional thinking (counteridentifying). However, this gendered standpoint epistemology leads to feminism's bizarre position with regard to other liberation movements, working inherently against the interests of non-white women and no one else. For example, Sandra Harding argues that oppositional thinking (counteridentification) with white men should be retained even though "[t]here are suggestions in the literature of Native Americans, Africans, and Asians that what feminists call feminine versus masculine personalities, ontologies, ethics, epistemologies, and world views may be what these other liberation movements call Non-Western versus Western personalities and world views. . . . I set aside the crucial and fatal complication for this way of thinking—the fact that one half of these people are women and that most women are not Western."[17] She further suggests that feminists respond by relinquishing the totalizing "master theory" character of our theory-making: "This response to the issue [will manage] to retain the categories of feminist theory. . .and simply set them alongside the categories of the theory making of other subjugated groups. . . . Of course, it leaves bifurcated (and perhaps even more finely divided) the identities of all except ruling-class white Western women."[18] The apperception of this situation is precisely what led to the choice of title for the book *All The Women Are White, All The Blacks Are Men, But Some of Us Are Brave*, edited by Gloria T. Hull, Patricia Bell Scott and Barbara Smith.[19]

Notwithstanding the power of *Bridge* to affect the personal lives of its readers, *Bridge*'s challenge to the Anglo-American subject of feminism has yet to effect a newer discourse. Women of color often recognize themselves in the pages of *Bridge*, and write to say, "The women writers seemed to be speaking to me, and they actually understood what I was going through. Many of you put into words feelings I have had that I had no way of expressing. . . . The writings justified some of my thoughts telling me I had a right to feel as I did."[20] On the other hand, Anglo-feminist readers of *Bridge* tend to appropriate it, cite it as an instance of difference between women, and proceed to negate that difference by subsuming women of color into the unitary category of woman/women. The latter is often viewed as the "common denominator" in an oppositional (counteridentifying) discourse with some white men, that leaves us unable to explore relationships among women.

Bridge's writers did not see the so called "common denominator" as the solution for the construction of the theoretical feminist subject. In the call for submissions the editors clearly stated: "We want to express to all women—especially to white middle class women—the experiences which divide us as feminists; we want to explore the causes, and sources of, and solutions to these divisions. We want to create a definition that expands what 'feminist' means to us."[21] Thus, the female subject of *Bridge* is highly complex. She is and has been constructed in a crisis of meaning situation which includes racial and cultural divisions and conflicts. The psychic and material violence that gives shape to that subjectivity cannot be underestimated nor passed over lightly. The fact that not all of this violence comes from men in general but also from women renders the notion of "common denominator" problematic.

It is clear, however, that even as *Bridge* becomes a resource for the Anglo-American feminist theory classroom and syllabus, there's a tendency to deny differences if those differences pose a threat to the "common denominator" category. That is, unity would be purchased with silence, putting aside the conflictive history of groups' interrelations and interdependence. In the words of Paula Treichler, "[h]ow do we address the issues and concerns raised by women of color, who may themselves be even more excluded from theoretical feminist discourse than from the women's studies curriculum?. . . Can we explore our 'common differences' without overemphasizing the division that currently seems to characterize the feminism of the United States and the world?"[22] Clearly, this exploration appears impossible without a reconfiguration of the subject of feminist theory, and her relational position to a multiplicity of others, not just white men.

Some recent critics of the "exclusionary practices in Women's Studies" have noted that its gender standpoint epistemology leads to a 'tacking on' of "material about minority women" without any note of its "significance for feminist knowledge."[23] The common approaches noted were the tendency to 1) treat race and class as secondary features in social organization (as well as representation) with primacy given to female subordination; 2) acknowledge that inequalities of race, class and gender generate different experiences and then set race and class inequalities aside on the grounds that information was lacking to allow incorporation into an analysis; 3) focus on descriptive aspects of the ways of life, values, customs and problems of women in subordinate race and class categories with little attempt to explain their source or their broader meaning. In fact, it may be impossible for gender standpoint epistemology to ever do more than a "pretheoretical presentation of concrete problems."[24] Since the subject of feminist theory and its single theme—gender—go largely unquestioned, its point of view tends to suppress and repress voices that question its authority, and as Jane Flax remarks, "The suppression of these voices seems to be a necessary condition for the (apparent) authority, coherence, and universality of our own."[25] This may account for the inability to include the voices of "women of color" into feminist discourse, though they are not necessarily under-represented in the reading list.

For the standpoint epistemologists, the desire to construct a feminist theory based solely on gender, on the one hand, and the knowledge or implicit recognition that such an account might distort the representation of many women and/or correspond to that of some men, on the other, gives rise to anxiety and ambivalence with respect to the future of that feminism, especially in Anglo-America. At the core of that attitude is the often unstated recognition that if the pervasiveness of women's oppression is virtually 'universal' on some level, it is also highly diverse from group to group and that women themselves may become complicitous with that oppression. "Complicity arises," says Macdonell, "where through lack of a positive starting point either a practice is driven to make use of prevailing values or a critique becomes the basis for a new theory."[26] Standpoint epistemologists have made use of the now gendered and feminist notion of consciousness, without too much question. (This notion, of course, represents the highest value of European culture since the Enlightenment.) The inclusion of other analytical categories such as race and class becomes impossible for a subject whose consciousness refuses to acknowledge that "one becomes a woman" in ways that are much more complex than in a simple opposition to men. In cultures in which "asymmetric race and class relations are a central organizing principle of society," one may also "become a woman" in opposition to other women. In other words, the whole category of woman may also need to be problematized, a point that I shall take up later. In any case, one should not step into that category nor that of man that easily or simply.

Simone de Beauvoir and her key work *The Second Sex* have been most influential in the development of feminist standpoint epistemology. She may even be responsible for the creation of Anglo-American feminist theory's "episteme": a highly self-conscious ruling class white Western female male subject locked in a struggle to the death with "Man." De Beauvoir has shaken the world of women, most especially with the ramification of her phrase, "One is not born, but rather becomes, a woman."[27] For over 400 pages of text after that statement, de Beauvoir demonstrates how a female is constituted as a "woman" by society as her freedom is curtailed from childhood. The curtailment of freedom incapacitates her from affirming "herself as a subject."[28] Very few women, indeed, can escape the cycle of indocrination except perhaps the writer/intellectual because "[s]he knows that she is a conscious being, a subject."[29] This particular kind of woman can perhaps make of her gender a project and transform her sexual identity.[30] But what of those women who are not so privileged, who neither have the political freedom nor the education? Do they now, then, occupy the place of the Other (the 'Brave') while some women become subjects? Or do we have to make a subject of the whole world?

Regardless of our point of view in this matter, the way to becoming a female subject has been effected through consciousness-raising. In 1982, in a major theoretical essay, "Feminism, Method and the State: An Agenda for Theory," Catharine A. MacKinnon cited *Bridge* as a book that explored the relationship between sex and race and argued that "consciousness-raising" was *the* feminist method.[31] The reference to *Bridge* was brief. It served as an example, along with other texts, of the challenge that race and nationalism have posed for Marxism. According to her, Marxism has been unable to account for the appearance of these emancipatory discourses nor has it been able to assimilate them. Nevertheless, MacKinnon's major point was to demonstrate the epistemological challenge that feminism and its primary method, "consciousness-raising," posed for Marxism. Within Marxism, class as method of analysis has failed to reckon with the historical force of sexism. Through "consciousness-raising" (from women's point of view), women are led to know the world in a different way. Women's experience of politics, of life as sex objects, gives rise to its own method of appropriating that reality: feminist method. It challenges the objectivity of the "empirical gaze" and "rejects the distinction between knowing subject and known object."[32] By having women be the subject of knowledge, the so-called "objectivity" of men is brought into question. Often, this leads to privileging women's way of knowing in opposition to men's way of knowing, thus sustaining the very binary opposition that feminism would like to change or transform. Admittedly, this is only one of the many paradoxical procedures in feminist thinking, as Nancy Cott confirms: "It acknowledges diversity among women while positing that women recognize their unity. It requires gender consciousness for its basis, yet calls for the elimination of prescribed gender roles."[33]

However, I suspect that these contradictions or paradoxes have more profound implications than is readily apparent. Part of the problem may be that as feminist practice and theory recuperate their sexual differential, through "consciousness-raising," women reinscribe such a differential as feminist epistemology or theory. With gender as the central concept in feminist thinking, epistemology is flattened out in such a way that we lose sight of the complex and multiple ways in which the subject and object of possible experience are constituted. The flattening effect is multiplied when one considers that gender is often solely related to white men. There's no inquiry into the knowing subject beyond the fact of being a "woman." But what is a "woman," or a "man" for that matter? If we refuse to define either term according to some "essence," then we are left with having to specify their conventional significance in time and space, which is liable to change as knowledge increases or interests change. The fact that Anglo American feminism has appropriated the generic term for itself leaves many a woman in this country having to call herself otherwise, i.e., "woman of color," which is equally "meaningless" without further specification. It also gives rise to the tautology "Chicana women." Needless to say, the requirement of gender consciousness only in relationship to man leaves us in the dark about a good many things, including interracial and intercultural relations. It may be that the only purpose this type of differential has is as a political strategy. It does not help us envision a world beyond binary restrictions, nor does it help us to reconfigure feminist theory to include the "native female." It does, however, help us grasp the paradox that within this cultural context one cannot be a feminist without becoming a gendered subject of knowledge, which makes it very difficult to transcend gender at all and to imagine relations between women.

In *Feminist Politics and Human Nature*, Alison M. Jaggar, speaking as a socialist feminist, refers repeatedly to *Bridge* and other works by women of color. In that work, Jaggar states that subordinated women are unrepresented in feminist theory. Jaggar claims that socialist feminism is inspired by Marxist and radical feminist politics though the latter has failed to be scientific about its insights. *Bridge* is cited various times to counter the racist and classist position of radical feminists.[34] Jaggar charges that "[r]adical feminism has encouraged women to name their own experience but it has not recognized explicitly that this experience must be analyzed, explained and theoretically transcended."[35] In a sense, Jaggar's charge amounts to the notion that radical feminists were flattening out their knowledge by an inadequate methodology, i.e. gender consciousness raising. Many of Jaggar's observations are a restatement of *Bridge*'s challenge to Anglo-American feminists of all persuasions, be it Liberal, Radical, Marxist, and Socialist, the types sketched out by Jaggar. For example, "[a] representation of reality from the standpoint of women must draw on the variety of all women's experience"[36] may be compared to Barbara Smith's view in *Bridge* that "Feminism is the political theory and practice to free *all* women: women of color, working-class women, poor women, physically challenged women, lesbians, old women, as well as white economically privileged heterosexual women."[37] Jaggar continues, "Since historically diverse groups of women, such as working class women, women of color, and others have been excluded from intellectual work, they somehow must be enabled to participate as subjects as well as objects of feminist theorizing."[38] Writers in *Bridge* did appear to think that "consciousness-raising" and the naming of one's experience would deliver some theory and yield a notion of "what 'feminist' means to us."[39] Except for Smith's statement, there is no overarching view that would guide us as to "what 'feminist' means to us." Though there is a tacit political identity gender/class/race-encapsulated in the phrase "women of color" that connects the pieces—they tend to split apart into "vertical relations" between the culture of resistance and the culture resisted or from which excluded. Thus, the binary restrictions become as prevalent between race/ethnicity of oppressed versus oppressor as between the sexes. The problems inherent in Anglo-American feminism and race relations are so locked into the "Self/Other" theme that it is no surprise that *Bridge*'s co-editor Moraga would remark, "In the last three years I have learned that Third World feminism does not provide the kind of easy political framework that women of color are running to in droves. The *idea* of Third World feminism has proved to be much easier between the covers of a book than between real live women."[40] She refers to the United States, of course, because feminism is alive and well throughout the Third World largely within the purview of women's rights, or as a class struggle.[41]

The appropriation of *Bridge*'s observations in Jaggar's work differs slightly from the others in its view of linguistic use, implying to a limited extent that language is also reflective of material existence. The crucial question is how, indeed, can women of color be subjects as well as objects of feminist theorizing? Jaggar cites María Lugones' doubts: "We cannot talk to you in our language because you do not understand it. . . . The power of white Anglo women vis-à-vis Hispanas and Black women is in inverse proportion to their working knowledge of each other. . . . Because of their ignorance, white Anglo women who try to do theory with women of color inevitably disrupt the dialogue. Before they can contribute to collective dialogue, they need to 'know the text,' to have become familiar with an alternative way of viewing the world. . . . You need to learn to become unintrusive, unimportant, patient to the point of tears, while at the same time open to learning any possible lessons. You will have to come to terms with the sense of alienation, of not belonging, of having your world thoroughly disrupted, having it criticized and scrutinized from the point of view of those who have been harmed by it, having important concepts central to it dismissed, being viewed with mistrust."[42] One of *Bridge*'s breaks with prevailing conventions is linguistic. Lugones' advice to Anglo women to listen was post *Bridge*. If prevailing conventions of speaking/writing had been observed, many a contributor would have been censored or silenced. So would have many a major document or writing of minorities. *Bridge* leads us to understand that the silence and silencing of people begins with the dominating enforcement of linguistic conventions, the resistance to relational dialogues, as well as the disenablement of peoples by outlawing their forms of speech. Anglo-American feminist theory assumes a speaking subject who is an autonomous, self-conscious individual woman. Such theory does not discuss the linguistic status of the person. It takes for granted the linguistic status which founds subjectivity. In this way it appropriates woman/women for itself, and turns its work into a theoretical project within which the rest of us are compelled to 'fit.' By 'forgetting' or refusing to take into account that we are culturally constituted in and through language in complex ways and not just engendered in a homogeneous situation, the Anglo-American subject of consciousness cannot come to terms with her (his) own class-biased ethnocentrism. She is blinded to her own construction not just as a woman but as an Anglo-American one. Such a subject creates a theoretical subject that could not possibly include all women just because we are women. It is against this feminist backdrop that many "women of color" have struggled to give voice to their subjectivity and which effected the publication of the writings collected in *Bridge*. However, the freedom of women of color to posit themselves as multiple-voiced subjects is constantly in peril of repression precisely at that point where our constituted contradictions put us at odds with women different from ourselves.

The pursuit of a "politics of unity" solely based on gender forecloses the "pursuit of solidarity" through different political formations and the exploration of alternative theories of the subject of consciousness. There is a tendency in more sophisticated and elaborate gender standpoint epistemologists to affirm "an identity made up of heterogeneous and heteronomous representations of gender, race, and class, and often indeed across languages and cultures"[43] with one breath, and with the next to refuse to explore how that identity may be theorized or analyzed, by reconfirming a unified subjectivity or "shared consciousness" through gender. The difference is handed over with one hand and taken away with the other. If it be true, as Teresa de Lauretis has observed, that "[s]elf and identity . . . are always grasped and understood within particular discursive configurations,"[44] it does not necessarily follow that one can easily and self-consciously decide "to reclaim [an identity] from a history of multiple assimilations,"[45] and still retain a "shared consciousness." Such a practice goes counter to the homogenizing tendency of the subject of consciousness in the United States. To be oppressed means to be disenabled not only from grasping an "identity," but also from reclaiming it. In this culture, to grasp or reclaim an identity means always already to have become a subject of consciousness. The theory of the subject of consciousness as a unitary and synthesizing agent of knowledge is always already a posture of domination. One only has to think of Gloria Anzaldúa's essay in *Bridge*, "Speaking in Tongues: A Letter to Third World Women Writers."[46] Though de Laureris concedes that a racial "shared consciousness" may have prior claims than gender, she still insists on unity through gender: "the female subject is always constructed and defined in gender, starting from gender."[47] One is interested in having more than an account of gender, there are other relations to be accounted for. De Laureris insists, in most of her work, that "the differences among women may be better understood as differences within women."[48] This position returns us all to our solitary, though different, consciousness, without noting that some differences are (have been) a result of relations of domination of women by women; that differences may be purposefully constituted for the purpose of domination or exclusion, especially in oppositional thinking. Difference, whether it be sexual, racial, social, has to be conceptualized within a political and ideological domain.[49] In *Bridge*, for example, Mirtha Quintanales points out that "in this country, in this world, racism is used *both* to create false differences among us and to mask very significant ones—cultural, economic, political."[50]

One of the most remarkable tendencies in the work reviewed is the implicit or explicit acknowledgement that women of color are excluded from feminist theory, on the one hand, and on the other the reminder that though excluded from theory, their books are read in the classroom and/or duly footnoted. It is clear that some of the writers in *Bridge* thought at some point in the seventies that feminism could be the ideal answer to their hope for liberation. Chrystos, for example, stares her disillusionment as follows: "I no longer believe that feminism is a tool which can eliminate racism or even promote better understanding between different races and kinds of women."[51] The disillusionment is eloquently reformulated in the theme poem by Donna Kate Ruchin, "The Bridge Poem."[52] The dream of helping the people who surround her to reach an interconnectedness that would change society is given up in favor of self-translation into a "true self." In my view, the speaker's refusal to play "bridge," an enablement to others as well as self, is the acceptance of defeat at the hands of political groups whose self-definition follows the view of self as unitary, capable of being defined by a single "theme." The speaker's perception that the "self" is multiple ("I'm sick of mediating with your worst self/on behalf of your better selves,"[53]) and its reduction harmful, gives emphasis to the relationality between one's selves and those of others as an ongoing process of struggle, effort and tension. Indeed, in this poem the better "bridging self" of the speaker is defeated by the overriding notion of the unitary subject of knowledge and consciousness so prevalent in Anglo-American culture. Consciousness as a site of multiple voicings is the theoretical subject, par excellence, of *Bridge*. Concomitantly, these voicings (or thematic threads) are not viewed as necessarily originating with the subject, but as discourses that transverse consciousness and which the subject must struggle with constantly. Rosario Morales, for example, says "I want to be whole. I want to claim myself to be

Puertorican, and U. S. American, working class and middle class, housewife and intellectual, feminist, marxist and anti-imperialist."[54] Gloria Anzaldúa observes, "What am I? *A third world lesbian feminist with marxist and mystic leanings.* They would chop me up into little fragments and rag each piece with a label."[55] The need to assign multiple registers of existence is an effect of the belief that knowledge of one's subjectivity cannot be arrived at through a single discursive "theme." Indeed, the multiple-voiced subjectivity is lived in resistance to competing notions for one's allegiance or self-identification. It is a process of disidentification[56] with prevalent formulations of the most forcefully theoretical subject of feminism. The choice of one or many themes is both theoretical and a political decision. Like gender epistemologists and other emancipatory movements, the theoretical subject of *Bridge* gives credit to the subject of consciousness as the site of knowledge but problematizes it by representing it as a weave. In Anzaldúa's terms, the woman of color has a "plural personality." Speaking of the new mestiza in *Borderlands/La Frontera*, she says, "[s]he learns to juggle cultures. . . .[the] juncture where the mestiza stands is where phenomena tend to collide."[57] As an object of multiple indocrinations that heretofore have collided upon her, their new recognition as products of the oppositional thinking of others can help her come to terms with the politics of varied discourses and their antagonistic relations.

Thus, current political practices in the United States make it almost impossible to go beyond an oppositional theory of the subject, which is the prevailing feminist strategy and that of others; however, it is not the theory that will help us grasp the subjectivity of women of color. Socially and historically, women of color have been now central, now outside antagonistic relations between races, classes, and gender(s); this struggle of multiple antagonisms, almost always in relation to culturally different groups and not just genders, gives configuration to the theoretical subject of *Bridge*. It must be noted, however, that each woman of color cited here, even in her positing of a "plurality of self," is already privileged enough to reach the moment of cognition of a situation for herself. This should suggest that to privilege the subject, even if multiple-voiced, is not enough.

NOTES

1. Moraga and Anzaldúa, 2–3.
2. Louis Althusser, *Lenin and Philosophy and Other Essays*, Ben Brewster, tr. (London: New Left Books, 1971).
3. Moraga and Anzaldúa, 23.
4. Moraga and Anzaldúa, 195.
5. Teresa de Lauretis, *Technologies of Gender* (Bloomington: Indiana University Press, 1987), 10.
6. Jane Flax, "Postmodernism and Gender Relations in Feminist Theory," *Signs* 12:4 (Summer 1987), 640.
7. Gayatri Chakravorty Spivak. "Three Women's Texts and a Critique of Imperialism," *Critical Inquiry* 12:1 (Autumn 1985), 243–44.
8. Flax, 640.

9. Julia Kristeva. "Women's Time," *Signs* 7:1 (Autumn 1981), 19.

10. Adrienne Rich, *On Lies, Secrets and Silence* (New York: W. W. Norton, 1979), 35.

11. Flax, 627.

12. Michel Pecheux, *Language, Semantics and Ideology* (New York: St. Martin's Press, 1982), 122.

13. Jean Bethke Elshtain, "Feminist Discourse and Its Discontents: Language, Power, and Meaning," *Signs* 7:3 (Spring 1981), 611.

14. Elshtain, 617.

15. Diane Macdonell, *Theories of Discourses: An Introduction* (New York: Basil Blackwell, 1986), 76.

16. For an intriguing demonstration of these operations, see Seyla Benhabib, "The Generalized and the Concrete Other: The Kohlberg-Gilligan Controversy and Feminist Theory" in Seyla Benhabib and Drucilla Cornell, *Feminism as Critique* (Minneapolis: University of Minnesota Press, 1987), 77–95.

17. Sandra Harding, "The Instability of the Analytical Categories of Feminist Theory," *Signs* 11:4 (Summer 1986), 659.

18. Harding, 660.

19. Gloria T. Hull, Patricia B. Scott and Barbara Smith, eds., *All The Women Are White, All The Blacks Are Men, But Some of Us Are Brave* (Westbury, N. Y.: Feminist Press, 1982).

20. Moraga and Anzaldúa, Foreword to the Second Edition, n.p.

21. Moraga and Anzaldúa, Introduction to the First Edition, xxiii.

22. Paula Treichler, "Teaching Feminist Theory," *Theory in the Classroom*, Cary Nelsen, ed. (Urbana: University of Illinois Press, 1986), 79.

23. Maxine Baca Zinn, Lynn Weber Cannon, Elizabeth Higginbotham and Bonnie Thornton Dill, "The Cost of Exclusionary Practices in Women's Studies," *Signs* 11:4 (Summer 1986), 296.

24. Baca Zinn *et al.*, 296–97.

25. Flax, 633.

26. Macdonell, 62.

27. Simone de Beauvoir, *The Second Sex* (New York: Vintage Books, 1974), 301.

28. de Beauvoir, 316.

29. de Beauvoir, 761.

30. For a detailed discussion of this theme, see Judith Butler, "Variations on Sex and Gender: Beauvoir, Wittig, and Foucault" in Benhabib and Cornell, 128–42.

31. Catharine MacKinnon, "Feminism, Marxism, Method and the State: An Agenda for Theory," *Signs* 7:3 (Spring 1982), 536–38.

32. MacKinnon, 536.

33. Nancy F. Cott, "Feminist Theory and Feminist Movements: The Past Before Us," *What Is Feminism: A Re-Examination*, Juliet Mitchell and Ann Oakley, eds. (New York: Pantheon Books, 1986), 49.

34. Alison M. Jaggar, *Feminist Politics and Human Nature* (Torowa, N. J.,: Rowman & Allanheld, 1983), 249–50; 295–96.

35. Jaggar, 381.

36. Jaggar, 386.
37. Moraga and Anzaldúa, 61.
38. Jaggar, 386.
39. Moraga and Anzaldúa, Introduction, xxiii.
40. Moraga and Anzaldúa, Foreword to the Second Edition, n.p.
41. Miranda Davies, *Third World: Second Sex* (London: Zed Books, 1987).
42. Jaggar, 386.
43. Teresa de Lauretis, "Feminist Studies/Critical Studies: Issues, Terms, and Contexts," *Feminist Studies/Critical Studies*, Teresa de Lauretis, ed. (Bloomington: Indiana University Press 1986), 9.
44. de Lauretis, *Feminist Studies*, 8.
45. de Lauretis, *Feminist Studies*, 9.
46. Moraga and Anzaldúa, 165–74.
47. de Lauretis, *Feminist Studies*, 14.
48. de Lauretis, *Feminist Studies*, 14.
49. Monique Wittig, cited in Elizabeth Meese. *Crossing the Double-Cross: The Practice of Feminist Criticism* (Chapel Hill: University of North Carolina Press, 1986), 74.
50. Moraga and Anzaldúa, 153.
51. Moraga and Anzaldúa, 69.
52. Moraga and Anzaldúa, xxi–xxii.
53. Moraga and Anzaldúa, xxii.
54. Moraga and Anzaldúa, 91.
55. Moraga and Anzaldúa, 205.
56. Pecheux, 158–59.
57. Gloria Anzaldúa, *Borderlands/La Frontera: The New Mestiza* (San Francisco: Spinsters/Aunt Lute, 1987), 79.

18

JUDITH BUTLER

Imitation and Gender Insubordination[1]

So what is this divided being introduced into language through gender? It is an impossible being, it is a being that does not exist, an ontological joke.

—Monique Wittig[2]

Beyond physical repetition and the psychical or metaphysical repetition, is there an *ontological* repetition?. . . This ultimate repetition, this ultimate theatre, gathers everything in a certain way; and in another way, it destroys everything; and in yet another way, it selects from everything.

—Gilles Deleuze[1]

TO THEORIZE AS A LESBIAN?

At first I considered writing a different sort of essay, one with a philosophical tone: the "being" of being homosexual. The prospect of *being* anything, even for pay, has always produced in me a certain anxiety, for "to be" gay, "to be" lesbian seems to be more than a simple injunction to become who or what I already am. And in no way does it settle the anxiety for me to say that this is "part" of what I am. To write or speak *as a lesbian* appears a paradoxical appearance of this "I", one which feels neither true nor false. For it is a production, usually in response to a request, to come out or write in the name of an identity which, once produced, sometimes functions as a politically efficacious phantasm. I'm not at ease with "lesbian theories, gay theories," for as I've argued elsewhere,[4] identity categories tend to be instruments of regulatory regimes, whether as the normalizing categories of oppressive structures or as the rallying points for a liberatory contestation of that very oppression. This is not to say that I will not appear at political occasions under the sign of lesbian, but that I would like to have it permanently unclear what precisely that sign signifies. So it is unclear how it is that I can contribute to this book and appear under its title, for it announces a set of terms that I propose to contest. One risk I take is to be recolonized by the sign under which I write, and so it is this risk that I seek to thematize. To propose that the invocation of identity is always a risk does not imply that resistance to it is always or only symptomatic of a self-inflicted homophobia. Indeed, a Foucaultian perspective might argue that the affirmation of "homosexuality" is itself an extension of a homophobic discourse. And yet "discourse," he writes on the same page, "can be both an instrument and an effect of power, but also a hindrance, a stumbling-block, a point of resistance and a starting point for an opposing strategy."[5]

So I am skeptical about how the "I" is determined as it operates under the title of the lesbian sign, and I am no more comfortable with its homophobic determination than with those normative definitions offered by other members of the "gay or lesbian community." I'm permanently troubled by identity categories, consider them to be invariable stumbling-blocks, and understand them, even promote them, as sites of necessary trouble. In fact, if the category were to offer no trouble, it would cease to be interesting to me: it is precisely the *pleasure* produced by the instability of those categories which sustains the various erotic practices that make me a candidate for the category to begin with. To install myself within the terms of an identity category would be to turn against the sexuality that the category purports to describe; and this might be true for any identity category which seeks to control the very eroticism that it claims to describe and authorize, much less "liberate."

And what's worse, I do not understand the notion of "theory," and am hardly interested in being cast as its defender, much less in being signified as part of an elite gay/lesbian theory crowd that seeks to establish the legitimacy and domestication of gay/lesbian studies within the academy. Is there a pregiven distinction between theory, politics, culture, media? How do those divisions operate to quell a certain intertextual writing that might well generate wholly different epistemic maps? But I am writing here now: is it too late? Can this writing, can any writing, refuse the terms by which it is appropriated even as, to some extent, that very colonizing discourse enables or produces this stumbling block, this resistance? How do I relate the paradoxical situation of this dependency and refusal?

If the potential task is to show that theory is never merely *theoria*, in the sense of disengaged contemplation, and to insist that it is fully political (*phronesis or even praxis*, then why not simply call this operation *politics*, or some necessary permutation of it?

I have begun with confession of trepidation and a series of disclaimers, but perhaps it will become clear that *disclaiming*, which is no simple activity, will be what I have to offer as a form of affirmative resistance to a certain regulatory operation of homophobia. The discourse of "coming out" has clearly served its purposes, but what are its risks? And here I am not speaking of unemployment or public attack or violence, which are quite clearly and widely on the increase against those who are perceived as "out" whether or not of their own design. Is the "subject" who is "out" free of its subjection and finally in the clear? Or could it be that the subjection that subjectivates the gay or lesbian subject in some ways continues to oppress, or oppresses most insidiously, once "outness" is claimed? What or who is it that is "out," made manifest and fully disclosed, when and if I reveal myself as lesbian? What is it that is now known, anything? What remains permanently concealed by the very linguistic act that offers up the promise of a transparent revelation of sexuality? Can sexuality even remain sexuality once it submits to a criterion of transparency and disclosure, or does it perhaps cease to be sexuality precisely when the semblance of full explicitness is achieved?[6] Is sexuality of any kind even possible without that opacity designated by the unconscious, which means simply that the conscious "I" who would reveal its sexuality is perhaps the last to know the meaning of what it says?

To claim that this is what I *am* is to suggest a provisional totalization of this "I". But if the I can so determine itself, then that which it excludes in order to make the determination remains constitutive of the determination itself. In other words, such a statement presupposes that the "I" exceeds its determination, and even produces that very excess in and by the act which seeks to exhaust the semantic field of that "I". In the act which would disclose the true and full content of that "I", a certain radical *concealment* is thereby produced. For it is always finally unclear what is meant by involving the lesbian-signifier, since its significantion is always to some degree out of one's control, but also because its *specificity* can only be demarcated by exclusions that return to disrupt its claim to coherence. What, if anything, can lesbians be said to share? And who will decide this question, and in the name of whom? If I claim to be a lesbian, I "come out" only to produce a new and different "closet." The "you" to whom I come out now has access to a different region of opacity. Indeed, the locus of opacity has simply shifted: before, you did not know whether I "am," but now you do not know what that means, which is to say that the copula is empty, that it cannot be substituted for with a set of descriptions.[7] And perhaps that is a situation to be valued. Conventionally, one comes out of the closet (and yet, how often is it the case that we are "outted" when we are young and without resources?); so we are out of the closet, but into what? what new unbounded spatiality? the room, the den, the attic, the basement, the house, the bar, the university, some new enclosure whose door, like Kafka's door, produces the expectation of a fresh air and a light of illumination that never arrives? Curiously, it is the figure of the closet that produces this expectation, and which guarantees its dissatisfaction. For being "out" always depends to some extent on being "in"; it gains its meaning only within that polarity. Hence, being "out" must produce the closet again and again in order to maintain itself as "out". In this sense, *outness* can only produce a new opacity; and *the closet* produces the promise of a disclosure that can, by definition, never come. Is this infinite postponement of the disclosure of "gayness," produced by the very act of "coming out," to be lamented? Or is this very deferral of the signified *to be valued*, a site for the production of values, precisely because the term now takes on a life that cannot be, can never be, permanently controlled?

It is possible to argue that whereas no transparent or full revelation is afforded by "lesbian" and "gay," there remains a political imperative to use these necessary errors or category mistakes, as it were (what Gayatri Spivak might call "catachrestic" operations: to use a proper name improperly[8]), to rally and represent an oppressed political constituency. Clearly, I am not legislating against the use of the term. My question is simply: which use will be legislated, and what play will there be between legislation and use such that the instrumental uses of "identity" do not become regulatory imperatives? If it is already true that "lesbians" and "gay men" have been traditionally designated as impossible identities, errors of classification, unnatural disasters within juridico-medical discourses, or, what perhaps amounts to the same, the very paradigm of what calls to be classified, regulated, and controlled, then perhaps these sites of disruption, error, confusion, and trouble can be the very rallying points for a certain resistance to classification and to identify as such.

The question is not one of *avowing* or *disavowing* the category of lesbian or gay, but, rather, why it is that the category becomes the site of this "ethical" choice? What does it mean to *avow* a category that can only maintain its specificity and coherence by performing a prior set of *disavowals*? Does this make "coming out" into the avowal of disavowal, that is, a return to the closet under the guise of an escape? And it is not something like heterosexuality or bisexuality that is disavowed by the category, but a set of identificatory and practical crossings between these categories that renders the discreteness of each equally suspect. Is it not possible to maintain and pursue heterosexual identifications and aims within homosexual practice, and homosexual identifications and aims within heterosexual practices? If a sexuality is to be disclosed, what will be taken as the true determinant of its meaning: the phantasy structure, the act, the orifice, the gender, the anatomy? And if the practice engages a complex interplay of all of those, which one of this erotic dimensions will come to stand for the sexuality that requires them all? Is it the *specificity* of a lesbian experience or lesbian desire or lesbian sexuality that lesbian theory needs to elucidate? Those efforts have only and always produced a set of contests and refusals which should by now make it clear that there is no necessarily common element among lesbians, except perhaps that we all know something about how homophobia works against women—although, even then, the language and the analysis we use will differ.

To argue that there might be a *specificity* to lesbian sexuality has seemed a necessary counterpoint to the claim that lesbian sexuality is just heterosexuality once removed, or that it is derived, or that it does not exist. But perhaps the claim of specificity, on the one hand, and the claim of derivativeness or non-existence, on the other, are not as contradictory as they seem. Is it not possible that lesbian sexuality is a process that reinscribes the power domains that it resists, that it is constituted in part from the very heterosexual matrix that it seeks to displace, and that its specificity is to be established, not *outside* or *beyond* that reinscription or reiteration, but in the very modality and effects of that reinscription. In other words, the negative constructions of lesbianism as a fake or a bad copy can be occupied and reworked to call into question the claims of heterosexual priority. In a sense I hope to make clear in what follows, lesbian sexuality can be understood to redeploy its 'derivativeness' in the service of displacing hegemonic heterosexual norms. Understood in this way, the political problem is not to establish the specificity of lesbian sexuality over and against its derivativeness, but to turn the homophobic construction of the bad copy against the framework that privileges heterosexuality as origin, and so 'derive' the former from the latter. This description requires a reconsideration of imitation, drag, and other forms of sexual crossing that affirm the internal complexity of a lesbian sexuality constituted in part within the very matrix of power that it is compelled both to reiterate and to oppose.

ON THE BEING OF GAYNESS AS NECESSARY DRAG

The professionalization of gayness requires a certain performance and production of a "self" which is the *constituted effect* of a discourse that nevertheless claims to "represent" that self as a prior truth. When I spoke at the conference on homosexuality in 1989,[9] I found myself telling my friends beforehand that I was off to Yale to be a lesbian, which of course didn't mean that I wasn't one before, but that somehow then, as I spoke in that context, I *was* one in some more thorough and totalizing way, at least for the time being. So I *am* one, and my qualifications are even fairly unambiguous. Since I was sixteen, being a lesbian is what I've been. So what's the anxiety, the discomfort? Well, it has something to do with that redoubling, the way I can say, I'm going to Yale to be a lesbian; a lesbian is what I've been being for so long. How is it that I can both "be" one, and yet endeavor to be one at the same time? When and where does my being a lesbian come into play, when and where does this playing a lesbian constitute something like what I am? To say that I "play" at being one is not to say that I am not one "really"; rather, how and where I play at being one is the way in which that "being" gets established, instituted, circulated, and confirmed. This is not a performance from which I can take radical distance, for this is deep-seated play, psychically entrenched play, *and this "I" does not play its lesbianism as a role*. Rather, it is through the repeated play of this sexuality that the "I" is insistently reconstituted as a lesbian "I"; paradoxically, it is precisely the *repetition* of that play that establishes as well the *instability* of the very category that it constitutes. For if the "I" is a site of repetition, that is, if the "I" only achieves the semblance of identity through a certain repetition of itself, then the I is always displaced by the very repetition that sustains it. In other words, does or can the "I" ever repeat itself, cite itself, faithfully, or is there always a displacement from its former moment that establishes the permanently non-self-identical status of that "I" or its "being lesbian"? What "performs" does not exhaust the "I"; it does not lay out in visible terms the comprehensive content of that "I," for if the performance is "repeated," there is always the question of what differentiates from each other the moments of identity that are repeated. And if the "I" is the effect of a certain repetition, one which produces the semblance of a continuity or coherence, then there is no "I" that precedes the gender that it is said to perform; the repetition, and the failure to repeat, produce a string of performances that constitute and contest the coherence of that "I."

But *politically*, we might argue, isn't it quite crucial to insist on lesbian and gay identities precisely because they are being threatened with erasure and obliteration from homophobic quarters? Isn't the above theory *complicitous* with those political forces that would obliterate the possibility of gay and lesbian identity? Isn't it "no accident" that such theoretical contestations of identity emerge within a political climate that is performing a set of similar obliterations of homosexual identities through legal and political means?

The question I want to raise in return is this: ought such threats of obliteration dictate the terms of the political resistance to them, and if they do, do such homophobic efforts to that extent win the battle from the start? There is no question that gays and lesbians are threatened by the violence of public erasure, but the decision to counter that violence must be careful not to reinstall another in its place. Which version of lesbian or gay ought to be rendered visible, and which internal exclusions will that rendering visible institute? Can the visibility of identity *suffice* as a political strategy, or can it only be the starting point for a strategic intervention which calls for a transformation of policy? Is it not a sign of despair over public politics when identity becomes its own policy, bringing with it those who would 'police' it from various sides? And this is not a call to return to silence or invisibility, but, rather, to make use of a category that can be called into question, made to account for what it excludes. That any consolidation of identity requires some set of differentiations and exclusions seems clear. But which ones ought to be valorized? That the identity-sign I use now has its purposes seems right, but there is no way to predict or control the political uses to which that sign will be put in the future. And perhaps this is a kind of openness, regardless of its risks, that ought to be safeguarded for political reasons. If the rendering visible of lesbian/gay identity now presupposes a set of exclusions, then perhaps part of what is necessarily excluded is *the future uses of the sign*. There is a political necessity to use some sign now, and we do, but how to use it in such a way that its futural significations are not *foreclosed*? How to use the sign and avow its temporal contingency at once?

In avowing the sign's strategic provisionality (rather than its strategic essentialism), that identity can become a site of contest and revision, indeed, take on a future set of significations that those of us who use it now may not be able to foresee. It is in the safeguarding of the future of the political signifiers-preserving the signifier as a site of rearticulation that Laclau and Mouffe discern its democratic promise.

Within contemporary U. S. politics, there are a vast number of ways in which lesbianism in particular is understood as precisely that which cannot or dare not *be*. In a sense, Jesse Helms's attack on the NEA for sanctioning representations of "homoeroticism" focuses various homophobic fantasies of what gay men are and do on the work of Robert Mapplethorpe.[10] In a sense, for Helms, gay men exist as objects of prohibition; they are, in his twisted fantasy, sadomasochistic exploiters of children, the paradigmatic exemplars of "obscenity"; in a sense, the lesbian is not even produced within this discourse as a prohibited object. Here it becomes important to recognize that oppression works not merely through acts of overt prohibition, but covertly, through the constitution of viable subjects and through the corollary constitution of a domain of unviable (un)subjects—*abjects*, we might call them—who are neither named nor prohibited within the economy of the law. Here oppression works through the production of a domain of unthinkability and unnameability. Lesbianism is not explicitly prohibited in part because it has not even made its way into the thinkable, the imaginable, that grid of cultural intelligibility that regulates the real and the nameable. How, then, to "be" a lesbian in a political context in which the lesbian does not exist? That is, in a political discourse that wages its violence against lesbianism in part by excluding lesbianism from discourse itself? To be prohibited explicitly is to occupy a discursive site from which something like a reverse-discourse can be articulated; to be implicitly proscribed is not even to qualify as an object of prohibition.[13] And though homosexualities of all kinds in this present climate are being erased, reduced, and (then) reconstituted as sites of radical homophobic fantasy, it is important to retrace the different routes by which the unthinkability of homosexuality is being constituted time and again.

It is one thing to be erased from discourse, and yet another to be present within discourse as an abiding falsehood. Hence, there is a political imperative to render lesbianism visible, but how is that to be done outside or through existing regulatory regimes? Can the exclusion from ontology itself become a rallying point for resistance?

Here is something like a confession which is meant merely to thematize the impossibility of confession: As a young person, I suffered for a long time, and I suspect many people have, from being told, explicitly or implicitly, that what I "am" is a copy, an imitation, a derivative example, a shadow of the real. Compulsory heterosexuality sets itself up as the original, the true, the authentic; the norm that determines the real implies that "being" lesbian is always a kind of miming, a vain effort to participate in the phantasmatic plenitude of naturalized heterosexuality which will always and only fail.[12] And yet, I remember quite distinctly when I first read in Esther Newton's *Mother Camp: Female Impersonators in America*[13] that drag is not an imitation or a copy of some prior and true gender; according to Newton, drag enacts the very structure of impersonation by which *any gender* is assumed. Drag is not the putting on of a gender that belongs properly to some other group, i.e. an act of *ex*propriation or *ap*propriation that assumes that gender is the rightful property of sex, that "masculine" belongs to "male" and "feminine" belongs to "female." There is no "proper" gender, a gender proper to one sex rather than another, which is in some sense that sex's cultural property. Where that notion of the "proper" operates, it is always and only *improperly* installed as the effect of a compulsory system. Drag constitutes the mundane way in which genders are appropriated, theatricalized, worn, and done; it implies that all gendering is a kind of impersonation and approximation. If this is true, it seems, there is no original or primary gender that drag imitates, but *gender is a kind of imitation for which there is no original*; in fact, it is a kind of imitation that produces the very notion of the original as an *effect* and consequence of the imitation itself. In other words, the naturalistic effects of heterosexualized genders are produced through imitative strategies; what they imitate is a phantasmatic ideal of heterosexual identity, one that is produced by the imitation as its effect. In this sense, the "reality" of heterosexual identities is performatively constituted through an imitation that sets itself up as the origin and the ground of all imitations. In other words, heterosexuality is always in the process of imitating and approximating its own phantasmatic idealization of itself—*and failing*. Precisely because it is bound to fail, and yet endeavors to succeed, the project of heterosexual identity is propelled into an endless repetition of itself. Indeed, in its efforts to naturalize itself as the original, heterosexuality must be understood as a compulsive and compulsory repetition that can only produce the *effect* of its own originality; in other words, compulsory heterosexual identities, those ontologically consolidated phantasms of "man" and "woman," are theatrically produced effects that posture as grounds, origins, the normative measure of the real.[14]

Reconsider then the homophobic charge that queens and butches and femmes are imitations of the heterosexual real. Here "imitation" carries the meaning of "derivative" or "secondary," a copy of an origin which is itself the ground of all copies, but which is itself a copy of nothing. Logically, this notion of an "origin" is suspect, for how can something operate as an origin if there are no secondary consequences which retrospectively confirm the originality of that origin? The origin requires its derivations in order to affirm itself as an origin, for origins only make sense to the extent that they are differentiated from that which they produce as derivatives. Hence, if it were not for the notion of the homosexual *as* copy, there would be no construct of heterosexuality *as* origin. Heterosexuality here presupposes homosexuality. And if the homosexual *as* copy *precedes* the heterosexual as *origin*, then it seems only fair to concede that the copy comes before the origin, and that homosexuality is thus the origin, and heterosexuality the copy.

But simple inversions are not really possible. For it is only *as* a copy that homosexuality can be argued to *precede* heterosexuality as the origin. In other words, the entire framework of copy and origin proves radically unstable as each position inverts into the other and confounds the possibility of any stable way to locate the temporal or logical priority of either term.

But let us then consider this problematic inversion from a psychic/political perspective. If the structure of gender imitation is such that the imitat*ed* is to some degree produced—or, rather, *re*produced—by imitation (see again Derrida's inversion and displacement of mimesis in "The Double Session"), then to claim that gay and lesbian identifies are implicated in heterosexual norms or in hegemonic culture generally is not to *derive* gayness from straightness. On the contrary, *imitation* does not copy that which is prior, but produces and *inverts* the very terms of priority and derivativeness. Hence, if gay identities are implicated in heterosexuality, that is not the same as claiming that they are determined or derived from heterosexuality, and it is not the same as claiming that that heterosexuality is the only cultural network in which they are implicated. These are, quite literally, *inverted* imitations, ones which invert the order of imitated and imitation, and which, in the process, expose the fundamental dependency of "the origin" on that which it claims to produce as its secondary effect.

What follows if we concede from the start that gay identities as derivative inversions are in part defined in terms of the very heterosexual identities from which they are differentiated? If heterosexuality is an impossible imitation of itself, an imitation that performatively constitutes itself as the original, then the imitative parody of "hetero-sexuality"—when and where it exists in gay cultures—is always and only an imitation of an imitation, a copy of a copy, for which there is no original. Put in yet a different way, the parodic or imitative effect of gay identities works neither to copy nor to emu-late heterosexuality, but rather, to expose heterosexuality as an incessant and *panicked* imitation of its own naturalized idealization. That heterosexuality is always in the act of elaborating itself is evidence that it is perpetually at risk, that is, that it "knows" its own possibility of becoming undone: hence, its compulsion to repeat which is at once a foreclosure of that which threatens its coherence. That it can never eradicate that risk attests to its profound dependency upon the homosexuality that it seeks fully to eradicate and never can or that it seeks to make second, but which is always already there as a prior possibility.[15] Although this failure of naturalized heterosexuality might constitute a source of pathos for heterosexuality itself—what its theorists often refer to as its constitutive malaise—it can become an occasion for a subversive and proliferat-ing parody of gender norms in which the very claim to originality and to the real is shown to be the effect of a certain kind of naturalized gender mime.

It is important to recognize the ways in which heterosexual norms reappear within gay identities, to affirm that gay and lesbian identities are not only structured in part by dominant heterosexual frames, but that they are *not* for that reason *determined* by them. They are running commentaries on those naturalized positions as well, parodic replays and resignifications of precisely those heterosexual structures that would con-sign gay life to discursive domains of unreality and unthinkability. But to be consti-tuted or structured in part by the very heterosexual norms by which gay people are oppressed is not, I repeat, to be claimed or determined by those structures. And it is not necessary to think of such heterosexual constructs as the pernicious intrusion of "the straight mind," one that must be rooted out in its entirety. In a way, the presence of heterosexual constructs and positionalities in whatever form in gay and lesbian identi-ties presupposes that there is a gay and lesbian repetition of straightness, a recapitula-tion of straightness—which is itself a repetition and recapitulation of its own ideality—within its own terms, a site in which all sorts of resignifying and parodic rep-etitions become possible. The parodic replication and resignification of heterosexual constructs within non-heterosexual frames brings into relief the utterly constructed status of the so-called original, but it shows that heterosexuality only constitutes itself as the original through a convincing act of repetition. The more that "act" is expro-priated, the more the heterosexual claim to originality is exposed as illusory.

Although I have concentrated in the above on the reality-effects of gender prac-tices, performances, repetitions, and mimes, I do not mean to suggest that drag is a "role" that can be taken on or taken off at will. There is no volitional subject behind the mime who decides, as it were, which gender it will be today. On the contrary, the very possibility of becoming a viable subject requires that a certain gender mime be already underway. The "being" of the subject is no more self-identical than the "being" of any gender; in fact, coherent gender, achieved through an apparent repeti-tion of the same, produces as its *effect* the illusion of a prior and volitional subject. In this sense, gender is not a performance that a prior subject elects to do, but gender is *performative* in the sense that it constitutes as an effect the very subject it appears to express. It is a *compulsory* performance in the sense that acting out of line with heterosexual norms brings with it ostracism, punishment, and violence, not to mention the transgressive pleasures produced by those very prohibitions.

To claim that there is no performer prior to the performed, that the performance is performative, that the performance constitutes the appearance of a "subject" as its effect is difficult to accept. This difficulty is the result of a predisposition to think of sexuality and gender as "expressing" in some indirect or direct way a psychic reality that precedes it. The denial of the *priority* of the subject, however, is not the denial of the subject; in fact, the refusal to conflate the subject with the psyche marks the psychic as that which exceeds the domain of the conscious subject. This psychic excess is precisely what is being systematically denied by the notion of a volitional "subject" who elects at will which gender and/or sexuality to be at any given time and place. It is this excess which erupts within the intervals of those repeated gestures and acts that construct the apparent uniformity of heterosexual positionalities, indeed which compels the repetition itself, and which guarantees its perpetual failure. In this sense, it is this excess which, within the heterosexual economy, implicitly includes homosexuality, that perpetual threat of a disruption which is quelled through a reinforced repetition of the same. And yet, if repetition is the way in which power works to construct the illusion of a seamless heterosexual identity, if heterosexuality is compelled to *repeat itself* in order to establish the illusion of its own uniformity and identity, then this is an identity permanently at risk, for what if it fails to repeat, or if the very exercise of repetition is redeployed for a very different performative purpose? If there is, as it were, always a compulsion to repeat, repetition never fully accomplishes identity. That there is a need for a repetition at all is a sign that identity is not self-identical. It requires to be instituted again and again, which is to say that it runs the risk of becoming *de*-instituted at every interval.

So what is this psychic excess, and what will constitute a subversive or *de*-instituting repetition? First, it is necessary to consider that sexuality always exceeds any given performance, presentation, or narrative which is why it is not possible to derive or read off a sexuality from any given gender presentation. And sexuality may be said to exceed any definitive narrativization. Sexuality is never fully "expressed" in a performance or practice; there will be passive and butchy femmes, femmy and aggressive butches, and both of those, and more, will turn out to describe more or less anatomically stable "males" and "females." There are no direct expressive or causal lines between sex, gender, gender presentation, sexual practice, fantasy and sexuality. None of those terms captures or determines the rest. Part of what constitutes sexuality is precisely that which does not appear and that which, to some degree, can never appear. This is perhaps the most fundamental reason why sexuality is to some degree always closeted, especially to the one who would express it through acts of self-disclosure. That which is excluded for a given gender presentation to "succeed" may be precisely what is played out sexually, that is, an "inverted" relation, as it were, between gender and gender presentation, and gender presentation and sexuality. On the other hand, both gender presentation and sexual practices may corollate such that it appears that the former "expresses" the latter, and yet both are jointly constituted by the very sexual possibilities that they exclude.

This logic of inversion gets played out interestingly in versions of lesbian butch and femme gender stylization. For a butch can present herself as capable, forceful, and all-providing, and a stone butch may well seek to constitute her lover as the exclusive site of erotic attention and pleasure. And yet, this "providing" butch who seems *at first* to replicate a certain husband-like role, can find herself caught in a logic of inversion whereby that "providingness" turns to a self-sacrifice, which implicates her in the most ancient trap of feminine self-abnegation. She may well find herself in a situation of radical need, which is precisely what she sought to locate, find, and fulfill in her femme lover. In effect, the butch inverts into the femme or remains caught up in the specter of that inversion, or takes pleasure in it. On the other hand, the femme who, as Amber Hollibaugh has argued, "orchestrates" sexual exchange,[16] may well eroticize a certain dependency only to learn that the very power to orchestrate that dependency exposes her own incontrovertible power, at which point she inverts into a butch or becomes caught up in the specter of that inversion, or perhaps delights in it.

PSYCHIC MIMESIS

What stylizes or forms an erotic style and/or a gender presentation—and that which makes such categories inherently unstable—is a set of *psychic identifications* that are not simple to describe. Some psychoanalytic theories tend to construe identification and desire as two mutually exclusive relations to love objects that have been lost through prohibition and/or separation. Any intense emotional attachment thus divides into either wanting to have someone or wanting to be that someone, but never both at once. It is important to consider that identification and desire can coexist, and that their formulation in terms of mutually exclusive oppositions serves a heterosexual matrix. But I would like to focus attention on yet a different construal of that scenario, namely, that "wanting to be" and "wanting to have" can operate to differentate mutually exclusive positionalities internal to lesbian erotic exchange. Consider that identifications are always made in response to loss of some kind, and that they involve a certain *mimetic practice* that seeks to incorporate the lost love within the very "identity" of the one who remains. This was Freud's thesis in "Mourning and Melancholia" in 1917 and continues to inform contemporary psychoanalytic discussions of identification.[17]

For psychoanalytic theorists Mikkel Borch-Jacobsen and Ruth Leys, however, identification and, in particular, identificatory mimetism, *precedes* "identity" and constitutes identity as that which is fundamentally "other to itself." The notion of this Other *in* the self, as it were, implies that the self/Other distinction is *not* primarily external (a powerful critique of ego psychology follows from this); the self is from the start radically implicated in the "Other." This theory of primary mimetism differs from Freud's account of melancholic incorporation. In Freud's view, which I continue to find useful, incorporation—a kind of psychic miming—is a response to, and refusal of, *loss*. Gender as the site of such psychic mimes is thus constituted by the variously gendered Others who have been loved and lost, where the loss is suspended through a melancholic and imaginary incorporation (and preservation) of those Others into the psyche. Over and against this account of psychic mimesis by way of incorporation and melancholy, the theory of primary mimetism argues an even stronger position in favor of the non-self-identity of the psychic subject. Mimetism is not motivated by a drama of loss and wishful recovery, but appears to precede and constitute desire (and motivation) itself; in this sense, mimetism would be prior to the possibility of loss and the disappointments of love.

Whether loss or memetism is primary (perhaps an undecidable problem), the psychic subject is nevertheless constituted internally by differentially gendered Others and is, therefore, never, as a gender, self-identical.

In my view, the self only becomes a self on the condition that it has suffered a separation (grammar fails us here, for the "it" only becomes differentiated through that separation), a loss which is suspended and provisionally resolved through a melancholic incorporation of some "Other." That "Other" installed in the self thus establishes the permanent incapacity of that "self" to achieve self-identity; it is as it were always already disrupted by that Other; the disruption of the Other at the heart of the self is the very condition of that self's possibility.[18]

Such a consideration of psychic identification would vitiate the possibility of any stable set of typologies that explain or describe something like gay or lesbian identities. And any effort to supply one—as evidenced in Kaja Silverman's recent inquiries into male homosexuality—suffer from simplification, and conform, with alarming ease, to the regulatory requirements of diagnostic epistemic regimes. If incorporation in Freud's sense in 1914 is an effort to *preserve* a lost and loved object and to refuse or postpone the recognition of loss and, hence, of grief, then to become *like* one's mother or father or sibling or other early "lovers" may be an act of love and/or a hateful effort to replace or displace. How would we "typologize" the ambivalence at the heart of mimetic incorporations such as these?[19]

How does this consideration of psychic identification return us to the question, what constitutes a subversive repetition? How are troublesome identifications apparent in cultural practices? Well, consider the way in which heterosexuality naturalizes itself through setting up certain illusions of continuity between sex, gender, and desire. When Aretha Franklin sings, "you make me feel like a natural woman," she seems at first to suggest that some natural potential of her biological sex is actualized by her participation in the cultural position of "woman" as object of heterosexual recognition. Something in her "sex" is thus expressed by her "gender" which is then fully known and consecrated within the heterosexual scene. There is no breakage, no discontinuity between "sex" as biological facticity and essence, or between gender and sexuality. Although Aretha appears to be all too glad to have her naturalness confirmed, she also seems fully and paradoxically mindful that that confirmation is never guaranteed, that the effect of naturalness is only achieved as a consequence of that moment of heterosexual recognition. After all, Aretha sings, you make me feel *like* a natural woman, suggesting that this is a kind of metaphorical substitution, an act of imposture, a kind of sublime and momentary participation in an ontological illusion produced by the mundane operation of heterosexual drag.

But what if Aretha were singing to me? Or what if she were singing to a drag queen whose performance somehow confirmed her own?

How do we take account of these kinds of identifications? It's not that there is some kind of *sex* that exists in hazy biological form that is somehow *expressed* in the gait, the posture, the gesture; and that some sexuality then expresses both that apparent gender or that more or less magical sex. If gender is drag, and if it is an imitation that regularly produces the ideal it attempts to approximate, then gender is a performance that *produces* the illusion of an inner sex or essence or psychic gender core; it *produces* on the skin, through the gesture, the move, the gait (that array of corporeal theatrics understood as gender presentation), the illusion of an inner depth. In effect, one way that gender gets naturalized is through being constructed as an inner psychic or physical *necessity*. And yet, it is always a surface sign, a signification on and with the public body that produces this illusion of an inner depth, necessity or essence that is somehow magically, causally expressed.

To dispute the psyche as *inner depth*, however, is not to refuse the psyche altogether. On the contrary, the psyche calls to be rethought precisely as a compulsive repetition, as that which conditions and disables the repetitive performance of identity. If every performance repeats itself to institute the effect of identity, then every repetition requires an interval between the acts, as it were, in which risk and excess threaten to disrupt the identity being constituted. The unconscious is this excess that enables and contests every performance, and which never fully appears within the performance itself. The psyche is not "in" the body, but in the very signifying process through which that body comes to appear; it is the lapse in repetition as well as its compulsion, precisely what the performance seeks to deny, and that which compels it from the start.

To locate the psyche within this signifying chain as the instability of all iterability is not the same as claiming that it is inner core that is awaiting its full and liberatory expression. On the contrary, the psyche is the permanent failure of expression, a failure that has its values, for it impels repetition and so reinstates the possibility of disruption. What then does it mean to pursue disruptive repetition within compulsory heterosexuality?

Although compulsory heterosexuality often presumes that there is first a sex that is expressed through a gender and then through a sexuality, it may now be necessary fully to invert and displace that operation of thought. If a regime of sexuality mandates a compulsory performance of sex, then it may be only through that performance that the binary system of gender and the binary system of sex come to have intelligibility at all. It may be that the very categories of sex, of sexual identity, of gender are produced or maintained in the *effects* of this compulsory performance, effects which are disingenuously renamed as causes, origins, disingenuously lined up within a causal or expressive sequence that the heterosexual norm produces to legitimate itself as the origin of all sex. How then to expose the causal lines as retrospectively and performatively produced fabrications, and to engage gender itself as an inevitable fabrication, to fabricate gender in terms which reveal every claim to the origin, the inner, the true, and the real as nothing other than the effects of *drag*, whose subversive possibilities ought to be played and replayed to make the "sex" of gender into a site of insistent political play? Perhaps this will be a matter of working sexuality *against* identity, even against gender, and of letting that which cannot fully appear in any performance persist in its disruptive promise.

NOTES

1. Parts of this essay were given as a presentation at the Conference on Homosexuality at Yale University in October, 1989.
2. "The Mark of Gender," *Feminist Issues* 5 no. 2 (1985): 6.
3. *Différence et répétition* (Paris: PUF, 1968), 374; my translation.
4. *Gender Trouble: Feminism and the Subversion of Identity* (New York and London: Routledge, 1990).
5. Michel Foucault, *The History of Sexuality, Vol. I*, trans. John Hurley (New York: Random House, 1980), 101.
6. Here I would doubtless differ from the very fine analysis of Hitchcock's *Rope* offered by D. A. Miller.
7. For an example of "coming out" that is strictly unconfessional and which, finally, offers no content for the category of lesbian, see Barbara Johnson's deftly constructed "Sula Passing: No Passing" presentation at UCLA, May 1990.
8. Gayatri Chakvavorty Spivak, "Displacement and the Discourse of Woman." In *Displacement: Derrida and After*, ed. Mark Krupnick (Bloomington: Indiana University Press, 1983).
9. Let me take this occasion to apologize to the social worker at that confrence who asked a question about how to deal with those clients with AIDS who turned to Bernie Segal and others for the purposes of psychic healing. At the time, I understood this questioner to be suggesting that such clients were full of self-hatred because they were trying to find the causes of AIDS in their own selves. The questioner and I appear to agree that any effort to locate the responsibility for AIDS in those who suffer from it is politically and ethically wrong. I thought the questioner, however, was prepared to tell his clients that they were self-hating, and I reacted strongly (too strongly) to the paternalistic prospect that this person was going to pass judgment on someone who was clearly not only suffering, but already passing judgment on him or herself. To call another person self-hating is itself an act of power that calls for some kind of scrutiny, and I think in response to someone who is already dealing with AIDS, that is perhaps the last thing one needs to hear. I also happened to have a friend who sought out advice from Bernie Segal, not with the belief that there is an exclusive or even primary psychic cause or solution for AIDS, but that there might be a psychic contribution to be made to surviving with AIDS. Unfortunately, I reacted quickly to this questioner, and with some anger. And I regret now that I didn't have my wits about me to discuss the distinctions with him that I have just laid out.

Curiously, this incident was invoked at a CLAGS (Center for Lesbian and Gay Studies) meeting at CUNY sometime in December of 1989 and, according to those who told me about it, my angry denunciation of the social worker was taken to be symptomatic of the political insensitivity of a "theorist" in dealing with someone who is actively engaged in AIDS work. That attribution implies that I do not do AIDS work, that I am not politically engaged, and that the social worker in question does not read theory. Needless to say, I was reacting angrily on behalf of an absent friend with AIDS who sought out Bernie Segal and company. So as I offer this apology to the social worker, I wait expectantly that the CLAGS member who misunderstood me will offer me one in turn.

10. See my "The Force of Fantasy: Feminism, Mapplethorpe, and Discursive Excess," *differences* 2, no. 2 (Summer 1990). Since the writing of this essay, lesbian artists and representations have also come under attack.

11. It is this particular ruse of erasure which Foucault for the most part fails to take account of in his analysis of power. He almost always presumes that power takes place through discourse as its instrument, and that oppression is linked with subjection and subjectivation, that is, that it is installed as the formative principle of the identity of subjects.

12. Although miming suggests that there is a prior model which is being copied, it can have the effect of exposing that prior model as purely phantasmatic. In Jacques Derrida's "The Double Session" in *Dissemination*, trans. Barbara Johnson (Chicago: University of Chicago Press, 1981), he considers the textual effect of the mime in Mallarmé's "Mimique." There Derrida argues that the mime does not imitate or copy some prior phenomenon, idea, or figure, but constitutes—some might say *performatively*—the phantasm of the original in and through the mime:

> He represents nothing, imitates nothing, does not have to conform to any prior referent with the aim of achieving adequation or verisimilitude. One can here foresee an objection: since the mime imitates nothing, reproduces nothing, opens up in its origin the very thing he is tracing out, presenting, or producing, he must be the very movement of truth. Not, of course, truth in the form of adequation between the representation and the present of the thing itself, or between the imitator and the imitated, but truth as the present unveiling of the present. . . . But this is not the case. . . . We are faced then with mimicry imitating nothing: faced, so to speak, with a double that couples no simple, a double that nothing anticipates, nothing at least that is not itself already double. There is no simple reference. . . . This speculum reflects no reality: it produces mere "reality-effects". . . . In this speculum with no reality, in this mirror of a mirror, a difference or dyad does exist, since there are mimes and phantoms. But it is a difference without reference, or rather reference without a referent, without any first or last unit, a ghost that is the phantom of no flesh. . .(206)

13. Esther Newton, *Mother Camp: Female Impersonators in America* (Chicago: University of Chicago Press, 1972).

14. In a sense, one might offer a redescription of the above in Lacanian terms. The

sexual "positions" of heterosexually differentiated "man" and "woman" are part of the Symbolic, that is, an ideal embodiment of the Law of sexual difference which constitutes the object of imaginary pursuits, but which is always thwarted by the "real." These symbolic positions for Lacan are by definition impossible to occupy even as they are impossible to resist as the structuring telos of desire. I accept the former point, and reject the latter one. The imputation of universal necessity to such positions simply encodes compulsory heterosexuality at the level of the Symbolic, and the "failure" to achieve it is implicitly lamented as a source of heterosexual pathos.

15. Of course, it is Eve Kosofsky Sedgwick's *Epistemology of the Closet* (Berkeley: University of California Press, 1990) which traces the subtleties of this kind of panic in Western heterosexual epistemes.

16. Amber Hollibaugh and Cherrie Moraga, "What We're Rollin Around in Bed With: Sexual Silences in Feminism," in *Powers of Desire: The Politics of Sexuality*, ed. Ann Snitow, Christine Stansell, and Sharon Thompson (New York: Monthly Review Press, 1983), 394–405.

17. Mikkel Borch-Jacobsen, *The Freudian Subject* (Stanford: Standford University Press, 1988); for citations of Ruth Leys's work, see the following two endnotes.

18. For a very fine analysis of primary mimetism with direct implications for gender formation, see Ruth Leys, "The Real Miss Beauchamp: The History and Sexual Politics of the Multiple Personality Concept," in *Feminists Theorize the Political* eds. Judith Butler and Joan W. Scott (New York and London: Routledge, forthcoming 1991). For Leys, a primary mimetism or suggestibility requires that the "self" from the start is constituted by its incorporations; the effort to differentiate oneself from that by which one is constituted is, of course, impossible, but it does entail a certain "incorporative violence," to use her term. The violence of identification is in this way in the service of an effort at differentiation, to take the place of the Other who is, as it were, installed at the foundation of the self. That this replacement, which seeks to be a displacement, fails, and must repeat itself endlessly, becomes the trajectory of one's psychic career.

19. Here again, I think it is the work of Ruth Leys which will clarify some of the complex questions of gender constitution that emerge from a close psychoanalytic consideration of imitation and identification. Her forthcoming book manuscript will doubtless galvanize this field: *The Subject of Imitation*.

The Question PART
of Essentialism 5

Luce Irigaray's essay "This Sex Which is Not One" exemplifies an important current in the debate around essentialism. This current, which is found in a strand of French feminist theorizing and in those elements of United States feminist theory that have been influenced by it, combines what I view as a curious blend of a radical feminist and deconstructionist perspective. The radical feminist element asserts women's total difference from men and gender as the fundamental dividing pole of the social order. The deconstructionist element disavows any positive content or identity to "woman" because the assertion of identity is seen as the hallmark of the discursive order associated with men. This combination of elements leads to a portrayal of "woman" as outside of the regime of the phallus; she is what resists capture by definition or quantification. Irigaray here describes a woman's sexual organs as that which can't be demarcated; they pervade her body. A woman's sex is not one, but neither is it two. It resists demarcation into separable, countable areas. Is this a form of essentialism? Yes and no. No, in so far as womanhood is portrayed as that which rejects essentialism. Yes, in so far as "woman" becomes a type of essence, a negative one.

More interesting than the question of whether this type of theory is or is not "essentialist," is where it leads politically. Many scholars have argued that it provides feminism with no place to stand. It eliminates essentialism, but it also prohibits any positive constructions of what women are. Without such positive constructions, how can we say what feminism stands for?

For those who saw this type of theory as the alternative to the essentialism of cultural feminism, the dilemma seemed the following: either we attribute some positive elements to the idea of "woman" and become essentialist, denying differences among women, or we abandon the possibility of saying anything positive about women and therefore deny the idea of feminism as a political movement committed to a specific agenda. One way out of this dilemma was associated with a phrase articulated by Gayatri Spivak: "strategic essentialism." This phrase seemed to suggest an essentialism that did not attribute any essence to womanhood in a real or ontological sense, but which employed positive ideas about being a "woman" for the sake of political action. In an interview held after that earlier remark, Spivak comments on problems in how this phrase has been interpreted. For one, it has tended to suggest to some that feminists can be essentialists at certain moments and not others, that is, that we can stop being anti-essentialists at certain times for the sake of political effectiveness. In contrast to such an interpretation, she claims that we need to think of strategic essentialism as entailing persistent critique, a continuous recognition of the dangers of that which is unavoidably useful. The phrase has tended to give what she calls a certain alibi to essentialism. For many the phrase has been interpreted as representing a theory rather than a strategy. But if recognized as a strategy, we have always to think about where the group is situated that is claiming feminism or womanhood in its name. Spivak emphasizes the necessity of "building for differences," not in the sense of proliferating multiplicity for its own sake but rather as "proceeding from an awareness of one's own power."

Linda Alcoff also takes up the dilemma created by the apparent contradiction between rejecting essentialism on the one hand and on the other leaving feminism with no place to stand. Essentialism, as reflected in the theory of much cultural feminism, seems to create homogeneous and ahistorical ideas about what it means to be a woman. It also reinforces the sexist idea of a naturalized womanhood. The poststructuralist alternative, however, eliminates the possibility of any positive conceptions upon which to base a politics. Also, the poststructuralist critique of subjectivity seems to deny the idea of agents capable of making change. In short, poststructuralism appears to leave nothing to struggle for and no one left to make the struggle.

Alcoff draws on the work of Teresa de Lauretis and Denise Riley to construct a way out of this dilemma. From de Lauretis she takes the idea of subjectivity positioned within specific discursive configurations but as also capable of reconstruction through reflective practice. From Riley she takes the idea of women's needs as emanating not from anything essential but from socially specific contexts. In short, Alcoff argues for a historicized subjectivity that is capable of rearticulating itself. This view of subjectivity makes possible a type of identity politics, where identity points to real patterns and needs but is also understood as "relative to a constantly shifting context." Thus the specific content of what a "woman" is will be relative to a given and changing context; from within that context, however, that content will be usable as the basis for political action.

Nancy Fraser begins with the assumption that the above type of position is what we need. But she raises the question of how the problematic aspects of the poststructuralist position even emerged. Fraser focuses on a strain in certain readings of poststructuralist thinkers, which she sees as the unexamined legacy of structuralism. This strain abstracts language from social practice and specific contexts of communication. Because it views language apart from specific social practices, it tends to generate monolithic views about language and meaning. Such abstraction gives it little to say about tensions and conflicts over meaning, within individuals and between social groups. Consequently, it has little to tell us about the complexities of individual identity, of how group identities emerge, and about conflict between social groups. Moreover, it brackets off the diachronic aspect of language. Therefore, it has little to say about how meaning shifts over time and tends to impute to language an ironclad determinism. In short, the legacy of structuralism in some poststructuralist theory is manifest in the tendency to create accounts that are frozen in time and all encompassing. Diverse linguistic practices are portrayed as homogeneous elements of "a monolithic and all pervasive symbolic order." Fraser points to certain interpretations of Lacan as an example of these tendencies. These interpretations, theory, she argues, remain caught within the heritage of structuralism. Moreover, feminist theorizing that has been influenced by these interpretations such as certain strains of Julia Kristeva's work, illustrate the specific problems this heritage generates.

In opposition to such tendencies, which Fraser captures in the phrase, "symbolicism," she points to the benefits of a pragmatic model of language. Such a model would treat language as manifest in diverse, contingent, discourses that change over time. It would enable us therefore to see individual identity and social group formation as complex and shifting. Thus, it would also allow us to thematize conflict and power among social groups.

Fraser claims that such a pragmatic model offers a way out of the two alternatives of essentialist conceptions of women's identity on the one hand and views of women's identity as sheer negation on the other. I agree with her and believe that we need to see gender identity as a complex assortment of a network of signifying practices, varying for individuals over time and among individuals, as gender identity intersects with such other networks of signifying practices as are captured in such concepts as class and race. This conception of gender identity points to a meaning of "woman" as always open to negotiation as diverse individuals and groups struggle over changes in its meaning to satisfy new needs. But as we come to recognize gender identity as the complex assortment of a network of signifying practices, so also do we need to see other forms of identity in similar ways. The essay by Uma Narayan points to the need for feminists and others to move away from essentialized conceptions of "nation" and "culture" as we move away from such ways of viewing gender. This becomes a particularly important issue as we move to the question of how differences among women are to be negotiated.

Narayan takes up the assertion often made that feminism is a western phenomenon and therefore has nothing to say to third world women. This is an assertion not only made by non-feminists against feminists but is sometimes believed by western feminists themselves. Western feminists are drawn to this position when they see it as the only alternative to a claim they reject, that women everywhere are the same and share common forms of oppression. But Narayan claims that the two alternatives of, on the one hand, thinking of feminism as uniform world wide and, on the other hand, seeing it as being limited to the west, do not exhaust the realm of possibilities. Moving away from these alternatives requires recognizing that third world societies are themselves internally heterogeneous and changing over time. Such heterogeneity and change lead to the creation of diverse messages in diverse contexts and between generations. The tensions generated by these differences make possible types of feminism that are specific to the societies from which they emerge.

Thinking about third world societies as heterogeneous and possessing histories is to reject the imperial view of such societies as homogeneous and without history. However, it is also to reject similar ways of thinking often found in those nationalist movements that have revolted against imperial domination. Such nationalist movements have tended to share in the imperial view of their own cultures as homogeneous and without history, only inverting the values given to their culture by the imperial view. But as the reifications of the imperial view were selective, so also are the idealizations of the nationalist movements. Thus, Hindu nationalists depict sati as a "native Indian" tradition, when, as Narayan points out, it has been a Hindu tradition practiced primarily in certain regions and by certain groups. Depicting it as a "native Indian" practice furthers the Hindu move for dominance over other groups. Similarly, while nationalist men reject changes in gender roles brought about by modernization, and label such changes a "western importation," they happily make use of technology such as television and computers, or subscribe to western generated ideologies such as Marxism, without describing them in these kinds of ways.

Thus, as we reject essentialist notions of "woman," so must we also reject essentialist notions of nation, culture, etc. This leads us not to a place where we have nothing to say, but to a multitude of places where we have much to say. It is only by recognizing the specificity of the places from which we speak and by creating the means through which we all are able to speak that we can begin to engage in true dialogue with each other.

19

LUCE IRIGARAY

"This Sex Which is Not One"

Female sexuality has always been theorized within masculine parameters. Thus, the opposition "viril" clitoral activity/"feminine" vaginal passivity which Freud—and many others—claims are alternative behaviors or steps in the process of becoming a sexually normal woman, seems prescribed more by the practice of masculine sexuality than by anything else. For the clitoris is thought of as a little penis which is pleasurable to masturbate, as long as the anxiety of castration does not exist (for the little boy), while the vagina derives its value from the "home" it offers the male penis when the now forbidden hand must find a substitute to take its place in giving pleasure.

According to these theorists, woman's erogenous zones are no more than a clitoris-sex, which cannot stand up in comparison with the valued phallic organ; or a hole-envelope, a sheath which surrounds and rubs the penis during coition; a nonsex organ or a masculine sex organ turned inside out in order to caress itself.

Woman and her pleasure are not mentioned in this conception of the sexual relationship. Her fate is one of "lack," "atrophy" (of her genitals), and "penis envy," since the penis is the only recognized sex organ of any worth. Therefore she tries to appropriate it for herself, by all the means at her disposal: by her somewhat servile love of the father-husband capable of giving it to her; by her desire of a penis-child, preferably male; by gaining access to those cultural values which are still "by right" reserved for males alone and are therefore always masculine, etc. Woman lives her desire only as an attempt to possess at long last the equivalent of the male sex organ.

All of that seems rather foreign to her pleasure however, unless she remains within the dominant phallic economy. Thus, for example, woman's autoeroticism is very different from man's. He needs an instrument in order to touch himself: his hand, woman's genitals, language—and this self-stimulation requires a minimum of activity. But a woman touches herself by and within herself directly, without mediation, and before any distinction between activity and passivity is possible. A woman "touches herself" constantly without anyone being able to forbid her to do so, for her sex is composed of two lips which embrace continually. Thus, within herself she is already two—but not divisible into ones—who stimulate each other.

This autoeroticism, which she needs in order not to risk the disappearance of her pleasure in the sex act, is interrupted by a violent intrusion: the brutal spreading of these two lips by a violating penis. If, in order to assure an articulation between autoeroticism and heteroeroticism in coition (the encounter with the absolute other which always signifies death), the vagina must also, but not only, substitute for the little boy's hand, how can woman's autoeroticism possibly be perpetuated in the classic representation of sexuality? Will she not indeed be left the impossible choice between defensive virginity, fiercely turned back upon itself, or a body open for penetration, which no longer recognizes in its "hole" of a sex organ the pleasure of retouching itself? The almost exclusive, and ever so anxious, attention accorded the erection in Occidental sexuality proves to what extent the imaginary that commands it is foreign to everything female. For the most part, one finds in Occidental sexuality nothing more than imperatives dictated by rivalry among males: the "strongest" being the one who "gets it up the most," who has the longest, thickest, hardest penis or indeed the one who "pisses the farthest" (cf. little boys' games). These imperatives can also be dictated by sado-masochist fantasies, which in turn are ordered by the relationship between man and mother: his desire to force open, to penetrate, to appropriate for himself the mystery of the stomach in which he was conceived, the secret of his conception, of his "origin." Desire-need, also, once again, to make blood flow in order to revive a very ancient—intrauterine, undoubtedly, but also prehistoric—relation to the maternal.

Woman, in this sexual imaginary, is only a more or less complacent facilitator for the working out of man's fantasies. It is possible, and even certain, that she experiences vicarious pleasure there, but this pleasure is above all a masochistic prostitution of her body to a desire that is not her own and that leaves her in her well-known state of dependency. Not knowing what she wants, ready for anything, even asking for more, if only he will "take" her as the "object" of *his* pleasure, she will not say what *she* wants. Moreover, she does not know, or no longer knows, what she wants. As Freud admits, the beginnings of the sexual life of the little girl are so "obscure," so "faded by the years," that one would have to dig very deep in order to find, behind the traces of this civilization, this history, the vestiges of a more archaic civilization which could give some indication as to what woman's sexuality is all about. This very ancient civilization undoubtedly would not have the same language, the same alphabet— Woman's desire most likely does not speak the same language as man's desire, and it probably has been covered over by the logic that has dominated the West since the Greeks.

In this logic, the prevalence of the gaze, discrimination of form, and individualization of form is particularly foreign to female eroticism. Woman finds pleasure more in touch than in sight and her entrance into a dominant scopic economy signifies, once again, her relegation to passivity: she will be the beautiful object. Although her body is in this way eroticized and solicited to a double movement between exhibition and pudic retreat in order to excite the instincts of the "subject," her sex organ represents the horror of having nothing to see. In this system of representation and desire, the vagina is a flaw, a hole in the representation's scoptophilic objective. It was admitted already in Greek statuary that this "nothing to be seen" must be excluded, rejected, from such a scene of representation. Woman's sexual organs are simply absent from this scene: they are masked and her "slit" is sewn up.

In addition, this sex organ which offers nothing to the view has no distinctive form of its own. Although woman finds pleasure precisely in this incompleteness of the form of her sex organ, which is why it retouches itself indefinitely, her pleasure is denied by a civilization that privileges phallomorphism. The value accorded to the only definable form excludes the form involved in female autoeroticism. The one of form, the individual sex, proper name, literal meaning—supersedes, by spreading apart and dividing, this touching of *at least two* (lips) which keeps woman in contact with herself, although it would be impossible to distinguish exactly what "parts" are touching each other.

Whence the mystery that she represents in a culture that claims to enumerate everything, cipher everything by units, inventory everything by individualities. *She is neither one nor two.* She cannot, strictly speaking, be determined either as one person or as two. She renders any definition inadequate. Moreover she has no "proper" name. And her sex organ, which is not *a* sex organ, is counted as *no* sex organ. It is the negative, the opposite, the reverse, the counterpart, of the only visible and morphologically designatable sex organ (even if it does pose a few problems in its passage from erection to detumescence): the penis.

But woman holds the secret of the "thickness" of this "form," its many-layered volume, its metamorphosis from smaller to larger and vice versa, and even the intervals at which this change takes place. Without even knowing it. When she is asked to maintain, to revive, man's desire, what this means in terms of the value of her own desire is neglected. Moreover, she is not aware of her desire, at least not explicitly. But the force and continuity of her desire are capable of nurturing all the "feminine" masquerades that are expected to her for a long time.

It is true that she still has the child, with whom her appetite for touching, for contact, is given free reign, unless this appetite is already lost, or alienated by the taboo placed upon touching in a largely obsessional civilization. In her relation to the child she finds compensatory pleasure for the frustrations she encounters all too often in sexual relations proper. Thus maternity supplants the deficiencies of repressed female sexuality. Is it possible that man and woman no longer even caress each other except indirectly through the mediation between them represented by the child? Preferably male. Man, identified with his son, rediscovers the pleasure of maternal coddling; woman retouches herself in fondling that part of her body: her baby-penis-clitoris.

What that entails for the amorous trio has been clearly spelled out. The Oedipal interdict seems, however, a rather artificial and imprecise law—even though it is the very means of perpetuating the authoritarian discourse of fathers—when it is decreed in a culture where sexual relations are impracticable, since the desire of man and the desire of woman are so foreign to each other. Each of them is forced to search for some common meeting ground by indirect means: either an archaic, sensory relation to the mother's body, or a current, active or passive prolongation of the law of the father. Their attempts are characterized by regressive emotional behavior and the exchange of words so far from the realm of the sexual that they are completely exiled from it. "Mother" and "father" dominate the couple's functioning, but only as social roles. The division of labor prevents them from making love. They produce or reproduce. Not knowing too well how to use their leisure. If indeed they have any, if moreover they want to have any leisure. For what can be done with leisure? What substitute for amorous invention can be created?

We could go on and on—but perhaps we should return to the repressed female imaginary? Thus woman does not have a sex. She has at least two of them, but they cannot be identified as ones. Indeed she has many more of them than that. Her sexuality, always at least double, is in fact *plural*. Plural as culture now wishes to be plural? Plural as the manner in which current texts are written, with very little knowledge of the censorship from which they arise? Indeed, woman's pleasure does not have to choose between clitoral activity and vaginal passivity, for example. The pleasure of the vaginal caress does not have to substitute itself for the pleasure of the clitoral caress. Both contribute irreplaceably to woman's pleasure but they are only two caresses among many to do so. Caressing the breasts, touching the vulva, opening the lips, gently stroking the posterior wall of the vagina, lightly massaging the cervix, etc., evoke a few of the most specifically female pleasures. They remain rather unfamiliar pleasures in the sexual difference as it is currently imagined, or rather as it is currently ignored: the other sex being only the indispensable complement of the only sex.

But *woman has sex organs just about everywhere*. She experiences pleasure almost everywhere. Even without speaking of the hysterization of her entire body, one can say that the geography of her pleasure is much more diversified, more multiple in its differences, more complex, more subtle, than is imagined—in an imaginary centered a bit too much on one and the same.

"She" is indefinitely other in herself. That is undoubtedly the reason she is called temperamental, incomprehensible, perturbed, capricious—not to mention her language in which "she" goes off in all directions and in which "he" is unable to discern the coherence of any meaning. Contradictory words seem a little crazy to the logic of reason, and inaudible for him who listens with ready-made grids, a code prepared in advance. In her statements—at least when she dares to speak out—woman retouches herself constantly. She just barely separates from herself some chatter, an exclamation, a half-secret, a sentence left in suspense—When she returns to it, it is only to set out again from another point of pleasure or pain. One must listen to her differently in order to hear an *"other meaning"* which is constantly in the process of weaving itself, at the *same time ceaselessly embracing words and yet casting them off to avoid becoming fixed, immobilized.* For when "she" says something, it is already no longer identical to what she means. Moreover, her statements are never identical to anything. Their distinguishing feature is one of contiguity. They touch (*upon*). And when they wander too far from this nearness, she stops and begins again from "zero": her body-sex organ.

It is therefore useless to trap women into giving an exact definition of what they mean, to make them repeat (themselves) so the meaning will be clear. They are already elsewhere than in this discusive machinery where you claim to take them by surprise. They have turned back within themselves, which does not mean the same thing as "within yourself." They do not experience the same interiority that you do and which perhaps you mistakenly presume they share. "Within themselves" means *in the privacy of this silent, multiple, diffuse tact.* If you ask them insistently what they are thinking about, they can only reply: nothing. Everything.

Thus they desire at the same time nothing and everything. It is always more and other than this *one*—of sex, for example—that you give them, that you attribute to them and which is often interpreted, and feared, as a sort of insatiable hunger, a voracity which will engulf you entirely. While in fact it is really a question of another economy which diverts the linearity of a project, undermines the target-object of a desire, explodes the polarization of desire on only one pleasure, and disconcerts fidelity to only one discourse—

Must the multiple nature of female desire and language be understood as the fragmentary, scattered remains of a raped or denied sexuality? This is not an easy question to answer. The rejection, the exclusion of a female imaginary undoubtedly places woman in a position where she can experience herself only fragmentarily as waste or as excess in the little structured margins of a dominant ideology, this mirror entrusted by the (masculine) "subject" with the task of reflecting and redoubling himself. The role of "feminity" is prescribed moreover by this masculine specula(riza)tion and corresponds only slightly to woman's desire, which is recuperated only secretly, in hiding, and in a disturbing and unpardonable manner.

But if the female imaginary happened to unfold, if it happened to come into play other than as pieces, scraps, deprived of their assemblage, would it present itself for all that as *a* universe? Would it indeed be volume rather than surface? No. Unless female imaginary is taken to mean, once again, the prerogative of the maternal over the female. This maternal would be phallic in nature however, closed in upon the jealous possession of its valuable product, and competing with man in his esteem for surplus. In this race for power, woman loses the uniqueness of her pleasure. By diminishing herself in volume, she renounces the pleasure derived from the nonsuture of her lips: she is a mother certainly, but she is a virgin mother. Mythology long ago assigned this role to her in which she is allowed a certain social power as long as she is reduced, with her own complicity, to sexual impotence.

Thus a woman's (re)discovery of herself can only signify the possibility of not sacrificing any of her pleasures to another, of not identifying with anyone in particular, of never being simply one. It is a sort of universe in expansion for which no limits could be fixed and which, for all that, would not be incoherency. Nor would it be the polymorphic perversion of the infant during which its erogenous zones await their consolidation under the primacy of the phallus.

Woman would always remain multiple, but she would be protected from dispersion because the other is a part of her, and is autoerotically familiar to her. That does not mean that she would appropriate the other for herself, that she would make it her property. Property and propriety are undoubtedly rather foreign to all that is female. At least sexually. *Nearness*, however, is not foreign to woman, a nearness so close that any identification of one or the other, and therefore any form of property, is impossible. Woman enjoys a closeness with the other that is *so near she cannot possess it, any more than she can possess herself.* She constantly trades herself for the other without any possible identification of either one of them. Woman's pleasure, which grows indefinitely from its passage in/through the other, poses a problem for any current economy in that all computations that attempt to account for woman's incalculable pleasure are irremediably destined to fail.

However, in order for woman to arrive at the point where she can enjoy her pleasure as a woman, a long detour by the analysis of the various systems of oppression which affect her is certainly necessary. By claiming to resort to pleasure alone as the solution to her problem, she runs the risk of missing the reconsideration of a social practice upon which *her* pleasure depends.

For woman is traditionally use-value for man, exchange-value among men. Merchandise, then. This makes her the guardian of matter whose price will be determined by "subjects": workers, tradesmen, consumers, according to the standard of their work and their need-desire. Women are marked phallically by their fathers, husbands, procurers. This stamp(ing) determines their value in sexual commerce. Woman is never anything more than the scene of more or less rival exchange between two men, even when they are competing for the possession of mother-earth.

How can this object of transaction assert a right to pleasure without extricating itself from the established commercial system? How can this merchandise relate to other goods on the market other than with aggressive jealousy? How can raw materials possess themselves without provoking in the consumer fear of the disappearance of his nourishing soil? How can this exchange in nothingness that can be defined in "proper" terms of woman's desire not seem to be pure enticement, folly, all too quickly covered over by a more sensible discourse and an apparently more tangible system of values?

A woman's evolution, however radical it might seek to be, would not suffice then to liberate woman's desire. Neither political theory nor political practice have yet resolved nor sufficiently taken into account this historical problem, although Marxism has announced its importance. But women are not, strictly speaking, a class and their dispersion in several classes makes their political struggle complex and their demands sometimes contradictory.

Their underdeveloped condition stemming from their submission by/to a culture which oppresses them, uses them, cashes in on them, still remains. Women reap no advantage from this situation except that of their quasi-monopoly of masochistic pleasure, housework, and reproduction. The power of slaves? It is considerable since the master is not necessarily well served in matters of pleasure. Therefore, the inversion of the relationship, especially in sexual economy, does not seem to be an enviable objective.

But if women are to preserve their auto-eroticism, their homo-sexuality, and let it flourish, would not the renunciation of heterosexual pleasure simply be another form of this amputation of power that is traditionally associated with women? Would this renunciation not be a new incarceration, a new cloister that women would willingly build? Let women tacitly go on strike, avoid men long enough to learn to defend their desire notably by their speech, let them discover the love of other women protected from that imperious choice of men which puts them in a position of rival goods, let them forge a social status which demands recognition, let them earn their living in order to leave behind their condition of prostitute—These are certainly indispensable steps in their effort to escape their proletarization on the trade market. But, if their goal is to reverse the existing order—even if that were possible—history would simply repeat itself and return to phallocratism, where neither women's sex, their imaginary, nor their language can exist.

—Translated by Claudia Reeder

20

LINDA ALCOFF

Cultural Feminism versus Post-Structuralism

The Identity Crisis in Feminist Theory

For many contemporary feminist theorists, the concept of woman is a problem. It is a problem of primary significance because the concept of woman is the central concept for feminist theory and yet it is a concept that is impossible to formulate precisely for feminists. It is the central concept for feminists because the concept and category of woman is the necessary point of departure for any feminist theory and feminist politics, predicated as these are on the transformation of women's lived experience in contemporary culture and the reevaluation of social theory and practice from women's point of view. But as a concept it is radically problematic precisely for feminists because it is crowded with the overdeterminations of male supremacy, invoking in every formulation the limit, contrasting Other, or mediated self-reflection of a culture built on the control of females. In attempting to speak for women, feminism often seems to presuppose that it knows what women truly are, but such an assumption is foolhardy given that every source of knowledge about women has been contaminated with misogyny and sexism. No matter where we turn—to historical documents, philosophical constructions, social scientific statistics, introspection, or daily practices—the mediation of female bodies into constructions of woman is dominated by misogynist discourse. For feminists, who must transcend this discourse, it appears we have nowhere to turn.[1]

Thus the dilemma facing feminist theorists today is that our very self-definition is grounded in a concept that we must deconstruct and de-essentialize in all of its aspects. Man has said that woman can be defined, delineated, captured—understood, explained, and diagnosed—to a level of determination never accorded to man himself, who is conceived as a rational animal with free will. Where man's behavior is under-determined, free to construct its own future along the course of its rational choice, woman's nature has over-determined her behavior, the limits of her intellectual endeavors, and the inevitabilities of her emotional journey through life. Whether she is construed as essentially immoral and irrational (à la Schopenhauer) or essentially kind and benevolent (à la Kant), she is always construed as an essential *something* inevitably accessible to direct intuited apprehension by males.[2] Despite the variety of ways in which man has construed her essential characteristics, she is always the Object, a conglomeration of attributes to be predicted and controlled along with other natural phenomena. The place of the free-willed subject who can transcend nature's mandates is reserved exclusively for men.[3]

Feminist thinkers have articulated two major responses to this situation over the last ten years. The first response is to claim that feminists have the exclusive right to describe and evaluate woman. Thus cultural feminists argue that the problem of male supremacist culture is the problem of a process in which women are defined by men, that is, by a group who has a contrasting point of view and set of interests from women, not to mention a possible fear and hatred of women. The result of this has been a distortion and devaluation of feminine characteristics, which now can be cor-rected by a more accurate feminist description and appraisal. Thus the cultural femi-nist reappraisal construes woman's passivity as her peacefulness, her sentimentality as her proclivity to nurture, her subjectiveness as her advanced self-awareness, and so forth. Cultural feminists have not challenged the defining of woman but only that def-inition given by men.

The second major response has been to reject the possibility of defining woman as such at all. Feminists who take this tactic go about the business of deconstructing all concepts of woman and argue that both feminist and misogynist attempts to define woman are politically reactionary and ontologically mistaken. Replacing woman-as-housewife with woman-as-supermom (or earth mother or super professional) is no advance. Using French post-structuralist theory these feminists argue that such errors occur because we are in fundamental ways duplicating misogynist strategies when we try to define women, characterize women, or speak for women, even though allowing for a range of differences within the gender. The politics of gender or sexual differ-ence must be replaced with a plurality of difference where gender loses its position of significance.

Briefly put, then, the cultural feminist response to Simone de Beauvoir's question, "Are there women?" is to answer yes and to define women by their activities and attributes in the present culture. The post-structuralist response is to answer no and attack the category and the concept of woman through problematizing subjectivity. Each response has serious limitations, and it is becoming increasingly obvious that transcending these limitations while retaining the theoretical framework from which they emerge is impossible. As a result, a few brave souls are now rejecting these choices and attempting to map out a new course, a course that will avoid the major problems of the earlier responses. In this paper I will discuss some of the pioneer work being done to develop a new concept of woman and offer my own contribution toward it.[4] But first, I must spell out more clearly the inadequacies of the first two responses to the problem of woman and explain why I believe these inadequacies are inherent.

CULTURAL FEMINISM

Cultural feminism is the ideology of a female nature or female essence reappropriated by feminists themselves in an effort to revalidate undervalued female attributes. For cultural feminists, the enemy of women is not merely a social system or economic institution or set of backward beliefs but masculinity itself and in some cases male biology. Cultural feminist politics revolve around creating and maintaining a healthy environment—free of masculinist values and all their offshoots such as pornography—for the female principle. Feminist theory, the explanation of sexism, and the justification of feminist demands can all be grounded securely and unambiguously on the concept of the essential female.

Mary Daly and Adrienne Rich have been influential proponents of this position.[5] Breaking from the trend toward androgyny and the minimizing of gender differences that was popular among feminists in the early seventies, both Daly and Rich argue for a returned focus on femaleness.

For Daly, male barrenness leads to parasitism on female energy, which flows from our life-affirming, life-creating biological condition: "Since female energy is essentially biophilic, the female spirit/body is the primary target in this perpetual war of aggression against life. Gyn/Ecology is the re-claiming of life-loving female energy."[6] Despite Daly's warnings against biological reductionism,[7] her own analysis of sexism uses gender-specific biological traits to explain male hatred for women. The childless state of "all males" leads to a dependency on women, which in turn leads men to "deeply identify with 'unwanted fetal tissue.'"[8] Given their state of fear and insecurity it becomes almost understandable, then, that men would desire to dominate and control that which is so vitally necessary to them: the life-energy of women. Female energy, conceived by Daly as a natural essence, needs to be freed from its male parasites, released for creative expression and recharged through bonding with other women. In this free space women's "natural" attributes of love, creativity, and the ability to nurture can thrive.

Women's identification as female is their defining essence for Daly, their haecceity, overriding any other way in which they may be defined or may define themselves. Thus Daly states: "Women who accept false inclusion among the fathers and sons are easily polarized against other women on the basis of ethnic, national, class, religious and other *male-defined differences*, applauding the defeat of 'enemy' women."[9] These differences are apparent rather than real, inessential rather than essential. The only real difference, the only difference that can change a person's ontological placement on Daly's dichotomous map, is sex difference. Our essence is defined here, in our sex, from which flow all the facts about us: who are our potential allies, who is our enemy, what are our objective interests, what is our true nature. Thus, Daly defines women again and her definition is strongly linked to female biology.

Many of Rich's writings have exhibited surprising similarities to Daly's position described above, surprising given their difference in style and temperament. Rich defines a "female consciousness"[10] that has a great deal to do with the female body.

> I have come to believe . . . that female biology—the diffuse, intense sensuality radiating out from clitoris, breasts, uterus, vagina; the lunar cycles of menstruation; the gestation and fruition of life which can take place in the female body—has far more radical implications than we have yet come to appreciate. Patriarchal thought has limited female biology to its own narrow specifications. The feminist vision has recoiled from female biology for these reasons; it will, I believe, come to view our physicality as a resource, rather than a destiny. . . . We must touch the unity and resonance of our physicality, our bond with the natural order, the corporeal ground of our intelligence.[11]

Thus Rich argues that we should not reject the importance of female biology simply because patriarchy has used it to subjugate us. Rich believes that "our biological grounding, the miracle and paradox of the female body and its spiritual and political meanings" holds the key to our rejuvenation and our reconnection with our specific female attributes, which she lists as "our great mental capacities . . . ; our highly developed tactile sense; our genius for close observation; our complicated, pain-enduring, multi-pleasured physicality."[12]

Rich further echoes Daly in her explanation of misogyny: "The ancient, continuing envy, awe and dread of the male for the female capacity to create life has repeatedly taken the form of hatred for every other female aspect of creativity."[13] Thus Rich, like Daly, identifies a female essence, defines patriarchy as the subjugation and colonization of this essence out of male envy and need, and then promotes a solution that revolves around rediscovering our essence and bonding with other women. Neither Rich nor Daly espouse biological reductionism, but this is because they reject the oppositional dichotomy of mind and body that such a reductionism presupposes. The female essence for Daly and Rich is not simply spiritual or simply biological—it is both. Yet the key point remains that it is our specifically female anatomy that is the primary constituent of our identity and the source of our female essence. Rich prophesies that "the repossession by women of our bodies will bring far more essential change to human society than the seizing of the means of production by workers. . . . In such a world women will truly create new life, bringing forth not only children (if and as we choose) but the visions, and the thinking, necessary to sustain, console and alter human existence—a new relationship to the universe. Sexuality, politics, intelligence, power, motherhood, work, community, intimacy will develop new meanings; thinking itself will be transformed."[14]

The characterization of Rich's and Daly's views as part of a growing trend within feminism toward essentialism has been developed most extensively by Alice Echols.[15]

Echols prefers the name "cultural feminism" for this trend because it equates "women's liberation with the development and preservation of a female counter culture."[16] Echols identifies cultural feminist writings by their denigration of masculinity rather than male roles or practices, by their valorization of female traits, and by their commitment to preserve rather than diminish gender differences. Besides Daly and Rich, Echols names Susan Griffin, Kathleen Barry, Janice Raymond, Florence Rush, Susan Brownmiller, and Robin Morgan as important cultural feminist writers, and she documents her claim persuasively by highlighting key passages of their work. Although Echols finds a prototype of this trend in early radical feminist writings by Valerie Solanis and Joreen, she is careful to distinguish cultural feminism from radical feminism as a whole. The distinguishing marks between the two include their position on the mutability of sexism among men, the connection drawn between biology and misogyny, and the degree of focus on valorized female attributes. As Hester Eisenstein has argued, there is a tendency within many radical feminist works toward setting up an ahistorical and essentialist conception of female nature, but this tendency is developed and consolidated by cultural feminists, thus rendering their work significantly different from radical feminism.

However, although cultural feminist views sharply separate female from male traits, they certainly do not all give explicitly essentialist formulations of what it means to be a woman. So it may seem that Echols's characterization of cultural feminism makes it appear too homogeneous and that the charge of essentialism is on shaky ground. On the issue of essentialism Echols states:

> This preoccupation with defining the female sensibility not only leads these feminists to indulge in dangerously erroneous generalizations about women, but to imply that this identity is innate rather than socially constructed. At best, there has been a curiously cavalier disregard for whether these differences are biological or cultural in origin. Thus Janice Raymond argues: "Yet there are differences, and some feminists have come to realize that those differences are important whether they spring from socialization, from biology, or from the total history of existing as a woman in a patriarchal society."[17]

Echols points out that the importance of the differences varies tremendously according to their source. If that source is innate, the cultural feminist focus on building an alternative feminist culture is politically correct. If the differences are not innate, the focus of our activism should shift considerably. In the absence of a clearly stated position on the ultimate source of gender difference, Echols infers from their emphasis on building a feminist free-space and woman-centered culture that cultural feminists hold some version of essentialism. I share Echols's suspicion. Certainly, it is difficult to render the views of Rich and Daly into a coherent whole without supplying a missing premise that there is an innate female essence.

Interestingly, I have not included any feminist writings from women of oppressed nationalities and races in the category of cultural feminism, nor does Echols. I have heard it argued that the emphasis placed on cultural identity by such writers as

Cherríe Moraga and Audre Lorde reveals a tendency toward essentialism also. However, in my view their work has consistently rejected essentialist conceptions of gender. Consider the following passage from Moraga: "When you start to talk about sexism, the world becomes increasingly complex. The power no longer breaks down into neat little hierarchical categories, but becomes a series of starts and detours. Since the categories are not easy to arrive at, the enemy is not easy to name. It is all so difficult to unravel."[18] Moraga goes on to assert that "some men oppress the very women they love," implying that we need new categories and new concepts to describe such complex and contradictory relations of oppression. In this problematic understanding of sexism, Moraga seems to me light-years ahead of Daly's Manichean ontology or Rich's romanticized conception of the female. The simultaneity of oppressions experienced by women such as Moraga resists essentialist conclusions. Universalist conceptions of female or male experiences and attributes are not plausible in the context of such a complex network of relations, and without an ability to universalize, the essentialist argument is difficult if not impossible to make. White women cannot be all good or all bad; neither can men from oppressed groups. I have simply not found writings by feminists who are oppressed also by race and/or class that place or position maleness wholly as Other. Reflected in their problematized understanding of masculinity is a richer and likewise problematized concept of woman.[19]

Even if cultural feminism is the product of white feminists, it is not homogeneous, as Echols herself points out. The biological accounts of sexism given by Daly and Brownmiller, for example, are not embraced by Rush or Dworkin. But the key link between these feminists is their tendency toward invoking universalizing conceptions of woman and mother in an essentialist way. Therefore, despite the lack of complete homogeneity within the category, it seems still justifiable and important to identify (and criticize) within these sometimes disparate works their tendency to offer an essentialist response to misogyny and sexism through adopting a homogeneous, unproblematized, and ahistorical conception of woman.

One does not have to be influenced by French post-structuralism to disagree with essentialism. It is well documented that the innateness of gender differences in personality and character is at this point factually and philosophically indefensible.[20] There are a host of divergent ways gender divisions occur in different societies, and the differences that appear to be universal can be explained in nonessentialist ways. However, belief in women's innate peacefulness and ability to nurture has been common among feminists since the nineteenth century and has enjoyed a resurgence in the last decade, most notably among feminist peace activists. I have met scores of young feminists drawn to actions like the Women's Peace Encampment and to groups like Women for a Non-Nuclear Future by their belief that the maternal love women have for their children can unlock the gates of imperialist oppression. I have great respect for the self-affirming pride of these women, but I also share Echols's fear that their effect is to "reflect and reproduce dominant cultural assumptions about women," which not only fail to represent the variety in women's lives but promote unrealistic expectations about "normal" female behavior that most of us cannot satisfy.[21] Our gender categories are positively constitutive and not mere hindsight descriptions of previous activities. There is a self-perpetuating circularity between defining woman as essentially peaceful and nurturing and the observations and judgments we shall make of future women and the practices we shall engage in as women in the future. Do feminists want to buy another ticket for women of the world on the merry-go-round of feminine constructions? Don't we want rather to get off the merry-go-round and run away?

This should not imply that the political effects of cultural feminism have all been negative.[22] The insistence on viewing traditional feminine characteristics from a different point of view, to use a "looking glass" perspective, as a means of engendering a gestalt switch on the body of data we all currently share about women, has had positive effect. After a decade of hearing liberal feminists advising us to wear business suits and enter the male world, it is a helpful corrective to have cultural feminists argue instead that women's world is full of superior virtues and values, to be credited and learned from rather than despised. Herein lies the positive impact of cultural feminism. And surely much of their point is well taken, that it was our mothers who made our families survive, that women's handiwork is truly artistic, that women's care-giving really is superior in value to male competitiveness.

Unfortunately, however, the cultural feminist championing of a redefined "womanhood" cannot provide a useful long-range program for a feminist movement and, in fact, places obstacles in the way of developing one. Under conditions of oppression and restrictions on freedom of movement, women, like other oppressed groups, have developed strengths and attributes that should be correctly credited, valued, and promoted. What we should not promote, however, are the restrictive conditions that gave rise to those attributes: forced parenting, lack of physical autonomy, dependency for survival on mediation skills, for instance. What conditions for women do we want to promote? A freedom of movement such that we can compete in the capitalist world alongside men? A continued restriction to child-centered activities? To the extent cultural feminism merely valorizes genuinely positive attributes developed under oppression, it cannot map our future long-range course. To the extent that it reinforces essentialist explanations of these attributes, it is in danger of solidifying an important bulwark for sexist oppression: the belief in an innate "womanhood" to which we must all adhere lest we be deemed either inferior or not "true" women. For many feminists, the problem with the cultural feminist response to sexism is that it does not criticize the fundamental mechanism of oppressive power used to perpetuate sexism and in fact reinvokes that mechanism in its supposed solution. The mechanism of power referred to here is the construction of the subject by a discourse that weaves knowledge and power into a coercive structure that "forces the individual back on himself and ties him to his own identity in a constraining way."[23] On this view, essentialist formulations of womanhood, even when made by feminists, "tie" the individual to her identity as a woman and thus cannot represent a solution to sexism.

This articulation of the problem has been borrowed by feminists from a number of recently influential French thinkers who are sometimes called post-structuralist but who also might be called post-humanist and post-essentialist. Lacan, Derrida, and Foucault are the front-runners in this group. Disparate as these writers are, their common theme is that the self-contained, authentic subject conceived by humanism to be discoverable below a veneer of cultural and ideological overlay is in reality a construct of that very humanist discourse. The subject is not a locus of authorial intentions or natural attributes or even a privileged, separate consciousness. Lacan uses psychoanalysis, Derrida uses grammar, and Foucault uses the history of discourses to attack and "deconstruct"[24] our concept of the subject as having an essential identity and an authentic core that has been repressed by society. There is no essential core "natural" to us, and so there is no repression in the humanist sense.

There is an interesting sort of neodeterminism in this view. The subject or self is never determined by biology in such a way that human history is predictable or even explainable, and there is no unilinear direction of a determinist arrow pointing from some fairly static, "natural" phenomena to human experiences. On the other hand, this rejection of biological determinism is not grounded in the belief that human subjects are underdetermined but, rather, in the belief that we are overdetermined (i.e., constructed) by a social discourse and/or cultural practice. The idea here is that we individuals really have little choice in the matter of who we are, for as Derrida and Foucault like to remind us, individual motivations and intentions count for nil, or almost nil, in the scheme of social reality. We are constructs—that is, our experience of our very subjectivity is a construct mediated by and/or grounded on a social discourse beyond (way beyond) individual control. As Foucault puts it, we are bodies "totally imprinted by history."[25] Thus, subjective experiences are determined in some sense by macro forces. However, these macro forces, including social discourses and social practices, are apparently not overdetermined, resulting as they do from such a complex and unpredictable network of overlapping and criss-crossing elements that no unilinear directionality is perceivable and in fact no final or efficient cause exists. There may be, and Foucault hoped at one point to find them,[26] perceivable processes of change within the social network, but beyond schematic rules of thumb neither the form nor the content of discourse has a fixed or unified structure or can be predicted or mapped out via an objectified, ultimate realm. To some extent, this view is similar to contemporary methodological individualism, whose advocates will usually concede that the complex of human intentions results in a social reality bearing no resemblance to the summarized categories of intentions but looking altogether different than any one party or sum of parties even envisaged and desired. The difference, however, is that while methodological individualists admit that human intentions are ineffective, post-structuralists deny not only the efficacy but also the ontological autonomy, and even the existence of intentionality.

Post-structuralists unite with Marx in asserting the social dimension of individual traits and intentions. Thus, they say we cannot understand society as the conglomerate of individual intentions but, rather, must understand individual intentions as constructed within a social reality. To the extent post-structuralists emphasize social explanations of individual practices and experiences I find their work illuminating and persuasive. My disagreement occurs, however, when they seem totally to erase any room for maneuver by the individual within a social discourse or set of institutions. It is that totalization of history's imprint that I reject. In their defense of a total construction of the subject, post-structuralists deny the subject's ability to reflect on the social discourse and challenge its determinations.

Applied to the concept of woman the post-structuralist's view results in what I shall call nominalism: the idea that the category "woman" is a fiction, and that feminsit efforts must be directed toward dismantling this fiction. "Perhaps. . . 'woman' is not a determinable identity. Perhaps woman is not some thing which announces itself from a distance, at a distance from some other thing. . . . Perhaps woman—a non-identity, non-figure, a simulacrum—is distance's very chasm, the out-distancing of distance, the interval's cadence, distance itself."[27] Derrida's interest in feminism stems from his belief, expressed above, that woman may represent the rupture in the functional discourse of what he calls logocentrism, an essentailist discourse that entails hierarchies of difference and a Kantian ontology. Because woman has in a sense been excluded from this discourse, it is possible to hope that she might provide a real source of resistance. But her resistance will not be at all effective if she continues to use the mechanism of logocentrism to redefine woman: she can be an effective resister only if she drifts and dodges all attempts to capture her. Then, Derrida hopes, the following futuristic picture will come true: "Out of the depths, endless and unfathomable, she engulfs and distorts all vestige of essentiality, of identity, of property. And the philosophical discourse, blinded, founders on these shoals and is hurled down these depths to its ruin."[28] For Derrida, women have always been defined as a subjugated difference within a binary opposition: man/woman, culture/nature, positive/negative, analytical/intuitive. To assert an essential gender difference as cultural feminists do is to reinvoke this oppositional structure. The only way to break out of this structure, and in fact to subvert the structure itself, is to assert total difference, to be that which cannot be pinned down or subjugated within a dichotomous hierarchy. Paradoxically, it is to be what is not. Thus feminists cannot demarcate a definitive category of "woman" without eliminating all possibility for the defeat of logocentrism and its oppressive power.

Foucault similarly rejects all constructions of oppositional subjects—whether the "proletariat," "woman," or "the oppressed"—as mirror images that merely recreate and sustain the discourse of power. As Biddy Martin points out, "The point from which Foucault deconstructs is off-center, out of line, apparently unaligned. It is not the point of an imagined absolute otherness, but an 'alterity' which understands itself as an internal exclusion."[20]

Following Foucault and Derrida, an effective feminism could only be a wholly negative feminism, deconstructing everything and refusing to construct anything. This is the position Julia Kristeva, herself an influential French post-structuralist, adopts. She says: "A woman cannot be; it is something which does not even belong in the order of being. *It follows that a feminist practice can only be negative*, at odds with what already exists so that we may say 'that's not it' and 'that's still not it.'"[30] The problematic character of subjectivity does not mean, then, that there can be no political struggle as one might surmise from the fact that post-structuralism deconstructs the position of the revolutionary in the same breath as it deconstructs the position of the reactionary. But the political struggle can have only a "negative function," rejecting "everything finite, definite, structured, loaded with meaning, in the existing state of society."[31]

The attraction of the post-structuralist critique of subjectivity for feminists is two-fold. First, it seems to hold out the promise of an increased freedom for women, the "free play" of a plurality of differences unhampered by any predetermined gender identity as formulated by either patriarchy or cultural feminism. Second, it moves decisively beyond cultural feminism and liberal feminism in further theorizing what they leave untouched: the construction of subjectivity. We can learn a great deal here about the mechanisms of sexist oppression and the construction of specific gender categories by relating these to social discourse and by conceiving of the subject as a cultural product. Certainly, too, this analysis can help us understand right-wing women, the reproduction of ideology, and the mechanisms that block social progress. However, adopting nominalism creates significant problems for feminism. How can we seriously adopt Kristeva's plan for only negative struggle? As the Left should by now have learned, you cannot mobilize a movement that is only and always against: you must have a positive alternative, a vision of a better future that can motivate people to sacrifice their time and energy toward its realization. Moreover, a feminist adoption of nominalism will be confronted with the same problem theories of ideology have, that is, Why is a right-wing woman's consciousness constructed via social discourse but a feminist's consciousness not? Post-structuralist critiques of subjectivity pertain to the construction of all subjects or they pertain to none. And here is precisely the dilemma for feminists: How can we ground a feminist politics that deconstructs the female subject? Nominalism threatens to wipe out feminism itself.

Some feminists who wish to use post-structuralism are well aware of this danger. Biddy Martin, for example, points out that "we cannot afford to refuse to take a political stance 'which pins us to our sex' for the sake of an abstract theoretical correctness. . . . There is the danger that Foucault's challenges to traditional categories, if taken to a 'logical' conclusion. . .could make the question of women's oppression obsolete."[32] Based on her articulation of the problem with Foucault we are left hopeful that Martin will provide a solution that transcends nominalism. Unfortunately, in her reading of Lou Andreas-Salome, Martin valorizes undecidability, ambiguity, and elusiveness and intimates that by maintaining the undecidability of identity the life of Andreas-Salome provides a text from which feminists can usefully learn.[33]

However, the notion that all texts are undecidable cannot be useful for feminists. In support of his contention that the meaning of texts is ultimately undecidable. Derrida offers us in *Spurs* three conflicting but equally warranted interpretations of how Nietzsche's texts construct and position the female. In one of these interpretations Derrida argues we can find purportedly feminist propositions.[34] Thus, Derrida seeks to demonstrate that even the seemingly incontrovertible interpretation of Nietzsche's works as misogynist can be challenged by an equally convincing argument that they are not. But how can this be helpful to feminists, who need to have their accusations of misogyny validated rather than rendered "undecidable"? The point is not that Derrida himself is antifeminist nor that there is nothing at all in Derrida's work that can be useful for feminists. But the thesis of undecidability as it is applied in the case of Nietzsche sounds too much like yet another version of the antifeminist argument that our perception of sexism is based on a skewed, limited perspective and that what we take to be misogyny is in reality helpful rather than hurtful to the cause of women.

The declaration of undecidability must inevitably return us to Kristeva's position, that we can give only negative answers to the question, What is a woman? If the category "woman" is fundamentally undecidable, then we can offer no positive conception of it that is immune to deconstruction, and we are left with a feminism that can be only deconstructive and, thus, nominalist once again.[35]

A nominalist position on subjectivity has the deleterious effect of de-gendering our analysis, of in effect making gender invisible once again. Foucault's ontology includes only bodies and pleasures, and he is notorious for not including gender as a category of analysis. If gender is simply a social construct, the need and even the possibility of a feminist politics becomes immediately problematic. What can we demand in the name of women if "women" do not exist and demands in their name simply reinforce the myth that they do? How can we speak out against sexism as detrimental to the interests of women if the category is a fiction? How can we demand legal abortions, adequate child care, or wages based on comparable worth without invoking a concept of "woman"?

Post-structuralism undercuts our ability to oppose the dominant trend (and, one might argue, the dominant danger) in mainstream Western intellectual thought, that is, the insistence on a universal, neutral, perspectiveless epistemology, metaphysics, and ethics. Despite rumblings from the Continent, Anglo-American thought is still wedded to the idea(l) of a universalizable, apolitical methodology and set of transhistorical basic truths unfettered by associations with particular genders, races, classes, or cultures. The rejection of subjectivity, unintentionally but nevertheless, colludes with this "generic human" thesis of classical liberal thought, that particularities of individuals are irrelevant and improper influences on knowledge. By designating individual particularities such as subjective experience as a social construct, post-structuralism's negation of the authority of the subject coincides nicely with the classical liberal's view that human particularities are irrelevant. (For the liberal, race, class, and gender are ultimately irrelevant to questions of justice and truth because "underneath we are all the same." For the post-structuralist, race, class, and gender are constructs and, therefore, incapable of decisively validating conceptions of justice and truth because underneath there lies no natural core to build on or liberate or maximize. Hence, once again, underneath we are all the same.) It is, in fact, a desire to topple this commitment to the possibility of a worldview—purported in fact as the best of all possible worldviews—grounded in a generic human, that motivates much of the cultural feminist glorification of femininity as a valid specificity legitimately grounding feminist theory.[36]

The preceding characterizations of cultural feminism and post-structuralist feminism will anger many feminists by assuming too much homogeneity and by blithely pigeonholding large and complex theories. However, I believe the tendencies I have outlined toward essentialism and toward nominalism represent the main, current responses by feminist theory to the task of reconceptualizing "woman." Both responses have significant advantages and serious shortcomings. Cultural feminism has provided a useful corrective to the "generic human" thesis of classical liberalism and has promoted community and self-affirmation, but it cannot provide a long-range future course of action for feminist theory or practice, and it is founded on a claim of essentialism that we are far from having the evidence to justify. The feminist appropriation of post-structuralism has provided suggestive insights on the construction of female and male subjectivity and has issued a crucial warning against creating a feminism that reinvokes the mechanisms of oppressive power. Nonetheless, it limits feminism to the negative tactics of reaction and deconstruction and endangers the attack against classical liberalism by discrediting the notion of an epistemologically significant, specific subjectivity. What's a feminist to do?

We cannot simply embrace the paradox. In order to avoid the serious disadvantages of cultural feminism and post-structuralism, feminism needs to transcend the dilemma by developing a third course, an alternative theory of the subject that avoids both essentialism and nominalism. This new alternative might share the post-structuralist insight that the category "woman" needs to be theorized through an exploration of the experience of subjectivity, as opposed to a description of current attributes, but it need not concede that such an exploration will necessarily result in a nominalist position on gender, or an erasure of it. Feminists need to explore the possibility of a theory of the gendered subject that does not slide into essentialism. In the following two sections I will discuss recent work that makes a contribution to the development of such a theory, or so I shall argue, and in the final section I will develop my own contribution in the form of a concept of gendered identity as positionality.

TERESA DE LAURETIS

Lauretis's influential book, *Alice Doesn't*, is a series of essays organized around an exploration of the problem of conceptualizing woman as subject. This problem is formulated in her work as arising out of the conflict between "woman" as a "fictional construct" and "women" as "real historical beings."[37] She says: "The relation between women as historical subjects and the notion of woman as it is produced by hegemonic discourses is neither a direct relation of identity, a one-to-one correspondence, nor a relation of simple implication. Like all other relations expressed in language, it is an arbitrary and symbolic one, that is to say, culturally set up. The manner and effects of that set-up are what the book intends to explore."[38] The strength of Lauretis's approach is that she never loses sight of the political imperative of feminist theory and, thus, never forgets that we must seek not only to describe this relation in which women's subjectivity is grounded but also to change it. And yet, given her view that we are constructed via a semiotic discourse, this political mandate becomes a crucial problem. As she puts it, "Paradoxically, the only way to position oneself outside of that discourse is to displace oneself within it—to refuse the question as formulated, or to answer deviously (though in its words), even to quote (but against the grain). The limit posed but not worked through in this book is thus the contradiction of feminist theory itself, at once excluded from discourse and imprisoned within it."[39] As with feminist theory, so, too, is the female subject "at once excluded from discourse and imprisoned within it." Constructing a theory of the subject that both concedes these truths and yet allows for the possibility of feminism is the problem Lauretis tackles throughout

Alice Doesn't. To concede the construction of the subject via discourse entails that the feminist project cannot be simply "how to make visible the invisible" as if the essence of gender were out there waiting to be recognized by the dominant discourse. Yet Lauretis does not give up on the possibility of producing "the conditions of visibility for a different social subject."[40] In her view, a nominalist position on subjectivity can be avoided by linking subjectivity to a Peircean notion of practices and a further theorized notion of experience.[41] I shall look briefly at her discussion of this latter claim.

Lauretis's main thesis is that subjectivity, that is, what one "perceives and comprehends as subjective," is constructed through a continuous process, an ongoing constant renewal based on an interaction with the world, which she defines as experience: "And thus [subjectivity] is produced not by external ideas, values, or material causes, but by one's personal, subjective engagement in the practices, discourses, and institutions that lend significance (value, meaning, and affect) to the events of the world."[42] This is the process through which one's subjectivity becomes en-gendered. But describing the subjectivity that emerges is still beset with difficulties, principally the following: "The feminist efforts have been more often than not caught in the logical trap set up by [a] paradox. Either they have assumed that 'the subject,' like 'man,' is a generic term, and as such can designate equally and at once the female and male subjects, with the result of erasing sexuality and sexual difference from subjectivity. Or else they have been obliged to resort to an oppositional notion of 'feminine' subject defined by silence, negativity, a natural sexuality, or a closeness to nature not compromised by patriarchal culture."[43] Here again is spelled out the dilemma between a post-structuralist genderless subject and a cultural feminist essentialized subject. As Lauretis points out, the latter alternative is constrained in its conceptualization of the female subject by the very act of distinguishing female from male subjectivity. This appears to produce a dilemma, for if we de-gender subjectivity, we are committed to a generic subject and thus undercut feminism, while on the other hand if we define the subject in terms of gender, articulating female subjectivity in a space clearly distinct from male subjectivity, then we become caught up in an oppositional dichotomy controlled by a misogynist discourse. A gender-bound subjectivity seems to force us to revert "women to the body and to sexuality as an immediacy of the biological, as nature."[44] For all her insistence on a subjectivity constructed through practices, Lauretis is clear that *that* conception of subjectivity is not what she wishes to propose. A subjectivity that is fundamentally shaped by gender appears to lead irrevocably to essentialism, the posing of a male/female opposition as universal and ahistorical. A subjectivity that is not fundamentally shaped by gender appears to lead to the conception of a generic human subject, as if we could peel away our "cultural" layers and get to the real root of human nature, which turns out to be genderless. Are these really our only choices?

In *Alice Doesn't* Lauretis develops the beginnings of a new conception of subjectivity. She argues that subjectivity is neither (over)determined by biology nor by "free, rational, intentionality" but, rather, by experience, which she defines (via Lacan, Eco, and Peirce) as "a complex of habits resulting from the semiotic interaction of 'outer world' and 'inner world,' the continouus engagement of a self or subject in social reality."[45] Given this definition, the question obviously becomes, Can we ascertain a "female experience"? This is the question Lauretis prompts us to consider, more specifically, to analyze "that complex of habits, dispositions, associations and perceptions, which en-genders one as female."[46] Lauretis ends her book with an insightful observation that can serve as a critical starting point:

> This is where the specificity of a feminist theory may be sought: not in feminity as a privileged nearness to nature, the body, or the unconscious, an essence which inheres in woman but to which males too now lay a claim; not in female tradition simply understood as private, marginal, and yet intact, outside of history but fully there to be discovered or recovered; not, finally, in the chinks and cracks of masculinity, the fissures of male identity or the repressed of phallic discourse; *but rather in that political, theoretical, self-analyzing practice* by which the relations of the subject in social reality can be rearticulated from the historical experience of women. Much, very much, is still to be done.[47]

Thus Lauretis asserts that the way out of the totalizing imprint of history and discourse is through our "political, theoretical self-analyzing practice." This should not be taken to imply that only intellectual articles in academic journals represent a free space or ground for maneuver but, rather, that all women can (and do) think about, criticize, and alter discourse and, thus, that subjectivity can be reconstructed through the process of reflective practice. They key component of Lauretis's formulation is the dynamic she poses at the heart of subjectivity: a fluid interaction in constant motion and open to alteration by self-analyzing practice.

Recently, Lauretis has taken off from this point and developed further her conception of subjectivity. In the introductory essay for her latest book, *Feminist Studies/Critical Studies*, Lauretis claims that an individual's identity is constituted with a historical process of consciousness, a process in which one's history "is interpreted or reconstructed by each of us within the horizon of meanings and knowledges available in the culture at given historical moments, a horizon that also includes modes of political commitment and struggle.... Consciousness, therefore, is never fixed, never attained once and for all, because discursive boundaries change with historical conditions."[48] Here Lauretis guides our way out of the dilemma she articulated for us in *Alice Doesn't*. The agency of the subject is made possible through this process of political interpretation. And what emerges is multiple and shifting, neither "prefigured... in an unchangeable symbolic order" nor merely "fragmented, or intermittent."[49] Lauretis formulates a subjectivity that gives agency to the individual while at the same time placing her within "particular discursive configurations" and, moreover, conceives of the process of consciousness as a strategy. Subjectivity may thus become imbued with race, class, and gender without being subjected to an overdetermination that erases agency.

DENISE RILEY

Denise Riley's *War in the Nursery: Theories of the Child and Mother* is an attempt to conceptualize women in a way that avoids what she calls the biologism/culturalist dilemma: that women must be either biologically determined or entirely cultural constructs. Both of these approaches to explaining sexual difference have been theoretically and empirically deficient, Riley claims. Biological deterministic accounts fail to problematize the concepts they use, for example, "biology," "nature," and "sex" and attempt to reduce "everything to the workings of a changeless biology."[50] On the other hand, the "usual corrective to biologism"[51]—the feminist-invoked cultural construction thesis—"ignores the fact that there really is biology, which must be conceived more clearly" and moreover "only substitutes an unbounded sphere of social determination for that of biological determination."[52]

In her attempt to avoid the inadequacies of these approaches, Riley states: "The tactical problem is in naming and specifying sexual difference where it has been ignored or misread; but without doing so in a way which guarantees it an eternal life of its own, a lonely trajectory across infinity which spreads out over the whole of being and the whole of society—as if the chance of one's gendered conception mercilessly guaranteed every subsequent facet of one's existence at all moments."[53] Here I take Riley's project to be an attempt to conceptualize the subjectivity of woman as a gendered subject, without essentializing gender such that it takes on "an eternal life of its own"; to avoid both the denial of sexual difference (nominalism) and an essentializing of sexual difference.

Despite this fundamental project, Riley's analysis in this book is mainly centered on the perceivable relations between social policies, popularized psychologies, the state, and individual practices, and she does not often ascend to the theoretical problem of conceptions of woman. What she does do is proceed with her historical and sociological analysis *without ever losing sight of the need to problematize her key concepts*, for example, woman and mother. In this she provides an example, the importance of which cannot be overestimated. Moreover, Riley discusses in her last chapter a useful approach to the political tension that can develop between the necessity of problematizing concepts on the one hand and justifying political action on the other.

In analyzing the pros and cons of various social policies, Riley tries to take a feminist point of view. Yet any such discussion must necessarily presuppose, even if it is not openly acknowledged, that needs are identifiable and can therefore be used as a yardstick in evaluating social policies. The reality is, however, that needs are terribly difficult to identify, since most if not all theories of need rely on some naturalist conception of the human agent, an agent who either can consciously identify and state all of her or his needs or whose "real" needs can be ascertained by some external process of analysis. Either method produces problems: it seems unrealistic to say that only if the agent can identify and articulte specific needs do the needs exist, and yet there are obvious dangers to relying on "experts" or others to identify the needs of an individual. Further, it is problematic to conceptualize the human agent as having needs in the same way that a table has properties, since the human agent is an entity in flux in a way that the table is not and is subject to forces of social construction that affect her subjectivity and thus her needs. Utilitarian theorists, especially desire and welfare utilitarian theorists, are particularly vulnerable to this problem, since the standard of moral evaluation they advocate using is precisely needs (or desires, which are equally problematic).[54] Feminist evaluations of social policy that use a concept of "women's needs" must run into the same difficulty. Riley's approach to this predicament is as follows: "I've said that people's needs obviously can't be revealed by a simple process of historical unveiling, while elsewhere I've talked about the 'real needs' of mothers myself. I take it that it's necessary both to stress the non-self-evident nature of need and the intricacies of its determinants, and also to act plitically as if needs could be met, or at least met half-way."[55] Thus Riley asserts the possibility and even the necessity of combining decisively formulated political demands with an acknowledgment of their essentialist danger. How can this be done without weakening our political struggle?

On the one hand, as Riley argues, the logic of concrete demands does not entail a commitment to essentialism. She says: "Even though it is true that arguing for adequate childcare as one obvious way of meeting the needs of mothers does suppose an orthodox division of labor, in which responsibility for children is the province of women and not of men, nevertheless this division is what, by and large, actually obtains. Recognition of that in no way commits you to supposing that the care of children is fixed eternally as female."[54] We need not invoke a rhetoric of idealized motherhood to demand that women here and now need child care. On the other hand, the entire corpus of Riley's work on social policies is dedicated to demonstrating the dangers that such demands can entail. She explains these as follows: "Because the task of illuminating 'the needs of mothers' starts out with gender at its most decisive and inescapable point—the biological capacity to bear children— there's the danger that it may fall back into a conservative restating and confirming of social-sexual difference as timeless too. This would entail making the needs of mothers into fixed properties of 'motherhood' as a social function: I believe this is what happened in postwar Britain."[57] Thus, invoking the demands of women with children also invokes the companion belief in our cultural conception of essentialized motherhood.

As a way of avoiding this particular pitfall, Riley recommends against deploying any version of "motherhood" *as such*. I take it that what Riley means here is that we can talk about the needs of women with children and of course refer to these women as mothers but that we should eschew all reference to the idealized institution of motherhood as women's privileged vocation or the embodiment of an authentic or natural female practice.

The light that Riley sheds on our problem of woman's subjectivity is three-fold. First, and most obviously, she articulates the problem clearly and deals with it head on. Second, she shows us a way of approaching child-care demands without essentializing femininity, that is, by keeping it clear that these demands represent only current and not universal or eternal needs of women and by avoiding invocations of motherhood altogether. Third, she demands that our problematizing of concepts like "women's needs" coexist alongside a political program of demands in the name of women, without either countermanding the other. This is not to embrace the paradox but, rather, to call for a new understanding of subjectivity that can bring into harmony both our theoretical and our political agendas.

Denise Riley presents a useful approach to the political dimension of the problem of conceptualizing woman by discussing ways to avoid essentialist political demands.

She reminds us that we should not avoid political action because our theory has uncovered chinks in the formulation of our key concepts.

A CONCEPT OF POSITIONALITY

Let me state initially that my approach to the problem of subjectivity is to treat it as a metaphysical problem rather than an empirical one. For readers coming from a post-structuralist tradition this statement will require immediate clarification. Continental philosophers from Nietzsche to Derrida have rejected the discipline of metaphysics in toto because they say it assumes a naive ontological connection between knowledge and a reality conceived as a thing-in-itself, totally independent of human practices and methodology. Echoing the logical positivists here, these philosophers have claimed that metaphysics is nothing but an exercise in mystification, presuming to make knowledge claims about such things as souls and "necessary" truths that we have no way of justifying. Perhaps the bottom line criticism has been that metaphysics defines truth in such a way that it is impossible to attain, and then claims to have attained it. I agree that we should reject the metaphysics of transcendent things-in-themselves and the presumption to make claims about the noumena, but this involves a rejection of a specific ontology of truth and particular tradition in the history of metaphysics and not a rejection of metaphysics itself. If metaphysics is conceived not as any particular ontological commitment but as the attempt to reason through ontological issues that cannot be decided empirically, then metaphysics continues today in Derrida's analysis of language, Foucault's conception of power, and all of the post-structuralist critiques of humanist theories of the subject. Thus, on this view, the assertion that someone is "doing metaphysics" does not serve as a pejorative. There are questions of importance to human beings that science alone cannot answer (including what science is and how it functions), and yet these are questions that we can usefully address by combining scientific data with other logical, political, moral, pragmatic, and coherence considerations. The distinction between what is normative and what is descriptive breaks down here. Metaphysical problems are problems that concern factual claims about the world (rather than simply expressive, moral, or aesthetic assertions, e.g.) but are problems that cannot be determined through empirical means alone.[58]

In my view the problem of the subject and, within this, the problem of conceptualizing "woman," is such a metaphysical problem. Thus, I disagree with both phenomenologists and psychoanalysts who assert that the nature of subjectivity can be discovered via a certain methodology and conceptual apparatus, either the epoch or the theory of the unconscious.[59] Neurophysiological reductionists likewise claim to be able to produce empirical explanations of subjectivity, but they will by and large admit that their physicialist explanations can tell us little about the experiential reality of subjectivity.[60] Moreover, I would assert that physicalist explanations can tell us little about how the concept of subjectivity should be construed, since this concept necessarily entails considerations not only of the empirical data but also of the political and ethical implications as well. Like the determination of when "human" life begins—whether at conception, full brain development, or birth—we cannot through science alone settle the issue since it turns on how we (to some extent) choose to define concepts like "human" and "woman." We cannot discover the "true meaning" of these concepts but must decide how to define them using all the empirical data, ethical arguments, political implications, and coherence constraints at hand.

Psychoanalysis should be mentioned separately here since it was Freud's initial problematizing of the subject from which developed post-structuralist rejection of the subject. It is the psychoanalytic conception of the unconscious that "undermines the subject from any position of certainty" and in fact claims to reveal that the subject is a fiction.[61] Feminists then use psychoanalysis to problematize the gendered subject to reveal "the fictional nature of the sexual category to which every human subject is none the less assigned."[62] Yet while a theorizing of the unconscious is used as a primary means of theorizing the subject, certainly psychoanalysis alone cannot provide all of the answers we need for a theory of the gendered subject.[63]

As I have already stated, it seems important to use Teresa de Lauretis's conception of experience as a way to begin to describe the features of human subjectivity. Lauretis starts with no given biological or psychological features and thus avoids assuming an essential characterization of subjectivity, but she also avoids the idealism that can follow from a rejection of materialist analyses by basing her conception on real practices and events. The importance of this focus on practices is, in part, Lauretis's shift away from the belief in the totalization of language or textuality to which most antiessentialist analyses become wedded. Lauretis wants to argue that language is not the sole source and locus of meaning, that habits and practices are crucial in the construction of meaning, and that through self-analyzing practices we can rearticulate female subjectivity. Gender is not a point to start from in the sense of being a given thing but is, instead, a posit or construct, formalizable in a nonarbitrary way through a matrix of habits, practices, and discourses. Further, it is an interpretation of our history within a particular discursive constellation, a history in which we are both subjects of and subjected to social construction.

The advantage of such an analysis is its ability to articulate a concept of gendered subjectivity without pinning it down one way or another for all time. Given this and given the danger that essentialist conceptions of the subject pose specifically for women, it seems both possible and desirable to construe a gendered subjectivity in relation to concrete habits, practices, and discourses while at the same time recognizing the fluidity of these.

As both Lacan and Riley remind us, we must continually emphasize within any account of subjectivity the historical dimension.[64] This will waylay the tendency to produce general, universal, or essential accounts by making all our conclusions contingent and revisable. Thus, through a conception of human subjectivity as an emergent property of a historicized experience, we can say "feminine subjectivity is construed here and now in such and such a way" without this ever entailing a universalizable maxim about the "feminine."

It seems to me equally important to add to this approach an "identity politics," a concept that developed from the Combahee River Collective's "A Black Feminist Statement."[65] The idea here is that one's identity is taken (and defined) as a political point of departure, as a motivation for action, and as a delineation of one's politics. Lauretis and the authors of *Yours in Struggle* are clear about the problematic nature of one's identity, one's subject-ness, and yet argue that the concept of identity politics is useful because identity is a posit that is politically paramount. Their suggestion is to recognize one's identity as always a construction yet also a necessary point of departure.

I think this point can be readily intuited by people of mixed races and cultures who have had to choose in some sense their identity.[66] For example, assimilated Jews who have chosen to become Jewish-identified as a political tactic against anti-Semitism are practicing identity politics. It may seem that members of more easily identifiable oppressed groups do not have this luxury, but I think that just as Jewish people can choose to assert their Jewishness, so black men, women of all races, and other members of more immediately recognizable oppressed groups can practice identity politics by choosing their identity as a member of one or more groups as their political point of departure. This, in fact, is what is happening when women who are not feminists downplay their identity as women and who, on becoming feminists, then begin making an issue of their femaleness. It is the claiming of their identity as women as a political point of departure that makes it possible to see, for instance, gender-biased language that in the absence of that departure point women often do not even notice.

It is true that antifeminist women can and often do identify themselves strongly as women and with women as a group, but this is usually explained by them within the context of an essentialist theory of femininity. Claiming that one's politics are grounded in one's essential identity avoids problematizing both identity and the connection between identity and politics and thus avoids the agency involved in underdetermined actions. The difference between feminists and antifeminists strikes me as precisely this: the affirmation or denial of our right and our ability to construct, and take responsibility for, our gendered identity, our politics, and our choices.[67]

Identity politics provides a decisive rejoinder to the generic human thesis and the mainstream methodology of Western political theory. According to the latter, the approach to political theory must be through a "veil of ignorance" where the theorist's personal interests and needs are hypothetically set aside. The goal is a theory of universal scope to which all ideally rational, disinterested agents would acquiesce if given sufficient information. Stripped of their particularities, these rational agents are considered to be potentially equally persuadable. Identity politics provides a materialist response to this and, in so doing, sides with Marxist class analysis. The best political theory will not be one ascertained through a veil of ignorance, a veil that is impossible to construct. Rather, political theory must base itself on the initial premise that all persons, including the theorist, have a fleshy, material identity that will influence and pass judgment on all political claims. Indeed, the best political theory for the theorist herself will be one that acknowledges this fact. As I see it, the concept of identity politics does not presuppose a prepackaged set of objective needs or political implications but problematizes the connection of identity and politics and introduces identity as a factor in any political analysis.

If we combine the concept of identity politics with a conception of the subject as positionality, we can conceive of the subject as nonessentialized and emergent from a historical experience and yet retain our political ability to take gender as an important point of departure. Thus we can say at one and the same time that gender is not natural, biological, universal, ahistorical, or essential and yet still claim that gender is relevant because we are taking gender as a position from which to act politically. What does position mean here?

When the concept "woman" is defined not by a particular set of attributes but by a particular position, the internal characteristics of the person thus identified are not denoted so much as the external context within which that person is situated. The external situation determines the person's relative position, just as the position of a pawn on a chessboard is considered safe or dangerous, powerful or weak, according to its relation to the other chess pieces. The essentialist definition of woman makes her identity independent of her external situation: since her nurturing and peaceful traits are innate they are ontologically autonomous of her position with respect to others or to the external historical and social conditions generally. The positional definition, on the other hand, makes her identity relative to a constantly shifting context, to a situation that includes a network of elements involving others, the objective economic conditions, cultural and political institutions and ideologies, and so on. If it is possible to identify women by their position within this network of relations, then it becomes possible to ground a feminist argument for women, not on a claim that their innate capacities are being stunted, but that their position within the network lacks power and mobility and requires radical change. The position of women is relative and not innate, and yet neither is it "undecidable." Through social critique and analysis we can identify women via their position relative to an existing cultural and social network.

It may sound all too familiar to say that the oppression of women involves their relative position within a society; but my claim goes further than this. I assert that the very subjectivity (or subjective experience of being a woman) and the very identity of women is constituted by women's position. However, this view should not imply that the concept of "woman" is determined solely by external elements and that the woman herself is merely a passive recipient of an identity created by these forces. Rather, she herself is part of the historicized, fluid movement, and she therefore actively contributes to the context within which her position can be delineated. I would include Lauretis's point here, that the identity of a woman is the product of her own interpretation and reconstruction of her history, as mediated through the cultural discursive context to which she has access.[68] Therefore, the concept of positionality includes two points: first, as already stated, that the concept of woman is a relational term identifiable only within a (constantly moving) context; but, second, that the position that women find themselves in can be actively utilized (rather than transcended) as a location for the construction of meaning, a place from where meaning is constructed, rather than simply the place where a meaning can be *discovered* (the meaning of femaleness). The concept of woman as positionality shows how women use their positional perspective as a place from which values are interpreted and constructed rather than as a locus of an already determined set of values. When women become feminists the crucial thing that has occurred is not that they have learned any new facts about the world but that they come to view those facts from a different position, from their own position as subjects. When colonial subjects begin to be critical of the formerly imitative attitude they had toward the colonists, what is happening is that they begin to identify with the colonized rather than the colonizers.[68] This difference in positional perspective does not necessitate a change in what are taken to be facts, although new facts may come into view from the new position, but it does necessitate a political change in perspective since the point of departure, the point from which all things are measured, has changed.

In this analysis, then, the concept of positionality allows for a determinate though fluid identity of woman that does not fall into essentialism: woman is a position from which a feminist politics can emerge rather than a set of attributes that are "objectively identifiable." Seen in this way, being a "woman" is to take up a position within a moving historical context and to be able to choose what we make of this position and how we alter this context. From the perspective of that fairly determinate though fluid and mutable position, women can themselves articulate a set of interests and ground a feminist politics.

The concept and the position of women is not ultimately undecidable or arbitrary. It is simply not possible to interpret our society in such a way that women have more power or equal power relative to men. The conception of woman that I have outlined limits the constructions of woman we can offer by defining subjectivity as positionality within a context. It thus avoids nominalism but also provides us with the means to argue against views like "oppression is all in your head" or the view that antifeminist women are not oppressed.

At the same time, by highlighting historical movement and the subject's ability to alter her context, the concept of positionality avoids essentialism. It even avoids tying ourselves to a structure of gendered politics conceived as historically infinite, though it allows for the assertion of gender politics on the basis of positionality at any time. Can we conceive of a future in which oppositional gender categories are not fundamental to one's self-concept? Even if we cannot, our theory of subjectivity should not preclude, and moreover prevent, that eventual possibility. Our concept of woman as a category, then, needs to remain open to future radical alteration, else we will preempt the possible forms eventual stages of the feminist transformation can take.

Obviously, there are many theoretical questions on positionality that this discussion leaves open. However, I would like to emphasize that the problem of woman as subject is a real one for feminism and not just on the plane of high theory. The demands of millions of women for child care, reproductive control, and safety from sexual assault can reinvoke the cultural assumption that these are exclusively feminine issues and can reinforce the right-wing's reification of gender differences unless and until we can formulate a political program that can articulate these demands in a way that challenges rather than utilizes sexist discourse.

Recently, I heard an attack on the phrase "woman of color" by a woman, dark-skinned herself, who was arguing that the use of this phrase simply reinforces the significance of that which should have no significance—skin color. To a large extent I agreed with this woman's argument: we must develop the means to address the wrongs done to us without reinvoking the basis of those wrongs. Likewise, women who have been eternally construed must seek a means of articulating a feminism that does not continue construing us in any set way. At the same time, I believe we must avoid buying into the neuter, universal "generic human" thesis that covers the West's racism and androcentrism with a blindfold. We cannot resolve this predicament by ignoring one half of it or by attempting to embrace it. The solution lies, rather, in formulating a new theory within the process of reinterpreting our position, and reconstructing our political identity, as women and feminists in relation to the world and to one another.

NOTES

In writing this essay I have benefited unmeasurably as a participant of the 1984–85 Pembroke Center Seminar on the Cultural Construction of Gender at Brown University. I would also like to thank Lynne Joyrich, Richard Schmitt, Denise Riley, Sandra Bartky, Naomi Scheman, and four anonymous reviewers for their helpful comments on an earlier draft of this paper.

1. It may seem that we can solve this dilemma easily enough by simply defining woman as those with female anatomies, but the question remains. What is the significance, if any, of those anatomies? What is the connection between female anatomy and the concept of woman? It should be remembered that the dominant discourse does not include in the category woman everyone with a female anatomy: it is often said that aggressive, self-serving, or powerful women are not "true" or "real" women. Moreover, the problem cannot be avoided by simply rejecting the concept of "woman" while retaining the category of "women". If there are women, then there must exist a basis for the category and a criterion for inclusion within it. This criterion need not posit a universal, homogeneous essence, but there must be a criterion nonetheless.

2. For Schopenhauer's, Kant's, and nearly every other major Western philosopher's conception of woman, and for an insight into just how contradictory and incoherent these are, see Linda Bell's excellent anthology, *Visions of Women* (Clifton, N.J.; Humana Press, 1983).

3. For an interesting discussion of whether feminists should even seek such transcendence, see Genevieve Lloyd, *The Man of Reason* (Minneapolis: University of Minnesota Press, 1984), 86–102.

4. Feminist works I would include in this group but which I won't be able to discuss in this essay are Elizabeth L. Berg, "The Third Woman," *Diacritics* 12 (1982) 11–20; and Lynne Joyrich. "Theory and Practice: The Project of Feminist Criticism," unpublished manuscript (Brown University, 1984). Luce Irigaray's work may come to mind for some readers as another proponent of a third way, but for me Irigaray's emphasis on female anatomy makes her work border too closely on essentialism.

5. Although Rich has recently departed from this position and in fact begun to move in the direction of the concept of woman I will defend in this essay (Adrienne Rich, "Notes toward a Politics of Location," in her *Blood, Bread, and Poetry* [New York: Norton, 1986]).

6. Mary Daly, *Gyn/Ecology* (Boston: Beacon, 1978), 355.

7. Ibid., 60.

8. Ibid., 59.

9. Ibid., 365 (my emphasis).

10. Adrienne Rich, *On Lies, Secrets, and Silence* (New York: Norton, 1979), 18.

11. Adrienne Rich, *Of Woman Born* (New York: Bantam, 1977), 21.

12. Ibid., 290.

13. Ibid., 21.

14. Ibid., 292. Three pages earlier Rich castigates the view that we need only release on the world women's ability to nurture in order to solve the world's problems, which may seem incongruous given the above passage. The two positions are consistent however: Rich is trying to correct the patriarchal conception of women as essentially nurturers with a view of women that is more complex and multifaceted. Thus, her essentialist conception of women is more comprehensive and complicated than the patriarchal one.

15. See Alice Echols, "The New Feminism of Yin and Yang," in *Powers of Desire: The Politics of Sexuality*, ed. Ann Snitow, Christine Stansell, and Sharon Thompson (New York: Monthly Review Press, 1983), 439–59, and "The Taming of the Id: Feminist Sexual Politics, 1968–83," in *Pleasure and Danger: Exploring Female Sexuality*, ed. Carole S. Vance (Boston: Routledge & Kegan Paul, 1984), 50–72. Hester Eisenstein paints a similar picture of cultural feminism in her *Contemporary Feminist Thought* (Boston, G. K. Hall, 1983), esp. xvii-xix and 105–45. Josephine Donovan has traced the more recent cultural feminism analyzed by Echols and Eisenstein to the earlier matriarchal vision of feminists like Charlotte Perkins Gilman (Josephine Donovan, *Feminist Theory: The Intellectual Traditions of American Feminism* [New York: Ungar, 1985], esp. chap. 2).

16. Echols. "The New Feminism of Yin and Yang," 441.

17. Ibid., 440.

18. Cherríe Moraga, "From a Long Line of Vendidas: Chicanas and Feminism," in *Feminist Studies/Critical Studies*, ed. Teresa de Lauretis (Bloomington: Indiana University Press, 1986), 180.

19. See also Moraga, "From a Long Line of Vendidas," 187, and Cherríe Moraga, "La Guera," in *This Bridge Called My Back: Writings by Radical Women of Color*, ed. Cherríe Moraga and Gloria Anzaldúa (New York: Kitchen Table, 1983), 32–33; Barbara Smith, "Introduction," in *Home Girls: A Black Feminist Anthology*, ed. Barbara Smith (New York: Kitchen Table, 1983), xix-ivi; "The Combahee River Collective Statement," in Smith, ed. 272–82; Audre Lorde, "Age, Race, Class, and Sex: Women Redefining Difference," in her *Sister Outsider* (Trumansburg, N. Y.: Crossing, 1984), 114–23; and bell hooks, *Feminist Theory: From Margin to Center* (Boston: South End, 1984). All of these works resist the universalizing tendency of cultural feminism and highlight the differences between women, and between men, in a way that undercuts arguments for the existence of an overarching gendered essence.

20. There is a wealth of literature on this, but two good places to begin are Anne Fausto-Sterling, *Myths of Gender: Biological Theories about Women and Men* (New

York: Basic, 1986); and Sherrie Ortner and Harriet Whitehead, eds., *Sexual Meanings: The Cultural Construction of Gender and Sexuality* (New York: Cambridge University Press, 1981).

21. Echols, "The New Feminism of Yin and Yang," 440.

22. Hester Eisenstein's treatment of cultural femicism, though critical, is certainly more two-sided than Echols's. While Echols apparently sees only the reactionary results of cultural feminism, Eisenstein sees in it a therapeutic self-affirmation necessary to offset the impact of a misogynist culture (see Einstein [n. 15 above]).

23. Michel Foucault, "Why Study Power: The Question of the Subject," in *Beyond Structuralism and Hermeneutics: Michel Foucault*, ed. Hubert L. Dreyfus and Paul Rabinow, 2d ed. (Chicago: University of Chicago Press, 1983), 212.

24. This term is principally associated with Derrida for whom it refers specifically to the process of unraveling metaphors in order to reveal their underlying logic, which usually consists of a simple binary opposition such as between man/woman, subject/object, culture/nature, etc. Derrida has demonstrated that within such oppositions one side is always superior to the other side, such that there is never any pure difference without domination. The term "deconstruction" has also come to mean more generally any exposure of a concept as ideological or culturally constructed rather than natural or a simple reflection of reality (see Derrida, *Of Grammatology*, trans. G. Spivak [Baltimore: Johns Hopkins University Press, 1976]; also helpful is Jonathan Culler's *On Deconstruction* [Ithaca, N. Y.: Cornell University Press, 1982]).

25. Michel Foucault, "Nietzsche, Genealogy, History," in *The Foucault Reader*, ed. Paul Rabinow (New York: Pantheon, 1984), 83.

26. This hope is evident in Michel Foucault's *The Order of Things: An Archaeology of the Human Sciences* (New York: Random House, 1973).

27. Jacques Derrida, *Spurs*, trans. Barbara Harlow (Chicago: University of Chicago Press, 1978), 49.

28. Ibid., 51.

29. Biddy Martin, "Feminism, Criticism, and Foucault," *New German Critique* 27 (1982); 11.

30. Julia Kristeva, "Woman Can Never Be Defined," in *New French Feminisms*, ed. Elaine Marks and Isabelle de Courtivron (New York: Schocken, 1981), 137 [my italics].

31. Julia Kristeva, "Oscillation between Power and Denial," in Marks and Courtivron, eds., 166.

32. Martin, 16–17.

33. Ibid., esp. 21, 24, and 29.

34. See Derrida, *Spurs*, esp. 57 and 97.

35. Martin's most recent work departs from this in a positive direction, in an essay coauthored with Chandra Talpade Mohanty, Martin points out "the political limitations of an insistence on 'indeterminancy' which implicitly, when not explicitly, denies the critic's own situatedness in the social, and in effect refuses to acknowledge the critic's own institutional home." Martin and Mohanty seek to

develop a more positive, though still problematized, conception of the subject as having a "multiple and shifting" perspective. In this, their work becomes a significant contribution toward the development of an alternative conception of subjectivity, a conception not unlike the one that I will discuss in the rest of this essay ("Feminist Politics: What's Home Got to Do with It?" In Lauretis, ed. (n. 18 above), 191–212, esp. 194).

36. A wonderful exchange on this between persuasive and articulate representatives of both sides was printed in *Diacritics* (Peggy Kamuf, "Replacing Feminist Criticism," *Diacritics* 12 [1982]: 42–47; and Nancy Miller, "The Text's Heroine: A Feminist Critic and Her Fictions," *Diacritics* 12 [1982]: 48–53).

37. Teresa de Lauretis, *Alice Doesn't* (Bloomington: Indiana University Press, 1984), 5.

38. Ibid., 5–6.

39. Ibid., 7.

40. Ibid., 8–9.

41. Ibid., 11.

42. Ibid., 159.

43. Ibid., 161.

44. Ibid.

45. Ibid., 182. The principal texts Lauretis relies on in her exposition of Lacan, Eco, and Peirce are Jacques Lacan, *Ecrits* (Paris: Seuil, 1966); Umberto Eco, *A Theory of Semiotics* (Bloomington: Indiana University Press, 1976), and *The Role of the Reader: Explorations in the Semiotic of Texts* (Bloomington: Indiana University Press, 1979); and Charles Sanders Peirce, *Collected Papers*, vols. 1–8 (Cambridge, Mass.: Harvard University Press, 1931–58).

46. Lauretis, *Alice Doesn't* (in. 37 above), 182.

47. Ibid., 186 (my italics).

48. Lauretis, ed. (n. 18 above), 8.

49. Ibid., 9.

50. Denise Riley, *War in the Nursery: Theories of the Child and Mother* (London: Virago, 1983), 2.

51. Ibid., 6.

52. Ibid., 2, 3.

53. Ibid., 4.

54. For a lucid discussion of just how difficult this problem is for utilitarians, *see* Jon Elster, "Sour Grapes—Utilitarianism and the Genesis of Wants," in *Utilitarianism and Beyond*, ed. Amartya Sen and Bernard Williams (Cambridge: Cambridge University Press, 1982), 219–38.

55. Riley, 193–94.

56. Ibid., 194.

57. Ibid., 194–95.

58. In this conception of the proper dimension of and approach to metaphysics (as a conceptual enterprise to be decided partially by pragmatic methods) I am following the tradition of the later Rudolf Carnap and Ludwig Wittgenstein, among others (Rudolf Carnap, "Empiricism, Semantics, and Ontology," and "On the Character of Philosophical Problems," both in *The Linguistic Turn*,

ed. R. Rorty [Chicago: University of Chicago Press, 1967]; and Ludwig Wittgenstein, *Philosophical Investigations*, trans. G. E. M. Anscombe [New York: Macmillan, 1958[).

59. I am thinking particularly of Husserl and Freud here. The reason for my disagreement is that both approaches are in reality more metaphysical than their proponents would admit and, further, that I have only limited sympathy for the metaphysical claims they make. I realize that to explain this fully would require a long argument, which I cannot give in this essay.

60. See, e.g., Donald Davidson, "Psychology as Philosophy," in his *Essays an Actions and Interpretations* (Oxford: Clarendon Press, 1980), 230.

61. Jacqueline Rose, "Introduction II," in *Feminine Sexuality: Jacques Lacan and the Ecole Freudienne*, ed. Juliet Mitchell and Jacqueline Rose (New York: Norton, 1982), 29, 30.

62. Ibid., 29.

63. Psychoanalysis must take credit for making subjectivity a problematic issue, and yet I think a view that gives psychoanalysis hegemony in this area is misguided, if only because psychoanalysis is still extremely hypothetical. Let a hundred flowers bloom.

64. See Juliet Mitchell, "Introduction I," in Mitchell and Rose, eds., 4–5.

65. This was suggested to me by Teresa de Lauretis in an informal talk she gave at the Pembroke Center, 1984–85. A useful discussion and application of this concept can be found in Elly Bulkin, Minnie Bruce Pratt, and Barbara Smith, *Yours in Struggle: Three Feminist Perspectives on Anti-Semitism and Racism* (Brooklyn, N.Y.: Long Haul Press, 1984), 98–99. Martin and Mohanty's paper (n. 35 above) offers a fruitful reading of the essay in *Yours in Struggle* by Minnie Bruce Pratt entitled "Identity: Skin Blood Heart" and brings into full relief the way in which she uses identity politics. See also "The Combabee River Collective" (n. 19 above).

66. This point has been the subject of long, personal reflection for me, as I myself am half Latina and half white. I have been motivated to consider it also since the situation is even more complicated for my children, who are half mine and half a Jewish father's.

67. I certainly do not believe that most women have the freedom to choose their situations in life, but I do believe that of the multiple ways we are held in check, internalized oppressive mechanisms play a significant role, and we can achieve control over these. On this point I must say I have learned from and admired the work of Mary Daly, particularly *Gyn/Ecology* (n. 6 above), which reveals and describes these internal mechanisms and challenges us to repudiate them.

68. See Teresa de Lauretis, "Feminist Studies/Critical Studies: Issues, Terms, Contexts," in Lauretis, ed. (n. 18 above), 8–9.

69. This point is brought out by Homi Bhabba in his "Of Mimicry and Man: The Ambivalence of Colonial Discourse," *October* 28 (1984): 125–33; and by Abdur Rahman in his *Intellectual Colonisation* (New Delhi: Vikas, 1983).

21

GAYATRI SPIVAK WITH ELLEN ROONEY

"In a Word": Interview

Ellen Rooney: *To undertake to place contemporary debates on essentialism in "context" is perhaps already to take sides in the controversy those debates have engendered. In some lexicons, at least, context is an anti-essentialist slogan; to contextualize is to expose the history of what might otherwise seem outside history, natural and thus universal, that is, the essence.*

As an idiom, "in a word" signals a moment of compressed and magically adequate expression. To summarize a matter "in a word" is to locate or hit upon its proper form, to capture its essential quality, and thus to say all that need be said. The problem of essentialism can be thought, in this way, as a problem of form, which is to say, a problem of reading. Context would thus emerge as a synonym for reading, in that to read is to demarcate a context. Essentialism appears as a certain resistance to reading, an emphasis on the constraints of form, the limits at which a particular form so compels us as to "stipulate" an analysis.

In "Rape and the Rise of the Novel," Frances Ferguson glosses stipulation as "trying to put a limit to ambiguity by defining the understanding of a term or a situation" (109); to put it in a word, perhaps. She argues that the "intense formality of the law of rape seems designed to substitute the reliability of invariable formulae for the manipulable terms of psychological states" (95); these "invariable formulae" ("rape," in a word) serve to foreclose the question of consent and to define rape in terms of compatible with phallocentrism. For the law and for some feminists as well, the victim's "body is thus converted into evidence, having become [a] text" (91). But while the body is formally legible, individual psychological states, specifically concerning consent and its absence, go unread. In a phallocentric context, this "intense formality" functions to exclude the victims entirely from the definition of rape; for example, "for ancient Hebrew law, the act of sex carries with it the inevitability of consent. For Brownmiller and Dworkin, it carries with it the impossibility of consent." The significance of form is thus stipulated in advance, an effect of the morphology of the body. Context is swallowed whole, and women, as subjects, disappear with it, absorbed entirely into their bodies.[1]

The body is of course essentialism's great text: to read in its form the essence of Woman is certainly one of phallocentrism's strategies; to insist that the body too is materially woven into social (con)texts is an anti-essentialism's reply. But feminism's persistent return to the body is only in part a rejoinder to the resilience of anti-feminism's essentialism. Caught between those who simply "read off" the body and those who take its ineluctable power to be a fragmentary social relation is the feminist who speaks "as a woman."

Feminists return to the problem of essentialism—despite their shared distaste for the mystifications of Woman—because it remains difficult to engage in feminist analysis and politics if not "as a woman." Elizabeth Spelman calls this phrase the "Trojan horse of feminist ethnocentrism," inevitably dissembling the differences among women (x). The body can figure here as a trump card, seeming literally to embody the womanness of woman, obscuring the fact that "only at times will the body impose itself or be arranged as that of a woman or a man."[2] We seem to desire that what unites us (as feminists) preexist our desire to be joined; something that stands outside our own alliances may authorize them and empower us to speak not simply as feminists but as women, not least against women whose political work is elsewhere. In the U.S., this is an old dream of "nonpartisanship" at the heart of politics, as well as what Donna Haraway calls "the feminist dream of a common language . . . a perfectly faithful naming of experience." In a word.[3]

Yet simply to label this political dream of women essentialism is to layer another political refusal over the rifts among us. The word essentialism can also work to conceal political divisions among women, insofar as it represents them as purely theoretical, questions of enlightenment. Political failures, if it be a failure not to unite all women under a single banner, are read as wholly intellectual failures—easily corrected. The original evasion is repeated; political difference is reduced to a matter of bad form, in a word, to essentialism.

In reading the body, to find "woman"; in "women," to secure feminism; to capture in a word the essence of a thing: essentialism is a dream of the end of politics among women, of a formal resolution to the discontinuity between women and feminisms. Antiessentialism may mimic this formalism, even as it seeks to diagnose it. Gayatri Spivak suggests—by turning repeatedly to the question of the word: which word to chose? to what end?—another reading.

ER: As you know, some current discussions of the topic of essentialism have resulted in calls for a new willingness to take the "risk of essentialism," and these calls include citations from some of your most recent remarks. I'm thinking here of Alice Jardine's comment in *Men in Feminism* that "one of the most thought-provoking statements of recent date by a feminist theorist [is] Gayatri Spivak's suggestion (echoing Heath) that women today may *have* to take 'the risk of essence' in order to think really differently,"[4] or of Bruce Robbins's interview with Edward Said, where Robbins asks: "One idea that has been much repeated in conversations about intellectuals and their relation to collectivity, especially among feminists, is the necessity to accept 'the risk of essence,' a phrase associated with Gayatri Spivak and Stephen Heath. Does it seem at all generalizable or useful in the case of the Palestinians?"[5]

You've examined the question of essentialism throughout your work, and you've said a number of different things about it, at times warning against defining women in terms of woman's putative essence and stressing the possibility that essentialism may be a trap, and, at other times, most recently in working on the text of the Subaltern Studies Group, talking about the "*strategic* use of a positivist essentialism in a scrupulously visible political interest." I'd like to talk about the necessary risks of taking what may seem to be essentialist positions; about how we can signal the difference between a strategic and a substantive or a real essentialism; about the possibility of mobilizing people to do political work without invoking some irreducible essentialism; ultimately, how we can determine when our essentializing strategies have become traps, as opposed to having strategic and necessary positive effects?[6]

GS: Strategy works through a persistent (de)constructive critique of the theoretical. "Strategy" is an embattled concept-metaphor and unlike "theory," its antecedents are not disinterested and universal. "Usually, an artifice or trick designed to outwit or surprise the enemy" (*Oxford English Dictionary*).

The critical moment does not come only at a certain stage when one sees one's effort succeeding. It is not only in that moment of euphoria that we begin to decide that we had been strategic all along. The strategic use of an essence as a mobilizing slogan or masterword like *woman* or *worker* or the name of a nation is, ideally, self-conscious for all mobilized. This is the impossible risk of a lasting strategy. Can there be such a thing? At any rate, the critique of the "fetish-character" (so to speak) of the masterword has to be persistent all along the way, even when it seems that to remind oneself of it is counterproductive. Otherwise the strategy freezes into something like what you call an essentialist position, when the situation that calls forth the strategy is seemingly resolved. The Subaltern Studies Group started working as a countermovement within South Asian history as written even by politically correct historians trying, among other things, to fabricate a national identity in decolonization: a different structural position from someone working from within the U. S. university. If one is considering strategy, one has to look at where the group—the person, the persons, or the movement—is situated when one makes claims for or against essentialism. A strategy suits a situation; a strategy is not a theory. And if one is considering "positivism," one might take into account the importance of positivism in the discipline of history in the nineteenth century.[7]

Within mainstream U. S. feminism the good insistence that "the personal is political" often transformed itself into something like "*only* the personal is political." The strategic use of essentialism can turn into an alibi for proselytizing academic essentialisms. The emphasis then inevitably falls on being able to speak from one's own ground, rather than matching the trick to the situation, that the word strategy implies. Given the collaboration between techniques of knowledge and structures of enablement, better I think to look for the bigger problem: that strategies are taught as if they were theories, good for all cases. One has to be careful to see that they do not misfire for people who do not resemble us and do not share the situation of prominent U. S. universities and colleges.

ER: Could I ask one further thing? When you spoke just then about noting our own essentialism, that sounded to me as if it were a reassertion of the need for the critique of essentialism. I think your description of the way in which your remark has been taken up in discourses that are produced from sites of influence and power is absolutely true. And the marking of the critical moment—what you call the strategic moment—is erased. What's reasserted then is actually the need for a kind of naïveté in the assertion of personal identity.

GS: Identity is a very different word from essence. We "write" a running biography with life-language rather than only word-language in order to "be." Call this identity! Deconstruction, whatever it may be, is not most valuably an exposure of error, certainly not other people's error, other people's essentialism. The most serious critique in deconstruction is the critique of things that are extremely useful, things without which we cannot live on, take chances; like our running self-identikit. That should be the approach to how we are essentialists.

A young man who knew Nietzsche better than he knew anything else thought that I was claiming that Derrida was "a poor man's Nietzsche." Isn't that the way many people read Derrida? If you knew Heidegger best, he would seem to be a poor man's Heidegger; if you knew Plato best, he would seem to be a poor man's Plato, and if a feminist, a rich woman's feminist? Perhaps what I'm saying here is that Derrida is a poor man's Althusser. In Althusser's naively powerful essay, "Marxism and Humanism," he writes that merely knowing an ideology does not dissipate its effect.[8] One of Derrida's most scandalous contributions is to begin with what is very familiar in many radical positions and to take it with the utmost seriousness, with literal seriousness, so that it questions the position (de)constructively as the wholly intimate other. One is left with the useful yet semimournful position of the unavoidable usefulness of something that is dangerous. Those might be the lineaments of the deconstructive critique of essence.

I have, then, reconsidered my cry for a strategic use of essentialism. In a personalist culture, even among people within the humanities, who are generally wordsmiths, it's the idea of a *strategy* that has been forgotten. The strategic has been taken as a point of self-differentiation from the poor essentialists. So long as the critique of essentialism is understood not as an exposure of error, our own or others', but as an acknowledgement of the dangerousness of something one cannot not use, I would stand by it as one stand among many. The critique of essentialism should not be seen as being critical in the colloquial, Anglo-American sense of being adversely inclined, but as a critique in the robust European philosophical sense.

ER: Could we pick up on the reference that you have made to deconstruction and talk about what you have called "the greatest gift of deconstruction: to question the authority of the investigating subject without paralyzing him, persistently transforming conditions of impossibility into possibility."[9] I think that one of the things that's most striking about your arguments about essentialism and about your work generally is the way you both assert the importance of positionality and refuse to essentialize it. How much would you say that your general thinking about essentialism is shaped by your conceptualization and your own practice of self-positioning or self-identification? What kind of relationship is there between the broad project to deconstruct—in the very precise sense that you were just invoking—identity, not to refuse identity but to deconstruct identity (a project you've participated in) and your own frequent concern to identify yourself, to position yourself, to refuse what you have pointed to most recently in "Can the Subaltern Speak?" as a tendency on the part of supposed critics of essentialism to make their own positions transparent and unproblematic?

GS: Assuming that there is such a thing as *the* story of a life (about which more later), it would sound rather different from all the other tellings about oneself that one engaged in. I believe that the way to save oneself from either objective, disinterested positioning or the attitude of there being no author (and these two opposed positions legitimize each other), or yet *the* story of one's life, is to "recognize" oneself as also an instantiation of historical and psychosexual narratives that one can piece together, however fragmentarily, in order to do deontological work in the humanities. When one represents oneself in such a way, it becomes, curiously enough, a deidentification of oneself, a claiming of an identity from a text that comes from somewhere else. I can compare this to the Derridean insight about the mother tongue that I discuss in Chapter Three: a mother tongue is something that has a history before we are born. We are inserted into it; it has the possibility of being activated by what can be colloquially called motives. Therefore, although it's unmotivated it's not capricious. We are inserted into it, and, without intent, we "make it our own." We intend within it; we critique intentions within it; we play with it through signification as well as reference; and then we leave it, as much without intent, for the use of others after our deaths. To an extent, the way in which one conceives of oneself as representative or as an example of something is this awareness that what is one's own, one's identity, what is proper to one, is also a biography, and has a history. That history is unmotivated but not capricious and is larger in outline than we are. This is different from the idea of talking about oneself. I have come to feel this more fully through the writings of Assia Djebar, the Algerian novelist. In *Anti- Oedipus*, Deleuze and Guattari talk about the way in which a socius is produced and then becomes a "miraculating" agency operating like a quasi cause.[10] The example they use is Capital, but in fact, culture, ethnos, sexuality, all of these things become miraculating agencies as if by a miracle one speaks as an agent of a culture or an agent of a sex or an agent of an ethnos et cetera.... A body without organs (necessary postsupposition of any sphere of agency?), has inscribed on its recording surface this miraculating agency, which seems like a quasi cause. What your re-cognize, or graph (a second time, something supposedly having *pre*existed) as representing, what your self represents, is that kind of a miraculating agency, a history, a culture, a position, an institutional position. But, via that persistent critique that I was talking about, you may be aware that this is miraculating you as you speak, rather than that you are speaking in unmediated identity. Of *course* that awareness is always beside, before, after the point, but that's life. The essence of life. These are uses of essence which you cannot go around. You are written into these uses of essence. This is the strategy by which history plays you, your language plays you, whatever the miraculating agency might be speaks you. It's not a question of choosing the strategy. You are, to an extent, distanced from it with humility and respect when you "build for difference."

ER: Yes, and given what you have said and in response both to that question and another, I'd like actually to skip to some things I thought we would talk about later, namely, why has antiessentialism been so powerful in the way you were just referring to, as a kind of term of abuse, and how important are the questions of the disciplines, the institutional constraints of the U. S. academy, and the interventions of cross- or counterdisciplinary discourses like women's studies or area studies? What is the purchase the essentialism debate has on the academy? How does its inflection differ from discipline to discipline? Is antiessentialism an effect of anti-disciplinary or cross-disciplinary work? Within feminism and within some other discourses, essentialism seems to be a kind of blind spot that won't go away. It hasn't, by and large, been historicized or related to the history of high philosophical essentialisms, but has been invoked to distance and disallow certain kinds of discourses. Why hasn't the response to that been a kind of philosophical essentialism that fights back, that resists this abuse, and the ahistorical and in some ways not very informed use of the word essentialism?

GS: And why there hasn't been a philosophical essentialism?

ER: In response, yes.

GS: Because essentialism is a loose-tongued phrase, not a philosophical school. It is used by nonphilosophers simply to mean all kinds of things when they don't know what other word to use. In disciplinary philosophy, Hilary Putnam, Nelson Goodman, et al. seem to be coping with the problem of the irreducibility of the mediation of the real without influencing the "essentialism debate." And they don't sound like post-structuralist feminists. In fact, when the question of essences is philosophically considered it doesn't seem very sexy. For example, nonfoundationalist ethics, which from the analytic ground cannot proceed very far: let us say, the work of a Thomas Nagel, or the more interesting work of a Bernard Williams. Nonfoundationalist moral philosophy doesn't look a bit like antiessentialism outside of philosophy. The question of antiessentialism and essentialism is not a philosophical question as such. Is essentialism a code word for a feeling for the empirical, sometimes? Even as antiessentialism is sometimes no more than an emphasis on the social? Why is the thought of the social free of essences? To worry about such distinctions too much might keep us from infiltrating the knowledge venture of imperialism, which was absolutely spectacular and which still holds institutional power—the establishment of anthropology, comparative literature, comparative philology, comparative religion, world history, et cetera: Eurocentric crossculturalism, and that's what we are, in fact, looking at, watered down and diluted in the house of a so-called interdisciplinary antiessentialism in the humanities and the social sciences. If these still dominate the techniques of knowledge, round about them is the operation of the structures of ennoblement, often tedious institutional skirmishes. If one establishes an interdisciplinary space which does not engage with this most important arena (a silent, unemphatic arena) of warring power in the disciplines themselves, where the people who don't publish much, who don't teach very well, engage day after day, with distribution requirements, let us say; if one doesn't budge them and consolidate ways of gathering the empirical, antiessentialism versus essentialism can prove a red herring.

ER: Your invocations of the knowledge venture and the philosophical discussion of the irreducibility of the essences reminds me of a passage from "A Literary Representation of the Subaltern," which speaks, I think, to the relationship between essentialism and the production of knowledge. It's one of your takes on the argument that "only a native can know the scene" and you say:

> The position that only the subaltern can know the subaltern, only women can know women and so on, cannot be held as a theoretical presupposition either, for it predicates the possibility of knowledge on identity. Whatever the political necessity for holding the position, and whatever the advisability of attempting to "identify" (with) the other as subject in order to know her, knowledge is made possible and is always in excess of knowledge. Knowledge is never adequate to its object. The theoretical model of the ideal knower in the embattled position we are discussing is that of the person identical with her predicament. This is actually the figure of the impossibility and non-necessity of knowledge. Here the relationship between the practical—need for claiming subaltern identity—and the theoretical—no program of knowledge production can presuppose identity, as origin—as, once again, of an "interruption" that persistently brings each term to crisis.[15]

This passage touches upon a number of issues I'd like to talk about: the first is deconstruction and what it's taught us about identity and difference, the proper and reading and their relationship as the production of knowledge. How would you say your interest in deconstruction has fed your thinking about essentialism? What's the importance of deconstruction in dismantling essentialism? How are essentialism and antiessentialism related in Derrida's text?

GS: In terms of the first bit that you read there is the further problem of "clinging to marginality." The trend speed in post-Fordist capitalism is superfast, and it is a truism to point out that tertiary education in the United States is run like the general economy, nearly 4,000 degree granting institutions, impossible telematic contact. Unless you have worked within other systems with equally intelligent colleagues and students, you don't realize how much some of the dogma on antiessentialism has been picked up by this political and economic structure. In the last decade, some of the "clinging to marginality" is being fabricated so that the upwardly mobile, benevolent student (the college is an institution of upward mobility; it would be ridiculous to deny that), the *so-called* marginal student, claiming validation, is being taught (because we don't have the sense of strategy that I was speaking of, what was good in strategy has now become a slogan, and we don't look at the years passing, the situation changing) speaking for oneself, which is then in fact, working precisely to contain the ones whom this person is supposed to represent. In other words, the miraculation is working as if it truly is a miracle, an academic miracle. Mariah speaks for Lucy as *Lucy* is taught in a too-benevolent class:

> "I was looking forward to telling you that I have Indian blood, that the reason I'm so good at catching fish and hunting birds and roasting corn and doing all sorts of things is that I have Indian blood. But now, I don't know why, I feel I shouldn't tell you that. I feel you will take it the wrong way."

This really surprised me. What way should I take this? Wrong way? Right way? What could she mean? To look at her, there was nothing remotely like an Indian about her. Why claim a thing like that? I myself had Indian blood in me. The Carib Indians were good sailors, but I don't like the sea; I only like to look at it. To me my grandmother is only a grandmother, not an Indian. My grandmother is alive; the Indians she comes from are all dead. If someone could get away with it, I am sure they would put my grandmother in a museum, as an example of something now extinct in nature, one of a handful still alive. In fact, one of the museums in which Mariah had taken me devoted a whole section to people, all dead, who were more or less related to my grandmother.

Mariah says, "I have Indian blood in me," and underneath everything I could swear she says it as if she were announcing her possession of a trophy. How do you get to be the sort of victor who can claim to be the vanquished also?"

Why should deconstruction "dismantle" essentialism? Deconstruction considers that the subject always tends toward centering and looks at the mechanism of centering among randomness; it doesn't say there *is* something called the decentered subject. When I say this, one rejoinder I often hear is: "Well, you just centered the subject in Derrida."[13]? To think about the danger of what is useful, is not to think that the dangerous thing doesn't exist. The former is the lesson of deconstruction for me. Thus does deconstruction teach me about the impossibility of antiessentialism. It teaches me something about essentialisms being among the conditions of the production of doing, knowing, being, but does not give me a clue to the real. The real in deconstruction is neither essentialist nor antiessentialist. It invites us to think through the counterintuitive position that there might be essences and there might not be essences. A "poor man's" agnosticism, all right? "Poor man's" there means to take literally, trivially, what is implicit in the radical moment. Deconstruction is not an essence. It is not a school of thought; it is a way of rereading. Deconstruction itself can lead to an essentialism. *Enlightened Absence* is an example, I think, of essentialist, humanist, deconstructivist feminism.[14] I think it can certainly become a viewpoint in deconstruction, a description of what it is to be feminine, how the antiessential feminine is the essence of the feminine.

ER: Moving in the other direction, off the same passage, and this is related to what you were saying earlier about how one talks about oneself: can you talk about your own history, or the trajectory of your own work, your earliest intellectual and political history, and its impact on your thinking about essentialism? Is your recent work and its partial focus on the problem of essentialism a reinscription of earlier concerns, concerns that perhaps predate your work on Derrida?

GS: One of the lessons learned early for a child in a colonial context, who comes from a background which has the full share of the ambivalence toward the culture of imperialism, is related to the fact that the native language operated very strongly in my part of India. Linguistic subnationalist essentialism informed the public and the private. In school, however, most of my teachers were tribal Christians. A caste Hindu child, secure within her native language, hegemonic Calcutta Bengali, being taught by tribal Christians, who were converted to Christianity from "below," turn "outside" the recognized religions of India. They were not Christianized, they *became* Christians. I still cannot think about my school days without an immense sense of gratitude to my parents for having thought to send me to such a school rather than to a less fashionable "native" school. In a situation like that, one begins to realize without realizing the extraordinary plurality of the source of enlightenment; in the very long haul, the general sources of our enlightenment were our race enemies. On the other hand, my direct teachers, who were not coreligionist, who were castewise lower, even outcasts, and yet my teachers, respected teachers, were Christians. Yet Christianity was also the religion of the hardly departed rulers. The sense of what a division there is in one's own making came early.

After independence, the idea of internationalism was under fire from the national party. The lines between socialist internationalism and the fabrication of national identity were finessed by the left in the era of the Third International. Forty years later, thirty years later, graphing one's bio, if one is asked why there is some sympathy for that word that I don't like—antiessentialism—in one's make-up, those are the things that one still thinks of. This indeed is the "experience" of the planned emergence into postcoloniality by a middle-class child in that part of India. The word *experience* is for me as mysterious as the mother tongue, something one is inserted in, self-representation, for example, antimiraculation. . . . That experience makes the strongest bond and also produces the greatest impatience with antiessentialism as a battle cry.

ER: Your reference to the left suggests another way of asking a question similar to the one I asked about deconstruction, a question about Marxism. That is, how has your interest in and your work on Marx influenced your thinking about essentialism? How does that Marxist tradition of antiessentialism fit into your own practice and thinking? Could you talk about a dynamic of essentialism and antiessentialism within Marxism?

GS: In Marx it is the slow discovery of the importance of the question of value that has opened up a lot of things for me. In Marx there is a strong sense that all ontological commitments (just as in our neck of the woods, all ontocultural commitments), that is to say, ontological commitments to political beings, historical agents, should be seen as negotiable, in terms of the coding of value.

I would draw your attention most strongly to, let's say, "The Trinity Formula" in *Capital*, volume 3, where Marx is mocking the idea that there is anything—in your own terms—essential about specific class formations.[15] And then also the final unfinished chapter on class. Unfortunately, the "Englishing" of Marx obliterated the trace of the counter-intuitive nature of Marx's exhortation to his implied reader—the worker. The worker has to be counter-intuitive in order to realize that he is the agent rather than the victim of Capital. The entire idea of agency is structurally negotiable.

The negotiability of commitment and the elusiveness of value are not popular ideas among Marxists. Marx calls the value-form "contentless and simple" (*inhaltlos und einfach*). The English translation is "slight in content."[16] There is a difference. Value is contentless yet not pure form. Marx is talking about something that cannot appear but must be presupposed to grasp the mechanics of the production of the world. It's the possibility of the possibility of mediation as it were, which establishes exchange, its appropriation and extraction as surplus and so on. This way of understanding Marx's project would not underestimate the importance of class, but would not see it as a trafficking in ineluctable essences.

ER: Could we move, then, to the relationship between the current and growing interest in materials from the so-called "third world" and essentialism? Is there a perception of a strategically essentialist moment that's located "out there" in the "third world," perhaps in the form of liberation struggles, which is related to the renewed interest, specifically among U. S. critics and scholars, in essentialism and in that—that benevolent, as you have called it, but problematic—desire for translations of "third world" texts and the production of new forms of knowledge about a "third world" which is also often rendered monolithically, both within feminism and outside of feminism? How much of the difficulty that academics in the U. S. have avoiding certain essentialist traps has to do with the displacement of questions of race and ethnicity into this monolithic and safely distanced "third world" and the consequent effacement of imperialism as such?

GS: It works both ways. You displace it into the third world, but, on the other hand, you again reconstruct the third world as people of color and marginalized people *in* the United States. These migrant communities become more real than the "original" cultures, to the great irritation of the activists as well as the intellectual elites in the "original" cultures, for different kinds of reasons. The concept of "decolonization" begins to combat only internal colonization in the first world. Between two texts like Frobel Folker's *The New International Division of Labour* and Nigel Harris's *The End of the Third World*, there is a decade.[17] And then read Chakravarthi Raghavan's *Recolonization*—published last year, but already out of date with the break up of the

U. S. S. R.[18] Plans for a very definite new economic program, after the Second World War and the accompanying change in global outlines, have now been scrapped. To use that as a culturalist description seems rather shabby. If the "third world" is used as a mobilizing slogan for the developing nations, that's fine, but that is rather different from essentialism. That is in response to specific policies of exploitation. In the arenas where this language is seriously used, each country comes asserting its difference. They really do know it's strategic. That is a strategy that changes moment to moment, and they in fact come asserting their differences as they use the mobilized unity to do some specific thing. I think one might keep that as a reminder.

On the ground of cultural politics as well, the third world and, today, the ruins of the second world are postcolonial worlds only in a highly diversified way. Consider, for example, the idea that magical realism is the paradigmatic style of the third world. What is the hidden ethical, political agenda behind claiming that a style practiced most spectacularly by some writers in that part of the third world which relates most intimately to the United States, namely Latin America (just as India used to relate to Britain), is paradigmatic of a space which is trying to cope with the problem of narrativizing decolonization? In Latin American space, one of the things that cannot be narrativized is decolonization, as the Ariel-Caliban debate and today's intimate involvement with the U. S. have clearly articulated for us.[19]

One might, then, look at the larger third world as diversely postcolonial, making catachrestic claims. . . . Political claims are not to ethnicity, that's ministries of culture. The political claims over which battles are being fought are to nationhood, sovereignty, citizenship, secularism. Those claims are catachrestic claims in the sense that the so-called adequate narratives of the concept-metaphors were supposedly not written in the spaces that have decolonized themselves, but rather in the spaces of the colonizers. There the question of essences becomes the question of regulative political concepts. I don't think about essentialism or antiessentialism when I look at what's going on in the third world and now the new second. I see either block unity, highly strategic in the strictest political sense, or these catachrestic claims negotiating questions like national language, nationhood, citizenship. Ethnicity and religion are negotiable signifiers in these fast-moving articulations. The question of essence is one of the players on this catachrestic chessboard.

One could look at it another way, as well. Capital is antiessentializing because it is the abstract as such. The essence of nations, cultures, et cetera, are deployed by capital*isms* for the political management of capital. The "politics of overdetermination" is the newest Anglo-U. S.-E. E. C. twist in that management, offering the idea of an antiessentialist multiplicity of agents. "The agent" cannot "be" overdetermined, you know. In order to consolidate the abstraction of agency overdetermination must *effectively* operate as condensation. These admirers of psychoanalysis trivialize it by equating it with deliberate psychodrama as a blueprint for social justice: traffic in antiessentialist essences.

ER: I take the force of your point, that when you think about the third world, especially politically, the problem of essentialism doesn't arise. But in what you have written, for example, about the Subaltern Studies Group, their practice, and their pursuit of an essential category or definition . . .

GS: . . . subaltern consciousness . . .

ER: . . . you describe a certain kind of project: they produce, in the process that you unpack, an antiessentialist encounter with radical textuality, I think that is the way you put it.

GS: Yes.

ER: That was part of what my question was directed at, the way in which your work on that group's work has gotten, at least in some ways, articulated in terms of the debate around essentialism and antiessentialism.

GS: Initially, my intervention made some members uncomfortable. I think I turned out to be more . . . well, I will use your word, antiessentialist . . .

ER: . . . in quotation marks . . .

GS: . . . than they had figured. They are, however, a volatile and singularly unmalicious group, so these differences are getting ironed out on both sides. I have a lot to learn from them. I do not monumentalize them. They are not a group of "third world" historians who are just wonderful and correctly strategically essentialist, et cetera. I think some of them had more invested in the subaltern consciousness than I had thought when I was welcomed in the group. But these are the breaks for a persistent critique. Most deconstructivists think the position too vulgar; most Marxists too elitist, too much in love with Parisian fads; many feminists, mainstream feminists, are beginning to feel that the position is somehow antifeminist. Outside in every machine! Perhaps for the Subaltern Studies Group, I am, occasionally, too much of a U. S. antiessentialist! I *am* one of the subalternists; I don't work *on* them. But they taught me to ask questions that I hadn't thought of myself. I'm against their grain as I am against the grain of the antiessentialist. But they taught me to ask questions that I hadn't thought of myself.

ER: You have made several references to the problem of theory, whether it's Marxists accusing you of being too attached . . .

GS: Not accusing—thinking of me.

ER: Thinking of you . . .

GS: I'm not so important that people are accusing me. . . . One of the subalternists did indeed accuse me of various things, but I've written about that in my book.

ER: (laughing) Okay . . .

GS: But that's an exception—no, when they think of me they think . . .

ER: (laughter)

GS: If my name comes up, let's put it that way . . .

ER: (laughing) Okay . . . in any case, there is one reading of essentialism in the U. S. context that suggests that it tends to be empirical, that it's a kind of practical rather than a theorized essentialism, or that it's essentialism by default. I wonder what you think of that reading, and that would return me to an earlier question about the absence of a kind of a philosophical rejoinder to antiessentialism. We've already talked about that, but I wonder if you think it's possible at present to construct a kind of self-consciously theorized essentialism, or if there would be any point in even trying to do that. There are, of course, discourses perhaps in the biological or the genetic sciences that seem to be seeking to isolate universal or essential human traits. Is the reductivness that tends to characterize those kinds of moves a primary strategy of essentialism? Do those kinds of reductions go against the grain or against the disciplinary prejudices and investments of literary and philosophical discourse and thus disable a substantive theoretical essentialism in the debate?

GS: Now, sociobiology, cognitive studies, artificial intelligence, which take something as the ground, they are exaggerated cases of most such discourses, hmmm?

ER: Right.

GS: These things become politically offensive, a way, precisely, of differentiating oppressive behavior. I have no problem there; I'm against that. And I don't particularly want to wait to theorize essentialism in order to say that; I really do believe in undermining the vanguardism of theory. I don't want a theory of essences. We have enough of those. We have nothing but the practice of essences. When I said strategy, I meant strategy. I don't even think I'm capable of thinking theory in that sense. With essences, at least I feel that they're so useful that they can become dangerous. With theory, I feel that, for the moment, for me, at least, it's best to keep it at a distance, see it as the practice of its production. Even so, I must ask why essentialism is confused sometimes with the empirical. Why do people make this terminological confusion? Earlier, in my school-teacherly voice, I said that this confusion is a way of not wanting to infiltrate the disciplines, the vested interests, the real problems. Instead, one says that the careful construction of an object of investigation in a field is essentialism. This has something like a relationship with confusing essentialism with the empirical. All we really want to claim is that there is no feminine essence; there's no essential class subject; the general subject of essence is not a good basis for investigation. This is rather different from being antiempirical.

We could base our ontological commitments on various forms of coding. It is, to me, spectacular that someone like Gayle Rubin, coming from a Freudian/Lévi-Straussian structuralist humanism should in fact get into the idea of value as coded in sex-gender systems.[20] Whether we declare ourselves as essentialists or antiessentialists, if we realize that our ontological commitments are dependent on various forms of coding, we can presuppose a variety of general catchrestic names as a grounding. Richard Rorty speaking about the nominalism in poststructuralism is right on target there.[21] What he does with it is something else. Assuming one's ontological commitment as susceptible to an examination of value coding and then to presuppose a catachrestic name in order to ground our project and our investigation allows us to be thoroughly empirical without necessarily being blind essentialists. Ultimately, if you will forgive me for saying so, a lot of self-consciously antiessentialist writing seems to be a bit useless and boring. It's often very derivative, resembling other and better models that are not as scared of essences. It seems to me that to be empirical in this way would be a much greater challenge, require much harder work, would make people read different things, primary texts of active social work. If you're reading development economics you sometimes don't read Cixous's latest thing. To confuse empirical work with the pursuit of essence is, in itself, something that should be examined, and I don't see any need for a substantive theory of essentialism.

ER: We've been talking about feminism all along, but to address it very directly, how would you say feminism, as such, which is already problematic . . . (laughs) . . . *feminisms!* . . . how have feminists influenced your thinking about essentialism? Did feminism or women's studies put essentialism on the agenda in the U. S. academy? And what would you say—you just now mentioned Cixous—about the way essentialism and antiessentialism are intertwined in the practice of feminist theory and women's studies, in the U. S. or in France, in the work of the antifeminist feminists like Cixous or Kristeva?

GS: I think in general women's studies philosophy is humanist. There is a piece by Jean Grimshaw in the current *Radical Philosophy* on Mary Daly's humanism.[22] Of course, Mary Daly is not representative of U. S. feminism, but I think some lessons can be learned there about the essentialist or antiessentialist debate.

When I began to write as a feminist, the idea of differences being unjustly made and unjustly not recognized needed the presupposition that what was self-same or identical was an essence. It was okay as a strategic presupposition; it certainly allowed me to learn and teach. But it does seem that like most strategies, for me at least, it has served its purpose, and at this point I can't go on beating that horse anymore. And as I say, my feminism now takes a distance from that debate.

As you know, feminism means something else in France. I really don't have much to do with it because that's very situation-specific. I like reading Irigaray, but I read her within the general tradition of French experimental writing, foregrounding rhetoric. It is only if she is read as the pure rhetorical prose of truth—whatever that might be—that she may seem essentialist when she talks about women. Broadly, Kojèvian

French intellectuals read Hegel and Marx with an eye to rhetoric. We know Derrida has to be read that way. Why do we become essentialist readers when we read someone like Irigaray?

I'm repelled by Kristeva's politics: what seems to me to be her reliance on the sort of banal historical narrative to produce "women's time"; what seems to me Christianizing psychoanalysis; what seems to me to be her sort of ferocious Western Europeanism; and what seems to me to be her long-standing implicit positivism: naturalizing of the chora, naturalizing of the presemiotic. I'm so put off by this that I can't read her seriously anymore, so it is more my problem. I mean, I'm not generous and catholic enough to learn from her anymore. I find Cixous much more risk-taking.

I think the kind of antiessentialism that I like these days is in the work of Kalpana Bardhan.[23] If you read her, you probably wouldn't see what I was talking about. One has to learn how to honor empirical work. Bardhan talks about how stratified the idea of women is in a place like India. In Bardhan's work (she's a development economist), you begin to see how impossible it is to focus, even within endogamous or exogamous marriage lines, on something called a space out of which you will define and articulate something called a woman. She even diversifies the radicals who can join in their struggle. She diversifies the people who study them. . . . In that kind of work which is not against essentialism but which completely pluralizes the grid, it is my task as a reader, as it is with deconstruction, to read and run with it somewhere else. It is my task as a reader to see where in that grid there are spaces where, in fact, "woman" oozes away. Essences, it seems to me, are just a kind of content. All content is not essence. Why be so nervous about it? Why not demote the word "essence," because without a minimalizable essence, an essence as *ce qui reste*, an essence as what remains, there is no exchange. Difference articulates these negotiable essences. There is no time for essence/anti-essence. There is so much work to be done.

ER: Yes, but it seems to me that the reason that can't be done across the board is teaching. I always have to "do" essentialism/antiessentialism with my students because in the first flush of feminist thought they become the most energetic essentialists, or personalists, perhaps. And that's, of course, a quite different thing from a research program or the kinds of books that one wants to write, but in my experience that's part of the reason that the question won't go away. It's a kind of initial question, politically and intellectually, when students discover the possibility of a feminist discourse.

GS: Rather than make it a central issue, work it into the method of your teaching so that the class becomes an example of the minimalizing of essences, the impossibility of essences; rather than talk about it constantly, make the class a proof of this new position. If we're talking strategy, you know as well as I do that teaching is a question of strategy. That is perhaps the only place where people like us actually get any experience in strategy. In that context, it seems to me that one can make a strategy of taking away from them the authority of their marginality, the centrality of their marginality, through the strategy of careful teaching, so that they come to prove that that authority will not take them very far because the world is a large place. Others are many. The self is enclosed; the concrete is fabricated. One can do it *in* teaching rather than talk about it *ad infinitum* because they're not ready to take sides.

ER: There has been, at least in literary studies, a kind of consensus that feminist critics have done exactly what you describe, taken a very small sample and then generalized about a "feminine aesthetic" or a "women's tradition"—produced ahistorical misrepresentation of things as feminine, feminine, you know, the Feminine, with a capital "F." Insofar as this criticism has been generally accepted, there's a kind of consensus in favor of pursuing specificity, multiplying differences. Is there a way in which multiplication can become pluralism? What are the consequences of that?

GS: The real problem, one of the reasons why it becomes pluralism, is that we live in a country which has pluralism—the pluralism of repressive tolerance—as the best of its political credo. Most of us are not interested in changing our social relations, and pluralism is the best we can do. Cultural Studies into multiculturalism.

Once we have established the story of the straight, white, Judeo-Christian, heterosexual man of property as the ethical universal, we must not replicate the same trajectory. We have limits; we cannot even learn many languages. This idea of a global fun-fair is a lousy teaching idea. One of the first things to do is to think through the limits of one's power. One must ruthlessly undermine the story of the ethical universal, the hero. But the alternative is not constantly to evoke multiplicity; the alternative is to know and to teach the student the awareness that this is a limited sample because of one's own inclinations and capacities to learn enough to take a larger sample. And this kind of work should be a collective enterprise. Other people will do some other work. This is how I think one should proceed, rather than make each student into a ground of multiplicity. That leads to pluralism. I ask the U. S. student: "What do you think is the inscription that allows *you* to think the world without any preparation? What sort of coding has produced *this* subject?" I think it's hard for students to know this, but we have a responsibility to make this lesson palliative rather than destructive. This is not a paralyzing thing to teach. In fact, when a student is told that responsibility means proceeding from an awareness of the limits of one's power, the student understands it quite differently from being told, "Look, you can't do all of this." I will share with you what I have learned about knowing, that these are the limitations of what I undertake, looking to others to each me. I think that's what one should do rather than invoke multiplicity.

ER: How is the problem of the subject related to the relationship between essentialism and the efforts to theorize the body, or bodies, as someone pointed out to me when I showed him this question? What kind of problem is this? Can we theorize our bodies without essentializing them as the body? Is our confusion about how to theorize bodies the root of the problem of essentialism? Insofar as there is another factor that keeps the question of essentialism kind of bubbling, I think it has to do with that fact that, at least in the U. S., the effort to biologize gender is not over in the general culture, polit-ical culture, for example, the front page of the *New York Times* a few weeks ago explain-ing why at certain times of the month we can't find our cars because of our . . .

GS: Really?

ER: . . . hormones raging. Yes.

GS: I didn't see that. It gives me an answer to my question!

ER: (laughs) How is your own effort to address bodies in some of your work part of your thinking about essentialism? And how do race and class actually enter in here, as well as the more obvious gender?

GS: The body, like all other things, cannot be thought, as such. I take the extreme ecological view that the body as such has no possible outline. As body it is a repetition of nature. It is in the rupture with Nature when it is a signifier of immediacy for the staging of the self. As a text, the inside of the body (imbricated with the outside) is mysterious and unreadable except by way of thinking of the systematicity of the body, value coding of the body. It is through the *significance* of my body and others' bodies that cultures become gendered, economicopolitic, selved, substantive.

ER: This is also a question that's not in here, per se, because when I looked again at that not very well formulated question about the unconscious and death, I realized that there is no question about psychoanalysis anywhere in here.

GS: That's okay.

ER: (laughs) Okay?

GS: Yah!

ER: (laughing) These are my last questions that didn't fit elsewhere. Is it possible to speak of a nonessential essence? Would that be a kind of gloss on strategic essential-ism?

GS: I don't think so.

ER: No?

GS: I mean one might just as well speak about an essential nonessence. It's possible to speak of everything. But an essence, if it's minimalizable, is also cross-hatched. Death as such can only be thought via essence or rupture of essence, that mother-tongue analogy that I gave earlier. . . . I cannot approach death as such. Death may be the catachresis that is indistinguishable from essence. May be.

ER: I've already asked about deconstruction as a kind of questioning of essences or of the relation between the essential and the antiessential, and as I look back I want to ask you about de Man as opposed . . . I was about to say as opposed to Derrida, but not necessarily as opposed to Derrida, but in his specificity as someone who can be of help.

GS: When I knew de Man, he was a phenomenologist, marked by people like Lévi-Strauss, Merleau-Ponty, Poulet. Deconstruction was a thing that appealed to him greatly later and he ran (or ambled off) with it in another direction. How can I call Lévi-Strauss a phenomenologist? Not within the bounds of an interview. De Man was also "interested" in a whole slew of German thinkers who inflected his understanding of deconstruction as a cousin of Romantic Irony. I see his work as lapidary and strong in its very limits. I don't believe he ever gave away his control in the writing. He talked *about* giving up his control, but he never really gave away his control in the way that Derrida constantly tries. De Man even writes about it in the introduction to *The Rhetoric of Romanticism*.[24] From de Man I learned the extreme importance of an absolutely literal-minded reading: To follow the logic of the rhetoric—the troplogy—wherever it might lead.

ER: You spoke earlier, several times, about other words that might be used rather than antiessentialist, and although I didn't know you were going to say that, as I was thinking about talking with you, I did fix on certain terms in your work, like "interruption," or "transactional," or "discontinuous." I don't mean that you were thinking of this when you made the earlier remarks, but are these perhaps other words that can serve the strategic, have strategic effects?

GS: The thinking of essences as what remains, the minimalizable, something with which we negotiate in the strategy of teaching in the broadest possible sense, without talking *about* the debate constantly does interrupt the teaching of cultural or literary *substance*, brings it to crisis.

"Transaction": now a transaction can be a transaction between essences, so it is not necessarily antiessentialist. Let's put that aside for a moment, we're running out of time. "Discontinuity," then. Radical discontinuity cannot appear, like pure difference; remember, essences cannot appear either. (There's not much *theoretical* difference between pure essence and pure difference.) Discontinuity must traffic in minimal continua. We go back to *ce qui reste*, fragments of essences to reckon with. That's where writing like Bardhan's is so interesting. Fragments of essences to reckon with rather than preserving myself from essences. If you see this as an antiessentialist project, I start running the other way again.

ER: (laughter). This is the whole business about strategy, asking what regulates your diagnosis, why do you want me with you, what claims me, what is claiming me?

ER: Can we talk, just because of the very last things that you've said, about the question of audience? When I thought about these questions, I also thought about my own work. I've been writing about pluralism. What I have been calling pluralism is partially what you were just referring to as corporatism. It's an essentialism that doesn't have to do so much with the object of study as with one's audience. The pluralism assumes not just her own transparency—in fact she may articulate her positionality—but the transparency and therefore the unity of one's audience. That's where essence resides, or is expressed, that is what pluralism doesn't acknowledge. Perhaps this isn't what you meant by anticorporatism. . . . I guess what I'm asking is for you to say a little bit more about it. What I see as the pluralist moment is the moment when one doesn't acknowledge—and I've learned this from you, at least I think I have learned it from you—the exclusions that fragment one's audience.

GS: Yes. When one takes the representative position—the homeopathic deconstruction of identity by identity—one is aware that outside of that representation of oneself in the middle of one stream, there are areas that are completely inaccessible to one. When I said "building for difference," the sense of audience is already assuming that the future is simply a future present. The most radical challenge of deconstruction is that notion of thought being a blank part of the text given over to a future that is not just a future present but always a future anterior. It never will be, but always will have been; that is the most practical assurance in view of which one works on, indefinitely outside in the teaching machine. The audience is not an essence, the audience is a blank. An audience can be constituted by people I cannot even imagine, affected by this little unimportant trivial piece of work, which is not just direct teaching and writing. That displaces the question of audience as essence or fragmented or exclusivist or anything. Derrida calls this a responsibility to the trace of the other, I think. . . . It's something that one must remind oneself of all the time. That is why what I cannot imagine stands guard over everything that I must/can do, think, live.

Yet, in the narrow sense, when an audience is responsible responding, invited, in other words, to coinvestigate, then positionality is shared with it. Audience and investigator: it's not just a binary opposition when an audience really is an audience. It now seems to me that many of the changes I've made in my position are because the audience has become a coinvestigator and I have realized what it is to have an audience. An audience is part of one. An audience shows one something. That may indeed be the transaction. It's a responsibility to the other taking on faces. It is not deessentializing, but attempting to deconstruct the binary opposition between investigator and audience.

Radically, then, one works not for a future present, but imagining the blank certitude of the future anterior. And the audience *is* the unimaginable; less radically in the second session, as it were, in the logical sphere, where one begins to imagine the audience responding, responsible, and invited to be coinvestigator, one starts owning the right to have one's invitation accepted, given that the invitation is, like all letters, open letters intercepted and that people turn up in other places for other occasions with that invitation, so that we begin to deconstruct that binary opposition bit by bit.[25] I don't see that particularly as dessentializing. It's something else. But yes, I think the question you've asked is very important.

ER: As you were answering it . . . you used the word "future"; after I had finished these questions, at the very end, I realized there was no question about history, either as a potentially essentializing discourse or as a potentially antiessentializing discourse. Actually, now these questions, with the words essentializing and antiessentializing . . .

GS: See what happens?

ER: . . . larded in so thickly, are no longer the right questions, having said that, what would you say about history?

GS: I'll give you a very short answer. It depends on your view of history as negotiable determinant or fact.

ER: Thank you.

GS: Thank you.

NOTES

This interview was held in Pittsburgh on December 9, 1988. The questions were crafted in consultation with Naomi Schor and Elizabeth Weed. We thank Erika Rundle for her heroic work of transcription and Nicole Cunningham for producing the final text.

1. Frances Ferguson, "Rape and the Rise of the Novel," *Representations 20 (Fall 1987): pp. 88–112*. Elizabeth V. Spelman, *Inessential Woman: Problems of Exclusion in Feminist Thought* (Boston: Beacon, 1988). Denise Riley, *"Am I That Name?" Feminism and the Category of "Women" in History* (Minneapolis: University of Minnesota Press, 1988). Donna J. Haraway, *Simians, Cyborgs, and Women: the Reinvention of Nature* (London: Free Association Books, 1991), pp. 109, 95, 91, 94.

    Space doesn't permit me to do justice to Ferguson's extraordinarily interesting and intricate essay. Her analysis reveals that the legal system's preference for addressing "stipulated states" enabled it to evade the systemic problem of the contempt for women's testimony on rape. Ferguson points out that it also makes it extremely difficult for women who are attacked by men they know to convince district attorneys even to press charges. (Ferguson cites Susan Estrich's discussion of "simple rape.") At the same time, in her analysis of *Clarissa*, Ferguson stresses that stipulation *can* be used, in particular cases, to combat phallocentric constructions of sexuality and sexual violence.

2. Denise Riley, *"Am I That Name?" Feminism and the Category of 'Women' in History* (Minneapolis: U of Minnesota Press, 1988), pp. 103, 92.

3. Donna Haraway, "A Manifesto for Cyborgs: Science, Technology and Socialist Feminism in the 1980s," *Socialist Review* 80 (1985) in *Coming to Terms: Feminism, Theory and Politics*, ed. Elizabeth Weed (New York: Routledge, 1989), p. 173.

4. Alice Jardine, "Men in Feminism: Odor di Uomo or Compagnons de Route?" *Men in Feminism*, ed. Jardine and Paul Smith (London: Methuen, 1987), p. 58.

5. Bruce Robbins, "American Intellectuals and Middle East Politics: Interview with Edward Said," *Social Text* 19/20 (1988), p. 51.

6. Kathy E. Ferguson has recently remarked: "Spivak's excessive self-referencing suggests. . .a claim to authority. . . While simpler considerations of vanity or convenience might also be at work, the politics of the gesture should not be overlooked" (Kathy E. Ferguson, *The Man Question: Visions of Subjectivity in Feminist Theory*, Berkeley: University of California Press, 1993, p. 201). This helpful analysis came too late for me to make serious changes to the footnote practice in this book. Indeed, beginning with an interview might itself be a sign of the sort of politics Ferguson exposes. I acknowledge my intention to be responsive to this warning in the future by attaching this codicil to my first self-reference, which comes, in this case, from Ellen Rooney. See Gayatri Chakravorty Spivak, *In Other Worlds: Essays in Cultural Politics* (New York: Methuen, 1987).

 We must of course remind ourselves, or positivist feminist colleagues in charge of creating the discipline of women's studies and our anxious students, that essentialism is a trap. It seems more important to learn to understand that the world's women do not relate to the privileging of essence, especially through "fiction," or "literature," in the same way (p. 89). Reading the work of Subaltern Studies from within but against the grain, I would suggest that elements in their text would warrant a reading of the project to retrieve the subaltern consciousness as the attempt to undo a massive historiographic metalepsis and "situate" the effect of the subject as a subaltern. I would read it, then, as a *strategic* use of positivistic essentialism in a scrupulously visible political interest. This would put them in line with the Marx who locates fetishization, the ideological determination of the "concrete," and spins the narrative of the development of the money-form; with the Nietzsche who offers us genealogy in place of historiography; the Foucault who plots the construction of "counter-money"; the Barthes of semitrophy; and the Derrida of "affirmative deconstruction." This would allow them to use the critical force of antihumanism, in other words, even as they share its constituting paradox: that the essentializing moment, the object of their criticism, is irreducible (p. 205).

7. See Spivak and Ranajit Guha, eds., *Selected Subaltern Studies* (New York: Oxford University Press, 1988).

8. Louis Althusser, "Marxism and Humanism," in *For Marx*, trans. Ben Brewster (London: Verso, 1985), p. 230.

9. Gayatri Chakravorty Spivak, *In Other Worlds: Essays in Cultural Politics* (New York: Menthuen, 1987), p. 201.

10. Gilles Deleuze and Felix Guattari, *Anti-Oedipus: Capitalism and Schizophrenia*, trans. Robert Hurley, Mark Seem, and Helen R. Lane (Minneapolis: University of Minnesota Press, 1983).

11. Spivak, *Worlds*, p. 253–54.

12. Jamaica Kincaid, *Lucy* (New York: Penguin, 1990), pp. 29–41.

13. Here is Derrida on the topic of the decentered subject: "one can doubtless decenter the subject, as is easily said, without challenging anew the bond between, on the one hand, responsibility, and on the other, freedom of subjective consciousness or purity of intentionality. This happens all the time, and is not altogether interesting, since nothing in the prior axiomatics is changed: one denies the axiomatics *en bloc* and keeps it going as a survivor, with minor adjustments *de rigeur*, and daily compromises lacking in rigor. Thus coping, thus operating at top speed, one accounts, and becomes accountable, for nothing; not for what happens, not for the 'why' of assuming responsibilities when lacking a concept" (Derrida, "The Conflict of the Faculties," in Richard Rand, ed., *The Conflict of the Faculties in America* [Lincoln: University of Nebraska Press, forthcoming]; "Mochlos ou le conflit des facultes," in Derrida, *Du droit a la philosophie* [Paris: Galilee, 1990], p. 408.

14. Ruth Salvaggio, *Enlightened Absence: Neo-Classical Configurations of the Feminine* (Urbana: University of Illinois Press, 1988).

15. Karl Marx, *Capital*, trans. David Fernback (New York: Vintage, 1981), vol. 3, pp. 953–970.

16. Marx, *Karl Marx Friedrich Engels Werke* (Berlin: Dietz, 1977), vol. 23, pp. 11–12; Karl Marx, *Capital*, trans. Ben Fowkes (New York: Vintage, 1977), vol. 1, pp. 89–90.

17. Frobel Folker, Jürgen Heinrichs, and Otto Kreve, *The New International Division of Labour: Structural Unemployment in Industrialized Countries and Industrialization in Developing Countries*, trans. Pete Burgess (Cambridge: Cambridge University Press, 1980), and Nigel Harris, *The End of the Third World: Newly Industrializing Countries and the Decline of Ideology* (London: Penguin, 1987).

18. Chakravarthi Raghaven, *Recolonization: GATT, The Uruguay Round and The Third World* (London: Zed Books, 1990).

19. I refer my readers to Jean Franco, *Border Trouble* (Harvard University Press, forthcoming), for a detailed study of this problematic.

20. Gayle Rubin, "The Traffic in Women: Notes on the 'Political Economy' of Sex," in *Toward an Anthropology of Women*, ed. Rayna Reiter (New York: Monthly Review, 1975), pp. 157–210.

21. Richard Rorty, "Philosophy As a Kind of Writing: An Essay on Derrida," in *Consequences of Pragmatism Essays: 1972–1980* (Minneapolis: University of Minnesota Press, 1982), pp. 90–109.

22. Jean Grimshaw, "'Pure Lust': The Elemental Feminist Philosophy of Mary Daly," *Radical Philosophy*, 49 (1988): pp. 24–30.

23. Kalpana Bardhan, "Women's Work, Welfare and Status: Forces of Tradition and Change in India," *South Asian Bulletin*, 6:1 (1986): pp. 3–16.

24. Paul de Man, *The Rhetoric of Romanticism* (New York: Columbia University Press, 1984), p. xi.

25. For the idea of two sessions, general and narrow, see Jacques Derrida, "The Double Session," in *Dissemination*, trans. Barbara Johnson (Chicago: University of Chicago Press, 1981).

22

NANCY FRASER

Structuralism or Pragmatics?

On Discourse Theory and Feminist Politics

This chapter grew out of an experience of severe puzzlement.[1] For several years I watched with growing incomprehension as a large and influential body of feminist scholars created an interpretation of Jacques Lacan's theory of discourse, which they sought to use for feminist purposes. I myself had felt (and still feel) a deep disaffinity with Lacan, a disaffinity as much intellectual as political. So while many of my fellow feminists were adapting quasi-Lacanian ideas to theorize the discursive construction of subjectivity in film and literature, I was relying on alternative models to develop an account of language that could inform a feminist social theory.[2] For a long while, I avoided any explicit, metatheoretical discussion of these matters. I explained neither to myself nor to my colleagues why it is that I looked to the discourse models of writers like Foucault, Bourdieu, Bakhtin, Habermas, and Gramsci instead of to those of Lacan, Kristeva, Saussure, and Derrida.[3] In this chapter, I begin to provide such an explanation. I will try to explain why I think feminists should have no truck with the versions of discourse theory that they attribute to Lacan and why we should have only the most minimal truck with related theories attributed to Julia Kristeva. I will also try to identify some places where I think we can find more satisfactory alternatives.

WHAT DO FEMINISTS WANT IN A DISCOURSE THEORY?

Let me begin by posing two questions, What might a theory of discourse contribute to feminism? and What, therefore, do feminists want in a discourse theory? I suggest that a conception of discourse can help us understand at least four things, all of which are interrelated. First, it can help us understand how people's social identities are fashioned and altered over time. Second, it can help us understand how, under conditions of inequality, social groups in the sense of collective agents are formed and unformed. Third, a conception of discourse can illuminate how the cultural hegemony of dominant groups in society is secured and contested. Fourth and finally, it can shed light on the prospects for emancipatory social change and political practice. Let me elaborate.

First, consider the uses of a conception of discourse for understanding social identities. The basic idea here is that people's social identities are complexes of meanings, networks of interpretation. To have a social identity, to be a woman or a man, for example, just is to live and to act under a set of descriptions. These descriptions, of course, are not simply secreted by people's bodies, nor are they simply exuded by people's psyches. Rather, they are drawn from the fund of interpretive possibilities available to agents in specific societies. It follows that in order to understand the gender dimension of social identity, it does not suffice to study biology or psychology. Instead, one must study the historically specific social practices through which cultural descriptions of gender are produced and circulated.[4]

Moreover, social identities are exceedingly complex. They are knit from a plurality of different descriptions arising from a plurality of different signifying practices. Thus, no one is simply a woman; one is rather, for example, a white, Jewish, middle-class woman, a philosopher, a lesbian, a socialist, and a mother.[5] Moreover, since everyone acts in a plurality of social contexts, the different descriptions comprising any individual's social identity fade in and out of focus. Thus, one is not always a woman in the same degree; in some contexts, one's womanhood figures centrally in the set of descriptions under which one acts; in others, it is peripheral or latent.[6] Finally, it is not the case that people's social identities are constructed once and for all and definitively fixed. Rather, they alter over time, shifting with shifts in agents' practices and affiliations. Thus, even the way in which one is a woman will shift, as it does, to take a dramatic example, when one becomes a feminist. In short, social identities are discursively constructed in historically specific social contexts; they are complex and plural; and they shift over time. One use of a conception of discourse for feminist theorizing, then, is in understanding social identities in their full sociocultural complexity, thus in demystifying static, single-variable, essentialist views of gender identity.

A second use of a conception of discourse for feminist theorizing is in understanding the formation of social groups. How does it happen, under conditions of inequality, that people come together, arrange themselves under the banner of collective identities, and constitute themselves as collective social agents? How do class formation and, by analogy, gender formation occur?

Clearly, group formation involves shifts in people's social identities and therefore also in their relation to discourse. One thing that happens here is that preexisting strands of identities acquire a new sort of salience and centrality. These strands, previously submerged among many others, are reinscribed as the nub of new self-definitions and affiliations.[7] For example, in the current wave of feminist ferment, many of us who had previously been "women" in some taken-for-granted way have now become "women" in the very different sense of a discursively self-constituted political collectivity. In the process, we have remade entire regions of social discourse. We have invented new terms for describing social reality, for example, "sexism," "sexual harassment," "marital, date, and acquaintance rape," "labor-force sex segregation," "the double shift," and "wife-battery." We have also invented new language games such as consciousness-raising and new, institutionalized public spheres such as the Society for Women in Philosophy.[8] The point is that the formation of social groups proceeds by struggles over social discourse. Thus, a conception of discourse is useful here, both for understanding social groups and for coming to grips with the closely related issue of sociocultural hegemony.

"Hegemony" is the Italian Marxist Antonio Gramsci's term for the discursive face of power. It is the power to establish the "common sense" or "doxa" of a society, the fund of self-evident descriptions of social reality that normally go without saying.[9] This includes the power to establish authoritative definitions of social situations and social needs, the power to define the universe of legitimate disagreement, and the power to shape the political agenda. Hegemony, then, expresses the advantaged position of dominant social groups with respect to discourse. It is a concept that allows us to recast the issues of social identity and social groups in the light of societal inequality. How do pervasive axes of dominance and subordination affect the production and circulation of social meanings? How does stratification along lines of gender, race, and class affect the discursive construction of social identities and the formation of social groups?

The notion of hegemony points to the intersection of power, inequality, and discourse. However, it does not entail that the ensemble of descriptions that circulate in society constitute a monolithic and seamless web, nor that dominant groups exercise an absolute, top-down control of meaning. On the contrary, "hegemony" designates a process wherein cultural authority is negotiated and contested. It presupposes that societies contain a plurality of discourses and discursive sites, a plurality of positions and perspectives from which to speak. Of course, not all of these have equal authority. Yet conflict and contestation are part of the story. Thus, one use of a conception of discourse for feminist theorizing is to shed light on the processes by which the sociocultural hegemony of dominant groups is achieved and contested. What are the processes by which definitions and interpretations inimical to women's interests acquire cultural authority? What are the prospects for mobilizing counterhegemonic feminist definitions and interpretations to create broad oppositional groups and alliances?

The link between these questions and emancipatory political practice is, I believe, fairly obvious. A conception of discourse that lets us examine identities, groups, and hegemony in the ways I have been describing would be a great aid to feminist practice. It would valorize the empowering dimensions of discursive struggles without leading to "culturalist" retreats from political engagement.[10] In addition, the right kind of conception would counter the disabling assumption that women are just passive victims of male dominance. That assumption overtotalizes male dominance, treating men as the only social agents and rendering inconceivable our own existence as feminist theorists and activists. In contrast, the sort of conception I have been proposing would help us understand how, even under conditions of subordination, women participate in the making of culture.

"LACANIANISM" AND THE LIMITS OF STRUCTURALISM

In light of the foregoing, what sort of conception of discourse will be useful for feminist theorizing? What sort of conception can best meet our needs to understand identities, groups, hegemony, and emancipatory practice?

In the postwar period, two general models for theorizing language emerged in France (and elsewhere). The first of these is the structuralist model, which studies language as a symbolic system or code. This model is derived from Saussure, presupposed in the version of Lacanian theory I shall be concerned with here, and abstractly negated but not entirely superseded in deconstruction and in related forms of French "women's writing." The second model, by contrast, I shall call the pragmatics model; it studies language at the level of discourses, as historically specific social practices of communication. This model is operative in the work of Mikhail Bakhtin, Michel Foucault, Pierre Bourdieu, and in some but not all dimensions of the work of Julia Kristeva and Luce Irigaray. In this section, I shall argue that the first, structuralist model is of only limited usefulness for feminist theorizing.

Let me begin by noting that there are good prima facie reasons for feminists to be wary of the structuralist model. This model constructs its object of study by abstracting from exactly what we need to focus on, namely, the social practice and social context of communication. Indeed, the abstraction from practice and context are among the founding gestures of Saussurean linguistics. Saussure began by splitting signification into langue, the symbolic system or code, and parole, speakers' uses of language in communicative practice or speech. He then made the first of these, langue, the proper object of the new science of linguistics, and relegated the second, parole, to the status of a devalued remainder.[11] At the same time, Saussure insisted that the study of langue be synchronic rather than diachronic; he thereby posited his object of study as static and atemporal, abstracting it from historical change. Finally, the founder of structuralist linguistics posited that langue was indeed a single system; he made its unity and systematicity consist in the putative fact that every signifier, every material, signifying element of the code, derives its meaning positionally by way of its difference from all of the others.

Together, these founding operations render the structuralist approach of limited utility for feminist theorizing.[12] Because it abstracts from parole, the structuralist model brackets questions of practice, agency, and the speaking subject. Thus, it does not engage with the discursive practices through which social identities and social groups are formed. Because this approach brackets the diachronic, moreover, it is not attuned to shifts in identities and affiliations over time. Similarly, because it abstracts from the social context of communication, the model brackets issues of power and inequality. Thus, it cannot illuminate the processes by which cultural hegemony is secured and contested. Finally, because the model theorizes the fund of available linguistic meanings as a single symbolic system, it lends itself to a monolithic view of signification that denies tensions and contradictions among social meanings. In short, by reducing discourse to a "symbolic system," the structuralist model evacuates social agency, social conflict, and social practice.[13]

Let me now try to illustrate these problems by means of a brief discussion of "Lacanianism." By "Lacanianism" I do not mean the actual thought of Jacques Lacan, which is far too complex to tackle here. I mean, rather, an ideal-typical neostructuralist reading of Lacan that is widely credited among English-speaking feminists.[14] In discussing "Lacanianism," I shall bracket the question of the fidelity of this reading, which could be faulted for overemphasizing the influence of Saussure at the expense of other, countervailing influences, such as Hegel.[15] For my purposes, however, this ideal, typical, Saussurean reading of Lacan is useful precisely because it evinces with unusual clarity difficulties that beset many conceptions of discourse that are widely considered "poststructuralist" but that remain wedded in important respects to structuralism. Because their attempts to break free of structuralism remain abstract, such conceptions tend finally to recapitulate it. "Lacanianism," as discussed here, is a paradigm case of "neostructuralism."[16]

At first sight, neostructuralist "Lacanianism" seems to promise some advantages for feminist theorizing. By conjoining the Freudian problematic of the construction of gendered subjectivity to the Saussurean model of structural linguistics, it seems to provide each with its needed corrective. The introduction of the Freudian problematic promises to supply the speaking subject that is missing in Saussure and thereby to reopen the excluded questions about identity, speech, and social practice. Conversely, the use of the Saussurean model promises to remedy some of Freud's deficiencies. By insisting that gender identity is discursively constructed, "Lacanianism" appears to eliminate lingering vestiges of biologism in Freud, to treat gender as sociocultural all the way down, and to render it in principle more open to change.

Upon closer inspection, however, these apparent advantages fail to materialize. Instead, "Lacanianism" begins to look suspiciously circular. On the one hand, it purports to describe the process by which individuals acquire gendered subjectivity through their painful conscription as young children into a preexisting phallocentric symbolic order. Here the structure of the symbolic order is presumed to constrain the development of individual subjectivity. But on the other hand, and at the same time, the theory purports to show that the symbolic order must necessarily be phallocentric because the attainment of subjectivity requires submission to "the Father's Law." Here, conversely, the nature of individual subjectivity, as dictated by an autonomous psychology, is presumed to determine the character of the symbolic order.

One result of this circularity is an apparently ironclad determinism. As Dorothy Leland has noted, the theory casts the developments it describes as necessary, invariant, and unalterable.[17] Phallocentrism, woman's disadvantaged place in the symbolic order, the encoding of cultural authority as masculine, the putative impossibility of describing a nonphallic sexuality, in short, any number of historically contingent trappings of male dominance now appear as invariable features of the human condition. Women's subordination, then, is inscribed as the inevitable destiny of civilization.

I can spot several spurious steps in this reasoning, some of which have their roots in the presupposition of the structuralist model. First, to the degree "Lacanianism" has succeeded in eliminating biologism, and that is dubious for reasons I shall not go into here,[18] it has replaced it with psychologism, the untenable view that autonomous psychological imperatives given independently of culture and history can dictate the way they are interpreted and acted on within culture and history. "Lacanianism" falls prey to psychologism to the extent that it claims that the phallocentricity of the symbolic order is required by the demands of an enculturation process that is itself independent of culture.[19]

If one half of "Lacanianism's" circular argument is vitiated by psychologism, then the other half is vitiated by what I should like to call "symbolicism." By symbolicism, I mean, first, the homogenizing reification of diverse signifying practices into a monolithic and all-pervasive "symbolic order," and, second, the endowing of that order with an exclusive causal power to fix people's subjectivities once and for all. Symbolicism, then, is an operation whereby the structuralist abstraction langue is troped into a quasi divinity, a normative "symbolic order" whose power to shape identities dwarfs to the point of extinction that of mere historical institutions and practices.

Actually, as Deborah Cameron has noted, Lacan himself equivocated on the expression "the symbolic order."[20] Sometimes he used this expression relatively narrowly to refer to Saussurean langue, the structure of language as a system of signs. If it followed this narrow usage, "Lacanianism" would be committed to the implausible view that the sign system itself determines individual's subjectivities independently of the social context and social practice of its uses. At other times, by contrast, Lacan used the expression "the symbolic order" far more broadly to refer to an amalgam that includes not only linguistic structures but also cultural traditions and kinship structures, the latter mistakenly equated with social structure in general.[21] If it followed this broad usage, "Lacanianism" would conflate the ahistorical structural abstraction langue with variable historical phenomena like family forms and child-rearing practices; cultural representations of love and authority in art, literature, and philosophy; the gender division of labor; forms of political organization and of other institutional sources of power and status. The result would be a conception of "the symbolic order" that essentializes and homogenizes contingent historical practices and traditions, erasing tensions, contradictions, and possibilities for change. This would be a conception, moreover, that is so broad that the claim that it determines the structure of subjectivity risks collapsing into an empty tautology.[22]

The combination of psychologism and symbolicism in "Lacanianism" results in a conception of discourse that is of limited usefulness for feminist theorizing. To be sure, this conception offers an account of the discursive construction of social identity. However, it is not an account that can make sense of the complexity and multiplicity of social identities, the ways they are woven from a plurality of discursive strands. Granted, "Lacanianism" stresses that the apparent unity and simplicity of ego identity is imaginary, that the subject is irreparably split both by language and drives. But this insistence on fracture does not lead to an appreciation of the diversity of the sociocultural discursive practices from which identities are woven. It leads, rather, to a unitary view of the human condition as inherently tragic.

In fact, "Lacanianism" differentiates identities only in binary terms, along the single axis of having or lacking the phallus. Now, as Luce Irigaray has shown, this phallic conception of sexual difference is not an adequate basis for understanding femininity[23]—nor, I would add, masculinity. Still less, then, is it able to shed light on other dimensions of social identities, including ethnicity, color, and social class. Nor could the theory be emended to incorporate these manifestly historical phenomena, given its postulation of an ahistorical, tension-free "symbolic order" equated with kinship.[24]

Moreover, "Lacanianism's" account of identity construction cannot account for identity shifts over time. It is committed to the general psychoanalytic proposition that gender identity (the only kind of identity it considers) is basically fixed once and for all with the resolution of the Oedipus complex. "Lacanianism" equates this resolution with the child's entry into a fixed, monolithic, and all-powerful symbolic order. Thus, it actually increases the degree of identity fixity found in classical Freudian theory. It is true, as Jacqueline Rose points out, that the theory stresses that gender identity is always precarious, that its apparent unity and stability are always threatened by repressed libidinal drives.[25] But this emphasis on precariousness is not an opening onto genuine historical thinking about shifts in people's social identities. On the contrary, it is an insistence on a permanent, ahistorical condition because, for "Lacanianism," the only alternative to conventional gender identity is psychosis.

If "Lacanianism" cannot provide an account of social identity that is useful for feminist theorizing, then it is unlikely to help us understand group formation. For "Lacanianism," affiliation falls under the rubric of the imaginary. To affiliate with others, then, to align oneself with others in a social movement, would be to fall prey to the illusions of the imaginary ego. It would be to deny loss and lack, to seek an impossible unification and fulfillment. Thus, from the perspective of "Lacanianism," collective movements would by definition be vehicles of delusion; they could not even in principle be emancipatory.[26]

Moreover, insofar as group formation depends on linguistic innovation, it is untheorizable from the perspective of "Lacanianism." Since "Lacanianism" posits a fixed, monolithic symbolic system and a speaker who is wholly subjected to it, it is inconceivable how there could ever be any linguistic innovation. Speaking subjects could only ever reproduce the existing symbolic order; they could not possibly alter it.

From this perspective, the question of cultural hegemony cannot be posed. There can be no question about how the cultural authority of dominant groups in society is established and contested, no question of unequal negotiations between different social groups occupying different discursive positions. For "Lacanianism," on the contrary, there is simply "the symbolic order," a single universe of discourse that is so systematic, so all-pervasive, so monolithic that one cannot even conceive of such things as alternative perspectives, multiple discursive sites, struggles over social meanings, contests between hegemonic and counterhegemonic definitions of social situations, conflicts of interpretation of social needs. One cannot even conceive, really, of a plurality of different speakers.

With the way blocked to a political understanding of identities, groups, and cultural hegemony, the way is also blocked to an understanding of political practice. For one thing, there is no conceivable agent of such practice. "Lacanianism" posits a view of the person as a nonsutured congeries of three moments, none of which can qualify as a political agent. The speaking subject is simply the grammatical "I," a shifter wholly subjected to the symbolic order; it can only and forever reproduce that order. The ego is an imaginary projection, deluded about its own stability and self-possession, hooked on an impossible narcissistic desire for unity and self-completion; it therefore can only and forever tilt at windmills. Finally, there is the ambiguous unconscious, sometimes an ensemble of repressed libidinal drives, sometimes the face of language as Other, but never anything that could count as a social agent.

This discussion shows, I think, that "Lacanianism" suffers from many conceptual shortcomings.[27] I have stressed those deficiencies that have their roots in the presupposition of the structuralist conception of language. "Lacanianism" seemed to promise a way to get beyond structuralism by introducing the concept of the speaking subject. This in turn seemed to hold out the promise of a way of theorizing discursive practice. However, as I hope I have shown, these promises remain unfulfilled. The speaking subject introduced by "Lacanianism" is not the agent of discursive practice. It is simply an effect of the symbolic order conjoined to some repressed libidinal drives. Thus, the introduction of the speaking subject has not succeeded in dereifying linguistic structure. On the contrary, a reified conception of language as system has colonized the speaking subject.

JULIA KRISTEVA BETWEEN STRUCTURALISM AND PRAGMATICS

So far, I have been arguing that the structuralist model of language is of limited usefulness for feminist theorizing. Now I want to suggest that the pragmatics model is more promising. Indeed, there are good prima facie reasons for feminists to prefer a pragmatics approach to the study of language. Unlike the structuralist approach, the pragmatics view studies language as social practice in social context. This model takes discourses, not structures, as its object. Discourses are historically specific, socially situated, signifying practices. They are the communicative frames in which speakers interact by exchanging speech acts. Yet discourses are themselves set within social institutions and action contexts. Thus, the concept of a discourse links the study of language to the study of society.

The pragmatics model offers several potential advantages for feminist theorizing. First, it treats discourses as contingent, positing that they arise, alter, and disappear over time. Thus, the model lends itself to historical contextualization, and it allows us to thematize change. Second, the pragmatics approach understands signification as action rather than as representation. It is concerned with how people "do things with words." Thus, the model allows us to see speaking subjects not simply as effects of structures and systems but, rather, as socially situated agents. Third, the pragmatics model treats discourses in the plural. It starts from the assumption that there is a plurality of different discourses in society, therefore a plurality of communicative sites from which to speak. Because it posits that individuals assume different discursive positions as they move from one discursive frame to another, this model lends itself to a theorization of social identities as nonmonolithic. Next, the pragmatics approach rejects the assumption that the totality of social meanings in circulation constitutes a single, coherent, self-reproducing "symbolic system." Instead, it allows for conflicts among social schemas of interpretation and among the agents who deploy them. Finally, because it links the study of discourses to the study of society, the pragmatics approach allows us to focus on power and inequality. In short, the pragmatics approach has many of the features one needs in order to understand the complexity of social identities, the formation of social groups, the securing and contesting of cultural hegemony, and the possibility and actuality of political practice.

Let me illustrate the uses of the pragmatics model for feminist theorizing by considering the ambiguous case of Julia Kristeva. Kristeva's case is instructive in that she began her career as a critic of structuralism and a proponent of a pragmatics alternative. Having fallen under the sway of "Lacanianism," however, she has not managed to maintain a consistent orientation to pragmatics. Instead, she has ended up producing a strange, hybrid theory, one that oscillates between structuralism and pragmatics. In what follows, I shall argue that the aspects of Kristeva's thought that are fruitful for political theory are linked to its pragmatics dimensions, while the impasses she arrives at derive from structuralist lapses.

Kristeva's intention to break with structuralism is most clearly and succinctly announced in a brilliant 1973 essay called "The System and the Speaking Subject."[28] Here she argues that, because it conceives language as a symbolic system, structuralist semiotics is necessarily incapable of understanding oppositional practice and change. To remedy these lacunae, she proposes a new approach oriented to "signifying practices." These she defines as norm-governed, but not necessarily all-powerfully constraining, and as situated in "historically determined relations of production." As a complement to this concept of signifying practices, Kristeva also proposes a new concept of the "speaking subject." This subject is socially and historically situated, to be sure, but it is not wholly subjected to the reigning social and discursive conventions. It is a subject, rather, who is capable of innovative practice.

In a few bold strokes, then, Kristeva rejects the exclusion of context, practice, agency, and innovation, and she proposes a new model of discursive pragmatics. Her general idea is that speakers act in socially situated, norm-governed signifying practices. In so doing, they sometimes transgress the established norms in force. Transgressive practice gives rise to discursive innovations and these in turn may lead to change. Innovative practice may subsequently be normalized in the form of new or modified discursive norms, thereby "renovating" signifying practices.[29]

The uses of this sort of approach for feminist theorizing should by now be apparent. Yet there are also some warning signs of possible problems. First, there is Kristeva's antinomian bent, her tendency, at least in this early quasi-Maoist phase of her career, to valorize transgression and innovation per se irrespective of its content and direction.[30] The flip side of this attitude is a penchant for inflecting norm-conforming practice as negative tout court, irrespective of the content of the norms. This attitude is highly problematic for feminist theorizing given that feminist politics requires ethical distinctions between oppressive and emancipatory social norms.

A second potential problem here is Kristeva's aestheticizing bent, her association of valorized transgression with "poetic practice." Kristeva tends to treat avant-garde aesthetic production as the privileged site of innovation. By contrast, communicative practice in everyday life appears as conformism simpliciter. This tendency to enclave or regionalize innovative practice is also problematic for feminist theorizing. We need to recognize and assess the emancipatory potential of oppositional practice wherever it appears—in bedrooms, on shop floors, in the caucuses of the American Philosophical Association.

The third and most serious problem that I want to discuss is Kristeva's additive approach to theorizing. By this I mean her penchant for remedying theoretical problems by simply adding to deficient theories instead of by scrapping or overhauling them. This, I submit, is how she ends up handling certain features of structuralism; rather than eliminating certain structuralist notions altogether, she simply adds other, antistructuralist notions alongside them.

Kristeva's additive, dualistic style of theorizing is apparent in the way she analyzes and classifies signifying practices. She takes such practices to consist in varying proportions of two basic ingredients. One of these is "the symbolic," a linguistic register keyed to the transmission of propositional content by means of the observance of grammatical and syntactical rules. The other is "the semiotic," a register keyed to the expression of libidinal drives by means of intonation and rhythm and not bound by linguistic rules. The symbolic, then, is the axis of discursive practice that helps reproduce the social order by imposing linguistic conventions on anarchic desires. The semiotic, in contrast, expresses a material, bodily source of revolutionary negativity, the power to break through convention and initiate change. According to Kristeva, all signifying practices contain some measure of each of these two registers of language, but with the signal exception of poetic practice, the symbolic register is always the dominant one.

In her later work, Kristeva provides a psychoanalytically grounded gender subtext to her distinction between the symbolic and the semiotic. Following "Lacanianism," she associates the symbolic with the paternal, and she describes it as a monolithically phallocentric, rule-bound order to which subjects submit as the price of sociality when they resolve the Oedipal complex by accepting the Father's Law. But then Kristeva breaks with "Lacanianism" in insisting on the underlying persistence of a feminine, maternal element in all signifying practice. She associates the semiotic with the pre-Oedipal and the maternal, and she valorizes it as a point of resistance to paternally coded cultural authority, a sort of oppositional feminine beachhead within discursive practice.

This way of analyzing and classifying signifying practices may seem at first sight to have promise for feminist theorizing. It seems to contest the presumption of "Lacanianism" that language is monolithically phallocentric and to identify a locus of feminist opposition to the dominance of masculine power. However, on closer inspection, this promise turns out to be largely illusory. In fact, Kristeva's analysis of signifying practices betrays her best pragmatics intentions. The decomposition of such practices into symbolic and semiotic constituents does not lead beyond structuralism.

The "symbolic," after all, is a repetition of the reified, phallocentric symbolic order of "Lacanianism." And while the "semiotic" is a force that momentarily disrupts that symbolic order, it does not constitute an alternative to it. On the contrary, as Judith Butler has shown, the contest between the two modes of signification is stacked in favor of the symbolic: the semiotic is by definition transitory and subordinate, always doomed in advance to reabsorption by the symbolic order.[31] Moreover, and more fundamentally problematic, I think, is the fact that the semiotic is defined parasitically over against the symbolic as the latter's mirror image and abstract negation. Simply adding the two together, then, cannot lead beyond structuralism to pragmatics. Rather, it yields an amalgam of structure and antistructure. Moreover, this amalgam is, in Hegel's phrase, a "bad infinity" that leaves us oscillating ceaselessly between a structuralist moment and an antistructuralist moment without ever getting to anything else.

Thus, by resorting to an additive mode of theorizing, Kristeva surrenders her promising pragmatics conception of signifying practice to a quasi-"Lacanianist" neostructuralism. In the process, she ends up reproducing some of "Lacanianism's" most unfortunate conceptual shortcomings. She, too, lapses into symbolicism, treating the symbolic order as an all-powerful causal mechanism and conflating linguistic structure, kinship structure, and social structure in general.[32] On the other hand, Kristeva sometimes does better than "Lacanianism" in appreciating the historical specificity and complexity of particular cultural traditions, especially in those portions of her work that analyze cultural representations of gender in such traditions. Even there, however, she often lapses into psychologism; for example, she mars her potentially very interesting studies of cultural representations of femininity and maternity in Christian theology and in Italian Renaissance painting by falling back on reductive schemes of interpretation that treat the historical material as reflexes of autonomous, ahistorical, psychological imperatives like "castration anxiety" and "feminine paranoia."[33]

All told, then, Kristeva's conception of discourse surrenders many of the potential advantages of pragmatics for feminist theorizing. In the end, she loses the pragmatics stress on the contingency and historicity of discursive practices, their openness to possible change. Instead, she lapses into a quasi-structuralist emphasis on the recuperating power of a reified symbolic order and thereby surrenders the possibility of explaining change. Likewise, her theory loses the pragmatics stress on the plurality of discursive practices. Instead, it lapses into a quasi-structuralist homogenizing and binarizing orientation, one that distinguishes practices along the sole axis of proportion of semiotic to symbolic, feminine to masculine, and thereby surrenders the potential to understand complex identities. In addition, Kristeva loses the pragmatics stress on social context. Instead, she lapses into a quasi-structuralist conflation of "symbolic order" with social context and thereby surrenders the capacity to link discursive dominance to societal inequality. Finally, her theory loses the pragmatics stress on interaction and social conflict. Instead, as Andrea Nye has shown, it focuses almost exclusively on intrasubjective tensions and thereby surrenders its ability to understand intersubjective phenomena, including affiliation, on the one hand, and struggle, on the other.[34]

This last point can be brought home by considering Kristeva's account of the speaking subject. Far from being useful for feminist theorizing, her view replicates many of the disabling features of "Lacanianism." Her subject, like its, is split into two halves, neither of which is a potential political agent. The subject of the symbolic is an oversocialized conformist, thoroughly subjected to symbolic conventions and norms. To be sure, its conformism is put "on trial" by the rebellious, desiring ensemble of bodily based drives associated with the semiotic. But, as before, the mere addition of an antistructuralist force doesn't lead beyond structuralism. The semiotic "subject" cannot itself be an agent of feminist practice for several reasons. First, it is located beneath, rather than within, culture and society; so it is unclear how its practice could be political practice.[35] Second, it is defined exclusively in terms of the transgression of social norms; thus, it cannot engage in the reconstructive moment of feminist politics, a moment essential to social transformation. Finally, it is defined in terms of the shattering of social identity, and so it cannot figure in the reconstruction of the new, politically constituted, collective identities and solidarities that are essential to feminist politics.

By definition, then, neither half of Kristeva's split subject can be a feminist political agent. Nor, I submit, can the two halves be joined together. They tend rather simply to cancel each other out, the first forever shattering the identitarian pretensions of the second, the second forever recuperating the first and reconstituting itself as before. The upshot is a paralyzing oscillation between identity and nonidentity without any determinate practical issue. Here, then, is another instance of a "bad infinity," an amalgam of structuralism and its abstract negation.

If there are no individual agents of emancipatory practice in Kristeva's universe, then there are no such collective agents either. This can be seen by examining one last instance of her additive pattern of thinking, namely, her treatment of the feminist movement itself. This topic is most directly addressed in an essay called "Women's Time" for which Kristeva is best known in feminist circles.[36] Here, she identifies three "generations" of feminist movements: first, an egalitarian, reform-oriented, humanist feminism, aiming to secure women's full participation in the public sphere, a feminism best personified in France perhaps by Simone de Beauvoir; second, a culturally oriented gynocentric feminism, aiming to foster the expression of a non-male-defined feminine sexual and symbolic specificity, a feminism represented by the proponents of écriture féminine and parler femme; and finally, Kristeva's own, self-proclaimed brand of feminism—in my view, actually postfeminism—a radically nominalist, antiessentialist approach that stresses that "women" don't exist and that collective identities are dangerous fictions.[37]

Despite the explicitly tripartite character of this categorization, the deep logic of Kristeva's thinking about feminism conforms to her additive, dualistic pattern. For one thing, the first, egalitarian humanist moment of feminism drops out of the picture in that Kristeva falsely—and astoundingly—assumes its program has already been achieved. Thus, there are really only two "generations" of feminism she is concerned with. Next, despite her explicit criticisms of gynocentrism, there is a strand of her thought that implicitly partakes of it—I mean Kristeva's quasi-biologistic, essentializing identification of women's femininity with maternity. Maternity, for her, is the way that women, as opposed to men, touch base with the pre-Oedipal, semiotic residue. (Men do it by writing avant-garde poetry; women do it by having babies.) Here, Kristeva dehistoricizes and psychologizes motherhood, conflating conception, pregnancy, birthing, nursing, and child-rearing, abstracting all of them from sociopolitical context, and erecting her own essentialist stereotype of femininity. But then she reverses herself and recoils from her construct, insisting that "women" don't exist, that feminine identity is fictitious, and that feminist movements therefore tend toward the religious and the prototolitarian. The overall pattern of Kristeva's thinking about feminism, then, is additive and dualistic: she ends up alternating essentialist gynocentric moments with antiessentialist nominalistic moments, moments that consolidate an ahistorical, undifferentiated, maternal feminine gender identity with moments that repudiate women's identities altogether.

With respect to feminism, then, Kristeva leaves us oscillating between a regressive version of gynocentric-maternalist essentialism, on the one hand, and a postfeminist antiessentialism, on the other. Neither of these is useful for feminist theorizing. In Denise Riley's terms, the first overfeminizes women by defining us maternally. The second, by contrast, underfeminizes us by insisting that "women" don't exist and by dismissing the feminist movement as a prototolitarian fiction.[38] Simply putting the two together, moreover, does not overcome the limits of either. On the contrary, it constitutes another "bad infinity" and so, another proof of the limited usefulness for feminist theorizing of an approach that merely conjoins an abstract negation of structuralism to a structuralist model left otherwise intact.

CONCLUSION

I hope the foregoing has provided a reasonably vivid and persuasive illustration of my most general point, namely, the superiority for feminist theorizing of pragmatics over structuralist approaches to the study of language. Instead of reiterating the advantages of pragmatics models, I shall close with one specific example of their uses for feminist theorizing.

As I argued, pragmatics models insist on the social context and social practice of communication, and they study a plurality of historically changing discursive sites and practices. As a result, these approaches offer us the possibility of thinking of social identities as complex, changing, and discursively constructed. This in turn seems to me our best hope for avoiding some of Kristeva's difficulties. Complex, shifting, discursively constructed social identities provide an alternative to reified, essentialist conceptions of gender identity, on the one hand, and to simple negations and dispersals of identity, on the other. They thus permit us to navigate safely between the twin shoals of essentialism and nominalism, between reifying women's social identities under stereotypes of femininity, on the one hand, and dissolving them into sheer nullity and oblivion, on the other.[39] I am claiming, therefore, that with the help of a pragmatics conception of discourse we can accept the critique of essentialism without becoming postfeminists. This seems to me to be an invaluable help, for it will not be time to speak of postfeminism until we can legitimately speak of postpatriarchy.[40]

NOTES

1. I am grateful for helpful comments and suggestions from Jonathan Arac, David Levin, Paul Mattick, Jr., John McCumber, Diana T. Meyers, and Eli Zaretsky.

2. See, for example, Fraser, "Struggle over Needs," in *Unruly Practices: Power, Discourse and Gender in Contemporary Social Theory* (Minneapolis: University of Minnesota Press, 1989).

3. I group these writers together not because all are Lacanians—clearly only Kristeva and Lacan himself are—but rather because, disclaimers notwithstanding, all continue the structuralist reduction of discourse to symbolic system. I shall develop this point later in this chapter.

4. Thus, the fund of interpretive possibilities available to me, a late-twentieth-century American, overlaps very little with that available to the thirteenth-century Chinese woman I may want to imagine as my sister. And yet in both cases, hers and mine, the interpretive possibilities are established in the medium of social discourse. It is in the medium of discourse that each of us encounters an interpretation of what it is to be a person, as well as a menu of possible descriptions specifying the particular sort of person each is to be.

5. See Elizabeth V. Spelman, *Inessential Woman* (Boston: Beacon Press, 1988).

6. See Denise Riley, *"Am I That Name?" Feminism and the Category of "Women" in History* (Minneapolis: University of Minnesota Press, 1988).

7. See Jane Jenson, "Paradigms and Political Discourse: Labour and Social Policy in the U. S. A. and France before 1914," Working Paper Series, Center for European Studies, Harvard University, winter 1989.

8. See Fraser, "Struggle over Needs," and Riley, *"Am I That Name?"*

9. Antonio Gramsci, *Selections from the Prison Notebooks of Antonio Gramsci*, ed. and trans. Quinton Hoare and Geoffrey Nowell Smith (New York: International Publishers, 1972).

10. For a critique of "cultural feminism" as a retreat from political struggle, see Alice Echols, "The New Feminism of Yin and Yang," in *Powers of Desire: The Politics of Sexuality*, ed. Ann Snitow, Christine Stansell, and Sharon Thompson (New York: Monthly Review Press, 1983).

11. Fernand de Saussure, *Course in General Linguistics*, ed. Charles Baily and Albert Sechehaye with the collaboration of Albert Riedlinger, trans. Roy Harris (LaSalle: Open Court, 1986). For a brilliant critique of this move, see Pierre Bourdieu, *Outline of a Theory of Practice* (Cambridge: Cambridge University Press, 1977). Similar objections are found in Julia Kristeva's "The System and the Speaking Subject," in *The Kristeva Reader*, ed. Toril Moi (New York: Columbia University Press, 1986), to be discussed below, and in the Soviet Marxist critique of Russian formalism from which Kristeva's views derive.

12. I leave it to linguists to decide whether it is useful for other purposes.

13. These criticisms pertain to what may be called "global" structuralisms, that is, approaches that treat the whole of language as a single symbolic system. They

are not intended to rule out the potential utility of approaches that analyze structural relations in limited, socially situated, culturally and historically specific sublanguages or discourses. On the contrary, it is possible that approaches of this latter sort can be usefully articulated with the pragmatics model discussed below.

14. In earlier versions of this chapter, I was not as careful as I should have been in distinguishing "Lacanianism" from Lacan. In taking greater pains to make this distinction here, however, I do mean to imply that I believe Lacan to be free of difficulties. On the contrary, I suspect that many of the basic critical points made here against "Lacanianism" tell against Lacan as well. But a much longer, more complex textual argument would be required to demonstrate this.

15. For the tensions between the Hegelian and Saussurean dimensions in Lacan's thought, see Peter Dews, *Logics of Disintegration: Post-Structuralist Thought and the Claims of Critical Theory* (New York: Verso, 1987).

16. For the notion of "neostructuralism," see Manfred Frank, *What is Neo-Structuralism?* trans. Sabine Wilke and Richard Gray (Minneapolis: University of Minnesota Press, 1989).

17. Dorothy Leland, "Lacanian Psychoanalysis and French Feminism," in *Revaluing French Feminism: Critical Essays on Difference, Agency, and Culture*, ed. Nancy Fraser and Sandra Bartky (Bloomington: Indiana University Press, 1991).

18. Here I believe one can properly speak of Lacan. Lacan's claim to have overcome biologism rests on his insistence that the phallus is not the penis. However, many feminist critics have shown that he fails to prevent the collapse of the symbolic signifier into the organ. The clearest indication of this failure is his assertion, in "The Meaning of the Phallus," that the phallus becomes the master signifier because of its "turgidity," which suggests "the transmission of vital flow" in copulation. See Jacques Lacan, "The Meaning of the Phallus," in *Feminine Sexuality: Jacques Lacan and the école freudienne*, ed. Juliet Mitchell and Jacqueline Rose (New York: Norton, 1982).

19. A similar argument is made by Leland in "Lacanian Psychoanalysis and French Feminism."

20. Deborah Cameron, *Feminism and Linguistic Theory* (New York: St. Martin's Press, 1985).

21. For an account of the declining significance of kinship as a social structural component of modern capitalist societies, see Linda J. Nicholson, *Gender and History: The Limits of Social Theory in the Age of the Family* (New York: Columbia University Press, 1986).

22. In fact, the main function of this broad usage seems to be ideological, for it is only by collapsing into a single category what is supposedly ahistorical and necessary and what is historical and contingent that "Lacanianism" could endow its claim about the inevitability of phallocentrism with a deceptive appearance of plausibility.

23. See "The Blind Spot in an Old Dream of Symmetry" in Luce Irigaray, *Speculum*

of the Other Woman, trans. Gillian C. Gill (Ithaca: Cornell University Press, 1985). Here she shows how the use of a phallic standard to conceptualize sexual difference casts woman negatively as "lack."

24. For a brilliant critical discussion of this issue as it emerges in relation to the very different—feminist object-relations—version of psychoanalysis developed in the United States by Nancy Chodorow, see Spelman, *Inessential Woman*.

25. Jacqueline Rose, "Introduction—II," in *Feminine Sexuality: Jacques Lacan and the école freudienne*.

26. Even Lacanian feminists have been known on occasion to engage in this sort of movement-baiting. It seems to me that, in Jane Gallop's introductory chapter to *The Daughter's Seduction: Feminism and Psychoanalysis* (Ithaca: Cornell University Press, 1982), she comes perilously close to dismissing the politics of a feminist movement informed by ethical commitments as "imaginary."

27. I have focused here on conceptual as opposed to empirical issues, and I have not directly addressed the question, is "Lacanianism" true? Yet recent research on the development of subjectivity in infants and young children seems not to support its views. It now appears that even at the earliest stages children are not passive, blank slates on which symbolic structures are inscribed but, rather, active participants in the interactions that construct their experience. See, for example, Beatrice Beebe and Frank Lachman, "Mother-Infant Mutual Influence and Precursors of Psychic Structure," in *Frontiers in Self Psychology, Progress in Self Psychology*, ed. Arnold Goldberg (Hillsdale N. J.: Analytic Press, 1988), 3–25. I am grateful to Paul Mattick, Jr., for alerting me to this work.

28. Kristeva, "The System and the Speaking Subject."

29. "Renovation" and "renewal" are standard English translations of Kristeva's term, "renouvellement." Yet they lack some of the force of the French. Perhaps this explains why readers have not always noticed the change-making aspect of her account of transgression, why they have instead tended to treat it as pure negation with no positive consequences. For an example of this interpretation, see Judith Butler, "The Body Politics of Julia Kristeva," in *Revaluing French Feminism*, ed. Nancy Fraser and Sandra Bartky (Bloomington: Indiana University Press, 1991).

30. This tendency fades in her later writings, where it is replaced by an equally one-sided, undiscriminating, neoconservative emphasis on the "totalitarian" dangers lurking in every attempt at uncontrolled innovation.

31. Butler, "The Body Politics of Julia Kristeva."

32. For an example, see Julia Kristeva, *Powers of Horror: An Essay on Abjection*, trans. Leon S. Roudiez (New York: Columbia University Press, 1982).

33. See Julia Kristeva, "Stabat Mater," in *The Kristeva Reader*, ed. Toril Moi (New York: Columbia University Press, 1986); and "Motherhood According to Giovanni Bellini" in Julia Kristeva, *Desire in Language: A Semiotic Approach to Art and Literature*, ed. Leon S. Roudiez, trans. Thomas Gora, Alice Jardine, and Leon S. Roudiez (New York: Columbia University Press, 1980).

34. For a brilliant critical discussion of Kristeva's philosophy of language, one to

which the present account is much indebted, see Andrea Nye, "Woman Clothed with the Sun," *Signs* 12, no. 4 (1987): 664–86.

35. Butler makes this point in "The Body Politics of Julia Kristeva."

36. Reprinted in *The Kristeva Reader*, ed. Toril Moi (New York: Columbia University Press, 1986).

37. I take the terms "humanist feminism" and "gynocentric feminism" from Iris Young, "Humanism, Gynocentrism and Feminist Politics," in Young, *Throwing Like a Girl and Other Essays in Feminist Philosophy and Social Theory* (Bloomington: Indiana University Press, 1990). I take the term "nominalist feminism" from Linda Alcoff, "Cultural Feminism versus Poststructuralism: The Identity Crisis in Feminist Theory," *Signs* 13, no. 3 (spring 1988): 405–36.

38. For the terms "underfeminization" and "overfeminization," see Riley, *"Am I That Name?"* For a useful discussion of Kristeva's neoliberal equation of collective liberation movements with "totalitarianism," see Ann Rosalind Jones, "Julia Kristeva on Femininity: The Limits of a Semiotic Politics," *Feminist Review* 18 (1984): 56–73.

39. This point builds on work that Linda Nicholson and I did jointly and that she is continuing. See our "Social Criticism without Philosophy: An Encounter between Feminism and Postmodernism," in *Feminism/Postmodernism*, ed. Linda Nicholson (New York: Routledge, 1993).

40. I borrow this line from Toril Moi, who uttered it in another context in her talk at the conference "Convergence in Crisis: Narratives of the History of Theory," Duke University, 24–27 September 1987.

23

UMA NARAYAN

Contesting Cultures

"Westernization," Respect For Cultures,

and Third-World Feminists[1]

INTRODUCTION

To try to define onself intellectually and politically as a Third World feminist is not an easy task. It is an unsettled and unsettling identity (as identities in general often are), but is also an identity that often feels forced to give an account of itself. There is nothing inherently wrong about the project of giving an account of oneself—of one's specific location as speaker and thinker, of the complex experiences and perceptions and sense of life that fuel one's concerns, of the reasons, feelings and anxieties that texture one's position on an issue, of the values that inform one's considered judgement of things.

What is strange, I believe, for many Third World feminists, is the sense that in our case, such an account is specially called for, *demanded* almost, by the sense that others have that we occupy a suspect location, and that our perspectives are suspiciously tainted and problematic because of our "Westernization." Many Third World feminists confront the attitude that our criticisms of our cultures are merely one more incarnation of a colonized consciousness, the views of "privileged native women in whiteface," seeking to attack their "Nonwestern culture" on the basis of "Western" values.[2] This essay attempts to reveal some of the problems and paradoxes embedded in these charges of "Westernization" as well as to understand what provokes them. I do not intend to provide an analysis of the term "Westernization," but rather to deconstruct some of the ways in which this term is rhetorically used against Third World feminist critiques by pointing to what strike me as selective and problematic applications of the term "Westernization." Although many of the concrete examples I use to make my points in this essay are from an Indian context, I believe parallel examples can be found in many other Third World contexts.

I should admit at the outset the pecularities of my own location. I have grown up and lived in a variety of places. I was born in India and lived there until I was eight, when I moved with my family to Uganda. I returned to India when I was fourteen and lived there until I was twenty-five. For the last dozen years I have lived in the United States, which makes my currently calling myself a Third World feminist problematic, in contrast, say, to feminists who live and function as feminists entirely within Third World contexts. I am also an academic, and academia is, in some ways, a world of its own.

However, I wish to speak as a Third World feminist in this essay for three important reasons. First, having lived the first quarter century of my life in Third World contexts, and having come of age politically in such contexts, a significant part of my sensibilities and political horizons are indelibly shaped by Third World realities. Second, this essay is an attempt to explicate the ways in which the concerns and analyses of Third World feminists are rooted in and responsive to the problems women face within their cultures, and to argue that they are not simple-minded emulations of Western feminist political concerns. I need to speak "as an insider" to make my point, even as I attempt to complicate the sense of what it is to inhabit a culture. Finally, though calling myself a Third World feminist is subject to qualification and mediation, it is no more so than many labels one might attach to oneself—no more than calling myself an Indian, a feminist, or a woman for that matter, because all these identities are not simple givens, but open to complex ways of being inhabited, and do not guarantee many specific experiences or concerns, even as they shape one's life in powerful ways.

SPEECH AND SILENCE IN THE MOTHER-TONGUE

Many feminists from Third World contexts confront voices that are eager to convert any feminist criticism they make of their culture into a mere symptom of their "lack of respect for their culture," rooted in the "Westernization" that they seem to have caught like a disease. These voices emanate from disparate sources, from family members, and ironically enough, from other intellectuals whose own political perspectives are indebted to political theories such as Marxism and liberalism that have "Western" origins. There is evidence that this tendency to cast feminism as an aping of "Westernized" political agendas is fairly commonplace in a number of Third World contexts.[3] I shall try to reveal the problematic assumptions that underlie these rhetorical dismissals of Third-World feminist voices as rooted in elitist and "Westernized" views of their cultures, and argue that, for many Third World feminists, their feminists consciousness is not a hot-house bloom grown in the arid atmosphere of "foreign" ideas, but has its roots much closer to home.

My very sense of my entitlement to contest my culture is threaded through with both confidence and doubt. I grew up in a fairly traditional, middle-class, South Indian family, in the urban milieu of Bombay. Besides my parents, both my paternal grandparents also lived in the household, making us what in India is called a "joint family." As the eldest grandchild, and for several years the only child, I was raised with considerable indulgence. And I also remember the boundaries and limits to this indulgence. I remember my mother saying "What sort of a girl are you to talk back like that to your father?" and my outraged child's sense of justice thinking "But his reprimand was not deserved, and he will not even listen to me, and she will not let me speak." I remember minding particularly that the reprimand to silence came from my mother, who told me so early, because she had no one else to tell, about all her sufferings in her conjugal home. I remember my mother's anger and grief at my father's resort to a silencing "neutrality" that refused to "interfere" in the domestic tyrannies that his mother inflicted on my mother. The same mother who complained about her silencing enjoined me to silence, teaching me that good daughters hold their tongues, doing what she had to do, because my failures to conform would translate as her failures to rear me well.

I also remember my mother saying years later, as a put down for my being argumentative and critical, contrasting my character unfavorably with hers, with a pride and satisfaction that were difficult for me to understand, "When I came to Bombay right after I was married, I was so innocent I did not know how to even begin to argue, or to complain or protest when they harassed me." That "innocence," that silence, indicated she was a good wife, a good daughter-in-law, well-brought up, a good Indian woman, a matter of pride, even to her whose "innocence" had not prevented her from recognizing that what she was being subjected to was wrong, but which had prevented her from explicitly contesting it.

And for once choosing to hold my tongue, I did not say, "But mother, you were not entirely silent. You laid it all on me. My earliest memory (you were the one who dated it after I described it to you, and were amazed that I remembered it) is of seeing you cry. I heard all your stories of your misery. The shape your 'silence' took is in part what has incited me to speech."

I am arguing that my eventual feminist contestations of my culture have something to do with the cultural dynamics of the family life that surrounded me as a child, something to do with my early sense of the "politics of home." My grandmother, whom I loved, and who was indulgent to me in her own way, tormented my mother, whom I also loved, in several petty and some not so petty ways, using her inventiveness to add color and detail to the stock repertoire of the domestic tyrannies available to Indian mothers-in-law. My father, clever and able and knowledgeable in so many other ways, would not "interfere." After all, "our" cultural traditions did not deem it appropriate for a son to reprimand his parents, providing a convenient cultural excuse for my father, (despite his having had a "Westernized education" not very different from that which would later be blamed for the intransigence of his daughter!) How could my loyalty and respect for "my culture" fail to be tainted by the clear fact that there was little justice or happiness for my mother in our house?

So it is strange, and perhaps not strange at all, that my mother adds her voice to so many others, that blame my being "Westernized" for my feminist contestations of my culture. And I want to remind her, and cannot bring myself to it, of her pain that surrounded me when I was young, a pain that was earlier than school and "Westernization," a call to rebellion that has a different and more primary root, that was not conceptual or English, but in the mother-tongue. One thing I want to say to all who would dismiss my feminist criticisms of my culture, using my "Westernization" as a whiplash, is that my mother's pain too has rustled among the pages of all those books I have read that partly constitute my "Westernization," and has crept into all the suitcases I have ever packed for my several exiles.

I would argue that, for many of us, women in different parts of the world, our relationships to our mothers has an interesting resemblance to our relationships to the motherlands of the cultures in which we were raised. Both our mothers and our mother-cultures give us all sorts of contradictory messages, encouraging their daughters to be confident, impudent, self-assertive and achieving, even as they attempt to instill conformity, decorum, and silence, seemingly oblivious to these contradictions. Thus, both my mother and the specific cultural context in which I was raised saw education as a good thing for daughters, encouraged us to do well at our studies, saw it as prudent that daughters have the qualifications necessary to economically support themselves, saw it as a good thing that we learned to master tasks in areas of life that had been closed to women of my mother's generation. At the same time, they were critical of the effects of the very things they encouraged—nervous about our intoxication with ideas and our insistence on using ideas acquired from books to question social rules and norms of life. And they were alarmed at our inclination to see careers as not something merely instrumentally valuable in the event that our marriages failed, but as essential elements of fulfilling lives, anxious about the fact that our independence and self-assertiveness seemed to be making us into women who lacked the compliance, deference, and submissiveness deemed essential in good wives.

It is not just that mothers and mother-cultures raise their daughters with contradictory messages, but that they often seem unaware of these contradictions. They give voice to the hardships and difficulties of being a woman that have marked their lives, teaching us the limitations and miseries of the routine fates that await us as woman, while also resisting our attempts to deviate from these cultural scripts. And so, they tend to regard their feminist daughters as symptoms of their failure to raise us with respect for "our" traditions, as daughters who have rejected the lessons they were taught by their mothers and mother-cultures. In seeing us in this mode, they fail to see how much what we are is precisely a response to the very things they have taught us, how much we have become the daughters they have shaped us into becoming. Thus, my mother insists on seeing my rejection of an arranged marriage, and my general lack of enthusiasm for the institution of marriage as a whole, as a "Westernized" rejection of Indian cultural values. But, in doing so, she forgets how routinely since my childhood she and many other women have complained in my presence about the oppressiveness of their marriages. She forgets how widespread and commonplace the cultural recognition is in India that marriage subjects daughters to difficult life-situations, and forgets that my childish misbehaviors were often met with the repri-mand "Wait till you get to your mother-in-law's house. Then you will learn how to behave."

I would argue that seeing the perspectives of feminist daughters simply as symp-toms of our "Westernization" and as "rejections of our cultures," constitutes a failure to perceive how capacious and complex cultural contexts are, and to see how cultures and their inhabitants often criticize the very institutions they endorse. It also consti-tutes a failure to see that motherlands are spaces where fathers still have most of the privileges and power, and that mothers and mother-cultures relate differently to their daughters than to their sons, imposing different demands and expecting different forms of conformity. Thinking about this difference may require us to rethink notions of what it is to "be at home" in a culture, and to redefine notions of cultural loyalty, betrayal, and respect in ways that do not privilege the experiences of men. Acquiring one's own "take" or perspective on one's mother-culture seems no less vital and inevitable than developing one's own sense of one's mother, perspectives where love and loyalty often co-exist, uneasily and painfully, with criticism. Just as daughters seldom tell their mothers' stories in the same terms as their mothers, feminist daugh-ters often have accounts of their mother-culture that differs in significant ways from its own accounts of itself. Retelling the story of a mother-culture in feminist terms is a *political* enterprise—an attempt to, publicly and in concert with others, challenge and redo dominant accounts that distort, misrepresent, and often intentionally fail to account for the interests and contributions of many inhabitants of the context. Those who perceive our feminism as merely a symptom of our "Westernization" fail to see how complicated are an individual's relationships to powerful influences that shape both their conformities and their conflicts, fail to see the closeness between us and the cultural contexts in which we have become both daughters and feminists.

Feminist movements in various parts of the world develop when historical and political circumstances encourage public recognition that many of the norms, insti-tutions, and traditions that structure women's personal and social lives are detrimen-tal to their well-being and enable political contestations in which these normative practices are critized and alternatives envisioned. I, like many feminists in Third World contexts, acquired a feminist politics in ways not very dissimilar to many fem-inists in Western contexts—by working with other women and participating in polit-ical activities designed to understand, call attention to, and remedy problems faced by women. Issues that feminist groups in India have politically engaged with include problems of dowry-deaths and dowry related harassment of women, police rape of women in custody, issues relating to women's poverty, work and health, and issues of ecology and communalism that affect women's lives.[4] Their political activities have ranged from public protests, publicizing and writing about these issues, to pressing for legal and public policy changes—activities that clearly make feminists and feminism part of the *national political landscape* of many Third World countries. Third World feminists have often been instrumental in making the systematic problems of unfair-ness, mistreatment, and devaluing that women face in their national contexts matters of general public concern, visible and objectionable even to many who do not call themselves feminists.

I am arguing that Third World feminism is not a mindless mimicking of "Western agendas" in one clear and simple sense—that, for instance, Indian feminism is clearly a response to issues confronting *Indian* women. For instance, the problem of "dowry deaths"—a phenomenon in which some middle-class families kill off a daughter-in-law, so that a son might remarry and procure another dowry—is an example of an issue that Indian feminists were crucial in calling to national attention. It is also an undoubtedly Indian problem, embedded in the Indian practices of dowry and arranged marriages. It cannot be argued that Indian feminists were endorsing "Western values" in condemning the phenomena, unless one wishes to suggest that "authentic Indian values" endorse the dowry murders of daughters-in-law! Though Indian feminists were instrumental in calling serious attention to this problem, many Indians who were not feminists had no difficulty in understanding why the phenomenon was objectionable.

If there seems to be a resemblance between the issues addressed by Third World feminists and those addressed by Western feminists, it is a result, not of faddish mimicry, but of the fact that women's inequality and mistreatment are, unfortunately, ubiquitous features of many "Western" and "Nonwestern" cultural contexts, even as their manifestations in specific contexts display important differences of detail. Thus, while women in Western contexts might be unfamiliar with violence against women rooted in the institutions of dowry and arranged marriages, they are no strangers to battery and violence prevalent within their own forms of marriage and family arrangements. They are no strangers either to the sense of shame that accompanies admitting victimization, or to a multiplicity of material, social, and cultural structures that pose serious impediments to their leaving abusive relationships or to seeking assistance. Given these similarities, there is considerable irony in the fact that our "Westernization" is blamed for our feminist cultural contestations, while this same "Western culture" has hardly displayed an easy willingness to take the fate of women seriously.

THE BURDENS OF HISTORY: COLONIALISM, NATIONALISM, FEMINISM, AND "WESTERNIZATION"

Why do terms such as "Westernized" or "Westernization" function as negative epithets in several Third World contexts? One cannot account for why these terms function as pejoratives without reference to the history of colonization of Third World countries by Western powers. Anticolonial struggles for national independence in many Third World countries rejected not only the legitimacy of Western colonial rule, but often constructed a nationalist political identify by contrasting indigenous values and cultural practices to those of the West, calling for a rejection of the latter. This valorization of the values and practices of the indigenous culture of the colony was often a response to colonial attempts to eradicate or regulate customs and practices in the colonies that Western colonial governments found unacceptable or inexpedient.

Ironically, the contrast between the values of "Western" culture and the values of colonized cultures was initially something insisted on by the colonizing powers, in whose rhetoric, the "superiority of Western civilzation" functioned as a rationale and justification for the colonial project, casting colonialism as an attempt to bestow the benefits of "Western civilization" on colonized peoples. One could say that anticolonial nationalist movements concurred with the colonizing powers about the differences in their values and cultures, but disagreed about the respective value of these values, inverting the colonialist contempt for indigenous cultures into a contempt for the culture of their colonizers. Both sides in the colonial encounter had different political reasons for this shared insistence on the "Otherness" of the other culture. This insistence on "Otherness," on the differences between the cultures that confronted each other in the colonial encounter, while not entirely false or fabricated, was often exaggerated in that it over-played differences while ignoring both similarities and assimilations.

I am arguing that the picture of "cultural differences" between "Western culture" and the cultures of various Third World colonies that was constructed in colonial times, and that persists in contemporary postcolonial incarnations, was never a simple descriptive project of describing "cultural differences." It was inevitably extricated in the *political and discursive struggles* that marked the colonial encounter, and was a product of attempts to justify, and interrelated attempts to resist, colonial rule. The pictures of both "Western" culture and particular "Third World" cultures that resulted were often marked by some interesting peculiarities.

For one thing, these pictures of different "cultures" and "cultural values" were *"idealized"* constructions, that were far from being faithful descriptions of the values that *actually pervaded* their institutional practices and social life. Thus, "Western culture" could see itself as staunchly committed to values like liberty and equality, a commitment that was often held up as a mark of its "superiority," even as Western powers engaged in slavery and colonization and resisted the granting of political and civil rights even to large numbers of Western subjects, including women. Anticolonial and nationalist visions of "national culture" were often equally distorted and problematic, converting the cultural perspectives and values of part of the national elite into an embodiment of "national culture." In the case of anticolonial Indian nationalism, "Indian culture" was often problematically equated with aspects of upper-caste Hindu culture, ignoring the actual cultural and religious diversity of the population.[5]

For another, both the pictures of "Western" culture and "Nonwestern cultures" were *"totalizations"*—pictures that cast values and practices that pertained to specific privileged groups within the community as values of the "Culture" as a whole. Thus, both Victorian British culture and the vision of many Indian nationalists constructed the "domestic realm" as a special domain insulated from "public life" within which women manifested their gender-specific virtues and social contributions, ignoring the fact that large numbers of poor and working class women in both contexts had always worked outside the "home." Finally, these contrasting pictures of "Western" and "Nonwestern" cultures not only tended to emphasize "cultural differences" but simultaneously cast these differences as symptoms of "cultural superiority."

All three features are evident in many of the cultural conflicts between Western colonizing powers and Third World nationalisms that involved issues pertaining to women's roles and female sexuality. Veiling, polygamy, child-marriage, and *sati* (a practice where a widow ritually immolates herself on her husband's funeral pyre as an indication of her devotion), were all significant points of conflict and negotiation between colonizing "Western" culture and different colonized Third World cultures. In these conflicts, the colonial powers often depicted these practices as symptoms of the backwardness and barbarity of Third World cultures in contrast to the "progressiveness of Western culture." Male-dominated Third World elites often responded by constructing these very practices as long-standing traditions that were constitutive of their values and world-views, as practices that were tied to the spiritual place of and respect for women in their cultures, any changes in which would be deeply corrosive of their ways of life and a capitulation to the cultural domination of a colonizing Western culture.

Given a background where colonial agendas faced off against anticolonial nationalist agendas, it often became virtually impossible to extricate discussions of indigenous practices that adversely affected women from this conflict-laden political and discursive background. Embroiled in issues of colonialism and nationalism, women and women's issues were vulnerable to co-optation by both colonialist and nationalist agendas, hostages to a discursive background of cultural muscle-flexing about the relative moral superiority of "Western" culture and the culture of particular colonies. The sound and fury of these "my culture is better than your culture" conflicts between male-dominated colonial governments and male-dominated Third World nationalisms often served to obscure the fact that women were clearly second-class citizens in *all* these cultural contexts.

Both colonial women (including feminists) and the women of the colonies participated in this complex process, playing their part in these games of cultural one-upmanship, pledging allegiance to their respective national cultures, and insisting on their difference from, and cultural superiority to, each other. For instance, Antoinette Burton shows how Victorian feminists often grounded their claims for political agency and rights in a reform ideology of women's special moral responsibility for the downtrodden, both at home and in the colonies. In domestic politics, they transformed "the poor into the symbolic nation that British women were responsible for saving."[6] In the colonial context, "Indian women appeared to them to be the natural and logical 'white woman's burden.'"[7] Indian nationalist men similarly saw their political role as crucially connected to "improving the status of Indian women."[8] Thus, both Victorian feminists and Indian nationalist men constructed "the Indian woman" as a site upon which to ground their own demands for political liberation and agency, giving them both an Other to "speak for" in a context where "speaking for" was "one of the prerequisites of political subjectivity."[9]

When one is confronted with a choice between two problematic pictures of one's political role it does not necessarily mean one has no reason to prefer one over the other. Thus, there were often aspects of nationalist discourse that made it more appealing to colonized women than the discourse of "imperial feminism." In a context where both Western colonial men and women participated in the construction of the women of the colonies as "cultural inferiors," it is not surprising that women from colonized cultures responded to the seduction of nationalist visions of their cultures, visions that, despite their problems, seemed to accord them a more "reverential" status and more of a political role and agency than did any of the visions of their colonizers.

Thus, in the Indian context, both nationalist men and women subscribed to a posited "dichotomy between the 'material' West and the 'spiritual' East," and nationalist women often embraced their roles as repositories of a "national spiritual essence" who "must remain untainted by "Westernization" and its implied pollution."[10] In the Indian nationalist agenda, women were "equated with motherhood and goddesses" and became the "last unpolluted sanctuary" who had the task of "guarding the essence of national culture."[11] Indian women often also subscribed to nationalist views that their cultures treated women with more veneration, regard, and honor than did "Western" culture. Gender thus played its part in the ideological service of both colonial Empires and of Third World nationalisms, helping to position "Western" and "non Western" women against each other as competing cultural embodiments of appropriate femininity and virtue. Simultaneously, colonialism and nationalism played their own ideological roles in the construction of gender roles, in both Western contexts and in the colonies.

The construction of national identity in opposition to "Westernization" and "Western culture" has continued into postcolonial times in a number of Third World contexts, partly as a result of the fact many Third World countries have remained vulnerable to economic exploitation and political manipulation by Western powers, even in the aftermath of colonialism. The rapid transformation of economic and social structures in many Third World contexts in recent decades has only intensified the feeling that the "traditional culture" is under threat. Among the more noticeable changes in recent decades in many Third World countries is the entry of increasing numbers of women from the ranks of local elites, predominantly middle-class urban women, into professional and public life, spheres of activity that used to be more exclusively male. The sense of cultural anxiety created by rapid social change results in responses that see changes in gender-roles as the paradigmatic symptom of cultural threat and loss, resulting in calls for a return to "our traditional way of life," a return that is primarily to be accomplished by returning women to their "traditional place."

The nationalist cultural pride that was predicated upon a return to "traditional values" and upon a rejection of "Westernization" that began under colonial rule thus re-emerges today in a variety of post-colonial "fundamentalist" movements, where returning women to their "traditional roles" continues to be defined as central to preserving national identity and cultural pride. In such contexts, the fact that many Third World feminists are women who have entered formerly male professional and political spheres, combined with the fact that they often demand greater equality and participation for women in various arenas of national life rather than a return to "traditional roles," facilitates casting them and their political visions as embodiments of the demon "Westernization." Third World feminist criticisms of practices and ways of life that are harmful and oppressive to women can then easily be dismissed as mere symptoms of their antinationalist cultural disloyalty, as forms of "cultural inauthenticity" rooted in their adoption of "Western" ways and values.

The peculiar features I mentioned with respect to the construction of "Western" and "Nonwestern" cultures under colonialism continue to manifest themselves in many of these postcolonial attempts to return to "traditional culture and values." For one thing, many of these visions of "national culture and traditional values" are totalized constructions that pick on certain values and practices that were not universally prevalent in these contexts, but only existed in specific "pockets" of the national landscape, depicting them as embodying "national" traditions or values. An illuminating example can be found in the construction of "Indian culture" that manifested itself in the late 1980s in the debate over the resurgence of the practice of *sati*. Indian feminist protests responded not only to the particular incident that captured national attention—the *sati* allegedly voluntarily committed by the 18-year old Roop Kanwar—but to the widespread adulation and public celebration her act provoked, which presented engaging in *sati* as conformity to "traditional" spiritual and religious values, and part of "Indian heritage." This construction of *sati* as a practice central to "Indian culture" flies in the face of historical facts. Even in colonial times, *sati* was practiced only in very limited areas of the country, and by women of some particular castes. The majority of the 8,134 *satis* recorded between 1815 and 1828 took place in the vicinity of Calcutta.[12] Three-fourths of the forty-odd *satis* recorded since Independence have occurred in a single district.[13] Thus, *sati* was never a widely practiced *Hindu* tradition, let alone an *Indian* one.

There are therefore multiple ironies in casting *sati* as a "traditional Indian cultural practice." The perception of *sati* as part of "traditional Hindu culture" has less to do with historical facts than with contemporary fundamentalist attempts to equate "Indian culture" with aspects of *Hindu* culture and with practices that embody *their* visions of "Indian womanhood." Contemporary supporters not only want to cast *sati* as definitive of "Indian values" but accuse Indian feminists who protested the Roop Kanwar incident as "being agents of modernity who were attempting to impose crass market-dominated values of equality and liberty on a society which once gave the noble, the self-sacrificing, and the spiritual the respect they deserve."[14] Radha Kumar adds, "Moreover, these views were defined as being drawn from the West, so Indian feminists stood accused of being Westernists, cultural imperialists, colonists, and indirectly—supporters of capitalist ideology."[15]

The political location of many Third World feminists makes it particularly clear that the scope of feminist struggles needs to include not only contestations of *particular practices and institutions* detrimental to women, but additionally to include challenges to the *larger pictures* of Nation, National History, and Cultural Traditions that serve to sustain and justify these practices and institutions. These are often "pictures of history" that *conceal their own historicity and their own status as representations*—suggesting that the Nation and its Culture are "natural givens" rather than historical inventions and constructions.

Such pictures of Nation, History, and Culture prove particularly problematic to a feminist politics that tends to challenge existing institutions and practices, and requires feminists to combine critical contestations of cultural practices with attempts to re-imagine their Nation, Culture, and History in ways that more adequately accommodate women's contributions as well as attention to their problems. Calling attention to the fact that these pictures are historically constituted representations, and deeply problematic ones at that, is of great importance to Third World feminists, because these representations not only function to exclude and marginalize large segments of the national community on class, ethnic, gender, and religious lines, but also to deny the legitimacy of Third World feminist agendas.

It is important to point out that these problematic pictures of Nation, Culture, and History are not unique to India or to the Third World. An investigation of past and present visions of the United States, of "American culture" and "the American way of life," reveal the same sorts of problems—often obscuring from national attention the contributions and problems of members of marginalized and powerless groups, as well as suggesting that feminist agendas are unpatriotic and "unAmerican." Totalizing and dangerous views of "culture" and "nationhood" can be found in current attempts to portray "Christian values" or particular constructions of "family values" as constitutive of "American culture" and "the American way of life"— attempts that function to variously stigmatize the predicaments and choices of single mothers, women on welfare, gays and lesbians, immigrants, and members of the "underclass" as "unAmerican." Representations of "American culture" have functioned and continue to function to marginalize members of racial and ethnic minorities and to legitimize anti-immigrant sentiments, while American nationalism continues to be deployed to justify problematic economic and political interventions in other parts of the world.

Feminists all over the world need to be suspicious of locally prevalent pictures of "national identity" and "national traditions" because they are used to privilege the views and values of certain parts of the heterogeneous national population as "definitive" of national life and culture. However, I do not think that feminists can escape the predicaments of nationalism, in Western or in Third World contexts, by appeals to an "international sisterhood of women." If nations are "imagined communities," then bigoted and distorted nationalisms must be fought with feminist attempts to *reinvent* and *re-imagine* the national community that is more genuinely inclusive and democratic. I believe feminists need to insist that *all* visions of "Nation" are constructs of political imagination, even though some of these visions see themselves as describing the Truth of some "National Essence." On the other hand, this similarity does not make all competing visions of "Nation" in any particular context morally equivalent, or leave us without ethical and political reasons for supporting one vision over others. Finally, national boundaries should not define the bounds of feminist imaginations, if we care about a more equitable and just global and international order.

SELECTIVE LABELING AND THE MYTH OF "CONTINUITY"

National cultures, in many parts of the world, seem susceptible to seeing themselves as *unchanging continuities* stretching back into a distant past. This picture of Nation, Culture, and History is often problematic in several ways. It tends to powerfully reinforce what I think of as the "Idea of Venerability"—making people susceptible to the suggestion that practices and institutions are valuable *merely* in virtue of the fact that they are of long-standing. It is a picture of Nation and Culture that stresses continuities of tradition, (often imagined continuities as the previously mentioned case of *sati* reveals) over assimilations, adaptations, and change. In some Third World contexts, the past history of colonization seems to exacerbate this problem. The Indian construction of anticolonial nationalism relied greatly on appeals to a totalizing vision of "our ancient civilization," casting independence from colonialism as a recovery of this "ancient civilization" while simultaneously casting "Western civilization" as an uppity and adolescent newcomer to the stage of world history and civilization. This background impedes calling attention to the extent to which actual cultural practices, as well as the place of particular practices in shared pictures of "our culture" have undergone substantial change.

A frequent and noticeable peculiarity in these portrayals of unchanging "national culture, traditions, and values" in Third World contexts is the degree to which there is an *extremely selective* rejection of "modernization" and "Westernization." What interests me is that while *some* cultural borrowings of Western artifacts and practices are perceived and castigated as "Westernization," not all are, making some of these cultural borrowings and changes contested and problematic in ways that other changes are not. I believe that the term "Westernization" functions in colonial and postcolonial Third World contexts less as a descriptive term and more as a rhetorical term. The logic of the ways in which the term is wielded is both interesting and deeply problematic. Certain artifacts and not others are "picked out" and labeled "Western," and certain changes and perspectives are conveniently attributed to "Westernization" and not others. This "selective labeling" of certain changes and not others as symptoms of "Westernization" permits Hindu fundamentalists to cast Indian feminists and their agendas as symptoms of "Westernization," even as they skillfully use contemporary media such as television to propagate their ideological messages, without losing sleep over whether the entry of television into Indian homes affects our "traditional way of life." Feminist commitment to liberty or equality for women can be portrayed as "Western values" by Hindu fundamentalists who feel no qualms or paradox in appropriating "the language of rights, asserting that they should have the right, as Hindus and as women"[16] to commit and propagate *sati*.

The selective labeling of certain changes and not others as symptoms of "Westernization" often proceeds hand in glove with the attitude that changes that are disapproved of constitute unforgivable betrayals of long-standing, deep-rooted and constitutive traditions of the culture. But changes that are approved of (often those not perceived as "Westernization") are seen as merely cosmetic changes, or pragmatic adaptations utterly consonant with the "preservation of our culture and values." It has often struck me that many in Third World contexts who condemn feminist criticisms and contestations as "Westernization" would like to believe that there has been a pristine and unchanging continuity in their tradition and way of life, until we feminist daughters provided the first rude interruption.

Both my grandmothers were married at the age of thirteen. I try not to think about what this meant to them, and above all what it could have meant to me if that particular tradition had continued. My mother was not married until she was twenty-one. Why did my maternal grandmother not do to her daughters what was done to her? How would she have explained so significant a change in the space of one generation, a change that, however else it is to be explained, cannot be explained in terms of her daughters' rebellions against the practice of marriage following on the heels of the first indications of puberty?

It is not clear to me how illuminating or intelligible it is to attribute such a change to "Westernization," given the complex interaction of local and colonial structures that probably operated to produce this change. For instance, there were colleges for women by the time my mother was in her teens ("Westernization"?) that did not exist in my grandmothers' youth. Perhaps a community that valued education as part of its particular caste-ethos (both my grandmothers had some schooling despite their early marriage and were literate), was thus encouraged to educate its daughters longer, postponing the age of marriage? Perhaps the voices of Hindu reformers (many of them men with "Westernized educations") whose attempts to "reform Hinduism" were linked to an attempt to create nationalist pride, and who attacked the practice of child-marriage, had some impact on this change?[17] Was this undeniably significant change explicitly seen by my mother's family as a "surrender of our traditions," as "Westernization"? I do not think it was, and wonder why, when so many of the cultural deviations of feminist granddaughters are perceived under these descriptions.

It is far from my intention to suggest that these changes that led to my mother not being married at thirteen have affected the lives of *all* Indian women. Class, caste, religious, and ethnic differences pose problems for attempts to make generalizations about women in Third World contexts, in much the same way as differences among women pose problems for generalizing about women in Western contexts. The forces of "modernization" that preserved my mother from being married at thirteen are, paradoxically, also responsible for marriages of some contemporary thirteen-year olds, as in the publicized recent case of Ameena. She was found sobbing in an Air India plane by an alert flight attendant, in the company of a sixty-three year old Saudi man, who was about to take her out of the country, and who claimed she was his legal wife.[18] For today, there are businesses, paradigms of efficiency, organization, and modern entrepreneurial spirit, where skillful middle-men mediate, for a price, between poor Indian families anxious to marry off their barely teenage daughters and those with the foreign currency to purchase them as "wives"—a complex interplay of tradition and modernity, poverty and perversity, that has hundreds of Ameenas sobbing on their way to foreign fates that make my grandmothers' fates seem enviable.

I have been struck by the fact that it is not only religious fundamentalists who believe they are continuing "ancient traditions" while ignoring the changes they have collaborated in and participated in within their life-times, but women like my mother. My mother's vision manages to ignore the huge difference between her marriage at twenty-one and her mother's marriage at thirteen, and sees both her life and her mother's as "upholding Indian traditions," while my life-choices are perceived to constitute a break with and rejection of tradition. My calling attention to the changes that mark the space between my mother's life and that of my grandmothers' is an attempt to drive home the fact that it is not merely Third World "intellectuals" or "Westernized feminists" who have been affected by profound changes in traditions, ways of life, and gender roles. Third World feminists, whose political agendas are constantly confronted with charges that they constitute betrayals of "our traditional ways of life," need to be particularly alert to how much relatively *uncontested change* in "ways of life" has taken place within these contexts. Some of these changes, while historically pretty recent, have become so "taken for granted" in our life-times that we are often amazed to confront the details and the extent of these changes.

I remember the surprise I felt in listening to one of my mother's stories about her girlhood, when her mother was a young wife and mother, married to my grandfather who was a lawyer. My mother recounted how my grandfather's clients would some-times come to the house hoping to meet with him, when he was away at the courts. It was then not deemed "proper" for my grandmother to directly meet or converse with these male clients, posing a "communication problem" that was rather ingeniously resolved, even though I do not know if the ingenuity was my grandmother's own or a solution that was generally "culturally available." My grandmother would stand behind the front door, and send her child, my mother, onto the front steps, where-upon the client would address the child, requesting her to ask her mother about her father's whereabouts. My grandmother behind the door would then tell her daughter to tell the client that her father was in court and would return at a particular time.

My mother's story was centrally motivated by the amused memory of standing on the front steps, saying nothing, while the entire conversation proceeded by means of the adults addressing her. What I registered in listening to this story were other facts—how the grandmother I knew two decades later no longer hid from her hus-band's clients; how my mother had, in sharp contrast to her mother, accompanied my father to mixed-gender gatherings where she socially interacted with his male col-leagues and co-workers; how many of the women of my generation had male col-leagues and clients of our own, taking our public lives and interactions with men for granted. Looking at these rapid generational changes, I find it impossible to describe "our traditional way of life" without seeing *change* as an ever-present constitutive ele-ment, affecting transformations that are most surprising when they seem to become "invisible" in their taken-for-grantedness.

The gender of the actors, not surprisingly, seems to be one factor that determines whether a particular change is regarded as "Westernization that is disrespectful of our traditions." My paternal grandfather wore trousers and shirts to work, not "Indian" clothes, as did my father. I have no idea if this particular transition was cat-egorized as problematic "Westernization" when it first took place. If it was, it was a characterization that seems to have disappeared. However, the women of my grand-mother's and mother's generations have worn traditional "Indian" dress all their lives, and I am sure that any attempt at a similar "transition" on their part would have been a matter of cultural consternation. Men seem to be permitted a greater degree of lat-itude for such cultural changes, changes that are often not labeled "Westernization," where parallel changes on the part of women are.

I have only fairly recently begun to see that one common thread that linked what was forbidden to me at various times under the rubric of "Westernization" involved cultural norms relating to female sexuality. When I was twelve and we went South to visit relatives who lived in much more "traditional" contexts than Bombay, my mother made it clear that, marked as I now was by puberty, I could not wear my "Western" skirts and dresses there, though they had seemed "Indian" enough to both me and her when I wore them in Bombay. The primary principle that seemed to determine what I could wear when I was South visiting my relatives was that it covered my legs. I have wondered in what sense this "culture" that was bothered by my knobbly twelve-year old legs was the "same" culture that produced the polymorphously perverse erotic sculptures on the temples of Khajuraho, festooned with dozens of sexually acrobatic "divine" bodies, in a variety of positions, some of which are undoubtedly only possible for the gods!

"Westernization" often seems simply a rhetorical label, used selectively to smear only those changes, those breaks with tradition, that those who have the authority to define "tradition" do not approve of. So what sets off our transgressions, our changes, the breaks we would make with our culture as "Third World feminists" from all these breaks, changes, and adaptations that have been going on all along? I believe there *is* something about the contestations of our cultures articulated in Third World feminist voices, that mark us, and the changes we would make, as targets for rhetorical attack. We are often young women, vocal and articulate, who clearly assert our entitlement to contest our cultures with a confidence that many cultures find unnerving in their women. And we have the temerity not just to make these breaks with "our" traditions in our own lives, but to *justify* these breaks, to justify our refusal to be "innocent" and silent. We arouse nervousness and resistance because we hold up to the culture the shame of what its traditions and cultural practices have so often done to its women, the deaths, the brutalities, and the more mundane and quotidian sufferings of women within "our" culture, that "our" culture is complicitous with. We arouse nervousness and resistance because we insist that the choices and happiness of women should matter considerably more than the preservation of traditions that ignore them.

Despite these accusations of "Westernization," our sorts of voices will not quietly vanish, shamed into silence. We are the sisters, the wives, the daughters of those who would dismiss us, and our points of view are no more able to be "outside" our cultural traditions, than the perspectives of those who label us "Westernized." We are very often no more products of a "Western" education than our critics, who position themselves as unproblematic preservers of "our traditions." And while we know only too well that our criticisms and contestations are not uniquely "representative" of our culture, we have the power and the ability to question whether the voices of our critics are any more uniquely "representative" of our complex and changing cultural realities. I firmly believe Third World feminists are entitled, in our own ways, to say what I said to my mother when she once accused me of being "decultured" (an English neologism that she seemed to invent in the heat of that argument-laden moment), that what she refused to see was that I was not just a feminist, but a different kind of Indian.

I do not wish to imply Third World feminists have *"the* right take" on their cultures. Feminist critiques of any culture, like other intellectual endeavors, might be mistaken in their assumptions, insensitive to context, inadequately attentive to the interests of those who are marginalized and powerless, and so forth. Such flaws, when perceived to be present, should elicit serious critical dialogue, instead of attempts to *dismiss* the views put forward by questioning the "authenticity" of the speaker or by characterizing feminism as a purely "Western" political agenda. These strategies of dismissal, where political positions are characterized as "alien," as "foreign," as "representing the views of Others," and whereby individuals who endorse these positions are simultaneously categorized as "traitors to their communities" and "betrayers" of their nation or of their communities of identity are not only deployed against Third World feminists, but seem fairly ubiquitous, used to de-legitimize numerous political groups, positions, and individuals.[19] These strategies of dismissal have also been used against feminists of color in Western contexts, where their perspectives are often dismissed as an espousal of a political agenda that is "White."[20]

I would argue that attempts to dismiss Third World feminist views and politics as "Westernization" should be combated partly by calling attention to the selective and self-serving deployments of the term, and partly by insisting that our contestations of our culture are no less rooted in our experiences within our cultures, no less "representative" of our realities than the views of our compatriots who do not share our perspectives. They need to point to how demands that they be deferential to their Culture, their Traditions, and Nations have always amounted to demands that they continually defer the articulation of issues affecting women. As an Algerian feminist puts it:

> (It is never, has been the right moment (to protest . . . in the name of women's interests and rights): not during liberation struggle against colonialism, because all forces should be mobilized against the principal enemy: French colonialism; not after Independence, because all forces should be mobilized to build up the devasted country; not now that racist imperialistic Western governments are attacking Islam and the Third World, etc.) Defending women's rights "now" (this "now" being ANY historical moment) is always a betrayal—of the people, of the nation, of the revolution, of Islam, of national identity, of cultural roots, of the Third World. . . .[21]

I am not suggesting that all the changes that have taken place within Third World contexts are for the better. I am not advocating that Third World feminists simplistically invert traditionalist, nationalist, or fundamentalist attempts to convey the message "Change is Bad, Traditions are Good," by insisting that "Traditions are Bad, Change is Good." While some of the changes that have taken place in Third World contexts arguably have improved the lives of women, others have made things worse. In Third World contexts, as elsewhere, changes that improve the lives of *some* women may do little for others, or might affect them adversely. Feminists need to be alert and attentive to all these various possibilities, and to encourage widespread and critical dialogue on various aspects of social change. All cultural contexts need to promote the abilities of their various members to think critically about the cultural elements that should be preserved and those that need to be challenged, opening up these questions to widespread political debate. The implication that Third World feminists lack the cultural legitimacy to name what is wrong about the ways in which their cultures treat women is often an attempt to curtail and cut short this political dialogue and to preserve a misguided sense of "cultural pride" that equates respect for a culture with blindness to its problems.

CONCLUSION

My intention has been to challenge the use of "Westernization" to delegitimize Third World feminist criticisms of their cultures. I believe that, instead of locating ourselves as "outsiders within" Third World cultures, Third World feminists need to challenge the notion that access to "Westernized educations" positions us "outside" of our home cultures. We all need to recognize that critical postures do not necessarily render one an "outsider" to what one criticizes, and that it is often precisely one's status as one "inside" the culture one criticizes, and deeply affected by it, that gives one's criticisms their motivation and urgency. We need to move away from a picture of cultural contexts as sealed rooms, with a homogenous space "inside" them, inhabited by "authentic insiders." Western feminist reflections on their own experiences should teach them that there are many ways to critically and creatively inhabit a culture.

Virginia Woolf's anti-nationalist assertion in *Three Guineas* that " . . . in fact, as a woman I have no country" needs to be supplemented by the insight that, as feminists, we have indeed many countries where the fates of women call out for critical thought and action for change. Neither Western feminists nor Third World feminists can simply side-step their complex insertions into national political contexts, but need to be alert to the fact that " . . . the nation cannot be taken for granted."[22] Feminists everywhere confront the conjoint tasks of selectively appropriating and selectively rejecting various facets of their complex cultural and political legacies, a critical engagement that can alone transform one's cultural inheritances into a culture of one's own.

NOTES

1. A much shorter version of this paper-in-progress, entitled "A Culture of One's Own: Situating Feminist Perspectives Inside Third World Cultures" was presented at the American Political Science Association meeting in Washington D. C., September 1993.
2. I have no desire to reify the category of "Third World feminist" by implying that all feminists from Third world backgrounds confront these voices or have the same responses to them. The term "feminism" has been questioned and

sometimes rejected by Third World women because of its perceived limitations. See for instance, Madhu Kishwar, "Why I do not Call Myself a Feminist," *Manushi*, No. 61, Nov.-Dec., 1990. Others refuse to surrender the term. See Cheryl Johnson-Odim's reasons for this position in "Common Themes, Different Contexts: Third World Women and Feminism", in Mohanty, Russo and Torres, (eds.), *Third World Women and the Politics of Feminism*, (Bloomington: Indiana University Press, 1991).

3. See the essays in *Identity Politics and Women: Cultural Reassertions and Feminisms in International Perspective*, edited by Valentine M. Moghadam, (Boulder: Westview Press, 1994).

4. See Mary Fainsod Katzenstein, "Organizing Against Violence: Strategies of the Indian Feminist Movement," Pacific Affairs, Vol. 62, No. 1, 1989.

5. Sucheta Mazumdar, "Women on the March: Right-Wing Mobilization in Contemporary India," *Feminist Review* 49, Spring, 4.

6. Ibid., 45.

7. Ibid., 211.

8. Ibid, 20.

9. Ibid., 31.

10. Sucheta Mazumdar, "Moving Away From A Secular Vision?: Women, Nation and the Cultural Construction of Hindu India," in *Identity Politics and Women: Cultural Reassertions and Feminisms in International Perspective*, edited by Valentine M. Moghadam, (Boulder: Westview Press, 1994), 257.

11. Ibid., 258, 260.

12. Ibid. 252.

13. Radha Kumar, "Identity Politics and the Contemporary Indian Feminist Movement", in *Identity Politics and Women: Cultural Reassertions and Feminisms in International Perspective*, edited by Valentine M. Moghadam, (Boulder: Westview Press, 1994), 286.

14. Ibid. 284.

15. Ibid.

16. Ibid. 284.

17. For a discussion of the complex nature of the nineteenth century Indian reformers and the colonial government's discourses on India, see the essays in Kumkum Sangari and Suresh Vaid (eds.), *Recasting Women: Essays in Indian Colonial History* (New Brunswick, N.J.: Rutgers University Press, 1990).

18. This case received a lot of attention in the Indian press, and was also the subject of a segment on *60 Minutes*, broadcast January 3, 1993.

19. For example, Aijaz Ahmed points out that "There is a powerful political movement in India which says . . . that Indian socialists are not true Indians because Marxism *originated* in Europe; that the Indian state should not be a secular state because secularism is a western construct." Aijaz Ahmad. "The Politics of Literary Postcoloniality," *Race and Class*, Vol. 36, January-March 1995, 5.

20. See Cherrie Moraga, "From a Long Line of Vendidas: Chicanas and Feminism," in *Theorizing Feminism: Parallel Trends in the Humanities and Social Sciences*, edited

by Anne C. Herman and Abigail J. Stewart, (Boulder, Colorado: Westview Press,) 1994, and Barbara Smith's "Introduction" to *Home Girls* (New York: Kitchen Table: Women of Color Press), 1983.

21. Marie-Aimee Helie-Lucas, quoted by Gayatri Chakravorti Spivak, "French Feminism Revisited" in *Feminists Theorize the Political*, edited by Judith Butler and Joan W. Scott, (New York: Routledge, 1992), 71.

22. Gayatri Chakravorti Spivak, "French Feminism Revisited" in *Feminists Theorize the Political*, edited by Judith Butler and Joan W. Scott, (New York: Routledge, 1992), 71.